Simon E. Overall
A Grammar of Aguaruna (Iiniá Chicham)

Mouton Grammar Library

Edited by
Georg Bossong
Bernard Comrie
Matthew S. Dryer
Patience L. Epps

Volume 68

Simon E. Overall

A Grammar of Aguaruna (Iiniá Chicham)

—

ISBN 978-3-11-063491-4
ISSN 0933-7636

Library of Congress Cataloging-in-Publication Data
A CIP catalog record for this book has been applied for at the Library of Congress.

Bibliographic information published by the Deutsche Nationalbibliothek
The Deutsche Nationalbibliothek lists this publication in the Deutsche Nationalbibliografie;
detailed bibliographic data are available in the Internet at http://dnb.dnb.de.

© 2018 Walter de Gruyter GmbH, Berlin/Boston
This volume is text- and page-identical with the hardback published in 2017.
Printing and binding: CPI books GmbH, Leck

♾ Printed on acid-free paper
Printed in Germany

www.degruyter.com

Dedicated to the Aguaruna people, with love and respect.

Acknowledgements

This book is the product of many years of work – recording, analysing, and poring over data – then writing, editing, rethinking and rewriting. I couldn't have completed it alone. At every stage of the process many people helped me immensely, and I take this opportunity to acknowledge them. Most importantly, this grammar would not have been possible without the enthusiasm and support of the *aents iiniá*: the Aguaruna people. Isaías Dati Puanchig, Pablo Santiak Kajekui, Arias Chamik Ukuncham, Elías Mañan Wamputsag, Abiut Nanchijam Jempets, Eduardo Cungumas Kujancham, Segundo Cungumas Kujancham, Liseth Atamain Uwarai, and Jessica Danducho Yampis all worked closely with me at various stages of the project, and their contributions are gratefully acknowledged. In the community of Centro Wawik, I had the privilege of recording traditional stories and songs with the following people: Tito Nanchijam Pegas, Benjamín Chamik Kujikat, Pascual Majuash Jiukam, Tsatsupig Akintui Daichap, and Rubio Akintui Daichap. In Tundusa, the following people generously provided autobiographical stories: Ana Nanantai Shawit, Alfredo Quiac Chuin, Nuria Wampash Chamikag, and Salomé Peas Agkuash. I remain in awe of their deep knowledge of Aguaruna oral tradition, and I hope that this work does justice to their contributions.

Successful fieldwork is not only about data and analysis. Consultants, their families, and others in the communities became good friends during my time in Centro Wawik and Tundusa. Many people helped me in innumerable ways, and although it would be impossible to list them all, a few deserve particular mention. Apu Abel Namarai Nanchijam in Centro Wawik and Apu Rafael Akuts in Tundusa, as the chief elected officials, gave permission for me to stay and work in their communities and happily provided all the assistance I required. Their personal interest in and support of my work was vital. The indigenous organization ASODEINI (*Asociación de Desarrollo Integral Iiniá*) provided excellent accommodation for my entire time in Centro Wawik along with generous help in all logistic matters. And I would especially like to acknowledge the generosity of the following people, in addition to those already mentioned: Doris Akintui, Prof Silvano Dati, Lucy Dekentai, and Pedro Nanchijam and family. *Yatsug aidautigmin, ubag aidautigminash, tuja muun aidautigminashkam see tajime.*

On the academic side, this work benefitted immeasurably from the excellent advice and encouragement of Sasha Aikhenvald and Bob Dixon, who supervised the dissertation on which it is based and also advised me during the revision process. Among the other people who were instrumental in my linguistics training, I take this opportunity to acknowledge two of my first linguistics teachers at the University of Auckland, the late W. Scott Allan and the late Frank Lichtenberk – inspiring mentors who introduced me to the possibilities of a career in linguistics and did everything they could to encourage and support my pursuit of it.

During the time that this grammar was a dissertation-in-progress at La Trobe University's Research Centre for Linguistic Typology, colleagues and visitors were invaluable sources of information and inspiration, and my unofficial mentors Dave Fleck and Gerd Jendraschek always found the time for enlightening discussion. I hope that some of their insight and academic rigour is reflected in these pages. Angel Corbera Mori, whose work on Aguaruna laid the foundations for much of this grammar, generously shared published and unpublished material with me, which I gratefully acknowledge. The research was funded by an Australian Postgraduate Award and the Research Centre for Linguistic Typology.

Of course, the grammar you are reading now has been greatly revised and updated from the dissertation version. The long revision process was guided by useful comments from the dissertation's examiners Willem Adelaar, Bernard Comrie and John Hajek, and Mouton Grammar Library's editor Pattie Epps read the full revised version and gave me many detailed and helpful comments. Adella Edwards prepared the maps with great patience and care. And finally, Jolene Overall unflinchingly proofread the entire manuscript with an incredible eye for detail.

Most importantly, throughout all of this work, my family have tolerated my long fieldwork absences and late nights spent writing, and I thank them with all my heart.

Simon E. Overall
Cairns, November 2016

Table of contents

Abbreviations and conventions

Examples, tables and figures are numbered consecutively within each chapter, in the form (1.2), which represents the second example in Chapter 1. Cited examples come from five sources:

1. Texts that were recorded, translated and glossed in the field. These are cited by the label given to the recording, of the form *agr041005_27*, where the first six digits represent the date of recording (*yymmdd*) – this example was recorded on 4 October 2005. The audio recordings and transcriptions are currently being prepared for archiving. Some examples are cross-referenced to the appended texts, and these are cited as e.g. "Text 1:2", representing line 2 of the first text. The full labels of these recordings are included with the metadata that accompanies each text.

2. Notes made in the field, including elicitation, teaching moments, and observation of interactions among native speakers. All of these examples were noted down in writing at the time and later double-checked with native speakers for accuracy. All examples that are unmarked for source are from field notes.

3. Examples from conversation data recorded and transcribed by Clarivel Tiinch and Jessica Danducho in the course of their own fieldwork, and shared with me in anonymized form. These are cited as *Tiinch & Danducho*. I have normalized the orthography in these examples, but only mark accent where the original transcriptions do so.

4. Personal correspondence. These are anonymized examples from written (email and chat) exchanges with native speakers, and are marked as such. The orthography has been normalized, and in most cases accent is unmarked.

5. Other written sources. A few examples have been taken from published or unpublished texts, and these are referenced to the source. The orthography in these examples follows that of the written source, but is normalized in the morphemic line.

Aguaruna words cited within the text are italicized and given in the citation form, e.g. *anɨn* 'magic song'. Accent is not marked unless it is relevant to the discussion. The underlying phonological form is included if it is relevant, e.g. *anɨn* /anɨnta/ 'magic song'. Since verb roots are obligatorily bound, they are cited in a nominalized form that includes the suffix -*ta*, e.g. *yuta* 'eat'; the suffix surfaces as /t/ when the root has two or more moras, e.g. *puhut* 'live'. This is the same citation form used in the dictionaries (Wipio 1996; Uwarai et al. 1998), and is described in §15.4.5. Where the internal morphology of a verb form is under discussion, however, I give the underlying stem, e.g. *i-waina-* (CAUS-see-) 'show'. All other bound forms are cited in the underlying form, for example the definite future suffix -*tata*, which surfaces as /tat/ or /tta/ depending on its position within the phonological word (§8.4.4.8).

Accent position is generally not marked in words cited in isolation, except where it is relevant to the discussion.

Cross-references to whole chapters are given as e.g. 'Chapter 2', while references to sections within chapters are given in the form e.g. '§2.3', which refers to section 3 in chapter 2. All citations in languages other than English are followed by translations in square brackets, and translations are mine unless otherwise noted. Examples in the text have four lines:

- The first line represents the surface, phonetic form
- The second line represents the morphemic form
- The third line gives interlinear morphemic glosses
- The fourth line is a translation into idiomatic English

The hyphen (-) separates roots and suffixes in examples and glosses, e.g. *nuwa-uchi* (woman-DIM) 'girl'. The equals sign (=) separates enclitics in examples and glosses, e.g. *nuwa=na* (woman=ACC). See §1.4.1 for a description of the criteria I use to distinguish enclitics from suffixes.

The colon (:) separates semantically identifiable morphemes in a portmanteau, in glosses only. For example, the suffix *-mĩ* marks recent past tense; third person subject; and declarative mood. These categories have distinct markers elsewhere in the paradigm, and as such can be analysed as distinct morphemes within Aguaruna grammar, but there is no principled way to identify underlying segmental markers in this suffix, so I gloss it as RECPST:3:DECL (§8.4.3.1).

The plus sign (+) separates phonologically identifiable forms that cannot be segmented, and is used in glosses only. There are three contexts where this symbol is used. The first involves suprasegmental morphemes. For example, genitive is marked with suppression of apocope in the stem and accent shift. This is a regular and identifiable phonological process, but there is no way to transcribe it separately, as with segmental markers, so it is transcribed as e.g. *atashú* (chicken+GEN) (§4.10.3). The second context is when vowel sandhi occurs. For example, the imperfective suffix *-a* fuses with the final vowel of the verb root *puhu-* 'live' to give *puha-* (live+IPFV-) (§8.3.2). The third function of the plus sign is to separate the glossing of a zero-marked morpheme – for example, third person subject is not overtly marked in speculative modality but contrasts with other persons that are marked: *puha-tai* (live+IPFV+3-SPEC) 'perhaps s/he is living' (§9.2.4).

An underscore (_) separates the two elements of a compound, in the morphemic line only. Compounds are glossed as one grammatical word: *ikama_yawaã* 'jaguar' (literally *forest_dog*).

For the English glosses, I have generally tried to remain consistent, so that e.g. *numi* 'tree, wood' is always glossed as 'tree' in examples, even where the free translation uses 'wood'. In other cases more than one gloss may be necessary, e.g. the verb root *ha-* generally translates as 'die' in perfective aspect, or 'be sick' in imperfective. The nominalized form *hata* may translate as 'death' or 'sickness', and I have selected the most appropriate gloss for the context in each example.

In phonological forms, the full stop (.) represents a syllable boundary and hash (#) a word boundary. A single asterisk (*) marks hypothetical reconstructed segments and morphemes, while two asterisks (**) mark an ungrammatical or otherwise impossible form. Syntactic constituents (NP, clause) are enclosed in square brackets '[]' in examples where this is necessary for clarity. Speech reports in examples are <u>underlined</u>. Spanish words in examples retain Spanish orthography, and are italicized in the morpheme line.

Glossing follows the Leipzig conventions as much as possible. A full list of abbreviations follows.

1, 2, 3	first, second, third person
1SG>2SG etc.	person of subject > person of object
SBJ>OBJ etc.	role in marked clause > role in controlling clause
A	most agentive argument of a transitive clause
ABL	ablative
ACC	accusative
ACT.NMLZ	action nominalizer
ADD	additive
ADJ	adjective
AGR	Aguaruna
ALL	allative
ANA	anaphoric pronoun
APPL	applicative
APPR	apprehensive
ATTRIB	attributive
BRIDGE	bridging construction
C	consonant
CA	current addressee
CAAAP	*Centro Amazónico de Antropología y Aplicación Práctica*
CAUS	causative
CC	copula complement
CNTR.EX	counter-expectation
COM	comitative
COMP	comparative
CONCESS	concessive
COND	conditional
COP	copula
CS	copula subject (only in glosses); current speaker (only in text and translations)
DECL	declarative

DESID	desiderative
DETRNS	detransitivizer
DIM	diminutive
DIST	distal demonstrative
DISTPST	distant past
DISTRIB	distributive
DR	diphthong reduction
DS	different subject
DUR	durative
E	recipient-like argument of a ditransitive clause
EP	epenthetic segment(s)
EVEN	counter-expectational adverbializer
EXCL	exclamative
EXPL	expletive
FAM	familiar
FIRST	'first' marker
FRUST	frustrative
FUT	future
GEN	genitive
HESIT	hesitation
HORT	hortative
IDEO	ideophone
IFUT	immediate future
IMP	imperative
INS	instrumental
INTENS	intensifier
INTENT	intentional
INTPST	intermediate past
INTR	intransitive
IPFV	imperfective
ITER	iterative
JUSS	jussive
LOC	locative
MED	medial demonstrative
N	noun; nasal consonant
NARR	narrative marker
NARR.PST	narrative past nominalizer
NEG	negative
NMLZ	nominalizer
NOM	nominative
NONVIS	non-visual

NORM	normative
NP	noun phrase
NSBJ	non-subject
O	least agentive/most patient-like argument of a transitive clause
OA	original addressee
OBJ	object (O/E)
OS	original speaker
PC	Proto-Chicham
PFV	perfective
PL	plural
POSS	possessive
POT	potential
PROH	prohibitive
PROX	proximal demonstrative
PRS	present tense
PSSD	possessed form of noun
PST	past tense
Q	question marker
Q.RHET	rhetorical question marker
Q.TAG	tag question marker
Q.TOP	topic in a question
Qu.	Quechua
RC	relative clause
RECIP	reciprocal
RECPST	recent past
REDUP	reduplicated material
REFL	reflexive
REL	relativizer
REMPST	remote past
REPET	repetitive
RESTR	restrictive
S	sole argument of an intransitive clause
SAP	speech act participant
SBD	non-temporal subordinator
SBJ	subject
SEQ	sequential
SG	singular
SIM	simultaneous
SIMIL	similative
Sp.	Spanish
SPEC	speculative

SS	same subject
TERM	terminative
TIME	time adverbial marker
TOP	topic marker
TR	transitive
V	vowel
VBLZ	verbalizer
VBLZ.INTR	intransitive verbalizer
VBLZ.TR	transitive verbalizer
VCC	verbless clause complement
VCS	verbless clause subject
VOC	vocative

Maps

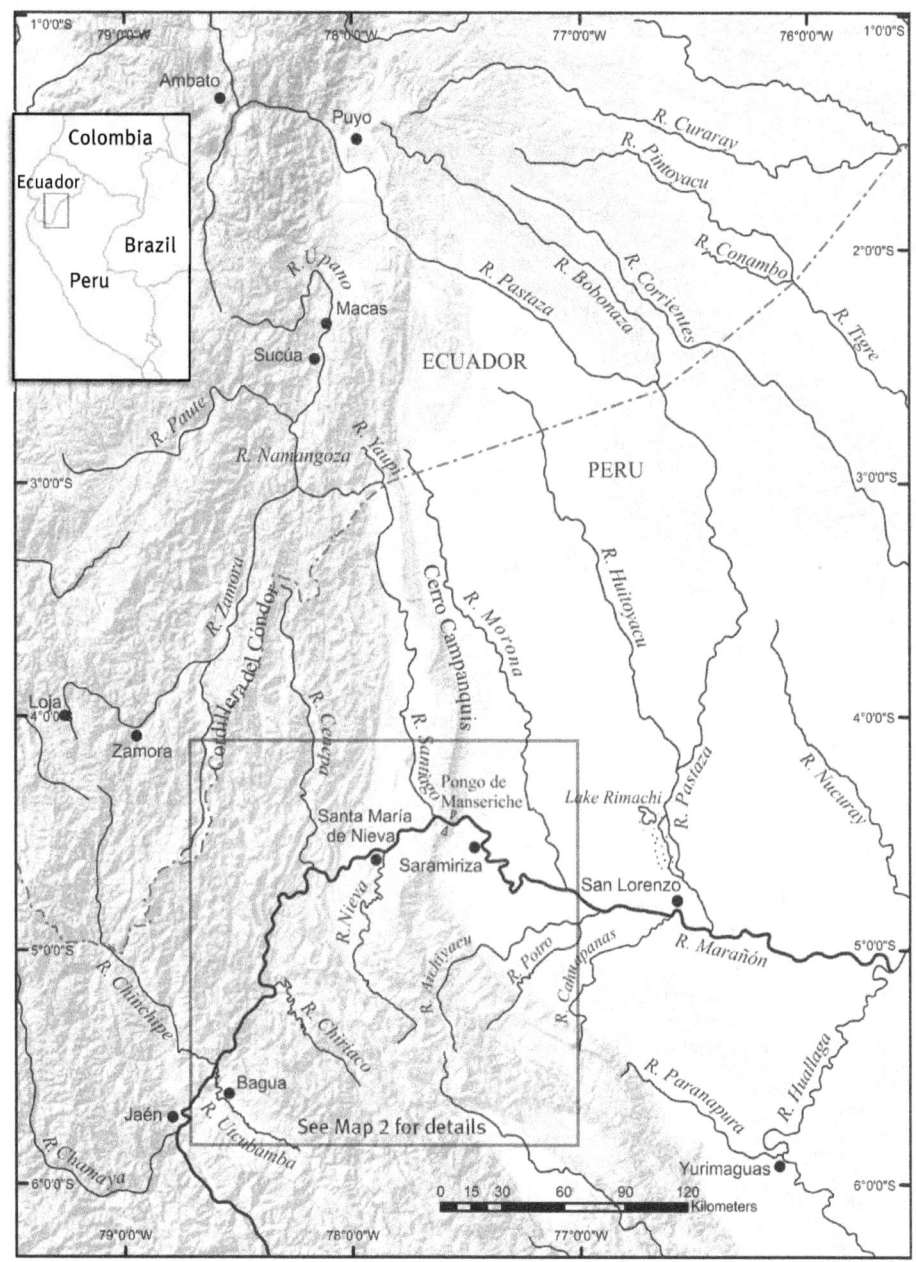

Map 1: The Chicham speaking area and surrounds, Peru and Ecuador

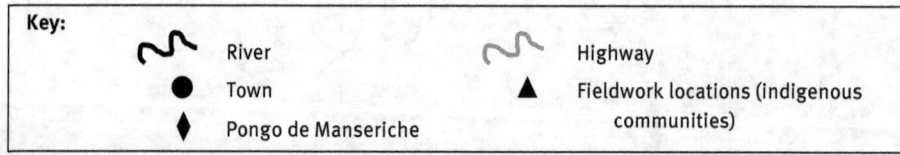

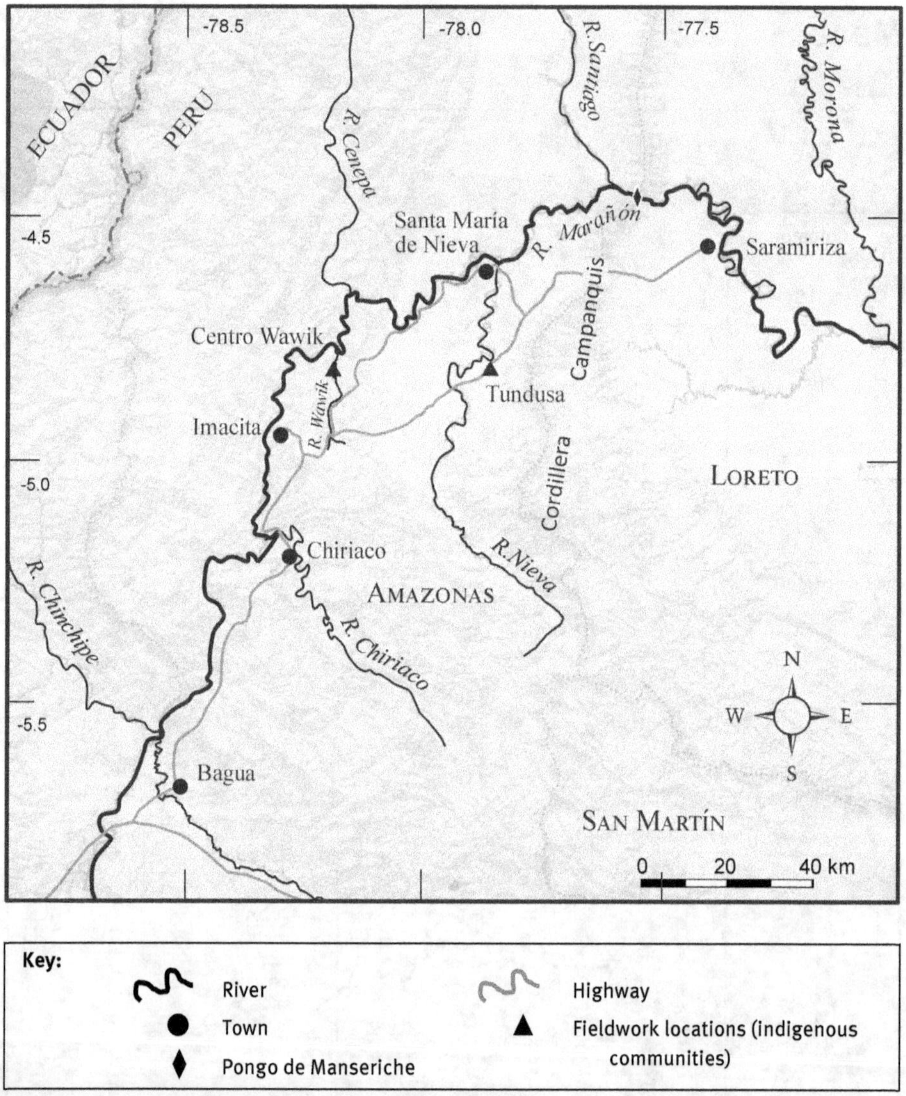

Map 2: Detail showing fieldwork locations

1 Introduction to the Aguaruna language

1.1 Preliminaries

This work is a description of Aguaruna, known to its speakers as *iiniá chicham* or *awajún chicham*. Aguaruna is spoken mainly in the Peruvian department of Amazonas along the Marañón River and its tributaries, of which the most important are the Cenepa, Santiago, Nieva and Chiriaco Rivers. Peruvian census data give a population of 55,000 for ethnic Aguaruna people (INEI 2009). Wise (1999: 309) suggested the following sociographic figures (for an estimated population of 39,000): 35% monolingual Aguaruna speakers; at least 80% literate in Aguaruna and perhaps 65% literate in Spanish (there are no more recent figures on bilingualism or literacy). Aguaruna is part of the small Chicham family (formerly known as Jivaroan – see §2.2), whose closely related members are all spoken in a single geographic area in northern Peru and southern Ecuador (§2.1). Within Aguaruna, speakers recognize two major varieties of the language: one spoken on the Nieva river and its tributaries, the other spoken in the remainder of the territory, that is, on the Marañón and its tributaries, including the Cenepa and Santiago rivers.[1] I refer to these as the Nieva and Marañón varieties, respectively; this grammar is based on the Marañón variety.

This first chapter provides a preliminary sketch of Aguaruna grammar, to familiarize the reader with the essential points and ease access to the more detailed discussion in subsequent chapters. It follows the same general structure as the grammar itself, consisting of the following sections: an introduction to orthographic practices, and briefly to phonology (§1.2); word classes (§1.3); morphological patterns (§1.4). Three sections outline the syntax: referring expressions (NPs) in §1.5, clause structure in §1.6 and grammatical relations in §1.7. Next I cover a few points from a more holistic, functional perspective than is possible elsewhere in the grammar: finiteness (§1.8); subordination and nominalization (§1.9); and clause combining (§1.10). A detailed description of the historical and ethnographic background is provided in Chapter 2.

---

1 A third variety of Aguaruna, spoken on the Chiriaco River in the Imaza district, was described to me by speakers of the Marañón variety as having a distinctive intonation (*medio cantando* 'almost singing'). I was unable to collect any data on this variety. Previous analysts have recognized two "dialects" that differ in their treatment of vowel elision, either devoicing or eliding completely. There is no evidence for this distinction in my data (see further discussion in §3.5.6).

1.2 Orthography and examples

A standard Aguaruna orthography was first developed in the 1950s by the SIL missionary Mildred Larson, and an official orthography was approved by the Peruvian government on 6 November 2009.[2] It is based on Spanish orthographic practices, and is mostly phonemic, except in a few respects. Orthographic <g> represents the phones [ɰ] (between vowels) and [ŋ] (syllable finally). This situation arises from an analysis by which the two were incorrectly considered allophones of one phoneme (Pike & Larson 1964). Although it misrepresents the phonology, there is no ambiguity because the two phones are in complementary distribution. Nasality is not indicated in standard orthography, although publications by the *Centro Amazónico de Antropología y Aplicación Práctica* (CAAAP) have used the convention of underlining nasal vowels, thus for example *yawaã* [ỹãɰ̃áã] 'dog' would be written <y̲a̲w̲áa>.[3] Standard orthography does distinguish (prenasalized) oral and nasal voiced stops, while I treat the former as allophones of the latter, as discussed in §3.4. Written accents are included in reference works or other material intended for use by non-native speakers,[4] but in normal usage they are only written where there is potential for ambiguity or where a word-final vowel is accented. The official Aguaruna alphabet is shown in Table 1.1, along with IPA equivalents.

Table 1.1: Standard Aguaruna orthography

Orthography	IPA equivalent
a	a
b	ᵐb
ch	t͡ʃ
d	ⁿd
e	ɨ
g	ɰ [between vowels]
g	ŋ [elsewhere]
h	ʔ
i	i

2 The relevant legislation is identified with the code 2554-2009-ED.
3 Although it does not form part of the standard orthography, the graph <ñ> is used by some speakers to represent the nasalized palatal glide [ỹ] that appears in nasal environments, so e.g. *yawaã* 'dog' would be written as <ñawaa>. This has the advantage of indicating nasality without requiring any vowel diacritic.
4 See for example the dictionaries Wipio (1996) and Uwarai et al. (1998), and CAAAP's pedagogical grammar (Regan et al. 1991).

Orthography	IPA equivalent
j	h
k	k
m	m
n	n
p	p
r	ɾ
s	s
sh	ʃ
t	t
ts	t͡s
u	u
w	w
y	j

I find the official orthography impractical for use in this grammar: the Spanish based orthography conflicts with both IPA and English orthographic norms (the graphs <h> and <j>, in particular, are potentially confusing); the dual function of <g> is not intuitively obvious, nor does it accurately reflect the Aguaruna phonemic system; and the use of underlining to mark nasality is awkward to implement, and conflicts with more widely used orthographic norms. In Chapter 3 on phonology I use standard IPA, although I follow established Americanist practice in transcribing the palatal glide as /y/ rather than /j/. In the rest of the grammar I use a blend of IPA and official orthography, aiming to provide a system that is both intuitively accessible and aesthetically more pleasing for a reader of English. The main departure from IPA is in my use of the digraphs <ch> and <sh> to represent the affricate /t͡ʃ/ and fricative /ʃ/, respectively. This use of <sh> brings with it the potential for ambiguity in a few examples where the phonemes /s/ and /h/ come together through elision of an intervening vowel; in those cases I separate the letters with an apostrophe; that is, <s'h> is to be read as IPA /sh/. Examples (1.1) and (1.2) illustrate the distinction.

(1.1)   káshai   [káʃɛi]
         'agouti'

(1.2)   díkas'hai   [ⁿdíkashɛi]
         dika-tsu-ha-i
         know+IPFV-NEG-1SG-DECL
         'I don't know'

Table 1.2 shows the graphs used in this grammar that differ from their IPA values.

Table 1.2: Non-IPA orthography used in this grammar

this grammar	IPA
b	^{m}b
ch	t͡ʃ
d	^{n}d
r	ɾ
sh	ʃ
s'h	sh
ts	t͡s
y	j

Full Aguaruna words in the text are given in the citation form, after the application of vowel elision, which is analysed as a synchronic process (see §3.5). Where relevant, the underlying form is also given. Bound morphemes are cited in the underlying form. Examples consist of four lines: the surface form (in italics), the underlying morphological form, a gloss line and a free translation. Spanish words in examples appear in Spanish orthography and are italicized in the morphological line, as in example (1.3). Note that consonant-final Spanish words typically require an epenthetic vowel /a/ prior to any further morphology being added. Loans that have been nativized to Aguaruna phonology are treated as native Aguaruna words, for example *bachit* < Sp. *machete*.

(1.3)   *dúka hospitalak*
           nu=ka   *hospital*-a=ka
           ANA=TOP   hospital-EP=TOP
           'that hospital'

Some predictable allophonic variants are not transcribed (see Chapter 3 for details), but allomorphs that are not strictly phonologically conditioned are transcribed distinctly. Nasality spreads across contiguous sequences of vowels and glides (§3.4), and all are transcribed as nasal in surface forms. Where one vowel can be identified as the source of nasality (by comparison with other forms), I transcribe just that vowel as nasal in underlying forms; otherwise I follow David Payne (1990b) in transcribing nasality on the rightmost segment with which it can be associated. There are some occurrences of /m/ and /n/ that are compulsorily denasalized at the lexical level, and I transcribe these using <b> and <d>. Those that are optionally denasalized are transcribed <m> and <n>.

1.3 Word classes

Open word classes in Aguaruna show a basic division between VERBAL and NOMINAL roots. The term nominal is used here in the classical sense, encompassing both nouns and adjectives; within this class, nouns and adjectives can be distinguished as they differ in their derivational possibilities, possessability, and ability to head an NP (although an adjective may be the only constituent of a headless NP – see Chapter 5 on NP structure, and §4.3 on the distinction between noun and adjective). The majority of their grammatical properties are shared, however, and the distinction is neutralized in their most typical functions: as the sole constituent of an NP and as the predicate in an equative or attributive clause. Because of this, nouns and adjectives are for most purposes best described as a single class of nominals.

Closed word classes are personal and demonstrative pronouns; numerals; quantifiers; adverbial words, with subclasses of manner adverbs, time words, location words, and a rich set of ideophones; a set of discourse particles; and interjections – the latter class runs through a continuum from more conventionalized words to involuntary vocalizations and many do not fit the standard phonology. Interrogative words are all members of other classes but share certain semantic and morphosyntactic properties, described in Chapter 10. There are no true conjunctions, but the discourse particle *tuhã* may function as a contrastive conjunction 'but', and the interjection *atsa* 'no' may function as a disjunction 'or' (see Chapter 12). Table 1.3 summarizes the functional slots that can be filled by the main word classes.

Table 1.3: Word classes and functional slots

	verb	noun	pronoun	dem	adjective	adverb
Core or oblique argument	–	✓	✓	✓	–	–
Equative clause complement	–	✓	✓	✓	✓	–
Head of predicate	✓	limited	–	–	limited	–
Head of NP	–	✓	✓	✓	–	–
Possessum in NP	–	✓	–	–	some	–
Possessor in NP	–	✓	✓	✓	–	–
Modifier in NP	–	some	–	✓	✓	some
Modifier of a verb	–	–	–	–	–	✓

Table 1.4 lists the word classes and the sections in which their properties are described. The remainder of this chapter gives a brief overview of these properties.

Table 1.4: Word classes

word class	described in
Noun	Chapter 4
Adjective	§4.3
Verb	Chapters 6, 8, 9, and 13
Personal and other pronouns	§4.6
Numerals	§5.3.1, §12.2.1
Quantifiers	§5.3.2, §12.2.2
Adverbial words	Chapter 12
Discourse particles	§12.4.1
Interjections	§12.4.2
Question words	Chapter 10

Word class changing derivation is described in the chapters relating to the target class. Table 1.5 lists the derivation types in terms of the source and target classes, and indicates where they are described.

Table 1.5: Word class changing derivations

source class	target class	described in
Verb	Nominal	Chapter 15
Verb, adverb	Adjective	§4.3.3
Noun	Verb	§6.6.1
Onomatopeia	Verb	§6.6.2
Pronoun	Verb	§6.6.2

1.3.1 Verbs

Verbs function as predicates. While nominals can function predicatively in equative/attributive clauses, they are restricted in their morphological possibilities (see Chapter 7). Verbs are obligatorily inflected for tense, mood, aspect, number, person OR subordination and switch reference. The only possibility of a bare verb root appearing is directly preceding an inflected auxiliary verb, and in that case the two form a single complex predicate (§6.7).

Semantically, verbs express actions, events and states. While there is an adjective class in Aguaruna, a number of property meanings are expressed with verbs, e.g. *tsɨtsɨmat* 'feel cold', *ishamat* 'be afraid'. Verb roots have inherent transitivity values, and there is a strong preference for divalent, transitive verbs. The language relies very heavily on verb roots in discourse, in particular in clause chaining constructions where many of the clauses consist only of a verb; the head-marking nature of the grammar means that overt NPs are not necessary to track referents. Verbs in this grammar are cited in a nominalized form, marked with final *-ta*, which surfaces as /t/ if the root is not monovocalic.

1.3.2 Nominals

Nominals form referring expressions, and syntactically they form noun phrases. Nouns head NPs while adjectives modify, but this distinction is not always clear, as headless NPs consisting only of a single adjective are possible. In discourse, adjectives most frequently function as predicates, and in that function they show identical formal properties to nouns. Nominals are inflected for case with phrase-level enclitics. There is no nominal number marking except with a nominalized plural-marked existential verb, syntactically a relative clause. There is no grammatical gender, nor noun classes beyond the distinction between alienably and inalienably possessible nouns.

1.3.3 Pronouns

Pronouns share most nominal morphology, and share with nouns the syntactic property of heading NPs. Unlike nouns, pronouns cannot be possessed, they do not take vocative forms, and they cannot be modified by adjectives within the NP. In discourse pronouns must have an accessible referent, whether already introduced in the discourse or introduced by a demonstrative pronoun itself through deictic reference. There is a set of personal pronouns, with distinct singular and plural forms (Table 1.7 in §1.8.2); these are the only nominals that vary for number. There is a set of demonstratives that also function anaphorically and as preposed determiners in the NP. The demonstratives form a three-way contrast between proximal *hu*, medial *anu* and distal *au*. There is a dedicated anaphoric pronoun *nu* which, like the demonstratives, may also function as a determiner. The demonstratives and the anaphoric pronoun also share the possibility of being postposed to a predicate to form a relative clause (see Chapter 16). There is one indefinite pronoun, *tikich* '(an)other'. Question words are not used with an indefinite sense, as they are in some (especially Indo-European) languages.

1.3.4 Adverbial words

In language descriptions 'adverb' tends to be a something of a disparate category. Adverbs typically divide into at least three subclasses, those of MANNER, TIME and LOCATION; and this is the case in Aguaruna. IDEOPHONES form an important fourth subclass in Aguaruna, behaving syntactically like manner adverbs but considered by native speakers to be a different class (see below). Adverbs modify predicates or clauses, and are distinguished by their very restricted range of morphology. A subset of manner adverbs is inflected for the person of the 'subject' (that is, the subject of the predicate they modify), using the same set of person markers as same-subject subordinate verbs (§12.3). Time and location words can take diminutive -*uchi* and the topic enclitic =*ka*. QUANTIFIERS typically modify NPs semantically, but pattern with adverbs in their morphology and syntax, as they are not formally part of the NP. They may also function as adverbs semantically, modifying a clause.

1.3.5 Ideophones

Ideophones are a distinct and important class, that have most in common with the manner adverbs in terms of their syntactic behaviour. Defined by Dingemanse (2012: 655) as "marked words that depict sensory imagery", ideophones in Aguaruna typically, but not always, represent sounds. For example *puhut* represents the sound of something heavy splashing into deep water, while *tapit* represents grabbing something. Ideophones cannot take any morphology, and most have the phonological form CVCVC.

1.4 Morphology

Aguaruna is both head and dependent marking at the NP and clause level. The morphology is almost entirely suffixing and basically agglutinating, although vowel elision can obscure the regularity in surface forms. There are a few cases of fusion and these are discussed below. The only trace of prefixing is a prefixed vowel that forms causative verbs. This is unproductive, the quality of the vowel is not predictable, and in some cases is accompanied by other phonological changes in the root – all very different from the generally regular and productive suffixing behaviour characteristic of the rest of the morphology. A productive suffix is also available to form causative verbs.

Phonological effects triggered by bound morphology include: accent shift; special 'combining forms' of pronominal hosts; and simplification of sequences of identical consonants. Both affixes and enclitics may trigger the first two of these effects, but enclitics do not trigger simplification of CC clusters.

1.4.1 Affix and clitic

Within the class of bound morphemes I distinguish between AFFIXES and CLITICS on syntactic grounds: affixes operate at the level of the word, while clitics operate at the phrasal or clausal level. Affixes are thus part of word formation in morphology while clitics are positioned by syntactic principles. The set of enclitics in Aguaruna is somewhat diverse, comprising five types that differ from one another in their morphological and phonological effects (Table 1.6). Those that can co-occur have strict ordering rules. The key parameters of variation are whether the enclitic has fixed or floating position, and whether it triggers accent shift in nominal stems. In addition, the case markers trigger the combining forms of pronominal hosts.

Table 1.6: Clitic types

clitic type	host	effects
accusative, locative, comitative, instrumental, ablative (§4.10)	NP; fixed position	combining form of pronominal hosts; accent shift for some
restrictive, additive, topic (§4.11, §4.12)	Constituent(s) in scope; floating	accent shift for ADDITIVE and RESTRICTIVE; no shift for TOPIC
question topic, speculative (§4.13)	Constituent(s) of marked clause; floating	accent shift
polar interrogative (§4.13)	NP or predicate; floating	accent shift on nominal
copula (§4.14)	Predicate NP; fixed	takes verbal suffixes

Fixed position enclitics are restricted to a particular constituent and are positioned by strict grammatical criteria. Case markers are enclitic to the final element of the NP, which is always a noun, adjective, personal or demonstrative pronoun. The copula enclitic must be attached to the final element of an NP functioning as the predicate of an equative/attributive clause.

Floating enclitics are more flexible in their positioning, following more pragmatic principles. The discourse markers (restrictive, topic and additive) appear on a constituent that the marker has scope over. The question topic and speculative markers are linked to specific clausal moods and are also apparently positioned according to scope. Both topic and question topic markers may appear on more than one constituent. The polar interrogative marker typically appears on the predicate, and forms part of the mood/modality paradigm, but may alternatively appear on a constituent that is the focus of the interrogation.

Those enclitics that can co-occur follow strict ordering: within case markers, locative and ablative may co-occur, in that order. Case markers may be followed by one of additive, restrictive, topic, question topic, speculative, polar interrogative, all of which are mutually exclusive. The copula enclitic may follow polar interrogative, but not any of the other enclitics, and in such cases the nominal stem may not include case marking.

Moving on to the discourse status markers, restrictive =kI is enclitic to the NP over which it has scope. The topic marker =ka is enclitic to the constituent(s) over which it has scope, or can be attached to a subordinate clause forming a conditional clause. Additive =sha(kama) is similarly enclitic to an NP constituent, but may have semantic scope over that NP or the whole clause. Encliticized to a subordinate clause, the additive marker forms a concessive clause. Interrogative and speculative clauses in addition to their verbal mood marking also involve enclitics that mark the focus of the mood operator. Polar interrogative is usually marked on the predicate, but the marker may instead be enclitic to the questioned constituent.

The copula is encliticized to nominal predicates, and is followed by verbal morphology. In some TAM combinations the copula must take the form of a separate verb.

There is one apparent and one actual case of endoclisis in the morphology of Aguaruna.[5] The apparent case is that of the enclitic copula, which may be followed by verbal suffixing morphology. In this case it is clear that the suffixes relate to the copula, that is, they are suffixed to the copula. This is clear from the fact that the copula enclitic alternates with a full morphologically free verb in some contexts.

The actual case of endoclisis involves the polar interrogative =ka. This enclitic functions as part of the verbal mood/modality paradigm, and normally appears in verbal slot G (see Chapter 6 on verbal morphology, and §10.4 on polar interrogative clauses). It may also appear on another constituent, in which case the verb takes no mood/modality marker. But when the verb is marked, and also includes the recent past tense marker -ma, polar interrogative must directly follow that suffix, in which case it precedes the person suffix. It is not clear how this unusual morphological behaviour came about. One could analyse polar interrogative as a suffix on verbs but an enclitic on other constituents (cf. Dixon's 2010: 21–22 analysis of Portuguese "endoclitic" pronouns), but this does not reflect the fact that it is clearly the same marker, whatever its position.

A final point regards the relativizing pronouns (Chapter 16). These may be EN-CLITICIZED to the predicate of the relative clause, and in previous work (Overall 2007) I treated these as the only examples of clitics. In fact, this is better described as a surface phonological process, and distinct from the morphological class of clitics.

---

5 I define endoclisis as the appearance of a clitic within a phonological word consisting of a root and affixes. In the examples discussed here, this means the clitic appears between a stem and suffixes. There are no examples of a clitic appearing within a root in Aguaruna.

1.4.2 Agglutination and fusion

Although mainly agglutinating, there is some fusion in the morphology. Before describing these cases, it is necessary to distinguish a few apparently fusional morphemes that are in fact the result of synchronic phonological processes. An illustrative example is in (1.4), where second person subject -mɨ in a declarative clause does not appear to be followed by the declarative suffix -i (compare example 1.5).

(1.4)   wɨɯamɨ
          wɨ-a-mɨ
          go-IPFV-2SG+DECL
          'you are going'

(1.5)   wɨɯahai
          wɨ-a-ha-i
          go-IPFV-1SG-DECL
          'I am going'

In this case, however, the non-appearance of the declarative suffix is due to a phonological rule, as the sequence /ɨi/ is disallowed. Despite not being manifested phonetically, the underlying presence of the suffix has a phonological effect: its presence blocks the application of apocope to the final CV syllable. Compare example (1.6), in which polar interrogative is marked on the questioned constituent leaving the verb unmarked for mood. In this case, the final syllable does undergo apocope.

(1.6)   pɨŋkɨhak puhám
          pɨŋkɨha=ka   puha-mɨ
          good=Q   live+IPFV-2SG
          'are you well?'

The same apparent fusion happens with the first person plural suffix -hi when followed by declarative -i.

   Genuine cases of fusion are associated mainly with the combination of tense markers + third person subject + declarative mood. Compare (1.7), in which tense, person and mood can be readily separated, to (1.8), in which a single suffix is the exponent of all three categories (see Chapter 8 for details of these markers).

(1.7)   wɨmahai
          wɨ-ma-ha-i
          go+PFV-RECPST-1SG-DECL
          'I went'

(1.8)   *wĩmĩ*
           wɨ-mĩ
           go+PFV-RECPST:3:DECL
           's/he went'

The most spectacular departures from straightforward agglutination involve supra-segmental morphs of two types: (i) suppression of apocope and (ii) nasality. As an example, first person plural subject in same-subject subordinate verbs is marked solely by non-application of apocope, as in example (1.9). Compare example (1.10), in which third person subject in the same context is marked by nasalization of the final vowel; as a result, both forms end in CV syllables underlyingly. Only the third person form undergoes apocope, however. Unlike the example in (1.4) above, there is no possibility of explaining this absence of apocope on purely phonological grounds.

(1.9)   *wɨɰaku*
           wɨ-a-ku
           go-IPFV-SIM+1PL:SS
           'as we were going, (we ...)'

(1.10)   *wɨɰak*
           wɨ-a-kũ
           go-IPFV-SIM+3:SS
           'as s/he was going, (s/he ...)'

Person marking in subordinate verbs is described in Chapter 13, and suppression of apocope is also a marker of some interrogative clause types, described in Chapter 10.

1.5 The noun phrase

The noun phrase consists minimally of a head noun, and may include preposed or postposed modifiers. The accusative, comitative, locative and instrumental case markers are enclitic to the final element of the NP, except where one of the following three determiners precedes the head: proximal demonstrative *hu*; distal demonstrative *au*; anaphoric pronoun *nu*. In that case all elements of the NP show case agreement. Possession is head-marked with a suffix and/or vowel change in the possessed noun, and the possessor, if it appears, takes the genitive form if it is a noun, or accusative case if it is a pronoun. Relative clauses are formed with nominalizations, or by means of pronouns postposed to a predicate (Chapter 16). Although most NPs have a simple structure, some more complex issues arise. Discontinuous

NPs are possible, and the modifier of a discontinuous NP may functionally simulate a separate argument. Headedness of NPs can be difficult to determine, as nouns and adjectives share morphology. All of these issues are discussed in Chapter 5.

1.6 Clause structure

The clausal unit describes a situation – an action, event or state. The clause consists of a single predicate, typically a verb, and its associated participants, which may be overt NPs. Clauses can be categorized by two sets of criteria: the first is finiteness, and relates to the the predicate itself, and the grammatical categories that are (or are not) associated with the predicate in any given clause. The second, grammatical relations and transitivity, is the relation between the predicate and its associated participants.

The syntactic constituents that combine to form a clause in Aguaruna are noun phrase(s) and predicate. Minor syntactic constituents are adjective phrase and manner adverb phrase: each consists of an optional modifier slot in pre-head position in addition to the head. Neither time words nor location words can be modified, thus always form single-word constituents. There is a strong verb-final tendency in all clause types. Subordinate clauses are always verb-final, while finite clauses show variation for pragmatic purposes. Constituent ordering is discussed in more detail in Chapter 18.

Subordinate clauses are embedded, to the extent that they are treated as syntactic constituents of the clause on a par with NP arguments. Only nominalized clauses can take case marking and function as core arguments (but see Chapter 17 for discussion of apparent examples of finite clause complements to the verb *wainat* 'see'). Floating enclitics marking discourse pragmatic status and focus of clausal mood operators can equally well attach to subordinate clauses as to NPs, and subordinate clauses can be centre-embedded.

Verbs can be categorized as intransitive, transitive, ditransitive or copula, on the basis of the number and type of arguments they subcategorize for. This then dictates the type of clause each verb can appear in. Valency changing derivation can be used to adjust a verb root's subcategorization profile. Subjects and speech act participant (SAP) objects are indexed with verbal suffixes and NP arguments are case-marked to show their role in the clause – core arguments take nominative or accusative case. Equative/attributive clauses and copular clauses headed by copula verbs all require two arguments, a subject and a complement. In the former, the complement is marked with an enclitic copula which hosts finite verbal morphology. Verbless equative/attributive clauses are possible within a highly restricted range of TAM values (§7.8).

The predicate may consist of just one verb, a predicate nominal, or a non-finite main verb and finite auxiliary. The main verb in an auxiliary construction may take one of several forms, and it is difficult to draw a sharp distinction between auxilia-tion and clause-combining constructions (§6.7). Nominalized verbs are widely used in relativization and complementation, and also function as finite verbs in some narrative genres.

1.7 Grammatical relations

Aguaruna follows a nominative-accusative alignment. Grammatical relations centre on SUBJECT and OBJECT, and participant nominalizations contrast SUBJECT with NON-SUBJECT – the latter includes objects and oblique participants such as location and instrument. Subjects take unmarked nominative case, and objects take accusative case, marked with the enclitic =na. There is a scenario-conditioned split in accusa-tive case marking (§7.3), whereby third person objects remain unmarked if the sub-ject is first person plural or second person. Case marking of all objects (notional direct (O) and indirect (E) objects as well as those added by applicative derivation) is identical. There is only one morphological slot for marking SAP objects on the verb, and clauses with more than one SAP object are avoided (§7.3).

There is no voice alternation in Aguaruna. Productive valency increasing deri-vations are applicative, which typically adds a semantic beneficiary or maleficiary, and causative; a few valency reducing derivations are unproductive (Chapter 6).

1.8 Finiteness

Finiteness can be defined functionally for clauses and formally for verbs. A finite clause is one that is specified for the categories of TENSE and MOOD. These categories allow cognitive grounding of the clause, deictically in time, and in reality status. Finite clauses also have fully specified arguments. Functionally, a finite clause can function independently, constituting a well-formed grammatical utterance. The finite verb in Aguaruna is defined as one which can head a finite clause, and is marked for the full range of verbal grammatical categories. In particular, the catego-ries of TENSE, PERSON and MOOD/MODALITY are obligatorily specified in finite verbs, distinct from non-finite verb forms and other word classes. Tense is definitional for finite verbs. Person of the subject is also marked on some subordinate verbs and manner adverbs, but using a different set of suffixes. Mood and modality form a single paradigm encompassing speech act distinctions, epistemicity and markers of speaker's attitude. There is an almost perfect co-occurrence of mood marking with finite verbs, but polar interrogative may be marked on constituents other than the verb – the clausal scope of speech act distinctions makes this possible. Aspect is not a definitional criterion of finiteness for Aguaruna verbs: some finite forms are un-marked for aspect, while some non-finite forms do take aspect marking. The basic template for a finite verb is given in Figure 1.1 (a more detailed schema appears in §6.1).

	A	B	C	D	E	F	G
ROOT	VALENCY	OBJECT	ASPECT	NEGATION	TENSE	SUBJECT	MOOD

Figure 1.1: Morphological structure of a finite verb

Verbal morphology may be added directly to the unmarked root plus any valency changing and object markers in slots A and B, or to one of the following four stems (all consisting of ROOT + (A) + (B) + C): IMPERFECTIVE; PERFECTIVE; POTENTIAL; DURATIVE. Some verbal suffixes always select a particular stem, others are more flexible and the choice of stem then alters the meaning of the form, as shown by the minimal pair (1.11), with perfective stem, and (1.12), with durative stem.

(1.11)   *yuwáta*
         yu-a-ta
         eat-PFV-IMP
         'eat (it)!'

(1.12)   *yuumatá*
         yu-ma-ta
         eat-DUR-IMP
         'keep on eating!'

Subordinate verbs have suffixes marking their subordinate status in slot E instead of tense, and lack mood marking (slot G). Most subordinate verbs and some manner adverbs take suffixes marking person of the subject, but these are a different set from the ones used in finite verbs. All subordinate verb forms are marked for SWITCH-REFERENCE, a category that is absent from finite verbs (Chapter 13).

While a finite verbal clause must be headed by a finite verb, the question remains what happens in clauses with non-verbal predicates. In copular clauses, the copula may be enclitic to the predicate nominal or it may be a separate fully inflected verb, depending on TAM and person values. Both enclitic and verbal copulas are marked with finite verbal morphology. In present tense, declarative copular clauses with third-person singular subject, a verbless construction is possible. This can be considered to still be specified for the clausal categories of tense and mood, as it is restricted to specific values of these categories. Non-verbal predication is discussed further in §7.9.

1.8.1 Tense and aspect

Aguaruna has four synthetic past tenses, plus a past tense nominalizer, and two synthetic future tenses, plus a future nominalizer. A range of periphrastic tensed constructions allows for expression of aspectual distinctions (Chapter 8). Most verb forms, whether finite or not, are formed on either a perfective or imperfective stem, and these aspect-marked stems may also mark number of the subject (§8.3).

1.8.2 Person and number

Verbal marking of subjects involves a number of distinct suffixes in slot F, which resemble the free pronouns only in second person. Table 1.7 shows the free pronouns, which distinguish three persons and two numbers. Bound person marking paradigms generally distinguish four persons: 1sg, 1pl, 2 and 3. Second person singular and plural are obligatorily distinguished only in finite verbs, while third person shows distinct plural marking in only a few contexts. First person plural is marked identically to second person in the object marking paradigm, and to third person in the possession paradigm (see Table 1.9).

Table 1.7: Free pronouns

	singular	plural
1	*wii*	*ii ~ hutii* (see §4.6)
2	*amɨ*	*atum* /atumɨ/
3	*nɨ̃ɨ*	*dita*

Morphological alternations show that the underlying forms of 1sg and 3sg are /wi/ and /nɨ̃/, respectively, with vowel lengthening in free forms to preserve a minimal word requirement (see §3.5.1). The final /mɨ/ of the second person pronouns surfaces throughout the subject paradigms, and changes to /mi/ when followed by certain bound morphemes. In contrast to the stability of the second person forms, first and third person are represented by remarkably diverse forms. There are also differences in the conditioning environments for the different allomorphs – second and third person subject markers in finite verbs differ depending on the tense of the verb, while first person singular and plural are not affected by this change (Table 1.8).

Table 1.8: Verbal subject markers

	finite verb		subordinate verb
	non-past tense	past tense	
1sg	-ha	-ha	-nu
1pl	-hi	-hi	zero / -i
2sg	-mɨ	-umɨ	-mɨ
2pl	-humɨ	-uhumɨ	-mɨ ~ -humɨ
3	-wa	portmanteau TENSE + PERSON	nasality

Verbal number is obligatorily marked for SAP subjects of finite verbs. There are also optional plural markers in slot C available for all persons, which can combine with the plural subject markers in slot F. Optional plural marking differs in imperfective and perfective stems, and does not appear in stems that lack aspect marking (see §8.3). In subordinate verbs, only first person makes an obligatory number distinction; use of the second person plural form is optional.

Verbal object marking (Table 1.9) is quite distinct from subject marking, and appears in slot B, except in the combination of first person subject with second person object, marked in slot F. Verb roots fall into two classes based on their marking of objects and the form of the applicative suffix, all of which take initial /h/ in the first class and /t/ in the second (§6.3). The applicative suffix is homophonous with the first person singular markers in both verb classes. Third person objects are not marked on the verb. The second person object markers when subject is third person include the sequence /ma/, which may relate to the /mɨ/ that marks second person in other paradigms (the allomorph -pa is a phonologically conditioned contraction of -tama). When the subject is first person, second person object is marked with the suffix -mɨ combined with the subject marker in slot F (analysed as a portmanteau in §6.3.1), and the verb class distinction is neutralized. First person plural objects are marked as second person, but a distinct suffix -kahatu may be used to mark first person plural exclusive object. This suffix is otherwise used to mark generic human objects.

Nominal possession markers have some similarity to verbal markers, but only the second person forms are clearly cognate (again we see the form /mɨ/). There are two possession classes, one signalled with vowel change and nasalization in third person and the other with a suffix. First person plural possessors are marked identically to third person. The distinction between classes is neutralized with first person singular possessor. First person singular -hu may be cognate with the verbal object marker in the hu verb class, or it may reflect an old possession marker – note that all the possession markers in the suffix class include initial /hu/ or /h/. See §4.8 for details of possession morphology.

Table 1.9: Verbal object markers and nominal possession markers

| | object on verb | | possessor on noun | |
	hu class	tu class	vowel change class	suffix class
1sg	-hu	-tu	-hu	-hu
1pl	(as 2) / -kahatu	(as 2) / -kahatu	(as 3)	(as 3)
2	-hama (3 subject) -mɨ (1 subject)	-tama / -pa (3 subject) -mɨ (1 subject)	vowel change + -mɨ	-humɨ
3	unmarked	unmarked	vowel change + nasality	-hĩ

In sum, person marking is disparate not just in the forms used, but also in the arrangement of the paradigms involved. There is no motivation to treat the verbal markers of subjects and objects or the nominal markers of possessors as bound forms of the pronouns, as they are quite distinct.

1.8.3 Mood and modality

In general, finite verbs are marked for mood/modality, a single paradigm that covers traditional speech acts as well as epistemic and attitudinal distinctions. Major mood types are declarative, interrogative, exclamatory and imperative; declarative and interrogative moods subsume various formally and functionally distinct subtypes.

Declarative is the basic form of a statement, and as such is functionally unmarked; formally, however, declarative is marked with a suffix while exclamative is zero-marked. The imperative marker is cognate with the future tense markers, and appears in a different morphological slot to the other mood/modality markers.

For some mood/modality values, the morphological marking may be distributed through the clause. Interrogative clauses mark one or more constituents with the question topic enclitic =sha, and in some cases this enclitic itself may mark interrogative mood. Speculative, an epistemic modality marker, utilizes both a verbal marker and a dedicated focus-marking enclitic. Polar questions are marked with the enclitic =ka which typically appears on the verb in slot G, but may also appear on a questioned constituent, leaving the predicate unmarked.

1.9 Subordinate and nominalized verbs

While finite verbs are obligatorily specified for tense and mood/modality, non-finite verbs never are; this is the criterial morphological distinction between the two groups. Subordinate verbs may take other inflectional categories such as aspect and person – although the person paradigm is distinct from that used in finite verbs (see Table 1.8 above). Non-finite verbs fall into two general groups: subordinate verbs and nominalizations. All subordinate verbs are obligatorily marked for switch-reference, and most also take aspect and person marking. A clause headed by a subordinate verb must be syntactically linked to a finite clause, although this link may be mediated by another subordinate clause; that is, subordinate clauses may be nested.

Nominalization is an important part of Aguaruna grammar. Nominalized verbs by definition function as constituents of a noun phrase, either heading or modifying. They generally take neither person nor switch-reference marking (see §15.3 for some exceptions to these generalizations), but some are marked for perfective/imperfective aspect. Nominalizations find use in clause combining as relative (Chapter 16) and complement clauses (Chapter 17), and one type of nominalization may also function as a finite verb, where it functions as a non-firsthand evidentiality strategy (§15.5.3).

1.10 Clause combining

Aguaruna can be characterized as a clause-chaining language. Texts in all genres have few finite verbs relative to non-finite forms. The non-finite verb forms are specified for fewer grammatical categories than finite forms, and are in that sense morphologically dependent. However, they do not necessarily share the operators of their associated finite clause. Unlike finite verbs, the verbs of subordinate clauses are marked for switch-reference. In terms of narrative structure, non-finite verb forms may be part of the main event line.

Syntactically, the non-finite clauses are treated as constituents of a matrix clause, and thus subordinate. The syntactic evidence for this comes from two sources: firstly, subordinate clauses may host floating mood enclitics and discourse enclitics; and secondly, subordinate clauses may be centre-embedded. Subordinate clauses may also be nested, in the sense that one may be dependent upon another, not necessarily directly upon a finite clause (§13.7).

The notion of SENTENCE is not particularly useful for Aguaruna grammar: the basic multiclausal construction is the clause chain, consisting of one finite clause and one or more associated subordinate clauses. The difficulty with identifying this construction with the sentence of traditional grammar is that the non-finite clauses, while subordinate by morpho-syntactic criteria, are not necessarily so by semantic or pragmatic criteria.

Bridging constructions, in which the first verb of a clause chain recapitulates the final verb of the preceding chain, are also widely used in texts (§14.8), and nominalizations may also function in clause chaining (see §15.5.2). Coordination of finite clauses is possible, though rare (§14.7).

1.10.1 Switch-reference

All subordinate clauses are marked for switch-reference. Most of the switch-reference marking involves a reflex of the 'different subject' suffix *-(n)ĩ*, and follow the canonical pattern of marking the subordinate clause as having the same or different subject from the controlling clause. This is a robust distinction in simple bi-clausal constructions in Aguaruna. Two subordinate clause markers do not follow the canonical pattern, instead requiring that a common argument appear in both the marked and controlling clause, in the specific grammatical functions shown in Table 1.10. This typologically unusual type of switch-reference is a notable feature of Panoan languages (Loos 1999; Valenzuela 2003). The non-inflecting subordinate verb forms do not receive any person marking, nor any reflex of the different subject suffix *-(n)ĩ*.

Table 1.10: Non-inflecting dependent verb markers

suffix	stem	role of common argument:	
		in marked clause	in controlling clause
-ma	perfective or imperfective	NON-SUBJECT	SUBJECT
-tatamana	unmarked	SUBJECT	OBJECT

The use of switch-reference marking in discourse goes beyond reference tracking and into narrative structure, as different-subject clauses correlate with background-ed information. Issues related to multiclausal constructions are discussed in Chapter 14, and narrative structure in Chapter 18.

2 Cultural and historical context

2.1 The Chicham languages

The Chicham language family is usually described as having four members: Shuar,[1] Achuar-Shiwiar,[2] Huambisa (or Wampis),[3] and Aguaruna (Wise 1999). Achuar and Shiwiar, although treated as two dialects of a single language in the literature (Fast et al. 1996), are considered to be distinct ethnic groups with distinct languages by their members (Martin Kohlberger, personal communication [Shiwiar]; Gerardo García Chinchay, personal communication [Achuar]). The precise details of the linguistic relationships within the family are not clear. Aguaruna is described as the "most diverse" by Wise (1999: 312), and phonologically it clearly stands apart from the other three languages due to a historic merger of Proto-Chicham (henceforth PC) */r/ and */h/ to give the phoneme /h/ in Aguaruna, where the other languages retain both /r/ and /h/. On the basis of this, the traditional approach has placed Aguaruna in opposition to a Shuar subgroup comprising the other languages (Fabre 2005; Wise 1999: 309; Stark 1985), but this division is based on an erroneous reconstruction of a PC phoneme */ŋ/ from which the languages of the Shuar subgroup innovated their /r/ (David Payne 1978, 1981b). On that basis, Aguaruna is seen as the most conservative language, and therefore an earlier split of Aguaruna from the rest of the family is implicated – see Figure 2.1.

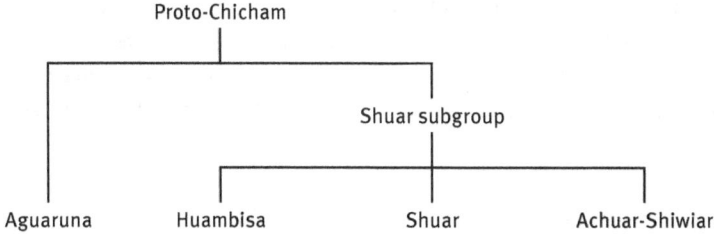

Figure 2.1: Chicham family tree including "Shuar subgroup" (after Stark 1985: 176)

---

1 Population 46,669 (http://www.ethnologue.org/show_language.asp?code=jiv); or 32,000 (Wise 1999: 309).

2 Population 5,000 (http://www.ethnologue.org/show_language.asp?code=acu); or 5,500 (Wise 1999: 309).

3 Population 9,333 (source: http://www.ethnologue.org/show_language.asp?code=hub); or 6,000 – 10,000 (Wise 1999: 309).

A revised reconstruction of PC */h/ and */r/ (see §3.2.4, and detailed discussion in Overall 2008) shows that in fact Aguaruna has innovated, and the /r/ of the other languages is a shared retention. In the absence of any shared innovation, there is no evidence to support any internal subgrouping. In fact, given the geographical proximity, high degree of mutual intelligibility, and sustained contact, any attempt at a family tree model of relationships within Chicham is probably futile (cf. Aikhenvald & Dixon 2001: 4). The following comment made by Fast et al. (1996) points toward the same conclusion.

> [E]n el dialecto shiwiar-maina que se habla por los ríos Corrientes y Macusari se hallan términos poco comunes en las áreas achuar, términos que, por increíble que parezca, también se hallan en el aguaruna … a pesar de que los shiwiar-maina viven más alejados de los aguaruna que los achuar.

> [In the Shiwiar-Maina dialect, spoken along the Corrientes and Macusari rivers, are found terms that are not common in the Achuar areas; terms that, incredible though it may sound, are also found in Aguaruna … in spite of the fact that the Shiwiar-Maina live further from the Aguaruna than do the Achuar.]

> Fast et al. (1996: 12)

Work currently underway suggests that Aguaruna is the only clearly demarcated linguistic group. Huambisa–Shuar is effectively a dialect continuum (Leandro Calvo, personal communication), as is Achuar–Shiwiar (Martin Kohlberger, personal communication). Furthermore, there is evidence for considerable mutual intelligibility between Aguaruna and Huambisa. This suggests that the Chicham family as a whole is better described as a cluster of dialects. As political units, the tribal groupings are well-established, and traditionally were in a permanent state of warfare with each other. In the modern era, intertribal warfare has been replaced with a sense of unity of the Chicham-speaking peoples, at least in Peru where the idea of an *etnia awajún-wampís* [Aguaruna-Huambisa ethnic group] has entered political discourse.

2.2 History

The Andes are at their lowest in the Cajamarca region of north Peru, thus forming a natural area of contact between coast, highland and lowland zones directly to the southwest of Chicham speaking area. The first Europeans to make contact with Chicham speakers travelled across the Andes from the coast, around the middle of the 16th century (Taylor & Descola 1981; Stirling 1938).

Until recently the language family has been known as Jivaroan, from the ethnonym *xíbaro* (modern Sp. *jívaro* or *jíbaro*). This term was introduced in the 16th century, and is a hispanification of the autodenomination **shiwar(a)* 'person', the source of the modern ethnonyms Shuar, Shiwiar and Achuar (< *achu* 'swamp-palm' + *shiwar(a)* 'people') (Gnerre 1973). The same etymon is present in modern Aguaruna as *shiwaŋ* 'enemy'. The term *jívaro/jíbaro* has become an offensive slur in modern Ecuador, and following Katan Jua's (2011) proposal, the linguistic family is now referred to as Chicham, the common word for 'language'.

Over the ensuing centuries, a multitude of more specific ethnonyms that were based on names of leaders or local watercourses gradually settled into the modern ethnonyms. A further group, the Antipas, were widely mentioned until the early 19th century, but disappeared from the record some time in the early 20th century, leaving no linguistic data (Loukotka 1968). Up de Graff (1923) spent some time living among Antipas in the late 19th century, and some linguistic information can be gleaned from his memoir. A list of names of Antipa men includes *Najáncos*, from the toponym *Naranjos* ('orange trees' in Spanish) and *Quiájui*, which is translated as 'darkness'. This can be clearly identified with the Aguaruna form in (2.1).

(2.1)   *kiyáhui*
          kĩya-ha-u=i
          become.dark-PFV-NMLZ=COP:3:DECL
          'it has become dark'

The two words *Najáncos* and *Quiájui* provide clear examples of [h] (orthographic <j>) < *r. In *Najáncos*, the <r> of Spanish appears as /h/ in the Antipa form. In *Quiájui*, the perfective suffix -*ha* has cognates -*ra* in the other Chicham languages and is the reflex of PJ *-ra. This evidence is enough to conclude that the Antipas spoke a Chicham language that shared the merger of */r/ and */h/ with Aguaruna. Up de Graff (1923) shows that Antipas and Aguarunas identified themselves as separate (and hostile) political units in the mid to late 19th century, and it is likely that there were some linguistic differences, given the common Chicham pattern of marking tribal identity by linguistic differences. It is not clear what happened to the Antipas, but the most likely explanation is that they were absorbed by the Aguarunas (see further discussion in Overall 2016b).

Early accounts of "Xibaros" (i.e. Chicham speakers) place them on the upper Santiago River, as with Rodriguez' (1684) account of a 1655 expedition:

[Padre Raymundo] Difpuſo ſus embarcaciones, y navegando el Marañon arriba, llegò à las juntas de el Rio de Santiago, y navegando por èl contra la corriente, dentro de pocos dias diò viſta à la Provincia de los Xibaros...

[Padre Raymundo set forth his vessels, and travelling up the Marañon River he arrived at the mouth of the Santiago River, and travelling up that river, after a few days the province of the Xibaros came into view]

Rodriguez (1684: 206)

Von Murr (1785) also places Chicham speakers on the Santiago River:

> Die Wohnsitze der Xibaros erſtrecken ſich durch meiſtens unwegſame Berge und Thäler, mit denen beyderſeits der obere Santyagofluß weit und breit umrungen iſt, und mit welchen ſie die Natur ſelbſt wider alle feindliche Anfälle beſtens verſchanzet hat.

> [The residences of the Xibaros stretch through mostly impenetrable mountains and valleys, with which both banks of the upper Santiago River are surrounded far and wide, and by means of which Nature itself has protected them very well against all enemy attacks.]
>
> von Murr (1785: 112)[4]

Maldonado's (1750) map places "Xibaros" on the mid and upper Santiago and "Ahuarunes" (i.e. Aguarunas) on the left bank of the Marañón, just upstream from the mouth of the Santiago. This was the first mention of the ethnonym *Aguaruna* (Guallart 1990: 13), and also the first evidence of a division between Aguaruna and the other Chicham groups. Later reports place Aguarunas and Antipas on the Marañón centred on the Pongo de Manseriche, which lies just downriver from the mouth of the Santiago. Rivet (1907) places Aguarunas further to the East, and Antipas in the Cordillera del Cóndor. Since then Aguaruna settlements have spread in all directions, as far as Bagua to the West, Moyobamba to the South and Saramiriza to the East, with titled communities in Cajamarca, Amazonas, San Martín and Loreto regions.

As for the etymology of the word *Aguaruna*, there is no consensus to be found. It does not seem to stem from any Chicham language. Naïve speculation suggests that the name means 'water people', combining Sp. *agua* 'water' with Qu. *runa* 'people'; but most authors consider a purely Quechuan etymology more likely, and a number of sources have been proposed. Uwarai et al. (1998: 3) suggest that:

> el término «aguaruna» proviene del quichua amazónico y significa «gente de las alturas». «Awa» significa «arriba» en el dialecto quichua del río Pastaza y «runa» significa «gente».

> [The term *aguaruna* comes from Amazonian Quechua and means 'people of the highlands'. *Awa* means 'above' in the Quechua dialect of the Pastaza River and *runa* means 'people'.]

Larson & Dodds (1985: 308) suggest that "[t]he name Aguaruna most likely comes from the Quechua words *awax* (weaving) *runa* (man) because the men are the weavers in this culture." Corbera (1994: 18-19) adds to these two suggestions the possibility that the first element comes from Qu. *háwa* 'foreign, stranger' (cf. *hawa runa* 'foreigner' in Hornberger & Hornberger 1977); and Gnerre (1976: 306) suggests a source in Qu. *auca-runa* 'savage man'. Given that there are as many proposed etymologies as there are analysts, the only clear conclusion to be drawn is that we

---

4 I am grateful to Gerd Jendraschek for his help in translating von Murr.

simply do not know the etymology of 'Aguaruna'; we do know, however, that his-panification or folk-etymological alteration of a Quechuan term is a likely source.[5]

The native autodenomination *awahun* /awahuni/ is a phonological adaptation of the Spanish term *aguaruna* (or its Quechuan source). In present day Peru this is the official demonym, with the orthographic form *awajún*. Amongst themselves, Aguaruna speakers more commonly use the autodenomination *iiniá* (< *ii=nĩ=ya* 1pl=LOC=ABL) '(one) of us' (Isaías Dati, personal communication); this term contrasts with *apach* 'non-Aguaruna' (< *apa-uchi* (father-DIM) 'grandfather'). In earlier usage *apach* generally referred to *mestizos*, or mixed-race Peruvians, while the term *kistian* (< Sp. *cristiano* 'Christian') was used for Europeans or Euro-Peruvians – the latter term is no longer in common use. Non-Peruvians may also be referred to with the term *iriŋku* from Spanish *gringo*. The Aguaruna language is referred to as *iiniá chicham* 'our language', in contrast to *apach chicham* 'Spanish'.

2.3 Traditional and modern culture

Chicham languages are closely related, and the groups share essentially the same culture. Karsten (1935), after visiting Shuar communites in Ecuador, says of his first encounter with Aguarunas:

> I soon found that the material culture of the Aguarunas was essentially the same as that of the Ecuadorian Jibaros [=Shuar] ... On the whole a great uniformity characterizes the Jibaro culture in spite of the enormous areas which it covers and the numerous sub-tribes into which the people is divided. The same seems to be true of their customs and religious beliefs, as far as I have been able to study them.
>
> Karsten (1935: 80)

The major anthropological works on Chicham culture are Karsten (1935), Stirling (1938) and Harner (1973), and the following brief overview represents a synthesis of the information in those three works.

Chicham speakers traditionally subsisted by swidden horticulture, hunting, and fishing, and most still do so today. Traditional *uum* (blowguns) and *tsɨntsak* (poisoned darts) have been largely replaced with shotguns, although blowguns are still used for small game. The same word *tsɨntsak* refers to blowgun darts and the magical "darts" that shamans use to cause sickness and death. Fish are caught using traps and poison *timu* (Sp. *barbasco*, *Lonchocarpus urucu*). The Aguaruna term is

---

5 Even so, it is important to bear in mind that the name may not be of Quechuan origin at all – like the ethnonym *Mayoruna*, which is probably a folk-etymological corruption of a Cocama word, and not Qu. *mayo* 'river' + *runa* 'people' as one might reasonably assume (David Fleck, personal communication).

shared by a number of languages in the area, and is probably originally from Tupí-Guaraní. Staple food crops are manioc and plantains, and corn, sweet potatoes, coconuts, papaya, peanuts among others are also cultivated. A large portion of the manioc is consumed in the form of *nihamanch* (Sp. *masato*), a beverage made from masticated and fermented manioc.

Households normally consist of a man and his wife or wives (formerly typically 2 or 3 – nowadays monogamy is the most common pattern) and children, and in some cases elderly parents. Each household traditionally lived at a distance of at least a few hundred metres from the nearest neighbour, and uxorilocality was the norm, with new husbands joining their father-in-law's household until the union produced the first child, at which point the young couple would set up their own household.

Prior to Christian missionary activity the Chicham people did not have a theistic religion. Their beliefs centred around a spirit world, which was visible only under the influence of plant-derived hallucinogens. The three most important plants are *datïm* (*Banisteriopsis spp.*; Sp. *ayahuasca, yagé*), *baikua* (angel's trumpet; *Brugmansia spp.* or *Datura spp.*; Sp. *toé*) and *tsaaŋ* (tobacco; *Nicotiana spp.*). While tobacco is a narcotic, not a hallucinogenic, it is often used in conjunction with the other two plants. All are traditionally consumed in liquid preparations. Young men would seek a vision of a spirit said to be the manifestation of ancestral warriors (*ahutap* in Aguaruna, *arutam* in the other Chicham languages). A person who has received such a vision is known as *waimaku* (< *waima-ka-u* = see.vision-PFV-NMLZ). The power thus obtained ensured success in battle, and once a man gained spirit power, he was seized with a desire to kill, and began to take part in head-hunting raids and warfare. Before the widespread use of shotguns, warfare was carried out with lances and wooden shields. Much scholarly and popular attention has focused on Chicham speakers' head-hunting, particularly the shrinking of a slain enemy's head to make a trophy called a *tsantsa*. It is enough to consider the titles of some works on Chicham culture to see how shrunken heads have piqued the interest of the reading public: *Head Hunters of the Amazon* (Up de Graff 1923); *Head-hunters of Western Amazonas* (Karsten 1935); *Off With Their Heads* (Von Hagen 1937); *Jivaro: Among the Headshrinkers of the Amazon* (Flornoy 1953); *Shrunken Heads* (Castner 2004). Details of the head-shrinking process and associated beliefs and rituals can be found in all the listed works, in particular Castner (2004). Shamans would obtain their power not just through visions, but also by learning from an older shaman. Shamans were divided into two types: cursing and healing. As the names imply, the aid of the former was sought when a man wished to have a curse placed on an enemy, while the latter were employed to combat sickness. Rubenstein (2002) reports that among the Shuar, Ecuadorian Quichua-speaking shamans are widely acknowledged to have superior shamanic skills, and most Shuar shamans studied with

Quichua-speaking teachers. Visions remain very important to the culture, and now-adays are used to gain insight into future events or to help solve difficult problems.

Starting in the early 20th century contact was made by evangelical missionaries, most importantly those working for the Summer Institute of Linguistics (Larson & Dodds 1985). Their efforts in conversion and education resulted in a high penetration of bilingual schools (the first school was established in 1953), high literacy in both Aguaruna and Spanish, and widespread acceptance of Christianity. Today the majority of Aguaruna people live in villages within areas of native title, most of which have primary schools and churches, along with a few secondary schools and health posts. The population has been expanding rapidly due to the introduction of modern health care and reduction in warfare. This growth, combined with the new village lifestyle, has led to a lack of resources, especially fish and game, in the more heavily-populated areas. As a result many Aguaruna leaders feel a strong motivation to find alternative forms of subsistence, such as raising livestock and fish farming. Production of cash crops and artefacts for trade has also increased. The Aguaruna are in general a very politically motivated people, and work actively to preserve their language, territory and culture. Many native political organizations in Peru have a large number of Aguaruna people in positions of power, and the Shuar are recognized as having a similar political presence in Ecuador (Rubenstein 2002). Early accounts of contact with Chicham speakers typically mention the egalitarian and fiercely independent nature of the societies, as in Colini's (1883: 339) statement: "Il carattere principale di questi selvaggi è un amore straordinario per la loro indipendenza e libertà." [The main characteristic of these savages is an extraordinary love for their independence and freedom.]

2.4 Indigenous linguistic tradition

Prior to the establishment of schools, Aguaruna culture was completely non-literate, with a rich body of traditional knowledge encoded in stories and songs. A detailed study of Aguaruna oral tradition lies beyond the scope of this work, however a brief outline follows. There are three important discourse genres: narrative, traditional songs and oratory. The bulk of the data I have collected is traditional narratives.

Narratives can be divided into two formally distinct categories: personal and reported. Personal narrative is presented as the speaker's firsthand experience, and implies that the speaker witnessed the events described; reported narrative by contrast implies that the speaker is relating information that they heard from elsewhere. This distinction is not overtly recognized in the native tradition, and all stories are grouped together under the label *auŋmatbau* 'things told'. Grammatically, there tend to be longer clause chains (more subordinate clauses) in narratives than in conversation. Because traditional stories are generally well known, reference tracking is not as important in this genre as one might expect. A distinct narrative modality, marked with the word *tuwahamĩ* (< *tuta* 'say'), is used only in stories and functions as a marker of genre, as well as marking the information as hearsay (Chapter 9). Nominalizations formed with the suffix -*u* may function as finite verbs, and this seems to be a marker of non-firsthand evidentiality (§15.5; Overall 2014a). Personal narrative has more finite verbs, and consequently a higher proportion of bridging constructions (described in §14.8).

There are two traditional song types: *nampɨt*, sung while drinking and dancing, and *anɨn*, magic songs. Since the introduction of Christianity, religious songs (with the borrowed Spanish name *himno* /imno/ 'hymn') have been added as a third song type. The religious songs use European tunes and the lyrics follow the same patterns as everyday language. There are also distinct verbs referring to performing the different song types: *nampɨt*, *anɨnhut*, *kantamat* (< Sp. *cantar* 'sing'), respectively. The verb *nampɨt* means 'drink *nihamanch* (manioc beer), dance and sing', all at the same time, the three activities being closely associated in Chicham culture. A traditional drinking party involves a group of people dancing and each singing their own song, set to the same basic rhythm. The lyrics are typically largely improvised on the spot, and the tune is based on a general template. The subject-matter of a *nampɨt* is typically flirtatious, as they are addressed to a dancing partner of the opposite sex. A nonsensical refrain *hanuyamayaa, yamayaaduu* is common to all *nampɨt*; it is sung to state the tune at the beginning of the song and as a kind of chorus between verses – this also allows the singer a brief break to compose the next verse. In spite of the introduction of modern recorded pop music, *nampɨt* remain an important part of contemporary Aguaruna culture, and a few Aguaruna pop bands have even used *nampɨt* style in their songs.

Anɨn magic songs were traditionally sung on many occasions, by both men and women, with the general goal of ATTRACTING something, be it a romantic partner, game animals or a good harvest. They are not intended to be performed for an audience, and may be hummed or even recited entirely in the "singer's" head; the lyrical content is typically addressed to the entity that the singer wants to influence: a potential romantic partner, game animals or *Nuŋkui*, the garden spirit. *Anɨn* are more formalized than *nampɨt*, and may be passed on from generation to generation, preserving archaic language. Converts to Christianity generally avoid singing *anɨn* as spells, but many still know the songs; Christian consultants were happy to find people to sing such songs for me to record. The tunes are similar to *nampɨt*, but instead of the nonsensical refrain characteristic of *nampɨt*, *anɨn* typically begin with a refrain of [wiyaa wiyaa] 'I, I' < *wi-yaa* (1SG-EP). Taylor & Chau (1983) give a fuller description of *anɨn* and other song types.

Oratorical ability is highly valued in Chicham society, and is remarked upon by observers almost as much as the head-hunting practices. Most anthropological works devote some space to a description of the prolonged and and forceful speeches that are characteristic of Chicham public speaking. Stirling (1938) describes one man's oratorical efforts as consisting of:

> ...shouting in a rhythmic manner, stamping his feet and making warlike gestures with his lance, which he brandished in his right hand.
>
> Stirling (1938: 98)

And he goes on to describe the following speaker:

> He likewise talked for more than half an hour while various of the seated men interjected occasional remarks, creating a terrific uproar; not unlike the effect produced by an evangelist haranguing his congregation, punctuated with the Amens and Hallelujahs of his listeners.
>
> Stirling (1938: 98)

In any group discussion, all of the men present will expect to be given an opportunity to speak as a point of etiquette (Larson & Dodds 1985). When schools were first being established in the early 1960s, after the first generation of Aguaruna teachers had been trained, delegations from Aguaruna communities gathered to request schools for their communities.

> Each member of each delegation insisted on giving a speech, Aguaruna style. If there were eight men in a delegation, their request was repeated eight times – in a loud oration, punctuated appropriately with spitting and foot stomping.
>
> Larson & Dodds (1985: 85)

Harner (1973: 139) reports that a *waimaku*, a man who has received spirit power, "tends to speak with great forcefulness" as a result of the increased strength, intelligence and self-confidence furnished by the *ahutap* spirit. A desire to advertise one's possession of spirit power has probably helped to drive the tradition of forcefulness in oratory.

Accounts of visitors to Chicham communities commonly describe a particular oratorical tradition of elaborate greeting rituals, the *inimat*. This ritual forms a special subtype of oratorical tradition. When a visitor arrives at a house, the host will sit in silence for anything from a few minutes to a whole day while the visitors are served *nihamanch* (manioc beer) by the women of the house. When ready, the host begins a long shouted conversation with each visitor in turn. The conversation combines a formulaic element, asking after the health of family members, and a more "free-form" element, in which important news is related. Larson & Dodds (1985) describe a traditional greeting ritual in about 1970; an Aguaruna man named Dantuchu visits the house of another Aguaruna man in the company of non-Aguaruna road workers. The host soon realizes that Dantuchu is Aguaruna:

> Immediately his host began the formal Aguaruna greeting process. Dantuchu and he exchanged names and the names of all their relatives.
>
> Larson & Dodds (1985: 152)

I have no recordings of such conversations, and the speakers I worked with no longer carry on the tradition.

2.5 Genetic relations

A number of languages, both living and extinct, have been linked to Chicham in the literature. Leaving aside the "macro-families" proposed by Greenberg (1987), among others (see Corbera 1994 for a thorough survey of these proposals, and Campbell 1988 for a refutation of the methods involved), only two had any reasonable evidence in their favour: Kandozi-Chapra (Candoshi-Shapra), an isolate spoken by about 3,000 people on the Morona and Pastaza rivers in Peru (Wise 1999) and Palta, an extinct language that was spoken in what is now the Ecuadorian province of Loja and the Peruvian department of Cajamarca (Adelaar & Muysken 2004: 396; Loukotka 1968: 157). In the following paragraphs I briefly discuss the two proposals.

Some works (e.g. Stark 1985) group Kandozi-Chapra with the Chicham languages. This was based on David Payne's (1981b) postulated relationship between Kandozi-Chapra and Chicham, but Payne himself has since rejected the idea (David Payne 1990a: 84). Tuggy (1992: 328) also notes that "el candoshi no es záparo, murato, maina ni jíbaro." [Kandozi is not Zaparoan, Murato, Maina, or Jivaroan (=Chicham)]. Taylor (1988: 16) includes Kandozi-Chapra in her *bloque Jívaro*, but notes that this is a cultural grouping, and makes no claim for linguistic affiliation. The connection continues to appear occasionally in the literature, for example Surrallés (2007: 267) specifically describes Kandozi as part of the Chicham language family.

There are clear examples of lookalikes in the lexicons of the two languages, but these must be loans (Table 2.1; it is not always clear which language is the source). There is no convincing evidence of grammatical similarity and no regular phonological changes apart from loss of intervocalic /ɾ/ in Chicham (cf. Kandozi *kawáaɾu*, Aguaruna *kawáu* 'parrot'), which also happens in loans from other languages. Very little linguistic material has been published on Kandozi-Chapra, and a full investigation of its possible genetic affiliation remains to be undertaken.

Table 2.1: Some lexical items shared between Kandozi-Chapra and Chicham

Kandozi-Chapra	Chicham	gloss
kaŋka	*kaŋka*	fish sp. (Sp. *boquichico*)
mantsʊ	*manchu*	mosquito
iichi	Huambisa *iichi*	uncle, father-in-law

The extinct language Palta was classified as a Chicham language by Loukotka (1968: 157–158), based on the four Palta vocabulary items in (2.2) (in the forms given by Adelaar & Muysken 2004: 396 and Taylor 1988: 80, both citing Jiménez de la Espada 1965, III: 143). These words comprise the only extant data on Palta.

(2.2) Palta
       yumé   'water'
       let   'firewood'
       xeme   'corn'
       capal   'fire'

The first word is clearly a possible cognate of Chicham *yumi* 'water'. Of the others, there is no good Chicham match for *let* 'firewood', but Gnerre (1975) suggests that *xemé* 'corn' could be metaphorically related to Chicham *himpïi* 'grey hairs' and that *capal* 'fire' may be related metonymically to Chicham *kapantu* 'red' < *kapaut* 'burn'. These lookalikes certainly hint at a Chicham association, and many toponyms in the area support this view, as they end in *-namá*, *-numa* – compare the Chicham locative case-marker *-numa*, *-nama* – and other toponyms ending in *-sa* are reminiscent of Chicham compounds with *intsa* 'stream', common in modern hydronyms (Adelaar & Muysken 2004: 396–397). Gnerre also links Malacato and tentatively Xiroa, relying on even less data than for Palta. Unfortunately there is little hope of any further data on these extinct languages coming to light.

In sum, there is not sufficient evidence to link Chicham genetically to any living language family, but the evidence does support the hypothesis that one or more languages formerly spoken in the highlands of what is now southern Ecuador were related to the modern Chicham languages.

2.6 The areal context

Dixon & Aikhenvald (1999: 8) give a list of areal features of Amazonian languages, contrasting them with Andean languages; and Aikhenvald (2007b: 193; 2012) gives updated versions. Of the latter list, Aguaruna appears to have more in common typologically with Andean than Amazonian languages. Dixon & Aikhenvald's (1999: 9–10) list of typological features that distinguish Andean from Amazonian languages are also a good fit for Aguaruna. As the authors themselves point out, "There is no sharp boundary between the Andean and Amazonian linguistic areas – they tend to flow into each other." (Dixon & Aikhenvald 1999: 10). Indeed, more recent work suggests that there is a more general East-West divide rather than Andes-Amazon (see for example the contributions in O'Connor & Muysken (eds.) 2014). This serves to highlight the important and under-investigated linguistic area of the eastern foothills of the Andes, and is particularly relevant to the Chicham languages in light of the long history of contact between coast, highland and lowland Amazonia in precisely the geographic area inhabited by Chicham speakers:

> (E)l Alto Amazonas ha sido, durante el período Formativo Temprano, un foco muy importante de influencias culturales, difundidas de este a oeste a lo largo de los valles transversales de los Andes ecuatoriales australes.

> [The upper Amazon was, during the Early Formative period,[6] a very important focal point for cultural influences, diffused from East to West along the valleys that transverse the southern equatorial Andes.]

Taylor (1988: 32)

Taylor & Descola (1981) suggest that Chicham languages were formerly spoken much further to the West than they currently are, perhaps into the coastal zone, and the linguistic evidence discussed above seems to support a historical presence of Chicham languages in the highlands.

2.7 Borrowing and codeswitching

Aguaruna is currently in a situation of intense contact with Spanish, and this is reflected in loans and calques in the language. There are also identifiable loans from Quechuan languages and a handful of other languages.

2.7.1 Spanish

Due to the ever-increasing presence of the Peruvian state and bilingual education in Aguaruna society, very many loans have entered Aguaruna from Spanish. There is no sharp line to be drawn between established loanwords and ad hoc cases of codeswitching – the very high degree of bilingualism means that Spanish words may be freely dropped into Aguaruna conversation. I heard many examples like those in (2.3 – 2.5) when visiting Aguaruna-speaking households.

(2.3)   *dúsɨ tostámu*
           dusɨ   *tosta*-mau
           peanut   toast:PFV-NSBJ.NMLZ
           'toasted peanuts'

---

6 The Formative period Taylor refers to is 3,500–500 years before the Christian Era (Taylor 1988: 23).

(2.4)   *fritáta*
           frita-ta
           fry:PFV-IMP
           'fry it!'

(2.5)   *ganáthai*
           gana-ta-ha-i
           earn:PFV-IFUT-1SG-DECL
           'I want to earn (money)'

The italicized verb roots, from Spanish *tostar* 'toast', *fritar* 'fry' and *ganar* 'earn'
respectively, have not been altered to fit Aguaruna phonology, nor do they use the
verbalizing suffix *-ma* that normally appears on verbs borrowed from Spanish (see
§6.6). But they do take native Aguaruna morphology. Compare the nominal examples in (2.6 – 2.8).

(2.6)   *jugadores áinau*
           jugadores   a-ina-u
           player+PL   COP-PL:IPFV-NMLZ
           'players'

(2.7)   *escuelanum*
           escuela=numa
           school=LOC
           'at school'

(2.8)   *tigren*
           tigre=na
           jaguar=ACC
           'the jaguar'

Note in particular that example (2.6) has both Spanish plural marking *-es* and the
Aguaruna relative-clause plural marker *ainau*. Appel & Muysken (1987: 172–173)
note a similar situation in Quechua, where Spanish nouns are borrowed along with
plural marking, and are then marked with the native plural suffix, for example
polisiya-s-kuna (police-PL-PL) 'policemen', where the underlined morphemes are
Spanish. Such examples are difficult to classify as code-switching or borrowings, as
they consist of a single Spanish word which doesn't have an Aguaruna equivalent in
(2.6) and (2.7), although it does in (2.8).

2.7.2 Quechuan

There are a number of loanwords from Quechuan languages in Aguaruna. There is no clear evidence to show which Quechuan language the words come from. There is no established Quechua speaking population near the modern day Aguaruna zone, but Quechua I was spoken on the upper Marañón River (Adelaar & Muysken 2004), so there is some possibility of early contact with Chicham. Any other contact would have been with Quechua II, in the Inca or post-colonial era. Adelaar (2006) says:

> Most Quechua loans in Amazonian languages are relatively recent and have their origin in lingua franca type varieties of Quechua associated with a short period of Inca expansion (roughly from 1470 to 1532) or with Spanish colonial and missionary policies (roughly from 1532 to 1770).

Adelaar (2006: 293)

Among the Shuar, Ecuadorian Quichua speakers are associated with shamanic power and are the most sought after teachers for apprentice shamans (Rubenstein 2002). Taylor & Chau (1983) note that Quechuan words may be introduced into Achuar shamans' songs, and, to a lesser degree, the magic songs (*anĩn*) traditionally used by all adults.

Table 2.2 lists the clear examples of Quechuan loans in Aguaruna. Because of the lack of information concerning contacts between Quechuan and Chicham speakers, and the often high degree of phonological change in naturalizing loans to Aguaruna phonology, it was impossible to ascertain an exact source for each word. The source orthography has been retained for all Quechuan words cited.

Table 2.2: Quechuan loans

Aguaruna	Quechuan	gloss (word class)	source
apu	*apu*	'chief' (N); 'big' (Adj)	Hornberger & Hornberger (1977: 10)
ima	*ima*	'very'; 'so much' (Adv); Qu. 'how' (question word)	Hornberger & Hornberger (1977: 70)
kuchi	*cuchi*	'pig' (N) (< Sp. *cochino*)	Stark & Muysken (1977: 169)
kuwichik(i)	*cuchqui*	'money'	Stark & Muysken (1977: 169)
mishu	*mishi*	'cat' (N) (< Sp.?)	Stark & Muysken (1977: 256)
pishak(a)	*pishcu*	'bird' (N)	Stark & Muysken (1977: 280)

Aguaruna	Quechuan	gloss (word class)	source
sinchi	*sinchi*	'strength' (N); 'strong' (Adj)	Stark & Muysken (1977: 313)
yaakat(a)	*llaqta*	'town' (N)	Hornberger & Hornberger (1977: 111)
yacha	*yachaj*	'clever person' (N); 'clever' (Adj)	Stark & Muysken (1977: 355)

Note that of the examples given, three may function as both noun and adjective – a common pattern in Quechuan but not in Aguaruna – and the intensifier *ima* is particularly versatile in Aguaruna (§12.3.6). This suggests that the Quechuan loans, although they appear on the surface to be well integrated into the language, are still a little short of complete assimilation in terms of word class behaviour.

2.7.3 Other languages

A number of vocabulary items, mostly flora and fauna, and some cultural items, are shared with other indigenous languages. Gnerre (1999: 116–117) identifies *tsukaŋka* 'toucan' (Carib *tukan*) and *yawaã* 'dog, jaguar' (Carib *yawar*) as having Carib sources, although both etyma may ultimately come from Tupí-Guaraní. Other words from Tupí-Guaraní (perhaps via some other language) are *timu* 'barbasco' and *kanu* 'canoe' – note that both of these etyma are also in use in Kandozi-Chapra. The vocabulary shared with Kandozi-Chapra in Table 2.1 (above) is mostly flora and fauna, and in rejecting the possibility of a genetic link these must be treated as loans, either from or into Chicham. Adelaar & Muysken (2004: 442) note the similarity of the Chicham verb *umu-* 'drink' to Aymara *uma*, and also show a number of grammatical lookalikes between Chicham and Aymara (2004: 436ff.). Although lookalikes are fairly easy to find, however, these are not necessarily proof of borrowing, any more than they are proof of genetic relationship. Much work remains to be done in the field of genetic and areal relations among South American languages, and the Chicham family is particularly interesting in this regard, as it sits both typologically and geographically right at the nexus of the Andean and Amazonian areas.

2.8 Previous research

The most substantial modern works on Aguaruna are:
Larson (1963): a description of morphology, cast in the tagmemics format.
Pike & Larson (1964): a discussion of some issues in phonology.
David Payne (1978): MA thesis, on nasality.
Larson (1978): PhD dissertation, on functions of reported speech in discourse.

David Payne (1990b): on accent in nouns and adjectives.

Corbera (1994): PhD dissertation. This work covers the whole grammar and is reasonably thorough, but does not always provide detailed argumentation and relies heavily on elicited data. It describes the Marañón variety of Aguaruna, but not from Wawik (Corbera 1994: 23).

There are also two dictionaries: Wipio (1996) and Uwarai et al. (1998). The compilers of material for CAAAP (such as Uwarai et al. 1998) have generally used information from speakers of the Nieva variety, while the dictionary published by SIL (Wipio 1996) reflects the Marañón variety; this explains differences in dictionary entries such as Nieva <ajéj> *ahɨh* vs. Marañón <ajég> *ahɨŋ* 'ginger'.

There is some variation between these analyses, and not just in minor details; from the number of phonemes to the nature of apocope and syncope processes, it is clear that there are still many important issues to be addressed. In addition, previous works have only lightly touched on morphophonology, and in many cases even the segmentation of morphs is erroneous. I shall discuss previous analyses in the body of this work only in cases where they present a viable alternative analysis to mine. The following works on other Chicham languages were also consulted:

Turner (1992): a sketch grammar of Shuar.

Gnerre (1999): a grammar of Shuar.

Pellizaro & Náwech (2005): a Shuar dictionary, with grammar notes.

Fast et al. (1996): a dictionary of Achuar-Shiwiar, with a grammar sketch.

Jakway et al. (1987): a dictionary of Huambisa

2.8.1 Present and future work

The primary goal of this grammar is to provide a detailed and accurate description of Aguaruna. On the basis of that description, I had the second goal of providing explanations, both synchronic and diachronic, for the observed phenomena. Throughout the grammar I have tried to strike a balance between keeping the descriptions and explanations typologically informed while remaining within the ambit of language-internal justification.

Many areas require future research. The two major areas which I hope will come under analysis in future works are (i) discourse structure and (ii) a comparative reconstruction of Proto-Chicham. In Chapter 18 I begin to address some issues in discourse organization based on the narratives I have analysed. There remains, however, much to be done. Reference tracking and source-of-information marking in particular are pervasive and subtle phenomena of which I have barely scratched the surface.

This study is based mainly on the contemporary speech of the Wawik River, where the Marañón variety is spoken, along with a small amount of data from the Nieva variety. With the exception of Huambisa, the other languages of the Chicham family have had grammar sketches published, and I have made use of those and the published dictionaries to formulate hypothetical historical scenarios where I felt it could shed light on issues under discussion. A major project for future research will be to document and describe the rest of the Chicham family so that comparative work can be confidently undertaken.

2.9 Fieldwork methodology and language data

The fieldwork upon which the bulk of this work is based was undertaken in two trips, the first from June 2004 to February 2005 and the second from June to August 2006. The majority of that time was spent living in Centro Wawik, a native community of about 420 people[7] in the Imaza district, province of Bagua, northern Amazonas (about 4.77°S, 78.19°W – see Map 2). The community is one of four on the Wawik river, a small tributary of the Marañón. The bulk of my data comes from speakers of the Marañón variety, as spoken on the Wawik river, and this work represents an analysis of Marañón Aguaruna. A further week was spent in Tundusa,[8] a native community situated on the highway to Saramiriza, in the Nieva district of Bagua province (approximately 4.78°S, 77.87°W), where I collected data on the Nieva variety of Aguaruna. Since the completion of the dissertation, I have undertaken further fieldwork, visiting communities around Imacita and the Santiago River, where I also collected data on Huambisa. Some further data has come from a Bible (YCA 2008) and other formal literature in Aguaruna; personal correspondence with native Aguaruna speakers; and transcripts of conversations made and very kindly shared with me by Clarivel Tiinch Ramírez and Jessica Danducho Yampis. The conversational data, involving exchanges of short sentences, were useful in particular for the analysis of information structure marking and question and answer constructions. The interactional nature of the exchanges also helped to inform the analysis of tense markers and deictic expressions, as narrative data tend to show little variation in temporal and spatial expressions. Note that while I have retained the source orthography of published data, the informal written examples have been normalized to use the same orthography as the rest of the grammar, unless otherwise indicated.

---

7 Fabre (2005: 8) gives the population as 289; the figure of 420 was provided to me by the Apu (Chief) Abel Namarai Nanchijam in 2004, and includes all people living within the area of his authority, including the outlying households.
8 Population 130 according to Fabre (2005: 9).

About 20 hours of audio was recorded, and about 10 hours' worth was transcribed, translated and glossed in the field with the help of native speakers. The texts are mainly traditional stories, with some procedural texts and one autobiographical narrative. Three texts are included in the appendices: a traditional story (Text 1); extracts from an autobiography (Text 2); and a procedural text (Text 3). Some examples also come from observations of day-to-day interaction, which provided many linguistic contexts that do not arise in recorded texts, and some from elicitation. Data were recorded from both male and female speakers, however the majority of consultants were male. Natural data from conversational interactions and observations are from speakers of both sexes, and varying ages.

I used elicitation to fill in paradigms and test hypotheses. The data used and cited in this work are mainly from spontaneous speech, and the advantage of this approach is a more natural data set, but a potential disadvantage is that there are very few examples that were judged ungrammatical by native speakers: while grammatical data can tell us a lot about a particular construction, only by taking into account forms judged to be ungrammatical can we clearly demarcate its limits.

3 Phonology

3.1 Introduction

The phoneme inventory of Aguaruna comprises 15 consonants and four vowels. Vowel nasality is phonemically contrastive, but complementary processes of nasal spreading and denasalization pose analytical challenges. A nasal feature may alternate between realization as vowel nasality or as [m], [n] or [ŋ], forming a homorganic cluster with a following consonant (§3.4.2). The phone [ŋ] also arises as a syllable-final allophone of the phoneme /h/; in §3.2.4 I show that there is no need to posit a phonemic velar nasal /ŋ/.

Vowel elision is a feature of the phonological word, and can obscure the basically agglutinating nature of the morphology. I analyse vowel elision as a synchronic process, and assume that underlying representations have a simpler syllable template than surface forms. Surface long vowels and diphthongs are treated as VV sequences phonologically. Accent placement is phonemically contrastive, and the motivations underlying accent placement in a phonological word are not yet fully clear. All of the examples in this Chapter use standard IPA. Examples in the rest of the grammar are transcribed in a slightly modified IPA, with the aim of being transparent and easily readable (§1.2).

3.2 Consonants

The consonant system of Aguaruna is presented in Table 3.1; major allophones are given in square brackets. Of the 15 consonants listed, the glottal stop /ʔ/ and the flap /ɾ/ have extremely limited distribution (appearing in <10 lexemes each). The nasal stops /m/ and /n/ have prenasalized oral allophones [ᵐb] and [ⁿd], and there is some evidence for these phones having phonemic status: their distribution is not entirely predictable on phonological grounds and there are apparent examples of surface minimal pairs. However, evidence is presented in §3.2.6 to support the more parsimonious analysis of [ᵐb] and [ⁿd] as synchronic allophones of /m/ and /n/. The three glides /y/, /w/ and /ɰ/ alternate with the vowels /i/, /u/ and /ɨ/ respectively when vowel elision allows them to function as syllable nuclei (§3.2.5). In the sections that follow I describe in detail all of the consonant phonemes.

Table 3.1: Aguaruna consonant phonemes

	bilabial	dental[1]	alveolar	palato-alveolar	velar	glottal
stop	p	t			k	ʔ
affricate[2]			ts [s]	tʃ [ʃ]		
fricative			s	ʃ		h [ŋ]
nasal	m [ᵐb]	n [ⁿd]				
glide	w [u]				y [i]	ɰ [ɨ]
flap			r [l]			

3.2.1 Oral stops

The oral stops are bilabial /p/, apico-dental /t/ and dorso-velar /k/. The oral stops appear word-initially, intervocalically, and following homorganic nasals. At the surface level, following vowel elision, they can also appear syllable and word-finally. Oral stops are voiceless, and are unreleased when they surface word-finally.

(3.1) a. [píŋ.kɨŋ]
       'good'

      b. [á.pa]
         'your father'

    c. [əɨp.sóu]
       'laid down'

      d. [kaŋ.káp̚]
         'root'

(3.2) a. [tɨ.máʃ]
       'comb'

      b. [há.ta]
         'sickness'

    c. [ɨ.sát.nɨ̃]
       'it bit me'

      d. [ta.kát̚]
         'work'

(3.3) a. [káŋ.ka]
       'fish sp.(*boquichico*)'

      b. [dú.ku]
         'your mother'

    c. [tsu.pík.ta]
       'cut it!'

      d. [pɨ.ɰák̚]
         'bed'

---

1 The dental phonemes /t/ and /n/ should strictly speaking be transcribed /t̪/ and /n̪/, however the diacritic is unnecessary as there is no contrast with alveolar consonants.

2 I transcribe the affricates /ts/ and /tʃ/ without the ligature, as they do not contrast with clusters.

Aspiration of voiceless stops is a marked feature of emphatic speech, usually accompanied by slight pauses between syllables and an exaggerated pitch accent.
Oral stops optionally exhibit the following allophonic variations when vowel elision
allows them to surface in syllable-final position preceding /h/:

A. $/p/ \rightarrow [\phi] / \_ h$

/p/ is fricativized when followed by the glottal fricative /h/.

(3.4)   [akuɸhúk]
         akupɨ-hu-kã
         let.go-APPL-PFV+SEQ+3:SS
         'having let go' (agr041102_08)

B. $/t/ \rightarrow [ɾ] / \_ h$

/t/ is realized as an alveolar flap when followed by /h/. The /h/ is often elided, and
the flap [ɾ] may be realized as [l], as is usual for phonemic /ɾ/ (§3.2.7).

(3.5)   [yuwárhɛi]~[yuwárɛi]~[yuwálɛi]
         yu-a-ta-ha-i
         eat-PFV-IFUT-1SG-DECL
         'I will eat (it)'

(3.6)   [uhaɾhúkta]~[uhaɾúkta]
         uha-tu-hu-ka-ta
         tell-APPL-1SG.OBJ-PFV-IMP
         'pass on a message for me'

C. $/k/ \rightarrow [x] / \_ h$

Similarly to /p/, the velar stop /k/ may be fricativized and surface as [x] when followed by /h/. Note that /k/ is elided when followed by /h/ in some morphological
environments (§3.5.4).

(3.7)   [ukúxhɛi]
         uku-ka-ha-i
         leave-PFV-1SG-DECL
         'I left' (agr041102_08)

Rules A and C (fricativization of /p/ and /k/) are rarely applied in my data. The most frequent examples are in traditional stories told by older men, suggesting that these processes are archaisms.[3] Rule B (change of /th/ to [ɾ]~[l]) is more common, and is typically encountered in casual (especially children's) speech. This process is considered informal by most speakers.

The earliest reports of Chicham languages describe voicing of stops when they form part of an NC cluster (rule D). Pike & Larson (1964: 57) report that /k/ has the postnasal allophone [g], but make no mention of similar allophony for /p/ and /t/.

D.   C → [+voice] / N._

There is no such voicing in my data, but hispanified forms of some Aguaruna personal names (e.g. *Cungumas*, pronounced [kuŋkúmas] in the contemporary language) and toponyms (e.g. *Tundusa*, a community in Nieva district – pronounced [tuntús] in contemporary Aguaruna) show that it must have been productive at some point. Karsten (1935) consistently transcribes voiced consonants following nasals, such as *kúndu* 'arm' (p. 561); *núnga* 'earth, country' (p. 566), where my data show *kúntu* and *núŋka* respectively. Such voicing appears to have been widespread in languages of the coast and highlands, including Quechua (Adelaar & Muysken 2004: 182). Martin Kohlberger (personal communication) reports that postnasal voicing is completely productive in Shiwiar.

Some positional restrictions apply to stops following vowel elision. The only sequences of identical consonants permitted at affix boundaries within a phonological word are the dentals /tt/ and /nn/. Any other CC sequence arising from vowel elision is simplified: CC → C. This simplification does not happen at clitic boundaries, however, where the sequence [kk] may also be encountered (there are no /p/ initial enclitics). Where a stop preceded by a homorganic nasal loses its following vowel after the application of apocope or syncope, the stop is elided: NC → N /_.{C, #}. Examples of both processes are included in the discussion on vowel elision in §3.5.5.

3.2.2 Glottal stop

The glottal stop /ʔ/ only appears intervocalically, and only in three roots in my corpus, listed in Table 3.2.

---

3 Pike & Larson (1964) mention the fricativization processes, but do not describe them as optional. The fact that they are optional now strongly supports the analysis as archaisms rather than innovations.

Table 3.2: Roots with glottal stop

word	gloss
āĩʔāĩ	'bee species'
āĩʔaiŋ(ku)	'mammal species (Sp. *zorrillo*)'
aiʔaɨt	'midnight'

The glottal stop also appears in some interjectional items such as *waʔ* 'oh!' and *hɨʔá ~ haʔá* 'yes'[4] (see also §12.4.2). Although it may appear word-finally in interjections, these fall outside of the regular phonological system and such examples cannot be considered phonemic. There are also examples of apparently epenthetic glottal stops following accented word-final vowels:

(3.8)   [ⁿdukuʃáʔ]
         duku=ʃa
         mother:PSSD:2=Q.TOP
         '(where is/what about) your mother?'

(3.9)   [apawáʔ]
         apa-wa
         father-VOC
         'father!'

(3.10)   [datɨmáʔikɨn]
         datɨma   ikɨnã
         ayahuasca+ACC   prepare+PFV+SEQ+3:SS
         'having prepared *ayahuasca*...' (agr040702_01)

Pike & Larson (1964: 60) treat the examples of glottal stop in (3.8) and (3.9) as phonemic, and translate them as '(where is) your mother?' and 'father (form used for calling)', respectively, without indicating any morpheme boundaries.[5] In my data there are examples of these forms without the glottal stops, and I prefer the more parsimonious analysis whereby the stops are epenthetic, appearing following a

---

4 Sadock & Zwicky (1985: 191) note that "[a]n interesting recurrent phenomenon in question-answering systems is that they are often peculiar with respect to their phonology; that is, they are often more like paralinguistic utterances than like ordinary morphemes." Also of note is Parker's (1996) "universal template" for 'yes': /heʔe/, which Aguaruna certainly approximates.
5 The Aguaruna Bible (YCA 2008) uses the graph <h> to mark vocative forms, e.g. *apuh* /apuʔ/ 'Lord!' < *apu* 'chief'.

word-final accented short vowel. This analysis also explains the form in (3.10) where there is a word-final accented vowel, but no particular grammatical function attributable to the glottal stop.

The phone [ʔ] occurs in one further morphological environment: when polar interrogative =ka is combined with third-person copula to give a question of the type "is it x?", the copula enclitic with underlying form =(a)ita loses its final vowel, and the final /t/ surfaces as an unreleased stop (3.11). Although the etymological source is /t/, this stop typically has velar or glottal articulation.

(3.11)   [pɨ́ŋkɨŋkɛik̚]~[pɨ́ŋkɨŋkɛiʔ̚]
           pɨŋkɨha=ka=ita
           good=Q=COP:3
           'is it good?'

Although there is no clear consensus between speakers on the precise nature of the phone, nor as to whether it should be represented orthographically as <k> or <h>=[ʔ], the majority of speakers I have discussed the issue with pronounce and transcribe it as velar <k>, likely by analogy with other polar questions in which the polar interrogative =ka is word-final and surfaces as /k/, as in (3.12).

(3.12)   [puhámɨk]
           puha-mɨ=ka
           live+IPFV-2SG=Q
           'are you there?'

The limited distribution of the glottal stop suggests it is effectively extrasystematic, but there is no satisfactory explanation for its presence in a few lexemes. No minimal pairs exist, but it is contrastive inasmuch as it cannot be omitted or replaced with any other phone. The three lexical items in Table 3.2 share a similar structure which looks as if it may have arisen from reduplication. The fact that Aguaruna presents other examples of glottal stop insertion as a pause phenomenon suggests that these words may not in fact contain glottal stops *per se*, but pauses. When transcribing a story, one consultant told me to write *aíʔaiŋ* 'zorrillo (mammal species)' as <ai aig>, that is, as two words with no orthographic representation of the glottal stop, which is normally written with orthographic <h>. This strongly suggests that he treated this word as being composed of two phonological words. None of the consulted works on the other Chicham languages mentions the existence of a glottal stop phoneme. The only lexeme that is potentially cognate with one of the Aguaruna forms is Shuar *aíaí* 'beetle' (*escarabajo*) in Pellizaro & Náwech (2005: 115). It is not clear precisely how this word should be pronounced – the grammar notes given (pp.15–16) suggest that it does not fit into the standard phonology, as <i> is said to alternate with <y> when followed by a vowel. For Achuar-Shiwiar, Fast et al. (1996: 136) give *ja ai* (<j>=/h/) 'yes' (*sî*) – perhaps the orthographic space here represents a glottal stop. This evidence suggests that if there are glottal stops in the other languages, they are even more marginal than that of Aguaruna.

3.2.3 Affricates and fricatives

The affricates and fricatives contrast on the two dimensions of place and manner of articulation, shown in Table 3.3.

Table 3.3: Place and manner distinctions between affricates and fricatives

	affricate	fricative
alveolar	ts	s
palato-alveolar	tʃ	ʃ

The manner distinction is neutralized when any of these phonemes surfaces syllable-finally or following a consonant, due to the processes of vowel elision. The neutralizations are shown in Table 3.4, and exemplified below.

Table 3.4: Manner neutralization in affricates and fricatives

underlying form	word-initial or intervocalic	syllable-final	following consonant
/s/	s	s	ts
/ts/	ts	s	ts
/ʃ/	ʃ	ʃ	tʃ
/tʃ/	tʃ	ʃ	tʃ

Affricates are realized as fricatives [s, ʃ] when they surface syllable-finally, neutralizing the distinction between affricate and fricative (3.13a and c; 3.14a and c). (3.13b) and (3.14b) show the affricate surfacing prevocalically.

(3.13) a. [tí.kiʃ]
tikitʃi
'another'

b. [ti.kí.tʃin]
tikitʃi=na
another=ACC

c. [ti.kíʃ.nak]
tikitʃi=na=ka
another=ACC=TOP

(3.14) a. [tɨn.tɨ́s]
tɨntɨtsa
'*Tentets* (proper name)'

b. [tɨn.tɨ.tsá]
tɨntɨtsa
Tentets+VOC
'Tentets!'

c. [ⁿdɨ́.kas.hɛi]
dɨka-tsu-ha-i
know+IPFV-NEG-1SG-DECL
'I don't know'

The manner distinction is also neutralized in syllable-initial position following consonants, in which case underlying fricatives surface as affricates. Compare (3.15a and b) with (c), and (3.16a) with (b).

(3.15) a. [aán.tʃa.kam]
aan=ʃakama
MED=ADD
'that one too'

b. [pi.ʃák.tʃa.kam]
piʃaka=ʃakama
bird=ADD
'also a bird'

c. [βí.ʃa.kam]
wi=ʃakama
1sg=ADD
'I too'

(3.16) a. [su.hut.tsá.ta]
            su-hu-tu-sa-ta
            give-APPL-1SG.OBJ-PFV-IMP
            'give (it) (to someone) for me!'

      b. [su.sá.ta]
            su-sa-ta
            give-PFV-IMP
            'give (it) (to someone)!'

Affricates trigger the formation of NC clusters when they follow nasal vowels, as described in §3.4.2, and illustrated in (3.17a). When the affricate /tʃ/ surfaces in syllable-final position, either NC cluster formation or fricativization may apply, resulting in surface [Vntʃ] or [Ṽʃ], apparently in free variation (3.17b, 3.18). This variation does not apply to the affricate /ts/, which always triggers NC cluster formation when preceded by a nasal vowel, giving surface [Vnts].

(3.17) a. [ku.hán.tʃam]
            kuhãtʃama
            'opossum (*Didelphis sp.*)'

      b. [ku.hántʃ.man]~[ku.hã́ʃ.man]
            kuhãtʃama=na
            opossum=ACC

(3.18)   [ni.ha.mántʃ]~[ni.ha.mã́ʃ]
            nihamãtʃi
            '*masato* (manioc beer)'

For the non-neutralized environments, that is, word-initial and intervocalic positions, the minimal pairs and near-minimal pairs presented in (3.19) and (3.20) demonstrate the phonemic status of both fricatives and affricates.

(3.19) a. kútʃi   b. kúʃi
            'pig'[6]   'coati'

      c. tʃúβi   d. ʃúβi
            '*paucar* (bird sp.)'   '*carachama* (small fish sp.)'

---

6 < Qu. *kutʃi* 'pig', ultimately from Sp. *cochino* 'pig'.

(3.20) a. tsiɨm   b. siɨmat
            'squirrel monkey'   'sweat (v.)'

        c. ɨtsát   d. ɨsát
            'peel (v.)'   'bite (v.)'

The alveolar and postalveolar sets show complementary phonotactic restrictions preceding /i/ and /ɨ/. In underived forms, the alveolars /s/ and /ts/ never appear preceding /i/, while the postalveolars /ʃ/ and /tʃ/ never appear preceding /ɨ/ (3.21).

(3.21)   **si   **tsi
            **ʃɨ   **tʃɨ

While **/si/, **/ʃɨ/ **/tʃɨ/ never appear in surface forms, the sequence /tsi/ does appear in derived words, and in one apparent loanword *durintsiu* 'conehead katydid' (see §3.2.7).

3.2.4 Glottal fricative /h/

In the Marañón variety of Aguaruna, upon which this grammar is based, the phoneme /h/ surfaces as a glottal fricative [h] syllable-initially and a velar nasal [ŋ] syllable-finally (the syllable-final allophone is [h] in the Nieva variety). Morphological alternations (3.22, 3.23) show that this typologically unusual distribution is genuine allophony rather than two phonemes with complementary phonotactic restrictions (as English /h/ and /ŋ/).

(3.22) a. [píŋkɨŋ]   b. [píŋkɨhɛi]
            piŋkɨha   piŋkɨha=i
            'good'   good=COP:3:DECL
                                                'it is good'

(3.23) a. [yatsúŋ]   b. [yatsuhú]
            yatsu-hu   yatsu-hu
            brother-PSSD:1SG   brother-PSSD:1SG+VOC
            'my brother'   'my brother!'

Of course, it is not obvious that the underlying phoneme should be /h/: the other option is that the underlying form is /ŋ/, with a syllable-initial allophone [h]. Either option appears equally plausible *a priori*, and in fact it has been generally assumed among linguists working with Chicham languages (Corbera 1994, David Payne 1978,

1981b, 1990b and cf. Wise 1999; all apparently following Pike & Larson 1964) that the underlying phoneme is /ŋ/, with syllable-initial allophone [h] or nasalized [h̃] (David Payne 1978, 1981b, 1990b and Corbera 1994), and furthermore that this phoneme is inherited from a Proto-Chicham (PC) phoneme */ŋ/. Overall (2008) shows that the data do not support this analysis. A reconstruction of the PC phoneme system, including evidence from loans, shows that PC */h/ and */r/ have merged in Aguaruna to produce the phoneme /h/, and that Marañón Aguaruna then innovated the syllable-final allophone [ŋ]. There is also some evidence for an intermediate stage where a distinction was made between plain [h] from PC */h/ and nasalized [h̃] from PC */r/, as hinted at by David Payne (1990b) and Pike & Larson (1964). This is discussed shown below to be untenable as a synchronic analysis, but a likely historical scenario.

A widely remarked-upon shibboleth for Aguaruna speakers is that syllable-final [ŋ] in Marañón Aguaruna corresponds to syllable-final [h] in Nieva Aguaruna. Table 3.5 shows some correspondences.

Table 3.5: Syllable-final [ŋ] and [h] in Aguaruna varieties

Marañon	Nieva	underlying form	translation
[pĩŋkɨn]	[pĩŋkɨh]	piŋkɨha	'good'
[dukún]	[dukúh]	duku-hu mother-PSSD:1SG	'my mother'
[tʃitʃasáŋmi]	[tʃitʃasáhmi]	tʃitʃa-sa-aha-mi converse-PFV-PL-HORT	'let's converse'

The [ŋ] allophone surfaces in Nieva Aguaruna apparently only when /h/ is directly followed by a second /h/, as in example (3.24).

(3.24)   Nieva Aguaruna
          [mína ⁿdukúŋhẽ̃ĩ puhúyahɛi]
          mi=na   duku-hu=haĩ   puhu-ya-ha-i
          1sg=ACC   mother-PSSD:1SG=COM live-REMPST-1SG-DECL
          'I lived with my mother' (agr060816_02)

The Marañón Aguaruna pattern must be the more innovative, because of the recency of vowel elision (see below): the syllable-final environment was the last to be created, so the syllable-final allophone must be the most recent. This is supported by the fact that the complementary distribution is not quite perfect: [ŋ] never appears in syllable-initial position, but just one verb, *auhut* 'read, study', can surface with [h] in syllable-final position after elision of its final vowel. In fact the root shows three syncopated allomorphs depending on the stem it is forming: [ouh] in the unmarked (example 3.25) and imperfective stems (3.26); [ouŋ] in the imperfective stem preceding the nominalizer *-mau* (3.27); and [ou] in the perfective stem, where the /h/ appears to have been elided preceding the perfective suffix *-sa* (3.28).

(3.25)   [naŋkámou áyahɛi papí óuhtan]
               naŋkama-u   a-ya-ha-i   papi
               begin+IPFV-NMLZ   COP-REMPST-1SG-DECL   book+ACC
               auhu-ta=na
               study-NMLZ=ACC
               'I began to study' (agr040824_02)

(3.26)   [nũw̃ĩ óuhkun wɨkə́ɨtiahɛi]
               nu=ĩ   auha-ku-nu   wɨkai-tu-ya-ha-i
               ANA=LOC   read+IPFV-SIM-1SG:SS   walk-APPL-REMPST-1SG-DECL
               'I went there to study' (agr040824_02)

(3.27)   [papí mína apáŋ óuŋ^mboun unuimátiahɛi ⁿdɨkasɨ]
               papi   mi=na   apa-hu   auha-mau=na
               book   1sg=ACC   father-PSSD:1SG   study+IPFV-NMLZ=ACC
               unuima-tu-ya-ha-i   dɨkasɨ
               learn-APPL-REMPST-1SG-DECL   a.few
               'I learned a few of the books that my father studied' (agr040824_02)

(3.28)   [ⁿdíta kounã́ papí óusatnumɨ̃]
               dita   kaunã   papi   au-sa-ti-numɨ̃
               3pl   come:PL+PFV+SEQ+3:SS   book+ACC   study-PFV-JUSS-3PL
               'let them come and study!' (agr040824_02)

The forms in Marañón Aguaruna with syllable-final [h] may have been introduced via the Nieva variety in the context of formal education. There is some variation among speakers, as shown by the fact that the speaker of (3.26) also produced (3.29), in which the imperfective stem followed by the simultaneous suffix surfaces as [ouŋ] rather than [ouh].

(3.29)   [papí óuŋku ^mbatsá^mbiahi]
               papi   auha-ku   batsama-maya-hi-i
               book   read+IPFV-SIM+1PL:SS   be:PL-INTPST-1PL-DECL
               'we were studying' (agr040824_02)

This could indicate that *auhut* 'study' is moving towards phonological regularity. In any case, I shall leave this one exception aside and assume for descriptive clarity that Marañón Aguaruna [h] and [ŋ] are in complementary distribution, representing an underlying phoneme /h/.

The phoneme /h/ is closely associated with nasality in adjacent vowels. As noted above, Aguaruna /h/ has arisen from a merger of PC */h/ and */r/, and there is some evidence that the two proto phonemes gave rise at an intermediate stage of development to plain */h/ and nasalized */h̃/ respectively, with only the nasal form triggering nasality in adjacent vowels. In the following paragraphs I give a histori-cal-comparative perspective on the phoneme /h/. In the course of this discussion, the allophony represented in the Marañón variety is used to represent Aguaruna as a whole.

As has been noted, the major phonological difference between Aguaruna and the other Chicham languages is that Aguaruna [h]/[ŋ] often corresponds to a rhotic[7] in the other languages. PC */r/ and */h/ have merged in Aguaruna: the reflexes of both are identical and show the same pattern of allophonic variation. Meanwhile both /r/ and /h/ have continued into Shuar, Achuar, Shiwiar and Huambisa. Phono-tactic restrictions on PC */r/, which does not appear word-initially, and */h/, which rarely appears word-finally, suggest that there may already have been some kind of neutralization in word-initial and word-final syllables in PC. It is clear that Aguaru-na, and particularly the Marañón variety, is the most innovative member of the fam-ily with respect to phonological development of PC */h/ and */r/. That the syllable-final allophone is the most recent development is apparent from the historical facts of vowel elision, as mentioned above: any positional allophony must postdate vowel elision, otherwise the prevocalic allophone would be universal.

3.2.4.1 Nasality associated with /h/

The nasal quality of the syllable-final allophone [ŋ] suggests a nasal component to Aguaruna /h/, and it frequently surfaces as [h̃], with a preceding vowel also surfac-ing as nasal. Matisoff (1975) shows that association of nasality with a glottal fricative is not uncommon, and such an association is also described for the Amazonian languages Warekena (Aikhenvald 1996: 498-9) and Jarawara (Dixon 2004b: 18). In many examples, the nasalized /h/ corresponds to /r/ in the other Chicham lan-guages, while the plain version corresponds to /h/ in those languages (the [ŋ] allo-phone does not trigger nasality). So perhaps in these examples the locus of nasality is not vowels but /h/ itself. However, while there is a high degree of coincidence between nasalizing /h/ and PC */r/, comparison with Shuar data from Pellizaro &

---

7 The rhotic is a flap /ɾ/ in Huambisa; I have not collected data on the other languages. I transcribe it simply as /r/ in the absence of reliable field data.

Náwech (2005) shows that this is not always the case. On the one hand, nasal vowels may surface in Aguaruna adjacent to /h/ that has arisen from PC */h/; in that case, the Shuar cognates show no nasality (Table 3.6).

Table 3.6: Nasality triggered by AGR /h/ < PC */h/

Aguaruna	Shuar	gloss
hãã	haa	'tear (cloth etc.)'
ũhutu	uhutu	'cough'
ãha	aha	'cook greens'

On the other hand, although Aguaruna /h/ from PC */r/ shows more consistent effects, there are at least two examples of /h/ < */r/ where no nasalization appears on adjacent vowels (Table 3.7).

Table 3.7: Lack of nasality in vowels adjacent to AGR /h/ < PC */r/

Aguaruna	Shuar	gloss
kakaham	kakaram	'powerful man'
ahutap	arutam	'spirit'

Many Aguaruna speakers preserve a distinction in nasality in reflexes of PC minimal pairs distinguished by */h/ versus */r/, such as the examples in Table 3.8. It is possible that these pairs are distinguished by the presence of /h/ vs. /h̃/, but equally plausible that the initial vowel is the locus of nasality, and is synchronically phonologically nasal. The latter option has the distinct advantage that it does not require positing a new phonemic distinction, given that vowel nasality is independently shown to be phonemically contrastive.[8]

---

8 Blust (1998) posits a remarkably similar historical scenario for the Oceanic language Seimat, with two glottal phonemes: plain /h/ arising from earlier */p/ and nasal /h̃/ arising from earlier */r/. Blust provides evidence that the glottal fricative, rather than the vowel, is the underlying locus of nasality in Seimat. (I am grateful to Mark Donohue for bringing the Seimat parallel to my attention.)

Table 3.8: Reflexes of PC minimal pairs

Aguaruna	Shuar	PC	gloss
aha	aha	*aha	'fell (trees)'
āha	ara	*ara	'sow seeds'
uha	uha	*uha	'tell'
ūha	ura	*ura	'open'

While discussing nasality, a native speaker told me that some speakers do nasalize the vowels of *uhat* 'tell', so that for example *uha-ka-ta-hamɨ-i* (tell-PFV-IFUT-1SG>2SG-DECL) 'I will tell you' surfaces as [ũh̃āktáhamɨ]. Other speakers, who preserve the distinction, may then laugh and say "you're going to *open* me?" (*ũhat* 'open') – but this is considered idiolectal variation rather than an error.

3.2.4.2 Summary

To summarize, while PC */h/ and */r/ have been retained in the other Chicham languages as distinct phonemes, they have undergone a merger in Aguaruna (Overall 2008). The evidence suggests that */r/ first became */h̃/ in Aguaruna, giving rise to minimal pairs distinguished only by nasality of the glottal fricative, which spread to the adjacent vowels. This must have quickly been reanalysed as vowel nasality, an already existing phonemic distinction. The development of a new allophone [ŋ] neutralized the already small contrast between */h/ and */h̃/ in syllable-final position, and evidence shows that many Aguaruna speakers either do not recognize the distinction, or ascribe it to vowel nasality. Based on evidence from the Nieva variety, in which syllable-final /h/ surfaces as [h] unless followed by another /h/, we can hypothesize that the [ŋ] allophone originally arose in this environment as a dissimilation to avoid an illegal identical /CC/ cluster, and has spread in the Marañón variety to all syllable-final /h/.

For a synchronic description of Aguaruna it is sufficient to posit just one phoneme /h/, which may phonetically nasalize adjacent vowels. Minimal pairs can be explained by assuming that the phonetic nasalization has given rise to phonemic vowel nasality for some speakers, and the instability of such minimal pairs only serves to strengthen the claim that they are not due to phonemically contrastive glottal fricatives.

3.2.5 Glides

There are three glide phonemes: /y/ is a voiced lamino-palatal approximant, /ɰ/ a voiced dorso-velar approximant and /w/ a voiced bilabial approximant, that appears to have no velar component – more accurately represented in IPA as /β/. Such a phoneme has been reported for other Amazonian languages such as Axininca Campa (David Payne 1981a) and Kashibo-Kakataibo (Zariquiey 2011). Overall (2007) analysed the glides as positional allophones of the vowels /i, ɨ, u/, respectively, however I find it more useful to treat them as distinct consonant phonemes. Treating the glides as syllable-initial allophones of vowels allows a more parsimonious phoneme inventory, and is attractive because they are in complementary distribution with vowels, but ignores the fact that glides behave as consonants for all phonological processes.

Glides do not count as moras for the purposes of the minimal word requirement. Consider, for example, the first person singular pronoun *wi*; the root is monomoraic and must have its vowel lengthened to form a valid independent phonological word: [βii]. This shows that the initial glide is not moraic. The underlying monovocalic root surfaces when further morphology is added, e.g. [βíka] *wi=ka* (1SG=TOP). By contrast, the first person plural pronoun *ii* is bimoraic and thus a valid phonological word [íi].

Glides count as consonants for accent shift, so they are skipped and not counted as moras. Example (3.30b) illustrates accent shift triggered by the accusative case enclitic *=na*. The shift is always one mora rightward, and in this example the glide [y] is skipped in favour of the following vowel, so must count as a consonant rather than a syllable nucleus (see §3.7 for details of accent shift).

(3.30) a. [táyu]
            tayu
            'oilbird'

       b. [tayún]
            tayu=na
            oilbird=ACC

More importantly, accent shift does not apply to words of more than four moras, and glides do not count for this purpose.

Glides act as consonants for syncope rules, but not for apocope (§3.5.1), and they have some phonotactic restrictions that also show they are not positional allophones.

3.2.5.1 Allophony of /w/

The glide /w/ is realized as a voiced bilabial fricative [β] when preceding the high front vowel /i/ in oral environments (3.31).

(3.31) a.   /wi=ka/ → [βí.ka]
                1sg=TOP

         b.   /kiiwi/ → [kíi.βi]
                centipede

3.2.5.2 Loss of intervocalic glides

The glides /w/ and /ɰ/ may optionally be elided in some environments.

A.   w → Ø /u_a

(3.32) a.   [puwántʃiŋ] ~ [puántʃiŋ]
                puwantʃiha
                Puanchig (proper name)

         b.   [yuwámi] ~ [yuámi]
                yu-a-mi
                eat-PFV-HORT
                'let's eat'

B.   ɰ → Ø /ɨ_a

(3.33) a.   [pɨɰák] ~ [pɨák]
                pɨɰaka
                'bed'

         b.   [wɨɰahɛi] ~ [wɨahɛi]
                wɨ-a-ha-i
                go-IPFV-1SG-DECL
                'I'm going'

In both of the above processes, the loss of the glide allows the two vowels to fuse into a single syllable nucleus, reducing the words from tri- to disyllables, as in (3.34).

(3.34)   /yu.wá.mi/ → [yuá.mi]
          'let's eat'

This process does not apply to glides in other positions. In all cases native speakers agree that the form with the glide is correct, and the form without it is a feature of rapid or casual speech.

Where syncope puts a glide into syllable-final position, or places a consonant immediately preceding a glide, the glide surfaces as a vowel. In other words, glides only surface as glides intervocalically. In (3.35), the ablative enclitic =ya surfaces as [ya] when it follows a vowel (a), and as [ia] when it follows a consonant due to elision of the preceding vowel (b).

(3.35) a.   [hɨ́ɰǎnmaya]
             hɨ́ɰa=numa=ya
             house=LOC=ABL
             'from the house'

        b.   [waβiknúmia]
             wawiku=numa=ya
             Wawik=LOC=ABL
             'from Wawik (river)'

Glides are treated as consonants in triggering syncope, but not apocope. The final /ya/ in (3.35a), although it surfaces as [ya], is not treated as a CV syllable; if it were, we would expect apocope to apply to the final vowel, giving a surface form **[hɨ́ɰǎnmɛi]. Compare example (3.36), in which the intermediate past tense marker -*maya* loses its final vowel to surface as [mɛi]. The intermediate form [ma.ya] is treated as two light syllables CV.CV, and the second of them ([ya]) loses its vowel. Because the glide [y] is placed into syllable-final position, it surfaces as [i].

(3.36)   [tsupíkmɛihɛi]
          tsupi-ka-maya-ha-i
          cut-PFV-INTPST-1SG-DECL
          'I cut it'

3.2.5.3 Phonotactic restrictions on glides and vowels
Glides have phonotactic restrictions based on syllable structure, and more specific restrictions based on the quality of adjacent vowels. [y] and [w] only appear word-initially or intervocalically. [ɰ] only appears intervocalically. Table 3.9 summarizes these restrictions.

Table 3.9: Phonotactic restrictions on glides based on syllable structure

glide	#_V	V_V	C_, _C, _#
/y/	✓	✓	–
/ɥ/	–	✓	–
/w/	✓	✓	–

In addition to these general restrictions, each has restrictions based on the vowels it may precede or follow. There is no /yi/ word-initially, but the sequence [yi] can appear word-internally. There is no surface /yɨ/ and no evidence for its underlying presence. There is evidence for underlying /ɥi/ in morphologically complex words, which surfaces as [yi] (note that the vowel sequences /iɨ/ and /ɨi/ never appear, see §3.3.1). There is no /wu/ in any position, word-initial or word-internal. The velar glide [ɰ] only appears in the environments /ɨ_u/, /ɨ_a/, /a_a/ and /u_a/. There is evidence from morphologically-conditioned vowel alternations that underlying [ɰ] is lost in the environments /a_u/ and /ɨ_ɨ/, and that it is realized as [y] when followed by /i/. There is no evidence for its underlying presence in any other environment. All of these restrictions are summarized in Table 3.10.

Table 3.10: Realizations of [ɰ] (empty cell = no evidence for underlying presence of ɰ)

first V	second V			
	i	ɨ	u	a
i	–	–	–	–
ɨ	–	∅	ɰ ~ ∅	ɰ ~ ∅
u	–	–	–	ɰ
a	y	–	∅	ɰ

Examples (3.37, 3.38) demonstrate the loss of [ɰ] in the two environments /ɨ_ɨ/ and /a_u/. In (3.37) the final vowel /a/ changes to /ɨ/ to mark first plural or third person possessor, and the glide is lost. In (3.38a), the glide surfaces in the imperfective stem, characterized by final /a/, but not in the unmarked stem with final /u/ (3.38b).

(3.37) a. [hɨ̃ɰ̃ã]
            'house'

        b. /hɨ̃ɰ̃ɨ/ → [hɨ̃ɨ̃]
            house+PSSD:1PL/3

(3.38) a. /kaɰa-mau/ → [kaɰamu]
            rot+IPFV-NMLZ

        b. /kaɰu-ta/ → [kout]
            rot-ACT.NMLZ

Example (3.39) illustrates the change of [ɰ] to [y] in the environment /a_i/, as the initial /i/ of the subject nominalizer -inu replaces the final vowel of the root.

(3.39)   /wɨkaɨɰa-inu/ → [wɨkəɨyin] NOT **[wɨkəɨɰin]
            walk-NMLZ
            'a walker'

The fact that the three glides have different phonotactic restrictions is further reason to treat them as phonemic: if they were allophones of the non-low vowels, we would expect to find more general rules governing their phonotactics.

3.2.6 Nasal stops

The nasal stops are bilabial /m/ and dental /n/. They are denasalized to [ᵐb, ⁿd] when they appear in non-nasal environments. Although this process is for the most part phonologically conditioned and optional, there are some morphological and lexical environments in which it is compulsory. The phenomenon is discussed at length in §3.4, in the wider context of nasal versus non-nasal articulations. There is no velar nasal phoneme /ŋ/ in Aguaruna, although the phone does surface syllable-finally, from two sources. Firstly, nasals [m, n, ŋ] may appear preceding a homor-ganic voiceless stop. Morphological evidence shows that some of these nasals alter-nate with vowel nasality, and can be analysed as arising from underlying nasal vowels – see discussion in §3.4. Secondly, the phone [ŋ] also arises as a syllable-final allophone of /h/, as described in §3.2.4 above.

3.2.6.1   Word-final loss of nasals
The nasal stops /m, n/ are optionally elided in word-final position (3.40, 3.41). The loss only happens in rapid speech, and does not appear to be conditioned by the initial phoneme of the following word.

(3.40)   [βíʃakam] ~ [βíʃaka]
            wi=ʃakama
            1sg=ADD
            'I too'

(3.41)   [datɨmán] ~ [datɨmá]
            datɨma=na
            ayahuasca=ACC

Loss of the [n] reflex of the accusative enclitic =*na* has led to the development of the
genitive form of the noun, as described in §4.10.3. The loss of nasal segments does
not leave any nasal quality in the preceding vowel, in keeping with the general observation that the nasal phonemes /m, n/ are not associated with vowel nasality.

3.2.7 Rhotic

Aguaruna has been described as lacking liquids (Wise 1999: 314), and neither
Corbera (1994) nor Wise (1999) includes a liquid phoneme in their inventories. This
is not the full story, however. Firstly, both [ɾ] and [l] are in common use in loans
from Spanish, including many proper names. Although most speakers preserve the
Spanish distinction of /ɾ/ versus /l/, for those who know less Spanish, especially
children, both sounds typically surface as [l]. Secondly, there is a native phoneme
/ɾ/, which typically surfaces as a voiced alveolar flap. It too varies freely with a lat-
eral [l] (example 3.42), but the [ɾ] pronunciation is considered by native speakers to
be more correct. The [l] pronunciation is typical in children's speech and only appears in very casual adult speech.

(3.42)   [piɾíya]~[pilíya]
            'variety of banana (Sp. *plátano guineo*)'

There are just four words in my corpus that contain the phoneme /ɾ/, listed in (3.43).
No minimal pairs exist, but other consonant phonemes are potentially contrastive in
intervocalic position.

(3.43) a. *piɾíya*
            'variety of banana (Sp. *plátano guineo*)'

        b. *suwákaɾɛip*
            'frog species' (where the noise made by the frog is said to be [kaɾéip])

    c.   *ʃaɾáʃam*
        'tree frog species'

    d.   *ⁿduɾíntsiu*
        'conehead katydid'

Example (b), and perhaps (c), are partially onomatopoetic, and (d) appears to be an adaptation of the Spanish *Lorenzo*, although it is not clear why the insect in question would be so named. No apparent cognates of these words appear in the published dictionaries of other Chicham languages. A few Aguaruna personal names have the phoneme /ɾ/, for example *Námarai*. All such names that I am aware of are also used in Huambisa communities, and it is reasonable to assume that these names have come from marriages with Huambisa speakers. Pike & Larson (1964: 56) say that the phoneme /ɾ/ "is present in the system only through loans from Spanish and Huambisa", but do not discuss it further. Note that the /ɾ/ of Aguaruna is not associated with the rhotic phoneme of Proto-Chicham described in §3.2.4.

3.2.8 Other consonantal allophony

When the vowel /ɨ/ follows one of the bilabial consonants /p/ or /m/, phonetic postlabialization typically occurs, as the vowel /ɨ/ requires spread lips.

(3.44)   [tɨpʷɨt]
           tɨpɨ-ta
           lie.down-ACT.NMLZ
           'lying down'

(3.45)   [ámʷɨ]
           amɨ
           'you (sg)'

This allophony is well-established, and represented in early transcriptions such as Karsten's (1935: 550) *amue* 'you (sg)'.

3.3 Vowels

There are four vowel phonemes, each with oral and nasal realizations, as shown in Table 3.11. Vowel nasality is phonemically contrastive, and spreads within a phonologically defined nasal domain (see §3.4 for a full description). Vowels therefore vary on three parameters: a two-way height distinction, a two-way nasality distinction, and a three-way backness distinction in the high vowels. A fourth parameter is rounding: only /u/ is rounded.

Table 3.11: Aguaruna vowel phonemes

	oral			nasal		
	front	central	back	front	central	back
high	i	ɨ	u	ĩ	ɨ̃	ũ
low		a			ã	

The high back vowel transcribed as /u/ typically has a somewhat lower realization than the cardinal vowel, and would be more accurately transcribed as /ʊ/. For consistency with the orthographic standard, I prefer to keep the symbol /u/.

In the diphthongs /ai/, /aɨ/ and /au/, the low vowel /a/ assimilates to immediately following high vowels: (A) it is raised and fronted when followed by /i/; (B) raised when followed by /ɨ/; (C) raised, backed and rounded when followed by /u/. This assimilation is obligatory in all speech registers.[9] The assimilations are exemplified in (3.46–3.48).

A.   /a/ → [ɛ] / _ i

(3.46)   [wɛinát]
            waina-ta
            see-ACT.NMLZ
            'seeing'

B.   /a/ → [ə] / _ ɨ

(3.47)   [əɨnts]
            aɨntsu
            'person'

---

9 Because the allophony of /a/ is completely predictable and obligatory, I transcribe it only in the present chapter; in the remainder of the grammar all underlying /a/ are transcribed as <a>.

C.   /a/ → [o] / _ u

(3.48)   [iⁿdóuk]
          inauka
          'sweet potato'

3.3.1 Vowel sequences

Any two-vowel sequence except **/ii/ and **/ɨi/ may form a surface long vowel or diphthong, and two-vowel sequences are frequent in both derived word forms and underived roots. In morphologically complex words triphthongs may be formed: the second vowel must be /a/ and the final vowel must be a vowel other than /a/, as in (3.49, 3.50).

(3.49)   [a.níou]
          anɨ-a-u
          remember-IPFV-NMLZ
          'one who remembers' (agr040712_02)

(3.50)   [taóu.mɨk]
          ta-a-umɨ=ka
          come-PFV-2SG=Q
          'have you arrived?' (typical greeting)

Triphthongs are infrequent, as the requisite morphological environment only rarely arises. The vast majority are word-final, as in example (3.49); example (3.50) is the only word-internal triphthong in my corpus – see further discussion in §3.5.

A glide, homorganic with the preceding vowel, appears between the first and second vowel in a word when (i) they are contiguous and (ii) the first is not /a/ and the second is /a/. This glide can be dropped in rapid speech, but native speakers consider it more correct to pronounce the glide, thereby putting the two vowels into separate phonetic syllables. This ensures that there are no *Va* diphthongs in initial syllables in careful speech.

Where morphological processes bring vowels together at morpheme junctures various sandhi rules are applied depending on the morphemes involved. Typically one of the vowels is deleted or an epenthetic glide is inserted. In addition, some morphemes have allomorphs involving consonants that surface to break up illegal vowel clusters. The various outcomes of vowel sandhi at morpheme boundaries are discussed in §3.6 on morphophonology.

Accent is assigned to one vocalic mora in every phonological word, and an ac-cented long vowel or diphthong will surface with a rising or falling pitch contour, reflecting the underlying accent position. I transcribe long vowels, diphthongs and triphthongs as sequences of vowels and mark the underlying accent position. So for example an underlying trisyllabic /ka.á.pɨ/ 'vine' after the application of apocope and synaeresis surfaces as a monosyllable, whose nucleus is phonetically a long vowel with a rising pitch contour: [kǎːp]. Transcribing the surface form as [kaáp] makes the phonology more transparent. There is no possibility of ambiguity in this transcription, because there is no possibility of contrast with a word-internal heter-osyllabic vowel sequence of the form **[ka.áp].

3.3.2 Elision and devoicing of vowels

Processes of apocope and syncope may operate on vowels according to their posi-tion in a phonological word. Vowel elision correlates with an earlier process of de-voicing, attested by previous analysts of Aguaruna and other Chicham languages, but absent from my data. Elision and devoicing are described in detail in the context of syllable structure in §3.5.

3.4 Nasal and oral prosodies

Nasal vowels contrast phonemically with oral vowels in roots and suffixes. The fol-lowing four observations form the basis of my analysis of nasality:

1. Nasality is a property of a phonological domain, defined as a contiguous se-quence of vowels and glides within a single phonological word. Morphophono-logical alternations show that nasality originating in a root or suffix spreads within the domain.
2. Nasal vowels may alternate with a syllable-final nasal consonant which takes its place of articulation from a following stop or affricate.
3. Nasal stops have oral counterparts that are for the most part phonologically conditioned allophones, but there is evidence that they are developing phone-mic status.
4. There is evidence to suggest that in addition to nasal articulation, oral articula-tion may also be treated as a marked feature of a nasal domain, and that in ad-dition to nasal spreading there is a complementary oral spreading phenomenon.

These phenomena are described in the following sections.

3.4.1 Nasality contrast, nasal domain and spreading

The nasal/oral contrast can be illustrated with minimal pairs in noun roots (3.51, 3.52) and verb roots (3.53). Note that the surface forms are given as examples, after nasal spreading has applied.

(3.51) a. [súw̃ɨ̃]   b. [súwɨ]
            'neck'   'dark'

(3.52) a. [ỹáỹã]   b. [yáya]
            'rat'   'star'

(3.53) a. [ũhát]   b. [uhát]
            ũha-ta   uha-ta
            open-ACT.NMLZ   tell-ACT.NMLZ
            'open'   'tell'

Bound morphemes may also be distinguished by nasality. The short allomorphs of the locative enclitic =(n)ĩ and instrumental =(a)i contrast only in nasality (3.54).

(3.54) a. [nṹw̃ĩ]   b. [ⁿdúβi]
            nu=ĩ   nu=i
            ANA=LOC   ANA=INS
            'in that place'   'by means of that'

Third-person subject in same-subject sequential subordinate verbs is marked solely by nasalization of the stem-final vowel. First person plural subject in the same environment is marked only by suppression of apocope, so the minimal pair in (3.55) is distinguished only by nasality of the final vowel.

(3.55) a. [húkĩ]   b. [húki]
            hu-kĩ   hu-ki
            take-PFV+SEQ+3:SS   take-PFV+SEQ+1PL:SS
            '(s/he) having taken...' '(we) having taken...'

A second morpheme marked with nasalization is first-person plural and third-person possessor in some vowel-changing nouns. Example (3.56a) shows third person possession marked with nasality, while the unpossessed root in (3.56b) has no nasal vowel, allowing the initial /n/ to be denasalized (§3.4.3; and see §4.8 for a description of nominal possession marking).

(3.56) a. [náw̃ĩ]   b. [ⁿdáwɨ]
            nawɨ̃   nawɨ
            foot+PSSD:1PL/3   foot
            'his/her foot', 'our feet'   'a foot'

Nasality spreads to contiguous vowels and glides, but spreading is blocked by any non-glide consonant or a word boundary. The domain of nasality is thus a sequence of contiguous vowels and glides within a single phonological word. In example (3.55) above, the domain of nasalization does not extend beyond the final vowel as it is blocked by the voiceless stop /k/; but in example (3.56), the nasal domain consists of two vowels and the glide between them. Nasal spreading is bidirectional, as can be seen in example (3.57), in which nasality spreads leftwards and rightwards from the underlyingly nasal locative enclitic =(n)ĩ:

(3.57)   [tũw̃ĩỹã]
            tu=ĩ=ya
            where=LOC=ABL
            'from where?'

Aguaruna is typical of the Amazonian area in showing nasal spreading, which has been noted as a potential areal feature by various authors: Doris Payne (2001: 595); Aikhenvald (2002: 45–46, 2006: 13 for Tucanoan and neighbouring Arawak languages); and see the contributions in Bruno et al. (2008).

3.4.2 Alternation of Ṽ with VN

Vowels which surface as nasal in word-final position surface as oral when followed by a consonant-initial suffix or enclitic, and the nasal component manifests as a nasal stop with the same place of articulation as the following consonant; this is illustrated by the alternations in (3.58). The consonants that trigger NC cluster formation are voiceless stops /p, t, k/ and affricates /ts, tʃ/.

(3.58) a. [ɨtsã]   b. [ɨtsantút]
            ɨtsã   ɨtsã-tu-ta
            'sun'   sun-VBLZ-ACT.NMLZ
                                            'shine'

(3.59) a. [yutéĩ]
   yu-taĩ
   eat-NSBJ.NMLZ
   'food'

       b. [yutéĩŋkɛit]
         yu-taĩ=ka=ita
         eat-NSBJ.NMLZ=Q=COP:3
         'is it food?'

Many roots contain homorganic NC clusters, and these nasals are the only permitted codas prior to the application of vowel elision; it would be useful to bring these into the same analysis as the NC clusters that alternate with nasal vowels. David Payne (1978) suggests an analysis whereby all nasal vowels arise from underlying syllable-final nasal segments which are unspecified for place of articulation; the alternation can then be explained with a rule which assimilates an underlying syllable-final nasal into a homorganic cluster with a following voiceless stop or affricate, or allows it to be realised as a nasal vowel otherwise. However, this analysis is unsatisfactory as it does not capture the observation that CVN syllables are treated as monomoraic, identically to CV syllables, for the purposes of the minimal word requirement (§3.5.1), and that nasal vowels can be freely elided while CVC syllables block vowel elision (§3.5.2).[10] Both of these phenomena are explained by assuming the converse, namely that all NC clusters arise from underlyingly nasal vowels, as illustrated in (3.60–3.62). (For the sake of simplicity, I transcribe these non-alternating NC clusters using the surface form in the rest of this grammar.)

(3.60) [kámpa]
    kãpa
    'ant sp. (*pucacuro*)'

(3.61) [tsúntsu]
    tsũtsu
    'snail sp.'

(3.62) [tʃĩŋki]
    tʃĩki
    'game bird (in general)'

The one exception is the action nominalizer *-ta*, which does not trigger NC cluster formation; compare (3.63a), with no NC cluster, with and (3.63b).

---

10 In the previous version of this grammar (Overall 2007: 60–61) I gave examples of CVN syllables apparently blocking vowel elision, but subsequent work has shown that these examples must involve exceptional non-eliding vowels (§3.5.2.1).

(3.63) a. [yɛ̃ĩ́t]
　　　　　yaĩ-ta
　　　　　help-ACT.NMLZ
　　　　　'helping'

　　　　b. [yɛimpákti]
　　　　　yaĩ-pa-ka-ti
　　　　　help-2.OBJ-PFV-JUSS
　　　　　'may (God) help you'

3.4.3 Denasalization

The nasal consonants /m, n/ are partially denasalized in non-nasal environments, that is where they are followed by a sequence of contiguous oral vowels and sonorants that is not followed by a nasal consonant (3.64–3.65).

(3.64) a. /míʃu/ → [bíʃu]~[ᵐbíʃu] 'cat'
　　　　b. /níka/ → [díka]~[ⁿdíka] 'know'

(3.65) a. /yamái/ → [yaᵐbéi] 'now, today'
　　　　b. /ináuk/ → [iⁿdóuk] 'sweet potato'

The denasalization is partial when word-internal, producing prenasalized voiced stops as in (3.65), but may be partial or full word-initially, producing prenasalized or fully oral stops (3.64).

The actual likelihood of denasalization also depends on the quality of the immediately following vowels and position in the word of the nasal stop. Denasalization typically does not occur when the nasal is followed by single word-final /a/. This predicts such alternations as those in (3.66) and (3.67).

(3.66) a. [mamá]
　　　　　mama
　　　　　mother
　　　　　'mother'

　　　　b. [maᵐbóu]
　　　　　mama-u
　　　　　mother+VOC-FAM
　　　　　'mummy!'

(3.67) a. [mína]
　　　　　mi=na
　　　　　1sg=ACC
　　　　　'me'

　　　　b. [míⁿdou]
　　　　　mi-nau
　　　　　1sg-POSS
　　　　　'mine'

The examples in (3.66b) and (3.67b) also show that only the environment *following* a nasal stop is relevant. They can be denasalized, even though the preceding syllable contains a nasal. The word-initial nasals cannot be denasalized because in both examples they are followed by nasal stops within the domain of nasal spreading.

Denasalization is more likely when preceding a high vowel, or when the nasal is word-initial and followed by a single vowel, as in (3.64) and the examples in (3.68).

(3.68) a. /núsɨ/   →   [dúsɨ]~[ⁿdúsɨ]   'peanut'
        b. /nátsa/   →   [dátsa]~[ⁿdátsa]   'youth'

But some words that appear to fulfil the criteria are typically not denasalized (3.69, 3.70).

(3.69)   [núwa] NOT **[ⁿdúwa]
            'woman'

(3.70)   [númi] NOT **[núᵐbi]
            'tree'

And some words are always associated with an oral stop: *dii* 'see'; *duku* 'mother'; *dika* 'know'; *dapa* 'bee'. Such words never surface with nasal stops in my data, unlike other forms, and literate native speakers prefer to write them using orthographic <b>, <d>. Here it is worth quoting David Payne (1978) at length:

> Pike y Larson manifiestan que las palabras [baku] 'muslo' y [duku] 'madre' no varian con las consonantes nasales. Varios de mis informantes usaban [maku] 'muslo'. Pese a que ninguno de ellos usaba [nuku] 'madre', escuché esto a menudo en el lenguaje infantil. Además, en los datos de Ray Wakelin [duku] 'madre' aparece en fluctuación con [nuku] 'madre'. Sin embargo, parece que, como Pike y Larson indicaron, hay algunas palabras con oclusivas sonoras iniciales en ambientes orales, para las cuales los hablantes rara vez, si alguna, usan consonantes nasales, excepto en el lenguaje infantil.

> [Pike and Larson state that the words [baku] 'thigh' and [duku] 'mother' do not alternate with nasal consonants. A number of my informants would use [maku] 'thigh'. Although none of them used [nuku] 'mother', I heard this often in children's speech. Furthermore, in Ray Wakelin's[11] data [duku] 'mother' appears in fluctuation with [nuku] 'mother'. However, it appears that, as Pike and Larson indicate, there are some words with initial voiced obstruents in oral environments, for which speakers rarely, if ever, use nasal consonants, except in children's speech.]

> (David Payne 1978: 54)

There are some lexical items in which denasalization is compulsory, while it remains optional in the rest of the lexicon. On the basis of this phenomenon, Corbera (1994) takes the position that [b] and [d] are recently established phonemes:

---

11 Payne here refers to Pike & Larson (1964). Ray Wakelin was an SIL missionary who worked with the Aguaruna before Larson. No bibliographical reference is given for the data attributed to Wakelin.

As plosivas sonoras /b/, /d/ diacronicamente não faziam parte do sistema fonológico do Agua-runa, porém no nível sincrônico elas podem ser consideradas como fonemas, pois esses seg-mentos sofrem um processo acelerado de fonologização, sobretudo na fala dos bilingües.

[The voiced plosives /b/, /d/ did not form part of the Aguaruna phonological system diachroni-cally, however at the synchronic level they must be considered phonemes, since these seg-ments are undergoing an accelerated process of phonologization, especially in the speech of bilinguals.]

(Corbera 1994: 31)

So Corbera interprets this as a case of a change in progress: [b] and [d] are in the process of becoming phonemes, and the phonologization is diffusing through the lexicon, in the sense of Chen & Wang (1975). Corbera (1994) also mentions the influ-ence of Spanish, and it is important to note that the alphabet of Aguaruna itself includes the letters <b, d> in addition to <m, n>. The majority of Aguaruna speakers are literate in Aguaruna, so the forced choice between nasal and non-nasal ortho-graphic representation may play some standardizing role for the more stable occur-rences of [b] and [d].

For the majority of cases, however, [b] and [d] remain purely phonologically-conditioned allophones of /m/ and /n/, and native speakers are generally accepting of nasal pronunciations even where they would not use such a form themselves, and vice versa.[12] Only two surface minimal pairs appear in my data:

(3.71) a. [yuwámi]
            yu-a-mi
            eat-PFV-HORT
            'let's eat'

        b. [yuwá^{m}bi]
            yu-a-mayi
            eat-PFV-INTPST:3:DECL
            'he ate'

(3.72) a. [númi]
            numi
            'tree'

        b. [nú^{m}bi]
            numi=i
            tree=INS
            'with a (piece of) wood'

But both oppositions arise from an underlying length distinction in the final sylla-ble: the underlying form of the intermediate past third person form is /mayi/ – the

---

12 This view is supported by Payne's observation (1978: 53): "Varios informantes que eran bastante elocuentes para corregir mis errores afirmaban que yo estaba diciendo una palabra correctamente si usaba una [m] allí donde ellos usaban de manera consistente [b]." [A number of informants who were quite vocal in correcting my mistakes affirmed that I was saying a word correctly if I used [m] where they consistently used [b].] If these words did in fact contain oral stops, in phonemic contrast to nasals, it is unlikely that a native speaker would accept the substitution as Payne describes.

/a/ is lost to syncope, giving an intermediate form /yuwamii/, which surfaces as [yuwábi]. Similarly the instrumental enclitic =(a)i fuses with the preceding /i/, but the denasalization appears to have had effect prior to that. So both minimal pairs can be explained by appealing to underlying phonological differences that trigger denasalization in one form but not the other. Given the lack of minimal pairs and the unstable realizations, I do not consider [b] and [d] to be phonemes. Instead, I treat all examples as allophones of /m/ and /n/ that surface in non-nasal environments. The oral allophones may be preferred in a few lexical items; those words where the nasal allophone is preferred all alternate morphologically with oral forms, giving rise to partial minimal pairs such as those in (3.73).

(3.73) a. [núwa]   b. [ⁿduwán̠]
            nuwa   nuwa-hu
            'a woman'   woman-PSSD:1SG
                                                'my wife'

Also compare *numi* 'tree, wood' (examples 3.72a and b above) where the nominative form is not denasalized, and contrasts with the denasalized instrumental form. The converse phenomenon can explain some (but not all) of the compulsorily denasalized forms too, such as those in (3.74).

(3.74) a. [ⁿdáwɨ]   b. [nãw̃ɨ]
            'a foot'   foot+PSSD:1PL/3
                                                'our/his/her/their feet'

These examples cannot be adduced as evidence of phonologization, as the alternation in all cases is still phonologically conditioned. What is unusual about them is the apparent lack of optionality in applying the denasalization rule, and this must be motivated by the alternation with denasalized or nasalized forms in the paradigm.

In my transcription of underlying forms, I transcribe the nasal form where the alternation is predictable from the rules, and the oral form where native speakers consistently pronounce and write the oral allophone. In surface forms, I use the symbols <b> and <d> to transcribe the denasalized segments.

A further perplexing phenomenon is the obligatory denasalization triggered by two /h/-initial suffixes. The first person singular possessor suffix -hu and pluractional perfective suffix -ha denasalize a preceding nasal domain of the stem to which they are attached, and if the consonant preceding the nasal domain is /m/ or /n/, it is also denasalized to [b] or [d] respectively; compare the (a) forms with the denasalized (b) forms in examples (3.75–3.77).

(3.75) a. [hĩ́ɰ̃ã]
            hĩɰa

            'house'

b. [hɨɰán]
    hɨɰa-hu
    house-PSSD:1SG
    'my house'

(3.76) a. [umáim]
            umai-mɨ
            sibling+PSSD-2
            'your sibling of the opposite sex'

b. [uᵐbán]
    uma-hu
    sibling-PSSD:1SG
    'my sibling of the opposite sex'

(3.77) a. [nihát]
            niha-ta
            wash-ACT.NMLZ
            'to wash'

b. [dihán̪tahɛi]
    niha-ha-ta-ha-i
    wash-PFV-IFUT-1SG-DECL
    'I'll wash (it)'

Both of these suffixes have cognates with initial /r/ in the other Chicham languages; elsewhere reflexes of PC */r/ tend to *nasalize* the preceding vowel (§3.2.4.1), making this phenomenon all the more mysterious. This is an issue that future comparative work may be able to explain.

Finally, some verbs that have final /u/ in the unmarked stem show nasal vowels when derivational morphology is added.[13]

(3.78) a. [móut]
            mau-ta
            kill-ACT.NR
            'to kill'

b. [mántin]
    mã-tu-inu
    kill-APPL-NMLZ
    'a good hunting dog' (i.e. one who kills (game) for someone)

This phenomenon, together with the loss of final /u/ in the derived form, suggest that the /u/ of these verbs may have originated as a verbal suffix. The /u/ is also lost in the perfective and imperfective stems (see discussion of verb conjugations in §6.2).

3.5 Syllable structure and vowel elision

A syllable nucleus may be monomoraic, consisting of a single short vowel; or it may be bimoraic, consisting of a long vowel (treated as a sequence of two identical vowels) or a diphthong. Because the target of the pitch accent is the vocalic mora, a

---

13 Also compare *kapau-* 'burn', *kapantu* 'red'.

syllable containing a diphthong or long vowel may have a falling or rising pitch contour if its first or second mora is accented (see §3.7). The vowels in complex nuclei participate in accent shift in the same way as heterosyllabic vowels. Vowel combinations other than /V₁V₁/ and /aV/ are typically avoided in the first syllable of a word, and are separated into two syllables by inserting a glide between them (§3.3.1). In morphologically complex forms the triphthong structure CV₁aV₃ is possible, where V₁ can be any vowel; V₂ must be /a/ and V₃ must be a high vowel (i.e. not /a/) (§3.5.4).

Surface forms allow frequent consonantal codas, but these arise from synchronic processes of vowel elision that operate on a simpler underlying syllable structure. The maximum syllable prior to the application of vowel elision is CVVN, where N represents the nasal stop in a homorganic, heterosyllabic NC cluster (§3.4). The onset consists of just one consonant; only word-initial syllables may lack an onset, so the minimum syllable is CV word-internally, and V word-initially. Apocope and syncope operate on CV syllables, and introduce consonantal codas into the surface syllable structure (§3.5.2).

There are just a few phonotactic restrictions on syllable structure: the velar glide /ɰ/ may not appear word-initially, and there are some restrictions on glide-vowel sequences (§3.2.5.3); the vowel combinations **ii̶ and **i̶i are disallowed (§3.3.1); and there are some restrictions on affricate-vowel sequences (§3.2.3).

In the following sections I first describe the minimal word restriction (§3.5.1), then in §3.5.2 to §3.5.5 I describe the vowel elision phenomena and their effects on the surface forms of words. Finally in §3.5.6 I address some previous analyses of the phenomena.

3.5.1 Minimal word

The minimal word in Aguaruna is two vocalic moras – only interjections can have fewer than two surface moras, and the first two moras of a word are never subject to elision. Syllable structure is irrelevant to the minimal word, which may be disyllabic (CV.CV, e.g. *ká.nu* 'canoe'), or monosyllabic with a long vowel or diphthong (CVV, e.g. *tʃúu* 'woolly monkey; *kái* 'avocado'). Codas are similarly irrelevant: CVN is a monomoraic syllable. This is illustrated in (3.79a): the final nasal /ŋ/ in the first syllable does not count as a mora, and apocope cannot apply to this form as the output would not fulfil the minimal word requirement. As noted above (§3.4), this is explained by assuming the CVN syllable is underlyingly CṼ. Examples (3.79b) and (c) show that apocope may result in monosyllabic or disyllabic words, so long as they fulfil the minimum two mora requirement.

(3.79) a. /tʃí.ki/ → [tʃĩŋ.ki] NOT **[tʃĩŋ]
            'game bird'

        b. /búu.kɨ/ → [ᵐbúuk]
            'head'

        c. /pí.ʃa.ka/ → [pí.ʃak]
            'bird'

Conversely, CV roots are lengthened when they appear without morphology, to fulfil the minimal word requirement (compare bare roots in 3.80a, 3.81a with the b forms).

(3.80) a. [βíi]   b. [βíka]
            wi   wi=ka
            1sg   1sg=TOP

(3.81) a. [núu]   b. [núna]
            nu   nu=na
            ANA   ANA=ACC

3.5.2 Vowel elision

There are three processes of vowel elision: APOCOPE, SYNCOPE[14] and DIPHTHONG REDUC-TION. That these are distinct processes can be seen from the fact that syncope is affected by the output of apocope. Vowel elision can freely apply to both oral and nasal vowels, and accented vowels may be elided. The repositioning of accent following elision follows different rules in nouns and verbs (§3.7).

Apocope operates first, eliding the nucleus of a final light (CV) syllable (3.82, 3.83; throughout the discussion of elision, vowels in **bold** type are those that are subject to elision). The minimal word requirement means that apocope does not apply to words of fewer than three moras.

(3.82)   [na.há.nat]
            na.ha.na.-**ta**
            create-ACT.NMLZ
            'to create'

---

14 I follow Payne (1990b) in using the term *syncope* slightly differently from the traditional definition of e.g. Matthews (1997: 367: "the loss of unstressed vowels in the middle of a word") – accent position is not a conditioning factor in the application of syncope in Aguaruna.

(3.83)   [pi.nín]
          pi.ni.**ha**
          'ceramic bowl'

Apocope does not apply to CV syllables where C is a glide; the final CV syllables in (3.84a) and (b) do not have their vowels elided, as they both have glides as onsets. Glides are treated the same as any other consonant for syncope – see example (3.86).

(3.84) a. [hĩꞯãnmaya]
            hĩ.ꞯa=**nu**.ma=ya
            house=LOC=ABL
            'from the house'

        b. [kíi.βi]
            kii.wi
            'centipede'

Syncope operates metrically, targetting alternate moras. Like apocope, syncope does not affect the first two moras of the word. Syncope also targets CV syllables. If the third mora is in a CV syllable, it is elided; likewise subsequent odd-numbered moras (3.85a, b).

(3.85) a. [nú.nik.tʃat.ta.kuik]
            nu-ni-**ka**-tʃa-**ta**.ta-ku-i=ka
            ANA-VBLZ.INTR-PFV-NEG-FUT-SIM-1PL:SS=COND
            'if we don't do that ...' (Text 3:17)

        b. [óuŋ.mat.ᵐbou]
            au.**hu**.ma-ta-mau
            tell.story-APPL+IPFV-NSBJ.NMLZ
            'a story'

If the third mora is not part of a CV syllable then it is skipped, and the fourth mora is targetted; the metrical application of the process is then "reset", and continues to apply to subsequent even-numbered moras in CV syllables (3.86).

(3.86)   [a.nɨn.téim.ta.kua]
          a.nɨn.tai.**ma**-ta-ka.wa
          think-APPL+IPFV-REPET+1PL:SS
          '(we) thinking ...' (Text 3:14)

Syncope follows apocope. If the vowel of a final CV syllable is elided, the erstwhile onset is resyllabified as a coda and blocks the application of syncope to the penultimate syllable; this can be seen in example (3.82) above, where the third syllable from the left fulfils the criteria for syncope to apply in the underlying representation, but after apocope of the final vowel the /t/ is resyllabified, closing the third syllable. As the third syllable is now CVC, it is not subject to syncope: the surface form is not **[na.hánt]. This effect can be readily seen in nouns which alternate between a citation form to which apocope has applied (3.87a) and forms with CV suffixes or enclitics, in which the final vowel of the root cannot be elided (3.87b).

(3.87) a.   [pí.ʃak]
            pi.ʃa.**ka**
            bird

        b.   [pi.ʃá.kan]
            pi.ʃa.ka=**na**
            bird=ACC

Nasal vowels can be elided (3.88a), (3.88b); as noted in §3.4.2, this makes an analysis deriving nasal vowels from underlying VN unsatisfactory, as closed syllables are expected to block vowel elision.

(3.88) a.   [nú.nik]
            nu-ni-**kã**
            ANA-VBLZ.INTR-PFV+SEQ+3:SS
            'having done that …'

        b.   [ni.hám.tʃĩn]
            ni.ha.mã.tʃi=**na**
            masato=ACC

3.5.2.1   Non-eliding vowels

There are some examples of vowels that do not elide as predicted by the process described above. Compare the examples in (3.89), with the action nominalizer suffix -*ta* in (a) and the homophonous imperative suffix in (b).

(3.89) a.   [ɨ.kɨ.mat]
            ɨ.kɨ.ma.-**ta**
            sit.down-ACT.NMLZ
            'to sit down'

b. [ɨ.kɨ́m.sa.ta]
i.kɨ.ma.-sa.-ta
sit.down-PFV-IMP
'sit down!'

In example (3.89b), the final vowel /a/ fulfils the criteria to undergo apocope – the output as predicted by the apocope rule should be **[ɨkɨ́msat]. But the full syllable /ta/ appears in the surface form. This and other non-eliding vowels must be lexically marked as such. There is no optionality to elision or non-elision: any given vowel in a particular root or suffix will either always undergo elision (when in the correct environment), or it never will. The action nominalizer -ta is always elided when it is in a position to do so, while the imperative suffix -ta NEVER undergoes vowel elision.

If the third vowel of a form is marked as non-eliding, then the fourth becomes the potential target of syncope, as we saw above when the third vowel is not part of a CV syllable. The process then moves to the sixth vowel and every alternate following vowel, as in example (3.90) where the third vowel of the root ikɨma- 'light (a fire)' is marked as never undergoing vowel elision.

(3.90) [ɨ.kɨ.mák.tat.hɛi]
i.kɨ.ma.-ka.-ta.ta.-ha.-i
light.fire-PFV-FUT-1SG-DECL
'I will light a fire'

Non-eliding vowels also appear within lexical roots, as in (3.91).

(3.91) /pa.ám.pa/ → [paámpa] NOT **[paám]
'plantain'

Note that paampa 'plantain' also does not undergo the accent shift expected in a nominal of three moras when the accusative enclitic is added (3.92).

(3.92) [paámpan yuwámhɛi]
paampa=na   yu-a-ma-ha-i
plantain=ACC   eat-PFV-RECPST-1SG-DECL
'I ate plantains'

Cognates in other Chicham languages suggest that some non-eliding vowels may have originated in CVC syllables that have since been simplified. For example, comparative data show that the frustrative suffix -takama (see §13.3) and intentional -tata (§8.4) historically had consonantal codas in their non-eliding first syllables. An example of how such a process can begin can be seen when the causative suffix *-mitika* surfaces as [mika] instead of expected [mitka] (§7.7). The existence of lexically defined exceptions to vowel elision shows that the processes are not purely phonologically conditioned synchronically. To capture the regularities of morphology, however, I use underlying representations in all examples.

3.5.3 Diphthong reduction

Diphthong reduction (DR) is a similar process to vowel elision, whereby a sequence /CaV/ (where V = {i, ɨ, u}) is reduced to /CV/. Some examples are in (3.93–3.95), again the elided vowels are bolded.

(3.93)   ami-n**a**u → [áminu]
             2sg-POSS
             'yours'

(3.94)   tsawa-ha-**ɨ** → [tsawáhɨ̃]
             dawn-PFV-3:DECL
             '(day) has dawned'

(3.95)   maa-n**a**i-a-mi → [maániami]
             kill-RECIP-PFV-HORT
             'let's fight'

In all instances of DR, the vowel /a/ is elided when it would be in a position to be syncopated if it were in a CV syllable. So in example (3.96), DR does not occur because the vowel /a/ is the second vowel in the word.

(3.96)   [míⁿdou]
             mi-nau
             1sg-POSS
             'mine'

DR is not purely phonologically conditioned, being limited to a few morphological environments. The nominalizer *-u*, third-person immediate past *-ɨ̃*, and past tense second person subject markers *-umɨ* (sg) and *-uhumɨ* (pl) all trigger DR when suffixed to a perfective stem that terminates in /Ca/, and a small set of suffixes shows internal DR.

3.5.3.1 DR with nominalizer -*u* and immediate past -*ɨ*

Perfective stems in combination with the nominalizer -*u* show diphthong reduction (3.97–3.99).

(3.97) [tɨpɨsú]
tɨpɨ-sa-u
lie.down-PFV-NMLZ
'lain down' (agr040723_29)

(3.98) [itʃiŋkú]
itʃĩ-ka-u
pull.apart-PFV-NMLZ
'pulled apart' (agr040723_29)

(3.99) [kuwáʃat wɨɰahui]
kuwaʃata   wɨ-aha-u=i
many   go+PFV-PL-NMLZ=COP:3:DECL
'many (people) went' (agr041005_14)

As noted above, DR only applies if the first vowel of the diphthong would be in a position to be syncopated. In the examples in (3.100, 3.101) the /a/ is the fourth vowel in each case and could not be syncopated; so DR also does not apply.

(3.100) [əɨpsóu]
aɨpɨ-sa-u
leave-PFV-NMLZ
'left' (agr040723_29)

(3.101) [akupkóu]
akupɨ-ka-u
release-PFV-NMLZ
'released' (agr040723_29)

The preceding examples also show that DR cannot be explained by assuming that apocope has applied before the nominalizer -*u* is added – if that were the case, we would expect the surface forms to be **[aɨpɨsu] and **[akupɨku] respectively. The phenomenon of morpheme-internal DR (described below) also argues against such a hypothesis. Following DR the short =*i* allomorph of the third person copula enclitic appears, which only follows single vowels (see §4.14), as in (3.102), also (3.99) above.

(3.102)   [atʃikuí]
            atʃi-**ka**-u=i
            grab-PFV-NMLZ=COP:3:DECL
            'grabbed' (Text 1:9)

Stems in which the perfective suffix -*a(w)* has fused with a root-final /a/ do not undergo DR, in keeping with the general observation that such forms always block elision (3.103).

(3.103)   [ahápouwɛi]
            ahapa-a-u=ai
            discard-PFV-NMLZ=COP:3:DECL
            'he threw (it) out'

But unsuffixed perfective stems do undergo DR (3.104).

(3.104)   [pɨmpɨ́ɨnun]
            pɨmpɨɨna-u=na
            turn.around+PFV-NMLZ=ACC
            '(one who) turned around' (agr040723_29)

Perfective stems terminating in /Ca/ and followed by the third-person perfective past suffix -*ɨ* are reduced in the same way to /Cɨ/ (3.105).

(3.105)   [tsawáhɨ̃]
            tsawa-**ha**-ɨ̃
            dawn-PFV-3:DECL
            '(day) has dawned'

Imperfective stems do not undergo DR when nominalizer -*u* is added, presumably because of the presence of the imperfective suffix -*a* (3.106).

(3.106)   [tupikóu] NOT **[tupikú]
            tupika-a-u
            run-IPFV-NMLZ
            'running' (agr040723_29)

And -*ina-u* (PL:IPFV-NMLZ) typically surfaces as [inau] not **[inu], although in rapid speech DR does occasionally apply (3.107).

(3.107)   [iᵐbáthuinu]
           imatu-hu-in**a**-u
           insist-APPL-PL:IPFV-NMLZ
           '(those who) were insisting' (agr041005_14)

Some apparently exceptional applications of DR arise from non-eliding vowels, as in example (3.108). Normally the third vowel would be elided by syncope, blocking the application of DR and giving the surface form **[apúttsauwai]. But the third vowel of the stem *aputu-* 'put+APPL' is a lexically marked non-eliding vowel, so the fourth vowel is available to be the target of DR, just as we saw above with syncope.

(3.108)   [apútusui]
           aputu-**sa**-u=i
           put+APPL-PFV-NMLZ=COP:3:DECL
           '(he) put (it)' (agr041005_15)

3.5.3.2   Suffix-internal diphthong reduction

Four suffixes, listed in Table 3.12, show diphthong reduction morpheme-internally.

Table 3.12: Diphthong reducing suffixes

underlying form	reduced form	gloss
-mau	*-mu*	non-subject nominalizer
-tʃau	*-tʃu*	negative nominalizer
-nau	*-nu*	possessor
-nai	*-ni*	reciprocal

The examples in (3.109–3.112) illustrate the forms where DR has applied.

(3.109)   [yúwamu]
           yu-a-**mau**
           eat-IPFV-NSBJ.NMLZ
           'what is eaten'

(3.110)   [ỹãw̃ã́ãtʃuithɛi]
           yawaã-tʃ**au**=ita-ha-i
           dog-NEG.NMLZ=COP-1SG-DECL
           'I am not a dog' (agr060816_01)

(3.111)   [íinu]
            ii-nau
            1pl-POSS
            'ours'

(3.112)   [máanit]
            maa-nai-ta
            kill-RECIP-ACT.NMLZ
            'fighting'

The three -*Cau* forms (-*mau*, -*tʃau* and -*nau*) are almost certainly historically derived from suffixes of the form /Ca/ combined with the nominalizer -*u*: -*ma* marks a switch of non-subject to subject (see §13.5), -*tʃa* marks negative (see §11.1), and accusative =*na* marks possessors (see §4.10). So their DR effects are diachronically similar to other applications of DR that are triggered by the nominalizer -*u*. There is no evidence, however, for historical morphological complexity to the reciprocal suffix -*nai*. Note also that I am not postulating synchronic morphological complexity in the -*Cau* forms. That this is not the case is demonstrated by the negative nominalizer -*tʃau*: the negative suffix -*tʃa* only appears with verb roots, but the negative nominalizer -*tʃau* appears with verbal, nominal and adjectival roots, so it must be a synchronically independent suffix.

3.5.4 The syllable following vowel elision

Three elision processes – apocope, syncope and diphthong reduction – have been described above. After the application of these processes, the surface-level syllable is minimally V word-initially and CV word-internally. The nucleus may consist of any long vowel or diphthong, or a triphthong which must be of the form /V_1aV_3/, where V_1 can be any vowel and V_3 can be any vowel other than /a/. Triphthongs are rare, appearing only in morphologically complex words and limited morphological environments. All consonants except glides can appear in the coda, so the maximum surface syllable is CVVV, CVVC or CVVNC$_{AFFRICATE}$ (see §3.5.5.1 for discussion of the final affricate). Allophony conditioned by position within the syllable demonstrates the phonological reality of this constituent.

Resyllabification apparently applies recursively throughout the processes of affixation and vowel elision. A consonant forms the onset of a syllable if it is followed by a vowel. No more than one consonant is permitted in the onset. A consonant which is not followed by a vowel is resyllabified into the coda of the preceding syllable if permitted, otherwise it is elided (§3.5.5.1). Sequences of two vowels fuse into the nucleus of a single syllable. Identical vowels form a long vowel (3.113), and non-identical vowels form a diphthong (3.114).

(3.113)   [háa.hɛi]
           ha-a-ha-i
           be.sick-IPFV-1SG-DECL
           'I'm sick' (Text 2:31)

(3.114)   [tóu]
           ta-u
           say+IPFV-NMLZ
           'saying' (agr041005_15)

Note that reduplicated material may terminate with a diphthong, but not a consonant, showing that the second element of a diphthong is part of the nucleus, and cannot be analysed as a glide forming a consonantal coda. Triphthongs may be formed in morphologically complex words only if the second element is /a/ and the third /i/, /ɨ/ or /u/ (3.115).

(3.115)   [a.nɨou]
           anɨ-a-u
           remember-IPFV-NMLZ
           'one who remembers' (agr040712_02)

An illustration of the surface syllable comes from the reduplication rule (§3.8.1), which copies the first syllable, plus the second syllable minus any coda, of the word to which it applies, as in (3.116).

(3.116)   [pampéi pampéinakŭã]
           pampai   pampa-ina-kawã
           REDUP   discuss-PL:IPFV-REPET+3:SS
           '(as they were) discussing and discussing...' (agr040719_01)

The verb root is disyllabic /pampa/, but the /i/ of the plural imperfective suffix /ina/ is included in the reduplicated element. This shows that the /i/ has been syllabified into the nucleus of the second syllable of the word. A further example is given by the resyllabification of a consonant after the application of apocope, closing the preceding syllable and blocking syncope (§3.5.2 above).

3.5.5 Syllable-position-conditioned consonantal effects

As shown above, vowel elision moves consonants into coda position in many syllables. In general these consonants form valid clusters, but there are some important effects arising from consonants being put into syllable-final position.

3.5.5.1   Elision of stops

Prior to the application of vowel elision, the only codas permitted are nasals in NC clusters. Vowel elision places other consonants into coda position, which gives rise to the possibility of having both members of an NC cluster in the same coda. However, there is a restriction prohibiting a stop from being the second element in a coda, so any stop that loses its syllable nucleus to elision, and cannot be resyllabified into a preceding coda, must be deleted. The examples in (3.117–3.119) illustrate this.

(3.117)   /u.kúm.pɨ/   →   *[u.kúm**p**]   →   [u.kúm]
            'blackfly (*manta blanca*)'

(3.118)   /mú.un.**ta**/   →   *[múun**t**]   →   [múun]
            'big', 'adult'

(3.119)   /wám.paŋ.**ku**/   →   *[wám.paŋ**k**]   →   [wám.paŋ]
            'morpho butterfly'

The same restriction applies word-internally (3.120).

(3.120)   /ti.hiŋ.**ka**.sá.=na/   →   *[ti.hiŋ**k**.sán]   →   [ti.hiŋ.sán]
            ribbon=ACC

But it does not apply to affricates in the same environments (3.121), (3.122).

(3.121)   /a.ɨn.**tsu**/   →   [ɘɨnts]
            'person'

(3.122)   /a.ɨn.**tsu**.=na.=ka/   →   [ɘɨnts.nak]
            person=ACC=TOP

3.5.5.2   Simplification of CC

The only identical CC clusters permitted at surface level are the dentals [tt] and [nn], shown in (3.123, 3.124).

(3.123)   [yuwáttahɛi]
            yu-a-tata-ha-i
            eat-PFV-FUT-1SG-DECL
            'I will eat'

(3.124)   [aánna]
            aanu=na
            MED=ACC

Such clusters are realized with a delayed release. Since voiceless stops surface as unreleased in syllable-final position (§3.2.1), the delayed release is essentially a manifestation of the same process: /t.t/ → [t'.t]; /n.n/ → [nʰ.n].

Where other CC clusters are formed through vowel elision they are simplified to C. In (3.125) underlying /kk/ is simplified to /k/.

(3.125)   [tupikámtikĩ] NOT **[tupikámtikkĩ]
            tupika-mɨtika-kĩ
            run-CAUS-PFV+SEQ+3:SS
            '(he) having made (him) run' (agr040723_29)

In (3.126) intermediate *[pɨŋkɨh-hu-n] surfaces as [pɨŋkɨhun].

(3.126)   [mína pɨŋkɨhun iwéintuktahɛi]
            mi=na   pɨŋkɨha-hu=na   i-waina-tu-ka-ta-ha-i
            1sg=ACC good-PSSD:1SG=ACC   CAUS-see-APPL-PFV-IFUT-1SG-DECL
            'I'll show my goodness'

And in (3.127) /ss/ is reduced to /s/.

(3.127)   [əɨsatatus]
            aisɨ-sa-tatus
            CAUS+bite-PFV-INTENT+3:SS
            'so as to cause to bite'

CC simplification does not operate at clitic boundaries, as shown in (3.128) where [kk] surfaces, and (3.129) with surface [ŋh] < /hh/.

(3.128)   [píʃakkɛit] NOT **[píʃakɛit]
            piʃaka=ka=ita
            bird=Q=COP:3
            'Is it a bird?'

(3.129) [ⁿdukúŋhẽ̃ĩ]
duku-hu=haĩ
mother-PSSD:1SG=COM
'with my mother'

3.5.5.3 Simplification of /kh/ → /h/

In verbal morphology at level I, when syncope forms a /kh/ cluster this is simplified
to /h/. This effect occurs with the transitive verbalizer -*tika* (3.130) and the causative
suffix -*mitika* (3.131), (3.132) when they are followed by /h/ initial applicative or
object suffixes, and suffix-internally with the first person plural object suffix -*kahatu*
when its first vowel is elided (3.133). I have no data to indicate whether or not the
same effect happens if the /k/ is part of the verb root.

(3.130) [ⁿdútihuamtẽ̃ĩ]
nu-**tika**-hu-a-**matai**
ANA-VBLZ.TR-1SG.OBJ-PFV+SEQ-1/3.DS
'when that happened to me...' (agr040824_02)

(3.131) [duʃ̃imtihamɨ]
duʃi-**mitika**-ha-mɨ-i
laugh-CAUS-1SG.OBJ+IPFV-2SG-DECL
'you're making me laugh'

(3.132) [kuŋkúumtihuttsata]
kuŋkuu-**mitika**-hu-**tu**-sa-ta
kiss-CAUS-APPL-1SG.OBJ-PFV-IMP
'have my child kiss (someone) for me!'

(3.133) [ᵐbukúhatin]
buku-**kahatu**-in**u**
suck-1PL.OBJ-NMLZ
'blood-sucking insect'

This simplification only happens in level I morphology (see §6.1 for a description of
the levels of verbal morphology). At level II the sequence /kh/ can freely occur,
alternating with /xh/ as described in §3.2.1 above (3.134), (3.135).

(3.134)   [atʃíkhɛi]
            atʃi-**ka**-ha-i
            grab-PFV-1SG-DECL
            'I've grabbed it' (agr041005_14)

(3.135)   [tímakham]
            ti-ma=**ka**-hamɨ
            say+PFV-RECPST=Q-1SG>2SG
            'did I say to you...?' (agr041006_04)

3.5.5.4   Other allophony

Two further allophonic variants determined by position within the syllable have
already been mentioned above: /h/ is realized as [ŋ] syllable-finally, and the affricates /ts/ and /tʃ/ surface as fricatives [s], [ʃ] respectively in syllable-final position.
The distinction is conversely neutralized in syllable-initial position following a consonant, where the fricatives /s/ and /ʃ/ surface as affricates [ts], [tʃ].

3.5.6 Comparison with prior analyses

In this section I briefly mention two phonological phenomena, namely devoicing of
vowels and metathesis, that have been mentioned by previous analysts but for
which there is no evidence in my data.

3.5.6.1   Devoicing of vowels

Pike & Larson (1964) refer to two "dialects" within Aguaruna, which differ in their
apocope effects. "Dialect A" loses vowels to apocope, while in "Dialect B" the same
vowels are not lost, but devoiced. The distribution of the two dialects is not clear:

> Dialect B is spoken by a minority in the same household, with no predictable basis for deter-
> mining which speaker will utilize Dialect A or B.
>
> (Pike & Larson 1964: 56)

It seems likely that dialect B reflects an intermediate stage in the apocope process,
in which the vowels are weakened but not entirely lost. Devoicing of word-final
vowels is attested for Achuar-Shiwiar (Fast et al. 1996) and Shuar (Pellizaro &
Náwech 2005). Amongst the speakers who provided the data for the present work,
there was none who consistently devoiced word-final vowels: they either elide them
completely or pronounce them fully, and the choice is morphologically conditioned,

not free variation; this supports the hypothesis that devoicing was an archaism or regionalism at the time Larson collected her data, and has now been lost.

3.5.6.2   Metathesis and vowel harmony

Previous researchers have stated that metathesis is common in morphophonological alternations in Chicham languages (cf. Adelaar & Muysken 2004: 435; Turner 1992: 28-29); but as we have seen, this is simply a product of identical vowels in the final two syllables, i.e. CV_iCV_i.[15] For example, the stem alternation in (3.136) looks as if metathesis applies to the final /VC/ of the stem when the accusative enclitic is added. In fact, however, the alternation arises from the elision of different vowels (the fourth in (a), the third in (b)), which gives the appearance of /am/ → /ma/ metathesis in this example simply because the final two syllables of the root happen to have identical vowels.

(3.136) a.   [kuhántʃam]   b.   [kuhántʃman]
             kuhantʃama   kuhantʃama=na
             'opossum'   opossum=ACC

In example (3.137) the final two syllables of the root have different vowels, and it is clear that the stem alternation is not metathesis of stem-final VC – if it were, the expected surface form of (3.137b) would be **[yuŋkípkan].

(3.137) a.   [yúŋkipak]   b.   [yuŋkípkin]
             yuŋkipaki   yuŋkipaki=na
             'collared peccary (*Pecari tajacu*)'   collared.peccary=ACC

A related process is a sporadic vowel harmony that arises in words of a particular phonological shape, such that only one of the last two vowels surfaces at a time. In such words the tendency is for the final two vowels to be identical. For example, in /muhuʃinimi/ 'tree species' the final /nimi/ must have come historically from the noun *numi* 'tree, wood', which appears frequently as the second element of compound plant names (e.g. *tsampaunum* 'manioc plant' – see §4.5 for a description of nominal compounding). In almost all surface forms, one of the final two syllables has its nucleus elided – compare (3.138a) and (b).

---

15 All apparent cases of metathesis are VC~CV, so Gnerre's historical reconstructions involving metathesis of C_1VC_2 → C_2C_1V, namely *ʃiwar* → *ʃirwa* (1973: 203) and *patal* → *palta* (1976: 307) are not justified by the synchronic data.

(3.138) a. [muhúʃinim]   b. [muhúʃinmin]
            muhuʃinimi   muhuʃinimi=na
            'tree species'   tree.sp=ACC

Presumably this lack of co-occurrence has allowed the "vowel harmony" to occur. This process is not at all regular, occurring in only a few noun roots of more than four moras.

3.6 Morphophonological processes

Certain phonological processes only occur in morphologically complex words, either because the phonological conditions for the processes are only met in morphologically complex words, or because of the presence of a particular suffix or enclitic. Common processes and the rules can be divided into three general groups, described in the following paragraphs:

A: Vowel sandhi, a collection of rules regarding whether the initial vowel of a vowel-initial suffix replaces the preceding vowel, forms a long vowel, diphthong, or triphthong, or triggers insertion of an epenthetic glide (§3.6.1)

B: Alternation of allomorphs: some suffixes have alternating long and short forms, and different combinations of phonological and morphological environments condition the choice of allomorph (§3.6.1)

C: "Other processes", effectively idiosyncratic properties of some suffixes (§3.6.2)

3.6.1 Vowel sandhi and alternation of allomorphs

The majority of bound morphemes are consonant-initial, but there are some vowel-initial forms, and when added to a stem (always vowel-final) they bring two or more vowels together. Most commonly this results in fusion of the stem-final vowel and the initial vowel of the suffix or enclitic, following the rule $V_1V_2 \rightarrow V_2$. When the initial /u/ of the diminutive suffix -utʃi fuses with a preceding vowel the resulting vowel has the quality of V_1, and if the sequence /ɨi/ fuses, the resulting vowel is /ɨ/, i.e. V_1. Similarly, if the sequence /ɨi/ does *not* fuse, it surfaces as [ɨi]. Two verbal suffixes (nominalizer -u and third person immediate past -ɨ) trigger diphthong reduction – DR is unlike fusion, as its occurrence is conditioned by syllable structure, the same conditions as syncope (see §3.5.2), while fusion is conditioned only by the immediate morphological and phonological environment. Table 3.13 summarizes the rules.

Table 3.13: Vowel-initial bound morphemes and their effects

morph	gloss	effects
-inu	subject nominalizer	fuses with any preceding vowel
-a(w)	'high affectedness' perfective	fuses with preceding /a/, then blocks further fusion and syncope
-i(ni)	'low affectedness' perfective	fuses with any preceding vowel in stems of more than two moras
-a	imperfective	fuses with preceding /u/ in morphologically complex stems; optionally fuses with preceding /a/; other effects determined by verb conjugation
-ina	plural imperfective	fuses with stem-final /i/ or /ɨ/, and the resulting vowel has the quality of V_1
-aha	plural	fuses with preceding /a/
-ama...ya	distant past	fuses with preceding /a/
-ɨ	third person, perfective stem	triggers DR; triggers long forms of 'low affectedness' *-i(ni)* and 'transferred action' *-ki(ni)*
-u	subject nominalizer	fuses with preceding /u/; triggers DR
-(a)i	apprehensive	never fuses; surfaces as [ɨ] following /ɨ/
-umɨ	second person singular, past tense	fuses with any preceding vowel in stems of more than two moras; triggers long form of *-i(ni)*
-uhumɨ	second person plural, past tense	as above
-i	declarative	fuses with preceding /ɨ/ or /i/
-utʃi	diminutive	may fuse with a preceding single vowel, and the resulting vowel has the quality of V_1
=(y)a	exclamative copula, third person	never fuses
=ɨ	non-visible copula, third person	never fuses, requires an epenthetic glide when preceded by a vowel other than /a/
=(a)i(ta)	copula	long form always requires epenthetic glide; short form fuses with stem-final /i/ or /ɨ/, and the resulting vowel has the quality of V_1
=(y)a	exclamative copula	never fuses
=(a)i	instrumental	short form fuses with preceding /i/
=(n)ɨ	locative/DS	never fuses

Some bound morphemes alternate between short and long allomorphs depending on the phonological and/or morphological environment. In all cases the short allomorph cannot be derived from the long allomorph by application of phonological rules, and the long allomorph cannot be derived from the short by appealing to euphonic epenthesis. Table 3.14 lists these forms.

Table 3.14: Short and long allomorphs

short form	long form	gloss	conditioning on long form
-a	-aw	'high affectedness' perfective	preceding /a/
-i	-ini	'low affectedness' perfective	preceding a vowel, with some exceptions
-ki	-kini	'transferred action' perfective	preceding 'immediate past, third person' -ɨ̃
-u	-wa	third person	following a vowel
-i	-ai	apprehensive	following 'high affectedness' -a(w)
-ɨ̃	-nɨ̃	different subject	following /i/ or /ɨ/
=ɨ̃	=nɨ̃	locative	following /i/ or /ɨ/
=i	=ai	instrumental	following a diphthong
=i, =ita	=ai,=aita	copula	following disyllabic stem except that short form always appears following /a/
=a	=ya	exclamative copula, third person	following /a/

The phonological conditioning for the alternations is rather different in each case. Below brief details are given for each morph from Table 3.13 and Table 3.14, roughly ordered along the following lines: verbal morphology is described first, in the order in which the morphs are affixed to the stem, then nominal morphology, also ordered according to their order in the stem.

3.6.1.1 Subject nominalizer *-inu*

The initial /i/ of the subject nominalizer *-inu* always fuses with the final vowel of the stem, regardless of the vowel's quality or the length of the stem (3.139), (3.140).

(3.139)   [hintínkaŋtin]
          hintina-kahatu-inu
          teach-1PL.OBJ-NMLZ
          'teacher'

(3.140)   [tínu]
             tu-inu
             say-NMLZ
             'a speaker'

In (3.141) the velar glide [ɰ] surfaces as [y] because of the following [i].

(3.141)   [wakɨyin]
             wakɨɰa-inu
             want-NMLZ
             'one who wants'

And the final /u/ of -*inu* surfaces as [a] when the copula enclitic follows – the copula
enclitic takes the postvocalic allomorph =*i* (3.142).

(3.142)   [hápak sɨntʃi tupikɛ́inɛi]
             hapa=ka   sɨntʃi   tupikau-inu=i
             deer=TOP   strongly   run-NMLZ=COP:3:DECL
             'the deer is a strong runner'(agr041005_26)

An alternative analysis would be loss of the final /u/ and addition of the postconsonantal allomorph =*ai* of the copula enclitic. This would be exceptional, however, as
no other stems drop their final vowels prior to the addition of the copula.

3.6.1.2   Perfective suffix -*a(w)*
Fuses with a stem-final /a/ (3.143), but then blocks further fusion or syncope (3.144).

(3.143)   [ahápata]
             ahapa-a-ta
             discard-PFV-IMP
             'throw it away!'

(3.144)   [ahápouwɛi]
             ahapa-a-u=ai
             discard-PFV-NMLZ=COP:3:DECL
             '(he) threw it away'

Note that the nominalizer -*u* normally triggers DR with a single preceding vowel.
The long form -*aw* appears when followed by /a/. In practice, this happens only

when it is followed by the plural suffix *-aha* (example 3.145) or the distant past suffix *-ama...ya* (example 3.146).

(3.145)   [mantuáwaŋtatuapi]
           man-tu-aw-aha-tata-wa-api
           kill-1SG.OBJ-PFV-PL-DESID-3-Q.TAG
           'they want to kill me' (agr041102_08)

(3.146)   [maáwabiahɛi]
           ma-aw-amaya-ha-i
           kill-PFV-DISTPST-1SG-DECL
           'I killed (it)'

3.6.1.3   Perfective suffix *-i(ni)*

Fuses with the final vowel in stems of more than two moras (3.147).

(3.147)a. paima-   b. paima-i   → [pɛimi]
           roll.up.sleeves   roll.up.sleeves-PFV

But not in stems of two moras or less (3.148).

(3.148) a. utu-   b. utu-i
            climb   climb-PFV

There are two exceptions in my data: *tu-* 'say' and *maa-* 'bathe', with perfective stems *ti(ni)* and *mai(ni)* respectively, showing fusion of *-i(ni)* with the stem.

    The long form *-ini* appears preceding two vowel-initial suffixes: third person immediate past *-ɨ* (3.149, 3.150); and distant past *-ama...ya* (3.151).

(3.149)   [ɨsátnɨ̃]
           ɨsa-tu-ini-ɨ̃
           bite-1SG.OBJ-PFV-3:DECL
           'it bit me' (agr041005_14)

(3.150)   [ɨhaphúkbou hɨɰántinɨ̃]
           ɨhaphu-ka-mau   hɨɰa-hu-tu-ini-ɨ̃
           give.birth-PFV-NSBJ.NMLZ   arrive-APPL-1SG.OBJ-PFV-3:DECL
           'the day of my giving birth has arrived' (agr041005_16)

(3.151)   [téiniaᵐbiahɛi]
            ta-ini-amaya-ha-i
            dig-PFV-DISTPST-1SG-DECL
            'I dug'

Conditioning is slightly different with the past tense second person suffixes *-umi* (singular) and *-uhumi* (plural): the long form appears only when a vowel precedes *-i(ni)*, that is, to avoid the illegal vowel sequence /Viu/ that would arise if the short form were used. So example (3.152) below takes the long form, but (3.153) takes the short form (unlike 3.149 above).

(3.152)   [méinumɨk]
            maini-umɨ=ka
            bathe+PFV-2=Q
            'have you bathed?'

(3.153)   [ɨsátiumɨ̃]
            ɨsa-tu-i-umɨ-i
            bite-1SG.OBJ-PFV-2-DECL
            'you bit me'

3.6.1.4   Perfective suffix *-ki(ni)*

The long form of the 'transferred action' perfective suffix *-kini* surfaces when followed by the immediate past third person suffix *-ĩ* (3.154).

(3.154)   [hukĩnĩ]
            hu-kini-ĩ
            take-PFV-3:DECL
            's/he's taken (it)'

3.6.1.5   Imperfective *-a*

Imperfective *-a* always fuses with final /u/ in morphologically complex stems (3.155).

(3.155)   [miníthawɛi]
            mini-tu-hu-a-wa-i
            arrive-APPL-1SG.OBJ-IPFV-3-DECL
            'it's coming towards me' (agr041005_14)

Following a stem-final /a/ the resulting /aa/ is *optionally* reduced to /a/ (3.156). The reduced form seems to be more common when the syllable is not accented.

(3.156)   [takáawɛi]~[takáwɛi]
            taka-a-wa-i
            work-IPFV-3-DECL
            'he/she is working'

In morphologically simple verb stems ending in vowels other than /a/, imperfective -*a* fuses with a stem final vowel in the second and third conjugations, but not in the first conjugation. Details of stem allomorphy conditioned by conjugation membership are in §6.2.

3.6.1.6   Plural imperfective -*ina*
Plural imperfective -*ina* always loses its initial /i/ following stem-final /i/ or /ɨ/ (3.157, 3.158).

(3.157)   [tsupínawɛi]
            tsupi-ina-wa-i
            cut-PL:IPFV-3-DECL
            'they are cutting'

(3.158)   [wɨnawɛi]
            wɨ-ina-wa-i
            go-PL:IPFV-3-DECL
            'they are going'

3.6.1.7   Plural -*aha*
Fuses with stem-final /a/, and the fused /a/ then blocks syncope (3.159) (but note that 'high affectedness' perfective suffix -*a(w)* takes the long form when followed by /a/, so never triggers fusion with -*aha*; see §3.6.1.2).

(3.159)   [tsupikáɳtatui]
            tsupi-ka-aha-tata-wa-i
            cut-PFV-PL-FUT-3-DECL
            'they will cut'

-*aha* never fuses with vowels other than /a/ – compare (3.160) where it follows stem-final /i/.

(3.160)   [ɨsápiaŋmɨ̃]
           ɨsa-pa-i-aha-mɨ̃
           bite-1PL.OBJ-PFV-PL-RECPST:3:DECL
           'they bit us'

3.6.1.8   Distant past *-ama…ya*

As with plural *-aha*, distant past *-ama…ya* fuses with stem-final /a/, and the resulting /a/ blocks syncope (3.161).

(3.161)   [takasá^mbiahɛi]
           taka-sa-amaya-ha-i
           work-PFV-DISTPST-1SG-DECL
           'I worked'

3.6.1.9   Third person *-ɨ̃*

The suffix *-ɨ̃* marks third person subject on perfective stems. It triggers diphthong reduction when suffixed to a perfective stem terminating in /Ca/ (3.162).

(3.162)   [pɨ́ŋkɨŋ tsawán tsawáhɨ̃]
           pɨŋkɨha   tsawanta   tsawa-ha-ɨ̃
           good   day   dawn-PFV-3:DECL
           'a fine day has dawned'

It also triggers long forms of 'low affectedness' *-i(ni)* and 'transferred action' *-ki(ni)* – see examples (3.149–3.151) and (3.154).

3.6.1.10   Nominalizer *-u*

Fuses with stem-final /u/ (3.163).

(3.163)   [ʃĩkitsuk]
           ʃiki-tsu-u=ka
           draw-NEG-NMLZ=TOP
           'without drawing water' (agr041005_14; see example 11.5)

There is no fusion with /i/ final stems (3.164), nor with /ɨ/ final stems (3.165).

(3.164)   [hiinkíu]
            hiina-ki-u
            go.out-PFV-NMLZ
            '(she) went out' (agr040721_07)

(3.165)   [wɨ́u]
            wɨ-u
            go+PFV-NMLZ
            's/he went'

This suffix triggers DR with perfective /Ca/ final stems, except where the /a/ arises from fusion of perfective -a(w) with a root final vowel /a/ (§3.5.2).

3.6.1.11   Apprehensive -(a)i

Apprehensive -(a)i never fuses with a preceding single vowel (3.166).

(3.166)   [hukíipa]
            hu-ki-i-pa
            take-PFV-APPR-2SG:PROH
            'don't take it!'

It surfaces as [ɨ] following stem-final /ɨ/ (3.167).

(3.167)   [wɨɨpa]
            wɨ-i-pa
            go+PFV-APPR-2SG:PROH
            'don't go!'

Note the difference between (3.167) and example (3.158) above, with plural imperfective -ina, which does fuse with preceding /ɨ/ so that wɨ-ina (go-PL:IPFV) surfaces as [wɨna]. The short form -i does fuse with a preceding diphthong /ai/ (3.168).

(3.168)   [ɨsɛ́ipa]
            ɨsa-i-i-pa
            get.burned-PFV-APPR-2SG:PROH
            'don't burn yourself!'

The long form -ai appears following perfective -a(w), which itself takes its long form -aw (3.169).

(3.169)   [yuwáwɛipa]
           yu-aw-ai-pa
           eat-PFV-APPR-2SG:PROH
           'don't eat (it)!'

3.6.1.12 Second person subject, past tense -umɨ, -uhumɨ
Both singular and plural forms fuse with a stem-final vowel in stems of more than
two moras (3.170).

(3.170)   [untsúkmumɨ]
           untsu-ka-ma-umɨ-i
           call-PFV-RECPST-2SG-DECL
           'you called'

Note that this is not DR, as shown by the fact that the /a/ of -ma 'recent past' in the
(3.170) is the fourth mora and would not be in a position to be syncopated.
   The second person past tense suffixes also trigger the long form of -i(ni), but only when this is necessary to break up an unacceptable vowel cluster (§3.6.1.3).

3.6.1.13 Third person subject suffix -wa / -u
Third person subject in present and future declarative, exclamative and interrogative verbs is marked with a suffix -wa (3.171), with short form -u that appears when
the preceding vowel is syncopated as in (3.172).

(3.171)   [ⁿdɨ́kawɛi]
           dɨka-a-wa-i
           know-IPFV-3-DECL
           'he/she knows'

(3.172)   [ᵐbúutui]
           buuta-u-i
           cry+IPFV-3-DECL
           'he/she is crying'

3.6.1.14 Declarative -i
Does not surface following stem-final /i/ or /ɨ/, but its underlying presence blocks
apocope (3.173, 3.174).

(3.173)   [puhámɨ]
            puhu-a-mɨ-i
            live-IPFV-2-DECL
            'you live'

(3.174)   [puháhi]
            puhu-a-hi-i
            live-IPFV-1PL-DECL
            'we live'

In non-declarative clauses, the person suffixes can undergo apocope because the declarative suffix is absent (3.175).

(3.175)   [amɨká wíɰam]
            amɨ=ka   wɨ-a-mɨ
            2sg=Q   go-IPFV-2
            'are *you* going?'

3.6.1.15 Diminutive *-utʃi*

The diminutive suffix may lose its initial /u/ following a vowel (3.176).

(3.176)   [apáʃ]
            apa-utʃi
            father-DIM
            'grandfather'

But other instances do not show fusion (3.177).

(3.177)   [ⁿdatsóuʃ]
            datsa-utʃi
            youth-DIM
            'youngster'

For some nouns consultants did not agree as to the correct formation of diminutive forms, that is, whether or not fusion should apply (3.178).

(3.178)   [katípiuʃ] ~ [katípiʃ]
            katipi-utʃi
            rat.sp-DIM
            'a little rat'

The diminutive suffix is prototypically derivational, as it changes the semantics of the root. It is likely therefore that diminutive-marked nouns are more lexicalized – note the semantic unpredictability of example (3.176) – and this may lead to the non-regularity of its phonological effects.

3.6.1.16 Copula

The enclitic copula has the long form *=aita* and short form *=ita*. Third person declarative copula is marked with a portmanteau enclitic with long form *=ai* and short form *=i* (see §4.14 for a full description of copula enclitics). Both enclitics show the same pattern of allomorphy. Stems ending in a single vowel /a/ always take the short form and stems ending in a diphthong always take the long form. With stems ending in a single vowel other than /a/, the long form appears following a disyllabic stem and the short form appears elsewhere, that is, following a single vowel in a stem of more than two moras. Table 3.15 exemplifies the various combinations of stem shape and stem-final vowel with the third-person declarative copula; the rows are ordered by the final vowel.

Table 3.15: Copula forms

2 mora stem	>2 mora stem	diphthong stem
[númiyai]	[apátʃi]	[naŋkéiyɛi]
numi=ai	*apatʃi=i*	*naŋkai=ai*
tree=COP:3:DECL	grandfather=COP:3:DECL	fruit=COP:3:DECL
'it's a tree'	'he's a grandfather'	'it's a fruit'
[húkɨɰɛi]	[wakámpɨ]	[pã́ɰ̃ə̃ɨ̃ỹ̃ɛ̃ĩ]
hu=kɨ=ai	*wakampɨ=i*	*paɰaɨ=ai*
PROX=RESTR=COP:3:DECL	fruit.sp=COP:3:DECL	rib+PSSD:1PL/3=COP:3:DECL
'it's only this'	'it's a fruit (*macambo*)'	'it's his rib'
[βisúwɛi]	[ɛ́iʃmaŋkui]	[mí^{n}douwɛi]
wisu=ai	*aiʃmaŋku=i*	*mi-nau=ai*
naked=COP:3:DECL	man=COP:3:DECL	1sg-POSS=COP:3:DECL
'he's naked'	'he's a man'	'it's mine'
[káyɛi]	[i^{n}dóukɛi]	[aŋsɨayɛi]
kaya=i	*idauka=i*	*ansɨa=ai*
stone=COP:3:DECL	sweet.potato=COP:3:DECL	fishhook=COP:3:DECL
'it's a stone'	'it's a sweet potato'	'it's a fishhook'[16]

---

16 *aŋsɨa* 'fishhook' < Sp. *anzuelo*.

The long form is always preceded by an epenthetic glide, and forms a separate syllable. Epenthetic glides following single vowels take their place of articulation from the preceding vowel: [y] following /i/; [ɰ] following /ɨ/; [w] following /u/. Following a diphthong the glide is [y] following all vowels except /u/, in which case it is [w].

Two exceptions to the rules are the singular SAP pronouns, which take the short form although first person singular has only one mora (3.179), and second singular only two (3.180).

(3.179)   [βíthɛi]
           wi=ita-ha-i
           1sg=COP-1SG-DECL
           'it is I'

(3.180)   [ámɨtmɨ]
           amɨ=ita-mɨ-i
           2sg=COP-2SG-DECL
           'you are you' (used in games of tag, "you're it!")

The copula enclitic is added after the application of diphthong reduction, so the short form is selected in example (3.181).

(3.181)   [tɨpɨsuí]
           tɨpɨ-sa-u=i
           lie.down-PFV-NMLZ=COP:3:DECL
           's/he lay down'

3.6.1.17   Third person exclamative copula =(y)a

The portmanteau enclitic =(y)a combines copula, third person and exclamative mood. Historically it has arisen from the long form of the third person declarative copula =ai with the final /i/ reanalysed as the declarative suffix and dropped. In all environments where the long form of declarative copula is used, the exclamative copula takes the same form minus the final /i/, including the same pattern of preceding epenthetic glides – compare (3.182a) and (b).

(3.182) a. [húkɨɰɛi]   b.   [húkɨɰa]
            hu=kɨ=ai   hu=kɨ=a
            PROX=RESTR=COP:3:DECL   PROX=RESTR=COP:3:EXCL
            'it's only this'   'it's only this!'

Stems of more than two moras with final vowel other than /a/, which take the short form of the declarative copula, are treated the same as stems of less than two moras by exclamative copula, except that stem-final /u/ does not trigger an epenthetic glide. Compare examples (3.183a) and (b).

(3.183) a.   [əɨntsui]
         aɨntsu=i
         person=COP:3:DECL
         'it's a person'

b.   [əɨntsua]
     aɨntsu=a
     person=COP:3:EXCL
     'it's a person!'

Following stem final /a/, the long form -*ya* always appears. Compare (3.184a) and (3.184b).

(3.184) a.   [túnɛi]
         tuna=i
         waterfall=COP:3:DECL
         'it's a waterfall'

b.   [túnaya]
     tuna=a
     waterfall=COP:3:EXCL
     'it's a waterfall!'

3.6.1.18   Past/non-visible, third person copula =ɨ̃

The past/non-visible copula =ɨ̃ is another portmanteau, combining third-person subject and non-visible (that is, either out of sight or past). The illocutionary force is exclamative, although there is no formally identifiable mood marking (see §4.14.4). There is no non-third form. Non-visible copula never fuses, and triggers an epenthetic glide when following a vowel other than /a/ (3.185).

(3.185)   [əɨntsũw̃ɨ̃]
          aɨntsu=ɨ̃
          person=NONVIS.COP:3
          'it was a person'

3.6.1.19   Instrumental =(a)i

The instrumental enclitic =*(a)i* takes the long form =*ai* following a diphthong (3.186, 3.187), and the short form =*i* elsewhere (3.188, 3.189).

(3.186)   [ɨkɨmtɛ̃ɨ̃ỹɛ̃ɨ̃]
          ɨkɨma-taɨ̃=ai
          sit.down-NSBJ.NMLZ=INS
          'with a stool'

(3.187)   [apahuíyɛi]
           apahui=ai
           god=INS
           'with God' (as complement of verb *suhumana* 'convert to' – see §4.10.6)

(3.188)   [maᵐbéi]
           mama=i
           manioc=INS
           'with manioc'

(3.189)   [nahánamui]
           nahana-mau=i
           make-NSBJ.NMLZ=INS
           'with the thing (you) made'

There are no examples of instrumental following stem-final /ɨ/ in my corpus. The short form fuses with a preceding /i/ (3.190, 3.191). The denasalization of preceding nasal stops associated with the short form is because of the underlying intermediate form ending in /ii/ (§3.4).

(3.190)   [nuᵐbí]
           numi=i
           tree=INS
           'with a piece of wood'

(3.191)   [uúᵐbi]
           uumi=i
           blowgun=INS
           'with a blowgun' (agr041005_14)

I have encountered one exception, with long form following /i/ (3.192).

(3.192)   [kutʃíyɛi]
           kutʃi=ai
           knife=INS
           'with a knife'

Perhaps this has something to do with the fact that the noun *kutʃi* 'knife' is a loan from Sp. *cuchillo* 'knife'.

3.6.1.20 Locative =*(n)ĩ*

Nominal locative enclitic =*ĩ* surfaces as =*nĩ* following /i/ or /ɨ/ (3.193), and verbal different subject suffix -*(n)ĩ* shows the same allomorphy (3.194).

(3.193)   [ámina hɨ̈min]
            ami=na   hɨ̈-mi=nĩ
            2sg=ACC   house-2=LOC
            'at your house'

(3.194)   [íi éidouti húwahin ámɨ wɨ́mumɨ̃]
            [ii   a-ina-u=ti   huwa-a-hi-nĩ]   amɨ
            [1pl   COP-PL:IPFV-NMLZ=SAP   stay-IPFV-1PL-DS]   2sg
            wɨ-ma-umɨ-i
            go+PFV-RECPST-2-DECL
            'while we stayed, you went away'

The allomorphs are identical for both the locative and DS markers, strongly suggesting a common origin – this is discussed further in §13.4.2.

3.6.2 Other processes

There are a few idiosyncratic processes that must be considered properties of the particular morphemes involved. The conditioning may have no phonological motivation at all.

3.6.2.1   Immunity to apocope

Perfective suffixes -*ki(ni)* and -*i(ni)* are immune to apocope, but not to syncope. So we find that the /i/ surfaces when word-final (3.195, 3.196), but is elided word-internally (3.197). This is unlike the non-eliding vowels discussed in §3.5.2.1, which never elide.

(3.195)   [pɨkamtɨ̃]
            pɨkama-tu-ĩ
            sit:PL-APPL-PFV+SEQ+3:SS
            '(they) having sat' (agr041005_14)

(3.196)   [hápikǐ]
           hapi-kǐ
           pull-PFV+SEQ+3:SS
           'having pulled' (agr041005_14)

(3.197)   [hapiktá]
           hapi-ki-ta
           pull-PFV-IMP
           'pull it!'

3.6.2.2   Vowel mutation triggered by -ki(ni)

The perfective suffix -*ki(ni)* triggers a change of /ɨ/ → /i/ in the verb root.

(3.198)   [naŋkɛ́ikǐ]
           naŋkaɨ-kǐ
           pass-PFV+SEQ+3:SS
           'having passed' (agr041005_26)

(3.199)   [wakítkittahɛi]
           wakɨtu-ki-tata-ha-i
           return-PFV-FUT-1SG-DECL
           'I'm going to go back' (agr060816_01)

3.6.2.3   Vowel lengthening triggered by durative -ma

The durative suffix -*ma* triggers lengthening of the final vowel in verb roots to which it is attached (3.200). Further examples are in §8.3.4.

(3.200)   [puhuumatá]
           puhu-ma-ta
           live-DUR-IMP
           'keep on living!' (leave-taking formula)

3.6.2.4   Action nominalizer -ta

The action nominalizer -*ta* does not trigger NC creation when suffixed to a verb root with a nasal vowel (§3.4.2).

3.6.2.5 Vowel harmony in restrictive =kI

The nominal restrictive enclitic =kI appears as [ki] when the preceding vowel is /i/ (3.201) and as [kɨ] elsewhere, that is, when the preceding vowel is /ɨ, u, a/ (3.202).

(3.201)   [βíki]
           wi=kI
           1sg=RESTR
           'I alone'

(3.202)   [ⁿdúkɨ]
           nu=kI
           ANA=RESTR
           'just that'

This vowel harmony is unique among bound morphs, although rather similar to the vowel change in roots conditioned by the presence of the suffix -ki(ni) as described in §3.6.2.2.

3.6.2.6 Combining form of SAP pronouns and person markers

The first person pronoun has the form wi, which is lengthened to wii when it appears without any affixes. With the addition of case-marking morphology, the stem takes the form mi-.[17] Similarly, the second person pronouns ami (singular) and atumɨ (plural) have the combining forms ami- and atumɨ-, respectively.

The case markers that trigger the combining pronominal forms are: accusative =na, comitative =haĩ and locative =(n)ɨ̃; and the verbal different subject suffix -(n)ɨ̃ triggers the combining form of a preceding second person subject suffix. Other bound morphology does not trigger the combining forms. Table 3.16 contrasts the combining forms, with accusative enclitic =na, with the non-combining forms with topic enclitic =ka.

---

17 This change of /w/ to /m/ is not reported for the other Chicham languages, and it is interesting to note that the verb minit 'arrive' has the form winit in the other languages, suggesting that Aguaruna has undergone a change of the sequence /win/ to /min/.

Table 3.16: Combining pronominal roots

person	accusative	topic
1sg	[mína] mi=na	[βíka] wi=ka
2sg	[ámina] ami=na	[ámɨk] amɨ=ka
2pl	[atúmin] atumi=na	[átumɨk] atumɨ=ka

Note that the locative form of first person singular is *minaĩ* – the expected form is
****minĩ*. This suggests that *=nĩ* may be a diphthong reducing morph; the only place
the unreduced form is expected to show up is when it is enclitic to a monovocalic
stem, and the only example of such a stem is *mi-* '1SG'.

The second person possessive suffix (*-mɨ*) has the combining form *-mi* when it is
followed by the same set of case markers (3.203, 3.204); and the subordinate verb
subject markers (*-mɨ, -humɨ*) have combining forms *-mi, -humi* when followed by the
'different subject' marker *-nĩ* (3.205; and see §13.5.2.5); this suffix is homophonous
with the locative enclitic, and probably etymologically related (§13.5.2.6).

(3.203)   [yatsúmin]
           yatsu-mɨ=na
           brother-2=ACC
           'your brother'

(3.204)   [wahɨŋmihẽĩʃ]
           wahɨ-hu-mɨ=haĩ=ʃa
           sister.in.law-PSSD-2=COM=Q.TOP
           'with your sister-in-law?' (agr041005_14)

(3.205)   [wɨɰakmin]
           wɨ-a-ku-mɨ-nĩ
           go-IPFV-SIM-2SG-DS
           'you going (different subject)…'

3.7 Accent

In every phonological word, one vocalic mora is prominent, and this prominence is
manifested in a higher pitch than the other moras in the word. In the previous version of this grammar I described this as a "pitch accent", however Hyman (2009)

shows that this term has little descriptive value as there is no clear cross-linguistic prototype. The Aguaruna system is neither a prototypical stress nor tone system, but shows a combination of properties typically associated with both types.

In common with tone systems, accent is manifested as a higher pitch (a high tone, H), and the tone bearing unit is the vocalic mora. Consequently, surface long vowels and diphthongs may show rising or falling intonation depending on the placement of a high tone. By definition, then, this cannot be analysed as a stress system:

> The stress-bearing unit is necessarily the syllable, as it is not possible for stress to contrast on the first vs. second mora of a long vowel
>
> Hyman (2009: 216)

In common with stress systems, on the other hand, and unlike prototypical tone systems, accent in Aguaruna is both CULMINATIVE and OBLIGATORY: every phonological word has one and only one primary accent. Roots and bound morphemes may have a maximum of one lexically specified H; if a morphologically complex phonological word has more than one underlying H, only the leftmost surfaces (culminativity). Conversely, if a phonological word has no underlying H, one is assigned by a default rule (obligatoriness). The principle of one H per word is thus an important criterion, and a diagnostic feature, of wordhood.

Beyond these general principles, accent assignment operates slightly differently in verbal and nominal words; the two systems are therefore described separately below, verbs in §3.7.1 and nominals in §3.7.2. Although the full details of accent assignment are not yet fully understood, a basic synopsis of the two systems is as follows:

- Some, but not all, verbal roots and suffixes have lexically specified accents; only the leftmost accent surfaces in the verbal word and if there is no underlying accent a default rule applies.
- Nominal roots may have lexically specified accents, but there is little evidence that nominal suffixes/enclitics do. Instead, most nominal morphology triggers rightward accent shift in the stem.

The two patterns are mostly distinct, with the exception of a few nominal enclitics that may take accent themselves (§3.7.2.1.2, §3.7.2.1.4), and a few verbal suffixes that can trigger accent shift (§3.7.1.2). Imperfective and perfective verb stems frequently differ in accent placement, but whether this is best analysed as productive accent shift or a lexically marked property of the stems is unclear.

Accent placement is potentially phonemically contrastive, with surface minimal pairs to be found, and both verbs and nouns show some morphological processes marked only by differing surface accent position. Such minimal pairs are more common in verbal than nominal roots. Some verb pairs that are homophonous except for the accent position also show remarkably similar semantics, suggesting that the relationship is more than simply chance similarity – it seems likely that these pairs result from some historical morphological process, which is no longer productive. Some examples of minimal pairs in verb roots are in (3.206–3.209).[18]

(3.206) a. *ʃíki-*
       'urinate on O'

      b. *ʃikí-*
       'draw water'

(3.207) a. *iháki-*
       'defecate on O'

      b. *ihakí-*
       'stain O'

(3.208) a. *ípɨna-*
       'fence in'

      b. *ipɨná-*
       'dam (stream etc.)'

(3.209) a. *ukáɨɰa-*
       'collapse'

      b. *ukaɨɰá-*
       'capsize'

Accent in nominal roots is not predictable, but minimal pairs distinguished by accent are rare. The minimal pair exemplified in (3.210) are both ultimately loanwords, although common enough in everyday use.

(3.210) a. *kútʃi*
       'pig' (< Qu. *kutʃi* < Sp. *cochino*)

      b. *kutʃí*
       'knife' (< Sp. *cuchillo*)

In general, final accent in nominals is confined to loans (as in 3.210b) and lexicalized nominalizations derived with the suffix *-u* (Chapter 15) e.g. *akahú* 'shotgun' < *aka-ha-u* 'light.fire-PFV-NMLZ'.

    The tone bearing unit is a vocalic mora. Consider the examples in (3.211), which constitute a minimal pair distinguished only by accent position once the final vowel is elided.

(3.211) a. [kâːp]
       ká.a.pi
       '*tamshi* vine'

---

18 Note that the accent marked in these examples is that which surfaces when the action nominalizer *-ta* is added to the unmarked stem.

b.   [kǎːp]
     ka.á.pɨ
     'fly'

The forms in (3.211) are illustrated in Figures 3.1 and 3.2 with images exported from PRAAT. Figure 3.1 shows the pitch contour of the word *káap* '*tamshi* vine' (example 3.211a), pronounced in isolation as a citation form. The falling pitch across the surface long vowel is clearly visible.

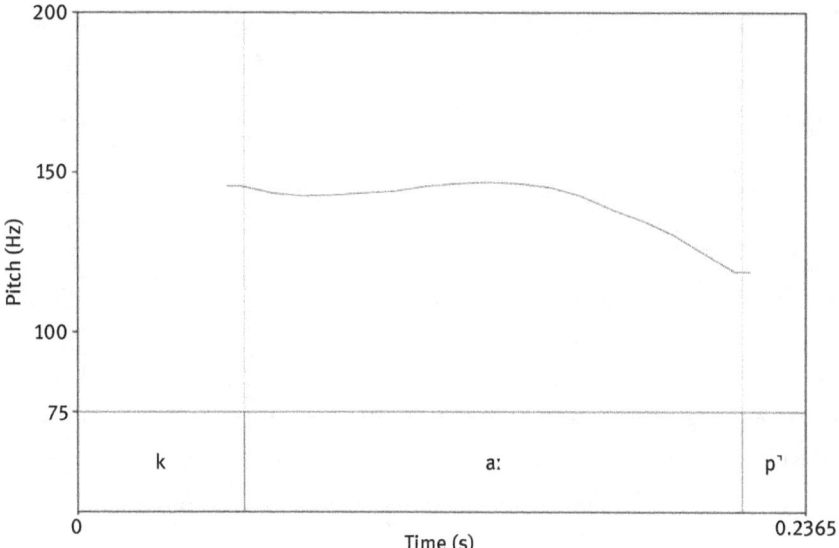

Figure 3.1: Pitch contour of /káap/ '*tamshi* vine'

Figure 3.2 shows the pitch contour of the word *kaáp* 'fly' (example 3.211b), similarly pronounced in isolation as a citation form. Again the pitch contour is clearly visible, and in this case shows a rising intonation.

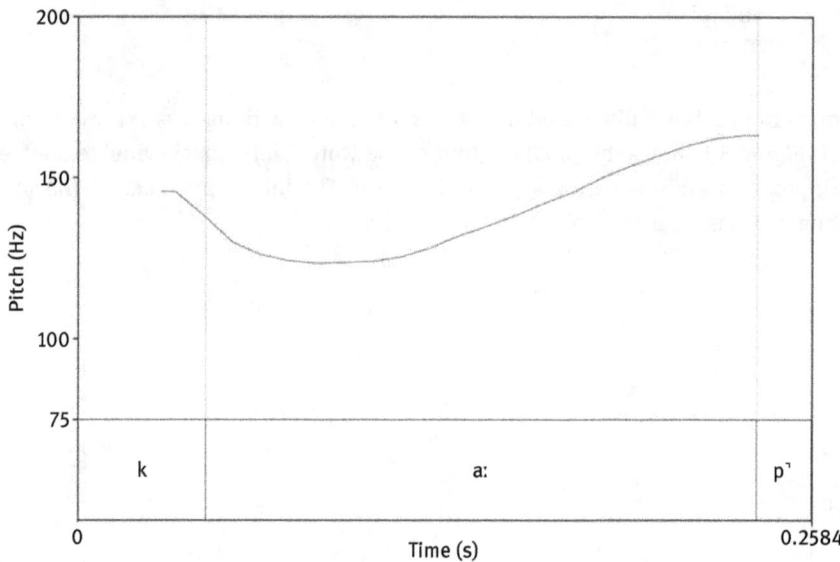

Figure 3.2: Pitch contour of /kaáp/ 'fly'

As noted in §3.3, the most useful way to transcribe surface long vowels, diphthongs and triphthongs is as sequences of vowels, allowing the accent position to be marked with a diacritic in the same way as it is in CV syllables. There is no possibility of ambiguity as all surface vowel sequences within a phonological word are homosyllabic. The surface minimal pair illustrated in (3.211a and b) are thus transcribed as (a) [káap] and (b) [kaáp].

Many nominal enclitics trigger an accent shift one mora rightward, and the accent shift effects are unaffected by syllable structure; for example, a CV.CV disyllable will show the same shifts as a CVV monosyllable. Table 3.17 illustrates accent shift with nominative and accusative forms of five nouns. Accusative is marked with the enclitic =na which shifts accent one mora rightward – in examples (c) and (d), the shift results in a changed pitch contour in the surface long vowel, and in example (e) the shift results in a changed pitch contour across the diphthong. Note that the minimal pair illustrated in (3.211) continue to be distinguished by accent placement after the shift (c and d in Table 3.17).

Table 3.17: Accent shift in accusative marked nouns

	nominative		accusative		
	underlying	surface	underlying	surface	gloss
a.	tsá.pa	[tsá.pa]	tsa.pá.=na	[tsa.pán]	'gourd bowl'
b.	kám.pa	[kám.pa]	kam.pá.=na	[kam.pán]	'*pucacuru* ant'
c.	ká.a.pi	[káap]	ka.á.pi.=na	[kaá.pin]	'*tamshi* vine'
d.	ka.á.pɨ	[kaáp]	ka.a.pɨ́.=na	[kaa.pɨ́n]	'fly'
e.	ká.i	[kéi]	ka.í.=na	[kɛín]	'avocado'

Accent shift in nominals is described in detail in §3.7.2.

3.7.1 Accent in verbs

3.7.1.1 Underlying accent

Some, but not all, verbal roots and suffixes have an underlying lexically-specified accent. In the surface form of a verbal word, the leftmost of these accents surfaces. If a verbal word contains no lexically-specified accent, whether in the root or a suffix, then accent falls on the root by default. The default root accent surfaces on the second vowel of underlyingly disyllabic roots, and the available evidence suggests that longer roots always have a lexically specified accent.

For example, the root *taka-* 'work' has no lexically-specified accent, while the imperative suffix *-ta* does – so the underlying accent of the imperative suffix surfaces in example (3.212a) (in examples in this section, lexically-specified accents are marked in the morphemic forms; elided vowels are in bold). The root *ɨ̈ma-* 'go ahead' does have a lexically specified accent, so this accent surfaces as it is the leftmost.

(3.212) a. [takastá]
taka-s**á**-tá
work-PFV-IMP
'work!'

b. [ɨ̈mkata]
ɨ̈ma-k**á**-tá
go.ahead-PFV-IMP
'go ahead!'

When a verbal word has no lexically specified accent, the accent defaults to the second vowel of the root (3.213).

(3.213)   [takáhɛi]
          taka-a-ha-i
          work-IPFV-1SG-DECL
          'I will work'

Example (3.212a) also illustrates the effects of vowel elision on verbal accent. When an accent-bearing vowel is elided, accent shifts to the next accent-bearing suffix, or again defaults to the root if there is no such suffix. Compare (3.214), where the accent of the perfective suffix -sa surfaces in (a), but not in (b) or (c).

(3.214) a.   [wahasá]
             waha-sá
             stand-PFV+SEQ+1PL:SS
             '(we) having stood...'

        b.   [wahastá]
             waha-sá-tá
             stand-PFV-IMP
             'stand (there)!'

        c.   [wahásmahɛi]
             waha-sá-ma-ha-i
             stand-PFV-RECPST-1SG-DECL
             'I stood'

The contrast between otherwise homophonous accent-bearing and non-accent-bearing suffixes can produce surface minimal pairs distinguished only by accent (3.215).

(3.215) a.   [yúwahɛi]
             yu-a-ha-i
             eat-IPFV-1SG-DECL
             'I am eating'

        b.   [yuwáhɛi]
             yu-á-ha-i
             eat-PFV-1SG-DECL
             'I'm finished eating'

Verbs with inherent root accent always result in rhizotonic words, while those with no inherent root accent only surface as rhizotonic if there is no accented suffix, through the application of the default rule (or one of the shifts described in §3.7.1.2 below).

3.7.1.2   Accent shift in verbs

A few suffixes and morphological combinations can trigger accent effects without actually taking the accent themselves. The perfective suffix -i(ni) forces accent onto the preceding vowel (3.216).

(3.216)   [wahéita]
          waha-i-tá
          stand-PFV-IMP
          'stand up!'

Negative -tʃa forces root accent (3.217, 3.218).

(3.217) a.   [takasmí]
             taka-sá-mí
             work-PFV-HORT
             'let's work'

        b.   [takástʃami]
             taka-sá-tʃa-mí
             work-PFV-NEG-HORT
             'let's not work'

(3.218) a.   [yuwámi]
             yu-á-mí
             eat-PFV-HORT
             'let's eat'

        b.   [yúwaʃmi]
             yu-á-tʃa-mí
             eat-PFV-NEG-HORT
             'let's not eat'

The plural familiar imperative -khua likewise forces root accent; compare (3.219a) and (b).

(3.219) a. [yuwátahum]
            yu-á-tá-humɨ
            eat-PFV-IMP-2PL
            'eat it!'

      b.   [yúwakhua]
            yu-á-khua
            eat-PFV-IMP:FAM:PL
            'eat it!' (agr040721_07)

There are two elision situations in which accent shifts to a normally non-accent-bearing suffix rather than to the root. Firstly, when DR triggered by the nominalizer -u reduces a perfective suffix that would otherwise take the accent, the accent surfaces on -u, despite its lack of underlying accent (3.220).

(3.220)   [tɨpɨsú]
          tɨpɨ-sá-u
          lie.down-PFV-NMLZ
          'lay down'

When such a form is followed by =i (short form) copula, the copula is accented, although it too lacks an underlying accent (3.221).

(3.221)   [tɨpɨsuí]
          tɨpɨ-sá-u=i
          lie.down-PFV-NMLZ=COP:3:DECL
          's/he lay down'

Secondly, some exceptional verbs can have the accent fall on the normally non-accent-bearing suffixes 'immediate future' -ta and 'intentional' -tasa / -tatus, as in (3.222, 3.223). The first person singular suffix -ha does not have an underlying accent, but when the intentional future suffix -ta has its vowel elided accent shifts to a following first singular suffix (3.222). The same phenomenon may allow accent to fall on the intentional subordinator -tasa / -tatus (3.223).

(3.222)   [utithéi]
          uti-tá-ha-i
          fetch+PFV-IFUT-1SG-DECL
          'I will fetch (it)' (agr041005_14)

(3.223)   [minitátus]
            mini-tatus
            arrive+PFV-INTENT+3:SS
            '(he) intending to arrive...'

With all other suffixes, accent defaults to the root as expected (3.224).

(3.224)   [miníttahɛi]
            mini-tata-ha-i
            arrive+PFV-FUT-1SG-DECL
            'I will arrive'

I assume that the verbs that allow such accent placement are lexically marked exceptions, but further data could show that there is a regular rule in play.

3.7.1.3   Further considerations

Verb forms incorporating the imperfective stem are always rhizotonic, with default or lexically-defined accent on the root, as no underlyingly accented suffixes combine with the imperfective stem. In addition, the imperfective stem often surfaces with accent one mora to the left of that in the unmarked stem. Because of the lack of morphophonological variation, it is impossible to judge whether this arises from a different lexically specified accent, a different default rule or some other cause. Accent on borrowed Spanish verbs tends to be on the second mora (3.225, 3.226).

(3.225)   [ganáthɛi]
            gana-tá-ha-i
            earn+PFV-IFUT-1SG-DECL
            'I want to earn (money)' (< Sp. *ganar*)

(3.226)   [ɸaltáawɛi]
            falta-a-wa-i
            be.lacking-IPFV-3-DECL
            'it's not enough' (< Sp. *faltar*)

And the perfective stem in example (3.227) shows apparent underlying root accent.

(3.227)   [ɸritáta]
            frita-tá
            fry+PFV-IMP
            'fry it!' (< Sp. *fritar*)

These examples suggest that accent on the second mora of the root is the default pattern for verbs.

3.7.2 Accent in nouns and adjectives

Accent assignment in nouns and adjectives shows a different pattern from that of verbs. Only three nominal enclitics can take accent themselves: =*numa* 'locative', =*(a)i* 'instrumental', and =*a* 'first'; but most trigger accent shift within the stem. There is some evidence for a default accent assignment in nouns, but not enough to state with certainty, nor is accent predictable. Accent shift rules for stems of two or three moras can be clearly formulated, and accent never shifts in stems of more than four moras; for stems of exactly four moras, however, the data are scarce and inconclusive. The following discussion is split into two parts, the first dealing with two and three mora stems and the second dealing with four mora stems.

3.7.2.1   Accent shift in two and three syllable stems

Accent in disyllabic and trisyllabic nominal roots may fall on the first or second mora. The overwhelming majority of two-mora words have initial accent. In trimoraic words accent generally falls on the second mora, but initial accent is not uncommon. Final accent is apparently only possible in morphologically complex forms. I have identified five patterns of accent shifting effects – the shift is always either one mora to the right or to the bound morph itself. Accent shifts operate on derived stems as well as underived roots, and some shift types are sensitive not only to the number of moras in the stem but also to the accent position prior to shifting, and to the syllable structure (i.e. whether there are surface long vowels or diphthongs in certain positions).

3.7.2.1.1 Simple shift

The most common pattern is to shift the accent one mora rightward in all dimoraic and trimoraic nominal stems, as exemplified by the accusative enclitic =*na*, in Table 3.18.

Table 3.18: Simple accent shift

NOM	ACC	**gloss**
píʃak	*piʃákan*	'bird'
dúku	*dukún*	'mother'
wíɨ	*wíɨn*	'salt'

Simple shift is triggered by the nominal suffixes and enclitics in (3.228).

(3.228)	*-hu*	First person singular possessor
	-hu	Possessed noun marker
	=na	Accusative
	=haĩ	Comitative
	=ya	Ablative
	=(n)ĩ	Locative
	=kI	Restrictive
	=ʃa	Question topic
	=tsu	Speculative
	=ʃa(kama)	Additive
	-nau	Possessive

The adjectival suffix *-(t)taku* 'partly' (§4.3.2) also triggers such a shift: *wíŋka* 'blue', *wiŋkáttaku* 'bluish'.

3.7.2.1.2 Simple shift except in trimoraic stems with second mora accent

The case markers in (3.229) trigger a simple rightward shift in all dimoraic and trimoraic stems except that when suffixed to a trimoraic stem with second mora accent in the unmarked form, accent surfaces on the enclitic itself.

(3.229)	*=numa*	Locative
	=(a)i	Instrumental

With dimoraic and trimoraic stems that show initial accent in the nominative, the effect is the same as the simple shift group, and accusative-marked forms are included in Table 3.19 for comparison.

Table 3.19: Locative type shift

NOM	ACC	INS	LOC	gloss
káya	kayán	kayái	kayánum	'stone'
píʃak	piʃákan	piʃákai	piʃáknum	'bird'
tʃĩmpúi	tʃimpuín	tʃĩmpuiyái	tʃĩmpuinúm	'stool'
wawík	wawikún	no data	wawiknúm	Wawik River

3.7.2.1.3 Shift in trimoraic stems only

The second person possessor suffix -mɨ is unique in its accent shift properties, triggering a simple rightward shift only in 3 mora stems, with no effect on 2 mora stems. Examples are given in Table 3.20 along with first singular possessor -hu, which triggers simple shift in 2 and 3 mora nouns, for comparison.

Table 3.20: Shift in 3 mora nouns only

NOM	1SG POSSESSOR	2 POSSESSOR	gloss
dáwɨ	dawíŋ	dáwɨm	'foot'
intáʃ	intaʃíŋ	intaʃím	'hair'

3.7.2.1.4 Always accented

The enclitic =a 'first' always takes the accent itself, and is always the last bound morpheme added. An epenthetic glide [y] is typically inserted between a stem-final /i/ and =a. Examples are in Table 3.21.

Table 3.21: Always accented

NOM	FIRST	gloss
tsúntsu	tsuntsuá	'snail'
tʃĩmpúi	tʃĩmpuiyá	'stool'

3.7.2.1.5 Final vowel accent

The vocative form may shift the accent to the final mora, and suppresses apocope (3.230).

(3.230) a. [yatsuhú]
yatsu-hu
brother-PSSD:1SG+VOC
'hey my brother!'

b. [simoŋká]~[simóŋka]
'hey Simon!'

This accent shift is not obligatory, and is probably better considered a product of the typically shouted delivery of vocative forms. Although David Payne (1990b) gives vocative forms for a variety of nouns, my consultants felt it was only compatible with names and kinship terms used for address. Shift types (4) and (5) are not limited to two and three mora stems.

3.7.2.2   Accent shift in four mora stems

Analysis of accent shift in four mora stems is hampered by the difficulty in finding illustrative examples. The shift apparently only occurs in four mora stems with paroxytonic (third mora) accent. Since four mora roots are rare, and nominals are not normally host to more than two bound morphs, such stems are uncommon in my corpus. Furthermore, in most instances vowel elision obscures accent shift. And finally, there is evidence for shortening of long vowels resulting in irregular roots.

David Payne (1990b) splits the 'simple shift' suffixes into two groups, based on their behaviour with four mora stems with third mora accent in nominative: accusative =*na*, possessive -*nau* and comitative =*haĩ* have no effect on four mora stems, while the rest trigger accent shift.

The possession suffixes (first singular -*hu* and second -*mɨ*) appear to shift accent only in roots whose second and third moras form a diphthong (Table 3.22).

Table 3.22: Shift in 4 mora noun with diphthong

NOM	1SG POSSESSOR	2 POSSESSOR	gloss
anɨntái	anɨntaíŋ	anɨntaím	'heart'

The only other example I have found of a shift in a four mora stem is with *tʃimpúi* 'stool' plus accusative =*na*: /tʃimpuína/. This is a four mora stem with third mora accent, and with the additive enclitic =*ʃakama*, the accent shifts: [tʃimpuináʃkam]. Note that the additive enclitic has the unusual effect of suppressing syncope in a preceding accusative enclitic =*na*, and compare the exceptional pronominal form *ámina* (2SG+ACC) that surfaces as *amináʃkam* with the additive enclitic – so there is something unusual about the combination of accusative and additive, making this example less useful for making generalizations. Now consider example (3.231), with no diphthong and no shift.

(3.231) a. [mamayák]
mamayaki
'fish sp. (*plateada*)'

b. [mamayákik]
mamayaki=kI
fish.sp=RESTR
'only a *plateada*'

This could be an exceptional noun – Wipio (1996) gives a form *mamayáaki*, and that form would not undergo accent shift because it has five moras. This underlying form would also explain the lack of syncope.

The only examples I have of accent shift in four mora stems are accented on the third mora, and the third and fourth moras form a diphthong. The only bound morphs for which my data provide evidence of accent shift in four mora stems are the possession suffixes: -*hu* first person possessor, -*hu* possessed and -*mɨ* second person; and the additive enclitic =ʃakama. More data, ideally naturally occurring, is required before we can be certain about the underlying patterns.

3.7.2.3   Accent shift with verbalizers -*ma* and -*maɰa*

The verbalizers -*ma* (manipulative) and -*maɰa* (inchoative) trigger accent shift in nominal stems. This can be seen in the imperfective stem of the derived verb – the unmarked stem then has the accent shifted one vowel rightwards.

Table 3.23: Accent shift with manipulative verbalizer -*ma*

noun	gloss	IPFV	unmarked	gloss
anɨntái	'heart'	anɨntái-ma-	anɨntaí-ma-	'think'
nánki	'spear'	naŋkí-ma-	naŋki-má-	'throw'

Inchoative -*maɰa*, -*mɨ* takes the accent itself in dimoraic and trimoraic roots, otherwise there is no shift. Verbs formed with the inchoative verbalizer do not show differing accent in different stems.

Table 3.24: Accent shift with inchoative verbalizer *-mauɟa*

noun	gloss	IPFV/unmarked	gloss
númi	'tree'	*numi-mí-*	'become a tree'
aíntsu	'person'	*aintsu-máuɟa-*	'become a person'
tsíuɟatik	'mythical bird'	*tsíuɟatik-mauɟa-*	'become a *tseatik*'

3.7.2.4　No shift

Two bound morphs never trigger accent shift (3.232).

(3.232)　　*=ka*　　　　　　topic
　　　　　-tʃau　　　　　negative

Some roots also appear to be lexically marked as non-shifting; in such cases it is generally possible to find evidence of historical change that explains this. For example, *tawás* 'feather crown' does not shift accent: the accusative form is *tawásan*. Its cognate in the other Chicham languages is *tawásapV*, a four mora stem which does not shift when accusative is added. Similarly, *paámpa* 'plantain' does not undergo apocope or accent shift, and is cognate with a form *paántama* in the other languages. Another possibility is that a historically long vowel has been shortened, as in /tsanimpa/ 'manioc plant', with surface nominative form *tsaním* and accusative form *tsanímpan*, lacking the expected shift – both David Payne (1990b) and Wipio (1996) give this word as /tsaniimpa/, with a long /i/ and consequently four moras.

3.7.3 Summary of accent

Accent in verbs has been shown to be determined by underlying accents in roots and bound morphs. Assuming that nominals are like verbs in having potentially more than one underlying accent in a morphologically complex form, of which the leftmost surfaces, the conclusion is that three mora roots with second mora accent in the nominative actually have no inherent accent, as these forms surface with accent on locative *=numa* and instrumental *=(a)i*, both of which must have underlying accent. This in turn implies that two mora roots all have lexically-specified underlying accent, as do three mora roots with initial accent in the nominative.[19]

---

19 Payne (1990b: 180) agrees that the default accent position is the second mora in nouns and adjectives: "[T]he basic pattern of accent assignment on Aguaruna substantives assigns high pitch

3.8 Phonological word

The phonological word in Aguaruna can be readily identified by phonotactic means. The first two criteria are the most important phonotactic cues, and are properties of all words:
– There is one primary accent per word
– There is potential for pause between words

The following criteria are also relevant, although their effects are apparent only in a subset of phonological words:
– Minimum word of two moras (§3.5.1)
– Word boundary blocks nasal spreading (§3.4)
– No Va diphthongs in initial syllable in careful speech (§3.5)
– No word-initial [ɯ] (§3.2.5)

3.8.1 Reduplication

The process of partial reduplication consists of copying and preposing the first syllable and the onset and nucleus – but not the coda – of the second syllable. The reduplicated material forms a separate phonological word, with an accent of its own. By far the most common occurrence of reduplication is in subordinate verbs formed with the repetitive suffix -*kawa*, which always involves reduplication (3.233).

(3.233)   [ásu asutínakũã]
            asu   asuti-ina-kawã
            REDUP   hit-PL:IPFV-REP+3:SS
            'hitting and hitting' (agr040723_29)

Where reduplication applies to a morphologically complex word, the reduplicated element consists of the first two syllables of the root, plus any material forming part of a diphthong with the second syllable (3.234); a consonantal coda on the second phonetic syllable is not included in the reduplicated element.

(3.234)   [pam.péi pam.péi.na.kũã]
            pampai   pampa-ina-kawã
            REDUP   discuss-PL:IPFV-REP+3:SS
            '(as they were) discussing and discussing...' (agr040719_01)

---

to the second mora from the beginning of the word. Certain exceptions have lexically marked accents on the first or third moras."

Example (3.234) shows a two mora verb root /pampa/, but the /i/ of the plural imperfective suffix is included in the reduplicated material. This can be explained by the fact that the /i/ is syllabified into the second syllable of the word, so the first two syllables are [pam.pai]; and these two syllables form the reduplicated element.

A coda on the second syllable never forms part of the reduplicated element; compare (3.235) below, where the reduplicated element is not **[awán]; also example (3.236), where the reduplicated element is not **[búut]:

(3.235)   [a.wá a.wán.ta.kũã]
            awa   awanta-a-kawã
            REDUP   fan.fire-IPFV-REP+3:SS
            'fanning and fanning (the fire)' (agr040723_29)

If the surface form of the verb root has fewer than two syllables, then the reduplicated element will also be monosyllabic (3.236).

(3.236)   [ᵐbúu ᵐbúut.kã.w̃ã]
            buu   buuta-kawã
            REDUP   cry+IPFV-REPET+3:SS
            'crying and crying' (agr041006_04)

Reduplication is less productive in non-verbal words. The nominal suffix -*ima* 'even' (probably < *ima* 'so much') is always accompanied by partial reduplication, following the same principles as described above. In (3.237) the root *nuwa* 'woman' is reduplicated as /nuwai/, including the /i/ of the suffix -*ima* 'even'.

(3.237)   [nuwéi nuwéima ipámatũã]
            nuwai   nuwa-ima   ipama-tu-ã
            REDUP   woman-EVEN   invite-APPL-PFV+SEQ+3:SS
            'having invited even the women...' (agr040723_12)

The same partial reduplication in numerals gives a distributive meaning (3.238).

(3.238)   [máki mákitʃik]
            maki   makitʃiki
            REDUP   one
            'one each'

3.8.2 Compound nouns

The two elements of a compound noun form a single grammatical word. Typically, compounds comprise two phonological words, but may fuse into one. Some freely vary, depending on factors such as speed of speech (3.239).

(3.239)   [íkamỹãw̃ãã]~[íkam ỹ̃ãw̃ãã]
            ikama   yawaã
            forest   dog
            'jaguar'

Many names of flora and fauna, as well as toponyms, are historically fused compounds. An illustrative example is *Bakants*, a community in Imaza district, historically from *baka* (< Sp. *vaca*) 'cow' + *intsa* 'stream' – so the name could be translated as 'Cow Creek'. The personal name *Jempets* [hɨmpɨs] also ultimately arises from a toponymic compound *hɨmpɨ* 'hummingbird' + *intsa* 'stream' (cf. Jijón y Caamaño 1919: 388ff, following Beuchat & Rivet 1909, 1910). Similarly there are many plant names ending in /numi/ < *numi* 'tree, wood'. Compounds show some phonological dependency even when they appear as two phonological words. Consider example (3.240).

(3.240)   [kã̃ỹũk wákam]
            kãyuka   wakampɨ
            agouti   macambo
            'variety of macambo fruit'

The form is pronounced as two phonological words, each carrying an accent. But the citation form of the noun *wakám* 'macambo' in isolation has second vowel accent. There is a rule for assigning the two accents to a compound: the first element surfaces with its usual nominative form, and the second element has initial accent, regardless of its accent in isolation. When the compound fuses into a single phonological word, only the leftmost accent surfaces (example 3.239, above). Compounds do not undergo accent shift triggered by addition of bound morphology (3.241).

(3.241)   [kã̃ỹũk wákampɨn]
            kãyuka   wakampɨ=na
            agouti   macambo=ACC
            'variety of macambo fruit (accusative form)'

This suggests that the whole compound is being treated as a single phonological word, so that accent shift does not apply because it is greater than four syllables (see §3.7.2).

The accent assignment rules show that there is some phonological fusion in all compounds, but there are still two accents, and apocope applies as if they are two words: so *aínts tʃápi* (person palm.species) 'variety of palm' surfaces with the final /i/, where we would expect apocope if the compound formed a single phonological word. Further details on the formation of compound nouns is in §4.5.

3.8.3 Encliticization of relativizers

The demonstrative pronouns *hu* (proximal) and *au* (distal) and the anaphoric pronoun *nu* may function as relativizers, in which role they directly follow a predicate which is unmarked for mood. The postposed relativizer may form a single phonological word with the predicate; in that case the relativizer carries the primary accent, but a secondary accent is also noticeable in the same position as the underlying accent of the host.

(3.242)   [ĩw̃ãntʃianúu]~[ĩw̃ãntʃia núu]
            ĩwantʃi=a   nu
            devil=COP:3   ANAᴿᴱᴸ
            'that which is the devil'

Forms derived from the intensifier *ima* 'so much' enter into a similar construction, forming adverbial expressions. Because the phonological fusion is optional, this process of *encliticization* is quite distinct from the morphological class of *clitics*, which are obligatorily phonologically bound. Although the actual phonological realization varies, for the sake of consistency all postposed relativizers and intensifiers are transcribed as separate words in the examples given. See §16.3 for a full description of the phenomenon, and further examples.

3.8.4 Interjections

Some members of the class of interjections do not fit into the usual phonological system. The four interjections in (3.243) violate the minimum word requirement described in §3.5.1, as they surface with only one vocalic mora; normally a phonological word must consist of at least two vocalic moras.

(3.243)   [tʃakˀ]   'boundary marker' in narratives
            [waʔˀ]   surprise
            [hɨʔˀ]   surprise
            [maʔˀ]~[máa]   hesitation

The glottal stop appears in five of eighteen interjections listed in §12.4.2, but in only three full lexemes, all nouns (§3.2.2).

3.9 Phonology of loans

Older Spanish loans are adjusted to Aguaruna phonology: *aaŋsɨa* < Sp. *anzuelo* 'fishhook'; *bátʃit* < Sp. *machete*. Since the mid-1950's, with the establishment of the bilingual education system, Spanish personal names have become common, and Spanish and Aguaruna phonologies basically coexist. Spanish words such as *grabadora* 'tape recorder', *bala* 'bullet, cartridge', *jugador* 'player (on a sports team)' are pronounced as in Spanish, even when they take Aguaruna morphology. Accent shift triggered by nominal suffixes applies to older loans (as in 3.244) and some newer ones (for example *bala* 'bullet, cartridge' undergoes shift), but *ad hoc* Spanish lexical items do not undergo accent shift (3.245).

(3.244) a.   [ᵐbátʃit]   b.   [ᵐbatʃitan]
             batʃita   batʃita=na
             'machete'   machete=ACC

(3.245) a.   [tígɾe]   b.   [tígɾen]
             tigre   tigre=na
             'jaguar'   jaguar=ACC

Loans from Quechuan are adjusted to fit Aguaruna phonology, for example *yáakat* < Qu. *llaqta* 'town'; *píʃak* < Qu. *pishcu*. Note especially the insertion of vowels to break up the consonant clusters. Some Quechuan loans are ambiguous as to word-class membership (see §2.7).

4 Morphology of nouns, adjectives and pronouns

4.1 Introduction

NOUN, ADJECTIVE and PRONOUN are the three word classes that can form referring expressions and be the sole constituent (but not necessarily head) of noun phrases. Noun and adjective are both open classes, and they coincide in most of their grammatical properties; they can therefore usefully be treated as a single class of NOMINALS for most descriptive purposes. Pronoun is a closed class whose members are syntactically and morphologically distinct from nominals; they do, however, share the majority of their morphology with the nominal class. The class of pronouns further subdivides into personal pronouns, demonstrative pronouns, and one dedicated anaphoric pronoun (the latter two classes also have adnominal functions, §5.2.1). In this chapter I describe the morphology of nouns, adjectives and pronouns, including the morphological criteria by which the three classes can be distinguished. The internal syntax of the NP is described in Chapter 5.

Nominal morphology serves four broad functions: it can alter the sense of the nominal itself (derivation); it can mark relations within the NP (possession markers); it can index the NP's function in the clause (case marking); and it can index the NP's pragmatic status (discourse markers). Nominal case markers are usually enclitic only to the final element of an NP, and are therefore an important diagnostic criterion for NP boundaries and membership (see Chapter 5). The encliticizing behaviour of nominal morphology also explains why so much of it is shared by the different word classes that can form NPs.

This chapter is structured as follows: first an overview of the morphology associated with NP constituents (§4.2). Next the criteria for distinguishing the classes of noun, adjective and pronoun are presented (§4.3). In §4.4 we describe some subclasses of nouns that are distinguished on morphological and syntactic grounds, and in §4.5 we describe the formation of compound nouns. Pronouns are the subject of §4.6. Derivational morphology is described in §4.7 and §4.9, and possession morphology in §4.8. Case marking enclitics are described in §4.10, and discourse enclitics in §4.11 to §4.13. Finally, the enclitic copulas are described in §4.14. The various functions of nominal morphology are discussed in relevant chapters, as shown in Table 4.1.

Table 4.1: Functions of nominal morphology

Morphology class	Functions described in
Possession	Chapter 5
Case marking	Chapter 5, Chapter 7
Discourse markers	Chapter 18
Mood/modality markers	Chapter 9
Copula enclitics	Chapter 7

The process of nominalization forms nominal stems from verbal roots. The details of nominalization, including restrictions on nominal morphology available to the resulting stems, are discussed in Chapter 15. Denominal derivation with verbalizing morphology is described in Chapter 6.

4.2 Structure of the nominal word

Nominal morphology is entirely suffixing/encliticized. The bound morphemes can be broadly divided on semantic and morphological grounds into derivational suffixes; possession suffixes; inflectional enclitics; and discourse enclitics. Inflectional morphology is marked with phrase-level enclitics, and appears on nouns, adjectives, pronouns and nominalizations. Discourse enclitics are more promiscuous and appear on NP constituents (nouns, adjectives, pronouns), as well as adverbial words and subordinate clauses. The structure of the nominal word is illustrated in Figure 4.1. The first three slots (A, B, C) are suffixes, except that the SAP marker in slot C is enclitic to the final constituent of the NP (§4.9.7). The following four slots (D – G) are NP enclitics.

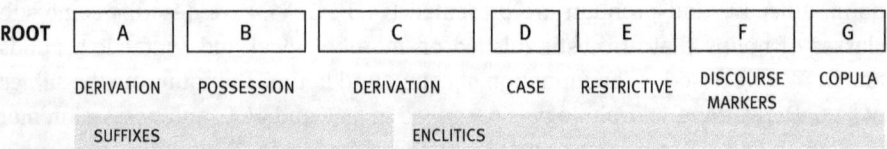

Figure 4.1: Nominal morphological slots

Figure 4.2 gives a more detailed breakdown of the morphology that appears in each slot. There is evidence for at least three sub-slots within slot C, but only those markers that co-occur can be confidently assigned to a sub-slot (§4.9). Slot D may be doubly filled, as locative and ablative markers may co-occur (§4.10.7).

SLOT	GROUP	SUFFIXES	GLOSS
		ROOT	
A:	Derivation	-uchi	Diminutive
B1:	Possession	-hu / vowel change	Possessed noun marker
B2:		(see §6.3.1)	Person of possessor
C1–3:	Derivation	-tinu	Attributive
	(see §4.9 for internal	-nau	Possessive
	ordering of slots)	-chau	Negative
		-uchi	Diminutive
		-mamtin	Similative
		-(a)ima	'Even'
		=ti(-humɨ)	SAP marker (-2pl)
	Verbalizing derivation	(see §6.6)	Verbalizers
D:	Case	Ø	Nominative
		=na	Accusative
		(see §4.10.3)	Genitive
		=hãĩ	Comitative
		=(n)ĩ / =numa	Locative
		=(a)i	Instrumental
		=ya	Ablative
		(see §4.10.8)	Vocative
E:	Restrictive	=kl	Restrictive
F:	Discourse markers	=ka	Topic
		=sha(kama)	Additive
		=a	First
	Mood/modality	=sha	Question topic
		=tsu	Speculative
		=ka	Polar interrogative
G:	Copula	(see §4.14)	Copula

Figure 4.2: Details of nominal morphological slots

Derivational suffixes fall in slot C, following possession marking, except that the diminutive suffix -*uchi* may also appear in slot A, preceding possession marking (but it cannot appear in slots A and C in the same word). Word-class-changing derivational suffixes relevant to nouns and pronouns are verbalizers, which are described in §6.6; the current chapter deals only with word-class-preserving derivational suffixes.

Pronominal words share a subset of nominal morphology. The same enclitics are compatible with pronouns, but they lack slot B possession morphology, and they are compatible only with 'possessive' and 'similative' from slot C. Diminutive in pronouns is only attested following the restrictive enclitic (4.1), unlike the pattern in nouns.

(4.1)   *níŋkiush*
          nĩ=ki-uchi
          3sg=RESTR-DIM
          'just him/her alone'

Certain suffixes and enclitics trigger a shift of accent in nouns and adjectives. The phenomenon of accent shift was discussed in detail in Chapter 3 along with all other morphophonological effects.

Denominalizing suffixes are added to a noun to create a new word of a different class. There are three verbalizers that can be added to nouns: manipulative *-ma*, attributive *-na* and inchoative *-maɰa*. Manipulative and attributive derivation may be added to nouns marked as possessed. There are also a number of noun-verb pairs in which there is no morphological marker of verbalization or nominalization. Verbalization is described in §6.6.

Nouns may also take an enclitic copula, which allows them to head a predicate. Copula enclitics are compatible with only a subset of nominal morphology, from slots A, B, C and E, and the polar interrogative enclitic from slot F. The copula enclitic can take a restricted range of verbal morphology, and alternates with a free copula verb. There is no motivation to treat the enclitic copulas as verbalizers, therefore I treat them as nominal morphology in §4.14 below. The syntax of copular clauses is described in Chapter 7.

4.3 Noun and adjective

Adjectives and nouns are distinguished from other lexical word classes by their ability to form part of an NP, taking case-marking morphology as appropriate, and by their ability to function as predicates in verbless equative clauses. The distinction between adjective and noun is a more subtle one, as they share a number of surface properties.[1] There is a distinction, however, that ultimately arises from the semantic distinction between nouns as referring words, denoting a bundle of properties, and adjectives as modifying words, denoting just one property. There are about 40 underived adjectives in my corpus. The morphological description in this section focuses on the properties that distinguish adjectives from nouns. In §4.3.1, I first discuss the semantic basis of adjectives as distinct from nouns, then describe the

---

1 Doris Payne (2001: 595) notes "weakness of a class of adjectives" as a possible areal Amazonian trait, and Krasnoukhova (2012) suggests that noun-like adjectives are more characteristic of the Andean sphere while verb-like adjectives are more likely to be found in the eastern Amazonian area – so both the Amazonian and Andean areas offer the possibility of influence on the Aguaruna pattern (see further discussion in Overall, in press-b).

grammatical properties of adjectives in §4.3.2, showing that certain grammatical differences arise from the underlying distinction between the two classes in Aguaruna. Jespersen tells us that:

> The adjective indicates and singles out one quality, one distinguishing mark, but each substantive suggests, to whoever understands it, many distinguishing features by which he recognises the person or thing in question.
>
> Jespersen (1958[1924]: 75)

Semantically, adjectives denote just one property, while nouns are characterized by a bundle of properties, of which more or fewer may be present depending on how closely the referent fits a prototype. This is the basic semantic distinction underlying the two word classes, and gives rise to the functional distinction between REFERENCE (nouns) and MODIFICATION (adjectives). Dixon tells us that adjectives have two functions:

> (a) In a statement that something has a certain property ... (b) As a specification that helps focus on the referent of the head noun in an NP.
>
> Dixon (2004a: 10)

These two functions are grammatically instantiated in Aguaruna by (a) copular clauses (as in 4.2, 4.3); and (b) NP modification (4.4, 4.5).

(4.2) *húka ollak múuntai*
  [hu=ka   olla=ka]   [muunta=i]
  PROX=TOP pot=TOP   big$_{ADJ}$=COP:3:DECL
  'this pot is big'

(4.3) *úchi píipish áinawai*
  [uchi]   [piipichi]   a-ina-wa-i
  child   small$_{ADJ}$ COP-PL:IPFV-3-DECL
  'the children are small' (agr060816_01)

(4.4) *wámpash muúntan tsukapɨak...*
  [wampachi   muunta=na]   tsukapɨ-a-kũ
  backpack   big$_{ADJ}$=ACC   carry.over.shoulder-IPFV-SIM+3:SS
  'carrying a big backpack over his shoulder...' (agr040720_02)

(4.5) *úchi píipichin sãã́sã...*
  [uchi   piipichi=na]   saã-sã
  child   small$_{ADJ}$=ACC   take-PFV+SEQ+3:SS
  'having taken the small children...' (agr060816_01)

However, the ability to form copular clauses is also a property of nouns, as in (4.6, 4.7).

(4.6)   *áanka wámpishkui*
          [aan=ka]   [wampishuku=i]
          MED=TOP   butterfly_NOUN=COP:3:DECL
          'that's a butterfly'

(4.7)   *áishmaŋ áinawai*
          [aishmaŋku]   a-ina-wa-i
          man_NOUN   COP-PL:IPFV-3-DECL
          'they are men'

And so, apparently, is the ability to modify NPs (4.8, 4.9).

(4.8)   *úchi kuwihá intsákan*
          [uchi   kuwiha]   intsa-ka-nu
          child   baby_NOUN+ACC   piggyback-PFV+SEQ-1SG:SS
          '(I) having carried the small child on my back...' (agr060816_01)[2]

(4.9)   *áishiŋtin núwa*
          [aishi-hĭ-tinu   nuwa]_NP
          husband-PSSD:1PL/3-ATTRIB   woman_NOUN
          'married women' (agr041005_19)

Conversely, there are examples of NPs consisting only of an adjective (4.10).

(4.10)   *wiŋkán hukíthai*
          [wiŋka=na]   hu-ki-ta-ha-i
          blue_ADJ=ACC   take-PFV-IFUT-1SG-DECL
          'I'll take the blue (one)'

In discourse, there is a typical functional division of labour:
–   Nouns introduce or refer to participants as arguments of verbs
–   Adjectives describe participants, as equative clause complements

---

2 The status of *kuwiŋ* 'baby, offspring' as a noun is confirmed by its possessability, as in *shaa kuwiŋ-hĭ* (corn+GEN baby-1PL/3) 'ear of corn' (Wipio et al. 1996: 85).

The similarities in surface distribution, combined with the large amount of morphology in common, mean that it can be difficult to determine the word class of any particular lexical NP constituent. Hengeveld (1992) notes that:

> Even if the attributive use of adjectives is not their prototypical use, it still is the use that distinguishes them from predicates of other classes.
>
> (Hengeveld 1992: 59)

It follows, then, that the more useful course of investigation is to disregard the neutralized distinction in predication and look elsewhere for criteria that differentiate nouns and adjectives. Although Aguaruna nouns can be predicated in the same way as adjectives, this is not their typical function; furthermore, only a few human nouns can appear in modifying function in an NP (as in 4.8 and 4.9 above; although nouns do function as modifiers in compounds, see §4.5), and the appearance of adjectives in headless NPs (as in 4.10 above) is highly contextually constrained. The semantic distinction between prototypical adjectives and nouns gives rise to two crucial grammatical distinctions:

– Nouns head NPs, while adjectives modify (reference versus modification functions)
– Adjectives, because they denote just one property, are gradable

Morphologically, evidence for distinguishing an adjective class from nouns comes from more general properties:

– Specifically adjectival morphology relating to gradability
– Low compatibility with possession morphology
– Unproductive adjectivalizing derivational morphology

There is a range of adjective-like behaviour based on at least two of the properties discussed here: (1) the ability to appear in headless NPs and (2) the ability to take possession marking. In the following three sections I discuss the grammatical distinctions listed above. The syntactic properties of NP modification are described in §5.4.

4.3.1 Adjectival morphology

Adjectives share almost all of their morphology with nouns. They share derivational suffixes (e.g. diminutive), inflectional case enclitics, NP-level discourse marking enclitics, and the copula enclitic. Nominal morphology not shared by adjectives includes that which pertains only to the NP head: the possession suffixes (see §4.8) are not compatible with most adjectives. Table 4.2 lists the nominal morphology shared by adjectives, and Table 4.3 lists those that are not shared.

Table 4.2: Nominal morphology shared by adjectives

form	gloss
-uchi	diminutive
-chau	negative
=na	accusative
=haî	comitative
(see §4.8)	possession (limited application)

Table 4.3: Nominal morphology not shared by adjectives

form	gloss
-nau	possessor
=ya	ablative
(accent shift and suppression of apocope)	genitive

As mentioned above, the one purely adjectival suffix is *-(t)taku* 'partly', described below.

Adjectives cannot head NPs. Headless constructions are limited to contexts in which a head noun can be retrieved, either from the preceding discourse or from general knowledge of the world. Compare (4.11a) and (b).

(4.11) a. *ámish atásh muúntan yuwáu*
amicha [atashu muunta=na] yu-a-u
fox chicken big=ACC eat-PFV-NMLZ
'a fox ate the big chicken'

b. *ámish muúntan yuwáu*
amicha [muunta=na] yu-a-u
fox big=ACC eat-PFV-NMLZ
'a fox ate the big (one)'

The NP in (4.11b) is only acceptable if an understood head such as *atash* 'chicken' has already been introduced into the discourse, hence the NP can be analysed as headless. Even given a context, this example was not acceptable for some native speakers in elicitation sessions, although (4.12) shows that such examples are encountered in more natural narrative contexts. This example comes from a narrative in which the noun *shinutaî* 'song' is topical and readily available to be interpreted as the understood referent of the headless NP.

(4.12)   *nínka muúntan shináu*
          nĩ=ka   [muunta=na]   shina-u
          3sg=TOP   big=ACC   sing+IPFV-NMLZ
          'it (the *kúgkup* bird) sang a big (song)' *i.e. it sang loudly* (agr041005_17)

Adjectives may be more or less acceptable in headless constructions, and may be incompatible with possession morphology. The most adjectival behaviour is displayed by *piŋkiŋ* 'good'. It can head an NP as a zero-derived abstract noun, meaning 'goodness', but apparently cannot be interpreted as modifying a headless NP (4.13).

(4.13)   *mína piŋkíhan iwaintúktahai*
          [mi=na   piŋkɨha-hu=na]   i-waina-tu-ka-ta-ha-i
          1sg=ACC   good-PSSD:1SG=ACC   CAUS-see-APPL-PFV-IFUT-1SG-DECL
          'I'll show my goodness'
          NOT
          ** 'I'll show my good (one)'

Core colour terms do not often combine with possession suffixes, even where an acceptable noun (such as *papí* 'book') is available from context, as shown by the unacceptability of (4.14) (and note that 4.10 above, with no possession suffix, is acceptable).

(4.14)   **winkáhun hukíthai*
          [wiŋka-hu=na]   hu-ki-ta-ha-i
          blue-PSSD:1SG=ACC   take-PFV-IFUT-1SG-DECL
          Intended reading: 'I'll take my blue (one)'

4.3.2 Gradability

Property concepts tend to be gradable, and the grammatical expression of gradation can be a useful criterion for distinguishing adjectives from other word classes (Dixon 2004a: 26). This is also the case in Aguaruna. Three modifiers can be used for grading adjectives, all three of which also operate on other word classes giving distinct senses, and one unproductive suffix is limited to a subset of adjectives. The constructions are summarized in Table 4.4.

Table 4.4: Modification of adjectives

	with adj	with noun	with verb	with adv
shiiŋ	'very'	–	'well'	'very'
sinchi	'too' (cannot be modified)	–	'strongly'	–
ima	'more'	'only' (with RESTR enclitic)	–	'more'
-(t)taku	'partly' (limited application)	–	–	–

The distinct patterns of applicability and meaning that arise from combinations of the four modification constructions with different word classes clearly distinguish adjectives as a separate class. Below I discuss the four strategies individually.

4.3.2.1 Gradation with *shiiŋ* 'very'

The adverb *shiiŋ* means 'well' when modifying a verb (4.15), and 'very' when modifying the adverb *sinchi* 'strongly' (4.16). Example (4.15) was uttered in the context of checking that a banknote is genuine: you give it a good pull, and a false note will rip in two.

(4.15) *shíiŋ hapiktá*
        shiiha   hapi-ka-ta
        well   pull-PFV-IMP
        'pull it well!'

(4.16) *shíiŋ sínchi ahániahai*
        [shiiha   sinchi]   ahantu-ya-ha-i
        very   strongly   be.shy-REMPST-1SG-DECL
        'I was really very shy' (agr040824_02)

shiiŋ also means 'very' when modifying an adjective, as in (4.17).

(4.17) *húka shíiŋ sútahuchi*
        [hu=ka]   [shiiha   sutahuchi=i]
        PROX=TOP   very   short=COP:3:DECL
        'this is very short'

The elicited example in (4.18) makes use of a modified attributive adjective, but no such constructions appear in my corpus of natural narrative.

(4.18)   *ỹã̄ũ ỹã̄w̃ã̄ã shíiŋ muúntan wainkámhai*
        yaũ   [yawaã   [shiiha   muunta=na]]
        yesterday   dog   very   big=ACC
        waina-ka-ma-ha-i
        see-PFV-RECPST-1SG-DECL
        'yesterday I saw a very big dog'

Similarly, example (4.19), in which a human noun that can function as an NP modifier is modified by *shiiŋ*, was elicited. No such examples appear in natural data, and I was unable to elicit such a construction with any other noun; so it would appear that its use is effectively incompatible with nouns.[3]

(4.19)   *nĩ̄ shíiŋ áishmaŋkui*
        [nĩ]   shiiha   aishmaŋku=i
        3sg   well   man=COP:3:DECL
        'he's very manly'

4.3.2.2 Gradation with *sinchi* 'too'

The adverb *sinchi* in combination with verbs means 'strongly' (4.20; and see 4.16 above).

(4.20)   *sinchi tupikákta*
        sinchi   tupika-ka-ta
        strongly   run-PFV-IMP
        'run fast!'

And with adjectives it means 'too (much)' – compare (4.21) with (4.17) above.

(4.21)   *húka sinchi sútahuchi*
        [hu=ka]   [sinchi   sutahuchi=i]
        PROX=TOP   too   short=COP:3:DECL
        'this is too short'

Although *sinchi* can be intensified with *shiiŋ* when it modifies a verb, it apparently cannot be further modified when modifying an adjective. Like *shiiŋ*, *sinchi* cannot be used to modify nouns;[4] nor can it modify adverbs.

---

3 This example could in fact be a calque from Spanish *él es muy hombre* 'he's very manly'.
4 Note, however, that the word *sinchi* is itself used as a noun meaning 'strength', and is probably a loan from Quechuan (§2.7.2).

4.3.2.3 Comparison with *ima* 'more'[5]

The intensifier *ima* means 'more' in combination with adjectives and adverbs, as in the following examples.[6]

(4.22)   *húu olla imá uchuchíhĩỹãĩ*
  [hu   *olla*]   ima   uchuchihĩ=ai
  PROX   pot   INTENS   small=COP:3:DECL
  'this pot is smaller'

(4.23)   *húu olla imá múuntai áuhãĩ (apátkam)*
  [hu   *olla*]   ima   muunta=i   [au=haĩ   (apatkama)]
  PROX   pot   INTENS   big=COP:3:DECL   DIST=COM   (COMP)
  'this pot is bigger than that one'

The standard of comparison appears in the comitative case, and is optionally followed by the comparative marker *apatkam*.[7]

The same intensifier *ima* combines with nouns marked with the restrictive enclitic =*kI* to give the sense of 'only' – that is, it intensifies the restrictive meaning (4.24, 4.25).

(4.24)   *imá biíknak yuwámhai*
  [ima   biika=na=kI]   yu-a-ma-ha-i
  INTENS   bean=ACC=RESTR   eat-PFV-RECPST-1SG-DECL
  'I only ate beans'

(4.25)   *wíka imá Chiriaconak wáinin áyahai*
  [wi=ka]   [ima   *Chiriaco*=na=kI]   waina-inu
  1sg=TOP   INTENS   Chiriaco=ACC=RESTR   see-NMLZ
  a-ya-ha-i
  COP-REMPST-1SG-DECL
  'I had only ever seen Chiriaco (a town in Bagua Province)'
  (agr040824_02)

---

5 There is a possibility that gradation is a historical development from a general intensifier under influence of the phonologically similar Spanish word *más* 'more', which similarly appears directly preceding an adjective or adverb. Also of interest is that the word *ima* is itself probably borrowed from the Quechuan *ima* 'how', which has a secondary use in intensification as in e.g. *ima sumaq* 'how beautiful!'.

6 Also *nuní* 'thus' can modify adverbs with the sense 'more' (§12.3.3).

7 < *apatu-ka-ma* 'compare-PFV-NSBJ>SBJ': so this is ultimately a subordinate clause, which could be translated as 'when (*comparand*) was compared with *standard*'.

The modified NP may include a possessor, as in (4.26).

(4.26)   *imá mína nuwahúk niŋkiúsh puhúmĩ*
           [ima   mi=na   nuwa-hu=kI]   nĩ=kI=uchi
           INTENS   1sg=ACC   wife-PSSD:1SG=RESTR   3sg=RESTR=DIM
           puhu-mĩ
           live-RECPST:3:DECL
           'only my wife stayed, alone'

The intensifier *ima* cannot directly modify a verb, but it can modify non-verbal adverbs, such as *sìnchi* in (4.27).

(4.27)   *húu imá sìnchi tupikáawai*
           [hu]   [ima   sìnchi]   tupika-a-wa-i
           PROX   INTENS   strongly   run-IPFV-3-DECL
           'this one runs faster'

In sum, the evidence provided by examples of modification with *ima* shows a clear distinction between adjective and noun.

4.3.2.4 Adjectival suffix -*(t)taku*

The suffix -*(t)taku* can be added to some colour terms and *udu* 'raw' to give the sense of 'partly', akin to the English suffix -*ish*. It is not clear what conditions the choice of allomorph. A selection of examples is given in Table 4.5.

Table 4.5: Adjectives with suffix -*(t)taku*

root		suffixed form	
wíŋka	'blue'	*wiŋká-ttaku*	'pale blue'
samíkmau	'green'	*samíkmau-ttaku*	'pale green'
udú	'raw'	*udú-taku*	'partly cooked'

The restriction of this suffix to members of the adjective class reflects the basic semantic fact that adjectives are gradable.

4.3.3 Adjectivalizing derivation

There is no productive adjectivalizing morphology, however there is evidence for etymological connections between some adjectives and words of other classes, and for a historically productive adjectivalizer.

4.3.3.1 Derivation between verb and adjective

Some adjectives have developed historically from verbs via nominalization, for example *mamukú* 'worn-out (of clothes etc.)' < *mamu-ka-u* 'wear.out-PFV-NMLZ'. Others are clearly related to verbs but not synchronically decomposable: *kapántu* 'red' < *kapáut* 'burn (intrans.)'; *kusú* 'dirty (water)' < *kusút* 'become dirty (of water)'; and *yapáu* 'bitter' is probably related to the verb *yapát* 'be salty'. Note that these adjectives end in /u/, suggesting that the nominalizer *-u* is etymologically part of their morphological makeup. The adjectives *udú* 'raw', *wisú* 'naked', have no corresponding verbs but also end in accented /u/, a pattern normally only associated with nominalization with *-u* (§3.7).

4.3.3.2 Derivation between noun and adjective

There are a few roots that function as both noun and adjective, shown in Table 4.6. The semantic distinction between the forms suggests that these are best analysed as zero-marked class changing derivation.

Table 4.6: Adjective – noun pairs

root	adjective	noun
pìŋkìŋ	'good'	'goodness'
muun	'big'	'adult'
apu[8]	'fat; big'	'chief'
aishmaŋ	'male'	'man'
nuwa	'female'	'woman'

It is difficult to say which is primary in each case. Only *pìŋkìŋ* 'good' ~ 'goodness' looks as if the adjectival meaning is clearly primary, as the nominal meaning refers to only one property, a typical function of adjectives. In the other examples, it looks

---

8 Borrowed from Quechua *apu* 'lord; chief; mountain spirit'.

rather as if the nouns are primary, as each denotes a cluster of properties, with the corresponding adjective referring to just one property – cf. Bhat (1994):

> [A] noun, when used in the modifier function of the adjective, or when adjectivalized, tends to attain this adjectival property of singling out one quality.
>
> Bhat (1994: 25)

In any case, the very possibility of derivation between noun and adjective presupposes two separate lexical classes. I am aware of just one possible example of an adjective derived from a noun morphologically: *yumiimitu* 'sweet', derived from *yumi* 'water, broth, juice, honey'.

4.3.3.3 Adjectivalizing suffix -*hama*

A number of adjectives terminate with the sequence /hama/, and some of them show a relationship to other word classes. Table 4.7 lists a selection of such words.

Table 4.7: Adjectives terminating in /hama/

adjective	gloss	possible source	gloss	word class
shaa-ham	'pale'	–	–	–
ɨsa-ham	'long, tall'	–	–	–
shii-ham	'pretty'	*shiiŋ* /ʃiiha/	'well, very'	adverb
yama-ham	'new'	*yama*	'now, recently'	adverb
duwɨ-ham	'fat'	*duwɨ-*	'get fat'	verb
kaka-ham	'valiant'	*kaka-*	'resist'	verb
katsū-ham	'hard'	*katsua-*	'ripen, harden'	verb

In the case of *shiiham* 'pretty', there has been haplological reduction from the expected form **shiiha-ham*. A similar haplology is also indicated in possession marking of some nouns (see §4.8), and the adjective *piŋkɨŋ* 'good' (with underlying form /piŋkɨha/) alternates with an adjective *piŋkɨham* 'perfecto, justo; santo' [perfect, just; holy] (Wipio et al. 1996: 100), showing the same haplology < **piŋkɨha-hama*. Although there is no corresponding verb ***piŋkɨt* in synchrony, there is a verb *ipiŋkɨt* 'to resolve' which appears to have a prefixed vowel marking causative (i.e. 'to make good'). These words thus appear to have a similar etymological relation with a verb root.

Finally, there are two other unproductively derived adjectives: *samɨkbau* 'green' is related to *samɨk* 'fresh'; and *bɨtɨk* 'equal, same' (adjective) is related to *bɨtɨ* 'fully, enough' (adverb).

4.4 Subclasses of nouns

There are two major subclasses of nouns in Aguaruna, based on their marking in possessive constructions, as described in §4.8. Some other minor subclasses can be distinguished, and are described in the following sections.

4.4.1 Gender

There is no grammatical gender in Aguaruna, but some kinship terms (§4.4.3 below) and five other nouns specify natural gender as part of their meaning. Four of these nouns form pairs: 'woman' – 'man' and 'sow' – 'boar'; but 'rooster' has no logical opposing term meaning 'hen' – the latter can only be expressed by the non-gender-specific *atash* 'chicken'. Table 4.8 is an exhaustive list of inherently gendered (non kinship) nouns in my data.

Table 4.8: Inherently gendered nouns

female form		male form	
nuwa	'woman'	*aishmaŋ(ku)*	'man'
shaŋkai	'sow'	*sukisik(i)*[9]	'boar'
–		*āyum(pa)*	'rooster'

Natural gender can be specified with the words *nuwa* 'woman' (4.28a, 4.29a) and *aishmaŋ* 'man' (4.28b, 4.29b) to specify female and male, respectively. These two nouns function as adjectives in this construction.

(4.28) a. *úchi núwa*
           uchi   nuwa
           child   woman
           'girl'

        b. *úchi áishmaŋ*
           uchi   aishmaŋku
           child   man
           'boy'

---

9 Perhaps derived from *suki* 'scrotum, testicles'

(4.29) a. *míshu núwa*
        mishu   nuwa
        cat   woman
        'female cat'

    b. *míshu áishmaŋ*
        mishu   aishmaŋku
        cat   man
        'male cat'

Corbera (1994: 137) mentions that in the case of male birds, *ãyum* 'rooster' is used instead of *aishmaŋ*. The native speakers I worked with rejected this and felt that *aishmaŋ* 'man' is the appropriate modifier for all animate males.

4.4.2 Proper names

Proper names form a class based on syntactic restrictions, as they cannot be modified, nor can they be possessed. Traditional Aguaruna names are often regular nouns such as names for animals or common cultural artefacts; or they may be formed on nominalized verb roots, e.g. *kahikui* < *kahi-ka-u=i* (become.angry-PFV-NMLZ=COP:3:DECL) 'he has become angry' (cf. Jimpikit & Antun' 2000: 48). Nicknames are common, and these follow the traditional pattern. Nowadays most names are Spanish, and follow the same pattern as other recent borrowings, in particular retention of Spanish phonology. One nativizing phenomenon is in vocative forms, which are marked by suppression of apocope and accent shift to the final vowel. Many Spanish names end in a consonant, and in such cases, an epenthetic final vowel /a/ is added, as in (4.30).

(4.30)   *aβelá*
        Abel.VOC
        'Abel!'

Traditional Aguaruna personal names are mostly used nowadays as surnames and nicknames. When the Peruvian naming system (given name, paternal surname, maternal surname) was first introduced to Aguaruna communities, people took their father's name as their first (paternal) surname and mother's name as second (maternal). These surnames are now passed on in the standard hispanic pattern; as a result, the traditional Aguaruna women's names dropped out of use as surnames after the first generation, and most modern surnames come from traditional men's names.

All proper names, including those borrowed from Spanish, can take all case markers but they cannot take possession morphology, as they cannot be possessed. Proper names, including toponyms and hydronyms, show a distinctive behaviour in NPs, where they can follow the head in modifer position but do not take case morphology, which typically appears on the final element of an NP. This is described and illustrated in §5.7.

4.4.3 Kinship terms

Kinship terms are the only nouns that can take both vocative and possession marking (often both at once) as in (4.31), where vocative is signalled by suppression of apocope and accent shift.

(4.31)   *yatsuhú*
           yatsu-hu
           brother-PSSD:1SG+VOC
           'my brother!'

Interlocutors are typically addressed by a kinship term, and those who are not blood relatives are addressed using the gender-appropriate term for sibling or parent, depending on their age relative to the speaker. Apparently this system is relatively recent and has been introduced in the context of christianity. Traditionally, the terms for siblings-in-law were used as general terms of address.

Some kinship terms are inherently gendered, and the three terms for siblings depend upon the gender of both siblings in the relationship: the relation between siblings of opposite sex is expressed by the term *uma*; that between two males by *yatsu-* (with first singular or second person possessor) or *yachĩ* (with first plural or third person possessor); and that between two females by *kai*. The terms are reciprocal: any two siblings address one another using the same word. The words are shown in Table 4.9.

Table 4.9: Gender-based terms for siblings and parallel cousins

relation	term
same sex, male	*yatsu-* / *yachĩ*
same sex, female	*kai*
opposite sex	*uma*

A similar pattern holds for siblings-in-law (Table 4.10).

Table 4.10: Gender-based terms for siblings-in-law and cross cousins

relation	term
same sex, male	*sai*
same sex, female	*yuwa*
opposite sex	*wahɨ* (sibling-in-law) / *antsu* (cross cousin, potential spouse)

The sibling terms also cover parallel cousins, while the sibling-in-law terms cover cross cousins, that is, potential siblings-in-law. However, opposite-sex siblings-in-law, that is, spouses of same-sex siblings and parallel cousins (*wahɨ*) are distinguished from opposite-sex cross cousins (*antsu*), as the latter are potential marriage partners for men and (not yet married) women. Table 4.11 lists the other gendered kinship terms.

Table 4.11: Gendered kinship terms

relation	male referent	female referent
Grandparent[10]	*apachi*	*dukuchi*
Parent or parent's same-sex sibling	*apa*	*duku*
Parent-in-law	*wɨuɲa*	*tsatsa*
Child	*uchi*	*nawanta*
Son of male's brother (*yatsu/yatʃɨ*)	*uchinu*	–
Child of sibling-in-law or cross-cousin[11]	*ahiku*	*nuwasu*

Non-gender-specific kinship terms are *awɨ* 'child of opposite-sex sibling' (i.e. child of *uma*, Table 4.9) OR 'spouse of child'; and *tihaŋki* 'grandchild'; and *uchi* 'child' is used as a general term. Because of changes to traditional marriage patterns and replacement of kinship terms with borrowed Spanish terms, many of these traditional kinship nouns appear to be falling into disuse in contemporary Aguaruna.

---

10 The terms for grandparents are decomposable as *apa-uchi* (father-DIM) and *duku-uchi* (mother-DIM).

11 Neither of these terms is in common use, according to my consultants.

4.4.3.1 Irregular nouns apa 'father' and duku 'mother'

The words *apa* 'father' and *duku* 'mother' form a subclass based on (i) irregular possession marking; and (ii) irregular vocative forms.

When the possessor is second person, these nouns ('father' and 'mother') take no possession morphology (4.32a, b). In all other persons, they behave morphologically as regular alienably possessed nouns (4.32c, d). See §4.8 for details of possession marking.

(4.32) a. *ámina ápa*
           ami=na   apa
           2SG=ACC   father:PSSD:2
           'your (sg) father'

      b. *atúmi ápa*
           atumi   apa
           2PL+GEN   father:PSSD:2
           'your (pl) father'

      c. *mína apáŋ*
           mi=na   apa-hu
           1sg=ACC   father-PSSD:1SG
           'my father'

      d. *áuna apahĩ́*
           au=na   apa-hĩ
           DIST=ACC   father-PSSD:1PL/3
           'his/her father'

The second-person possessor forms are not deficient in other morphology.

The second irregularity is that these two nouns do not take regular vocative marking, instead adding the suffix *-wa* (4.33). Accent is typically shifted to the final vowel, as with other vocative forms.

(4.33) a. *apawá*
           apa-wa
           father-VOC
           'father!'

b. *dukuwá*
   duku-wa
   mother-VOC
   'mother!'

4.4.4 Locational nouns

Nouns with inherent locational meaning can take the ablative marker =*ya* directly, while other nouns must have the locative enclitic =*numa* added first – see examples in §4.10.7. A group of seven nouns take an exceptional locative form, marked with accent shift instead of a suffix. They are described in §4.10.5.

4.5 Compound nouns

Compound nouns are common in Aguaruna and evidence of fossilized compounds shows that this is well-established as a productive process. All compound nouns are endocentric and head-final. Compounds differ from modified NPs in the following ways:

- Semantically: the modifying noun is in a delimiting function.
- Syntactically: with respect to external syntax, the modifying noun precedes the head; with resepect to external syntax, a compound noun heads an NP and functions as a single constituent.
- Phonologically: the two nouns show phonological dependency in accent assignment, and may fuse into one phonological word.

Some forms that must have originated as compounds are no longer parseable into two words, having fused completely into one grammatical and phonological word.

4.5.1 Semantic properties of compounds

All compound nouns are endocentric, that is, they denote a class of items described by one of the elements, which is the head (Aikhenvald 2007a: 30). The head is always the second element. Typically, the first element modifies the head with respect to one particular property. The most common semantic domain for compounding is in names of flora and fauna, as in examples (4.34–4.36).

(4.34)   *dápi mánchi*
            dapi   manchi
            snake   locust
            'type of locust that has a venemous bite'

(4.35)   *ípak hɨmpɨ*
            ipaka   hɨmpɨ
            annatto   hummingbird
            'type of hummingbird with a red chest (the colour of annatto)'

(4.36)   *aɨnts ũỹũsh*
            aɨntsu   ũyushi
            person   sloth
            'type of sloth that is thought to look human'

Some examples of compounds do not involve the same relation of modification between the two elements. In example (4.37) the referent is a type of dog (in the general Amazonian sense of predatory carnivore), but it does not resemble a forest in any respect; instead, it is a *dog from the forest*.

(4.37)   *íkam ỹãw̃ãã*
            ikama   yawaã
            forest   dog
            'jaguar'

In other examples (4.38, 4.39), the relation between the two nouns is more like possession (compare pseudo compounds, in which a possession relationship is overtly marked, §4.5.5).

(4.38)   *kístian chícham*
            kistian   chichama
            mestizo   language
            'Spanish (language)'

(4.39)   *shiwáŋ báikua*
            shiwaha   baikua
            enemy   angel's.trumpet
            'variety of angel's trumpet (*Brugmansia sp.*) said to have been stolen from enemies during raids'

And in some cases, such as (4.40), the relation is unclear.

(4.40)   *númpa wíchiŋ*
          numpa   wichiŋku
          blood   squirrel
          'type of squirrel'

Of course, there must be some historical reason for the choice of determining noun that is simply not known to the present researcher. Other examples that appear equally opaque prove to have logical motivation on further investigation. For example, *wakam* 'macambo' (*Theobroma bicolor*, a fruit related to cacao) heads compounds in combination with three animal names (4.41). The motivation for the names was a mystery to me until a speaker explained that it relates to the size of the fruits: the relative size is matched to the relative size of the animal specifier.

(4.41) a.   *kã́ỹŭk wákam*
             kãyuka   wakampɨ
             agouti   macambo
             'variety of macambo'

        b.   *káshai wákam*
             kashai   wakampɨ
             paca   macambo
             'variety of macambo'

        c.   *pabáu wákam*
             pabau   wakampɨ
             tapir   macambo
             'variety of macambo'

4.5.2 Syntactic properties of compounds

As the preceding examples have shown, the modifying element of a compound always precedes the head. This contrasts with the internal syntax of a modified NP, in which the modifier always follows the head (see §5.4; and see Overall, in press-b for a diachronic account of word order in compound nouns and modified NPs).

4.5.3 Phonological properties of compounds

As noted above, compounds show a continuum of phonological fusion. All compounds show some phonological dependency, manifested in accentuation effects, but only in the most fused is vowel elision affected. The accent in the second (head) element of a compound is always on the first syllable, regardless of the accent in isolation: example (4.41a) above has the surface pronunciation [káỹũk wákam], but the head noun in isolation surfaces as [wakám].

Compounds tend to become a single phonological word. The form in (4.37) above, *ikám yawaã* 'jaguar', appears in my data as one or two phonological words, apparently depending on such factors as speed of speech and emphasis. Some synchronically monomorphemic nouns appear to have arisen historically from compounds. For example *yuŋkipák* /yuŋkipaki/ 'collared peccary' appears to be formed from *páki* 'white-lipped peccary', but the first element *yuŋki* has no synchronic meaning and does not appear outside of this one compound.[12] Similarly, many names of flora end with /numi/, apparently arising from compounds headed by *numi* 'tree, wood' (as in 4.42).

(4.42)   *tsampáunum*
          tsampau-numi
          ?-tree
          'manioc plant'

Some nouns end in /nimi/ (example 4.43), showing the sporadic vowel harmony described in §3.6.2, clear evidence that they are no longer parsed by speakers into their two constituent parts.

(4.43)   *páunim*
          pau-nimi
          sapodilla-tree
          'tree with leaves similar to *sapodilla* (*Manilkara zapota*)'

Apocope applies in fused forms where it would not in those consisting of two phonological words. So for *yuŋkipák* < /yuŋkipaki/ 'collared peccary' apocope applies to the citation form, but for *múun páki* /muunta paki/ (big white.lipped.peccary) 'type of white-lipped peccary' the head element *páki* is an independent phonological word, and because it has only two syllables apocope does not apply.

---

12 There is a word *yuŋki* 'queen leafcutter ant', but there is no evidence to suggest that this is involved in the compound. The compound must be old: it has cognates in the other Chicham languages, all of which end in /piki/, applying the sporadic 'vowel harmony' discussed in §3.6.2, and attesting to the fact that the word is not synchronically considered a compound. Further phonological changes in Achuar-Shiwiar have produced the two dialectal variants *yaŋkipík* and *naŋkipík*. Also of interest is Gnerre's (1999: 119) suggestion that the word *paki* 'white-lipped peccary' is itself a Carib loan.

Fused forms clearly consist of one phonological word: there is just one, stable accent; vowel elision applies where it would not if these were two words; literate native speakers write them as one word. It appears that the most phonologically bound compounds are also the most difficult to parse, normally because the first element no longer exists as an independent word. Whether the phonological cohesion arises as a result of the difficulty in parsing or vice versa is hard to tell. A full description of the phonology of compounds is in §3.8.2. Compounds are lexicalized, and cannot be nonce formations. The meaning is generally not immediately predictable from the sum of the parts. For the most part compounds tend to be names of flora and fauna – using the compounding strategy, a number of similar species can be named based on a prototype system.

4.5.4 Adjective-noun compounds

Adjective-noun compounds are rare, totalling only four in my data, listed in Table 4.12.

Table 4.12: Adjective-noun compounds

compound	gloss		translation
múun páki	muunta big	paki peccary	'large species of peccary'
múun uwíŋ	muunta big	uwɨha hand	'thumb'
ɨsáham uwíŋ	isahama tall	uwɨha hand	'middle finger'
sútaŋ uwíŋ	sutaha short	uwɨha hand	'ring finger'

Firstly note that all but one are names of digits. Secondly, note that two are formed with *muun* 'big', 'adult' which functions as a noun as well as an adjective, so they are not definitive examples of adjective-noun compounding. This leaves two fingers: 'tall' and 'short'. The other two fingers are *tsɨŋkɨ uwɨŋ* 'index finger' (cf. *tsɨŋkɨn* 'fork in branch') and *uchi uwɨŋ* (child hand) 'little finger'. See Overall (in press-b) for further discussion of these forms.

4.5.5 Pseudo compounds

A few terms for body parts appear at first glance to be compounds in terms of their semantic unity, but are in fact normal possessive NPs. In examples (4.44, 4.45), the overt marking on both nouns (genitive (§4.10.3) and possession (§4.8)) shows that these are possessive NPs. The phonological fusion characteristic of compounds is not in evidence: there are two stable accents that are just as expected for the constructions.

(4.44) *numpá híntĩ*
        numpa   hintĩ
        blood+GEN   path+PSSD:1PL/3
        'vein' lit. *blood's path*

(4.45) *duhí w̃ããhí*
        duhi   waã-hĩ
        nose+GEN   hole-PSSD:1PL/3
        'nostril' lit. *nose's hole*

4.6 Pronominal words

Like nouns, pronouns may head NPs. Unlike nouns, they cannot be possessed, they do not take vocative forms, and they cannot be modified or specified within the NP. In discourse, pronouns must have a recoverable referent, whether already introduced in the discourse, available from context, or introduced by a demonstrative pronoun itself through deictic reference. The following sections first describe personal pronouns (§4.6.1), followed by the demonstrative and anaphoric pronouns (§4.6.2).

4.6.1 Personal pronouns

Personal pronouns show a number distinction, with singular and plural forms for each. They are listed in Table 4.13. These are the only nominals to show a number distinction.

Table 4.13: Personal pronouns

person	singular		plural
1	*wi-* / *wii*	**specific**	*ii*
		non-specific	*hutii*
2	*amɨ*		*atum(ɨ)*
3	*nɨ̃-* / *nɨ̃ɨ̃*		*dita*

The first and third singular pronouns have their vowels lengthened and surface as [wíi] and [nɨ̃ɨ̃] respectively when they appear unsuffixed, to fulfil the two-syllable minimal word requirement. The distinction between the two first person plural forms has its basis in specificity: *ii* refers to a specific set of participants, while *hutii* is non-specific. This is not an inclusive/exclusive distinction, as both *ii* and *hutii* can exclude second person: compare examples (4.46) and (4.47).

(4.46) *ii áinauti ɨ̃ɣ̃ãkmáhimɨ ámɨ*
    [ii   a-ina-u=ti]ₙₚ:ₐ   ɨɰa-ka-ma-himɨ
    1pl   COP-PL:IPFV-NMLZ=SAP   search-PFV-RECPST-1PL>2SG+DECL
    [amɨ]ₙₚ:ₒ
    2sg
    'we searched for you (sg)'

(4.47) *hutíi áidauti dakastáthimɨ ámina*
    hutii   a-ina-u=ti   daka-sa-tata-himɨ
    1pl   COP-PL:IPFV-NMLZ=SAP   wait.for-PFV-FUT-1PL>2SG+DECL
    ami=na
    2sg=ACC
    'we will wait for you (sg)'

In example (4.48), taken from a natural narrative, *ii* explicitly excludes second person.

(4.48) *íik hṹw̃ĩ íi núwati máinahi, ámik wɨ́mɨ ã́w̃ĩ amɨ́sh máita*
    [ii=ka   hu=ĩ   ii   nuwa=ti   ma-ina-hi]
    1pl=TOP   PROX=LOC 1pl   woman=SAP   bathe-PL:IPFV-1PL+DECL
    [amɨ=ka   wɨ-mɨ   au=ĩ   ami=sha   mai-ta
    2sg=TOP   go+PFV -2:SS   DIST=LOC   2sg=ADD   bathe+PFV-IMP
    'we women are bathing here, you go and bathe over there'
    (agr041005_19)

The standard way of inviting someone to do something together with the speaker uses *ii* marked with comitative case, as in (4.49). In this example *ii* must include second person, as there are only two participants involved: the speaker is asking the addressee to 'dance with me', not 'dance with us'.

(4.49)   *íihãĩ nantsɨmámi*

            ii=haĩ   nantsɨma-mi

            1pl=COM   dance+PFV-HORT

            'let's dance together'

Example (4.50) similarly shows *ii* including the addressee. It is taken from a story in which a dog falls in love with a woman, so her husband kills the dog. The woman asks him 'have you killed our dog?', using the pronoun *ii*.[13]

(4.50)   *ỹãw̃ắã íinu maáshmakum*

            [yawaã   ii-nau]   maa-cha-ma=ka-umɨ

            dog   1pl-POSS   kill+PFV-NEG-RECPST=Q-2SG

            'have you killed our dog?' (agr041005_15)

In example (4.51) both *ii* and *hutii* are used in combination with the word *iinia* 'one of us' carrying the SAP marker, giving the meaning 'we being us' (*iinia* probably comes from *ii=nĩ=ya* (1PL=LOC=ABL) '(a person) from our place').

(4.51)   *yatsúŋ Simón wakɨɰawai íi hutíi iiniáti kúntin maátasa wahúk*

            wɨkáitayamɨ̃ nunúna

            yatsu-hu   *Simón*   wakɨɰa-wa-i   [ii   hutii

            brother-PSSD:1SG   Simon   want+IPFV-3-DECL 1PL   1PL

            iinia=ti   kuntinu   maa   maa-tasa   wahuka

            one.of.us=SAP animal   REDUP kill+PFV-INTENT+1PL:SS how

            wɨkaɨɰa-tayamɨ̃   nunu=na]

            walk-NORM   ANA=ACC

            'My brother Simon wants (to know): how do we, (people) from around here, go hunting?' (Text 3:1)

So the evidence from actual usage suggests that the meanings of the two 1PL pronouns are basically the same, but *ii* refers to a more-or-less specified set of people, while *hutii* is non-specific. Importantly, although the use of *ii* can be characterized as excluding some potential referent(s), it is not *exclusive* in the generally accepted

---

13 For the use of negative polarity in polar questions see Chapter 10.

sense of excluding second person. Instead, it may exclude second or third person referent(s), and in the latter case second person is included.

A relatively recent development of *hutii* is indicated by the fact that no cognates appear in the dictionaries of other Chicham languages, all of which give only the one form *ii*. The fact that *ii* enters into the semantically non-compositional idiom *ii=haĩ* (1PL=COM) 'you and I together' also suggests this is an older form. *hutii* may have ultimately arisen from the proximal demonstrative *hu* with the speech-act participant marker =*ti* (§4.9.7), meaning 'we here'. Further study of conversational data should help to pin down the precise semantic differences between *ii* and *hutii*. The current work is based mostly on narrative data, in which first person plural reference is rare. The first person plural verbal object marker is used to indicate a generic human object (§6.3.1), but the pronouns are not used with such a generic sense.

4.6.1.1 Combining stems of SAP pronouns

The first person singular and second person singular and plural pronouns have combining forms that appear when some case enclitics are added, shown in Table 4.14.

Table 4.14: Combining pronominal stems

person	underlying root	combining form
1sg	*wi*	*mi-*
2sg	*amɨ*	*ami-*
2pl	*atumɨ*	*atumi-*

The case enclitics are added to the combining stems, but there is one exceptional form: first person with locative surfaces as *mináĩ*, not the expected ****mi=nĩ*, as discussed in §3.6.2.

4.6.1.2 Interrogative Pronouns

Interrogative pronouns are formed from three roots: *tu* 'which', 'where'; *wahĩ* 'what (non-human)'; and *ya* 'who (human)'. Interrogative pronouns take the same morphology as other pronouns, in addition to having some distinct morphological properties which are shared with other interrogative forms. The properties of interrogatives are described in Chapter 10.

4.6.2 Demonstrative pronouns

Demonstrative pronouns exhibit a three-way spatial distinction: proximal, medial and distal. All appear to be relative to the speaker, regardless of addressee's position. There is also a general anaphoric pronoun *nu*, which is used for non-deictic reference. Table 4.15 lists the surface realizations of the case-marked forms of the demonstrative pronouns, along with those marked with the 'first', 'topic' and 'additive' enclitics.

Table 4.15: Demonstrative and anaphoric pronouns

	proximal	medial	distal	anaphoric
NOM	*húu*	*anú*	*áu*	*núu*
ACC	*húna*	*aánna*	*áuna*	*núna*
LOC	*hū́w̃ī*	*aaní̃*	*ā́w̃ī*	*nū́w̃ī*
ALL	*huní*	*aán*	*aní*	*nuní*
INS	*húwi*	*adúi*	*áwi*	*dúwi*
FIRST	*huwá*	*anuwá*	*auwá*	–
TOP	*húka*	*aánka*	*áuk*	*dúka*
ADD	*húshakam*	*aánchakam*	*aúshkam*	*dúshakam*

The proximal and general anaphoric pronouns have reduplicated variants *huhú* and *nunú* respectively, which can be freely substituted for the simple forms. The reduplicated forms are attested in nominative, accusative (*huhú=na*, *nunú=na*) and locative (*huhū́=ĩ*, *nunū́=ĩ*) case in my corpus. In addition, the same two pronouns have long variants that appear only with locative and instrumental case: *huwahū́=ĩ* (PROX=LOC), *huwahú=i* (PROX=INS); *nuwanū́=ĩ* (ANA=LOC), *nuwanú=i* (ANA=INS). These forms must be based on the 'relativized copula' focussing construction (§18.2.3), with the structure shown in (4.52).

(4.52) *huwahū́w̃ī*
       hu=a   hu=ĩ
       PROX=COP:3   PROX_REL=LOC
       'at this place that is here'

The medial demonstrative *anu* is morphologically quite irregular, varying between stems *anu* and *aa(n)* through the paradigm. It is also the least common form in narratives, and is rare in my data. The examples I do have are in reported speech, such as example (4.53), spoken by a rat who teaches a human woman how to give birth.

(4.53)   *diiŋsákia, anú mína uchíŋ*
           dii-hu-sa-kia   [**anu**]vcs   [mi=na   uchi-hu]vcc
           look-1SG.OBJ-PFV-IMP:FAM   MED   1sg=ACC   child-PSSD:1SG
           'look at me; those are my children' (agr041005_16)

In example (4.54) the referent identified deictically with the medial demonstrative ('that naked one') is anaphorically referred to with the distal demonstrative *au* in the following verbless clause.

(4.54)   *anu wisu puha nu, au uchuchihĩã nu*
           [**anu**   wisu   puha   nu]NP   [**au**]vcs
           MED   naked   live+IPFV   ANAREL   DIST
           [uchuchi-hĩ=a   nu]vcc
           child+DIM-PSSD:1PL/3=COP:3   ANAREL
           'that naked one, that's her child' (Tiinch & Danducho)

Example (4.55) is the response to a question about the location of a community.

(4.55)   *anu carretera nima duki, au Santa Rosa tawa atu*
           anu   carretera   nima   nu=kI
           MED   highway   follow+IPFV+3   ANA=RESTR
           [**au**]vcs   [Santa Rosa   ta-wa   atu]vcc
           DIST   Santa Rosa   say+IPFV-3   near
           'just following that highway, it's near a place called Santa Rosa' (Tiinch & Danducho)

Although the medial demonstrative does not necessarily denote addressee's location, in some contexts this association does happen. Compare (4.56) with (4.57): in both exchanges, the writer is located in Lima (referred to with proximal) and the addressee in Melbourne (referred to with medial).

(4.56)   *huhuiŋ bachik ĩtsã hiinui yabaik*
           huhu=ĩ=ka   bachika   ĩtsã   hiina-wa-i   yamai=ka
           PROX=LOC=TOP   a.little   sun   come.out+IPFV-3-DECL   today=TOP
           'here (Lima) the sun is out a bit today' (personal correspondence)

(4.57) a. *yabai Lima tsĩtsĩkaya*
            yamai   Lima   tsĩtsĩka=ya
            now   Lima   cold=COP:3:EXCL

b.   *aanĩsha?*
   aan=ĩ=sha
   MED=LOC=Q.TOP
   '^{a.}Lima is cold now, ^{b.}how about over there (Melbourne)?' (personal
   correspondence)

In (4.58), the speaker is in Nieva and the addressee in Melbourne. The city of
Chiclayo, distant from both, is referred to using the distal demonstrative.

(4.58) a.   *wika Chiclayo wɨmainaithai*
      wi=ka   *Chiclayo*   wɨ-mai-na=it-ha-i
      1sg=TOP   Chiclayo   go-POT-NMLZ=COP-1SG-DECL
   b.   *ãwĩ awai Western Union*
      au=ĩ   a-wa-i   *Western Union*
      DIST=LOC   exist-3-DECL   Western Union
   c.   *hũwĩ Nieva atsawai*
      hu=ĩ   *Nieva*   atsa-wa-i
      PROX=LOC   Nieva   exist:NEG+IPFV-3-DECL
      '^{a.}I can go to Chiclayo, ^{b.}there's a Western Union there, ^{c.}here in Nieva
      there isn't one' (personal correspondence)

Demonstratives have an allative form that does not appear with lexical nominals,
marked with the enclitic *=n(i)* and giving a directional meaning (4.59, 4.60). With all
other nominals, locative case covers this allative sense.

(4.59)   *hunɨ́ wɨmɨ́*
      hu=ni   wɨ-mi
      PROX=ALL   go+PFV-HORT
      'let's go this way'

(4.60)   *aán wainkámumɨ*
      aan   waina-ka-ma-umɨ
      MED+ALL   see-PFV-RECPST-2SG+DECL
      'you saw it over in that direction'

All of the nominal demonstratives can function as determiners within an NP, as in
(4.61, 4.62), or occur alone as head of an NP, as in (4.63, 4.64). A nominal demonstrative heading an NP cannot be modified.

(4.61)   *nunú aínts*
         [nunu   aintsu]_{NP}
         ANA   person
         'that person'

(4.62)   *núna nuwán húwaya túwahamĭ*
         [nu=na   nuwa=na]_{NP}   hu-a-ya   tuwahamĭ
         ANA=ACC   woman=ACC   take-IPFV-REMPST   NARR
         'they took those women' (agr040723_29)

(4.63)   *húsha wahimpáya*
         [hu=sha]_{NP}   wahimpaya
         PROX=Q.TOP   what+COP:3:Q
         'what is this?'

(4.64)   *núna húkĭ wĭµa wĭµakŭã*
         [nu=na]_{NP}   hu-kĭ   wĭµa   wĭ-a-kawã
         ANA=ACC   take-PFV+SEQ+3:SS   REDUP   go-IPFV-REPET+3:SS
         'having taken that (child) she was going and going...' (agr040721_07)

When one of the demonstratives *hu* 'proximal', *au* 'distal' and *nu* 'anaphoric' modifies a case-marked NP, it shows case agreement with the head noun, as in (4.62) above. It is likely that the medial demonstrative *anu* shows the same phenomenon, but there are no examples in my data. Case agreement is described fully in §5.2.1.

The pronouns *hu*, *au*, and *nu* also function as relativizers, and derivatives of the intensifier *ima* enter into the same construction – see Chapter 16 for a detailed description. The demonstrative *hu*, anaphoric *nu*, demonstrative adverb *aa* and intensifier *ima* take special verbalizers *-ni* and *-tika* to form pro-verbs with meanings 'do this', 'do that', 'do thus', 'do so much', respectively. The pro-verbs are widely used in bridging constructions in narrative. They are described in §6.6, and their functions in §14.8.

4.6.2.1 Textual anaphora

Textual anaphora is frequent with the anaphoric pronoun *nu*, especially in reported speech and narratives. The example in (4.65) is the last line of a narrative. The demonstrative *nu=na* (ANA=ACC) refers back to the entire story. Similar formulae are commonly used to end traditional stories.

(4.65)   *wíi anɨau asán, núna wíi ɨtsɨŋhai*
           [wi   anɨ-a-u   asa-nu]   [nu=na]
           1sg   think.about-IPFV-NMLZ   COP+SBD-1SG:SS   ANA=ACC
           wi   ɨtsɨha-ha-i
           1sg   relate+IPFV-1SG-DECL
           'being one who remembers, I tell that (story).' (agr040712_02)

Such anaphora can also refer to a section of discourse that is not in the form of a narrative. Example (4.66) comes from a story where a young man has just passed on to his sister-in-law a long series of instructions from his brother. The anaphoric pronoun *nunu* refers to the instructions.

(4.66)   *nunú dútikami*
           nunu   nu-tika-mi
           ANA   ANA-VBLZ.TR+PFV-HORT
           'let's do that' (agr041005_14)

Similarly, an agreement will often be concluded with the formula in (4.67).

(4.67)   *núu atí*
           nu   a-ti
           ANA   exist-JUSS
           'let it (i.e. what has just been agreed) be'

4.6.2.2 Textual cataphora
Textual cataphora is rare in narrative but more common in conversation. The device uses the distal demonstrative pronoun *au*, which always carries the restrictive enclitic *=kI* in such constructions. This is immediately followed by a clause which is apparently in apposition to the pronoun. The pronoun *au=kɨ* (DIST=RESTR) in example (4.68) cannot refer to the object argument, as it does not carry the expected accusative marking.

(4.68)   *aúk kaŋkapɨ íhuahai*
           au=kI   [kaŋkapɨ   ihu-a-ha-i]
           DIST=RESTR   *Kagkap*+VOC   stab-IPFV-1SG-DECL
           'Kagkap! I (will) stab it (the jaguar)!' (agr041005_14)

Use of textual cataphoric *auk* expresses the unexpectedness of the information conveyed. Example (4.69) is taken from a story in which a woman had been sexually penetrated by an unknown assailant, which turns out to be an evil spirit (*ɨ̃wanch*) that has taken the form of a monkey. Her husband stays awake the next night to see who has done this to his wife, and when he sees what he thinks is a monkey, he says this to his wife.

(4.69)   *aúk wáshi áikaŋmawai*
       au=kI   [washi   aika-hama-a-wa-i]
       DIST=RESTR   spider.monkey   thus+VBLZ.TR-2.OBJ-IPFV-3-DECL
       'a spider monkey is doing that to you!' (agr040723_29)

The context of example (4.70) is that a woman is living in an agouti's house, and has been told she cannot accompany the agouti to the garden because the path is too steep and dangerous. Later, however, the agouti's child tells the woman that she has been lied to, with this exclamation.

(4.70)   *aúk píŋkɨhai híntak*
       au=kI   píŋkɨha=i   hinta=ka
       DIST=RESTR   good=COP:3:DECL   path=TOP
       'it's a good path!' (agr040721_07)

Textual cataphora has some semantic overlap with discourse particles (§12.4) and with mood/modality (Chapter 9) as it expresses the speaker's attitude towards the proposition expressed in the clause.

4.7 Nominal derivational morphology, first level

The first level of derivational morphology consists of only one suffix, *-uchi* 'diminutive'. Diminutive may precede possession marking, unlike other derivational suffixes (4.71).

(4.71)   *yaápchiŋmin*
       yaapɨ-uchi-hu-mɨ=na
       nerve-DIM-PSSD-2=ACC
       'your little nerves' (agr040720_02)

However, the diminutive suffix may also appear in slot C, following other slot C suffixes – see examples in §4.9.4. As noted above (see example 4.1), diminutive is only attested following the restrictive enclitic in pronouns.

4.8 Possession morphology

The relationship of possession consists of one noun (the possessor) modifying a second (the possessum). In Aguaruna possession is typically double-marked, on the head (the possessum) and the dependent (the possessor), but there is also a derivational possessive marker that marks possessors without requiring any marking on the possessum (see §4.9.2). Possession morphology marks a noun as possessed, and also indexes the person of the possessor. Possession suffixes form a distinct group based on their morphological characteristics, preceding case enclitics. When the possessor is second person, there are two clearly identifiable morphological slots, the first filled by a marker of possession and the second marking second person. The other persons are marked with portmanteau suffixes, although it is possible to analyse these as morphologically complex, at least historically.

Possession is marked with a combination of vowel change in the root and suffixes. There is a three-way distinction in possession marking, contrasting first person singular with second person and third person. First person plural possessor is marked identically to third person possessor, and no number distinction is made in marking second and third person possessors. Nouns fall into two classes based on the marking they take when possessed. The vowel-changing group uses a combination of suffixes and root apophony in second person, and root apophony only in first plural and third persons, while the suffixing group marks possession entirely with suffixes in all persons. The two classes are not distinguished when the possessor is first person singular, which is marked for all nouns with a suffix -*hu*. Table 4.16 shows the person markers for possessed nouns. Possession class membership is not readily predictable on semantic grounds – see discussion in §4.8.2.

Table 4.16: Morphological marking of possessed nouns

	vowel-changing class	suffixing class
1sg	-*hu*	-*hu*
2	-*mɨ*	-*hu-mɨ*
1pl/3	nasality of final vowel	-*hĩ*

Table 4.17 exemplifies possession paradigms for a vowel-changing noun *númpa* 'blood' and a suffixing noun *súsu* 'beard'.

Table 4.17: Possession paradigms

	vowel-changing	suffixing
1sg	numpáŋ numpa-hu blood-PSSD:1SG	susúŋ susu-hu beard-PSSD:1SG
2	númpɨm numpɨ-mɨ blood+PSSD-2	susuhúm susu-hu-mɨ̄ beard-PSSD-2
1pl/3	númpɨ̄ numpɨ̄ blood+PSSD:1PL/3	susuhɨ̂ susu-hɨ̄ beard-PSSD:1PL/3

Nouns of the vowel-changing class with final /a/ or /u/ undergo vowel changes when the possessor is a person other than first singular. Roots ending in /i/ and /ɨ/ never show vowel changes. There is a basic regularity to the vowel changes, althhough a few exceptions must be admitted. There is also some phonological basis for subgroups of vowel-changing nouns based on the changes:

- Roots ending in /a/ show regular vowel change, with the final vowel becoming /ɨ/ or /i/ depending on the quality of the preceding vowel.
- Roots ending in /hV/ always show irregularities, probably arising from haplology in the first-person singular possessed form, which is marked with the fix -hu.
- Roots ending in /u/ are the least common, and data are insufficient to support a rule-based analysis: of three examples, one changes /u/ to /i/, one shows the same change but only in the non-second form, and the third adds final /i/ in the non-second form, while still retaining /u/.
- Patterns of apophony are described below. Table 4.18 exemplifies vowel-changing nouns ending in /i/ and /ɨ/, with no vowel change with any possessor.

Table 4.18: Possessed forms of vowel-changing nouns with final /i/ and /ɨ/

root	1sg	2	1pl/3	gloss
anɨntai	anɨntai-hu	anɨntai-mɨ	anɨntaī	'heart'
kai	kai-hu	kai-mɨ	kaī	'sister of female'
awɨ	awɨ-hu	awɨ-mɨ	awɨ̄	'child of sibling of opposite sex'/ 'spouse of child'
dɨtsɨpɨ	dɨtsɨpɨ-hu	dɨtsɨpɨ-mɨ	dɨtsɨpɨ̄	'chest'

Vowel changes with final /a/ are phonologically conditioned. Final /a/ becomes /ɨ/ if the preceding syllable contains the vowel /u/ or /ɨ/ (Table 4.19).

Table 4.19: Change of final /a/ to /ɨ/ following /ɨ/ and /u/

root	1sg	2	1pl/3	gloss
duka	duka-hu	dukɨ-mɨ	dukɨ̃	'leaf'
numpa	numpa-hu	numpɨ-mɨ	numpɨ̃	'blood'
nuwa	nuwa-hu	nuwɨ-mɨ	nuwɨ̃	'woman'
nuŋka	nuŋka-hu	nuŋkɨ-mɨ	nuŋkɨ̃	'ground'
hɨɰa	hɨɰa-hu	hɨ̃-mɨ	hɨ̃̃	'house'

Elsewhere, that is, following a syllable with nucleus /a/ or /i/, /a/ becomes /i/ (Table 4.20). The single exception to these rules in my data is the noun *chicham* /chichama/ 'speech', which takes the possessed form *chichamɨ̃* 'our/his/her speech', rather than the expected **chichamĩ*.

Table 4.20: Change of final /a/ to /ĩ/ following /i/ and /a/

root	1sg	2	1pl/3	gloss
kata	kata-hu	kati-mɨ	katĩ	'penis'
yawaã	yawaã-hu	yawai-mɨ	yawayĩ	'dog'[14]
hinta	hinta-hu	hinti-mɨ	hintĩ	'path'
iha	iha-hu	ihi-mɨ	ihĩ	'shit'

There appears to be no regular rule to the /u/-final vowel-changing nouns. If more examples can be found, perhaps a regular rule can be induced, but my data contain only the three nouns shown in Table 4.21.

---

14 But 'dog' also appears as suffixing: *yawaã-hĩ* (dog-PSSD:1PL/3) 'his/her/our dog'.

Table 4.21: Possessed forms of vowel-changing nouns ending in /u/

root	1sg	2	1pl/3	gloss
wɨnu	wɨnu-hu	wɨni-mɨ	wɨnɨ̄	'mouth'
baku	baku-hu	baku-mɨ	bakuɨ̄	'thigh'
yatsu	yatsu-hu	yatsu-mɨ	yachɨ̄	'brother of male'

Roots that end in /hV/ give rise to some confusion (Table 4.22).

Table 4.22: Possessed forms of nouns ending in /hV/

root	1sg	2	1pl/3	gloss
uhahi	uha-hu	uhahi-mɨ	uhahɨ̄	'pubic hair'
kaŋkaha	kaŋka-hu	kaŋkahi-mɨ	kaŋkahɨ̄	'lower leg'
uwɨha	uwɨ-hu	uwɨ-hu-mɨ	uwɨ-hɨ̄	'hand'
numpiha	numpi-hu	numpi-hu-mɨ	numpi-hɨ̄	'anus'

There are two patterns here: the first two nouns are treated as regular vowel-changing nouns, but the first singular form has the suffix -*hu* added to the root without its final /hV/ – presumably a haplological deletion.[15] The second pattern sees the noun treated as a suffixing noun but throughout the paradigm the suffixes are added to the root minus its final /hV/ syllable; this looks like a more general deletion, by analogy with the first person singular forms.

4.8.1 Morphological analysis of possession marking

There is good evidence that both the vowel changing and the suffixing paradigms can be analysed as morphologically complex, consisting of two levels: the first marking the noun as possessed, and the second marking the person of the possessor – this approach is taken by David Payne (1990b), and Corbera (1994: 124ff.), although their analyses need to be altered slightly to explain all of the observed facts. It is clear that the second person suffixing form must be morphologically complex: -*mɨ* marks second person throughout the grammar, including on vowel-changing nouns, so it is safe to assume the -*hu* element marks the noun as possessed. What of the 1PL/3 form -*hɨ̄*? Previous analysts (David Payne 1990b, Corbera

---

15 The proposed haplology would apply to /hV-hV/ regardless of vowel quality.

1994: 124ff) have decomposed this into *-hu* and a 1PL/3 marker *-(i)ĩ*, with subsequent fusion of the vowels. By this analysis, the same suffix *-(i)ĩ* also triggers the vowel changes and nasalization in vowel-changing nouns. Further support for this hypothesis comes from the accent shifting effects: *-hu* shifts accent in 2 and 3 vowel nouns, and *-(i)ĩ* shifts accent in 3 vowel nouns. Another piece of evidence for the hypothesized morphologically complex origin of *-hĩ* comes from the word *apahúi* 'God', presumably a fossilized example of an earlier stage of development decomposable as **apa-hu-(i)ĩ* (father-PSSD-1PL/3) 'our father'. In the modern language, 'our father' is *apa-hĩ* (father-PSSD:1PL/3). The problem with the prior analyses is that vowel change also happens in second person forms, so it cannot be triggered simply by fusion of 1PL/3 *-(i)ĩ* with the root-final vowel. The following set of rules adequately predicts the regular possession marking described above:

1. The possessed form of the noun is marked in vowel-changing nouns with root apophony for non-first-singular possessor and zero-marked for first singular possessor. In suffixing nouns, possession is marked with the suffix *-hu*.
2. Person is marked in all possessed nouns with the suffixes *-hu* 1SG, *-mi* 2 and *-ĩ* 1PL/3.
3. The combination *-hu-hu* (-PSSD-1SG) is reduced haplologically to *-hu*.
4. The combination *-hu-ĩ* (-PSSD-1PL/3) fuses to surface as *-hĩ*.

These rules explain all apart from the exceptional nouns already described. Support for the phonological rules in 3 and 4 comes from the word *apahúi* 'God' and the examples of haplology in noun roots that end in /hV/. While this hypothesis is certainly of value as a historical explanation, and reduces the observed data to a relatively simple set of rules, it has the problem in a synchronic description of postulating a hypothetical morpheme *-ĩ* that never actually surfaces in that form.

4.8.2 Semantic correlates of class membership

The two classes of nouns basically distinguish inalienable and alienable possession, represented by vowel-changing and suffixing nouns, respectively; however, the assignment of any given noun to one or the other class is not readily predictable on semantic grounds. The extra phonological material involved in marking alienable possession can be seen as iconic, inasmuch as the possession bond is seen to be weaker (T. Payne 1997: 105). The vowel-changing/inalienable class includes body parts (including part-whole relations such as 'leaf', 'root', and 'branch'), kinship terminology, and a few other nouns such as 'house', 'land', 'path', 'shit' – all readily acceptable semantically as inalienably possessed. But within the important semantic areas of body parts and kinship terminology we find many suffixing nouns too, as illustrated in Table 4.23 and Table 4.24.

Table 4.23: Suffixing body-part nouns

root	gloss
ampu	'guts'
kuntu	'arm'
muntsu	'nipple'
susu	'facial hair'
chuki	'vulva'

Table 4.24: Suffixing kinship nouns

root	gloss
pata	'relative'
apach	'grandfather'
dukuch	'grandmother'
diich	'uncle'
wɨuʝa	'father-in-law'
tsatsa	'mother-in-law'
yuwa	'female cross-cousin of female'
antsu	'cross-cousin of opposite sex'
wahɨ	'sibling-in-law of opposite sex'
uchi	'child'
nawanta	'daughter'
uchinu	'son of brother of male'
ahik	'nephew' (archaic/jocular)
nuwas	'niece' (archaic/jocular)
tihaŋ	'grandchild'

In fact, there are more suffixing than vowel-changing kinship nouns in my corpus: all of the regular vowel-changing kinship nouns I am aware of are listed in Table 4.25.

Table 4.25: Vowel-changing kinship nouns

root	gloss
kai	'sister of female'
sai	'brother-in-law of male'

root	gloss
uma	'sibling of opposite sex'
awɨ	'child of *uma* or spouse of child'

There are three exceptional kinship nouns: *yatsu* 'brother of male' has the partially-suppletive vowel-changing 1PL/3 form *yachĩ*, while *duku* 'mother' and *apa* 'father' are unmarked for second person possessor but suffixing for other persons.

Vowel-changing body-part nouns are more common than suffixing forms; a selection is presented in Table 4.26.

Table 4.26: Vowel-changing body-part nouns

root	gloss
baku	'thigh'
ditsɨpɨ	'chest'
iha	'shit'
intashi	'hair of the head'
iyāshi	'body'
kaŋkahi	'lower leg'
nanchiki	'fingernail, claw, hoof'
nuhi	'nose'
numpa	'blood'
suwɨ	'throat'
chiŋkuni	'elbow'
tikishi	'knee'
uhahi	'pubic hair'
ūhɨ	'body hair'
wɨnu	'mouth'
yapi	'face'

Possession is not obligatory or inherent: nouns of both classes can appear outside of a possessive construction. Possession can also be indicated with the possessive suffix on the possessor noun or pronoun, which derives a nominal modifying the possessum; the latter is unmarked. This strategy is obligatory for at least two nouns when the possessor is human: *dúka* 'leaf' and *tsúntsu* 'snail'. The reason for this is that *dúka* has the extended meaning 'labia' and *tsúntsu* the extended meaning 'vulva of an animal'; use of possession-marking morphology implies these senses, so the unmarked form is used to avoid embarrassing double meanings. At least one noun, ỹãw̃áã 'dog', can be marked as either class.

4.8.2.1 Exceptional nouns

A few nouns do not fit into the patterns described above. The irregular *chicham* 'speech' has already been mentioned. *áishĩ* 'husband' appears only in the vowel-changing possessed form, but Uwarai et al. (1998: 11) give *áishhĩ* as the possessed form, that is, a suffixed form *aishi-hĩ* (husband-PSSD:1PL/3). Perhaps this is a similar situation to the noun *ỹãw̃áã* 'dog', which may be declined as either type. The noun *úma* 'sibling of opposite sex' has second person form *umáim < umai-mɨ* (sibling+PSSD-2) and third person form *úmayĩ* (sibling+PSSD:1PL/3). As mentioned above, *duku* 'your mother' and *apa* 'your father' take no possession marking with second person possessor, but are declined as regular suffixing nouns for all other persons.

All nouns marked with the diminutive suffix -*uchi* are suffixing, regardless of the class of the underived root. For example, *yaapɨ̃* 'nerve+PSSD:1PL/3' is of the vowel-changing class, but compare example (4.71) above, in which the diminutive-marked form *yaapɨ-uchi* (nerve-DIM) is followed by the possession morphology proper to the suffixing class. This suggests that suffixing is the default class, but it could also be the case that diminutive forms take their class from that of the noun *úchi* 'child', which is clearly related etymologically to the diminutive suffix.

The possessor may take one of two forms, genitive, described in §4.10.3, or possessive, described in §4.9.2. The structure of the possessive NP as a whole is described in §5.6.

4.9 Derivational morphology, second level

Slot C contains derivational suffixes and the SAP enclitic. These markers do not typically co-occur, but occasionally do so, giving evidence for subordering within slot C as shown in Figure 4.3. The other suffixes (similative, 'even') and the SAP enclitic are not attested in combination with any other slot C morphology.

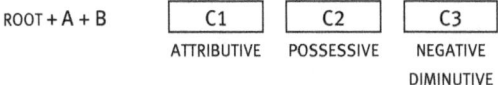

ROOT + A + B   C1   C2   C3
               ATTRIBUTIVE POSSESSIVE NEGATIVE
                                        DIMINUTIVE

Figure 4.3: Ordering within nominal morphology slot C

Examples (4.72–4.75) illustrate these orderings.

(4.72)   *mídauchu*
           mi-nau-chau
           1sg-POSS-NEG.NMLZ
           'not mine'

(4.73)   *mínaush*
           mi-nau-uchi
           1sg-POSS-DIM
           'my little one'

(4.74)   *apáɳtinush*
           apa-hĩ-tinu-uchi
           father-PSSD:1PL/3-ATTRIB-DIM
           'a child who has a father (living)'

(4.75)   *uchíɳtinnau*
           uchi-hĩ-tinu-nau
           child-PSSD:1PL/3-ATTRIB-POSS
           'belonging to a parent'

I have no examples of similative *-mamtin*, 'even' *-(a)ima*, or the SAP marker *=ti* co-occurring with other suffixes of slot C, nor of negative and diminutive co-occurring.

4.9.1 Attributive

The attributive suffix *-tinu* gives the meaning 'possessor of X', where X is the root noun. Attributive is suffixed to a stem with 1PL/3 possessor marking, either with the suffix *-hĩ* (PSSD:1PL/3) or with root apophony and nasalization according to its class. The following examples illustrate attributive marking with a suffixing noun (4.76) and a vowel-changing noun (4.77).

(4.76)   *uchíɳtin*
           uchi-hĩ-tinu
           child-PSSD:1PL/3-ATTRIB
           'a parent'(agr040723_29)

(4.77)   *núwɨntin*
           nuwɨ-tinu
           woman+PSSD+1PL/3-ATTRIB
           'a married man'

Attributive marking is only possible with nouns, as adjectives and pronouns cannot be possessed. When followed by the negative suffix *-chau*, attributive appears as *-tu* (4.78, 4.79).

(4.78)   *aháŋtuchu*
           aha-hĭ-tu-chau
           garden-PSSD:1PL/3-ATTRIB-NEG.NMLZ
           'one who does not have a garden'

(4.79)   *núwɨnchau*
           nuwɨ-tu-chau
           woman+PSSD+1PL/3-ATTRIB-NEG.NMLZ
           'an unmarried man'

And the final /u/ changes to /a/ when followed by the copula enclitic (4.80).

(4.80)   *núwɨnnai*
           nuwɨ-tinu=i
           woman+PSSD:1PL/3-ATTRIB=COP:3:DECL
           'he has a wife'

This suggests that the suffix must be complex, composed of an element *-tu* followed by the subject nominalizer *-inu*, which always fuses with the preceding vowel and appears as *-ina* when followed by the copula enclitic.

4.9.2 Possessive

The possessive suffix *-nau* combines with nouns and pronouns that are semantically possessors, and forms a nominal that refers to the thing possessed (4.81–4.83). The resulting nominal may head or modify an NP, or function as a predicate.

(4.81)   *isaíasnau*
           isaias-nau
           Isaías-POSS
           'Isaías' one'

(4.82)   *húu mínauwai*
           hu   mi-nau=ai
           PROX   1sg-POSS=COP:3:DECL
           'this is mine'

(4.83)　*ỹãw̃ǽǽ ĩinu maáshmakum*
　　　　[yawaã　ii-nau]　　ma-a-cha-ma=ka-umɨ
　　　　[dog　　1pl-POSS]　kill-PFV-NEG-RECPST=Q-2SG
　　　　'have you killed our dog?' (agr041005_15)

Example (4.84) comes from a story in which dogs and men swapped penises. Note that the speech verb is functioning as a narrative modality marker (see §9.2.3).

(4.84)　*yamái ỹãw̃ǽǽnua núu ĩinu ahakú táwai*
　　　　yamai　　[yawaã-nau=a　　nu]　　[ii-nau]　　a-haku
　　　　now　　　dog-POSS=COP:3　　ANAREL　1pl-POSS　COP-NARR.PST
　　　　ta-wa-i
　　　　say+IPFV-3-DECL
　　　　'now the dog's one was ours, so the story goes' (agr041005_20)

The possessive suffix may be added to nouns and pronouns, including proper nouns (4.85) and the interrogative pronoun (4.86).

(4.85)　*huhú isaíasnau*
　　　　[huhu]　[*Isaías*-nau]
　　　　PROX　　Isaias-POSS
　　　　'this is Isaias' one', 'this belongs to Isaías'

(4.86)　*yánauwaita*
　　　　ya-nau=aita
　　　　who-POSS=COP:3
　　　　'whose is it?'

Unlike other NP modifiers, a possessive marked pronoun can precede rather than follow the head noun, presumably influenced by the functionally similar genitive form, which always precedes the noun – see §4.10.3.

4.9.3 Negative

The negative suffix -*chau* combines with nouns (4.87) and adjectives (4.88).

(4.87)　*wíka ỹãw̃ǽǽchuithai*
　　　　wi=ka　　　　yãwaa-chau=aita-ha-i
　　　　1sg=TOP　　　dog-NEG.NMLZ=COP-1SG-DECL
　　　　'I am not a dog' (agr060816_01)

(4.88)   *píŋkìŋchau*
          piŋkɨha-chau
          good-NEG.NMLZ
          'bad, ugly'

The same suffix combines with verb stems to form negative nominalizations. Although historically composed of the verbal negative suffix *-cha* plus the nominalizer *-u*, the fact that it applies to verbal, nominal and adjectival roots shows that it must be a synchronically distinct suffix. I use the gloss NEG.NMLZ to reflect the etymology, including for consistency those examples in which it is suffixed to already nominal stems (as in 4.87 and 4.88). Further discussion and examples are in Chapter 11 and Chapter 15.

4.9.4 Diminutive

The diminutive suffix *-uchi* is clearly related to the noun *uchi* 'child'. Diminutive implies smallness or emotional connection or both.

(4.89)   *datsáush*
          natsa-uchi
          youth-DIM
          'youth'

(4.90)   *shíiŋbaush*
          shiihama-uchi
          pretty-DIM
          'pretty'

Diminutive is compatible with nouns, adjectives and adverbs (4.91).

(4.91)   *ãɰ̃áũsh*
          ãɰa-uchi
          outside-DIM
          'just outside'

The use with adverbs may be influenced by the local Spanish. Diminutive marking with adverbs (e.g. *aquicito* 'here-DIM'; *despuecito* 'later-DIM') is a marked regionalism in Peru, associated with Andean and Amazonian Spanish (Roberto Zariquiey, personal communication). The emotional connotation of the diminutive suffix has a parallel in verbs with the perfective marker *-sa* (see §8.3). As mentioned in §4.7, the diminutive suffix appears in slot A, preceding possession morphology, when the two markers co-occur.

4.9.5 Similative

The similative suffix *-mamtin* combines with nominal roots and the anaphoric pronoun *nu* to give the meaning 'similar to X'.

(4.92)   *aíntsmamtin*
         aintsu-mamtin
         person-SIMIL
         'something like a person'

(4.93)   *hímpɨa númamtin*
         hɨmpɨ=a   nu-mamtin
         hummingbird=COP:3   ANAREL-SIMIL
         'something like a hummingbird'

Similative may also combine with the adverb *maak* 'fine' (4.94).

(4.94)   *yamaik maakmamtin puhahai*
         yamai=ka   maakɨ-mamtin   puha-ha-i
         now=TOP   fine-SIMIL   live+IPFV-1SG-DECL
         [I was sick but] 'now I am more or less fine' (personal correspondence)

4.9.6 'Even'

The nominal suffix *-(a)ima*, which is always accompanied by reduplication, gives a form with the meaning 'even X' where X is the noun root.

(4.95)   *ashí tíkichik uchí úchima hinámtãĩ...*
         ashi   tikichi=ka   [uchi   uchi-ima]   hina-matãĩ
         all   other=TOP   REDUP   child-EVEN   die:PL+PFV+SEQ-1/3:DS
         'all the others, even the children, having died...' (agr040723_29)

The syntactic status of the 'even' form is unclear. In (4.95) it could be part of the subject NP, although the topic enclitic on *tikish* 'other' suggests that that word is the end of the NP. In example (4.96) the noun *nuwa* 'woman' is the semantic object of the verb, but it takes no accusative marking, also suggesting that the 'even' form is not part of a core argument NP.

(4.96)   *nuwái nuwáima ipámatũã...*
        [nuwai   nuwa-ima]   ipama-tu-ã
        REDUP   woman-EVEN   invite-APPL-PFV+SEQ+3:SS
        'having invited even the women...' (agr040723_12)

The same suffix takes the form *-aima* following /ɨ/ in example (4.97).

(4.97)   *kɨŋkɨ́ kɨŋkɨ́ɰaima*
        [kɨŋkɨ   kɨŋkɨ-aima]
        REDUP   wild.potato-EVEN
        'even wild potato (*sachapapa*)' (agr040723_13)

The 'even' form is very rare in my data, and I cannot be certain of the conditioning factors in choice of allomorph.

4.9.7 SAP marker

The SAP marker is an enclitic *=ti* that attaches to the final element of an NP and marks reference to a plural speech act participant (4.98, 4.99).

(4.98)   *uchitísh shiyáku áhabiahi*
        uchi=ti=sha   shiya-ka-u   aha-amaya-hi
        child=SAP=ADD   go:PL-PFV-NMLZ   COP:PL-DISTPST-1PL+DECL
        'we children went too' (agr040824_02)

(4.99)   *íik hũ̃wĩ íi núwati máinahi*
        ii=ka   hu=ĩ   [ii   nuwa=ti]   ma-ina-hi
        1pl=TOP   PROX=LOC   1pl   woman=SAP   bathe-PL:IPFV-1PL+DECL
        'we women are bathing here' (agr041005_19)

When the referent is second-person plural, *=ti* is followed by the second person plural marker *-humɨ* (4.100).

(4.100)   *átum áinautihum*
        [atumɨ   a-ina-u=ti-humɨ]ₙₚ
        2pl   COP-PL:IPFV-NMLZ=SAP-2PL
        'you all'

The addition of person marking to an NP enclitic is reminiscent of the copula enclitic described below (§4.14), but unlike the copula, SAP marking does not form a predicate. NPs marked with the SAP enclitic function as core arguments, taking case marking and discourse enclitics. NPs marked with ablative case also occasionally include person marking – see §4.10.7.

The SAP marker appears with nouns and the relative-clause plural marker *ainau*. It is not attested with any other relative clause. It also appears with the noun *iinia* 'one of us' (as in Text 3:1). One of the first person plural pronouns, *hutii*, may have historically come from the proximal demonstrative *hu* plus the SAP marker, which would have the meaning 'we here' (§4.6.1).

4.10 Case marking

Aguaruna is a nominative–accusative language, and uses inflectional morphology to mark core and peripheral cases. Subjects of transitive and intransitive verbs (A and S) take nominative case, which is unmarked; this is also the citation form of the noun. Objects (O and E) are marked with the accusative enclitic. Nominal morphology does not distinguish O from E. Non-core cases are: comitative; locative; ablative; instrumental and vocative. The inflectional enclitics are generally mutually exclusive, except that ablative can co-occur with other case markers: locative and ablative typically appear together in that order, and the ablative marker also functions as derivational, and in that role it can be followed by other case markers. There is also a genitive form, which is not strictly a case as it marks relations within the NP rather than grammatical relations. Genitive has developed historically from accusative marking. Although nominative case is not marked, the lack of marking is incompatible with other enclitics (apart from derivational ablative marking); so an NP in subject position cannot carry any of the inflectional enclitics listed above.

Case markers are generally enclitic to the final constituent of an NP, unless a demonstrative pronoun is present – then all constituents are case-marked. Full details of marking patterns conditioned by NP structure are in Chapter 5. Nominals and pronouns are marked identically for nominative, accusative, comitative, ablative and instrumental cases. They are distinct for genitive and locative. Only nouns take vocative case and only pronouns take allative. Locative is marked as for pronouns following nominal possession marking. Table 4.27 summarizes the differences in case marking.

Table 4.27: Nominal and pronominal case marking

	nominal	pronoun
nominative	unmarked	unmarked
accusative	=na	=na
genitive	accent shift, suppression of apocope	=na
comitative	=haĩ	=haĩ
locative	=numa	=(n)ĩ
ablative	=ya	=ya
instrumental	=(a)i	=(a)i
vocative	accent shift, suppression of apocope	–
allative	–	=ni

Proper names borrowed from Spanish do not undergo accent shift, although they do show non-application of apocope. When the name ends in a consonant in Spanish, word-final /a/ is added (essentially an underlying form with final /a/ is "reconstructed"), as shown in Table 4.28.

Table 4.28: Genitive forms of Spanish names

NOM	GEN	Spanish
dóris	dórisa	Doris
árias	áriasa	Arias

Native proper names behave as regular nouns (many names *are* regular nouns, such as names of animals or cultural artefacts).

4.10.1 Nominative

Nominative case is not marked formally. Nouns and pronouns in subject position appear in the unmarked citation form. The examples in (4.101, 4.102) show a noun (*nuwa* 'woman') and a pronoun (*wi* '1sg') in subject position.

(4.101)   *núwa hapímkuchin iŋkɨau*
            nuwa   hapimuku-uchi=na   iŋkɨ-a-u
            woman   broom-DIM=ACC   put-IPFV-NMLZ
            'the women put their brooms (in baskets)' (agr040723_29)

(4.102)   *wíi iwasán díik ma? tipistáhai*
          wi   iwa-sa-nu   diik   ma?
          1SG   wake-SBD-1SG:SS   watching   HESIT
          tipi-sa-ta-ha-i
          lie.down-PFV-IFUT-1SG-DECL
          'I will lie awake watching' (agr040723_29)

Example (4.103) illustrates the noun *tsampáunum* 'manioc leaves' in its citation form (underlined).

(4.103)   *núna tsanímpan dukɨn "tsampáunum" múuntak túu ahakú áinawai*
          [nu=na   tsanimpa=na   dukɨ=na]   tsampaunumi
          ANA=ACC   manioc.plant=ACC leaf+PSSD:1PL/3=ACC   *tsampaunumi*
          muunta=ka   tu   a-haku   a-ina-wa-i
          adult=TOP   say   COP-NARR.PST   COP-PL:IPFV-3-DECL
          'the elders used to call those manioc leaves "*tsampaunum*"'
          (agr040723_29)

The name in apposed name NPs also appears in citation form (§5.7), and some object NPs also appear in nominative rather than accusative case. Split marking of objects is described in detail in Chapter 7.

4.10.2 Accusative

The accusative case enclitic *=na* marks object NPs. Example (4.104) shows that both "gift" and "recipient" type objects receive accusative case,[16] and also illustrates the case agreement in an NP with a determiner.

(4.104)   *tsúŋki áidau kuwáshat namakán núna datsáuchin anɨntáŋ susáhui*
          [tsuŋki   a-ina-u]NP:A   [kuwashata   namaka=na]NP:O
          mermaid   COP-PL:IPFV-NMLZ   many   fish=ACC
          [nu=na   datsauchi=na]NP:E   anɨntaha
          ANA=ACC   youth=ACC   as.a.gift
          su-sa-aha-u=i
          give-PFV-PL-NMLZ=COP:3:DECL
          'the mermaids gave that youth many fish as a gift' (agr040824_01)

---

16 This case enclitic in fact merges the functions of traditional accusative and dative cases, and might be better labelled *objective* case, but I have followed previous authors in retaining the label *accusative*.

The same form marks pronominal possessors (4.105).

(4.105)   *mína dukúŋ*
        [mi=na   duku-hu]_{NP}
        1sg=ACC   mother-PSSD:1SG
        'my mother'

An optional but common phonological process of word-final nasal deletion may affect the post-apocope reflex of the accusative enclitic, [n]. The accusative enclitic apparently historically marked possessors in possessive NPs, but synchronically the form with deleted nasal has developed into a distinct genitive marker, which I describe in the following sections.

4.10.3 Genitive

An overt possessor is not required within a possessive NP. When the possessor NP is expressed, it directly precedes the possessed noun, and typically appears in the genitive form, giving an NP of the form [*possessor*+GEN *possessum*-(PSSD)-PERSON]_{NP}. In most examples genitive is not marked segmentally, but is distinguished from the unmarked root by non-application of apocope and accent shift in nouns of 2 or 3 vowels (4.106–4.108).

(4.106)   *washí yakahí̃*
        [washi   yaka-hĩ]_{NP}
        monkey+GEN   arm-PSSD:1PL/3
        'the monkey's arm' (agr040723_29)

(4.107)   *atashú yumíhĩ*
        [atashu   yumi-hĩ]_{NP}
        chicken+GEN   water-PSSD:1PL/3
        'chicken broth'

(4.108)   *nátsatsama dukɨ́n*
        [natsatsama   dukɨ=na]_{NP}
        Santa.Maria.plant+GEN   leaf+PSSD:1PL/3=ACC
        'leaves of the Santa Maria plant' (agr040723_29)

In all examples, the genitive form is identical to the accusative form except that it lacks the final /n/, as shown in Table 4.29.

Table 4.29: Accusative and genitive forms

nominative	accusative	genitive	gloss
wáshi	*washín*	*washí*	'monkey'
atásh	*atashún*	*atashú*	'chicken'
nátsatsam	*nátsatsaman*	*nátsatsama*	'Santa Maria plant'

In fact, it appears that the genitive form is derived historically from the accusative form, and the possessor in a possessive NP was originally marked with the accusative enclitic. The evidence for this hypothesis is:

1. Dropping of final nasals is well attested, particularly from accusative forms that directly precede their governing element
2. Pronominal possessors are always marked accusative
3. Lexical noun possessors may be marked with accusative if the NP is a verbal object

The phenomenon of word-final nasal deletion has already been shown to operate (§3.2.6), and needs no further discussion here. In the following two sections I shall elaborate on points (2) and (3) above, which relate to the overlap between accusative and genitive marking.

When the possessor is a singular pronoun, it is marked with accusative case, and clearly carries the enclitic =*na* (example 4.105 above). This phenomenon can be explained phonologically, as none of the singular pronouns undergoes apocope in the accusative form, and consequently nasal deletion cannot apply.

Example (4.109) illustrates the phenomenon of case agreement when the NP has a determiner. In this example, the possessor is a complex NP *nu nuwa* (ANA woman) 'that woman', and we see that the anaphoric pronoun takes accusative case, to "agree" with the genitive marking of its head noun.

(4.109)   *núna nuwá patahĩ*
        [nu=na   nuwa]_{NP:POSSESSOR}   pata-hĩ
        ANA=ACC   woman+GEN   family-PSSD:1PL/3
        'that woman's family' (agr060816_01)

Example (4.110) shows a possessive object NP 'that (man) Kagkap's wife'; accusative case is marked throughout the NP, including the possessor (Kagkap).

(4.110)   *núna kaŋkapín nuwín intsámhuinaushkam*
        [[nu=na   kaŋkapɨ=na   nuwɨ=na]
        ANA=ACC   Kagkap=ACC   woman+PSSD:1PL/3=ACC

intsamahu-ina-u=shakama]_{NP}
have.sex-PL:IPFV-NMLZ=ADD
'also those who were having sex with Kagkap's wife' (agr041005_14)

Both the phonological similarities and the interchangeability suggest that genitive is historically derived from accusative, through reanalysis of the form without final /n/. The pronominal forms *mi=na* (1SG=ACC) and *nĩ=na* (3SG=ACC), in which the accusative enclitic is added to a monosyllabic root, are not of the right phonological shape to have their final vowel elided, and so they have not undergone the split of genitive from accusative. Their genitive and accusative forms are identical, and both show the *=na* enclitic. The second person singular pronoun *ami=na* (2SG=ACC) and distal demonstrative *au=na* (DIST=ACC) show the same behaviour, although their final vowels are in a position to be elided – presumably by analogy with the other singular pronouns.

4.10.4 Comitative

Comitative case, marked with the enclitic *=haĩ*, forms an oblique NP and is typically used as a coordination strategy to link two subject NPs, as in examples (4.111, 4.112). The subject of the verb is first person singular, as evidenced by the agreement on the verb, showing that the comitative-marked NP is not part of the subject.

(4.111)　　*mína nuwáhãĩ taáttahai*
　　　　　　[mi=na　　　nuwa=haĩ]　　　ta-a-tata-ha-i
　　　　　　1sg=ACC　　wife=COM　　　　come-PFV-FUT-1SG-DECL
　　　　　　'I will come (back) with my wife'

(4.112)　　*nṹwĩ áuhkun wikáitiahai yatsún áidauhãĩ*
　　　　　　nu=ĩ　　　　　auha-ku-nu　　　　　　　wakɨtu-ya-ha-i
　　　　　　ANA=LOC　　　study+IPFV-SIM-1SG:SS　　return-REMPST-1SG-DECL
　　　　　　[yatsu-hu　　　　　　a-ina-u=haĩ]
　　　　　　brother-PSSD:1SG　　COP-PL:IPFV-NMLZ=COM
　　　　　　'I went back there to study with my brothers' (agr040824_02)

The verb may also be inflected as plural in such constructions, as in example (4.113).

(4.113)　　*hintínkaŋtin kistiánhãĩ chicháinakũĩ...*
　　　　　　hintintu-kahatu-inu　　　[kistianu=haĩ]
　　　　　　teach-1PL.OBJ-NMLZ　　　non.Aguaruna=COM

chicha-ina-ku-ĩ
speak-PL:IPFV-SIM+1/3-DS
'as the teacher was speaking with some non-Aguarunas...'
(agr040824_02)

In example (4.114) the comitative marked NP is functioning like an object semantically, although the verb is etymologically reciprocal, coming from *mau-* 'kill' + *-nai* RECIP (§7.7.3).

(4.114)   *maanihakuí hũw̃ĩỹã aínts kanús'hãĩ*
           maani-haku=i   [hu=ĩ=ya   aíntsu]
           fight-NARR.PST=COP:3:DECL   PROX=LOC=ABL   person
           [kanusa=haĩ]
           Santiago.River=COM
           'the people from here used to fight with (the people from) the Santiago River (i.e. Huambisas)' (agr041005_18)

Similarly the verb *chichat* 'speak' takes a comitative-marked NP referring to the conversation partner, which is typically not equally agentive, rather, more like an addressee. However, example (4.113) above, in which the presence of a comitative marked NP triggers plural subject marking on *chichat* 'speak', shows that this is not always the case.

    Comitative case is also used to mark the standard of comparison in a comparative construction, as in example (4.115) (repeated from §4.3.2):

(4.115)   *húu olla imá múuntai áuhãĩ apátkam*
           [hu   olla]   ima   muunta=i   [au=haĩ
           PROX   pot   INTENS   big=COP:3:DECL   DIST=COM
           apatu-ka-ma]
           compare-PFV-NSBJ>SBJ
           'this pot is bigger than that one'

The word *apatkam* is optional, and comitative case is sufficient to mark the standard of comparison. In a comparison of equality, as in (4.116), comitative case is also used.

(4.116)   *úchi kása áuk túnchihãĩ bitɨkai*
           [uchi   kasa=a   au=ka]   [tunchi=haĩ]
           child   thief=COP:3   DIST_REL=TOP witch.doctor=COM
           bitɨka=i
           equal=COP:3:DECL
           'a child who is a thief is the same (i.e. as bad) as a witch-doctor'
           (agr040712_01)

4.10.5 Locative

There are two locative enclitics: *=(n)ɨ* and *=numa*. The choice of marker is morphologically conditioned, as *=(n)ɨ* appears only on pronouns (4.117) and following possession suffixes (4.118), while *=numa* is the default, appearing elsewhere (4.119,
4.120).[17] Locative case can be used to express motion towards or into, as in (4.117–
4.120).

(4.117)   *húw̃ĩ taáta*
           hu=ɨ̃   ta-a-ta
           PROX=LOC   come-PFV-IMP
           'come here'

(4.118)   *hɨɰahúĩ w̃ɨɰahai*
           hɨɰa-hu=ɨ̃   wɨ-a-ha-i
           house-PSSD:1SG=LOC   go-IPFV-1SG-DECL
           'I'm going to my house'

(4.119)   *wãã́num chaát akunáu*
           waã=numa   chaat   akuna-u
           cave=LOC   IDEO   CAUS+enter+PFV-NMLZ
           'he made it go *zip!* into the cave' (agr040723_29)

(4.120)   *ahánum w̃ɨɰahai*
           aha=numa   wɨ-a-ha-i
           garden=LOC   go-IPFV-1SG-DECL
           'I'm going to the garden' (agr040721_07)

---

17 Corbera (1994: 119ff) suggests that *=numa* is a 'general locative', expressing the spatial relation
of 'being inside' or 'being in a place', while *=(n)ɨ* is adessive, expressing location 'nearby'. My data
do not support any analysis involving a semantic distinction.

And locative case also expresses static location, as in (4.121–4.124).

(4.121) *húẁ̃ĩ ukúkmĩ̆*
hu=ĩ̆   uku-ka-mĩ̆
PROX=LOC   leave-PFV-RECPST:3:DECL
'he left it here' (agr040723_29)

(4.122) *hĩ̆ɥahúĩ̆ puháwai*
hĩ̆ɥa-hu=ĩ̆   puha-wa-i
house-PSSD:1SG=LOC   live+IPFV-3-DECL
'he is at my house'

(4.123) *pĩ̆ɥaknúm tĩ̆pĩ̆stá*
pĩ̆ɥaka=numa   tĩ̆pĩ̆-sa-ta
bed=LOC   lie-PFV-IMP
'lie down on the bed!'

(4.124) *wawiknúm puhúhai*
wawiku=numa   puhu-ha-i
Wawik=LOC   live-1SG-DECL
'I live in Wawik (village)'

The locative enclitic =*numa* has some extended uses. In example (4.125) it expresses an instrumental-type meaning.

(4.125) *nawĩ̆num miná minákuan Mesones taáwabiahai*
nawĩ̆=numa   mina   mina-kawa-nu   *Mesones*
foot=LOC   REDUP   arrive+IPFV-REPET-1SG:SS Mesones.Muro
ta-aw-amaya-ha-i
come-PFV-DISTPST-1SG-DECL
'arriving on foot, I came to Mesones Muro (a settlement in Imaza district)' (Text 2:15)

And in (4.126) it expresses reason when attached to a nominalized clause.

(4.126) *yáakat puhústasan wakĩ̆ɥamunum tíu áyahai*
[yaakata   puhu-sa-tasa-nu   waki-a-mau=numa]
city   live-PFV-INTENT-1SG:SS   want-IPFV-NSBJ.NMLZ=LOC
ti-u   a-ya-ha-i
say+PFV-NMLZ   COP-REMPST-1SG-DECL
'I said (it) out of a desire to live in the city' (agr040824_02)

Example (4.127) shows a locative-marked nominalization expressing an imminent action.

(4.127) *Arias wɨtánum puháwai*
       Arias   wɨ-ta=numa   puha-wa-i
       Arias   go-ACT.NMLZ=LOC   live+IPFV-3-DECL
       'Arias is about to go'

The ablative case enclitic *=ya* is typically added to a locative-marked stem, as in (4.128, 4.129).

(4.128) *chapínmaya*
       chapi=numa=ya
       Chapi=LOC=ABL
       'from the village of Chapi'

(4.129) *hũw̃ɨ́ỹã*
       hu=ɨ́=ya
       PROX=LOC=ABL
       'from here'

This double case marking is discussed in §4.10.7.

4.10.5.1 Exceptional locative marking

Seven nouns mark locative case not with an enclitic, but instead with accent shift; Table 4.30 is an exhaustive list of such exceptional locative forms in my corpus. These lexemes could be considered inherently locational, and all are of relatively high frequency.

Table 4.30: Exceptional locative forms

nominative	locative	gloss
áũɲã	āũɲã́	'porch, outside'
hɨ́ũɲã	hɨ̃ũɲã́	'house'
hínta	hintá	'path'
íkam	ikám	'forest'
náin	naín	'hill'
namák	namaká	'river'
núŋka	nuŋká	'ground'

Example (4.130) illustrates such a form.

(4.130)   *kaŋkáp naín wahakmā́ antúkui*
           kaŋkapɨ   nainta   waha-kamā̃   antu-ka-u=i
           Kagkap   hill+LOC   stand-TERM+3:SS   hear-PFV-NMLZ=COP:3:DECL
           'When Kagkap got to the top of the hill, he heard (people calling him)'
           (agr041005_14)

The accent shift is of the 'simple accent shift' pattern (§3.7.2), typically triggered by enclitics, and suggests that a historically present case marker has been lost from these words, leaving only the accent shift (compare genitive marking (§4.10.3), where accent shift correlates with the historical presence of accusative enclitic).

Locative *=numa* appears to be the more recently grammaticalized form. It is longer, it can take accent, and it is more general in its application. The expectation is that a locative marker would develop from a general noun meaning 'place' and support for this comes from the fact that many older toponyms end in *-numa* or *-nama*, while more recent toponyms do not. This suggests that the general noun was used in compounds to form toponyms, but that this usage stopped once it had fully grammaticalized into a locative case marker.

4.10.6 Instrumental

The instrumental enclitic is *=(a)i*, illustrated in (4.131, 4.132).

(4.131)   *cámarai dakumkámi*
           cámara=i   dakuma-ka-mi
           camera=INS   imitate-PFV-HORT
           'Let's take a photo with the camera.'

(4.132)   *ikɨmtãĩỹãĩ kasán maámhai*
           [ikɨma-taĩ=ai]   kasa=na   maa-ma-ha-i
           sit-NSBJ.NMLZ=INS   thief=ACC   kill+PFV-RECPST-1SG-DECL
           'I killed the thief with a wooden stool'

Instrumental-marked nouns form oblique NPs, and function adverbially. Its use is relatively rare in texts. Example (4.133) shows an extended function of instrumental case.

(4.133) *dɨkás apahuíyai suhumánkathai*
        dɨkas   [apahui=ai]   suhumana-ka-ta-ha-i
        truly   [god=INS]   convert-PFV-IFUT-1SG-DECL
        'I will certainly convert to God (i.e. Christianity)' (agr040824_02)

A further extended function involves some time words, which are derived with instrumental case. As can be seen from the examples in Table 4.31, the semantic effect of this derivation is not entirely predictable.

Table 4.31: Time words with instrumental case

root	gloss	root=INS	gloss
mihan	'year' (noun)	*mihadai*	'for a year'
tsawan	'day' (noun)	*tsawantai*	'by day'
yama	'recently' (time word)	*yabai*	'now'

4.10.7 Ablative

The ablative enclitic *=ya* marks a source or origin. It can be attached directly to nouns with inherently locational meanings, as in examples (4.134, 4.135).

(4.134) *muháya*
        muha=ya
        mountain.range=ABL
        'from the mountains'

(4.135) *kanúsia*
        kanusa=ya
        Santiago.River=ABL
        'from the Santiago River'

But with other nouns it must follow a locative enclitic (4.136, 4.137).

(4.136) *kuwáshat aɨnts tíkish nuŋkánmaya*
        [kuwashata   aɨntsu   tikichi   nuŋka=numa=ya]ₙₚ
        many   person   other   land=LOC=ABL
        'many people from other lands'

(4.137)   *belénnumiaŋ minám*
           Belén=numa=ya=ka   mina-mɨ
           Belén=LOC=ABL=Q   arrive+IPFV-2
           'are you arriving from Belén (village)?'

Ablative-marked nouns may function as oblique NPs, as in (4.138).

(4.138)   *haánchin ukukíu asán mína hɨɰahṹɨ̃ỹã utithái*
           [haanchi=na   uku-ki-u   asa-nu]   [mi=na
           clothes=ACC   leave-PFV-NMLZ   COP+SBD-1SG:SS   1sg=ACC
           hɨɰa-hu-ɨ̃=ya   uti-ta-ha-i]
           house-PSSD:1SG=LOC=ABL   fetch+PFV-IFUT-1SG-DECL
           'I left my clothes behind, so I'll get them from my house' (Text 2:16)

But they may also function as derived nominals in core grammatical roles, and then take further case marking (4.139).

(4.139)   *wawiknúmian wainkámhai*
           [wawiku=numa=ya=na]   waina-ka-ma-ha-i
           Wawik=LOC=ABL=ACC   see-PFV-RECPST-1SG-DECL
           'I saw the (person) from Wawik village'

And an ablative marked NP may function as a predicate, marked by the copula en-clitic (4.140).

(4.140)   *wĩka Pablo puhámunmayaithai*
           wi=ka   Pablo   puha-mau=numa=ya=ita-ha-i
           1sg=TOP   Pablo   live-NSBJ.NMLZ=LOC=ABL=COP-1SG-DECL
           'I am from (the place) where Pablo lives'

Note that even when functioning as a core argument, the ablative-marked noun tends to be clause-initial or clause-final, and often forms a discontinuous constitu-ent with its head, so has the flavour of an oblique NP (see further examples in §7.5).

    Ablative-marked nouns also occasionally take subordinate clause person suf-fixes (4.141, 4.142), a property shared with some adverbs and derived nominals.

(4.141)   *ishámainnumian hiinkímhai*
           isha-mai-inu=numa=ya-nu   hiina-ki-ma-ha-i
           fear-POT-NMLZ=LOC=ABL-1SG:SS   go.out-PFV-RECPST-1SG-DECL
           'I got out of danger'

(4.142)   *chapínmayamɨk minám*
          chapi=numa=ya-mɨ=ka   mina-mɨ
          Chapi=LOC=ABL-2:SS=Q   arrive+IPFV-2
          'are you arriving from *Chapi* (village)?'

4.10.8 Vocative

Vocative is unlike other nominal cases, as a vocative-marked noun functions like an interjection: it does not play any grammatical role in the sentence, and may appear as a stand-alone utterance. Vocative does, however, enter into the system of oppositions with other case inflections, as its presence excludes the other markers. David Payne (1990b) gives vocative forms for a variety of nouns, but consultants I worked with felt that the form is compatible only with human referents. Spontaneous examples in my data are all personal names and kinship terms; vocative forms of some nominalized verbs were also given in elicitation sessions (see Chapter 15). Vocative is marked productively with suppression of apocope, and there are two unproductive suffixes that appear with certain kinship terms. All vocative-marked nouns typically involve accent shift to the final syllable, but this is not obligatory and is probably a product of the typically shouted delivery rather than a morphological process.

The first unproductive suffix is -*ta*. This suffix normally takes the accent, and is never subject to apocope. Table 4.32 illustrates surface nominative and vocative forms of the only two nouns that take this suffix in my data.

Table 4.32: Vocative formed with -*ta*

nominative	vocative	gloss
úchi	*uchitá*	'child'
yátsu	*yatsutá*	'brother'

The second suffix -*wa* appears only with *apa* 'father' and *duku* 'mother'. As with other vocative forms accent typically shifts to the final syllable (Table 4.33).

Table 4.33: Vocative formed with *-wa*

nominative	vocative	gloss
ápa	*apawá*	'father'
dúku	*dukuwá*	'mother'

These two forms are rarely used for addressing one's parents in the modern language, having been replaced with *papá* and *mamá* from Spanish. They are still used as terms of respect when addressing one's elders, and among Christians, *apa-wa* (father-VOC) is used to address God in prayers.

The only productive vocative form is marked with suppression of apocope and, typically, accent shift to the final vowel. Table 4.34 presents some examples.

Table 4.34: Vocative formed with suppression of apocope and accent shift

	nominative	vocative	gloss
a.	*tihiŋkás*	*tihiŋsá*	'female name'
b.	*díích*	*diichí*	'uncle'
c.	*páblo*	*pabló*	Pablo
d.	*dóris*	*dorisá*	Doris

Note in example (a) that suppression of apocope allows syncope to operate on the vowel of the third syllable. Nowadays most personal names are from Spanish. These follow the same pattern of accent shift to the final vowel, thus in example (c) *Pablo* [páblo] becomes [pabló]. Where a Spanish name does not end in a vowel, final /a/ is added, simulating suppression of apocope (example d).

When used as terms of address, kinship terms typically appear with the first person possessor suffix, and also show suppression of apocope and accent shift – compare nominative (4.143a) and vocative (4.143b) forms.

(4.143) a. *yatsúŋ*
        yatsu-hu
        brother-PSSD:1SG
        'my brother'

    b. *yatsuhú*
        yatsu-hu
        brother-PSSD:1SG+VOC
        'my brother!'

4.10.8.1 Familiar vocative

The vowel /u/ may be added to regular vocative forms to give a familiar vocative –
compare (4.144a) and (b).

(4.144) a.   *mamá*
        mama
        mother+VOC
        'mum!'

     b.   *mamáu*
        mama-u
        mother+VOC-FAM
        'mummy!'

With Spanish proper names ending in a consonant, /u/ replaces the final /a/ that is
usually added, exemplified in Table 4.35.

Table 4.35: Familiar vocative in Spanish names

regular vocative	familiar vocative	gloss
dorisá	*dorisú*	Doris
simoŋká	*simoŋkú*	Simón

4.11 Restrictive =*kɨ*

The restrictive enclitic =*kɨ* can be translated into English as 'only'. There are two
allomorphs, /ki/ and /kɨ/, and the choice of allomorph depends on the final vowel of
the stem to which the enclitic is attached: /ki/ following /i/ (4.145) and /kɨ/ elsewhere (4.146; and 4.149 below).

(4.145)   *núnikmatãĩ níŋki huwák...*
      nu-ni-ka-matãĩ   nĩ=kɨ   huwa-a-kũ
      ANA-VBLZ.INTR-PFV+SEQ-1/3:DS 3sg=RESTR   be.left-IPFV-SIM+3:SS
      'so while she was left alone...' (agr040721_07)

(4.146)   *dúkɨ*
      nu=kɨ
      ANA=RESTR
      'just that'

Note in example (4.147) that both topic *=ka* and restrictive *=kI* surface as /k/ after the application of apocope. They can be distinguished, however, by the fact that restrictive triggers accent shift while topic does not.

(4.147) *núwak puhuumatí, amík utitá*
       [nuwa=ka   puhu-ma-ti]   ami=kI   uti-ta
       woman=TOP   live-DUR-JUSS   2sg=RESTR   fetch+PFV-IMP
       'let the woman stay (here), you fetch (the water) by yourself!'
       (agr041005_14)

Restrictive often appears in combination with the intensifier *ima* (example 4.148).

(4.148) *imá biíknak yuwámhai*
       [ima   biika=na=kI]   yu-a-ma-ha-i
       INTENS   bean=ACC=RESTR   eat-PFV-RECPST-1SG-DECL
       'I only ate beans'

Restrictive appears on nominals and pronouns and at least one time word (see §12.3.4), but not verbs. A particular idiomatic use of restrictive is with the textual cataphoric distal demonstrative *au*, used to preface an exclamation; see examples in §4.6.2.

The restrictive enclitic is the only one that can appear in slot E, between case markers in slot D and the discourse markers in slot F. Restrictive can co-occur with enclitics from both slots, as in example (4.149) where it is preceded by accusative *=na* and followed by additive *=sha(kama)*. Note in this example that restrictive in combination with negative polarity translates as 'not even'.

(4.149) *mína saíŋnakish úhatsuk...*
       [mi=na   sai-hu=na=kI=sha]
       1sg=ACC   brother.in.law-PSSD:1SG=ACC=RESTR=ADD
       uha-tsu-u=ka
       tell-NEG-NMLZ=TOP
       'without telling even my brother-in-law...' (agr040824_02)

4.12 Discourse enclitics

The discourse and mood/modality enclitics form the outermost layer of nominal morphology. These clitics are mutually exclusive, but do not express obligatory grammatical categories. They express meanings that are ancillary to the inflectional system, and can be added to nouns already carrying inflectional markers. The use of discourse enclitics is subject to semantic and pragmatic restrictions, not grammatical ones, although it may be conditioned to some extent by the mood or polarity of the controlling verb. Typically they express speaker attitude or information structure. None of the discourse enclitics appears in subordinate clauses, and topic marker =*ka* does not appear in interrogative clauses, where its function is fulfilled by a dedicated 'question topic' marker =*sha*. In addition to forming the outermost morphological layer on NPs, discourse enclitics may appear on adverbs and, with some limitations, subordinate verbs. Table 4.36 summarizes the compatibility of discourse enclitics with word classes.

Table 4.36: Compatibility of discourse markers with word classes

	nominal	pronoun	adverb	subordinate clause
topic	✓	✓	✓	✓
question topic	✓	✓	✓	✓
additive	✓	✓	✓	✓
first	✓	✓	–	✓
speculative	✓	✓	?	✓
polar interrogative	✓	✓	?	✓

4.12.1 Topic =*ka*

The topic marker =*ka* can be encliticized to any nominal or pronoun (4.150), and also appears on time words and subordinate clauses, where it marks conditional clauses (§14.6).

(4.150) *íik aáttsa wáittsa iɰamsá yúwaithi*
  ii=**ka**   aatusa   [waitu-sa]   [iɰama-sa]
  1pl=**TOP**   thus+1PL   suffer-SBD+1PL:SS   search-SBD+1PL:SS
  yu-u=aita-hi
  eat-NMLZ=COP-1PL+DECL
  'and so, suffering while searching, we are ones who eat' (Text 3: 23)

In a complex NP, topic may appear on more than one constituent. Example (4.151) shows topic marking on both elements of a full NP. Typically it will appear on both of a pronominal determiner plus lexical noun.

(4.151) *úchi ichinkám, dúka úchik tsíkɨa tsíkɨakũã hákã tɨpisú túwahamɨ̃*
  uchi   [ichina-ka-ma]   [[nu=**ka**   uchi=**ka**]
  child   pull.apart-PFV-NSBJ>SBJ   ANA=**TOP**   child=**TOP**

tsɨkɨa   tsɨkɨ-a-kawã   ha-kã
REDUP   jump-IPFV-REPET+3:SS   die-PFV+3:SS
tɨpɨ-sa-u   tuwahamɨ̃
lie.down-PFV-NMLZ   NARR
'the child, when (the devil) pulled it apart, that child jumped about then lay down dead' (agr040723_29)

Topic marking also typically appears on both the head noun and a modifying relative clause (4.152). When the final element is the plural marking nominalization *aidau*, however, topic marking typically only appears on that word (4.153). Possessors in possessive NPs cannot take topic marking (4.154).

(4.152)   *ikámyawaŋ aɨntsún yuwáuk*
       [ikam_yawaã=ka   [aɨntsu=na   yu-a-u=ka]]ₙₚ
       jaguar=TOP   person=ACC   eat-PFV-NMLZ=TOP
       'the jaguar that ate a person' (agr041005_14)

(4.153)   *ashí yutã̃ɨ aídaunak*
       [ashi   yu-taɨ̃   a-ina-u=na=ka]ₙₚ
       all   eat-NSBJ.NMLZ   COP-PL:IPFV-NMLZ=ACC=TOP
       'all edible things' (agr040721_07)

(4.154)   *mína apáhuk*
       [mi=na   apa-hu=ka]ₙₚ
       1sg=ACC   father-PSSD:1SG=TOP
       'my father'

More than one NP in a clause may be marked with the topic enclitic, including those marked with case enclitics such as accusative or locative. In example (4.155) both an accusative marked object and locative marked oblique NP are marked with the topic enclitic.

(4.155)   *aɨntsnak kanúnmak tuntúnmitkainau*
       aɨntsu=na=**ka**   kanu=numa=**ka**   tuntuna-mitika-ina-u
       person=ACC=**TOP**   canoe=LOC=**TOP**   make.noise-CAUS-PL:IPFV-NMLZ
       'they caused the people to make noise in the canoe' (that is, they killed them so they fell into the canoe with a crash) (agr041005_18)

Examples of topic marking on non-nominal constituents and discussion of its role in narrative structure are in Chapter 18.

4.12.2 Additive =sha(kama)

The additive enclitic =shakama, with short form =sha, combines the meaning of 'also' and 'even'. That is, it indicates that the marked constituent is included in the situation described by the clause, and that this is somehow counter to what is expected. The long and short allomorphs are apparently in free variation; examples (4.156a and b) are semantically identical.

(4.156) a.   *mináshkam*
           mi=na=shakama
           1sg=ACC=ADD
           'me too' / 'even me'

      b.   *minásh*
           mi=na=sha
           1sg=ACC=ADD
           'me too' / 'even me'

Additive and topic are mutually exclusive, but their distribution is slightly different. Unlike topic, additive does not appear on more than one constituent of an NP, and typically only appears once in a clause. The additive enclitic may have a wider scope than the host constituent. In example (4.157) from Text 3, the sense is not that 'he in addition to someone else' wants to know, rather it is one of 'and he wants to know…'; that is, the 'also' sense has clausal rather than phrasal scope (see also example 15.103).

(4.157)   *nĩshkam dɨkátatus wakɨ̧ɥau asámtãĩ, nína uháhai yabái*
        [nĩ=shakama   dɨka-tatus   wakɨɥa-u
        3sg=ADD   know+PFV-INTENT+3:SS   want+IPFV-NMLZ
        asa-mataĩ]   [nĩ=na   uha-ha-i   yamai]
        COP+SBD-1/3:DS   3sg=ACC   tell+IPFV-1SG-DECL   now
        'and because he wants to know, I am telling him now' (Text 3:3)

When combined with a negative verb, additive is interpreted as 'not even' (4.158).

(4.158)   *makíshkish ayamhúkchahui*
        makichiki=sha   ayamhu-ka-cha-aha-u=i
        one=ADD   defend-PFV-NEG-PL-NMLZ=COP:3:DECL
        'not even one defended (him)' (agr041005_14)

Additive also appears on adverbial words (Chapter 12) and subordinate verbs, marking concessive clauses (§14.6).

4.12.3 First =a

The enclitic =a marks an NP and gives the sense of 'first'. It is always the final enclitic, and always takes the accent. The scope seems to be phrasal, as in examples (4.159, 4.160).

(4.159) *nĩỹấ káshikmas tãấ...*
  nĩ=a   kashikmas   ta-ã
  3sg=FIRST   early   come-PFV+3:SS
  'he having come first, early in the morning...' (agr041005_15)

(4.160) *mantinná hukíthai*
  mantu-inu=na=a   hu-ki-ta-ha-i
  kill.APPL-NMLZ=ACC=FIRST   take-PFV-IFUT-1SG-DECL
  'I'll take the good hunting dog (lit. *the killer*) first'

'First' only appears with nouns and pronouns, and does not appear to be compatible with adjectives. I have no examples of complex NPs marked with =a.

4.13 Mood/modality markers

Mood/modality enclitics mark constituents in clauses with interrogative mood or speculative modality. Interrogative clauses of all kinds take the question topic marker =sha, speculative modality takes the speculative enclitic =tsu, and polar interrogative is marked with =ka. In the case of polar interrogative, the enclitic itself marks the clausal mood, and may appear on the verb or on a constituent that is the focus of the interrogation. For the other two, clausal mood must also be marked elsewhere in the clause. The mood/modality markers appear on nouns, pronouns and adverbs, and may also appear on various types of subordinate clauses – see Chapter 13 for details.

4.13.1 Question topic =sha

The question topic marker =sha optionally marks NPs in interrogative clauses (4.161). More than one constituent may be marked with this enclitic, as in (4.162).

(4.161) *yatsuhú amɨsh puhámɨk?*
         [yatsu-hu]   [amɨ=**sha**]   puha-mɨ=ka
         brother-PSSD:1SG+VOC   2sg=**Q.TOP**   live+IPFV-2SG=Q
         'my brother, are you alive?' (typical greeting)

(4.162) *kiíwish yutáɨŋkait iísh?*
         [kiiwi=**sha**]   [yu-taɨ=ka=aita   ii=**sha**]
         centipede=**Q.TOP**   eat-NSBJ.NMLZ=Q=COP:3   1pl=**Q.TOP**
         'do we (i.e. people) eat centipedes?' (agr040721_07)

I have no examples of NPs in which more than one constituent is marked (unlike with topic =*ka*); but there are very few examples of complex NPs marked with question topic =*sha*. Example (4.163) shows a pronoun and coreferent nominalized clause both marked with =*sha*, but in this case the nominalization is also marked with first person singular -*nu*, showing that it is being treated as a dependent clause.

(4.163) *wɨsha huní wɨkáɨ̵unush, wahúk wakɨtkithaki ataktú mína nuŋkahṹɨsh?*
         wi=**sha**   hu-ni   wɨkaɨ̵a-u-nu=**sha**   wahuka
         1sg=**Q.TOP**   PROX-ALL   wander-NMLZ-1SG:SS=**Q.TOP**   how
         wakitu-ki-ta-ha=ki   ataktu   mi=na
         return-PFV-IFUT-1SG=Q.RHET   again   1sg=ACC
         nuŋka-hu=ĩ=**sha**
         land-PSSD:1SG=LOC=**Q.TOP**
         'having travelled all this way, how will I ever return again to my home?'
         (agr040824_02)

A single noun or pronoun marked with =*sha* can form a clause on its own, in which case accent falls on the enclitic, and apocope does not apply.

(4.164) *Elishá?*
         *Eli=**sha***
         Elí=**Q.TOP**
         '(where is/what about etc.) Elí?'

(4.165) *hushá?*
         hu=**sha**
         PROX=**Q.TOP**
         '(what about) this?'

This type of clause is highly contextually restricted, and cannot contain anything other than a single word.

4.13.2 Speculative =*tsu*

Speculative modality involves an enclitic =*tsu*, which appears on an NP (as in 4.166) or dependent clause. Unlike the topic markers =*ka* and =*sha*, the speculative enclitic appears only once in a clause.

(4.166)   *pisháknas wainkámaɲtai*
           pishaka=na=**tsu**   waina-ka-ma-ha-tai
           bird=ACC=**SPEC**   see-PFV-RECPST-1SG-SPEC
           'I probably saw a bird'

Speculative induces accent shift in the stem to which it is attached. When the speculative enclitic =*tsu* appears, the verb is marked with the speculative mood suffix -*tai*. However, a verbal suffix -*tsa* may appear together with -*tai*, in which case the enclitic =*tsu* does not appear. A full description of speculative modality marking is in §9.2.4.

4.13.3 Polar interrogative

The polar interrogative enclitic =*ka* most commonly appears on predicates. It can, however, appear on the NP that is the focus of the interrogation, in which case the predicate is unmarked (4.167). When polar interrogative appears on a pronoun, it takes the accent and apocope does not apply (4.168). The polar interrogative enclitic always precedes the copula enclitic when they co-occur (4.169).

(4.167)   *amísh piŋkɨhak puhám?*
           amɨ=sha   piŋkɨha=**ka**   puha-mɨ
           2sg=Q.TOP   good=**Q**   live+IPFV-2SG
           'are you well?' (greeting formula)

(4.168)   *huká?*
           hu=**ka**
           PROX=**Q**
           'this one?'

(4.169)   *píŋkɨŋkait?*
           piŋkɨha=**ka**=ita
           good=**Q**=COP:3
           'is it good?'

4.14 Copula enclitics

Copula enclitics mark predicate nominals in equative/attributive clauses. There are two copula enclitics available for SAP subjects, distinguished on the basis of tense: =(a)ita for present tense and =ya for remote past. For third person subjects, there are three basic forms. Two correspond to the tense distinctions made with SAP subjects, namely present and remote past. Within the present tense form, however, third person distinguishes five variants, used with different modalities. The third person copulas are all portmanteaux, with fused person marking. The remote past is =yi. The third copula available for third person subjects is the non-visible exclamative form =ĩ. This form is used to convey the same effect as exclamatory mood but further indicates that the referent is not present.

Equative/attributive clauses with any tense value other than present or remote past use a full copula verb rather than the enclitic forms. Table 4.37 summarizes the forms of SAP and third person copula enclitics.

Table 4.37: Copula enclitics

clause type	3 subject	SAP subject
declarative	=(a)i	=(a)ita + subject + mood
non-declarative	=a	=(a)ita + subject + mood
exclamative	=(y)a	=(a)ita + subject + mood
polar interrogative	=(a)it	=ka=ita +subject
content interrogative	=(a)ita	=(a)ita + subject
remote past declarative	=yi	=ya + subject + mood
non-visible	=ĩ	–

Negative and polar interrogative are expressed by NP enclitics that precede the copula enclitic. In the sections below I discuss the properties of the various forms.

4.14.1 General copula enclitic, SAP subject =(a)ita

The copula enclitic has long and short allomorphs in all persons, distinguished by presence or absence of the initial /a/. Conditioning for this allomorphy is described in §3.6.1. The =(a)ita form appears with SAP subjects, followed by person and mood suffixes.

4.14.2 Copula enclitic, third person subject

The =*(a)i* form appears with third-person subjects in declarative mood. The full form =*(a)ita* surfaces when it is enclitic to an interrogative lexeme (example 4.170); this is in keeping with the general observation that apocope does not operate on the predicate when there is an interrogative lexeme in the clause, and shows that the basic form of the enclitic is =*(a)ita*, and the final /t/ is lost in third-person forms.

(4.170)   *yádauwaita?*
          ya-nau=**aita**
          who-POSS=**COP:3**
          'whose is it?'

The polar interrogative enclitic =*ka* precedes the copula enclitic, which then undergoes apocope, and appears as =*ait*.

(4.171)   *píŋkiŋkait?*
          piŋkɨha=ka=**aita**
          good=Q=**COP:3**
          'is it good?'

The final /t/ is unreleased and glottalized. In addition to the pronunciation given above, some speakers feel that the correct pronunciation is [píŋkɨŋkaik] while for others it is [píŋkɨŋkaiʔ]. Since the actual pronunciation is so heavily obscured, the 'correct' form only becomes an issue in writing. Although all three pronunciations appear to be about equally represented among speakers I worked with, I prefer to transcribe the enclitic as =*(a)it*, to reflect the etymology.

Plural cannot be marked on a predicate nominal, and to specify plural subject the full copula verb *ata* must be used; compare (4.172a and b).

(4.172) a.   *áishmaŋkui*
             aishmaŋku=i
             man=COP:3:DECL
             'he is a man'

       b.   *áishmaŋ áinawai*
             aishmaŋku   a-ina-wa-i
             man   COP-PL:IPFV-3-DECL
             'they are men'

The non-declarative copula form is =*a*. The final /i/ of the copula enclitic has been reanalysed as the declarative suffix and is dropped in non-declarative clauses. Note however that the non-declarative form always surfaces as =*a*, even where the short declarative form =*i* appears; compare (4.172a) above, with (4.173), in which the relativizing pronoun *nu* is postposed to the non-declarative form of the predicate.

(4.173)   *áishmaŋkua nú*
           aishmaŋku=**a**   nu
           man=**COP:3**   ANA_{REL}
           'one who is a man'

This shows that although it has historically arisen from the declarative form through dropping the final /i/, the non-declarative copula is synchronically distinct – otherwise we would expect the non-declarative form of (4.172a) to surface as *áishmaŋku*. Note that I gloss the non-declarative form simply as 'COP:3', to contrast with the declarative form glossed 'COP:3:DECL'.

4.14.3 Exclamative copula enclitic =*(y)a*

Exclamatory mood is generally zero marked in verbs (§9.2.5), making it identical to the non-declarative form. However, the exclamative copula enclitic has slightly different allomorphy to the non-declarative form described above. The exclamative form never fuses with a preceding vowel, instead appearing as =*ya* when it follows a stem-final /a/. Compare the examples in (4.174) below: (a) is declarative, and surfaces with the short form =*i*. (b) is non declarative and surfaces as =*a*, fusing with the preceding /a/. The exclamative form in (c), however, does not fuse, instead surfacing as =*ya*.

(4.174) a.   *túnai*
              tuna=i
              waterfall=COP:3:DECL
              'it's a waterfall'

        b.   *túnaa nu*
              [tuna=a   nu]_{NP}
              waterfall=COP:3   ANA_{REL}
              'that which is a waterfall'

c.   *túnaya*
     tuna=ya
     waterfall=COP:3:EXCL
     'it's a waterfall!'

As with the non-declarative copula described above, the exclamative copula enclitic shows a distinct pattern of allomorphy and is synchronically a separate form.

4.14.4 Past/non-visible copula =ɨ̃

The past/non-visible copula =ɨ̃ has equivalent illocutionary force to the exclamative copula, but is used in contexts where the referent is not present, whether in space or time. This may be related to the third-person immediate past suffix -ɨ̃, or it may represent a mutation of the exclamative copula above.

(4.175)   *aɨ́ntsũw̃ɨ̃*
          aɨntsu=ɨ̃
          person=NONVIS.COP:3
          'it was a person!'
          OR
          'it's a person (not visible)'

4.14.5 Remote past copula =ya

The remote past copula has the same form as the remote past verbal suffix, and shows the same fusional third person singular allomorph =yi. It shows the same TAM restrictions as the other copula enclitics, only appearing in declarative and polar interrogative clauses. Unlike the other copula markers, the remote past copula enclitic can take the third person plural suffix -numɨ – the same third person plural suffix appears with the verbal remote past suffix and with jussive and apprehensive verbs.

(4.176)   *pɨŋkɨ́hayanumɨ*
          pɨŋkɨha=ya-numɨ
          good=COP:REMPST-3PL+DECL
          'they were good'

As with other copula markers, negative (4.177) and polar interrogative (4.178) precede the remote past copula enclitic.

(4.177)   *píŋkiŋchauyahai*
            piŋkɨha-chau=ya-ha-i
            good-NEG.NMLZ=COP:REMPST-1SG-DECL
            'I was not good'

(4.178)   *píŋkiŋkaya*
            piŋkɨha=ka=ya
            good=Q=COP:REMPST:3
            'was it good?'

The syntax of copular and related clauses is described in §7.8.

5 The noun phrase

5.1 Preliminary remarks

The noun phrase is a syntactic constituent that forms referring expressions and encodes arguments of verbs. The possibility of pronominal substitution clearly demonstrates the status of the NP as a syntactic unit, and the case markers, which are enclitic to the final element of the NP, provide a diagnostic test for internal constituency. Pronouns may function as determiners and also head NPs, and adjectives may modify a head noun or be the only element in an NP, as may nominalized relative clauses. Quantifiers and numerals tend to be adjacent to the NP that they semantically modify, but remain separate by formal morphological criteria. I begin by describing the core properties of the NP, illustrating with analytically straightforward examples. In the remainder of this section I describe the internal syntax of the NP and the morphological marking with phrase level enclitics. Sections 5.2 to 5.7 describe the various NP operators and in sections 5.8 to 5.10 I address the more difficult questions of constituency raised by the existence of complex and non-integral NPs. The final section, §5.11, addresses coordination of NPs.

5.1.1 Internal syntax of the NP

The NP consists minimally of a single lexical noun (*naŋkai=na* in 5.1), pronoun (5.2), adjective (5.3) or a nominalization (5.4). The examples in (5.1–5.4) are all marked with accusative case, showing that these NPs are core arguments, namely objects.

(5.1)   *núwa mákichik naŋkaín usupáŋ...*
          [nuwa   makichiki]ₙₚ:ₐ   [naŋkai=na]ₙₚ:ₒ   usupa-hã
          woman   one   fruit=ACC   crave-PFV+SEQ+3:SS
          'a woman, having craved fruit...' (agr040721_07; see example 5.30)

(5.2)   *núna múun áuŋmatuinakũĩ...*
          [nu=na]ₙₚ:ₒ   muunta   auhumatu-ina-ku-ĩ
          ANA=ACC   elder   tell-PL:IPFV-SIM+1/3-DS
          'when the elders were telling that (story)...' (agr040723_29; see example 9.32)

(5.3)   *níŋka muúntan shináu*
          [nĩ=ka]_{NP:A}   [muunta=na]_{NP:O}   shina-u
          3sg=TOP   big=ACC   sing+IPFV-NMLZ
          'it (the *kúgkup* bird) sang a big (song)' *i.e. it sang loudly* (agr041005_17)

(5.4)   *yakí wakã̂ ĩkĩtun yunúmtukui*
          [yaki   wa-kã   iki-ta-u=na]_{NP:O}
          above   go.up-PFV+SEQ+3:SS   sit-APPL+IPFV-NMLZ=ACC
          yunuma-tu-ka-u=ai
          approach-APPL-PFV-NMLZ=COP:3:DECL
          'he approached (the boa) that was sitting up above' (Text 1:8)

An NP headed by a lexical noun can take an initial DETERMINER, one of the demonstrative and anaphoric pronouns. One or more MODIFIERS may follow the head. Adjectives, a small set of human nouns, and relative clauses may modify NPs. The
canonical structure of a simple NP can be represented as in (5.5), exemplified in
(5.6), with a pre-head determiner; and (5.7), with a post-head adjectival modifier. As
noted in §4.5, the two elements of a compound noun function as a single constituent, not as a complex NP.

(5.5)   [(Determiner) N (Modifier)]_{NP}

(5.6)   *núna kãỹũkan pĩit ĩtsĩkĩ*
          [nu=na   kãyuka=na]_{NP:O}   piit   i-tsikĩ
          ANA=ACC   agouti=ACC   IDEO   CAUS-jump+PFV+SEQ+3:SS
          'having made that agouti jump: "boing!"' (agr040721_07)

(5.7)   *wámpash muúntan tsukapĩak...*
          [wampachi   muunta=na]_{NP:O}   tsukapi-a-kũ
          backpack   big_{ADJ}=ACC   carry.over.shoulder-IPFV-SIM+3:SS
          'carrying a big backpack over his shoulder...' (agr040720_02)

Relative clauses typically follow the head, but may precede it. The determiner is
optional, and only one can appear in any NP. More than one modifier can appear in
an NP, but in practice NP modification is rare. Only lexical heads may be modified
with adjectives or nouns. Proper names may take a demonstrative determiner, and
may be modified by a relative clause. NPs headed by pronouns can also be modified
by a relative clause. Relative clauses are discussed briefly in §5.5 and in more detail
in Chapter 16.

   Two further types of NP can be recognized by their distinct morphosyntax: POS-
SESSIVE and APPOSED NAME NPs. In a possessive NP, the possessed noun is marked to

show that it is possessed. The possessed noun is the head and the possessor need not be overtly included. If it is, it takes genitive marking if it is a lexical noun or accusative case if it is a pronoun. This is represented schematically in (5.8), and described in detail, with examples, in §5.6.

(5.8)   [(Det) (NP_POSSESSOR) N_POSSESSUM]_NP

The third NP type is the apposed name NP, with the structure in (5.9). This is different from a modified NP, as the case marking enclitics appear on the head, while the apposed name always appears in the unmarked citation form. The apposed name NP is described in §5.7.

(5.9)   [N_HEAD N_PROPER.NAME]_NP

5.1.2 NP enclitics

Case markers and discourse level enclitics apply at the phrase level, and appear on the final word in a complex NP (see Chapter 4 for details of the morphology). The following examples illustrate accusative marking in a modified NP (5.10) and a head-final NP (5.11); and comitative marking (5.12) and locative marking on a modifier (5.13) and head (5.14).

(5.10)   *hiŋkái áinaun*
            [hiŋkai   a-ina-u=na]
            fruit   COP-PL:IPFV-NMLZ=ACC
            'fruits' (agr040721_07)

(5.11)   *tíkish intsán*
            [tikichi   intsa=na]
            other   stream=ACC
            'another stream' (agr040723_29)

(5.12)   *mína nuwáhãɨ̃*
            [mi=na   nuwa=haɨ̃]
            1sg=ACC   woman=COM
            'with my wife' (agr041005_14)

(5.13)   *íntsa tsíhiŋnum*
           [íntsa   tsíhiŋka=numa]
           stream   narrow=LOC
           'in a narrow stream' (agr040719_13)

(5.14)   *mína ahahű́ĩ*
           [mi=na   aha-hu=ĩ]
           1sg=ACC   garden-PSSD:1SG=LOC
           'in my garden'

There are two exceptions to this pattern: (i) when a pronominal determiner precedes the head, all elements in the NP receive case marking (discussed in §5.2); (ii) when a possessive NP is a verbal object, a lexical possessor is marked with accusative (rather than genitive), that is, both elements of the NP receive accusative marking (discussed in §5.6). The discourse-level enclitics (topic =*ka*, additive =*shakama*, restrictive =*kI*) generally follow the same patterns as the case markers, but are somewhat variable.

The rarity of modification contrasted with the elaborateness of some modified NPs, and the multiple case-marking when pronominal determiners are present, all suggest a relatively loose structure to the NP in Aguaruna. This is also suggested by the existence of non-integral NPs, where two identically case-marked constituents may have the same referent (as in 5.15).[1]

(5.15)   *yutáĩnmayan hiíkmahai dukán*
           [yu-taĩ=numa=ya=na]   hii-ka-ma-ha-i   [duka=na]
           eat-NSBJ.NMLZ=LOC=ABL=ACC take.out-PFV-RECPST-1SG-DECL   leaf=ACC
           'I took the leaf out of the food' lit. *I removed the from-the-food leaf*

Rather than a straightforward NP constituent, such examples appear to consist of two NPs in apposition, each with its own head. Further evidence for looseness of the NP is the ambiguous behaviour of quantifiers and especially numerals, which tend to be positioned near to the noun that they semantically modify but resist formal inclusion in the NP. This is discussed further in §5.8.

---

1 Krasnoukhova (2012) distinguishes between discontinuous NPs, which clearly form a single constituent (as identified by gender agreement, for example), and appositional NPs, which consist of two potentially independent NPs that are to be understood as having the same referent.

5.2 Pre-head NP operators

The pre-head operators fall into three groups: (i) demonstrative and anaphoric pronouns functioning as determiners; (ii) *tikish* 'another'; and (iii) *tuki* 'like'. Of these, the pronouns and *tikish* 'another' can head NPs, while *tuki* cannot. Numerals and quantifiers may also appear in pre-head position, but are more flexible in their positioning. They cannot head NPs and do not normally take case marking, and they may also function adverbially. Table 5.1 summarizes the morphosyntactic properties of the pre-head operators, and numerals and quantifiers are included for comparison. Note that *tuki* may function adverbially, but in that case is a time word meaning 'always'.

Table 5.1: Morphosyntactic properties of determiners

	DEM/ANA	*tikich*	*tuki*	numeral/ quantifier
Can head NP	✓	✓	–	–
Can function adverbially	–	–	(✓)	✓
Case agreement[2]	✓	–	–	–
May follow head	–	–	–	✓

In the following sections I describe only the pre-head operators. Numerals and quantifiers are described in §5.3 below.

5.2.1 Determiners

The most noticeable property of the determiners (proximal demonstrative *hu*, medial demonstrative *anu*, distal demonstrative *au*, anaphoric pronoun *nu*) is that they trigger agreement throughout the NP in case-marking. I only have examples of accusative (5.16–5.19) and locative (5.20, 5.21) case following this pattern of agreement, but it is likely that other cases behave similarly. Example (5.18), with a pre-head determiner and post-head relative clause, shows that all elements of the NP receive case marking when a pre-head determiner is present. Also of note is example (5.21), in which the two distinct locative markers appear: *=ĩ* on the pronominal determiner and *=numa* on the lexical head noun (see §4.10.5 for details of the two locative markers).

---

2 See §5.2.1 for discussion.

(5.16)   *núna kãỹúkan pɨ́ɨt ɨ́tsɨkɨ̃*
           [nu=**na**   kãyuka=**na**]ₙₚ   pɨ̃ɨt   ɨ-tsɨkɨ̃
           ANA=**ACC**   agouti=**ACC**   IDEO   CAUS-jump+PFV+SEQ+3:SS
           'having made that agouti jump: "boing!"' (agr040721_07)

(5.17)   *núwa núna ỹãw̃ãã́n kamɨ̃́ pakihíbauwai*
           nuwa   [nu=**na**   yawaã=**na**]ₙₚ   kamɨ̃
           woman   ANA=**ACC**   dog=**ACC**   truly
           pakihima-u=ai
           fall.in.love.with+PFV-NMLZ=COP:3:DECL
           'the woman actually fell in love with that dog' (agr041005_15)

(5.18)   *úchi húna saɨpchíhin iyaunakɨ́sh yuwáwaiŋka*
           uchi   [hu=**na**   saɨpɨ-uchi-hɨ̃=**na**
           child   PROX=**ACC**   rind-DIM-3=**ACC**
           iya-u=**na**=kI=sha]ₙₚ   yu-aw-aɨ̃-ka
           fall+IPFV-NMLZ=**ACC**=RESTR=ADD   eat-PFV-APPR+3SG-PROH
           'lest the child eat this rind that is falling' (agr040721_07)

(5.19)   *núna kaŋkapɨ́n nuwɨ́n ɨntsamhuídaushkam*
           [nu=**na**   kaŋkapɨ=**na**   nuwɨ̃=**na**]ₙₚ
           ANA=**ACC**   Kagkap=**ACC**   wife+PSSD:1PL/3=**ACC**
           ɨntsamahu-ina-u=shakama
           have.sex.with-IPFV.PL-NMLZ=ADD
           'those who were having sex with Kagkap's wife, too' (agr041005_14)

(5.20)   *ã́w̃ɨ̃ minã́ɨ̃ áuwɨ̃*
           [au=**ɨ̃**   **minaɨ̃**]ₙₚ   au=ɨ̃
           DIST=**LOC** 1sg+**LOC**   DIST=NONVIS.COP:3
           'it's there, where I live' (agr040723_29)

(5.21)   *nṹw̃ɨ̃ waánum duháhũã*
           [nu=**ɨ̃**   waã=**numa**]ₙₚ   duhahu-ã
           ANA=**LOC**   cave=**LOC**   flood-PFV+SEQ+3:SS
           'having flooded in that cave...' (agr040723_29)

The same agreement happens with NPs expressing the possessor in possessive NPs. In this case, the determiner takes accusative case to agree with the genitive form of a lexical head (example 5.22). This is unsurprising given that pronominal possessors always take accusative case, and genitive is itself historically derived from accusative marking.

(5.22)   *núna nuwá patahĩ*
           [[nu=na   nuwa]_{NP:POSSESSOR}   pata-hĩ]_{NP}
           ANA=ACC   woman+GEN   family-PSSD:1PL/3
           'that woman's family' (agr060816_01)

The discourse-level enclitics may also agree, as shown by the NP [*nu=ka uchi=ka*] (ANA=TOP child=TOP) 'that child' in example (4.151) in Chapter 4. But example (5.23) shows that the agreement is not obligatory, and examples in examples in §4.11 and §4.12 show that restrictive *=kĩ* and additive *=sha(kama)* also do not take part in obligatory agreement.

(5.23)   *ashí yutãĩ aídaunak*
           [ashi   yu-taĩ   a-ina-u=na=ka]_{NP}
           all   eat-NSBJ.NMLZ   COP-PL:IPFV-NMLZ=ACC=TOP
           'all edible things' (agr040721_07)

5.2.2 *tikish* 'another'

The pronoun *tikish* /tikichi/ 'another' shares almost all properties of the demonstratives: it can modify a following noun (5.24) or head an NP (5.25).

(5.24)   *tíkish intsán*
           [**tikichi**   intsa=na]
           another   stream=ACC
           'another stream' (agr040723_29)

(5.25)   *núu tíkish áidau*
           [nu   **tikichi**   a-ina-u]_{NP}
           ANA   **another**   COP-PL:IPFV-NMLZ
           'those others' (agr041005_14)

Unlike the demonstratives, *tikish* 'another' does not trigger obligatory case agreement (cf. 5.24), although occasional examples of agreement do show up. Example (5.26) is from the same story as (5.24), told by a different speaker.

(5.26)   *tikíchin intsán*
           [tikichi=**na**   intsa=**na**]
           other=**ACC**   stream=**ACC**
           'another stream' (agr040719_13)

While (5.24) does not show case agreement, (5.26) does. Given that the grammatical and textual contexts are the same, this may be free variation or it may be entirely a matter of variation between speakers. Note that the two examples show the same intonation profile, and in particular there is no pause or other intonational phenomenon that might suggest (5.26) consists of two NPs.

Another difference between *tikish* and the demonstratives is that when heading an NP, *tikish* may itself take a demonstrative determiner, as in example (5.25) above.

5.2.3 *tukɨ* 'like'

The word *tukɨ* typically functions as a time word meaning 'always' (§12.3.4), but also may function as an NP operator, where it translates as 'like'. As an NP operator *tukɨ* always precedes the head noun. The following two examples come from a story about a man who tries to kill a powerful enemy. As he approaches the intended victim's house, he is described (5.27) as being like a *macana* fish (*Adontosternarchus sp.*), which is known for rapidly zig-zagging through the water making it hard to catch – in the attacker's case, he wants to be safe from marksmen. After entering the house, the attacker's gun fails to fire, because the intended victim has spirit power which makes him invulnerable. The attacker then panics and flees, this time running straight back into the forest as fast as he can, like a hummingbird (5.28).

(5.27)   *túkɨ kantásh akuŋkáuwai*
          [**tukɨ**   kantashi]   aku-hu-ka-u=ai
          like   fish.sp   approach-APPL-PFV-NMLZ=COP:3:DECL
          'he approached (the house) like a *macana* fish' (agr041005_23)

(5.28)   *túkɨ hɨmpɨ wakɨ́tkɨuwai*
          [**tukɨ**   hɨmpɨ]   wakitu-ki-u=ai
          like   hummingbird   return-PFV-NMLZ=COP:3:DECL
          'he went back like a hummingbird' (agr041005_23)

These examples suggest that the NP functions as a manner adverbial when preceded by *tukɨ*, but I do not have sufficient examples to be certain of this.

5.3 Numerals and quantifiers

5.3.1 Numerals

Numerals (see §12.2 for a list) typically function as NP operators, and may precede or follow the noun. Examples (5.29, 5.30) show the numeral *makichik* 'one' functioning as an indefinite article.

(5.29) *nű̃wĩ makichík aínts wakắ, núna hiŋkahín akákɨak...*
     nu=ĩ   [**makichiki**   aɨntsu]   wa-kã
     ANA=LOC   **one**   person   go.up-PFV+SEQ+3:SS
     [nu=na   hiŋka-hĩ=na]   akakɨ-a-kũ
     ANA=ACC   seed-PSSD:1PL/3=ACC   drop-IPFV-SIM+3:SS
     'one man having gone up there, he was dropping those seeds...'
     (agr041005_19)

(5.30) *núwa mákichik naŋkaín usupáŋ, hiinkíu túwahamĩ*
     [nuwa   **makichiki**]   naŋkai=na   usupa-hã
     woman   **one**   fruit.sp=ACC   crave-PFV+SEQ+3:SS
     hiina-ki-u   tuwahamɨ
     go.out-PFV-NMLZ   NARR
     'a woman, having craved fruit, went out, they say' (agr040721_07)

Unlike the pronominal determiners, case agreement does not occur with pre-head numerals (5.31).

(5.31) *iŋkúŋmahai makichík aɨntsún*
     iŋku-ha-ma-ha-i   [makichiki   aɨntsu=na]ₙₚ:ₒ
     meet-PFV-RECPST-1SG-DECL   one   person=ACC
     'I met a person'

Numerals do not generally take case enclitics. In (5.32), the Spanish numeral *cuatro* 'four' does not seem to be a constituent of the NP, as the accusative enclitic =na appears on the preceding word.

(5.32) *mamayák múun áina núna cuatro húkĩ...*
     [mamayaki   muunta   a-ina   nu=na]ₙₚ:ₒ   ***cuatro***
     fish.sp   big   COP-PL:IPFV+3   ANAREL=ACC   **four**
     hu-kĩ
     take-PFV+SEQ+3:SS
     'having taken four of those big fish (*plateada*) ...' (agr040713_10)

The absence of case marking suggests that the numeral is not part of the NP, and instead is functioning adverbially. Other examples show unambiguously adverbial uses of numerals, as in (5.33) where there is no overt NP for the numerals to be associated with.

(5.33)   *yuhastáhum, hímaŋ kampáatum imánitahum yuhátahum*
          yuha-sa-ta-humɨ   **himaha**   **kampaatuma**
          go:PL-PFV-IMP-2PL   **two**   **three**
          ima-ni-ta-humɨ   yuha-ta-humɨ
          INTENS-VBLZ.INTR+PFV-IMP-2PL   go:PL+PFV-IMP-2PL
          'go together, in twos and threes, go together!' (agr041005_14)

Quantifiers show the same ambiguity with respect to NP membership, as described below. Unlike the quantifiers, occasional examples appear of case marking on numerals. Example (5.34) is an elicited example with the numeral *makichik* 'one' as the only constituent of a headless NP; and see example (12.6) in Chapter 12, where a distributive numeral takes accusative case.

(5.34)   *makíshkin yuwámhai*
          [makichiki=na]~NP~   yu-a-ma-ha-i
          one=ACC   eat-PFV-RECPST-1SG-DECL
          'I ate one (of them)'

5.3.2 Quantifiers

Quantifiers (see §12.2 for a list) have essentially the same syntactic properties as numerals, that is, they may precede or follow an NP head or function adverbially. Unlike numerals, quantifiers never take case marking, and cannot be the sole constituent of an NP. Examples (5.35, 5.36) are similar to (5.32) above, in that the quantifiers *mái* 'both' and *kuwáshat* 'many' appear to be outside the NP according to the diagnostic of case marking. This suggests that the quantifiers are syntactically adverbial modifiers of the verb, rather than NP modifiers, although semantically they are clearly associated with the NP.

(5.35) *ikám wíꭚaun mái ímiŋkak...*

       [ikama   wɨ-a-u=na]_{NP:O}   **mai**

       forest+LOC   go-IPFV-NMLZ=ACC   **both**

       ɨ-miŋka-kã

       CAUS-disappear-PFV+SEQ+3:SS

       'having kidnapped both of the ones who went to the forest...'
       (agr040712_02)

(5.36) *yakumán kuwáshat tukuí*

       [yakuma=na]   **kuwashata**   tuku-u=i

       monkey=ACC   **many**   shoot+PFV-NMLZ=COP:3:DECL

       'he shot many monkeys' (agr041005_28)

Other examples show unambiguously that quantifiers, like numerals, may function adverbially. The verb *áyampat* 'look around' in example (5.37) is intransitive, so *mái* 'both' cannot refer to an O argument; and we know from the context that the S is singular.

(5.37) *mái áyampã̃...*

       mai   ayampã̃

       both   look.around+PFV+SEQ+3:SS

       '(he) having looked around on both sides...' (agr040712_02)

Example (5.38) illustrates the use of *ashí* 'all' as an NP operator.

(5.38) *ashí aínts áidau*

       [**ashi**   aɨntsu   a-ina-u]_{NP}

       all   person   COP-PL:IPFV-NMLZ

       'all the people' (agr041005_14)

In (5.38) the quantifier *ashí* 'all' looks like a determiner, as it directly precedes the head noun. But case-marking again shows that post-head *ashí* is not part of the NP. Similarly to *mái* 'both' in example (5.35) above, examples (5.39, 5.40) show that *ashí* cannot be part of the object NP, because it does not carry the accusative or discourse enclitics.

(5.39) *nűꭓĩ aínts utsáutainashkam ashí wainák...*

       nu=ĩ   [aɨntsu   utsau-taĩ=na=shakama]_{NP:O}

       ANA=LOC   person   throw.away:PL-NSBJ.NMLZ=ACC=ADD

> ashi   waina-kã
> all   see-PFV+SEQ+3:SS
> 'having seen the whole place there where (dead) people were disposed
> of...' (agr040712_02)

(5.40)   *húnak ashí amútuk...*
          [hu=na=ka]   **ashi**   amu-tu-kã
          PROX=ACC=TOP   **all**   finish-APPL-PFV+SEQ+3:SS
          'having finished (eating) all of this...' (agr041005_14)

In example (5.41), *ashí* is unambiguously adverbial. It cannot be referring to any NP
because the verb is intransitive and S singular (note that this is a hyberbolic use,
with the literal meaning "I died completely").

(5.41)   *dútihuamtãĩ, ashí hakábiahai*
          nu-tika-hu-a-mataĩ   **ashi**   ha-ka-maya-ha-i
          ANA-VBLZ.TR-1SG.OBJ-PFV+SEQ-1/3:DS   **all**   die-PFV-INTPST-1SG-DECL
          'when that happened to me, I almost died' (agr040824_02)

In spite of the adverbial profile exhibited by quantifiers, they are semantically typically NP operators, and the pair of examples in (5.42, 5.43) demonstrates that the
association of a quantifier with an NP may be reflected syntactically: with two potential referents in the clause, *ashí* 'all' is considered to be modifying the NP head
that it directly precedes.

(5.42)   *ashí úchi áidau tsabáun yuwáwaŋmĩ*
          [**ashi**   uchi   a-ina-u]   [tsamau=na]
          all   child   COP-PL:IPFV-NMLZ   banana=ACC
          yu-a-aha-mĩ
          eat-PFV-PL-RECPST:3:DECL
          'all the children ate bananas'

(5.43)   *úchi áidau ashí tsabáun yuwáwaŋmĩ*
          [uchi   a-ina-u]   [**ashi**   tsamau=na]
          child   COP-PL:IPFV-NMLZ   **all**   banana=ACC
          yu-a-aha-mĩ
          eat-PFV-PL-RECPST:3:DECL
          'the children ate all the bananas'

Finally, the distribution of *kuwáshat* 'many' is analogous to the other two quantifiers. In example (5.44), additive *=shakama* is enclitic to the nominalized form *áidau*

which shows that this is the boundary of an NP, and *kuwáshat* must be outside that NP.

(5.44)   *aínts áidaushkam kuwáshat wíɥahui*
          [aintsu   a-ina-u=shakama]ₙₚ   **kuwashata**
          person   COP-PL:IPFV-NMLZ=ADD   **many**
          wɨ-aha-u=i
          go+PFV-PL-NMLZ=COP:3:DECL
          'many people also went' (agr041005_14)

It does seem to be the case that the quantifiers typically precede the head when functioning as NP operators, but typically directly precede the verb when functioning adverbially.

The nominalized form *áidau* (*a-ina-u* 'COP-PL:IPFV-NMLZ') functions as a plural marker in NPs. Synchronically this is a relative clause, and not a quantifier, and it is discussed in §5.5 below.

5.4 NP modification

Adjectives and some nouns can modify the head noun in an NP, as in examples (5.45) and (5.46), respectively. Modifiers attribute some property to the head noun, unlike the determiners, numerals and quantifiers described above. Modifying nominals always follow the head noun, while relative clauses typically follow but may precede the head (§5.5; and see Overall, in press-b, for a historical-comparative analysis of NP modification).

(5.45)   *ỹãw̃ãã pɨŋkɨŋ*
          [yawaãₙ   pɨŋkɨhaₐDJ]ₙₚ
          dog   good
          'a good dog'

(5.46)   *úchi núwa*
          [uchiₙ   nuwaₙ]ₙₚ
          child   woman
          'a girl' lit. *a female child*

Compound nouns, consisting of two noun roots functioning as a single nominal constituent, show quite different properties to modified NPs, both in their [modifier-head] order and in their lack of phonological independence (§4.5).

Modification within the NP is relatively uncommon in texts, as adjectives typically function predicatively. This neutralizes the syntactic distinction between noun and adjective in most contexts. When it does occur, however, attributive adjectival modification can be quite elaborate, as in examples (5.47, 5.48).

(5.47) *carabina pɨŋkɨŋ yamáŋbauchin balan "shakaut, shakaut!" ashí dɨkapɨs...*
      [*carabina*   pɨŋkɨha   yamahama-uchi=na]ₙₚ   [*bala*=na]ₙₚ
      rifle   good   new-DIM=ACC   bullet=ACC
      shakaut   shakaut   ashi   dɨkapɨ-sã
      IDEO   IDEO   all   check-SBD+3:SS
      'checking everything, a good new rifle, bullets: *chk chk* (sound of bolt sliding)...' (agr041005_23)

(5.48) *ỹãw̃ãhɨ́ pɨŋkɨŋ áishmaŋ duwɨham áhakui*
      [yawaã-hɨ̃   pɨŋkɨha   aishmaŋku   duwɨhama]ₙₚ
      dog-PSSD:1PL/3   good   man   fat
      a-haku=i
      exist-NARR.PST=COP:3:DECL
      'she had a good fat male dog' lit. *her good male fat dog existed* (agr041005_15)

I do not have sufficient data to say whether there are any rules to the ordering of multiple modifiers, on semantic or other principles. There does seem to be a tendency for plural marking *aidau* to be the final modifying element, but I have not tested whether this is is actually a grammatical requirement. Further discussion of more complex NPs is in §5.8.

5.5 Relative clauses

A relative clause is a clause that modifies an NP. There are two construction types in Aguaruna that allow a clause to function this way: the first involves nominalization, and the second uses a pronoun (anaphoric *nu*, proximal demonstrative *hu* or distal demonstrative *au*) or a derivative of the intensifier *ima* postposed to the predicate, which must be clause-final in such a construction. Both strategies form a nominal that can head as well as modify an NP, and there is no purely relativizing construction. Nominalized relative clauses are typically externally headed, with the relative clause following the head; those formed with pronouns are internally headed. Further discussion of the internal syntax of relative clauses is taken up in Chapter 16, following the description of nominalization in Chapter 15.

Examples (5.49) and (5.50) show nominalized relative clauses referring to the subject and object of the relative clause.

(5.49)   *ikámyawaŋ aɨntsún yuwáuk*
           [ikam_yawaã=ka   [aɨntsu=na   yu-a-**u**=ka]]_{NP}
           jaguar=TOP   person=ACC   eat-PFV-**NMLZ**=TOP
           'the jaguar that ate a person' (agr041005_14)

(5.50)   *níhamanch yahámushkam*
           [nihamanchi   [yaha-**mau**=shakama]]_{NP}
           masato   prepare+PFV-**NSBJ.NMLZ**=ADD
           'also *masato* (manioc beer) that had been prepared' (agr040721_07)

The typical position for externally headed relative clauses is following the head, as is the case for other modifiers, however there is some variation. Example (5.51) shows a nominalized relative clause preceding the head noun.

(5.51)   *ĩwanch yáunchuk húkimu núwa*
           [[ĩwanchi   yaunchukɨ   hu-ki-mau]   nuwa]_{NP}
           devil   long.ago   take-PFV-NSBJ.NMLZ   woman
           'women that the devil had taken long ago' (agr040723_29)

Examples in which an NP that includes a nominalized relative clause takes accusative marking are very rare except with plural marking *a-ina-u* (COP-PL:IPFV-NMLZ), which behaves like any regular modifier in that it takes the accusative enclitic while the head noun remains unmarked (5.52).

(5.52)   *hiŋkái áidaun utuák*
           [hiŋkai   a-ina-u=na]   utua-kã
           fruit   COP-PL:IPFV-NMLZ=ACC   pile.up-PFV+SEQ+3:SS
           'having piled up fruits...' (agr040721_07)

Among the few other examples of nominalized relative clauses in object NPs, marking is variable, and both elements may be marked accusative as in example (5.53). A nominalization is potentially referential, and as such appears to be less tightly integrated into the NP structure than an adjective.

(5.53)   *saɨpín iyáhun yuwáu túwahamĩ*
           [saɨpi=**na**   iyã-ha-u=**na**]   yu-a-u   tuwahamĩ
           peel=**ACC**   fall-PFV-NMLZ=**ACC**   eat-PFV-NMLZ   NARR
           'he ate the (manioc) peelings that had fallen (on the ground), they say'
           (agr040721_07)

Example (5.18) above showed an NP with pre-head determiner and post-head relative clause, with accusative case agreement throughout.

The word *aidau* frequently appears as a plural marker in modifer position. This word is decomposable as a nominalized relative clause with the morphological structure *a-ina-u* (COP-PL:IPFV-NMLZ). Examples (5.54) and (5.55), in which the same verb stem *a-ina-* (COP-PL:IPFV-) is relativized with the postposed anaphoric pronoun *nu(nu)*, show that the word *aidau* is synchronically morphologically analysable.

(5.54) *nuwán ìntsámhin áina nunú*
[nuwa=na   ìntsamahu-inu   a-ina   nunu]ₙₚ
woman=ACC   have.sex-NMLZ   COP-PL:IPFV+3   ANAʀᴇʟ
'those (men) who were having sex with the woman' (agr041005_14)

(5.55) *kíiwi áina núna yúwau ásã...*
[kiiwi   a-ina   nu=na]ₙₚ   yu-a-u
centipede COP-PL:IPFV+3   ANAʀᴇʟ=ACC   eat-IPFV-NMLZ
asã
COP+SBD+3:SS
'as (the armadillo) was eating those centipedes...' (agr040721_07)

There is, however, some evidence that the word *aidau* is being reanalysed as a morphologically simple plural marker, as it seems to be the case that the only possibility of having two nominalized relative clauses in a single NP is if one of them is *aidau* (as in 5.56).

(5.56) *wainkábiahai kuwáshat aìnts háau aídaun*
waina-ka-maya-ha-i   kuwashata [aìntsu   ha-a-u
see-PFV-INTPST-1SG-DECL   many   person   be.sick-IPFV-NMLZ
a-ina-u=na]
COP-PL:IPFV-NMLZ=ACC
'I saw many sick people' (agr040824_02)

Examples (5.57) and (5.58) show relative clauses formed with pronouns, demonstrative *au* and anaphoric *nu*, respectively (also see 5.54 and 5.55 above).

(5.57) *úchi kása áuk túnchihãĩ bitíkai*
[uchi   kasa=a   au=ka]ₙₚ   tunchi=haĩ
child   thief=COP:3   DISTʀᴇʟ=TOP   witch.doctor=COM

bɨtɨka=i
equal=COP:3:DECL
'a child who is a thief is the same (i.e. as bad) as a witch-doctor'
(agr040712_01)

(5.58)   *tsuŋkí áishĩ datsáuchia núna dukuhĩ́*
         [[tsuŋki   aishĩ   datsauchi=a
         mermaid+GEN   husband+PSSD:1PL/3   youth=COP:3
         nu=na]ₙₚ:ₚₒₛₛₑₛₛₒᵣ   duku-hĩ]ₙₚ
         ANAREL=ACC   mother-PSSD:1PL/3
         'the mother of the mermaid's young husband' lit. *the mermaid's hus-*
         band who is a youth (agr040824_01)

The NP in (5.58) is rather complex: the head is the possessed noun *dukuhĩ* 'his mother', and the rest is the possessor NP, which itself is headed by a possessed noun
aishĩ 'her husband', preceded by the possessor *tsuŋki* 'mermaid' and followed by the
relative clause. The relative pronoun is marked with accusative case, as is appropriate for pronominal possessors (see §5.6).

   Although the head, that is, the semantic referent, typically directly precedes or
follows a nominalized relative clause, it may be embedded within a pronominal
type, as in the elicited example (5.59) where the head is the object of the relative
clause, *aɨntsu=na* 'person=ACC'.

(5.59)   *wíi aɨntsún wainkámha dúka chapínum puhúwai*
         [wi   aɨntsu=na   waina-ka-ma-ha   nu=ka]ₙₚ
         1sg   person=ACC   see-PFV-RECPST-1SG   ANAREL=TOP
         chapi=numa   puhu-wa-i
         Chapi=LOC   live-3-DECL
         'the person that I saw lives in Chapi (village)'

The internal syntax of relative clauses is discussed in more detail in Chapter 16.

5.6 Possessive NP

The possessive NP consists minimally of a head noun marked with possession morphology. The possessor need not be overtly expressed, and the possession morphology indicates (to some extent) person and number of the possessor. If it is expressed, the possessor takes the form of an NP which must directly precede the
possessum, and is marked with the genitive form if it is a lexical noun, or with accusative case if it is a pronoun.

Possessive NPs typically appear unmodified, but examples such as (5.48) above, with three modifying adjectives, and (5.60) with a relative clause, show that there is no syntactic restriction on modification within the possessive NP.

(5.60)   *patahî áidau*
            [pata-hĩ   a-ina-u]
            family-PSSD:1PL/3   COP-PL:IPFV-NMLZ
            'his family members' (Text 1:18)

The possessor NP typically consists of a single noun or pronoun, but may be more complex. Example (5.61) illustrates the possibility of recursive possessive NPs, and example (5.58) above shows a recursive possessor modified by a relative clause.

(5.61)   *nína wɨɰahî hɨ̈n*
            [[[nĩ=na]NP:POSSESSOR   wɨɰa-hĩ]NP:POSSESSOR
            3sg=ACC   father.in.law-PSSD:1PL/3+GEN
            hɨ̈=nĩ]NP
            house+PSSD:1PL/3=LOC
            'at his father-in-law's house' (Text 2: 26)

Lexical possessors appear with genitive marking, but singular pronouns take accusative marking (5.62, and 5.58 above).

(5.62)   *mína apáŋ*
            [mi=na   apa-hu]NP
            1sg=ACC   father-PSSD:1SG
            'my father'

The possessor may be marked with the possessive suffix *-nau*, instead of the genitive form, in which case the possessum does not take possession morphology, as in (5.63).

(5.63)   *mídau piníŋ*
            [mi-nau   piniha]NP
            1sg-POSS   bowl
            'my bowl'

In effect this is a simple modified NP. The possessor-marked forms function adjectivally, and as such are expected to follow the noun, but often precede a possessum, presumably by analogy to genitive-marked possessors. The construction with possessive-marked possessor and unmarked possessum is preferred for two nouns: *duka* 'leaf' and *tsuntsu* 'snail', as described in §4.8.

Finally, occasional examples of semantically possessive NPs appear in my data in which the possessum does not carry the expected possession marking, as in (5.64). All of the examples I have involve first person singular possessors, which are marked with accusative case as expected in a possessive NP.

(5.64)   *mína núwa*
        [mi=na   nuwa]_{NP}
        1sg=ACC   woman
        'my wife' (agr040721_07)

5.7 Apposed name NP

The apposed name NP consists of two coreferential elements: the head noun and a proper name, which always follows the head. The relationship is not one of modification, but of identity. In addition to this semantic distinction, apposed name NPs differ morphologically from simple modified NPs in that the apposed name never takes any morphology. Examples (5.65, 5.66) show apposed name NPs in which the head is marked as possessed.

(5.65)   *ubáŋ chihĭȁp*
        [uma-hu   chihĭap]_{NP}
        sibling-PSSD:1SG   Chijiap
        'my brother Chijiap (female speaker)' (agr060816_01)

(5.66)   *yuwáŋ kȁỹŭk*
        [yuwa-hu   kȁyuka]_{NP}
        sister.in.law-PSSD:1SG   agouti
        'my sister-in-law, the agouti (female speaker)' (agr040721_07)

In example (5.67), the proper name *kanus* refers metonymically to the Huambisa people who live on the Santiago River, rather than the river itself. It follows the relativizing pronoun *nunu*, which is marking a focus construction (see §16.3, §18.2.3).

(5.67)   *tsumúnumia shiwáha nunú kanús*
        [tsumu=numa=ya   shiwaha=a   nunu   kanusa]_{NP}
        downriver=LOC=ABL   enemy=COP:3   ANA_{REL}   Santiago.River
        'those enemies from downriver, (those from the) Santiago River'
        (agr041005_18)

In example (5.68), the locative case marker =*numa*, which normally appears on the final element of the NP, is enclitic to the head rather than the phrase-final apposed name.

(5.68)　　　*iŋkúnikui namaknúm mahanú*
　　　　　　iŋku-nai-ka-u=ai　　　　　　　　　[namaka=numa　　mahanu]
　　　　　　meet-RECIP-PFV-NMLZ=COP:3:DECL　river=LOC　　　　Marañón
　　　　　　'they met at the river Marañón' (agr041005_18)

Proper names do receive case markers and other morphology when they head NPs, as in example (5.69), from a story in which a devil drinks dry a number of streams then vomits up the Marañón and Santiago Rivers.

(5.69)　　　*mahanún "kutút" iyáak nahánau túwahamĩ*
　　　　　　[mahanu=na]　　kutut　iya-a-kũ　　　　　　　nahana-u
　　　　　　Marañón=ACC　　IDEO　vomit-IPFV-SIM+3:SS　　create+PFV-NMLZ
　　　　　　tuwahamĩ
　　　　　　NARR
　　　　　　'vomiting "*kutut!*" (the devil) created the Marañón River' (agr040723_29)

Example (5.70) apparently shows a discontinuous apposed name NP. The job title *coordinador de centro sectorial de Centro Wawik* 'coordinator of Centro Wawik' is coreferential with the nominal *taka-ta=na* (work-ACT.NMLZ=ACC) 'work'; but it is not marked with accusative case, in keeping with the pattern in apposed name NPs, but unlike other discontinuous NPs, which take case marking on both elements (see §5.9 below).

(5.70)　　　*iglesianmaya takatá suhusáhabi coordinador de centro sectorial de centro wawík*
　　　　　　[*iglesia*=numa=ya　　taka-ta=na]NP:O
　　　　　　church=LOC=ABL　　　work-ACT.NMLZ=ACC
　　　　　　su-hu-sa-aha-amayi
　　　　　　give-1SG.OBJ-PFV-PL-DISTPST:3:DECL
　　　　　　[*coordinador de centro sectorial de Centro Wawik*]NP:O
　　　　　　coordinator of Centro Wawik
　　　　　　'they gave me a church-related job, coordinator of Centro Wawik' (agr040824_02)

A possible use of a discontinuous apposed-name NP with the verb *anaiyat* 'name' is discussed in §7.6.2.2.

5.8 More complex issues of NP constituency

The questions that arise regarding NP constituency relate to the existence of head-less NPs and to the integrity of complex NPs as syntactic units. The first question was addressed in §4.3, where I concluded that NPs consisting of a single adjective are best analysed as headless. The complex NPs present a different problem. Some phenomena suggest that coreferential elements may be appositional rather than forming a single syntactic unit, and constructions involving multiple case marking may be seen as comprising two NPs. Consider the case agreement described above (§5.2.1). Demonstrative pronouns can also head NPs, so it is possible that a construction as in (5.71) actually comprises two NPs in apposition – one headed by the demonstrative and the second by the lexical noun:

(5.71)   [nu=**na**]ₙₚ   [kãyuka=**na**]ₙₚ
            ANA=**ACC**   agouti=**ACC**
            'that one, the agouti' (cf. example 5.16)

However there is a strong argument against the "two NPs" hypothesis: where an object NP is composed of the three elements [Demonstrative Noun Modifier], as in (5.72), all three elements carry the accusative marker.

(5.72)   *núna nɨhɨn akaŋkɨn inaŋtúk...*
            [nu=**na**   nɨhɨ=**na**   akaŋkɨ=**na**]
            ANA=**ACC**   meat+PSSD:1PL/3=**ACC**   abdomen+PSSD:1PL/3=**ACC**
            inahũ-tu-kã
            cook-APPL-PFV+SEQ+3:SS
            'having cooked the meat from the abdomen...' (literally *that abdomen meat*) (agr041005_15)

If such examples involved two NPs, i.e. [Demonstrative]ₙₚ [Noun Modifier]ₙₚ, we would expect the [Noun Modifier] NP to mark accusative only on the final element. As example (5.72) shows, all three elements are marked, showing that all three are constituents of a single NP, with case agreement triggered by the presence of a pronominal determiner.

In §5.4 some examples of NPs with multiple modifiers were presented. Although these examples are atypical, there is no justification for considering them to consist of more than one NP. In particular, note that the NP in (5.47 – repeated below), with two modifying adjectives, has accusative case marking only on the final element, showing clearly that it must be a single NP.

(5.73)   *carabina píŋkɨŋ yamáŋbauchin*
          [*carabina*   pɨŋkɨha   yamahama-uchi=na]ₙₚ
          rifle   good   new-DIM=ACC
          'a good new rifle' (repeated from 5.47)

The use of nominalizations as standalone verbs in addition to their function as relative clauses means that some apparent highly complex NPs can be analysed as more than one clause, as in example (5.74) where the nominalized verb *batsata-u* (live:PL-NMLZ) functions as a finite verb, and sits between two NPs. The alternative analysis, whereby all the nominal elements including *batsata-u* form a single NP, does not make sense as the head noun *nuwa* 'woman' and the plural marker *a-ina-u* (COP-PL:IPFV-NMLZ) would each appear twice in the same NP. Note that this example does show a single rising intonation contour.

(5.74)   *núniamunum, áishiŋtin núwa áidau batsátu shíiham áidau núwa ayáu*
          nu-ni-a-mau=numa   [aishi-hĩ-tinu
          ANA-VBLZ.INTR-IPFV-NSBJ.NMLZ=LOC   husband-PSSD:1PL/3-ATTRIB
          nuwa   a-ina-u]ₙₚ   batsata-u   [shiihama
          woman   COP-PL:IPFV-NMLZ   live:PL-NMLZ   pretty
          a-ina-u   nuwa]ₙₚ   aya-u
          COP-PL:IPFV-NMLZ   woman   exist:PL+IPFV-NMLZ
          'in the place where that happened there were many [married women] living, [pretty women]' (agr041005_19)

5.9 Discontinuous NPs

NPs may apparently be split into two discontinuous parts, typically appearing on either side of the verb. In example (5.75), two coreferential nominals are marked as objects of one verb. This type of construction is most common with object NPs, but example (5.77) below, with a discontinuous NP in S role, shows that subject NPs may also be split in this way.

(5.75)   *ámina yawáimin wainkámhai mantínun*
          [ami=na   yawaĩ-mi=na]   waina-ka-ma-ha-i
          2SG=ACC   dog+PSSD-2=ACC   see-PFV-RECPST-1SG-DECL
          [mantu-inu=na]
          kill+APPL-NMLZ=ACC
          'I saw your good hunting dog'
          or
          'I saw your dog, the good hunter'

The final element in (5.75) could be considered an afterthought. In example (5.76), however, it is the head noun that follows the verb, presumably to focus it, leaving the modifier 'out of the food' in preverbal position.

(5.76) *yutáinmayan hiíkmahai dukán*
[yu-taĩ=numa=ya=na]   hii-ki-ma-ha-i
eat-NSBJ.NMLZ=LOC=ABL=ACC   take.out-PFV-RECPST-1SG-DECL
[duka=na]
leaf=ACC
'I took the leaf out of the food'

The accusative marking shows that the two elements must form a single NP – the verb *hiit* 'take out' is a simple transitive and only licences one object NP. By morphological criteria this is a single, discontinuous NP. Syntactically, however, the two elements are treated as discrete units, and both elements function as clausal participants. Compare example (5.77), in which the head is the focus of interrogation, and is in clause-initial position (and marked with the polar interrogative enclitic), while the modifying relative clause is in final position and marked with the question topic enclitic, as it is treated as presupposed.

(5.77) *uchík áya wainkámush*
[uchi=ka]   a-ya   [waina-ka-mau=sha]
child=Q   COP-REMPST:3   see-PFV-NSBJ.NMLZ=Q.TOP
'was it a child you saw?'

The two parts of a discontinuous NP may functionally simulate separate arguments as in (5.78) in which the modifying possessor NP *mina nuwanun* 'my wife's (one)' is semantically a beneficiary.

(5.78) *numín tsupíktahai mína nuwánun*
[numi=na]   tsupi-ka-ta-ha-i   [mi=na
tree=ACC   cut-PFV-IFUT-1SG-DECL 1sg=ACC
nuwa-nau=na]
woman-POSS=ACC
'I'll cut wood for my wife' lit. *I'll cut my wife's wood*

As with the examples above, the morphology dictates that [*numi=na* ... *mi=na nuwa-nau=na*] (tree=ACC 1SG=ACC woman-POSS=ACC) 'my wife's wood' must be analysed as one NP, as the verb is a simple transitive and cannot license more than one accusative-marked NP. Semantically, however, 'my wife' is functioning as a beneficiary type argument. Coreferentiality of discontinuous NPs may be better treated as a pragmatic rather than a syntactic phenomenon, as Doris Payne (1993) does for Cariban languages. The use of discontinuous NPs as a strategy to control the number of arguments in a clause is discussed in §7.2.

5.10 Headless NPs

Headedness of NPs can be difficult to determine, as nouns and adjectives share morphology. Doris Payne (1990) addresses a similar analytical problem in Yagua, and identifies a PRAGMATIC HEAD on the basis of discourse properties: the pragmatic head is discourse manipulable, in that it can be reintroduced later in a narrative. For example, in an Aguaruna story the NP in (5.79) appears. Later in the narrative, the same participant is restated as simply *tsuŋki* '(the) mermaid'. Because the adjective *shiiŋbauch* 'pretty' is not referential in (5.79), it cannot be used to reactivate the participant.

(5.79)   *tsúŋki shíiŋbauch*
          [tsuŋki   shiihama-uchi]
          mermaid   pretty-DIM
          'a pretty mermaid' (agr040824_01)

As Doris Payne puts it:

> In sum, a sentence or phrase-based view of headship breaks down in Yagua. But a discourse perspective as to what is, or is not, further manipulable (or pragmatically referential) disambiguates the head noun from the modifying noun.
>
> Doris Payne (1990: 110)

By contrast, a headless NP consisting only of an adjective may appear only where the ellipted head noun is readily recoverable from the discourse context; example (5.80) comes from a narrative in which the noun *shinutaĩ* 'song' is topical and readily available to be interpreted as the understood referent of the headless NP.

(5.80)   *níŋka muúntan shináu*
          nĩ=ka   [muunta=na]$_{NP:O}$ shina-u
          3sg=TOP   big=ACC   sing+IPFV-NMLZ
          'it (the *kúgkup* bird) sang a big (song)' *i.e. it sang loudly* (agr041005_17)

5.11 NP coordination

The basic coordination construction is simply to list the coordinate NPs. It is typically asyndetic, but may make use of the adverb *aatus* 'thus' to mark the end of the list. A second NP coordination strategy uses the comitative case-marker *=haĩ*.

5.11.1 Listing coordination

Listing coordination typically has no overt morphological marker, and consists, as the name suggests, in simply listing the coordinate NPs (5.81).

(5.81) *kábau áinaun, tsaáŋ áinaun, híma áinaun, chihunkán pasuhűắ...*
        [kabau   a-ina-u=na]   [tsaaŋku
        termite.nest   COP-PL:IPFV-NMLZ=ACC   tobacco
        a-ina-u=na]   [hima   a-ina-u=na]
        COP-PL:IPFV-NMLZ=ACC   chilli   COP-PL:IPFV-NMLZ=ACC
        [chihunaka=na]   pasu-hu-ã
        dry.leaf=ACC   put.in-APPL-PFV+SEQ+3:SS
        'having put (into the cave) termite nests, tobacco, chillies and dry leaves (to set a fire and smoke out the devil)...' (agr040723_29)

In example (5.82), the first coordinate NP precedes the verb, forming a stylistically unmarked AOV clause, while three other NPs follow. The postverbal NPs thus resemble afterthoughts. It is also noteworthy that the coordinated NPs in this example are not completely parallel: the last NP 'all kinds of food' is a superordinate term that includes the previous three.

(5.82) *kắỹŭkak mamának útua útuamã, paámpanak, piríanak, ashí yutắĩ aídaunak...*
        kãyuka=ka   [mama=na=ka]   utua   utuama-ã
        agouti=TOP   manioc=ACC=TOP   REDUP   pile.up-PFV+SEQ+3:SS
        [paampa=na=ka]   [piria=na=ka]
        plantain=ACC=TOP   banana.sp=ACC=TOP
        [ashi   yu-taĩ   a-ina-u=na=ka]
        all   eat-NSBJ.NMLZ   COP-PL:IPFV-NMLZ=ACC=TOP
        'the agouti, having piled up manioc, plantains, bananas, all kinds of food...' (agr040721_07)

Although the listing construction is essentially asyndetic, it may include the adverb *aatus* 'thus' to mark the end of the list. This is more common in examples such as (5.83), where the two coordinate NPs are not obviously presented as a list.

(5.83) *nĩ yachín ãỹãũ̃ãĩ, nuwín aátus*
         nĩ   [yachĩ=na]   ayã-u=ai
         3sg   brother+PSSD:1PL/3=ACC   take.with+PFV-NMLZ=COP:3:DECL
         [nuwĩ=na]   aatusã
         woman+PSSD:1PL/3=ACC   thus+3
         'he took his brother and his wife too' (agr041005_14)

Asyndetic coordination may also apply within the NP. In example (5.84), two Spanish nouns *coro* 'religious song' and *himno* 'hymn' share a single modifying adjective and relative clause.

(5.84) *coro, himno yamáham unuimáŋmau kánta kantamáinkawa miníyahi*
         [coro   himno   yamahama   unuima-ha-mau]
         song   hymn   new   learn-PFV-NSBJ.NMLZ
         kanta   kantama-ina-kawa   mini-ya-hi
         REDUP   sing-PL:IPFV-REPET+1PL:SS   arrive-REMPST-1PL+DECL
         'we arrived, singing new songs and hymns that we had learned'
         (agr040824_02)

Similarly, in example (5.85) three nouns share a single postposed plural marker *a-ina-u* (COP-PL:IPFV-NMLZ).

(5.85) *naŋkámauwai píshak, chíŋki, kúntin áidau tukután*
         naŋkama-a-u=ai   [[pishaka   chiŋki   kuntin
         begin-PFV-NMLZ=COP:3:DECL   small.bird   game.bird   animal
         a-ina-u]   tuku-ta=na]
         COP-PL:IPFV-NMLZ   shoot-ACT.NMLZ=ACC
         'he began to shoot small birds, game birds and animals' (agr040724_01)

Asyndetic NP coordination can make it difficult to judge the transitivity of some verbs, and this is discussed in detail in Chapter 7.

5.11.2 Coordination strategy with comitative case

Listing coordination is typically used to coordinate object NPs, as in the above examples. Subject NPs, by contrast, do not normally appear in coordinate constructions. Comitative case marking can be used to functionally coordinate subject NPs. The comitative-marked NP becomes an oblique participant, and the verbal subject marking reflects only the grammatical subject, as in example (5.86) in which the verb is marked for first person singular subject.

(5.86) *mína nuwáhãĩ taáttahai*
mi=na   nuwa=haĩ   ta-a-tata-ha-i
1sg=ACC   wife=COM   come-PFV-FUT-1SG-DECL
'I will come (back) with my wife'

Other examples of comitative case marked NPs may be interpretable as subjects but are semantically better considered oblique participants, and in such constructions comitative case marking cannot be said to simulate coordination. In particular, the verb *chichat* 'converse' takes a comitative marked complement but frequently context suggests that the two NPs are not symmetrical subjects. Compare example (5.87), where the wife is not an equal subject in a conversation, rather she is the addressee (but see example (4.113) in Chapter 4, where the verb is marked for plural subject).

(5.87) *dikatkau nuwáhãĩ chichasá, "kashín wikáikun wítathai" tusá...*
dikatkau   nuwa=haĩ   chicha-sa   <u>kashini</u>
first   woman=COM   converse-PFV+SEQ+1PL:SS   <u>tomorrow</u>
<u>wikaiuja-a-ku-nu</u>   <u>wi-tata-ha-i</u>   tu-sa
walk-IPFV-SIM-1SG:SS   go+PFV-FUT-1SG-DECL   say-SBD+1PL:SS
'first, having spoken to our wives, saying "tomorrow I will go walking (i.e. hunting)"...' (Text 3:5)

Comitative case may be used to coordinate object NPs, but as a general rule, comitative marking is preferred for coordination of subject NPs, and a listing construction for object NPs. Example (5.88), where comitative case coordinates two object NPs, was judged infelicitous by native speakers, although grammatical. A more acceptable formulation would couch both object NPs in accusative case, as in (5.89) – a listing construction.

(5.88) *? ámi nahánamun wíi nahánamuhãĩ wainkámhai*
[ami   nahana-mau=na]   [wi
2sg   make+PFV-NSBJ.NMLZ=ACC   1sg
nahana-mau=**haĩ**]   waina-ka-ma-ha-i
make+PFV-NSBJ.NMLZ=**COM**   see-PFV-RECPST-1SG-DECL
?'I saw the one that you made, along with the one that I made'

(5.89) *ámɨ nahánamun, wíi nahánamun wainkámhai*
    [amɨ   nahana-mau=na]   [wi
    2sg   make+PFV-NSBJ.NMLZ=ACC   1sg
    nahana-mau=**na**]   waina-ka-ma-ha-i
    make+PFV-NSBJ.NMLZ=**ACC**   see-PFV-RECPST-1SG-DECL
    'I saw the one that you made and the one that I made'

6 The verb

6.1 Introduction

The verb is the most morphologically complex word class in Aguaruna. Verb roots are characterized by the obligatory presence of morphology, with the bare root appearing only in a very restricted auxiliary construction (§6.7). Verbal morphology is almost entirely suffixing but there is one unproductive prefix slot; this is the only trace of prefixing in Aguaruna (§7.7.1). I find it convenient to distinguish two levels of verbal morphology, of which the first mainly consists of prototypically derivational morphemes, while the second mainly contains prototypically inflectional morphemes. However, the traditional division into derivational and inflectional morphology is not a very useful one for Aguaruna verbs (this has been noted as a property of agglutinating languages in general by Plungian, 2001); consider, for example, the fact that the first level of morphology includes object but not subject marking, and number but not person of the subject. Nominalization, on the other hand, traditionally considered derivational because it is class-changing, is at the second level and is completely productive.

Morphological level I consists of the sole prefix position and all suffix positions up to and including the negative markers. The verb root together with any affixes at this level form the level I stem, to which level II morphology is attached. The morphology at level II can be divided into three groups: two sets of inflectional morphology associated with finite and dependent verbs, and the nominalizers. Figure 6.1 presents a simplified schema of the two morphological levels.

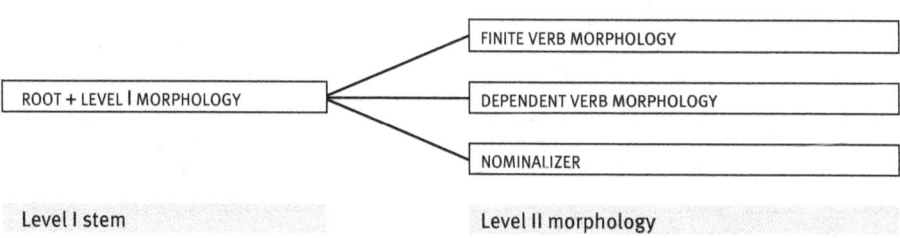

Figure 6.1: Levels of verbal morphology

In finite verbs level II is composed almost exclusively of tense, subject and mood markers, as shown in Figure 6.2. These three categories are obligatory, although only the subject suffixes form an equipollent system, as tense and mood may be zero-marked. In inflecting subordinate verbs, level II consists of subordinating suffixes, person, and switch-reference marking. Subordinate verbs may also take clause-level mood/modality enclitics. Nominalized verbs take nominal morphology, and may also take clause-level enclitics.

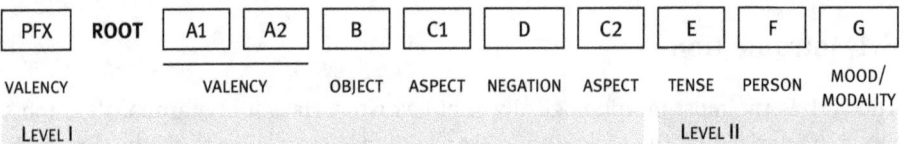

PFX	ROOT	A1	A2	B	C1	D	C2	E	F	G
VALENCY		VALENCY		OBJECT	ASPECT	NEGATION	ASPECT	TENSE	PERSON	MOOD/MODALITY
LEVEL I								LEVEL II		

Figure 6.2: Level I and II morphological slots in finite verbs

The division in Figures 6.1 and 6.2 is somewhat idealized: some level II suffixes are added to stems that cannot include the full complement of level I suffixes, so there is not a single unique "level I stem". It is useful to divide the morphology this way for descriptive clarity, however. Level I can be more precisely characterized as in Figure 6.3.

SLOT	GROUP	SUFFIXES	GLOSS
PFX:	Causative	V-	Causative
ROOT			
A1:	Valency	-mitika	Causative
		-na, -ki, -ka, -pa	Unproductive valency changers
		-ma	Reflexive
		-nai	Reciprocal
A2:	Valency	-hu / -tu	Applicative
B:	Object	(see §6.3.1)	SAP object markers
		-ma	Reflexive
		-nai	Reciprocal
C1:	Aspect	-ka, -sa, -ki(ni), -a(w), -i(ni), -ha	Perfective
		-a	Imperfective
		-ina	Imperfective + plural subject
		-mai	Potential
		-ma	Durative
D:	Negative	-tsu, -cha	Negative
C2:	Aspect (plural)	-aha	Plural subject (with perfective suffix in slot C1)

Figure 6.3: Level I affixes

Reflexive and reciprocal can appear in slot A, where they function as derivational valency changers, or in slot B, where they function as part of the object-marking paradigm. Object-marking suffixes appear in slot B, except that second-person object is marked at level II when the subject is first person; this is explained in §7.3 as an effect of a person hierarchy. In addition to the obligatory number distinction for first and second person subjects, plural subject is optionally marked along with imperfective or perfective aspect (slot C1 or C2, respectively) for all persons. Of the traditional TAM categories, tense and mood combine with person to form tidy inflectional sets at level II, while aspect is quite separate. Number is marked differently depending on (imperfective versus perfective) aspect, and the two negative markers are distributed according to (present versus non-present) tense.

There is no straightforward way to integrate the formal and functional aspects in a description of Aguaruna verbal morphology, and in the chapters that follow I have aimed for a middle ground: the description is couched in functional terms but also roughly follows the formal ordering in which affixes appear. Some important morphological issues are discussed in the remainder of this chapter. Verb conjugations, defined by phonological changes to the root when forming various stems, are described in §6.2. Both the applicative suffix of slot A and the object marking suffixes of slot B show lexically conditioned allomorphy, giving two sets of suffixes characterized by initial /h/ or /t/, and this is described in §6.3. Morphologically irregular verbs are described in §6.4, and a set of verbs with inherent plural number in §6.5. Derivation of verbs from other word classes is described in §6.6. Finally, §6.7 describes the formation of auxiliary constructions.

Valency and object marking are taken up again in Chapter 7. Chapters 8 and 9 describe the TAM morphology of finite verbs: Chapter 8 covers the aspect markers of slot C and the tense and person markers of slots E and F, while Chapter 9 covers mood and modality, marked in slot G. Chapter 10 describes question formation, also marked in slot G. Negation, including the verbal suffixes of slot D, is described in Chapter 11. Subordinate verb morphology is described in Chapter 13, and deverbal nominalization in Chapter 15.

6.2 Verb conjugations

Verbs fall into five conjugations based on changes in the root between the unmarked, perfective and imperfective stems. The morphological phenomena that define the conjugations cannot be explained in purely phonological terms. Unmarked verb roots terminate in a single vowel, two identical vowels, or /a/ followed by a non-identical vowel. All verbs ending in /a/, /i/ and /ɨ/ in the unmarked form, whether preceded by a vowel or not, fall into the first two conjugations. Some of those ending in /u/ fall into the first two conjugations, with the rest making up three "u-dropping" conjugations that lose their final /u/ in the perfective and imperfective stems.[1] Table 6.1 summarizes the conjugation membership of roots based on their phonological shape.

Table 6.1: Root terminations and conjugation membership

conjugation	final vowel(s) of unmarked root					
	/i/, /ai/, /ii/	/ɨ/, /aɨ/, /ɨɨ/	/a/, /aa/	/u/	/uu/	/au/
1	some	some	all	some	–	–
2	some	some	–	–	all	–
3A	–	–	–	some	–	–
3B	–	–	–	some	–	some
3C	–	–	–	–	–	some

There are some patterns based on phonological forms. All roots terminating in /a/ and /aa/ are first conjugation and all in /uu/ are second conjugation. The single-/u/ roots are the most disparate, some falling in the first conjugation, the rest in the first and second u-dropping sets (3A and 3B). The first u-dropping set (3A) contains only /u/ verbs, the third (3C) only /au/ verbs, the second a mix of /u/ and /au/. We will see below that 3A and 3B are analogous to 1 and 2, as 2 and 3B add /a/ in the perfective stem, while 1 and 3A do not. The first two conjugations between them contain about 90% of verbs, with the majority (perhaps 80% of the total) in the first conjugation. Of the third conjugation, 3C appears to be the largest by a small margin.

In the following sections I describe the morphological properties of the five conjugations. In the examples, verbs are quoted in three forms, giving the unmarked, perfective and imperfective stems respectively. The quoted perfective stems include the default perfective suffix if the verb has one (§8.3.1), and imperfective stems include the (singular subject) imperfective marker -*a* (§8.3.2). Accent position is marked in exemplified stems.

6.2.1 First conjugation

The first conjugation is the most regular, in that there is a single root that remains unchanged in all stems, and any changes to the stems can be accounted for by the following phonological rules.

---

1 I label this "u-dropping" because I treat the unmarked stem as basic. In fact, there is some evidence that the /u/ of the "u-dropping" verbs may be an old "infinitive" marker (cf. §6.2.5, §3.4.3).

1. If the root ends with two identical vowels, one is dropped in perfective and imperfective stems **unless** the root is underlyingly disyllabic (cf. *kɨɨ-*, *dii-*)
2. In monosyllabic roots ending in a vowel other than /a/, an epenthetic glide appears preceding the perfective suffix *-a* and imperfective *-a* (cf. *wɨ-* 'go')
3. In /a/-final roots, imperfective *-a* typically fuses with final /a/ **unless** the root is underlyingly monovocalic (cf. *ha-* 'be sick')

Table 6.2: First conjugation verbs, /a/ final root

	unmarked	perfective	imperfective	gloss
a.	áɰa	aɰá-ha	áɰa	'write'
b.	hiiná	hiina-kí	hiína	'go out'
c.	há	ha-ká	há-a	'be sick; die'
d.	maá	ma-í²	ma-á	'bathe'

Table 6.3: First conjugation verbs, /ɨ/ final root[3]

	unmarked	perfective	imperfective	gloss
a.	mahɨ	mahɨ-ha	mahɨ-a	'clean up'
b.	kɨɨ	kɨɨ-ka	kɨɰ-á	'burn (intr.)'
c.	wɨ	wɨ	wɨɰ-a	'go'
d.	kǎɨ	kǎɨ	kǎɰa	'have someone fold their knees to their chest'

Table 6.4: First conjugation verbs, /i/ final root`

	unmarked	perfective	imperfective	gloss
a.	tsúpi	tsupí-ka	tsúpi-a	'cut'
b.	kāhíi	kāhí-ha	kāhí-a	'sleep (plural subject)'
c.	dií	dií-s	diy-á	'look at'
d.	pǎi	pǎi	pǎy-a	'roll tips of darts in venom'

---

2 Note that the perfective suffix *-i(ni)* replaces the final /a/ of the root.
3 Final /ɨ/ becomes /i/ when preceding perfective suffix *-ki(ni)* (even if an elided syllable intervenes).

Table 6.5: First conjugation verbs, /u/ final root

	unmarked	perfective	imperfective	gloss
a.	ahakú	ahaku-há	aháku-a	'lose a child'
b.	aáŋku	aáŋku-a	áaŋku-a	'leave a space'

Note that there are no /uu/ endings in the first conjugation. In the second conjugation, however, there are no roots ending in single /u/, although there are some ending in double /uu/.

6.2.2 Second conjugation

Second conjugation verbs differ from the first conjugation in that their perfective form is characterized by the presence of stem-final /a/. There are no /a/ stems in this conjugation, and all of the /u/ final roots involve double /uu/. An interesting point to note is that the perfective suffix associated with second conjugation verbs is almost always -*ha*. The phonological changes that characterize the second conjugation are:

1. /a/ is added to the root in the perfective stem; if the root has more than two vowels, /a/ replaces the final vowel
2. If the root ends in two identical vowels, one is dropped in imperfective stems unless the root is underlyingly disyllabic (cf. first conjugation rule 1)

Table 6.6: Second conjugation verbs, /ɨ/ final root

	unmarked	perfective	imperfective	gloss
a.	tamɨ̵	tamɨá-ha	tamɨ-a	'become greasy'
b.	ahápɨ	ahápa	ahápɨ-a	'throw away'
c.	aɨpɨ	aɨpa-sá	aɨpɨ-a	'throw on the ground'

Table 6.7: Second conjugation verbs, /i/ final root

	unmarked	perfective	imperfective	gloss
a.	ahɨ̄ɨ	ahɨ̄á-ha	ahɨ́-a	'knock down'
b.	kɨ̄ɨ	kiyá-ha	kíy-a	'become evening'

Table 6.8: Second conjugation verbs, /u/ final root

	unmarked	perfective	imperfective	gloss
a.	katsúu	katsuá-ha	katsú-a	'ripen; harden'
b.	kuŋkúu	kuŋkuá-sa	kuŋkú-a	'kiss; smell'

6.2.3 Third (u-dropping) conjugation type A

The third conjugation is characterized by a final /u/ in the unmarked root that is lost in the imperfective stem. The phonological rules are as for the first conjugation with the addition of:

1. Final /u/ is lost preceding the imperfective suffix -*a*

Table 6.9: Third conjugation type A verbs

	unmarked	perfective	imperfective	gloss
a.	puhú	puhú-sa	puh-á	'be/live'
b.	a(ɰ)ú	a(ɰ)w-í	aɰ-á	'cook in a pot'
c.	ka(ɰ)ú	ka(ɰ)ú-ha	kaɰ-á	'rot (of meat)'

Note in examples (b) and (c) that the underlying velar glide is lost between /a/ and /u/ in the unmarked and perfective stems (see §3.2.5).

6.2.4 Third (u-dropping) conjugation type B

As with the other third conjugation verbs, final /u/ is lost in the imperfective stem. Unlike the 3A forms, final /u/ becomes /a/ in the perfective stem. This could be analysed as a combination of two processes: (1) loss of the final /u/, as in 3C verbs, and (2) addition of /a/, as in second conjugation verbs.

Table 6.10: Third conjugation type B verbs

	unmarked	perfective	imperfective	gloss
a.	kánu	kaná-ha	kán-a	'sleep (singular subject)'
b.	kaŋkáu	kaŋkaá-ha	kaŋká-a	'darn'

6.2.5 Third (u-dropping) conjugation type C

The third conjugation type C is characterized by a final /u/ in the unmarked form that is not present in the perfective and imperfective stems; unlike 3B there is no added /a/ in the perfective stem. All 3C verb roots end in /au/ in the unmarked form. The rules are:

1. In perfective and imperfective stems the /u/ of the unmarked stem does not appear; the root behaves as a regular (first conjugation) /a/ stem

Table 6.11: Third conjugation type C verbs

	unmarked	perfective	imperfective	gloss
a.	tupikáu	tupiká-ka	tupiká	'run'
b.	máu	ma-á	má-a	'kill'
c.	kakáu	kaká-ha	kaká	'cause an argument'

Two phonological peculiarities are distinctive of 3C conjugation verbs. Firstly, the /u/ of the unmarked stem is replaced by derivational suffixes applicative *-hu* / *-tu* and causative *-mitika* (example 6.1). Secondly, the presence of final /u/ apparently denasalizes a preceding nasal domain, given that some forms where /u/ is replaced by applicative *-tu* show nasality, as in example (6.2). Both properties suggest that the /u/ of the unmarked stems is the reflex of a historical suffix.

(6.1)   /tupikamitika/
         tupikau-mitika-
         run-CAUS-
         'chase'

(6.2)   /mantu/
         mau-tu-
         kill-APPL-
         'kill (game) for someone'

6.2.6 Final /hu/, /tu/

Verb stems that include either allomorph of the homophonous applicative or first person singular object suffixes, *-hu* / *-tu*, form a conjugation of their own with the following rules:

1. Imperfective -*a* always fuses with final /u/
2. Perfective suffix -*i(ni)* always fuses with final /u/

These rules apply to other verbs ending in /hu/ and /tu/, as in Table 6.12, even where the applicative suffix is not present, presumably by analogy to the suffixed forms. Monovocalic roots normally do not undergo any fusion, and the root /hu/ 'take' has the expected imperfective stem /húwa/; but /tu/ 'say' is exceptional in allowing fusion in its perfective and imperfective stems, as shown in Table 6.12, and discussed further in §6.4.

Table 6.12: Morphologically simple verb roots ending in /hu/ and /tu/

	unmarked	perfective	imperfective	gloss
a.	kantaúhu	kantaúhu-ka	kantáuh(a)	'belch'
b.	utú	uti < utu-i(ni)	utá	'fetch'
c.	tú	tí < tu-i(ni)	tá⁴	'say'

This conjugation differs from 3A only in its treatment of perfective -*i(ni)*.

The first conjugation is completely regular, and contains the overwhelming majority of verbs. The oldest verbal loanwords from Spanish use the third infinitive form of the Spanish verb, minus the final /r/, and suffixed with the manipulative verbalizer -*ma* (see §6.6), thus forming first conjugation /a/ stems. Some examples are shown in (6.3).

(6.3) a. *kuita-ma-* (< *cuidar*)   'care for'
   b. *diwi-ma-* (< *deber*)   'owe'
   c. *kanta-ma-* (< *cantar*)   'sing (in church)'

Contemporary borrowings simply take the truncated infinitive form of the Spanish verb as the root, without adding the verbalizer -*ma*. The only examples I have of such borrowings are -*ar* verbs in Spanish, so they become regular first conjugation /a/ stems in Aguaruna (examples in 6.4).

(6.4) a. *frita-*   'fry'
   b. *gana-*   'earn'

---

4 I have one example of an imperfective form: *tuwa* < *tu-a* (say-IPFV), characterized by a consultant as an "old people's" form.

So it seems that the default conjugation is the first, and all examples of borrowed verbs, whether nativized with a verbalizer or borrowed directly, are /a/ stems.

6.3 Verb classes: *hu* verbs and *tu* verbs

Verbs fall into two classes, manifested in the forms of the object markers and the applicative suffix. In the following sections I describe the object markers (§6.3.1) and discuss the allomorphy that defines the two classes (§6.3.2). Applicative marking is described in more detail in §7.7.2.

6.3.1 Object marking

Only SAP objects are indexed with verbal suffixes. Third person objects are always zero-marked. Furthermore, only one object is ever indexed on the verb. The choice of which object to mark obeys a person hierarchy with the ranking 1 > 2 > 3, so if one SAP object is present, it will be indexed with a suffix. I have no natural examples with two SAP objects; even in elicitation such forms are very rare, and there exists a range of strategies to avoid them, by encoding one participant as something other than a grammatical object. There is no difference in object markers arising from the O/E distinction, but the distinction can play a role in deciding which semantic object will be encoded as something other than a grammatical object, as there is a general avoidance of higher-ranked O than E arguments. A full discussion of grammatical relations and their effects on object marking is in Chapter 7.

The object-marking suffixes themselves vary according to the verb class and the person and number of both subject and object, and their ordering with respect to other suffixes also varies depending on the participants involved. The forms of the object suffixes in the two classes are shown in Table 6.13, along with the applicative suffix for comparison. The basic pattern is that applicative and first singular object are homophonous, and marked with *-hu* or *-tu*; second person object is marked with *-hama* or *-tama* (*-pa* is a phonologically conditioned contraction of *-tama*), which may be decomposable as **-ha* / **-ta* plus a second person marker **-ma*. First plural object is generally marked identically to second person, except that the form *-kahatu* can be used where second person is specifically excluded, and is also used to mark generic human objects. Some of the variation in the forms shown in Table 6.13 may be morphologically or phonologically conditioned. Most of the data for first person plural object were elicited, and this may also have affected the amount of variation seen.

Table 6.13: Object suffixes

verb class	applicative	1sg object	2 object	1pl object
hu	*-hu*	*-hu*	*-hama*	*-hama* *-pa* *-kahatu*
tu	*-tu*	*-tu*	*-tama* *-pa*	*-tama* *-pa* *-tVpa* *-hama* *-kahatu*

6.3.1.1 First person singular object

In the *hu* class, first person singular object is marked with *-hu* (6.5, 6.6).

(6.5)   *dakumhúkta*
        dakuma-**hu**-ka-ta
        copy-**1SG.OBJ**-PFV-IMP
        'take my photo' lit. *make a copy of me*

(6.6)   *mína suhustá*
        mi=na   su-**hu**-sa-ta
        1sg=ACC   give-**1SG.OBJ**-PFV-IMP
        'give it to me'

In the *tu* class, first person object is marked with *-tu* (6.7, 6.8).

(6.7)   *isatkáttawai*
        isa-**tu**-ka-tata-wa-i
        bite-**1SG.OBJ**-PFV-FUT-3-DECL
        'it's going to devour me' (agr041005_14)

(6.8)   *ũỹúntusta*
        ũyuna-**tu**-sa-ta
        accompany-**1SG.OBJ**-PFV-IMP
        'come with me!' (agr040721_07)

6.3.1.2 Second person object

In *hu* verbs with third person subject, second person object is marked with -*hama* (6.9, 6.10).

(6.9)   *túhamui*
           tu-**hama**-wa-i
           say-**2.OBJ**+IPFV-3-DECL
           '(she) says to you' (agr040721_07)

(6.10)   *áikaŋmawai*
           aika-**hama**-wa-i
           do-**2.OBJ**+IPFV-3-DECL
           '(it) is doing that to you' (agr040723_29)

The same relation in the *tu* class is marked with -*tama* (6.11) or -*pa* (6.12). The -*pa* form is a contraction of -*tama* when the first vowel is elided; that is, intermediate /tma/ surfaces as /pa/. There is no number distinction made in second person object marking when the subject is third person.

(6.11)   *súŋka dushíktamui*
           suŋka   dushiki-**tama**-a-wa-i
           Sugka   laugh.at-**2.OBJ**-IPFV-3-DECL
           'Sugka is laughing at you'

(6.12)   *wáipakmĩ*
           wai-**pa**-ka-mĩ
           see-**2.OBJ**-PFV-RECPST:3:DECL
           'he saw you'

First person subject and second person object are marked with portmanteau level II suffixes (6.13). This is the only object marking that appears at level II.

(6.13)   *tímakham*
           ti-ma=ka-**hami**
           say+PFV-RECPST=Q-**1SG>2SG**
           'did I tell you?' (agr041006_04)

The suffix -*hami* appears to be decomposable as first person singular subject -*ha* and second person -*mi*. When a first person plural subject acts on a second person singular object, the suffix is -*himi*, which seems to combine first plural -*hi* and second person -*mi*. However, when the first person subject is singular and the second person object plural, the marker is still *-himɨ*, so it appears that the person distinction is neutralized at the expense of number marking. The marking is set out in Table 6.14.

Table 6.14: Marking of first person subject / second person object

	2sg object	2pl object
1sg subject	*-hamɨ*	*-himɨ*
1pl subject	*-himɨ*	*-himɨ*

Because of the neutralization, I analyse this as a system of two portmanteau suffixes, which both indicate first person subject and second person object, and have a singular/plural distinction that is sensitive to either participant (cf. Larson 1963).

6.3.1.3 First person plural object

The choice of suffix for marking first person plural object is similarly lexically specified, and most of the markers are shared with second person object; but the distinction between the two classes of verbs is not as clear. Both classes have verbs that take first person plural object markers *-hama* (6.14), *-pa* (6.15) and *-kahatu*, and in the *tu* class there are also verbs that take the markers *-tama* and *-tpa*.

(6.14) *hunásh ya hútihamawa?*
        hu=na=sha   ya   hu-tika-hama-a-wa
        PROX=ACC=Q.TOP   who   PROX-VBLZ.TR-1PL.OBJ-IPFV-3
        'who is doing this to us?' (agr040712_02)

(6.15) *amúpawai*
        amu-pa-a-wa-i
        terminate-1PL.OBJ-IPFV-3-DECL
        '(he) is killing us all' (agr040712_02)

As can be seen from Table 6.13 above, first person plural object basically follows the forms of second person object, but with more variation in forms – although note that, as with all the object markers, any given verb will always take the same form. First plural object is the only one to break the pattern whereby the *hu* class takes objects in /h/ and the *tu* class takes objects in /t/. This may be a result of elicitation with verbs that are infrequently used, resulting in confusion as to their class membership.

The *-kahatu* marker is not part of the *hu/tu* system, and is used in contexts where second person is specifically excluded. This form also marks generic human objects, as in *hintinkaŋtin* 'teacher' (< *hintintu-kahatu-inu* 'teach-1PL.OBJ-NMLZ', lit. *one who teaches us*); *maŋkaŋtin* 'murderer' (< *mã-kahatu-inu* 'kill-1PL.OBJ-NMLZ', lit. *one who kills us*). That this is a generic object can be seen from the following examples. Example (6.16) comes from a story in which the narrator's father had killed a stranger, so the only way that the object of 'kill' could be construed as 'one of us' is in the generic sense of 'a person'.

(6.16) *mína apáŋ maŋkaŋtuáu áyi*
        [mi=na   apa-hu]   mã-kahatu-a-u
        1sg=ACC   father-PSSD:1SG   kill-1PL.OBJ-PFV-NMLZ
        a-yi
        COP-REMPST:3:DECL
        'my father had killed someone' (agr040824_02)

Example (6.17) describes the speaker working as a teacher for two years. He is not included in the group of people being taught, so the object marker *-kahatu* must refer to a generic 'people' rather than first person plural 'us'.

(6.17) *múun hintínbaun hintínkaŋtu áyahai hímaŋ mihadái*
        muunta   hintintu-mau=na   hintintu-kahatu   a-ya-ha-i
        adult   teach-NMLZ=ACC   teach-1PL.OBJ   COP-REMPST-1SG-DECL
        himaha   mihana=i
        two   year=INS
        'I taught in adult education for two years' (agr040824_02)

When the first vowel of *-kahatu* is elided, it surfaces as /hatu/, rather than the expected /khatu/ (example 6.18, and see §3.5.4).

(6.18) *bukúhatin*
        buku-kahatu-inu
        suck-1PL.OBJ-NMLZ
        'insects that suck human blood'

6.3.1.4 Alternation of forms

Applicative and object suffixes can co-occur, and in that case show alternation. Table 6.15 shows this for the combination of applicative and first singular object.

Table 6.15: 'Applicative' and 'first person singular object' allomorphs

class	APPL	1SG.OBJ	APPL-1SG.OBJ
hu	*-hu*	*-hu*	*-hu-tu*
tu	*-tu*	*-tu*	*-tu-hu*

The two homophonous forms never co-occur in a word. When a verb takes both applicative and first singular object suffixes, the object suffix switches its form, as shown in the fourth column of Table 6.15, and in examples (6.19–6.21) with *tsupi-* 'cut', a *hu* class verb, and (6.22–6.24) for *ɨ̃ɰã-* 'look for', a *tu* class verb.

(6.19) *wíi numín tsupíŋkathimɨ*
        wi   numi=na   tsupi-**hu**-ka-ta-himɨ
        1sg   tree=ACC   cut-**APPL**-PFV-IFUT-1SG>2PL+DECL
        'I will cut wood for you~PL~'

(6.20) *áu tsupíŋkamɨ̃*
        au   tsupi-**hu**-ka-mɨ̃
        DIST   cut-**1SG.OBJ**-PFV-RECPST:3:DECL
        's/he cut me'

(6.21) *mínau númi tsupíŋtuktahum*
        [mi-nau   numi]   tsupi-**hu**-**tu**-ka-ta-humɨ
        1sg-POSS tree   cut-**APPL**-**1SG.OBJ**-PFV-IMP-2PL
        'cut my wood for me'

(6.22) *ɨ̃ɰã́tak yuháawai*
        ɨɰa-**tu**-a-kũ   yuha-a-wa-i
        look.for-**1SG.OBJ**-IPFV-SIM+3:SS   go:PL-IPFV-3-DECL
        'they're looking for me'

(6.23) *nína ɨ̃ɰã́tkámɨ̃*
        nɨ̃=na   ɨɰa-**tu**-ka-mɨ̃
        3sg=ACC   look.for-**APPL**-PFV-RECPST:3:DECL
        's/he looked (for it) on someone's behalf'

(6.24) *ɨ̃ɰã́thúkmɨ̃*
        ɨɰa-**tu**-**hu**-ka-mɨ̃
        look.for-**APPL**-**1SG.OBJ**-PFV-RECPST:3:DECL
        's/he looked for (it) on my behalf'

Because of the homophony of applicative and first person singular object, examples such as (6.20) are ambiguous out of context; the example is repeated below (6.25) with the second possible gloss:

(6.25)   *áu tsupíŋkamĩ*
         au   tsupi-**hu**-ka-mĩ
         DIST   cut-**APPL**-PFV-RECPST:3:DECL
         's/he cut (it) for someone'
         OR
         's/he cut me' (with gloss as in 6.20)

Typically, the out-of-context reading for an ambiguous form is as first person singular object (i.e. 's/he cut me' in example 6.20). In example (6.23) the third-person accusative pronoun *nĩ=na* (3SG=ACC) is used to avoid ambiguity. Of course, in actual use truly context-free examples are extremely rare.

The other object suffixes also take part in the same pattern of alternating allomorphs.

6.3.2 Source of the allomorphy

There are two unusual aspects of this allomorphy that currently defy explanation. The first is the allomorphy itself: such variants are very unusual in Aguaruna morphology, which in general is agglutinating with fairly transparent phonological conditioning of allomorphy. The second unusual aspect is the fact that object and applicative suffixes share the same pattern of allomorphy. This is addressed in §6.3.2.3 below.

With respect to the allomorphy itself, there are two possible explanations: either the variants could have arisen from an earlier phonological conditioning, or they could have arisen from two different morphemes. Tables 6.16 and 6.17 give some examples of verbs from both sets, with the action nominalizer *-ta* suffixed to the unmarked stem. The following sections consider the possibility of phonological (§6.3.2.1) or semantic (§6.3.2.2) conditioning of the allomorphs.

Table 6.16: *hu* verbs

verb	gloss	transitivity
achít	grab	TRANS
achít	nail	TRANS
ahamát	make a garden	INTRANS

verb	gloss	transitivity
ahápɨt	throw away	TRANS
ántut	listen	INTRANS
díit	look at	TRANS
kuitámat	care for	TRANS
súmat	ask for	TRANS
súta	give	DITRANS
suwimát	punish	TRANS
tsupít	cut	TRANS
tukút	pierce ears	TRANS
túta	say	INTRANS/TRANS
umít	do	TRANS
untsút	call	TRANS
wɨ́ta	go	INTRANS
yúta	eat	TRANS

Table 6.17: *tu* verbs

verb	gloss	transitivity
sɨɰát	ask for	DITRANS
wainát	see	TRANS
ɨsát	bite	TRANS
nihát	wash	TRANS
ɨɰát	look for	TRANS
hiŋkát	tie up	TRANS
inahút	cook	TRANS
achihút	roast	TRANS
uhát	tell	TRANS
awɨ́-tut	send	DITRANS
ahákmatut	plant	TRANS
táut	dig out	TRANS
ahát	plant a garden	TRANS
ahít	throw down	TRANS
íŋkut	meet	TRANS
ayámhut	defend	TRANS
húwat	stay	INTRANS

6.3.2.1 Phonological conditioning of the alternants

There is no apparent phonological conditioning on the allomorphy. Both variants appear in essentially the same environments with respect to syllable structure, accent placement and final vowel of the root. There are four monovocalic roots, and all are *hu* verbs. There are no *tu* verbs with final vowel /ɨ/, but this is probably an accident of the data, as verb roots ending in /ɨ/ are rare in any case.

6.3.2.2 Semantic conditioning of the alternants

Semantically there are two possibilities: the allomorphy could be based on the semantics of the verb, or based on the semantic role of the participant referenced. Simple transitive, ditransitive and intransitive examples appear in both groups, and as can be seen from the examples given in Table 6.16 and Table 6.17, neither type stands out as forming a semantic group distinct from the others. The object suffixes can refer to patient or recipient like objects, but this has no bearing on which class they are part of (cf. examples 6.5 and 6.6, above).

To summarize, there is no synchronic phonological or semantic conditioning of the variants, and all that can be said is that these are two lexically-conditioned allomorphs.

6.3.2.3 Relationship between applicative and object morphemes

The second element of the allomorphy problem is the relationship between the two homophonous forms 'applicative' and 'first singular object'. Both show the same unusual allomorphy but this allomorphy is interrupted when both appear in the same word. There is a clear requirement for alternation of /h/ and /t/, which is carried over to the other object suffixes. For the present, the only solution is to describe the two groups of forms and leave an explanation until more data, historical and comparative, can be added to the equation.

6.4 Irregular verbs

Because of the agglutinating nature of the morphology, there are very few irregular verbs in Aguaruna. I identify four roots that are morphologically exceptional: *tuta* 'say'; *ata* 'exist'; *ata* copula; *puhut* 'live'.

6.4.1 *tuta* 'say'

tuta 'say' is morphologically irregular in that its vowel is elided when forming perfective and imperfective stems, unlike other monosyllabic roots. Table 6.18 compares the stems of *tuta* 'say' and two regular monosyllabic roots.

Table 6.18: Stems of monosyllabic verb roots

unmarked	perfective	imperfective	gloss
tu	*tu-i* > [ti]	*tu-a* > [ta]	'say'
hu	*hu-ki* > [húki]	*hu-a* > [húwa]	'take'
yu	*yu-a* > [yuwá]	*yu-a* > [yúwa]	'eat'

This verb is also unusual in having no fixed transitivity value, as described in §7.6.3.

6.4.2 Existential *ata* and copula *ata*

Two irregular verbs are homophonous, having the form *ata*. They are probably historically related, but synchronically can be distinguished. The existential verb *ata* 'exist' is intransitive, taking just an S argument, while the copula takes two arguments (copula subject and copula complement), both in nominative case. Neither existential nor copula takes any aspect marking apart from the imperfective plural *-ina*, and this is possible only with copula, while existential has a suppletive plural S form *aya* 'exist:PL'. Copula *ata* is restricted to subordinate clauses and finite clauses that are not present tense declarative, polar interrogative or tag questions – in those clause types the copula complement is marked with an enclitic copula (see §7.9 for TAM restrictions on copula verb, and §4.14 for morphology of the enclitic copula). Existential has no TAM restrictions. Copula *ata* cannot take negative marking, instead negation is marked with the suffix *-chau* on the predicate nominal (6.26). For existential *ata* there is a suppletive negative existential verb *atsut* 'exist:NEG' (6.27) – note that this verb does take imperfective aspect marking.

(6.26)   *wíka ỹãw̃ą́ą̃chuithai*
      [wi-ka]cs   [yawaã-chau=ita-ha-i]cc
      1sg=TOP   dog-NEG.NMLZ=COP-1SG-DECL
      'I am not a dog' (agr060816_01)

(6.27)   *yúmi atsáwai*
           [yumi]ₛ   atsa-wa-i
           water   exist:NEG+IPFV-3-DECL
           'there's no water'

Interrogation is marked with nominal enclitics in copular clauses (6.28), but with a verbal enclitic in existential clauses (6.29) (see Chapter 10 for details).

(6.28)   *húsha nihámchikait*
           [hu=sha]cs   [nihamanchi=ka=ita]cc
           PROX=Q.TOP   *masato=Q=COP:3*
           'is this *masato* (manioc beer)?'

(6.29)   *nihamã́sh áwak*
           nihamanchi   a-wa=ka
           masato   exist-3=Q
           'is there any *masato*?'

Both copula and existential *ata* share a suppletive subordinate form *asa-* which is always treated morphologically as a perfective stem, taking sequential suffixes which differ from those of non-temporal subordinate suffixes in DS clauses (§13.4.2). No distinction is made between non-temporal and sequential clauses, as can be seen from example (6.30), which semantically is clearly not a sequential linkage; that is, the "not knowing Spanish" does not represent a sequential clause that is prior to "being unable to take me to Lima".

(6.30)   *mína apahúsh kistián chichamán díkachu asámtãĩ, ítúmainchau áyi*
           mi=na   apa-hu=sha   kistian_chichama=na
           1sg=ACC   father-PSSD:1SG=ADD   Spanish.language=ACC
           dɨka-chau   asa-matãĩ   ɨ-tu-mai-inu-chau
           know-NEG.NMLZ COP+SBD-1/3:DS   take-1SG.OBJ-POT-NMLZ-NEG.NMLZ
           a-yi
           COP-REMPST:3:DECL
           'because my father didn't know Spanish either, he couldn't take me (to Lima)' (agr040824_02)

While the subordinate form *asa-* behaves morphologically like a perfective stem, both verbs lack a distinct perfective stem. The imperative form in (6.31) and jussive in (6.32) are formed on the unmarked stem *a-*. There are no imperative forms for existential.

(6.31) *áishmaŋ atá*
aishmaŋku   a-ta
man   COP-IMP
'be a man!'

(6.32) *núu atí*
nu   a-ti
ANA   exist-JUSS
'let that be'

Although existential and copula *ata* are homophonous in many forms, and share the irregular subordinate form and lack of perfective form, they are distinguished in the plural subject forms, by their different behaviour in interrogation and negation, and by their differing TAM restrictions.

6.4.3 *puhut* 'live'

The intransitive verb *puhut* 'live' has three major senses. Firstly, it simply means 'to be alive'; secondly, it can be used with a locational complement to express either temporary location or permanent dwelling; thirdly, it is used as an auxiliary to form progressive constructions. In the second sense, the distinction between temporary location and permanent dwelling is reflected in the formation of present tense, which takes the imperfective stem if the state is temporary, or the unmarked stem if the state is permanent (example 6.33). As far as I am aware, this is the only verb that can appear in present tense without using the imperfective stem.

(6.33) *chapínum puhúwai*
chapi=numa   puhu-wa-i
Chapi=LOC   live-3-DECL
's/he lives in Chapi (village)'

6.5 Inherently plural verbs

A subclass of verb roots are inherently specified for plurality. That is, there are pairs of verbs that have the same meaning except that one requires plural S (if intransitive) or O (if transitive). The plural argument is always S or O, never A (Durie 1986 and Dixon 1994: 55 point out that this pattern is probably universal in verb roots with inherent number specification). Table 6.19 and Table 6.20 give examples of some intransitive and transitive plural verbs, and their non-plural counterparts.

Table 6.19: Plural S intransitive verb roots

non-plural S	plural S	gloss
puhut	batsat	'live', 'be'
wɨta	ashinat[5]	'go'

Table 6.20: Plural O transitive verb roots

non-plural O	plural O	gloss
maut	amut	'kill'
apuhut[6]	chimpit	'put'

These are not suppletive roots: verbal number marking is always optional in Agua-runa, and the non-plural roots can refer to singular or plural S or O participants, as in the elicited example (6.34) where a non-plural intransitive root takes plural sub-ject marking.

(6.34)   *yúwak puhúinawai*
          yu-a-kũ   puhu-ina-wa-i
          eat-IPFV-SIM+3:SS   live-PL:IPFV-3-DECL
          'they are eating'

There may be more to the distinction than number: *amut* 'kill (plural O)' could be better translated as 'finish off' (it is typically translated by native Aguaruna speakers with the Spanish verb *terminar*) – the choice is similar to that between the English verbs 'kill'/'massacre', of which the second must have a plural object, but the first may have singular or plural. The Aguaruna verb *amut* 'finish off' can also take food or drink as object, e.g. *amuktá* < *amu-ka-ta* (finish.off-PFV-IMP) 'finish (the food or drink) up!', showing that it differs semantically from *maut* 'kill' in more than just number.

---

5 Perhaps < *ashi-na-* (all-VBLZ-)?
6 < *a-puhu-* (CAUS-live)

6.6 Verbalization

Verbs can be derived from nouns (§6.6.1) and from some pronouns and adverbs (§6.6.2).

6.6.1 Verbalization from nouns

There are six processes by which verbs are derived from nouns, listed in Table 6.21 along with the semantic properties of the derived verb and a comment on the productivity of the process.

Table 6.21: Denominal verbalization

suffix	semantics	productivity
-∅	'typical' action (often manipulative)	unproductive
-ma	manipulative – derives a transitive verb	unproductive
-na	attributive – 'to get *noun*'	unproductive
-maɯa	inchoative – 'become *noun*'	productive? but uncommon
-tu	meteorological phenomena	unproductive, only two examples
-tu	onomatopoetic verbs	unproductive

Zero derivation may produce verbs of any transitivity type (examples in 6.35). There is not enough evidence to say for certain which direction the derivation works: perhaps the verb is primary, with a zero-derived noun.

(6.35) hĩɯa 'house' → hĩɯa- 'arrive' (intransitive)
        timashi 'comb' → timashi- 'comb O's hair' (transitive)
        naŋki 'spear' → naŋki- 'throw O at O' (ditransitive)

Verbalization with manipulative -ma always produces a transitive verb. The derived verb has the sense of some typical action associated with the noun, and there is no flexibility. So for example, naŋki-ma (spear-VBLZ) in (6.36) always means 'throw O', and could not mean 'stab'. Example (6.37) shows that manipulative may be added to the possessed form of the noun.

(6.36) hĩɯa 'house' → hĩɯa-ma- 'build O (must be 'house')'
        naŋki 'spear' → naŋki-ma- 'throw O' (cf. naŋkit 'throw at' in 6.35)

(6.37) *paki-hĩ* (lover-PSSD:1PL/3) → *paki-hĩ-ma-* 'fall in love with O'

Manipulative *-ma* was also used to accommodate verbs borrowed from Spanish, as in examples in (6.38), although in contemporary Aguaruna this suffix is not used to nativize borrowed verbs.

(6.38) *kanta-ma* < *cantar* 'sing'
        kuita-ma < *cuidar* 'care for'
        diwi-ma   < *deber*   'owe'

Attributive *-na* derives an intransitive verb meaning 'to get a *noun*'. As with the attributive nominal suffix (see §4.9.1), it is suffixed to the first person plural/third person possessed form of the noun.

(6.39) *paki-hĩ* (lover-PSSD:1PL/3) → *paki-hĩ-na-* 'fall in love'
        nuwĩ   (wife+PSSD:1PL/3)   → *nuwĩ-na-*   'get married'

The first example contrasts with manipulative *-ma* added to the same stem, the latter deriving the transitive verb *paki-hĩ-ma-* (lover-PSSD:1PL/3-VBLZ) 'to fall in love with O'.

Inchoative derives a verb that means simply 'become x' (6.40). It is not very common in my data, but appears in traditional stories in which animals may appear as humans, and origin myths in which people get turned into trees, birds and animals.

(6.40) *aintsu* 'person' → *aintsu-maɰa-* 'become human'
        numi   'tree'   → *numi-maɰa-*   'become a tree'

Two meteorological verbs are derived with the suffix *-tu* (6.41).

(6.41) *ĩtsã* 'sun'   → *itsan-tu-*   'shine (of sun or moon)'
        nasĩ 'wind' → *nasin-tu-*   'blow (of wind)'

The meteorological forms are typically used with an overt cognate subject as in (6.42).

(6.42) *dásĩ dásĩntui*
        dasĩ   dasinta-wa-i
        wind   blow+IPFV-3-DECL
        'the wind is blowing', 'it's windy'

Five onomatopoetic verbs derived with *-tu* represent involuntary oral actions (Table 6.22). The suffix *-tu* is from the verb *tuta* 'say', and the verbs are fossilized speech reports consisting of onomatopoetic representations of the sound described, for example *hachi* represents a sneeze, *hiki* a hiccup.

Table 6.22: Onomatopoetic 'oral action' verbs

verb	gloss
búu-tu-	cry
hachi-tú-	sneeze
hɨkɨ-tú-	hiccup
hukaá-tu-	snore
ūhu-tú-	cough

6.6.2 Derived pro-verbs

Pro-verbs are formed on demonstratives and adverbs, by means of two verbalizers: *-ni* and *-tika*. The derived forms are shown in Table 6.23.

Table 6.23: Derived pro-verbs

root		*-ni*	*-tika*	gloss
proximal demonstrative pronoun	*hu*	*hu-ni-*	*hu-tika-*	'this' / 'do this'
anaphoric pronoun	*nu*	*nu-ni-*	*nu-tika-*	'that' / 'do that'
intensifying adverb	*ima*	*ima-ni-*	*ima-tika-*	'so' / 'do so much'
demonstrative adverb	*aa*	*aa-ni-*	*a-ika-*[7]	'thus' / 'do thus'

The pro-verbs differ in transitivity: those formed with *-ni* are intransitive, those with *-tika* transitive, and they generally agree in transitivity with the verb that they anaphorically represent. In example (6.43), the pro-verb *hunit* refers anaphorically to a description of a dog wandering off instead of staying with his master, and the relevant verb is the intransitive *wita* 'go'. This contrasts with (6.44), referring to a discussion about an unknown assailant who has been killing people, using the

---

7 It is not clear why the /t/ of *-tika* does not appear in this form.

transitive verb *imiŋkaut* 'kidnap'. The pro-verb is transitive *hutikat*, and it includes an object marking suffix, as well as an overt anaphoric object pronoun.[8]

(6.43) *wáŋka húniawa*
       waŋka   hu-ni-a-wa
       why   PROX-VBLZ.INTR-IPFV-3
       'why does (he) do this?' (agr041005_15)

(6.44) *húnash ya hútihamawa*
       hu=na=sha   ya   hu-tika-hama-a-wa
       PROX=ACC=Q.TOP   who   PROX-VBLZ.TR-1PL.OBJ-IPFV-3
       'who is doing this to us?' (agr040712_02)

The pro-verbs are very common in narratives, and are used in bridging constructions to track participants and provide a conceptual link between finite clauses. In addition to the transitivity distinction, the two sets of pro-verbs indicate the anticipated discourse prominence of the subject or object: the *-ni* forms are used where the subject of the verb is to be more topical in what follows, and the *-tika* forms where the object is to be more topical. An illustration of this distinction can be found in the fact that the subordinator *-ma*, which indicates a switch whereby a non-subject of the subordinate verb becomes subject of the controlling verb, only appears with *-tika* forms. On the other hand, the subject nominalizer *-inu* only appears with the *-ni* pro-verbs. Bridging constructions are described more fully in the context of clause combining in §14.8 and in the context of discourse structure in §18.5.

6.7 Auxiliation

Aguaruna makes frequent use of auxiliary verb constructions, by means of which two verbs form a complex predicate. The full verb carries the semantic content of the predicate, while the auxiliary indicates aspectual distinctions and, to some extent, body posture. The auxiliary verb is typically finite, and is marked for tense, person and number, and mood/modality; it may also take a subordinate or other dependent form, as in example (6.55) below. The full verb typically appears in a dependent form, and for most examples it is impossible to tell by grammatical criteria alone whether a given construction is auxiliation or general clause-combining. True auxil-

---

8 Given that the object pronoun is anaphorically referring to the previous stretch of discourse and is not coreferent with the object marked on the verb, this appears to be a ditransitive clause. I do not have sufficient data to comment any further on this.

iary constructions can be shown by morphological evidence to form a single predicate, under the right combination of subject and object (§6.7.2), or when the full verb appears as an unmarked root (§6.7.3). Auxiliation is the only construction in which a bare verb root can appear,[9] and it is clear that such examples must form a single complex predicate since neither finite nor subordinate clauses may be headed by a bare verb root. There is apparently no semantic or structural distinction arising from the form of the full verb, whether dependent-marked or unmarked. There is, however, a two-way distinction between what I label STRONG and WEAK auxiliary constructions which can be observed in the treatment of transitive full verbs (§6.7.4). There are three parameters of variation in auxiliary constructions:

(i)   Choice of auxiliary verb – the copula verb *ata* is distinct from the other types
(ii) Form of the full verb
(iii) Strong versus weak auxiliation

These parameters are apparently unrelated except that use of the copula *ata* as auxiliary limits the possible forms for the full verb.

6.7.1 Auxiliary verbs

Six lexical verbs are used as auxiliaries – there are no exclusively auxiliary verbs. The copula *ata* appears only with nominalized full verbs, forming compound tenses. Five others may be used with all the possible full verb forms described in §6.7.3, and add aspectual senses to the predicate. They are listed in Table 6.24.

Table 6.24: Verbs used as aspectual auxiliaries

verb	lexical meaning	aspect
puhut	'live'	stative
wɨta	'go'	intention
wɨkałɨɰat	'walk'	persistent action
wahat	'stand'	stative + posture
tɨpɨt	'lie down'	stative + posture

---

9 *Pace* Corbera (1994: 220), who states that "uma raiz verbal não aparece sozinha ou despida" [a verbal root does not appear alone or bare].

The auxiliaries are not equally represented in my data: *puhút* 'live' is much more common than the others, and appears more likely to form strong auxiliation constructions.

6.7.2 Clause combining and auxiliation

Given that the full verb may appear in subordinate form, one may wonder why this should be considered auxiliation at all. Consider the examples (6.45, 6.46).

(6.45)   *iháakun mináhai*
          iha-a-ku-nu   mina-ha-i
          visit-IPFV-SIM-1SG:SS   arrive+IPFV-1SG-DECL
          'I have arrived to visit' lit. *I arrive visiting*

(6.46)   *máitasan wɨᶙahai*
          mai-tasa-nu   wɨ-a-ha-i
          bathe+PFV-INTENT-1SG:SS go-IPFV-1SG-DECL
          'I'm going to bathe'

Example (6.45) is a clause-combining construction both morphosyntactically and semantically. Both predicates have semantic content: I am simultaneously visiting and arriving. In (6.46), the relationship is a little less clear. Based on semantics, the independent verb 'go' could be considered to be functionally an auxiliary, parallel to the English intentional/future construction 'I'm going to bathe'. The intentional suffix forms a subordinate verb in Aguaruna, and there is no way to express intention with just one, independent, verb. The question is whether the action of 'going' is a separate proposition, as 'visiting' is in example (6.45), or whether it is there solely to provide a future and intentional sense. Note that there *is* a way to unambiguously indicate that 'going' and 'bathing' are separate propositions, using a sequential temporal clause as in example (6.47).

(6.47)   *wɨnu máithai*
          wɨ-nu   mai-ta-ha-i
          go+PFV+SEQ-1SG:SS   bathe+PFV-IFUT-1SG-DECL
          'I'm going to bathe' lit. *having gone, I'll bathe*

Now consider example (6.48).

(6.48)   *dosmilseistin graduaciónnum wɨtasan puháhai*
          dosmilseis-tin   *graduación*=numa   wɨ-tasa-nu
          2006-TIME   graduation=LOC   go+PFV-INTENT-1SG:SS
          puha-ha-i
          live+IPFV-1SG-DECL
          'I am intending to go to my graduation in 2006' (agr040824_02)

This is clearly an example of auxiliation. As above, it is an intentional subordinate construction, but in (6.48) the finite verb is *puhút* 'live', the semantic content of which is not part of the proposition; it is there to provide a stative aspect to the predicate. A similar structure is used in example (6.49) below. Here, however, the full verb *túta* 'say' is marked with the non-temporal subordinator *-sa*, so there is no morphosyntactic motivation to use an auxiliary, as in the examples above.

(6.49)   *tíma "ayú" tus puháu*
          ti-ma   <u>ayu</u>   tus   puha-u
          say+PFV-NSBJ>SBJ   ok   say+SBD+3:SS   live+IPFV-NMLZ
          'when he said that (to her), she was saying "ok"' (agr040721_07)

The examples just discussed contain two predicates by morphological and syntactic criteria, but semantically appear to consist of just one predication. Now consider example (6.50).

(6.50)   *dakasú áyahai*
          daka-sa-u   a-ya-ha-i
          wait-PFV-NMLZ   COP-REMPST-1SG-DECL
          'I had waited (for someone)'

This is semantically an example of a single predication, namely a periphrastic past tense formed with two verbs. But in example (6.51) a second-person object is added, and here the morphological evidence shows that this is a single predicate.

(6.51)   *dakasú áyahamɨ*
          daka-sa-u   a-ya-hamɨ
          wait-PFV-NMLZ   COP-REMPST-1SG>2SG+DECL
          'I had waited for you'

The combination of first person subject and second person object is marked with a level II suffix (§6.3.1), but the full verb in (6.51) is nominalized and cannot take level II suffixes. So the object marker cannot appear on the full verb, and instead appears on the auxiliary verb. The auxiliary verb *áta* is a copula, and cannot take an object argument, so the construction must derive its transitivity from the main verb. Such examples clearly show that the construction forms a single complex predicate. Unfortunately, such diagnostic cases are not frequent in the data: only with first person subject and second person object is the object marked at level II. Compare example (6.52), with a first-person singular object which is marked at level I and therefore appears on the full verb.

(6.52)   *wáitkau áyumɨ*
          wai-tu-ka-u   a-ya-umɨ-i
          see-1SG.OBJ-PFV-NMLZ   COP-REMPST-2SG:PST-DECL
          'you saw me'

When the full verb consists only of the unmarked root, however, all object suffixes must appear on the auxiliary, as in example (6.53). Note again that the auxiliary does not normally take object markers, as it is intransitive when used as a lexical verb.

(6.53)   *auká túu wɨkáɨtam*
          au=ka   tu   wɨkaɨɯa-tu-a-mɨ
          3=Q   say   walk-1SG.OBJ-IPFV-2
          'Is it him you keep talking to me about?'

We have seen that there are multiverbal constructions that consist of a full verb plus auxiliary, and morphology shows that they form a single predicate when either the object of a transitive full verb is marked on an intransitive auxiliary, or when the full verb appears as a bare root (or both). Constructions that are semantically similar but have no morphological evidence for being a single predicate can be considered to be auxiliation constructions by analogy. In the following sections I consider the possible forms of the full verb and the distinction between strong and weak auxiliation, which hinges on the way mismatches in transitivity between full verb and auxiliary are handled.

6.7.3 Forms of the full verb

The full verb may be:
  (i)   Nominalized
  (ii) Subordinated with *-ku* 'simultaneous'
  (iii) Unmarked root

Of the three possible forms, only the unmarked root is unambiguously auxiliation. In example (6.54), the auxiliary construction with copula *ata* is monoclausal. The full verb is nominalized, and syntactically is part of the subject NP.

(6.54)   *wíi aníau asán, núna wíi ítsiŋhai*
         [wi   ani-a-u   asa-nu]   nu=na   wi
         1sg   think.about-IPFV-NMLZ   COP+SBD-1SG:SS   ANA=ACC   1sg
         itsiha-a-ha-i
         tell-IPFV-1SG-DECL
         'being one who remembers, I tell that (story)' (agr040712_02)

Example (6.55), with a nominalized full verb, shows that the object may come between the full verb and the auxiliary.

(6.55)   *áuhtsuk papínak puhúyahai*
         auhu-tsu-u=ka   papi=na=ka   puhu-ya-ha-i
         study-NEG-NMLZ=TOP   book=ACC=TOP   live-REMPST-1SG-DECL
         'I was not studying books' (agr040824_02)

In example (6.56), the verb *tipa-ĩ* (lie+IPFV+1SG/3-DS) 'lying' functions as an auxiliary to the semantically more contentful but morphologically simple *iwa* 'be awake'.

(6.56)   *káhĩ maám shinták iwá tipǎĩ...*
         [kahĩ   maa-ma]   [shinta-kũ]
         sleep+PSSD:1PL/3   kill+IPFV-NSBJ>SBJ   wake+IPFV-SIM+3:SS
         [iwa   tipa-ĩ]
         be.awake   lie+IPFV+1SG/3-DS
         'when he got sleepy (lit. *when his sleepiness was killing him)*, waking up and lying awake...' (agr040723_29)

Note that the auxiliary verb may still require the applicative suffix, as described below.

6.7.4 Strong and weak auxiliation

In examples (6.57, 6.58) an intransitive auxiliary takes the applicative suffix when combined with a transitive full verb.

(6.57)　　*isák, yúwak puhúhakũĩ...*

isa-kã	[yu-a-kũ	puhu-ha-ku-ĩ]
bite-PFV+SEQ+3:SS	eat-IPFV-SIM+3:SS	live-APPL+IPFV-SIM+1/3-DS

'having bitten (the possum), (the jaguar) was eating it...' (agr041005_21)

(6.58)　　*sínchi puyathúsan díi ikímtuyahai*

sinchi	puyathu-sa-nu	[dii	ikima-tu-ya-ha-i]
strongly	take.interest-SBD-1SG:SS	look	sit-APPL-REMPST-1SG-DECL

'I sat looking at it with great interest' (agr040824_02)

In example (6.58), the full verb is the bare root *dii* 'look', showing that this is true auxiliation. But the use of the applicative suffix to license the (implicit) object shows that the auxiliary verb *ikimat* 'sit' has not been entirely semantically bleached, and still retains its lexical transitivity value.

So there are two levels of auxiliation that are potentially morphologically distinguished: strong auxiliation takes its transitivity from the main verb, while in weak auxiliation the auxiliary verb must agree with the main verb in transitivity. All of the verbs used as auxiliaries are intransitive, so any time one of them is used in a weak auxiliation construction with a transitive main verb, it requires the applicative marker to increase its valency.

In general, the more contentful auxiliaries, particularly those referring to body posture, are less likely to form strong auxiliary constructions. Examples (6.59, 6.60) illustrate weak auxiliation with the auxiliary *tipít* 'lie down'.

(6.59)　　*ámina kuitámkun tipíŋhami*

ami=na	kuitama-a-ku-nu	tipi-hu-a-hami
2sg=ACC	care.for-IPFV-SIM-1SG:SS	lie.down-APPL-IPFV-1SG>2SG+DECL

'I'm lying down looking after you'

(6.60)　　*ámina kuitámhamak tipíŋtamui*

ami=na	kuitama-hama-a-kũ	tipi-hu-tama-a-wa-i
2sg=ACC	care.for-IPFV-2.OBJ-SIM+3:SS	lie.down-APPL-2.OBJ-IPFV-3-DECL

'he's lying down looking after you'

However there is not a clear division between verbs that can take part in strong auxiliation constructions; with *puhút* 'live', for example, the strong auxiliation construction in example (6.61) was judged ungrammatical (compare example 6.51 above, with copula *áta* as auxiliary):

(6.61)   ****dakasú puhúyahami**
           daka-sa-u   puhu-ya-hami
           wait-PFV-NMLZ   live-REMPST-1SG>2SG+DECL
           'I was waiting for you'

But the strong auxiliation in example (6.62) has the same auxiliary verb, *puhút* 'live'.

(6.62)   *ukúu puhám...*
           uku-u   puha-ma
           leave-NMLZ   live+IPFV-NSBJ>SBJ
           'when (the agouti) left (the woman) behind...' (agr040721_07)

The subordinator -*ma* indicates that a non-subject argument of the marked verb is the subject of the controlling verb (see §13.5). In example (6.62), the subject of the controlling verb (the woman) is the object of *ukút* 'leave', while the subordinating suffix is on the intransitive auxiliary *puhút* 'be/live'. Probably also of relevance is the fact that the construction in (6.61) requires the object to be marked with the level II portmanteau suffix -*hami* (1SG>2SG) while that in (6.62) makes use of the subordinator -*ma* that can be used with intransitive verbs.

One could argue that only the strong construction is true auxiliation, while the weak type is actually clause combining. However, examples such as (6.58) provide evidence that weak auxiliation constructions really are monoclausal, as the full verb appears as a bare root, which cannot head a clause of its own. Of course, there will always be a "grey area", as mentioned above, of constructions that are syntactically clause-combining and semantically ambiguous.

7 Grammatical relations and transitivity

Clauses can be broadly classified by two parameters: transitivity and mood. This chapter addresses the first parameter, and describes grammatical relations, transitivity and valency-changing processes in Aguaruna. Mood and modality are addressed in Chapter 9. Grammatical relations in Aguaruna centre on SUBJECT and OBJECT, and the language has a basically nominative-accusative profile. Nominalization, however, contrasts subject with NON-SUBJECT, a grouping which includes oblique roles such as location and instrument (§7.2.2). The same non-subject relation is apparently involved in one of the non-canonical switch-reference markers, although it is less clear in that case (see §13.6). The object relation includes not only semantic patients, but also recipients and beneficiaries, and the two objects of a ditransitive clause share the same morphological and syntactic properties. Verb roots have inherent transitivity values (with some ambitransitivity), and valency can be changed with derivational morphology (§7.7). Objects added by derivation show the same morphological and syntactic properties as those of underived monotransitive and ditransitive clauses. Subjects and SAP objects are indexed with verbal suffixes, and NP arguments are case-marked to show their role in the clause – core arguments take nominative or accusative case. The effects of a person hierarchy can be seen throughout the marking of grammatical relations. There is a preference for divalent, transitive verbs, in which the most agentive participant is mapped to the grammatical role of subject. Semantic experiencers are generally encoded as subjects, and stimuli as objects (like English but unlike Spanish). Verbs of bodily sensation ('be cold', 'be hungry') are generally intransitives, as are meteorological verbs ('the sun shines', 'the wind blows'). Equative/attributive clauses may be verbless, consisting of a subject and a nominal predicate, or copular, with a copula subject and copula complement argument. In equative and attributive clauses the copula is enclitic to the predicate nominal in most TAM configurations, and may be omitted altogether to give a verbless clause in present tense (§7.9).

The predicate itself may consist of just one verb, or a predicate nominal, or it may be a complex predicate consisting of a non-finite main verb and finite auxiliary. The main verb in an auxiliary construction may take a subordinate or nominalized form, and it is difficult to draw a sharp distinction between auxiliation and clause-combining constructions in which both verbs carry semantic content. Auxiliary constructions consisting of a main verb and an auxiliary verb are monoclausal, the two verbs form a complex predicate, and transitivity is determined by the main verb. What I label weak auxiliary constructions are similarly monoclausal, but the transitivity value is not shared between the two verbs. Both types of auxiliary constructions have grammaticalized from multiclausal constructions, and some synchronically multiclausal constructions are very similar on the surface. See §6.7 for a full description of auxiliation.

There is a strong predicate-final tendency in all clause types: this is obligatory in subordinate clauses, while finite clauses show variation for pragmatic purposes. Constituent ordering is discussed in more detail in §18.1. In the following sections I first discuss syntactic constituency (§7.1), then go on to describe the properties of core arguments (§7.2, §7.3). In §7.4 I discuss oblique participants. §7.6 and §7.7 address transitivity and valency changing, and §7.8 and §7.9 describe copular and verbless clauses.

7.1 Syntactic constituency

A clause consists of a single predicate and its associated arguments. Overt expression of arguments as NPs is not obligatory, so a clause may consist minimally of just the predicate; it is very common for subordinate clauses in clause chains to consist of only an appropriately inflected verb. The basic multi-clause unit is a CLAUSE CHAIN, consisting of one or more subordinate clauses associated with a single finite clause. Typically, every clause in a narrative is linked to the preceding and following clause, either through subordination or a bridging construction, and there is no clear line to be drawn between syntactic and pragmatic levels of linking. Judging by semantic criteria, it is difficult to treat a clause chain as equivalent to the *sentence* of traditional grammar, as the subordinate clauses may form part of the main event line; consequently I avoid the term *sentence* in my description of Aguaruna. Issues related to multiclausal constructions are all discussed in Chapter 14, while the present chapter focuses on relations within the clause.

7.2 Grammatical relations

Aguaruna has a robust nominative-accusative profile manifested through case marking of noun phrases (dependent marking), verbal marking of objects (head marking), and also apparent in switch-reference behaviour and participant nominalizations. For the following discussion I find it useful to label grammatical functions following Dixon's (1994, 2010) terminology: S is defined as the single core participant of an intransitive clause; A the most agentive participant of a transitive clause; O the second core participant of a transitive clause, and the most patient-like participant of a ditransitive clause; and E the third, recipient-like, participant of a ditransitive clause. I also use the label E_{APPL} to designate the argument added by applicative derivation. Figure 7.1 sets out the grammatical roles of Aguaruna as groupings of grammatical functions. The primary distinction is between subject (S and A, as well as Copula Subject) and object (O, E and E_{APPL}). A second, less pervasive, grammatical opposition is that of subject versus non-subject; this is exploited in forming nominalizations using the non-subject nominalizers *-taĩ* and *-mau* (§15.4.2) (and perhaps in non-canonical switch reference with the marker *-ma*, §13.5). The resulting forms can refer to any non-subject participant of the clause, whether object or oblique (typically location or instrument). The recipient-like E argument projected by ditransitive verbs, and the beneficiary-like E$_{APPL}$ argument added by the applicative derivation are treated identically, but some object-marking strategies can be shown to be manifestations of a preference for E/E$_{APPL}$ to be higher on a person hierarchy than O arguments (discussed in §7.3).

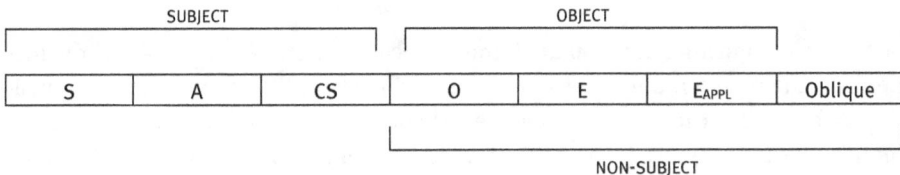

Figure 7.1: Grammatical roles and their groupings

There are just two grammatical phenomena where S and A do not pattern together: inherently plural verbs are selected for plural S or O (see §6.5), and two perfective suffixes *-a* 'high affectedness' and *-i(ni)* 'low affectedness' are selected based on the affectedness of S or O (see §8.3.1).

The marking of grammatical roles shows some effects of the person hierarchy in Figure 7.2.[1]

1 > 2 > 3

Figure 7.2: Person hierarchy

Effects of this hierarchy are manifested in two areas relating to object marking. Firstly, verbal object marking appears in morphological slot B (see Figure 6.2 in §6.1) only when the subject is lower on the hierarchy than the object. When the subject outranks the object, the object marker follows the subject marker in slot F (in practice this applies only to clauses with first person subject and second person object, as third person objects are not overtly marked on the verb). This effect is discussed further in §7.3. Secondly, there is a preference in ditransitive clauses for the E or E$_{APPL}$ object to be higher ranked than the O, and various strategies are applied to

---

1 In the previous version of this grammar (Overall 2007) I proposed a hierarchy that separated 1sg and 2sg from 1pl/2pl, but subsequent research has shown that this was unnecessary.

avoid violations of this preference. A third phenomenon is only partially attributable to the hierarchy: there is a scenario-conditioned split in accusative case marking of objects when the subject is first plural or second person. In such clauses, lower ranked objects (i.e. third person) are unmarked while higher ranked objects (i.e. first person) are marked. As the effects of the hierarchy are seen in object marking, they are described in section §7.3 below. In the remainder of this section I define the grammatical relations of Aguaruna.

7.2.1 Subject

SUBJECT is the most readily apparent grammatical relation. No grammatical distinction is made between the subject of an intransitive verb (S) and subject of a transitive verb (A), both receive the same verbal subject markers and nominative case-marking, as in examples (7.1) and (7.2) where the same pronominal form *wi* and the same suffix *-ha* encode first person singular subject.

(7.1)   *wíi wíɯahai*
         [wi]ₙₚ:ₛ wɨ-a-ha-i
         1sg   go-IPFV-1SG-DECL
         'Is am going'

(7.2)   *wíi atashún yuwáthai*
         [wi]ₙₚ:ₐ [atashu=na]ₙₚ:ₒ   yu-a-ta-ha-i
         1sg   chicken=ACC   eat-PFV-IFUT-1SG-DECL
         'Iₐ am going to eat chicken'

Similarly, the subject of an equative/attributive or copula clause is treated identically to S and A, as in example (7.3).

(7.3)   *wíi awahúnithai*
         [wi]ₙₚ:ₒₛ awahuni=ita-ha-i
         1sg   Aguaruna=COP-1SG-DECL
         'Ics am (an) Aguaruna'

The same identity of S, A and CS holds for all persons and all types of noun phrase, whether lexical or pronominal. The following morphosyntactic properties are criterial for subjecthood:
A. Verbal suffixes cross-reference the subject in finite clauses.
B. Subject NPs appear in the unmarked nominative case.

C. Canonical and non-canonical switch-reference are sensitive to subjects (see Chapter 13).
D. The participant nominalizers *-inu* and *-u* refer to the subject of the verb (see Chapter 15).

Semantically, the subject is prototypically an agent, and always encodes the most agentive or animate participant. For verbs of emotion and perception the experiencer is the subject, and the stimulus, if present, the object. For meteorological verbs, the weather phenomenon is the subject, as in example (7.4).

(7.4)   *yúmi yútawai*
         [yumi]_{NP:S}   yuta-wa-i
         rain_{NOUN}   rain_{VERB}+IPFV-3-DECL
         'it's raining' lit. *rain is raining*

Subjects typically appear in clause-initial position, and subjects of verbless clauses typically take the topic enclitic *=ka* (Chapter 18).

7.2.2 Object and non-subject

The OBJECT relation covers the grammatical functions O and E, that is, notional direct and indirect objects, as well as those added by applicative (E_{APPL}) and causative derivation. Semantically, objects include patients and themes as well as recipients and beneficiaries/maleficiaries, and also stimuli of verbs of perception. Objects are distinguished by the following morphosyntactic properties:
A. Accusative case marking (with regular exceptions, described below).
B. SAP objects marked on verb.
C. Controller of non-canonical switch-reference subordinator *-tatamana*: subject of the marked clause is coreferent with an object of the controlling clause (§13.5).

The three properties A–C also distinguish objects from oblique arguments. Objects and obliques are grouped together into a general NON-SUBJECT role through the following shared properties:
A. Potential target for non-subject nominalization with *-taĩ* and *-mau* (Chapter 15).
B. Controller of non-canonical switch-reference subordinator *-ma*: a non-subject in the marked clause is coreferent with subject of the controlling clause (§13.5).

In the following sections I describe the morphological marking of objects and the person hierarchy effects evident in the system.

7.3 Object marking and hierarchy effects

In keeping with the mixed head and dependent-marking nature of Aguaruna grammar, objects are indexed through a combination of verbal suffixes and case marking on the object noun phrase. The following sections describe both marking strategies in turn.

7.3.1 Verbal marking of objects in monotransitive clauses

SAP objects are indexed with verbal suffixes, but third-person objects never are; compare (7.5a) and (7.5b) with (7.5c).[2]

(7.5) a. *isatkáttawai*
         isa-tu-ka-tata-wa-i
         bite-1SG.OBJ-PFV-FUT-3-DECL
         'it will bite me'

     b. *isaŋpáktatui*
         isa-hapa-ka-tata-wa-i
         bite-2.OBJ-PFV-FUT-3-DECL
         'it will bite you'

     c. *isáktatui*
         isa-ka-tata-wa-i
         bite-PFV-FUT-3-DECL
         'it will bite (him/her/it/them)'

The object markers appear close to the verb root (slot B in Figure 6.2), preceded by valency changing morphology and followed by aspect marking. The exception is the combination of first person subject and second person object, which is marked with a portmanteau suffix in the subject marking slot (slot F in Figure 6.2). This suffix has the form *-hami* if both arguments are singular, as in example (7.6), and *-himi* otherwise, as in example (7.7).

(7.6)   *wainkáthami*
          waina-ka-ta-hami
          see-PFV-IFUT-1SG>2SG+DECL
          'I will see you (sg.)'

---

2 See §6.3.1 for details of the object marking suffixes.

(7.7)   *wainkáthimɨ*
         waina-ka-ta-himɨ
         see-PFV-IFUT-[1>2]PL+DECL
         'I will see you (pl.)' or 'we will see you (sg.)' or 'we will see you (pl.)'

The distinct marking strategy for situations in which a first person subject acts on a second person object can be attributed to the person hierarchy (Figure 7.2) and a corresponding grammatical role hierarchy that ranks transitive subjects over objects (Figure 7.3).

A > O

Figure 7.3: Role hierarchy in transitive clause object marking

These hierarchies together define DIRECT and INVERSE situations, which in turn predict the marking pattern. A direct situation is one in which the hierarchies harmonize, and an inverse situation is one in which they do not, as shown schematically in Figure 7.4. The values "high" and "low" relate to the position on the person hierarchy.

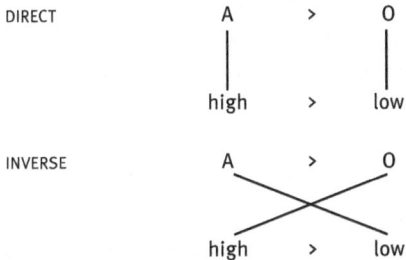

Figure 7.4: Direct and inverse situations (after Zúñiga 2006: 24)

In Aguaruna, inverse situations are characterized by the presence of an object suffix in slot B. In direct situations, when the hierarchies do harmonize, the object is marked along with the subject in slot F if it is second person, or unmarked if it is third person. We will see below that for multiple object clauses, E and E_APPL are ranked above O and a similar pattern of marking disharmonic configurations holds.

7.3.2 Verbal marking of objects in multiple object clauses

Where a verb takes more than one object, only the highest of them (according to the person hierarchy) is indexed on the verb, whether O, E or E_APPL. In example (7.8) there are two objects: third person O and first singular E, and first singular is marked.

(7.8)   *mína suhustá*
          [mi=na]_E   su-hu-sa-ta
          1sg=ACC   give-1SG.OBJ-PFV-IMP
          'give (it) to me'

Example (7.9) has three objects: third person O ('the book') and E ('your father'), and first singular E_APPL, a beneficiary added by the applicative derivation. Again the first person object is marked on the verb.

(7.9)   *huhú papí ápa suhuttsáta*
          [huhu   papi]_O   [apa]_E   su-hu-tu-sa-ta
          PROX   book   father:PSSD:2   give-APPL-1SG.OBJ-PFV-IMP
          'give this book to your father for me'

The choice of which object to mark obeys the person hierarchy in Figure 7.2, such that first person arguments will be given preference, followed by second person. This is expressed with rule (A):

(A)   The highest ranked object is marked on the verb

The role hierarchy that defines direction in simple transitive clauses (Figure 7.3) can be extended to the other object grammatical functions, with E_APPL ranked highest, and E outranking O (Figure 7.5).

$$E_{APPL} > E > O$$

Figure 7.5: Hierarchy within object functions

The preference is for this hierarchy to harmonize with the person hierarchy. A disharmonic configuration, in which the O outranks the E, is a DITRANSITIVE INVERSE situation (following Haspelmath's 2007 terminology); in such situations the applicative marker appears. Use of the applicative marker can be seen as a syntactic promotion (from O to E_APPL), with the marked SAP object being interpreted by preference as E_APPL, therefore the highest role. At the same time as this promotion strategy, a notional E argument may be demoted to an oblique NP with locative case marking (example 7.11); this process can also be seen as non-canonical object marking. Because the rearrangement of roles is purely syntactic, however, I prefer to analyse the applicative marker as explicitly marking a ditransitive inverse situation. That is, the applicative marker signals that the marked object does not occupy the highest ranked grammatical function. Use of the applicative marker to mark inversion means that it is no longer available for its usual function of adding a beneficiary type object, and some examples below illustrate strategies to express a notional beneficiary without adding a grammatical object. These include placing a notional beneficiary into a different (subordinate) clause, so that it is no longer within the valency of the same verb as the higher-ranked O (example 7.13), and placing a notional beneficiary in an oblique locative-marked noun phrase translating as "in X's name" (example 7.16).

We saw above examples with SAP O (7.5), and with SAP E and third person O (7.8), and in both types it was the SAP object that was marked on the verb. This is hardly surprising, since third person objects are never marked; but the question remains, what happens in clauses with two SAP objects? In seeking to answer this question through elicitation, I found that in general, such configurations are simply avoided (avoidance strategies are discussed below). This preference for no more than one SAP object of a clause can be expressed as (B).

(B)   Avoid clauses with more than one SAP object.

(B) is apparently not an absolute rule, but a preference. Consider example (7.10), obtained through elicitation, which has two SAP objects: second person O and first singular E. As predicted by rule (A), the first singular object is the one marked on the verb, and as this is a direct scenario there is no applicative marking or non-canonical object marking.[3]

---

3 Note that there are no natural examples in my corpus of two SAP objects co-occurring in one clause, and the bulk of the data for this discussion were gathered from elicitation. I was fortunate enough to work with some highly imaginative and insightful Aguaruna speakers during the elicitation process, and I acknowledge in particular the input of Abiut Nanchijam to this section. The reader is reminded that the elicited sentences relate to hypothetical and often fanciful situations and must not be read as representative of Aguaruna cultural values.

(7.10)   *ápa ámina "míhãĩ nuwȋnati" tus suhustínȋ*

[apa]	[ami=na]	mi=haĩ	nuwȋna-ti
father:PSSD:2	2sg=ACC	1sg=COM	marry+PFV-JUSS

tus	su-hu-sa-tinu=ȋ
say+SBD+3:SS	give-1SG.OBJ-PFV-FUT+NMLZ=NONVIS.COP:3

'your father will give you to me to marry' lit. *saying "let her marry me"*[4]

In contrast, in example (7.11) the underlying semantic structure has first person singular O and second person E, an inverse scenario. The first person singular O is the one marked on the verb, as the highest ranked participant on the person hierarchy, and the applicative suffix is used to mark this as a ditransitive inverse situation. (Alternatively, one could say that the notional 1sg O is recast as an E$_{APPL}$ argument through the use of the applicative suffix.) At the same time, the semantic recipient (and notional E) is marked as an oblique NP with locative case.

(7.11)   *mína apáŋ áminȋ suhutkáttawai "nuwȋnati" tus*

[mi=na	apa-hu]	[ami=nȋ]
1sg=ACC	father-PSSD:1SG	2sg=LOC

su-hu-tu-ka-tata-wa-i		
give-APPL-1SG.OBJ-PFV-FUT-3-DECL	nuwȋna-ti	tus
	marry+PFV-JUSS	say+SBD+3:SS

'my father will give me to you to marry'

Note that the semantic roles have not been rearranged: the verb *suta* 'give' still requires two object arguments, and both are represented in the clause structure. The rearrangement of grammatical functions is purely syntactic. Because of this, the use of applicative marking is best analysed as a marker of ditransitive inversion rather than as true valency increasing derivation in this example.

In the similar example (7.12), the context is that a girl's father tells her he is planning to give her away in marriage, and she expresses her desire to marry José. The third person E takes locative case, and the first person O requires the applicative marker.

(7.12)   *"Joséyãĩ suhutkáti" tusán wakȋɰahai*

José=ĩ	su-hu-tu-ka-ti	tu-sa-nu
José=LOC	give-APPL-1SG.OBJ-PFV-JUSS	say-SBD-1SG:SS

wakȋɰa-a-ha-i
want-IPFV-1SG-DECL

'I want you to give me to José' lit. *I want, saying "let him give me to José"*

---

4 The current speaker is referred to with a first person pronoun in the speech report – see §17.1 for a description of deictic-centre shift in speech reports.

In (7.13), the notional E, the jaguar, is not overtly included in the same clause as the first singular O. Instead, it appears in a speech report encoding a purpose clause (described in §14.4). Regular marking of O and E, both verbal and nominal, is completely absent, but as with the previous examples the underlying semantic argument structure remains.

(7.13)   *wáŋka "ikámȳãw̃ãã yuwáti" túsamɨsh suhútkattamɨ*
           waŋka   [ikam yawaã   yu-a-ti   tu-sa-mɨ=sha]
           why   jaguar   eat-PFV-JUSS   say-SBD-2=Q.TOP
           su-hu-tu-ka-tata-mɨ
           give-APPL-1SG.OBJ-PFV-FUT-2
           'why are you going to give me to the jaguar to eat?'

As noted above, the extended function of the applicative suffix as a marker of ditransitive inverse situations means that it is not available to mark applicativization. Consequently, there is a preference to avoid adding an applicative object to a clause that already has a SAP object. Consider example (7.14), in which a third person E_APPL is added to a clause with second person O, producing a disharmonic clause.

(7.14)   *wíi ámina suwímhuattahamɨ*
           [wi]   [ami=na]   suwima-hu-a-tata-hamɨ
           1sg   2sg=ACC   beat-APPL-PFV-FUT-1SG>2SG+DECL
           'I will beat you for him/her'

Out of context, the preferred reading for example (7.14) is 'I will beat someone for you', interpreting the second person object as E_APPL and assuming a third person O. This ambiguity explains why adding an E_APPL to a clause that already contains a SAP object is generally avoided. This preference can be expressed as (C):

(C)   Avoid adding applicative derivation to a clause with a SAP object.

Consider example (7.15), with a second person O and first singular notional beneficiary. Although the notional beneficiary outranks the O, if it were marked as E_APPL there would be competition for the object marking slot and the second person O would have to go unmarked. This is avoided by placing the first singular argument in a subordinate purpose clause – note that this is the same construction used in example (7.13) above.

(7.15)　　　*ámina ináŋtamkattawai "mína yuwáti" tus*
　　　　　　[ami=na]　　inahu-tama-ka-tata-wa-i　　[mi=na　　　yu-a-ti
　　　　　　2sg=ACC　　cook-2.OBJ-PFV-FUT-3-DECL　　1sg=ACC　　eat-PFV-JUSS
　　　　　　tus]
　　　　　　say+SBD+3:SS
　　　　　　's/he will cook you for me to eat'

In example (7.16), the notional beneficiary ('my wife') is marked in an oblique NP, as the E_{APPL} slot is already filled by first singular.

(7.16)　　　*mína duwahún náahin huhú papí ápa suhuttsáta*
　　　　　　[mi=na　　　nuwa-hu=na　　　　　naa-hĩ=nĩ]　　　　　　　[huhu
　　　　　　1sg=ACC　　woman-PSSD:1SG=ACC　　name-PSSD:1PL/3=LOC　　PROX
　　　　　　papi]　　　[apa]　　　　　su-hu-tu-sa-ta
　　　　　　book　　　father:PSSD:2　　give-APPL-1SG.OBJ-PFV-IMP
　　　　　　'give this book to your father for me, on my wife's behalf' lit. *in my wife's name*

Similarly, in example (7.17) the second person notional beneficiary appears in an oblique NP.

(7.17)　　　*mína suwímhuattawai ámina náaŋmin*
　　　　　　[mi=na]　　suwima-hu-a-tata-wa-i　　　[ami=na
　　　　　　1sg=ACC　　beat-1SG.OBJ-PFV-FUT-3-DECL　　2sg=ACC
　　　　　　naa-hu-mi=nĩ]
　　　　　　name-PSSD-2=LOC
　　　　　　'he will beat me for you' lit. *in your name*

This construction using the noun *naa* 'name' as a locative marked argument is perhaps calqued from the structurally identical Spanish usage, for example *en su nombre* 'in his/her name'.

I noted above that the strategy of marking ditransitive inverse with the applicative suffix and non-canonical locative case marking of O were purely syntactic, as they do not rearrange the underlying argument structure of the clause. It is possible, however, to avoid potentially ambiguous clause structures entirely in some cases. Example (7.18) illustrates a semantic beneficiary (and potential E_{APPL}) couched in a subordinate clause. The semantic import of this example could be paraphrased 'he will tell you for his mother', but this would involve an E_{APPL} object being added to a clause that already contains a SAP O.

(7.18)   *"dukuhǐ uhathúkta" tíma, uhapáktatui*
           [duku-hǐ   uha-tu-hu-ka-ta   ti-ma]
           mother-PSSD:1PL/3   tell-APPL-1SG.OBJ-PFV-IMP   say+PFV-NSBJ>SBJ
           uha-pa-ka-tata-u-i
           tell-2.OBJ-PFV-FUT-3-DECL
           'his mother having said "tell him for me!", he will tell you'

Example (7.19) illustrates a similar strategy: the notional beneficiary is represented as part of the O NP, that is, "our (baby, dog etc.)".

(7.19)   *átum hutínu kuitámkattahumɨ*
           [atumɨ]   [huti-nau]   kuitama-ka-tata-humɨ
           2pl   1pl-POSS   care.for-PFV-FUT-2PL+DECL
           'you_PL will look after our one (for us)'

Finally, in example (7.20), the O argument is a discontinuous NP, with the post-verbal part representing the beneficiary; so the possessive marker is functionally simulating a 'benefactive' case (see discussion in §5.9).

(7.20)   *numín tsupíktahai mína nuwánun*
           [numi=na]   tsupi-ka-ta-ha-i   [mi=na   nuwa-nau=na]
           tree=ACC   cut-PFV-IFUT-1SG-DECL   1sg=ACC   woman-POSS=ACC
           'I'll cut wood for my wife' lit. *I'll cut my wife's wood*

It would be stretching the facts to describe these as examples of non-canonical beneficiary marking, however they do give some idea of how speakers of Aguaruna can communicate situations involving semantic beneficiaries without violating the grammatical preferences described above.

    The data presented in this section have demonstrated the effects of a hierarchy that distinguishes three types of object: O, E and E_APPL. The distinction is only apparent through testing of very subtle properties, and in the case of the data above, through elicitation of examples – I have found no naturally occurring examples that demonstrate these effects. For all other grammatical purposes, O, E and E_APPL are treated identically as members of the OBJECT grammatical relation, and I find this to be the most useful label to apply in this grammar.

7.3.3 Case marking of object NPs

Object NPs are marked with the accusative case enclitic =*na*, except where a second person or first plural subject acts on a third person object. When the subject is first person singular or third person, all object NPs take accusative case, but when the subject is first person plural or second person, third person objects appear in the unmarked nominative case. Compare the examples in (7.21–7.23), with accusative marking, with those in (7.24–7.26), in which the object NPs lack accusative case.

(7.21) *tsabaún yuwáti*
        [tsabau=na]$_{NP:O}$ yu-a-ti
        banana=ACC   eat-PFV-JUSS
        'let him/her eat a banana!'

(7.22) *kuchín maáŋmɨ*
        [kuchi=na]$_{NP:O}$ maa-aha-mɨ
        pig=ACC   kill+PFV-PL-RECPST:3:DECL
        'they killed a pig'

(7.23) *atashún yuwáttahai*
        [atashu=na]$_{NP:O}$ yu-a-tata-ha-i
        chicken=ACC   eat-PFV-FUT-1SG-DECL
        'I will eat chicken'

(7.24) *nɨ̃ ɨ̈mata*
        [nɨ̃]$_{NP:O}$ ɨɨma-ta
        3sg   carry+PFV-IMP
        '(you$_{SG}$) carry him!'

(7.25) *kúchi maámuŋmɨ*
        [kuchi]$_{NP:O}$ maa-ma-uhumɨ
        pig   kill+PFV-RECPST-2PL
        'you$_{PL}$ killed a pig'

(7.26) *atásh yuwáttahi*
        [atashu]$_{NP:O}$ yu-a-tata-hi
        chicken   eat-PFV-FUT-1PL
        'we will eat chicken'

SAP objects are marked on the verb and with accusative case on the pronoun (7.27–7.29).

(7.27)   *mína huhuktá*
        [mi=na]_{NP:O}   hu-hu-ki-ta
        1sg=ACC   carry-1SG.OBJ-PFV-IMP
        'carry me!'

(7.28)   *mína suhustá*
        [mi=na]_{NP:E}   su-hu-sa-ta
        1sg=ACC   give-1SG.OBJ-PFV-IMP
        'give (it) to me!'

(7.29)   *hutíi áidauti dakastáthimi ámina*
        [hutii   a-ina-u=ti]_{NP:A}   daka-sa-tata-himi
        1pl   COP-PL:IPFV-NMLZ=SAP   wait.for-PFV-FUT-1PL>2PL+DECL
        [ami=na]_{NP:O}
        2sg=ACC
        'we will wait for you'

Objects in nominative case saturate the valency of a transitive verb; there is no possibility of adding another core argument, whether unmarked or accusative-marked. With respect to switch-reference and nominalization, unmarked objects behave identically to other objects, and there is no motivation to recognize them as anything other than object arguments.

It is tempting to try to derive the split accusative marking from the same hierarchy (Figure 7.2) that was shown to motivate the direct/inverse pattern of verbal object marking, and at first glance this looks like a viable analysis. Consider the pattern of accusative case marking in two argument configurations involving second person subject, as in Table 7.1: when the object outranks the subject (i.e. 2sg A > 1sg O), accusative case marking is present, but when the subject outranks the object (2sg A > 3sg O) it is not.

Table 7.1: Accusative case marking in clauses with second person subject

subject	object	direction	ACC marking
2sg	1sg	inverse	yes
2sg	3sg	direct	no

This fragment of the paradigm suggests that it is the direct/inverse distinction that motivates the presence or absence of accusative marking on object NPs. But the analysis breaks down in clauses with first person singular subject, in which all object NPs are marked with accusative case (Table 7.2). The data from verbal object marking clearly indicate first person as the highest ranked value on the hierarchy, and we would therefore expect that it would never trigger accusative case marking.

Table 7.2: Accusative case marking in clauses with first person singular subject

subject	object	direction	ACC marking
1sg	2sg	direct	yes
1sg	3sg	direct	yes

Furthermore, first person plural and second person do not show any asymmetry – all SAP objects always receive accusative case marking. In short, there is simply no way to relate the whole phenomenon of split accusative marking to the person hierarchy without some unwarranted analytic contortions. The fact remains, however, that unmarked objects only ever appear in (a subset of) direct clauses, with SAP subject and third person object; and all inverse clauses involve accusative marked objects.[5]

7.4 Covert core participants

Subject and object NPs are not obligatorily overt. Aguaruna is a largely head-marking language, with extensive switch-reference marking, and this combined with context are typically sufficient to avoid ambiguity of reference. There is apparently no syntactic context in which an NP argument of a finite verb is obligatorily covert. In same-subject complement clauses the tendency is that the common argument will not surface, but this is probably not a strict rule (see discussion in §17.2). The potential absence of overt object arguments raises the question of how to define transitivity, and this question is addressed in §7.6 below. Switch-reference is described in general terms in Chapter 13, and its functions Chapter 14. Reference tracking in discourse is described in §18.3.

7.5 Oblique participants

An oblique participant is one that is neither subject nor object by the definitions given above. Four oblique nominal cases are morphologically marked: comitative,

---

5 The previous version of this grammar (Overall 2007) included examples that suggested some asymmetry between second person singular and first person plural. Subsequent work has shown that these examples were an artefact of elicitation and not a feature of natural discourse.

locative, instrumental and ablative (see §4.10). A noun phrase marked with any of these cases may function as a clausal modifier. In addition, an ablative-marked noun may function as an oblique NP or as an NP modifier, in which case the ablative marked noun may take nominative or accusative case. Ablative-marked nouns also occasionally appear marked with subordinate verbal person suffixes. Finally, there is a vocative form, normally marked by suppression of apocope and accent-shift to the final vowel (§4.10.8). A vocative-marked noun stands outside the grammatical relations of a clause, even when it is coreferential with a core participant, as in (7.30): the verb *puhut* 'live' is a one-place predicate, and the subject role is filled by the nominative case-marked pronoun. There is no core syntactic role available for the vocative-marked noun. Typically there is some intonational disconnect between a vocative form and the rest of the clause.

(7.30) *yatsuhú, amísh puhámɨk*
        yatsu-hu   amɨ=sha   puha-mɨ=ka
        brother-PSSD:1SG+VOC   2sg=Q.TOP   live+IPFV-2=Q
        'my brother, are you alive?' (typical greeting)

NP arguments may be conjoined through simple juxtaposition (§5.11), and such examples must be distinguished from those verbs that can genuinely take more than two core arguments. Comitative case may conjoin NP arguments, as in (7.31), and it is also used to mark the standard of comparison in a comparative construction (7.32).

(7.31) *wɨ́ mɨ́na nuwáhãɨ̃ mɨnɨ́ttahai*
        wɨ   [mi=na   nuwa=haɨ̃]   mini-tata-ha-i
        1sg   1sg=ACC   woman=COM   arrive+PFV-FUT-1SG-DECL
        'I will arrive with my wife'

(7.32) *úchi kása áuk tunchɨhãɨ̃ bɨtɨkai*
        uchi   kasa=a   au=ka   [tunchi=haɨ̃]
        child   thief=COP:3   DISTREL=TOP   witch.doctor=COM
        bɨtɨka=ai
        equal=COP:3:DECL
        'a child who is a thief is the same (i.e. as bad) as a witch-doctor'
        (agr040712_01)

Oblique cases and their functions are described in Chapter 4.

7.6 Transitivity

Clauses with basic underived verbs may be intransitive, with a single nominative marked subject argument; transitive, with one subject and one object argument; or ditransitive, with one subject and two object arguments. Copular clauses take one nominative marked subject argument, and a second nominal as predicate – this may be a noun, adjective or nominalization. The majority of underived verbs (about two-thirds in text counts) are two-place (transitive) predicates, and almost all the rest are one-place (intransitive) predicates. All one and two-place predicates project the same basic argument structures: S (subject), or A (subject) and O (object); and case-marking is always nominative for subject, and accusative or nominative for object (with the selection of case according to the principles described in §7.3.3 above). There are just three underived ditransitive predicates that I know of (listed in Table 7.3 below). The two object arguments of underived ditransitive clauses are for the most part grammatically identical but evidence presented above (§7.3.2) shows that O and E can be differentiated. Applicative and causative derivations add a grammatical object, and can be applied to all types of verbs, giving up to three objects in a clause. These added objects also pattern in the same way as other objects.

A further semantic property of transitive verbs is relevant to a discussion of valency: a number of verbs are quite flexible in the semantic role of the arguments selected. In particular, two verbs of 'making' and 'building' (what Fleck 2003 calls "artefact construction verbs") may take either the raw material or the artefact as their object. This flexibility combined with the possibility of asyndetic NP coordination can produce constructions such as (7.41) below, which looks on the surface like a "double O" construction. This semantic flexibility is also possible with subjects, for example *tsawaut* can mean 'dawn', with 'day' as its subject, or with a human subject it means 'stay awake until dawn' or 'wake up'. This semantic flexibility is distinct from ambitransitivity, as the argument structure remains the same. Table 7.3 summarizes the possible transitivity values in the language.

Table 7.3: Transitivity values of underived verbs

type	arguments	number in lexicon
Intransitive	S	about 33%
Transitive	A, O	about 66%
Ditransitive *suta* 'give'	A, O, E	1
Double object	A, O_1, O_2	3+
anaiyat 'name'	A, O, <name>	1
Copula	CS, CC	3

The three underived ditransitive verbs are listed in Table 7.4. Note that only for *suta* 'give' do I have evidence to distinguish an O and E argument.

Table 7.4: Underived ditransitive verbs

verb	gloss
suta	'give O to E'
siṷat	'ask O_1 for O_2'
naŋkit	'throw O_1 at O_2'
hǐṷamat	'build O_1 out of O_2'

The three copula verbs are listed in Table 7.5.

Table 7.5: Copula verbs

verb	gloss
ata	'be'
nahanɨt	'<subject> become <complement>'
dɨkapɨt	'<subject> feel oneself to be <complement>'

Two other verbs appear with three core arguments: *hǐṷamat* 'build a house', with one nominative marked subject and two accusative marked objects, and *anaiyat* 'name' with one subject, one accusative marked object and one unmarked object. These unusual case frames are discussed with three-place predicates in §7.6.2, where I suggest that their unusual surface form arises from principles of NP structure.

7.6.1 Basic one and two place predicates

The distinction between one and two-place predicates can be difficult to ascertain, as third-person objects are unmarked on the verb and often not explicitly stated. Clearly then the best test of transitivity is to check the possibility of including an overt object noun phrase in the clause: an intransitive verb will be ungrammatical with an object noun phrase. For example, the verb *kitamat* 'be thirsty' typically appears with no overt object, and an English-speaking analyst might assume it to be intransitive. But an overt object noun phrase is grammatical (7.33), showing that this verb can appear in transitive clauses.

(7.33)   *nihámchin kitámahai*
          nihamanchi=na   kitama-a-ha-i
          masato=ACC   be.thirsty-IPFV-1SG-DECL
          'I'm thirsty for *masato* (manioc beer).'

From this it could be assumed that all instances of the verb *kitamat* 'be thirsty' have an understood object, but in the majority of examples it has no overt NP realization. The situation is more complicated than this, however. Taking as a starting point the idea that "the core arguments must be stated – or else be understood – for the clause to be acceptable and to have sense." (Dixon & Aikhenvald 2000: 2), it is clear that there is no specific understood object in a context-free statement of the clause "I'm thirsty". Instead, we must entertain the possibility that this verb (and others like it) are ambitransitive. To anticipate the more detailed discussion in §7.6.3 below, there are a few verbs, including *kitamat* 'be thirsty', that are best analysed as S=A ambitransitive. For all other transitive verbs, an O argument must be stated or understood; this means it is either already activated (zero anaphora) or is accessible from the extralinguistic context. Inherent transitivity of verb roots is demonstrated by the following factors:

–   Valency-changing derivational processes (§7.7).
–   'High/low affectedness' perfective markers refer to O or S (§8.3).
–   Some verbs subcategorize for plural O or S – never A (§6.5).

The following sections describe the structure of intransitive, transitive and ditransitive clauses.

7.6.1.1 Intransitive clauses
An intransitive clause consists of one core participant, the subject (S), and the predicate. Intransitive predicates can take oblique arguments, as in (7.34a), but these are never obligatory (compare 7.34b).

(7.34) a.   *namaká wíɰahai*
             namaka   wɨ-a-ha-i
             river+LOC   go-IPFV-1SG-DECL
             'I'm going to the river'

       b.   *wíɰahai*
             wɨ-a-ha-i
             go-IPFV-1SG-DECL
             'I'm going'

Because these are one-place predicates, they never appear with an accusative-marked NP, nor is any non-subject participant marked on the verb.

Goal arguments of motion verbs are typically marked with locative case, but some may be unmarked. This could be considered a property of the nouns themselves, rather than the verbs: that is, one could say that there is a class of inherently locational nouns that do not require locative marking. Demonstrative pronouns function the same way, as in (7.35).

(7.35)   *wɨkaɨtáiŋ húu wɨháma*
            wɨkaɨɯa-taɨ̃=ka   hu   wɨ-hama
            walk-NSBJ.NMLZ=TOP   PROX   go+PFV+3-CNTR.EX
            'the path went here!' (Text 1:19)

There is no other evidence for a privileged status for locative arguments of motion verbs.

7.6.1.2 Transitive clauses

A transitive clause has two core participants: the subject (A) and the object (O). As shown above, transitivity is a lexical property of verbs. Thus a transitive clause can be defined as one whose verb is transitive, whether inherently or through the addition of valency-increasing derivation (§7.7). As with the intransitive clause, the NP arguments are not obligatorily overt, but they must be recoverable either anaphorically or from the physical context.

7.6.2 Three-place predicates

Three-place predicates take one subject argument and two objects. There are just three underived three-place predicates. Derived three-place predicates are most commonly formed with the applicative suffix *-hu* / *-tu* (§7.7.2). As discussed above, valency increasing derivation to introduce a semantic beneficiary is avoided in transitive clauses that already have a SAP object (§7.3.2).

7.6.2.1 Ditransitive verbs

A ditransitive verb takes two objects, without requiring any kind of valency increasing operation. Aguaruna has three ditransitive roots that I am aware of: *suta* 'give' (7.36, 7.37), *sɨɯat* 'ask for' (7.38), and *naŋkit* 'throw' (7.39).

(7.36)   *húna ámina dukún susáthai*
          [hu=na]_{NP:O}   [ami=na   duku=na]_{NP:E}   su-sa-ta-ha-i
          PROX=ACC   2sg=ACC   mother:PSSD:2=ACC   give-PFV-IFUT-1SG-DECL
          'I'll give this to your mother'

(7.37)   *mína suhustá*
          [mi=na]_{NP:E}   su-hu-sa-ta
          1sg=ACC   give-1SG.OBJ-PFV-IMP
          'give it to me!'

(7.38)   *uchín awɨmáthai Pablon sɨu̧áti kuchín*
          uchi=na   awɨma-ta-ha-i   [*pablo*=na]_{NP:E?}
          child=ACC   send+PFV-IFUT-1SG-DECL   Pablo=ACC
          sɨu̧a-ti   [kuchi=na]_{NP:O?}
          ask.for+PFV-JUSS   knife=ACC
          'I'll send a child to ask Pablo for a knife'

(7.39)   *machiŋkín naŋkiámhai kayán*
          [machiŋki=na]_{NP:E?}   naŋki-a-ma-ha-i   [kaya=na]_{NP:O?}
          spider.monkey=ACC   throw-PFV-RECPST-1SG-DECL   stone=ACC
          'I threw stones at a spider monkey'

The verb *suta* 'give' is the best attested underived ditransitive verb in my data. In example (7.36), the verb *suta* 'give' takes two NP arguments: *hu* 'this' and *amina duku* 'your mother'. The verb subcategorizes for three arguments, semantically the giver (A), the gift (O) and the recipient (E). The subject appears in nominative case, while the object arguments both take accusative case, and are treated equally with respect to nominalization and switch reference. The distinction between O and E only shows up clearly in the hierarchy effects discussed in §7.3. Although there is no strong evidence to show which argument is O and which E for the verbs *sɨu̧at* 'ask for' and *naŋkit* 'throw at', one potential piece of evidence is that the high-affectedness perfective marker *-a* is used with *naŋkimat* 'throw O' (a simple transitive verb), and the same perfective marker applies to *naŋkit* 'throw at' suggesting that the missile must be the O, i.e. 'throw O at E'.

Other cross-linguistically typical ditransitive verbs are derived stems, e.g. *a-wɨ-tu-* (CAUS-go-APPL-) 'send O to E_{APPL}' (i.e. 'cause O to go for the benefit of E_{APPL}') as in example (7.40); and *i-waina-* (CAUS-see-) 'show O₁ to O₂' (i.e. 'cause O₂ to see O₁').

(7.40)   *wɨi awɨtímhai mína duwahún papín*
          wi   a-wɨ-tu-i-ma-ha-i   [mi=na
          1sg   CAUS-go-APPL-PFV-RECPST-1SG-DECL   1sg=ACC

nuwa-hu=na]_{NP:E.APPL}   [papi=na]_{NP:O}
woman-PSSD:1SG=ACC   letter=ACC
'I sent a letter to my wife'

I have encountered one other apparent 'double O' verb (cf. Fleck 2003: 864ff): *hɨɯãmat* (< *hɨɯã-ma* house-VBLZ) 'make O₁ (must be *hɨɯã* 'house') out of O₂', exemplified in (7.41). Semantically the two object NPs do not fit the prototypical theme and recipient pattern.

(7.41)   *hɨ̃ɯ̃ãmkahai hɨ̃ɯ̃ã́n numín*
         hɨɯãma-ka-ha-i   [hɨɯã=na]_{NP:O}   [numi=na]_{NP:O}
         build-PFV-1SG-DECL   house=ACC   tree=ACC
         'I built a house out of wood'

In example (7.41), both object NPs are semantically patients. Which one should be considered O and which E is not *a priori* apparent, and perhaps both are actually best treated as O arguments. Compare the examples in (7.42) and (7.43).

(7.42)   *wĩi nahánamhai naŋkín*
         wi   nahana-ma-ha-i   [naŋki=na]_{NP:O}
         1sg   make+PFV-RECPST-1SG-DECL   spear=ACC
         'I made a spear'

(7.43)   *shiŋkín nahánamhai*
         [shiŋki=na]_{NP:O}   nahana-ma-ha-i
         stilt.palm=ACC   make+PFV-RECPST-1SG-DECL
         'I made (something) out of stilt palm (Sp: *topa*)'

The verb *nahanat* 'make', like *hɨɯãmat* 'build', can take either the artefact made ('make O') or the material ('make something out of O') as its object. But it is a simple transitive verb, and only one object can appear in a clause. Now compare example (7.44).

(7.44)   *nĩ awɨtími uchihín paámpan yuhúmkan*
         nĩ   a-wɨ-ti-mɨ   [uchi-hĩ=na]_{NP:O}
         3sg   CAUS-go-APPL+PFV-RECPST:3:DECL   child-PSSD:1PL/3=ACC
         [paampa=na]_{NP:O}   [yuhumaka=na]_{NP:O}
         plantain=ACC   manioc=ACC
         'he sent plantains and manioc to his son'

Here we have a derived ditransitive verb *awɨtut* 'send O to E_APPL' (< *a-wɨ-tu* 'CAUS-go-APPL'), but there are three accusative-marked NPs in the clause. The first, *uchihɨ̃* 'his child', is semantically the recipient, the added E_APPL argument. The other two are semantically theme arguments. In fact, this construction is best analysed as asyndetic NP coordination. So the structure is as in (7.45).

(7.45) nĩ   a-wɨ-ti-mɨ̃   [uchi-hɨ̃=na]
        3sg   CAUS-go-APPL+PFV-RECPST:3:DECL   child-PSSD:1PL/3=ACC
        [[paampa=na]   [yuhumaka=na]]_NP:O
        plantain=ACC   manioc=ACC
        'he sent plantains and manioc to his son'

A single object NP is composed of two asyndetically coordinated NPs. Now, if we look back at example (7.41), we can apply the same analysis: there is just one object NP, consisting of two coordinated NPs: *hɨɯ̃ã* 'house' and *numi* 'tree, wood'. This analysis has the advantage that it does not require us to posit any grammatical phenomenon that is not already attested: I noted above that there are some simple transitive verbs that have a certain semantic flexibility, selecting different semantic roles as O. In combination with the "listing" NP coordination strategy [NP ... NP (*aatus*)] described in §5.11, this gives rise to apparent double object constructions. This analysis would mean there is no need to posit a 'double O' transitivity value for the verb *hɨɯ̃ãmat* 'build a house', but it is not clear whether it could apply to the other ditransitive verbs.

7.6.2.2 The verb *anaiyat* 'name'
The verb *anaiyat* 'name' takes three nominal arguments: the name-giver (which takes nominative case), the name-receiver (accusative case), and the name (nominative), as exemplified in (7.46).

(7.46) *wii mína uchihún anáiyakmahai Pablo*
        [wi]_NP:A   [mi=na   uchi-hu=na]_NP:O   anaiya-ka-ma-ha-i
        1sg   1sg=ACC   child-PSSD:1SG=ACC   name-PFV-RECPST-1SG-DECL
        [*pablo*]_NP:NAME
        Pablo
        'I named my son Pablo'

The 'name' argument is similar to a speech report, as it is being used as the word itself, rather than referring to a participant, and the citation form is used. This apparent three-place predicate can be analysed as arising from the apposed name type of NP; compare example (7.47) (repeated from §5.7).

(7.47) *iŋkúnikui namaknúm mahanú*

iŋku-nai-ka-u=ai   [namaka=numa   mahanu]
meet-RECIP-PFV-NMLZ=COP:3:DECL   river=LOC   Marañón
'they met each other at the river Marañón' (agr041005_23)

The name *mahanu* 'Marañón' is treated as being outside of the NP, as can be seen
from the fact that the phrase-level locative case enclitic *=numa* is attached to *namak*
'river' (see §5.7 for details). By this analysis example (7.46) would be a simple transitive, but the O is a discontinuous apposed name NP. We have seen above that the
two parts of a discontinuous NPs may function like separate arguments (cf. §5.9).
The intuitive problem with this analysis is that it does not capture the semantics of
the clause adequately. The concept of naming is much more like a ditransitive than
a simple transitive, implying the argument structure in (7.48).

(7.48)   [I]$_A$ gave [my son]$_E$ [the name Pablo]$_O$

So a more appropriate analysis might be that this is a ditransitive verb that takes an
unmarked O argument, which must be a proper name. By this analysis, the verb
anaiyat 'name' is unique in being the only one to take a non-canonically marked
argument. It bears repeating here that proper names, including those borrowed
from Spanish, are not deficient in case morphology when heading NPs (§4.4), so the
lack of marking on *Pablo* as an O argument is not a property of the name itself, and
must arise from the construction in which it appears.

7.6.3 Ambitransitivity

As mentioned above, first and second-person objects are marked on the verb, but
third-person objects are not. Thus a clause with a third-person object that is not
manifested by an overt object NP does not exactly wear its transitivity on its sleeve:
if there are two overt objects (that are not coordinated), the verb must be ditransitive; if there is one, it could be a simple transitive or ditransitive; and if there is
none, it could be any of the three. There are, however, certain contexts in which the
transitivity distinction is clearly apparent. The clearest is that of valency-changing
derivation. Verbs can be transitivized or (less commonly) detransitivized with derivational suffixes, showing clearly that underived roots must have inherent transitivity values.

The only object-like properties of a non-subject participant of an intransitive
clause relate to: (i) the non-subject nominalizers *-taĩ* and *-mau* which form nominals
referring to a participant associated with the action of the verb (typically instrument, location or O); (ii) the subordinator *-ma*, which indicates that a non-subject

argument of the subordinate clause (typically an object) is coreferential with the subject of the controlling clause.

Because of the possibility of NP ellipsis and the fact that third-person objects are zero-marked on the verb, many instances of lexically transitive verbs could be considered intransitive, and the verbs would thus be S=A ambitransitives. In fact, however, only a few verbs are truly ambitransitive. Non-overt objects may be topical and accessible from the preceding discourse, or pragmatically accessible from the physical context; in those cases we can say that the clause is transitive, with an understood O argument. Consider example (7.49).

(7.49)   *hukíta*
          hu-ki-ta
          take-PFV-IMP
          'take it!'

There are no overt argument NPs in the clause. Second person singular subject is indexed by the use of the imperative suffix, but there is no indexing of an object. For this clause to make sense, however, there must be an understood object; an appropriate context would be if a visitor was admiring some item in the host's house, and the host offered it as a gift. The appropriate translation into English must include the object pronoun 'it'. A few verbs do allow both transitive and intransitive uses. Consider (7.50).

(7.50)   *yuwáumïk*
          yu-a-umï=ka
          eat-PFV-2SG=Q
          'have you eaten?'

There is no object to be understood from context here; 'eating' is treated as a purely subject oriented activity. The same verb can be used transitively with covert objects. Example (7.51) is something a parent might say to a child who is about to put something inedible in its mouth – the object is inferred from the physical context. In (7.52) the object is overtly mentioned in the subordinate clause, and is therefore anaphorically accessible.

(7.51)   *yuwáwaipa*
          yu-aw-ai-pa
          eat-PFV-APPR-2SG:PROH
          'don't eat (it)!'

(7.52)   *kúntin maá yuwámi*
          [kuntinu   ma-a]   [yu-a-mi]
          animal   kill-PFV+1PL:SS   eat-PFV-HORT
          'let's kill and eat animals!' (agr041005_14)

The verbs that I am aware of that do allow S=A ambitransitivity are in the semantic domain of eating and drinking: *yuta* 'eat', (perhaps *umut* 'drink'?), *kitamat* 'be thirsty', *yapahut* 'be hungry' and *ushumat* 'be hungry for meat'.

7.6.3.1 S=O ambitransitivity

There is just one verb in my data for which S=O ambitransitivity can be demonstrated: *isat* translates as 'bite' (example 7.53, with low affectedness perfective suffix *-i(ni)*) or 'devour' (example 7.54, with intensive perfective suffix *-ka*) in its transitive use.

(7.53)   *mína ɨsátnɨ̃*
          mi=na   ɨsa-tu-ini-ɨ̃
          1sg=ACC   bite-1SG.OBJ-PFV-3+DECL
          'it bit me'

(7.54)   *ikámỹãw̃ãã kuchín ɨsákmɨ̃*
          ikam_yawaã   kuchi=na   ɨsa-ka-mɨ̃
          jaguar   pig=ACC   bite-PFV-RECPST:3:DECL
          'the jaguar devoured the pig'

The same verb is used intransitively with the meanings 'burn oneself' (example 7.55, with attenuative *-sa*) or 'burn up' (example 7.56, with intensive *-ka*; note that this example refers metaphorically to a "burned out" (flat) battery). While there is a clear metaphorical path between being bitten or devoured and being burned or consumed by flames, this is also a significant semantic change.

(7.55)   *ɨsáipa*
          ɨsa-i-i-pa
          burn.self-PFV-APPR-2SG:PROH
          'don't burn yourself!'

(7.56)   *pila ɨsakɨ̃*
          pila   ɨsa-ka-ɨ̃
          battery   burn.up-PFV-3:DECL
          'the battery has gone flat'

The perfective suffix *-ka* typically correlates with a high degree of effort on the part of the subject, and thus seems incongruent with an intransitive verb meaning 'burn up' – this suggests that the transitive sense 'devour', which takes the same perfective marker, must be prior to the intransitive.

While there are other examples of related verb pairs differing in transitivity, the majority involve phonological adjustments to the root, most of which are synchronically unproductive (see §7.7). Given the general lack of productivity of valency-reducing morphology, it is perhaps more useful to consider the transitive/intransitive alternation in *ɨsat* to be an unproductive zero-marked detransitivization combined with a metaphorical extension of 'bite'/'devour' > 'get burned'/'be consumed by fire'. In any case, this verb is unique in having two such distinct senses.[6]

7.6.3.2 Ambitransitivity in derived verb forms

Two verb forms always make transitive verbs S=O ambitransitive: the potential stem formed with the suffix *-mai* (examples 7.57, 7.58); and deverbal nouns formed with the future nominalizer *-tinu*, which may refer to either the A or the O of the nominalized verb (example 7.59).

(7.57) *nĩ wainmáinai*
   nĩ   waina-mai-inu=ai
   3sg   see-POT-NMLZ=COP:3:DECL
   'she can see'

(7.58) *píshakak shĩiŋ paán wainmáinai*
   pishaka=ka   shiiha   paanta   waina-mai-inu=ai
   bird=TOP   very   clearly   see-POT-NMLZ=COP:3:DECL
   'the bird can be easily seen'

(7.59) *uwáŋtinun wainkámhai*
   uwa-ha-tinu=na   waina-ka-ma-ha-i
   drink-PFV-FUT+NMLZ=ACC   see-PFV-RECPST-1SG-DECL
   'I saw the beverage that was to be drunk'
   OR
   'I saw the person who will drink'

---

6 Olawsky (2006: 385) notes that Urarina (an isolate also spoken in Northwest Peru) has only one S=O ambitransitive verb, *mukua* which translates as 'burn'.

These examples show another peculiarity of the potential stem, that it typically appears as a nominalized form. Other examples show that it is the stem itself, rather than the nominalized form, that triggers ambitransitivity – compare (7.60) and (7.61).

(7.60)   *antúmaitsui áu kantámauk*
           antu-mai-tsu-u-i   [au   kantama-mau=ka]ₙₚ:ₛ
           hear-POT-NEG-3-DECL   DIST   sing-NSBJ.NMLZ=TOP
           'that song cannot be heard'

(7.61)   *áuk antúmaitsui*
           [au=ka]ₙₚ:ₛ   antu-mai-tsu-u-i
           DIST=TOP   hear-POT-NEG-3-DECL
           'that person cannot hear'

The morphological similarity of the nominalized form *-mai-inu* (POT-NMLZ) to the future nominalizer *-tinu* (<-*ta-inu* IFUT-NMLZ) has probably contributed to the ambitransitivity of nominalizations formed with the future nominalizer. In addition, the fact that *-tinu* is not synchronically parseable into a future marker and a nominalizer must have helped the change, as the nominalizer *-inu* in other uses refers strictly to the subject.

7.6.3.3 Transitivity of *tuta* 'say'

The verb *tuta* 'say' is exceptional, in that it is truly multitransitive. It may appear as transitive, with the object being the speech report, or the object may be the address-ee, or a person about whom the subject says something (as in 7.62).

(7.62)   *tumámiuwai yúwachu*
           tu-mami-u=ai   yu-a-chau
           say-REFL+PFV-NMLZ=COP:3:DECL   eat-IPFV-NEG.NMLZ
           'he said he hadn't eaten anything' (agr041005_28)

The same verb may be applicativized, with the addressee as the added object (7.63).

(7.63)   *minaká túhutam*
           mi=na=ka   tu-hu-tu-a-mɨ
           1sg=ACC=Q   say-APPL-1SG.OBJ-IPFV-2
           'are you talking to me?'

And it may be ditransitive, with the thing said and the addressee as the two objects (7.64).

(7.64)   *mína apahún húna chicháman titáhai*
           [mi=na   apa-hu=na]ₑ   [hu=na   chichama=na]ₒ
           1sg=ACC   father-PSSD:1SG=ACC   PROX=ACC   word=ACC
           ti-ta-ha-i
           say+PFV-IFUT-1SG-DECL
           'I'll say this word to my father'

Given this variation, it must be concluded that the verb *tuta* 'say' functions both as a simple transitive and as a ditransitive verb, uniquely among Aguaruna verbs.

7.7 Valency changing derivation

There are two productive valency-increasing derivations marked in slot A, causative and applicative. Both increase the valency of the verb by one, adding an object to the clause. In the case of causative, there is a rearrangement of roles from the un-derived clause, as the added argument is the subject and the erstwhile subject becomes an object. Applicative straightforwardly adds an object argument, semantically typically a beneficiary but also sometimes maleficiary. Reflexive and reciprocal can function unproductively as valency reducing derivation, and in that role they appear in slot A; they can also appear in slot B, as part of the object marking paradigm. A few verb roots show unproductive phonological alternants with differing transitivity values. In general, the intransitive variant is the more marked member of such pairs. These are described in §7.7.4. Slot A is split into A1, which contains all the forms except applicative, and A2, with applicative. Both slots may be filled.

7.7.1 Causative

Causative verbs are formed by either prefixing a vowel (7.65) or by means of the suffix *-mitika* (7.66).

(7.65)   *atashún ayúhathai*
           [atashu=na]ₒ:CAUS   ayuhu-a-ta-ha-i
           chicken=ACC   CAUS+eat-PFV-IFUT-1SG-DECL
           'I'm going to feed the chickens' (cf. *yu-* 'eat')

(7.66) *anú tawás atsɨ́mtihukta*
        [anu   tawasa]ₒ   atsɨ-mitika-hu-ka-ta
        MED   feather.crown   wear-CAUS-1SG.OBJ-PFV-IMP
        'put that *tawas* on me'

Both have the same effect of increasing valency by adding a subject argument, the causer, while the semantic actor (which would be the subject in a non-causative clause) becomes an object, the causee. The prefixed form seems to be older and more lexicalized: the quality of the vowel is unpredictable on phonological grounds; there may be other phonological changes to the root in addition to the prefixed vowel; and the resulting form may be semantically unpredictable. The suffixing operation is the default, and is generally available only to those verbs that do not have a prefixed causative form, although some verbs may be compatible with both processes. David Payne (1990a) notes both a prefixed vowel and a suffix involving /mV/ as widespread forms marking causative in South American languages.

When a transitive verb is causativized it creates a ditransitive clause, as in (7.67 – note the object *Arias' tawas* is a discontinuous NP). (In the glosses I label the underived object with subscript O, and the derived arguments A:CAUS (causer) and O:CAUS (causee).)

(7.67) *húna uchín tawásan atsɨ́mtikathai Ariasnaun*
        [hu=na   uchi=na]ₒ:CAUS   [tawasa=na]ₒ
        PROX=ACC   child=ACC   feather.crown=ACC
        atsɨ-mitika-ka-ta-ha-i   [*Arias*-nau=na]ₒ
        wear-CAUS-PFV-IFUT-1SG-DECL   Arias-POSS=ACC
        'I'll make this child put on Arias' *tawas* (feather crown)'

Table 7.6 schematically shows the changes in grammatical roles when intransitive and transitive verbs are causativized.

Table 7.6: Changes in grammatical roles under causativization

underived clause	causative clause	meaning
–	Subject (A:CAUS)	Causer
Subject (A/S)	Object (O:CAUS)	Semantic actor, causee
Object (O)	Object (O)	Semantic object

7.7.1.1 Prefixed causative

Table 7.7 lists all the prefixed causative verbs that I am aware of, although this is unlikely to be all that exist in the language.

Table 7.7: Prefixed causative verbs

underived	gloss	causativized	gloss
kɨ̄-	'become night'	i-kin-tu-	'do something every second day'
chicha-	'speak'	i-chachi-	'cause to speak'
kahɨ̄-	'ferment'	i-kahɨ̄-	'make ferment'
waina-	'see'	i-waina-	'show'
kanu-	'sleep'	i-kana-	'give a bed'
ta-	'arrive'	i-ta-	'bring'
tsɨkɨ-	'jump'	i-tsɨkɨ-	'make jump', 'startle'
mɨna-	'be lacking'	i-mɨna-	'reduce'
mɨŋkaɨɰa-	'get lost'	i-mɨŋkau-	'lose'
hɨɰa-	'arrive'	i-hɨɰa-	'cause to arrive, bring to light'
watsa-	'get thin'	i-watsɨ-	'cause to become thin'
chupi-	'get wet'	u-chupi-	'make something wet'
dupa-	'become overgrown'	u-dupɨ-	'allow to become overgrown'
kuŋkuu-	'smell, kiss'	u-kuŋku-	'perfume, season'
kuwa-	'boil'	u-kuwa-	'boil'
kuyū-	'become low (water)'	u-kuyu-	'cause to dry out'
suu-	'suffer'	u-suwa-	'cause to suffer'
ikɨ́-	'fart at someone'	a-íki-	'take a child outside to defecate'
iháŋma-	'diet'	a-íhi-	'put someone on a diet'
nihɨ́-	'have sex with'	a-díhi-	'cause animals to mate'
tipɨ-	'lie down'	a-ipɨ-	'throw down'
puhu-	'live'	a-puhu-	'put'
umu-	'drink'	a-mu-	'give to drink'
wɨ-	'go'	a-wɨɨma-	'send'
ha-	'be sick; die'	a-haku-	'suffer death of a child'
yu-	'eat'	a-yuhu-	'feed'

The prefixed vowel is not predictable on the basis of the phonological shape of the root, but the pattern shown in Table 7.8 suggests that historically the prefixed vowel repeated the first vowel of the root.

Table 7.8: Root vowels and causative prefix

first vowel of root	prefixed vowel
/i/	*i*- or *a*-
/ɨ/	mostly *ɨ*-, some *a*-
/u/	mostly *u*-, some *a*-
/a/	*i*-, *ɨ*- or *a*-

Some of the prefixed causatives show changes to the root in addition to the prefix. *a-haku-* 'cause the death of a child' must be derived from the verb root *ha-*, which means 'be sick' in the imperfective form (*ha-a-* 'be.sick-IPFV') but 'die' when the perfective stem (*ha-ka-* 'die-PFV-') is used. The prefixed causative form is derived from the perfective stem rather than the unmarked root, as it refers to causing death, not illness. *a-ipɨ-* 'lay down' is a causative counterpart to *tipɨ-* 'lie down'. In this example, loss of the initial /t/ is apparently simply an irregular phonological change in a high-frequency verb. The three forms *kɨ̃-* 'become night', *yu-* 'eat', and *wɨ-* 'go' have suffixed syllables added in the causative forms: *i-kin-tu-* 'do every second day'; *a-yu-hu-* 'feed'; and *a-wɨ̈-ma-* 'send'. And there are a few sporadic vowel changes, including a metathetic change of the root *chicha-* 'speak' to causative *i-chachi-*. Finally, there is one example of a prefixed causative verb apparently formed from an adjective: *piŋkɨŋ* /piŋkɨha/ 'good' has the causative verbal counterpart *i-piŋkɨ-* 'resolve' i.e. 'make good'.

Semantically, the prefixed causatives are not always compositional. The form *a-haku-* 'suffer death of a child' was already mentioned; this is clearly more specific than simply 'cause to die'. Another example is *i-kin-tu-* 'do every second day', which does not mean 'cause to become night' (an impossibility in any case), although the semantic relation between the underived and causative forms is quite easy to see.

7.7.1.2 Suffixed causative

For those verbs that do not have a prefixed causative counterpart, causative is formed with the suffix *-mitika* (7.68–7.70).

(7.68) *uchín tsɨɰáŋmitkatãĩ tupikáu*
  [uchi=na]o:CAUS tsɨɰaha-mitika-taĩ tupika-u
  child=ACC cry-CAUS-SBD:1/3:DS run+IPFV-NMLZ
  'when heᵢ made the children cry, heⱼ came running' (agr040723_29)

(7.69)   *dɨkachu ahakúi uchíŋmitkatnak*
dɨka-chau   a-haku=i
know-NEG.NMLZ   COP-NARR.PST=COP:3:DECL
uchiha-mitika-ta=na=ka
give.birth-CAUS-ACT.NMLZ=ACC=TOP
'(they) didn't know how to make her give birth' (agr041005_16)

(7.70)   *ɨmpɨmtikatakamã...*
ɨmpɨ-mitika-takamã
become.deaf-CAUS-FRUST+3:SS
'trying in vain to deafen (him)...' (agr041005_04)

When causative is followed by a suffix with initial /h/ and its final /a/ is elided, the resulting /kh/ cluster is reduced to /h/ (7.71 and 7.72, and see §3.5.4).

(7.71)   *ámɨ mína dushímtihamɨ̃*
[amɨ]A:CAUS   [mi=na]O:CAUS   dushi-mitika-ha-mɨ
2sg   1sg=ACC   laugh-CAUS-1SG.OBJ+IPFV-2SG+DECL
'you are making me laugh'

(7.72)   *kuŋkúumtihuttsata mína uchíŋ*
kuŋkuu-mitika-hu-tu-sa-ta   [mi=na   uchi-hu]O:CAUS
kiss-CAUS-APPL-1SG.OBJ-PFV-IMP   1sg=ACC   child-PSSD:1SG
'have my child kiss (somebody)'

The causative suffix occasionally surfaces as [mika] where [mitka] is expected (7.73).

(7.73)   *nínak nína nuwɨ̃n ahápmikathai*
[nɨ̃=na=ka]O:CAUS   [nɨ̃=na   nuwɨ̃=na]O
3sg=ACC=TOP   3sg=ACC   woman+PSSD:1PL/3=ACC
ahapa-mitika-ta-ha-i
discard-CAUS-IFUT-1SG-DECL
'I'll make him leave his wife'

That this is a surface-level simplification of the cluster /tk/ is apparent from the fact that neither of the vowels is elided. If the underlying form were /ahapa-**mika**-ta-ha-i/, the expected surface form would be **[ahápmiktahai]. Similar simplification of consonant clusters is evident in the historical development of the desiderative suffix *-tata* < *-taŋta* / *-tatta* (§8.4.4) and frustrative *-takama* < *-tatkama* (§13.3.3). Also see the discussion in §3.5.1.

7.7.1.3 Combination of causative and applicative

As I mentioned above, causative in slot A1 can combine with applicative in slot A2, as in example (7.72) above, where applicative adds a beneficiary object. The prefixed causative can also combine with applicative adding a beneficiary, as in (7.74).

(7.74)   *ayuhuthuáta mína atashún*
           ayuhu-tu-hu-a-ta   [mi=na   atashu-hu]o
           CAUS+eat-APPL-1SG.OBJ-PFV-IMP   1sg=ACC   chicken-PSSD:1SG
           'feed my chickens for me!'

7.7.1.4 Further issues in causative semantics

The prefixing and suffixing causatives are not semantically equivalent. While a suffixed form's meaning is essentially the sum of its parts, corresponding to a semantic higher predicate of causation plus the meaning of the original verb, the prefixed forms rather denote a single event, and some show unexpected semantic narrowing, as noted above. The prefixed causatives tend to involve culture-specific meanings and actions. *a-yuhu-* 'feed' < *yu-* 'eat'; *a-mu* 'offer to drink' < *umu-* 'drink'; and *i-kana-* 'give a bed, put up for the night' < *kanu-* 'sleep' all have the sense of offering the means for the causee to do the action of the verb, but not directly causing them to do it; and these are all actions that a host is expected to perform for a guest. *a-haku-* 'suffer death of a child' and *i-tsiki-* 'cause to jump, startle' do not involve control or intention on the part of the causer, but they are common enough experiences for mothers and hunters, respectively.

A given verb will typically have either a prefixed or a suffixed causative form, but I have found one verb that may take both: *tsiki-* 'jump' has the prefixed causative form *i-tsiki-* 'startle' and the suffixed form *tsiki-mitika-* 'make jump'. The choice in this case correlates with a semantic distinction: the prefixed form refers to startling a game animal, without intention from the causer, while the suffixed form is more deliberate, for example one might use it to describe playing with a domestic dog. Example (7.75) is from a text about hunting, describing the process of stalking an animal. Example (7.76) was offered as a possible use of the suffixed causative, where the context would be that someone is showing a dog trained to jump.

(7.75)   *núwĩ shitá shitámhakua "ĩtsikíshtahash" túsa anɨntáimtakua...*
           nu=ĩ   shita   shitama-ha-kawa
           ANA=LOC   REDUP   crawl-APPL+IPFV-REPET+1PL:SS
           i-tsɨkɨ-cha-ta-ha=sha   tu-sa
           CAUS-jump+PFV-NEG-IFUT-1SG=ADD   say-SBD+1PL:SS

anɨntaima-ta-kawa

think-APPL+IPFV-REPET+1PL:SS

'crawling and crawling there, thinking "I won't startle it"' (Text 3:14)

(7.76)   *ỹãw̃ǎ̃ã tsɨkɨ́mtikbau diismí*

yawaã   tsɨkɨ-mitika-mau   dii-sa-mi

dog   jump-CAUS-NSBJ.NMLZ   look-PFV-HORT

'let's see the dog being made to jump!'

The causative construction typically downgrades the causee's volition or choice. A speech report construction may be used to encode causative-like situations in which the (intended) causee has greater choice over whether or not to perform the action (7.77, 7.78).

(7.77)   *nɨ̃́ túhutmɨ̃ "nampɨktá" túsã*

nɨ̃   tu-hu-tu-mɨ̃   [nampɨ-ka-ta

3sg   say-APPL-1SG.OBJ-RECPST:3:DECL   dance-PFV-IMP

tu-sã]

say-SBD+3:SS

'he had me dance / he asked me to dance'

(7.78)   *wíi "susáta" titáhai*

wi   su-sa-ta   ti-ta-ha-i

1sg   give-PFV-IMP   say+PFV-IFUT-1SG-DECL

'I'll make him give it away' lit. *I'll say "give it away"*

7.7.2 Applicative

The applicative derivation can be applied to intransitive, transitive and ditransitive verb roots, as well as to causativized stems, and is marked with a suffix in slot A2. In all cases it increases the valency of the verb, adding an object (labelled E:APPL). Semantically, the added object is typically a beneficiary (as in 7.79) or maleficiary (7.80).

(7.79)   *minásh batáɨ ukuithúkta*

[mi=na=sha]E:APPL   [bataɨ]O   ukui-tu-hu-ka-ta

1sg=ACC=ADD   chambira   detach-APPL-1SG.OBJ-PFV-IMP

'get some *chambira* (fruit) for me too!'

(7.80)　　*wíi huhúkmahai papín yatsuhún*

      wi　　　　hu-hu-ki-ma-ha-i　　　　　　　　　[papi=na]ₒ

      1sg　　　take-APPL-PFV-RECPST-1sg-DECL　　book=ACC

      [yatsu-hu=na]ₑ:APPL

      brother-PSSD:1SG=ACC

      'I took a book from my brother'

Applicative has two allomorphs, *-hu* and *-tu*. They are in complementary, lexically-conditioned distribution, this differentiation also affects the object marking suffixes in slot B, and the phenomenon as a whole defines two verb classes which I label '*hu* verbs' and '*tu* verbs'. The allomorphy of applicative and object suffixes is discussed in detail in §6.3.

7.7.2.1 Semantics of applicative

Although the added argument is most commonly a beneficiary, maleficiary objects are also relatively common (7.81, 7.82).

(7.81)　　*ámish mína atashún yuhutũáĩ*

      [amichi]ₐ　[mi=na]ₑ:APPL　[atashu=na]ₒ　yu-**hu**-tu-a-ĩ

      fox　　　　1SG=ACC　　　chicken=ACC　eat-APPL-1SG.OBJ-PFV-3+DECL

      'a fox ate my chicken'

(7.82)　　*ámina balán iŋkithámkamĩ*

      [ami=na]ₑ:APPL　[bala=na]ₒ　iŋki-**tu**-hama-ka-mĩ

      2sg=ACC　　　　bullet=ACC　put.in-APPL-2.OBJ-PFV-RECPST:3:DECL

      'he's loaded his gun (to shoot) you'

When applicative is added to intransitive verbs of motion the added object may be a beneficiary or maleficiary, as in (7.83), or it may relate to a goal or purpose of the motion, as in (7.84, also 7.89 below).

(7.83)　　*ihaphúkbau hiɰáŋtinĩ*

      ihaphu-ka-mau　　　　　　　　hĩɰa-**hu**-tu-ini-ĩ

      give.birth-PFV-NSBJ.NMLZ　arrive-APPL-1SG.OBJ-PFV-3+DECL

      'the day of my giving birth has arrived' (agr041005_16)

(7.84)　　*tsampáunumin wihák uchín batsakíu túwahamĩ*

      [tsampaunumi=na]ₑ:APPL　wi-**hu**-a-kũ　　　　uchi=na

      manioc.leaf=ACC　　　　　go-APPL-IPFV-SIM:3:SS　child=ACC

batsa-ki-u tuwahami̇̃
leave-PFV-NMLZ NARR
'going to get manioc leaves, they left the children behind, so the story goes' (agr040721_07)

With *tu-* 'say' the added object may be the addressee (7.85), despite the fact that that semantic role may also be filled by an underived object (7.86).

(7.85) *mína túhutmi̇̃*
[mi=na]ᴇ:ᴀᴘᴘʟ   tu-**hu**-tu-mi̇̃
1sg=ACC   say-**APPL**-1SG.OBJ-RECPST:3:DECL
'(she) told me'

(7.86) *túhamui*
tu-hama-wa-i
say-2.OBJ+IPFV-3-DECL
'(she) says to you'

Applicative is used with the existential *a-* to express possession (7.87).

(7.87) *mínau kuwáshat káŋka ahútui*
[mi-nau   kuwashata   kaŋka]ᴀ   a-hu-tu-a-u-i
1sg-POSS   many   boquichico   exist-APPL-1SG.OBJ-IPFV-3-DECL
'I have many *boquichico* (fish sp.)'

Some examples are conventionalized to some extent. The verb *chicha-* 'speak' has an applicativized form *chicha-hu-* 'advise' (7.88).

(7.88) *wíi uchín chicháhin atáhai*
wi   [uchi=na   chicha-hu-inu]   a-ta-ha-i
1sg   child=ACC   speak-APPL-NMLZ   COP-IFUT-1SG-DECL
'I will be the children's advisor' (agr040723_29)

And the verb *kauna-* 'arrive (plural subject)' in its applicativized form *kau-tu-* refers specifically to animals gathering to eat a particular type of food (7.89).[7]

---

7 *kaunat* 'arrive (plural subject)' loses its final /na/ when a suffix from slot A or B is added (§7.7.4).

(7.89)   <Nején káyuk, pambaúshkam kaútui>

        [nɨhɨ=na]$_{E:APPL}$ kãyuka   pabau=shakama

        fruit=ACC   agouti   tapir=ADD

        kau-ta-wa-i

        arrive.PL-APPL+IPFV-3-DECL

        'El fruto es comestible para el añuje y el sachavaca.' [The fruit is edible to agoutis and tapirs] lit. *agoutis and tapirs arrive for the fruit*

                                                      (Jernigan 2006: 248)

There is no evidence, however, of more opaque lexicalized forms like those formed with the prefixed causative construction in §7.7.1.

In weak auxiliation constructions applicativization is used to transitivize an intransitive auxiliary to harmonize with a transitive main verb (see description and examples in §6.7). In this case, there is no semantic value to the applicative construction, as it is being used solely to increase valency.

7.7.2.2 Morphosyntactic properties of applicative objects

The added object has the same morphological and syntactic properties as the O or E of an underived verb, including accusative case marking (examples 7.81, 7.82, 7.89, among others) and verbal marking if the object is a SAP (examples 7.81 and 7.82). Applicative objects may be relativized upon in the same way as other objects, using a non-subject nominalization: in example (7.90), the common argument is E$_{APPL}$ in the nominalized relative clause.

(7.90)   *mína kumpáŋ tawás sumáŋkamun wainkáttawai*

        [[mi=na   kumpa-hu]$_{E:APPL}$ [tawasa]$_{O}$

        1sg=ACC   friend-PSSD:1SG   feather.crown

        suma-hu-ka-mau=na]$_{NP:O}$ waina-ka-tata-wa-i

        buy-APPL-PFV-NSBJ.NMLZ=ACC   see-PFV-FUT-3-DECL

        'she will see my friend, for whom I bought a *tawas*'

And applicative marked objects may control the "subject=object" switch-reference marker *-tatamana* (§13.6.1). Applicativized verbs are subject to the general restriction whereby no more than one SAP object can be marked on the verb. The only phenomenon that distinguishes E$_{APPL}$ from O and E relates to the restriction on clause structure described in §7.3, that requires avoidance of clauses with an E$_{APPL}$ object that is higher on the person hierarchy than the O or E.

7.7.3 Reflexive and reciprocal

Reflexive *-ma* and reciprocal *-nai* are used to mark situations in which subject and object are coreferential, and in this respect they are functionally part of the object-marking paradigm. They are formally unlike the object markers, however, in that overt object NPs are incompatible with reflexive and reciprocal, so syntactically they are valency-decreasing derivations. Many examples of reflexive and reciprocal are semantically non-compositional, and the morphology shows that in these examples the suffixes appear in slot A1, along with other valency-decreasing derivation. In their productive function as semantically transparent markers of subject/object coreference they appear in slot B, with the object markers. Because applicative appears in slot A2, its presence can provide a morphological test: derivational reflexive and reciprocal in slot A1 precede the applicative suffix, while object marking forms in slot B follow it. In the discussion that follows, reflexive is used to illustrate many points, as I have only limited data on reciprocal constructions. All the data that I do have suggests that reciprocal behaves the same as reflexive, and I assume that this holds true for all properties of reflexive.

7.7.3.1 Reflexive and reciprocal in slot B

First let us consider some straightforward object marking examples. The verb *timashit* 'comb someone's hair' is transitive. In example (7.91) it takes the reflexive suffix, marking coreference of subject and object. Note, as mentioned above, that a subject pronoun may be overt but not an object pronoun, showing that this is formally an intransitive clause.

(7.91)   *wíi (**mína) timáshmahai*
           wi   (mi=na)   timashi-ma-ha-i
           1sg   1sg=ACC   comb-REFL+IPFV-1SG-DECL
           'I am combing my hair'

Like reflexive, the reciprocal suffix *-nai* also involves coreferentiality of subject and object, however in this case the members of the (necessarily plural) subject group perform the action on each other, rather than on themselves. Also like reflexive, reciprocal is in complementary distribution with the object-marking suffixes and may function to derive new lexemes (see below). Reciprocal contrasts with plural reflexive, in which a number of subjects perform the action on themselves, independently of each other. Compare the following examples of (7.92a) simple transitive; (7.92b) plural reflexive; and (7.92c) reciprocal.

(7.92) a.   *timashínawai*
            timashi-ina-wa-i
            comb-PL:IPFV-3-DECL
            'they are combing (other people's) hair'

       b.   *timáshmainawai*
            timashi-ma-ina-wa-i
            comb-REFL-PL:IPFV-3-DECL
            'they are combing their own hair'

       c.   *timashnáyainawai*
            timashi-nai-ina-wa-i
            comb-RECIP-PL:IPFV-3-DECL
            'they are combing each other's hair'

The minimal pair in examples (7.93a and b) shows that reflexive and object marking clearly function as part of the same paradigm.

(7.93) a.   *tsupímakmĩ*
            tsupi-ma-ka-mĩ
            cut-REFL-PFV-RECPST:3:DECL
            'he has cut himself'

       b.   *tsupíŋmakmĩ*
            tsupi-hama-ka-mĩ
            cut-2.OBJ-PFV-RECPST:3:DECL
            'he has cut you'

Example (7.94) shows the combination of applicative in slot A2 and reflexive in slot B, and the semantics is clearly compositional: reflexive marks the identity of the subject with the object added by the applicative derivation.

(7.94)   *wikaiɯák wíuwai kuntínun mantumaátatus*
         wikaiɯa-kũ   wi-u=ai   [kuntinu=na
         walk+IPFV-SIM+3:SS go+PFV-NMLZ=COP:3:DECL   animal=ACC
         mantu-ma-a-tatus]
         kill+APPL-REFL-PFV-INTENT+3:SS
         'he went walking to kill animals for himself' (i.e. 'he went hunting')
         (Text 1:3)

Reflexive reduces the valency by exactly one: in (7.94) the E$_\text{APPL}$ object is coreferent with the subject and no longer treated as an argument of the verb, but the O object (*kuntin* 'animal') is retained.

As with all object markers (see §7.3), the object referred to by the reflexive marker in slot B is by preference the highest ranked in the role hierarchy E$_\text{APPL}$ > E > O (Figure 7.5 above). So when reflexive is added in slot B to an applicativized stem, it targets the E$_\text{APPL}$ object (as in 7.94). By contrast, when reflexive appears in slot A1, applicative follows it in slot A2 and adds an E$_\text{APPL}$ object to the already reflexivized stem. In other words, the ordering of the suffixes iconically reflects their scope. Note that derivational reflexive may be added to an underived ditransitive, in which case the same hierarchy effect is evident, as it targets the E rather than the O argument (see example 7.99 and discussion).

Some examples indicate a reflexive suffix of the form *-mama*, as in (7.95). I do not have enough evidence to say any more about this.

(7.95)   *kashín dɨkápmamsathai*
         kashini   dɨkapi-mama-sa-ta-ha-i
         tomorrow   test-REFL-PFV-IFUT-1SG-DECL
         'tomorrow I will try my luck (lit. *test myself*)' (agr041005_28)

Example (7.96) refers to an old belief that a hunter would have bad luck if he had eaten beans prior to hunting. Although the man in the story had eaten beans, he claimed he had not and went hunting anyway. The rest of the story describes how a jaguar ate him, providing a very clear moral for the audience.

(7.96)   *nɨ̃ tumámiuwai yúwachu*
         nɨ̃   tu-mama-i-u=ai   yu-a-chau
         3sg   say-REFL-PFV-NMLZ=COP:3:DECL   eat-IPFV-NEG.NMLZ
         'he₁ said he₁ hadn't eaten (beans)' lit. *he said about himself (that he was) a non-eater* (agr041005_28)

7.7.3.2 Reflexive and reciprocal in slot A1

In slot B, the reflexive suffix indexes the object of the verb in a contrastive paradigm with the other object-marking suffixes. When it appears in slot A1, reflexive has a more derivational feel, as it creates new lexemes whose meaning is not entirely predictable from the semantics of the underived verb. Consider the verb *iki-* 'move something into another position', which is reflexivized to become *iki-ma-* 'sit down' (example 7.97). Semantically this is more specific than the expected "move oneself into another position". It cannot mean 'lie down', for example (this would be expressed with the verb *tipi-*).

(7.97) *ikímsata chimpuinúm*
        iki-ma-sa-ta   chimpui=numa
        move.into.position-REFL-PFV-IMP   stool=LOC
        'sit on the stool!'

In addition to this semantic narrowing characteristic of derivation, morphology shows that reflexive takes slot A1 in this stem. In example (7.98), the applicative suffix *-tu* appears in slot A2, and follows the reflexive suffix.

(7.98) *nuwán ikímtawai*
        [nuwa=na]E:APPL   iki-ma-ta-wa-i
        woman=ACC   move.into.position-REFL-APPL+IPFV-3-DECL
        'he is sitting right up next to the woman'

The same applicativized form can mean 'sit on O', where the thing sat on is a grammatical object, marked with accusative case, in contrast to the intransitive form in (7.97) in which the thing sat on (*chimpui* 'stool') is marked with locative case.

A somewhat more opaque derivation involves the verb *su-* 'give', which is reflexivized to give *su-ma-* 'buy'. This can be analysed as 'give to oneself', although the semantics is not compositional. The underived verb *su-* 'give' is ditransitive, and as noted above, the object that is coreferent with the subject in the reflexivized form is the highest ranked, that is, the E. The O object is retained, as the thing bought (7.99), and the derived form is monotransitive.

(7.99) *sandía sumákta*
        [sandía]O   su-ma-ka-ta
        watermelon   give-REFL-PFV-IMP
        'buy some watermelon!'

As with example (7.98) above, the reflexivized form can be applicativized to add a beneficiary EAPPL argument (7.100).

(7.100) *wíi haánchin sumáŋkathami*
        wi   [haanchi=na]O   su-ma-hu-ka-ta-hami
        1sg   clothes=ACC   give-REFL-APPL-PFV-IFUT-1SG>2SG+DECL
        'I will buy you clothes' (agr040824_02)

In addition to the non-compositional semantics, derivational reflexive may differ from slot B reflexive syntactically, as it does not appear to reduce valency in some examples. Consider *yumpu-* 'move a mass (e.g. of soil)' (example 7.101); detransitivized *yumpu-na-* 'collapse (e.g. soil in a landslide)' (7.102); reflexivized *yumpu-ma-* 'fall and bring a mass (such as soil) down with oneself' (7.103). The reflexivized form still allows an accusative marked O in the clause, and seems to have the same valency as the underived form in (7.101).

(7.101)   *nuŋkán yúmpuahai*
          [nuŋka=na]ₒ   yumpu-a-ha-i
          ground=ACC   move.mass-IPFV-1SG-DECL
          'I'm moving soil'

(7.102)   *núŋka yumpúnãĩ̃*
          [nuŋka]ₛ   yumpu-na-ĩ
          ground   move.mass-DETRNS+PFV-3+DECL
          'the soil has slipped (i.e. in a landslide)'

(7.103)   *áu nuŋkán yumpúmãĩ̃*
          au   [nuŋka=na]ₒ   yumpu-ma-ĩ
          DIST   ground=ACC   move.mass-REFL+PFV-3+DECL
          'that person slipped and brought down a mass of soil with them'

Although these examples make it look as if the verb *yumpu-* has a very specific meaning that requires 'soil' as the object, it can be used with other nouns, such as *paampa* 'plantain' in (7.104).

(7.104)   *paámpa yumpúnãĩ̃*
          [paampa]ₛ   yumpu-na-ĩ
          plantain   move.mass-DETRNS+PFV-3+DECL
          'the stacked-up plantains fell down'

There is also an applicativized form based on the *-na* form: *yumpu-na-tu-* refers to a crowd of people moving towards someone or something (7.105).

(7.105)   *áuna ashí yumpúntawai*
          [au=na]ₑ:APPL ashi   yumpu-na-ta-wa-i
          DIST=ACC   all   move.mass-DETRNS-APPL+IPFV-3-DECL
          'everyone's going towards that person'

Although I have fewer examples of reciprocal, it can also apparently function to derive new lexemes. The transitive root *mau-* 'kill' becomes *maa-ni-* 'fight' with the addition of the reciprocal suffix. While it is easy to see the semantic connection here, it is also apparent that *maa-ni-* does not simply mean 'kill each other'; consider example (7.106), in which the subjects (a woman and her husband) clearly did not kill each other – rather, they fought then resolved their problems.

(7.106)   *aíshihãĩ maá maániakũã nuwanũĩ chicháman ɨpɨŋkã huwáku túwahamɨ*
           [aishɨ=haĩ   maa   maa-nai-a-kawã]
           husband+PSSD:1PL/3=COM   REDUP   kill-RECIP-IPFV-REPET+3:SS
           nuwanu=ĩ   [chichama=na   ɨpɨŋkɨ-kã]   huwa-ka-u
           ANA=LOC   problem=ACC   resolve-PFV+SEQ+3:SS   stay-PFV-NMLZ
           tuwahamɨ
           NARR
           '(the woman) fighting with her husband, they then resolved their problems, so the story goes' (agr040721_07)

And in example (7.107) the verb takes singular subject marking, making a reciprocal reading impossible.

(7.107)   *kashín wíi maániktathai*
           kashini   wi   maa-nai-ka-tata-ha-i
           tomorrow   1sg   kill-RECIP-PFV-FUT-1SG-DECL
           'tomorrow I'm going to fight'

This clearly shows that the form derived from *mau-* 'kill' goes beyond simple reciprocal-marking, and has derived a new lexeme 'fight' with prototypically reciprocal meaning. The lexicalization affects the semantics as the subjects do not in fact have to kill each other for the verb *maa-ni-* 'fight' to be appropriately used.

I have no examples that include both reciprocal and applicative in the same stem, so I cannot say for certain that it shows the same possibility as reflexive of appearing in slot A1 or B; but the fact that it shares the possibility of derivational and object marking functions suggests that it is also morphologically parallel.

7.7.3.3 O → S detransitivizer -na

The suffix *-na* in slot A1 derives an intransitive verb, whose S argument is the O argument of the corresponding transitive. This derivation can only be applied to transitive verb roots. Example (7.108) shows the underived transitive verb *aima-* 'fill container with liquid', where the liquid is the O argument and the container takes locative case; the derived form in (7.109) is *aim-na-* 'fill container', where the S argument is the liquid and the container again takes locative case.

(7.108)   *yumín tsapánum aimkáthai*
           [yumi=na]ₒ   tsapa=numa   aima-ka-ta-ha-i
           water=ACC   cup=LOC   fill-PFV-IFUT-1SG-DECL
           'I'll fill the cup with water'

(7.109)   *yúmi tsapánmak aimnákmɨ̃*
           [yumi]ₛ   tsapa=numa=ka   aima-na-ka-mɨ̃
           water   cup=LOC=TOP   fill-DETRNS-PFV-RECPST:3:DECL
           'The cup is full of water' lit. *the water has filled the cup*

In example (7.110), the transitive verb *kupi-* 'break a bone' takes a suffix in slot B marking first person O object. The derived form in (7.111) is intransitive, and the S argument is the person who suffered the broken bone.

(7.110)   *kupiŋkã̂ɨ̃*
           kupi-hu-ka-ɨ̃
           break.bone-1SG.OBJ-PFV-3+DECL
           'He's broken my bone'

(7.111)   *kupinkáhai*
           kupi-na-ka-ha-i
           break.bone-DETRNS-PFV-1SG-DECL
           'I've suffered a broken bone'

Similarly, the verb *hii-* 'take out, extract' is transitive, but the derived form *hii-na-* (take.out-DETRNS-) 'go out' is intransitive. Unlike the derivational reflexive and reciprocal forms, those derived with *-na* are not semantically opaque, and the S=O rearrangement of roles is perfectly regular.

Detransitivizing *-na* in slot A1 can co-occur with applicative in slot A2. Example (7.112) illustrates the underived verb *pɨmpɨ-* 'wrap up O by turning it'. In this case the verb refers to a boa wrapping up a person to kill him.

(7.112)   *maáuwai pɨmpɨáŋ pɨmpɨáŋ*
           maa-u=ai   pɨmpɨa-hã   pɨmpɨa-hã
           kill+PFV-NMLZ=COP:3:DECL   wrap-PFV+SEQ+3:SS   wrap-PFV+SEQ+3:SS
           '(the boa) killed (the man) by wrapping him up' (Text 1:11)

The detransitivized form in (7.113) refers to the motion of S turning away.

(7.113)   *tuhintúk pɨmpɨɨnakɨ̃...*
tuhintu-kã   pɨmpɨ-na-kɨ̃
be.unable-PFV+SEQ+3:SS   turn-DTRNS-PFV+SEQ+3:SS
'being unable to do it, he turned to go...' (agr040723_29)

This form may then be applicativized, with the meaning of turning towards the added E_{APPL} object (7.114).

(7.114)   *uchín pɨmpɨntikiu túwahamɨ̃*
uchi=na   pɨmpɨ-na-tu-ki-u   tuwahamɨ̃
child=ACC   turn-DTRNS-APPL-PFV-NMLZ   NARR
'(the devil) turned towards the child, they say' (agr040723_29)

Detransitivizing *-na* is probably related to the 'attributive' verbalizer *-na* which derives an intransitive verb from a noun (§6.6.1).

7.7.3.4 Loss of root-final /na/ triggered by slot A and B suffixes

Verb roots ending in /na/ lose the final /na/ when a suffix of slot A or B is added, although they never alternate with unmarked stems, and show no semantic indication that they have undergone a detransitivizing derivation. The verb *ipɨna-* 'block' is transitive; in (7.115) it takes *waiti* 'door' as its object. In (7.116), the applicative marker appears in slot A2, and adds an E_{APPL} object (*uwɨŋ hinaina nuna* 'sheep that are going out'). In this form the final /na/ of the root is lost, suggesting that it is also a derivational suffix. But the form with final /na/ is transitive, and there is no related verb **ipɨ-*, so this is clearly not the detransitivizer *-na*.

(7.115)   *waítin ɨpɨntahai*
[waiti=na]_O   ipɨna-ta-ha-i
door=ACC   block+PFV-IFUT-1SG-DECL
'I'll block the door'

(7.116)   *tadíshan uwíŋ hiináina núna ɨpɨttahai*
[tanisha=na]_O   [uwiha   hiina-ina   nu=na]_{E:APPL}
fence=ACC   sheep   go.out-PL:IPFV+3   ANA_{REL}=ACC
ipɨ-tu-ta-ha-i
block-APPL-IFUT-1SG-DECL
'I'll block the fence so the sheep don't get out'

Examples (7.117, 7.118) show a similar alternation of root-final /na/ with the applicative suffix, in the verb *ukuina-* 'gather'.

(7.117)   *batáɨn ukuínkathai*
          [bataɨ=na]ₒ   ukuina-ka-ta-ha-i
          chambira.fruit=ACC   gather-PFV-IFUT-1SG-DECL
          'I'll get some chambira fruit'

(7.118)   *minásh batáɨ ukuíthukta*
          [mi=na=sha]ₑ:APPL   [bataɨ]ₒ   ukui-tu-hu-ka-ta
          1sg=ACC=ADD   chambira.fruit   gather-APPL-1SG.OBJ-PFV-IMP
          'get some chambira fruit for me too!'

Both (7.116) and (7.118) involve /na/ being lost in applicativized stems. The same
effect happens when object markers appear in slot B: compare *waina-* 'see' in (7.119)
with *wai-* 'see' in (7.120) and (7.121).

(7.119)   *wíi wainkámhai áu aídaun*
          wi   waina-ka-ma-ha-i   [au   a-ina-u=na]ₒ
          1sg   see-PFV-RECPST-1SG-DECL   DIST   COP-PL:IPFV-NMLZ=ACC
          'I saw them'

(7.120)   *áu áidau mína waitkáŋmĩ*
          au   a-ina-u   [mi=na]ₒ   wai-tu-ka-aha-mĩ
          DIST   COP-PL:IPFV-NMLZ   1sg=ACC   see-1SG.OBJ-PFV-PL-RECPST:3:DECL
          'they saw me'

(7.121)   *áu waipákmĩ*
          au   wai-pa-ka-mĩ
          DIST   see-2.OBJ-PFV-RECPST:3:DECL
          's/he saw you'

The loss of /na/ is purely morphological, triggered by the presence of suffixes in
slots A and B, rather than by the functional category of valency markers. This is
shown by (7.122), in which second person object is marked in slot F with the portmanteau suffix *-hamɨ* (1SG>2SG), and the final /na/ of the root surfaces.

(7.122)   *waínhamɨ*
          waina-a-hamɨ
          see-IPFV-1SG>2SG+DECL
          'I see you'

Examples (7.123a and b) illustrate the same alternation with the verb *bukuna-* 'suck'
and the first person plural object suffix *-kahatu* marking generic human object.

(7.123) a. *bukunín*
bukuna-inu
suck-NMLZ
'one who sucks' (may refer to a baby, mammals, a smoker)

b. *bukúhatin*
buku-kahatu-inu
suck-1PL.OBJ-NMLZ
'insects that suck human blood'[8]

The alternation also happens with reflexive marking: transitive *unuina-* 'teach' alternates with intransitive reflexivized *unui-ma-* 'get accustomed to, learn' (< teach-REFL).

It is clear from all these examples that the presence or absence of /na/ has no effect on transitivity, and these are regular verb roots that just happen to end in /na/. Presumably the loss of /na/ is motivated by analogy to valency-changing *-na*, which can alternate with suffixes from slots A and B (although the suffix *-na* can co-occur with applicative, as shown in 7.114). Table 7.9 lists all the /na/ verbs I have encountered; as far as I am aware, all underived verb roots terminating in /na/ show this behaviour.

Table 7.9: Verbs with 'placeholding' *-na*

root	gloss
bukuna-	'suck'
ípína-	'fence in'
kauna-	'arrive (plural subject)'
nahana-	'make'
ukuina-	'pick fruit'
unuina-	'teach'
waina-	'see'

7.7.3.5 Alternation of *-na* and *-ma*

In §6.6.1 I described two verbalizing suffixes *-ma* and *-na*, which derive transitive and ditransitive verbs respectively from nouns, and can apply to the same nominal

---

8 The loss of initial /ka/ from the suffix *-kahatu* is a regular phonological process, described in §3.5.5.3.

stem. I have also described two detransitivizing suffixes, reflexive -*ma* and S=O detransitivizer -*na* , as well as the interaction of root-final /na/ with valency related morphology. Because of these homophonies it is not immediately clear, when presented with a pair of related verb stems terminating in /ma/ and /na/, what the relationship between them is; one needs to know the full paradigm to be certain of which suffix(es) are involved. This potential ambiguity of stems is probably what made the /na/ dropping possible in the first place.

7.7.4 Unproductive valency effects

Three further forms are involved in valency alterations, but are extremely limited in their application, and therefore may not be morphemes synchronically.

7.7.4.1 S → A transitivizer -*ki*

A transitivizing suffix -*ki* appears in only two verbs in my data: *dushi*- 'laugh' is intransitive, while *dushi-ki*- 'laugh at' is transitive. The same suffix alternates with -*pa* (perhaps the same suffix as described in §7.7.4.3 below) in the pair *iha-pa*- 'defecate' versus *iha-ki*- 'defecate on O' (both < *iha* (noun) 'shit').

7.7.4.2 S → O causativizer -*ka*

The causative transitivizer -*ka* appears in only one verb in my data: *waitu*- 'suffer' is intransitive, while *wait-ka*- 'torment, annoy' is transitive.

7.7.4.3 A → S detransitivizer -*pa*

The transitive verb *shiki*- 'urinate on O' (< *shiki* 'urine') has an intransitive alternant *shiki-pa*- 'urinate'. The only other possible appearance of this suffix is in *iha-pa*- 'defecate' < *iha* 'shit'; but there is no zero-marked transitive, instead the suffix -*ki* (above) is used: *iha-ki*- 'defecate on O'. Probably related are *iha-hii*- 'strain to defecate or give birth'; *iha-hu*- 'have diarrhoea'; and possibly related *iha-ki*- 'stain O' (note the difference in accent between *ihákit* 'defecate on O' and *ihakít* 'stain O').

7.7.4.4 Accent shift, vowel change, and zero derivation

A further unproductive derivational process among verbs is accent shift. I have encountered a number of verbs that are semantically related and differ only in accent placement: *ihákit* defecate on O' and *ihakít* 'stain' were already mentioned; other examples are *shíkit* 'urinate on something' and *shikít* 'draw water'; *nihát* 'wash' and *níhat* 'poison fish using *barbasco*' (the action of releasing the poison into the river is similar to washing clothes, and native speakers translate this process into Spanish as *lavando el río* 'washing the river'). A few other examples were given in §3.7.

The copula verb *nahanɨt* 'become' is related to the transitive verb *nahanat* 'make' through an unproductive process of vowel-change (see §7.8). The same phonological relation holds between transitive *dɨkapat* 'count, measure' and copula *dɨkapɨt* 'feel', although I treat both as suffixed derivatives of *dɨkat* 'know' in Table 7.10, below.

Finally, a few verbs have different senses, with different transitivity values, without any morphological change. I mentioned the case of *ɨsat* 'bite; devour' (transitive) and 'burn oneself; burn up' (intransitive) in §7.6.3. The verb *dɨkapɨt*, already mentioned above, has two senses: transitive 'try, test, taste, confirm' and copula 'feel (oneself to be)', and two other intransitive verbs *wahat* 'stand' and *huwat* 'stay' can also be used as copulas (§7.9). Another example is the existential *ata* 'exist' and homophonous copula, although this pair is distinct in other parts of the paradigm (§6.4.2).

7.7.4.5 Derivation from *dɨkat* 'know'

The transitive verb *dɨkat* 'know' has a number of derived forms, which are not entirely semantically compositional, shown in Table 7.10. This verb is not unusual, but just happens to be one for which I have encountered a good number of examples. It is clear that there remains much work to be done in the area of lexical derivation.

Table 7.10: Derivation from *dɨkat* 'know'

verb stem	composition	gloss
dɨka-pɨ-	know-?-	try, test, taste, confirm (trans.)
dɨka-pɨ-	know-?-	feel, know oneself to be (copula)
dɨka-pɨ-nai-	know-?-RECIP-	compete (intrans.)
dɨka-pɨ-tu-ma-	know-?-APPL-REFL-	find one's bearings (intrans.)
dɨka-pa-	know-?-	count, measure (trans.)
dɨka-ma-	know-REFL-	find out by spying (intrans.)
dɨka-ma-hu-	know-REFL-APPL-	spy on someone (trans.)

7.8 Copular clauses

Aguaruna has two full copula verbs: *nahanit* 'become' (example 7.124) and *dikapit* 'feel' (7.125). Both take two nominative marked arguments, the copula subject (CS) and the copula complement (CC) (as do clauses formed with the copula enclitic, described in §7.9).

(7.124) *nunú namák áina dúka ... máma naháni̱aku áinawai*
         [nunu   namaka   a-ina   nu=ka]cs   ...   [mama]cc
         ANA   fish   COP-PL:IPFV   ANA$_{REL}$=TOP   ...   manioc
         nahani̱a-ka-u   a-ina-wa-i
         become-PFV-NMLZ   COP-PL:IPFV-3-DECL
         'those fish (when the young man took them out of the water) turned into manioc' (agr040824_01)

(7.125) *ashí ai̱nts áidau ikámyawanak kákahus maanimáinchau dikapi̱dau*
         [ashi   ai̱ntsu   a-ina-u]cs   [ikam_yawaã=na=ka
         all   person   COP-PL:IPFV-NMLZ   jaguar=ACC=TOP
         kakahus   maani-mai-inu-chau]cc   dikapi̱-ina-u
         easily   fight-POT-NMLZ-NEG.NMLZ   feel-PL:IPFV-NMLZ
         'all the people felt that they were unable to fight a jaguar' (agr041005_14)

Both *nahanit* and *dikapit* are related to other verbs (*nahanat* 'make' and *dikat* 'know') through unproductive derivation. The two nominative arguments of *nahanit* 'become' are readily distinguishable semantically as 'source' and 'outcome', and the related verb *nahanat* 'make' can take two types of O: the material or the artefact produced (but not both at once) (§7.6.2). *dikapit* can also be used transitively, and then means 'try, test, taste, confirm'.

7.9 Non-verbal predicates

Equative/attributive clauses take two arguments: a subject (CS) and a predicate noun or adjective complement (CC). The predicate nominal is marked with the copula enclitic (7.126a), or the copula verb *ata* is used, depending on tense, mood, and number of the subject (7.126b) (see §4.14 for a detailed description of the copula enclitic).

(7.126) a. *wíi awahúnithai*
        wi   awahuni=ita-ha-i
        1sg   Aguaruna=COP-1SG-DECL
        'I am Aguaruna'

    b. *íi awahún áinahi*
        ii   awahuni   a-ina-hi
        1pl   Aguaruna   COP-PL:IPFV-1PL+DECL
        'we are Aguaruna'

The copula enclitic may optionally be omitted in present tense declarative clauses with third person subject, resulting in a verbless construction (7.127, 7.128) in which the two arguments are simply juxtaposed. Note that the subject of a verbless clause normally takes the topic enclitic *=ka* (also see §18.2).

(7.127) *dúka shukuím akapín yúwa nunú*
        [nu=ka]cs [shukuima akapɨ=na   yu-a   nunu]cc
        ANA=TOP   boa.sp   liver=ACC   eat-IPFV+3   ANAREL
        'that was a *shukuim* boa, that eats livers' (Text 1:13)

(7.128) *mina dukuhuk apash*
        [mi=na   duku-hu=ka]cs   [apachi]cc
        1sg=ACC   mother-PSSD:1SG=TOP   non.Aguaruna
        'my mother is non-Aguaruna' (Tiinch & Danducho)

The enclitic copula appears in: present tense, indicative and interrogative mood, generally only with singular CS; and in simultaneous subordinate clauses. In any other type of clause, the copula verb *ata* must be used. These include non-present tenses (7.129); subordinate clauses other than simultaneous (7.130); and with plural subject (7.131; also 7.126b above).

(7.129) *dúka hospitalak Dos de Mayo áyi*
        [nu=ka   *hospital*-a=ka]cs [*Dos de Mayo*]cc a-yi
        ANA=TOP hospital-EP=TOP   Dos de Mayo   COP-REMPST:3:DECL
        'that hospital was (named) *Dos de Mayo*' (agr040824_02)

(7.130)   *wíi aníau asán, núna wíi ítsiɲhai*

[wi]cs	[ani-a-u]cc	asa-nu	nu=na	wi
1sg	remember-IPFV-NMLZ	COP+SBD-1SG:SS	ANA=ACC	1sg

ítsihũ-a-ha-i
tell-IPFV-1SG-DECL
'being one who remembers, I tell that (story)' (agr041005_14)

(7.131)   *átumik yabáik áishmaɲ áinahumi*

[atumi=ka]cs	yamai=ka	[aishmaɲku]cc	a-ina-humi
2pl=TOP	now=TOP	man	COP-PL:IPFV-2PL+DECL

'you are men now'

There is also a remote past copula enclitic, that can be used in remote past tense; it is not clear what conditions its selection over a separate verb as in (7.129). The remote past copula is rare in my data – some examples are in §4.14.

The copula root *ata* is homophonous with the existential verb *ata* 'exist', and probably historically connected (see §6.4.2). The positional verb *wahat* 'stand' also occasionally functions as a copula in equative/attributive clauses (7.132–7.134).

(7.132)   *iiniá kakákchau wahasuí*

[iinia]cs	[kaka-ka-chau]cc	waha-sa-u=ai
1pl	be.strong-PFV-NEG.NMLZ	stand-PFV-NMLZ=COP:3:DECL

'our people were not strong' (agr041005_18)

(7.133)   *núu aínts puhú wahás*

[nu	aintsu]cs	[puhu]cc	waha-sã
ANA	person	white	stand-SBD+3:SS

'that person being pale...' (Text 1:35)

(7.134)   *secundaria ashímkan, hintínkaɲtin wahasábiahai hímaɲ mihadái*

secundaria	ashima-ka-nu	[hintinkaɲtinu]cc
secondary.school	finish-PFV+SEQ-1SG:SS	teacher

waha-sa-amaya-ha-i	himaha	mihana=i
stand-PFV-DISTPST-1SG-DECL	two	year=INS

'after I finished secondary school, I was a teacher for two years' (agr040824_02)

The verb *huwat* 'remain' may also function as a copula, though rarely (7.135).

(7.135)   *wíi wákɨ bɨ́sɨmaŋ huwáktathai*
           [wi]cs [wakɨ_bɨsɨmaŋ]cc huwa-ka-tata-ha-i
           1sg   sad   stay-PFV-FUT-1SG-DECL
           'I will be sad'

Like the existential *ata, wahat* 'stand' and *huwat* 'remain' project just one S argument when used with their lexical meanings and two arguments (CS and CC) as copulas.

The conditioning for the three different morphosyntactic realizations of equative/attributive clauses are set out in Table 7.11. The overlap between enclitic copula and verbless constructions is apparently free variation. In all types, the relation described may be one of identity, class membership or attribution of a property.

Table 7.11: Conditioning on equational/attributive clause types

	verbless	enclitic	verb
Present tense; declarative; third person singular subject	✓	✓	–
Present (or remote past) tense; indicative; interrogative; simultaneous subordinate clauses; singular subject	–	✓	–
Tenses other than present (or remote past); imperative; plural subject	–	–	✓

8 Tense, aspect and person in finite verbs

8.1 Introduction

As we saw in Chapter 6, the first level of verbal morphology contains all of the derivational suffixes, almost all of the object-marking suffixes, and the negative suffixes. The root plus any suffixes at this level form a stem to which the level II suffixes associated with finite verbs are attached. The present chapter deals with these suffixes, which can loosely be termed inflectional.

Level II morphology in Aguaruna is characterized by two interesting tendencies. The first is fusion; this appears to be the only area of the grammar where truly fusional morphemes occur, particularly in third-person forms, and in contrast to the generally agglutinating nature of Aguaruna morphology. The second characteristic is a tendency to recycle grammaticalization paths. Consider the examples in (8.1a) and (8.1b).

(8.1)   a.   *yuwáttahai*
             yu-a-**tata**-ha-i
             eat-PFV-**FUT**-1SG-DECL
             'I will eat'

        b.   *yuwátatahai*
             yu-a-**tata**-ha-i
             eat-PFV-**DESID**-1SG-DECL
             'I want to eat'

The two forms glossed FUT ('definite future') and DESID ('desiderative') have the homophonous form /tata/ at the morphemic level, but constitute a minimal pair at the surface level, based on whether or not syncope applies to the vowel of the first syllable. The absence of syncope in the desiderative suffix is due to its being a recently fused periphrasis from a construction which couches an 'intentional future' marked verb in a speech report: **yu-a-ta-ha ta-ha-i* (eat-PFV-IFUT-1SG say+IPFV-1SG-DECL) 'I intend to eat, I say'. This is apparent from descriptions of other Chicham languages and other varieties of Aguaruna, where the desiderative suffix contains the phoneme /h/, the reflex of first person singular -*ha* – so we can infer a prior stage of example (8.1b) having the form **[yuwáta**h**tahai]* (cf. Fast et al. 1996: 46; Corbera 1994: 266). It is highly likely that the future form has derived from an earlier instance of the same fusion, and synchronically forms an unexceptional part of the phonological word. So there is a synchronic contrast between two forms representing points on a grammaticalization path *intention* > *desiderative* > *future*. Similar examples are evident among past tense forms, where a periphrastic construction with the copula *ata* as auxiliary coexists with two forms showing different levels of fusion, and the three forms differ semantically (see §8.4.3). Historical grammaticalization of various periphrastic forms has increased the number of tense marking suffixes, of which three show evidence of being older than the rest: immediate future *-ta*, recent past *-ma* and remote past *-ya* (along with the formally unmarked present tense).

8.2 Morphological positions

Level two consists of three suffix positions, as shown in Figure 8.1.

SLOT	GROUP	SUFFIXES	GLOSS
LEVEL I			
PFX:	Valency		
	ROOT		
A:	Valency		
B:	Object		
C:	Aspect	(see §8.3)	
D:	Negative		
LEVEL II			
E:	(i)	(see §8.4)	Tense
		-tata	Desiderative
		-ta	Imperative
		-ti	Jussive
	(ii)	*-(a)i* (§8.5)	Apprehensive
	(iii)	*-mi* (§8.6)	Hortative
F:	Person	(see §8.7)	Subject
			First person subject + second person object
G:	Mood/modality	(see Chapter 9)	

Figure 8.1: Level II morphology in finite verbs

Slot E is obligatorily filled, and contains the tense markers, including zero-marked present tense; also desiderative, imperative (second person only) and jussive (third person only), all historically derived from the future primary tense marker. Suffixes of this group may be followed by person markers. Apprehensive combines with the same person markers as set (i) for all persons, and may also combine with distinct person markers to form prohibitive (second and third person only) and negative jussive (third person only). Hortative never combines with any other level II suffix, and is only used with first person plural subject. Imperative and jussive correlate historically with future in the tense paradigm, but unlike future tense they impart imperative mood to the clause, thus preventing any mood suffix from appearing. Apprehensive, prohibitive, negative jussive and hortative likewise impart mood to the clause and block the addition of any further mood marking in slot G. All finite verbs must be specified for subject. First and second persons have distinct singular and plural forms, third person marks plural only in jussive, apprehensive, prohibitive and remote past. Second and third persons take different markers depending on tense and mood, and some third person markers are fused with tense markers. Plural subject for all persons is optionally marked with level I suffixes in slot C (see §8.3). Second person object is marked in slot F only when the subject is first person. All other object suffixes, including second person object with third person subject, are at level I in slot B (§6.3.1; §7.3). Mood is obligatorily marked in finite clauses, and all clause types are marked with suffixes in slot G except imperative, marked in slot E, and polar interrogative. The polar interrogative enclitic =*ka* normally appears in slot G, but in recent past, intermediate past and distant past tenses, the enclitic immediately follows the primary past suffix -*ma* of slot E, and may then be followed by the remote past primary tense suffix -*ya*, and a subject suffix in slot F. As a floating clitic, =*ka* may also appear on some other clausal constituent leaving the predicate unmarked (§10.4).

Although a bare verb root can appear as the full verb in an auxiliary construction, any other verb form must have at least one suffix. Tense, person and mood are all obligatorily specified, but they may be zero-marked: a verb that has no overt tense suffix is interpreted as present; person of the subject is implicit in imperative clauses; and in non-interrogative, non-imperative clauses lack of a mood/modality suffix indicates exclamative mood. Zero-marking forms a paradigmatic opposition with the segmentally-marked tense and mood/modality suffixes, and we can say that level II suffixes obligatorily mark finite independent verbs for person of the subject (and number for first and second person subjects), tense and mood.

There are some incongruities in level II morphology: desiderative appears as part of the tense paradigm (explained by origins in primary future), and second person objects are marked at level II only with first person subjects. All other object markers are at level I. The quirky requirement that polar interrogative must immediately follow the primary recent past suffix invites speculation, but at present there is not sufficient evidence to form a viable explanation.

8.3 Aspect

Verbs have five stem types, all of which may host further morphology. These are shown in Table 8.1. In addition to the unmarked stem there are a perfective and an imperfective stem,[1] a potential stem and a durative stem. Perfective and imperfective forms are contrastive in present-tense independent clauses and some nominalizations, while in non-present tenses and dependent clauses the choice of stem is morphologically conditioned; that is, certain suffixes always select one particular stem. The unmarked stem appears with some nominalizers, some dependent suffixes and one tensed form. The potential stem typically appears nominalized with the subject nominalizer -inu, but also may take tense and person markers to form a finite verb. The durative stem only ever appears directly followed by an imperative suffix. Three verbs are irregular with respect to aspect marking, as described in §6.4. As was noted in Chapter 6, a bare verbal root can appear only in an auxiliary construction (§6.7).

Table 8.1: Verb stems

stem	slot C suffix	comments
unmarked	none	
perfective	(see §8.3.1)	may undergo vowel change in the root
imperfective	-a (sg), -ina (pl)	marks singular/plural subject
potential	-mai	all verbs become S=O ambitransitive
durative	-ma	triggers lengthening of preceding vowel

The five stems are illustrated in examples (8.2–8.7). Perfective and imperfective are aspectual distinctions. Perfective is temporally bound; the action of the verb is seen as a complete whole. Imperfective is temporally unbound, and makes no reference to an endpoint (Dik 1989: 187; Comrie 1976: 3–4, 18). A present perfective form refers to a just-completed action, while an imperfective form refers to an ongoing or habitual action: compare (8.3) and (8.4).

(8.2)   *yutãĩ*
          yu-taĩ
          eat-NSBJ.NMLZ
          'food'

---

1 I follow the compilers of the dictionary published by CAAAP (Uwarai et al. 1998) in listing the three major stems in the order unmarked, perfective, imperfective.

(8.3)   *yuwáhai*
         yu-a-ha-i
         eat-PFV-1SG-DECL
         'I'm done eating', 'I've just eaten'

(8.4)   *yúwahai*
         yu-a-ha-i
         eat-IPFV-1SG-DECL
         'I'm eating', 'I eat'

(8.5)   *yúinawai*
         yu-ina-wa-i
         eat-PL:IPFV-3-DECL
         'they are eating'

(8.6)   *yumáinkait*
         yu-mai-inu=ka=it
         eat-POT-NMLZ=Q=COP:3
         'is it edible?'

(8.7)   *yuumatá*
         yu-ma-ta
         eat-DUR-IMP
         'keep on eating!'

Slot C contains suffixes that formally differentiate imperfective and perfective stems. A perfective stem typically includes one of a set of suffixes whose selection is mostly lexically conditioned. Consequently, previous analysts have considered these suffixes to be the markers of perfective aspect (Larson 1963: 15–16, 18; Corbera 1994: 268–269); however this is not the full story. Firstly, some verbs have perfective stems that do not include a suffix in slot C; and secondly, the perfective stems of second and third conjugation verbs differ phonologically from the unmarked root, regardless of the presence or absence of a perfective suffix. So although the majority of verbs manifest the distinction between perfective and imperfective stems entirely in the presence or absence of a suffix in slot C, the aspectual distinction may still be present even in the absence of formal differentiation; and the formal distinction itself may involve more than just the addition of a perfective suffix.

8.3.1 The perfective stem

The six perfective suffixes are listed in Table 8.2. The selection of perfective suffix appears to be mostly lexically conditioned, based on the semantics of the verb root. There is limited potential to switch suffixes, giving distinct semantic effects. The glosses and meanings ascribed to the perfective suffixes are intentionally vague, and have no real predictive power; that is, one cannot know the appropriate perfective suffix for a given verb on the basis of semantics alone.

Table 8.2: Perfective suffixes

suffix	gloss	meaning
-ka	intensive	intensive effort by subject (whether A or S)
-ki(ni)	transferred	associated change of location
-sa	attenuative	attenuative or diminutive
-ha	pluractional	plural action (iterative), or involving liquid – distributed(?) complex actions(?)
-a(w)	high affectedness	change of state of O or location of S
-i(ni)	low affectedness	no change of state for O or location of S

All of the perfective suffixes except -i(ni) 'low affectedness' can take accent. The initial vowel of the low affectedness suffix -i(ni) replaces the final vowel of the stem (§3.6.1) and the accent falls on the preceding vowel if the root is polysyllabic (§3.7.1). The perfective suffixes form a paradigm, and are not all available for use with any given verb root; a given verb will have a typical association with one perfective suffix, or with none. The most common example of substitution of one suffix for another is with -sa 'attenuative', which frequently appears in imperative forms, and has the effect of softening the request. The semantic range of perfective suffixes is vague, and it is very difficult to pin down a meaning for each one. It may be that some are historically derived from two or more homophonous forms, for example the suffix -ha is used for non-punctual actions such as 'sleep', 'dawn', but also appears with many verbs involving liquid (e.g. 'rain', 'drink', 'wash ones hands') that do not appear to fit the "non-punctual" prototype. In the following sections I illustrate the typical uses of each suffix, based on the two available sources of information: those verbs that take a suffix as their default, and the semantic effects of swapping suffixes while keeping the same verb root.

Attenuative -sa
The attenuative perfective suffix has the semantic effect of reducing the force of the verb. A common use is to make requests more polite – compare (8.8a), with the

default suffix for the verb *umut* 'drink', and (8.8b), where the default has been replaced with attenuative *-sa*.

(8.8) a.   *uwáṇta*
            uwa-**ha**-ta
            drink-PFV-IMP
            'drink!'

       b.   *uwásta*
            uwa-**sa**-ta
            drink-PFV-IMP
            'please drink!'

Native speakers consider the effect to be equivalent to the diminutive suffix on nouns, and the two forms frequently co-occur in clauses. The diminutive use is illustrated in (8.9). In (8.9b) the perfective stem including the attenuative suffix is nominalized with the non-subject nominalizer *-mau*. The diminutive suffix *-uchi* is not compatible with the aspect-marked nominalizers, so using the attenuative perfective suffix is the only strategy available to achieve the same effect.

(8.9) a.   *isástatui*
            isa-**sa**-tata-wa-i
            bite-PFV-FUT-3-DECL
            'it'll bite (you)' (said of a cute puppy or baby)

       b.   *ámi nahánsamu*
            amɨ   nahana-**sa**-mau
            2sg   make-PFV-NSBJ.NMLZ
            'the little thing you made' (cf. Sp. *la cosita que hiciste*)

Attentuative may also convey a stative sense with bodily action verbs: compare (8.10a) and (8.10b). Other verbs involving *-sa* like *chichat* 'speak, converse' suggest that it relates to personal involvement of the subject.[2]

(8.10) a. *waháita*
            waha-**i**-ta
            stand-PFV-IMP
            'stand up!'

---

[2] This is rather similar to the semantic domain of middle voice (Kemmer 1993), which is also associated with verbs of speaking and posture.

b. *wahastá*
    waha-**sa**-ta
    stand-PFV-IMP
    'stand (there)!'

Intensive -*ka*

Use of the intensive perfective suffix denotes a high level of effort on the part of the subject. This is most clearly observed when -*ka* is contrasted with another perfective suffix, as in (8.11a), with the default attenuative suffix, and (8.11b) with the intensive suffix.

(8.11) a. *chichastá*
            chicha-**sa**-ta
            speak-PFV-IMP
            'speak' (i.e. 'converse')

        b. *chichaktá*
            chicha-**ka**-ta
            speak-PFV-IMP
            'speak' (forcefully, e.g. giving a speech)

In some cases the intensity arises from repetition of the verbal action, as in (8.12b, 8.13b).

(8.12) a. *kantamáta*
            kantama-**a**-ta
            sing-PFV-IMP
            'sing!'

        b. *kantamkáta*
            kantama-**ka**-ta
            sing-PFV-IMP
            'sing (many songs)!'

(8.13) a. *uwáŋta*
            uwa-**ha**-ta
            drink-PFV-IMP
            'drink!'

b. *uwákta*
uwa-**ka**-ta
drink-PFV-IMP
'drink (an unusual amount, e.g. more than one vessel)!'

Some verbs that take -*ka* as default are *tupikaut* 'run'; *wata* 'go up'; *antut* 'listen'. Of particular note are the pro-verbs formed with -*ni*, that are used when the subject is more relevant to the context, and all take intensive -*ka* as their default perfective suffix (§6.6.2).

Pluractional -*ha*

The suffix -*ha* is the most difficult to furnish with a single gloss. It is quite possible that this suffix arises historically from a merger of two suffixes representing something like 'liquid action' and 'complex action'. The pluractional suffix appears with many verbs involving water, such as *ikiŋmat* 'wash one's hands', *yutut* 'rain', *umut* 'drink'. This use may be considered to mark 'liquid action'. The same suffix can also indicate plurality or repetition of an action (8.14b).

(8.14) a. *isáittawai*
isa-**i**-tata-wa-i
bite-PFV-FUT-3-DECL
'it will bite (him/her)'

b. *isáŋtatui*
isa-**ha**-tata-wa-i
bite-PFV-FUT-3-DECL
'it will bite (him/her) repeatedly'

Another possibility is that the original sense is of non-punctual action. Some other verbs that typically take -*ha*, such as *hiŋkat* 'tie up', *kanut* 'sleep', *tsawaut* 'dawn' could be seen as fitting this description.

Transferred action -*ki(ni)*

The transferred action suffix -*ki(ni)* is perhaps the most straightforward in its semantics, adding the sense of 'associated motion'. The word 'associated' is key: this suffix is not used with verbs whose core meaning involves motion; instead, it adds the sense of motion to a verb, indicating that the action is completed in a different location from that in which it was begun. A verb that typically takes -*ki(ni)* is *huta* 'take'. An example with change of suffix involves *tupikaut* 'run', which typically takes -*ka* 'intensive action', but can take -*ki(ni)* to emphasize running to somewhere. The vowel of the short form -*ki* does not elide in word-final position, although it does do so word-internally.

High affectedness -*a(w)*

The high affectedness suffix accentuates the affectedness of the object when used with transitive verbs. Compare the effect of high-affectedness (8.15a) versus low-affectedness (8.15b) forms.

(8.15) a. *pelotan umpuáhai*
            pelota=na   umpu-**a**-ha-i
            ball=ACC   blow-**PFV**-1SG-DECL
            'I've inflated the ball' (change of state)

        b. *hiín umpúihai*
            hii=na   umpu-**i**-ha-i
            fire=ACC   blow-**PFV**-1SG-DECL
            'I've blown on the fire' (no change of state)

Typical verbs that take high-affectedness are *yuta* 'eat' and *maut* 'kill'. Note in particular that the pro-verbs formed with -*tika*, that indicate relevance of the object, take -*a*; by contrast, the subject relevant pro-verbs formed with -*ni* take the intensive suffix -*ka*, which emphasizes the subject's role in the action (§6.6.2).

The 'high affectedness' marker may appear with intransitive verbs; typically verbs of motion such as *hɨꞷat* 'arrive'; *tata* 'come'. In example (8.16), it appears with the intransitive verb *tɨpɨt* 'lie down', presumably to highlight the fact that the jaguar submerged itself completely. This verb takes attenuative -*sa* as its default, as is typical for posture verbs.

(8.16)   *íkamỹãw̃ãã tɨpɨámɨ̃*
            ikam_yawaã   tɨpɨ-**a**-mɨ̃
            jaguar   lie.down-**PFV**-RECPST:3:DECL
            'the jaguar submerged itself (in water)'

Low affectedness -*i(ni)*

Use of the low affectedness suffix is characterized by an unchanged state of the object of a transitive verb, as in example (8.15b) above. When used with an intransitive verb (e.g. *maat* 'bathe'), the sense is again non-change of state, but of the S argument. Example (8.17) contrasts the verb *isat* in combination with low affectedness (8.17a), where it translates as 'bite', and intensive -*ka* (8.17b), in which case it translates as 'devour'.

(8.17) a. *dápi uchín isáinɨ̃*

        dapi   uchi=na   isa-**ini**-ɨ̃

        snake   child=ACC   bite-**PFV**-3+DECL

        'the snake has bitten the child'

     b. *ĩkamỹãw̃ãã kuchín isakɨ̃́*

        ikam_yawaã   kuchi=na   isa-**ka**-ɨ̃

        jaguar   pig=ACC   bite-**PFV**-3+DECL

        'the jaguar has devoured the pig'

The verb *isat* is the only attested S=O ambitransitive verb, and examples in §7.6.3 show that the same two perfective suffixes contrast in its intransitive uses: 'low affectedness' *-i(ni)* gives the sense of 'burn oneself' while 'intensive' *-ka* gives the sense of 'be consumed by fire'.

Some typical verbs that take *-i(ni)* are *maat* 'bathe'; *isat* 'bite'; *taut* 'dig (an animal) out (of the ground)'. The long form *-ini* appears when followed by some vowel-initial suffixes – see §3.6.1.

8.3.1.1 Exceptional perfective stems

In addition to the root alternations involving addition of /a/ and/or loss of /u/ that define the five conjugations (§6.2), some other phonological changes can affect perfective stems. The first is clearly phonologically motivated, and involves a kind of vowel harmony (8.18). This is not a productive phonological process, however, and is limited to this morphological environment.

(8.18)   /ɨ/ → [i] when *-ki(ni)* 'associated motion' perfective suffix is added

Others involve consonantal changes, shown in Table 8.3. These verbs are both members of the 3B conjugation, with change of root-final /u/ to /a/ in perfective stems and loss of /u/ in imperfective stems (§6.2). They must be lexically-marked exceptions, as there is no phonological motivation for the changes.

Table 8.3: Consonant change in perfective roots

unmarked	perfective	imperfective	gloss
shimu-	shiya-ka- go:PL-PFV-	shim-a- go:PL-IPFV-	'go (plural S)'
umu-	uwa-ha- drink-PFV-	um-a- drink-IPFV-	'drink'[3]

8.3.2 The imperfective stem

The imperfective stem is marked with the suffix -*a* when the verb has singular subject.[4] The singular imperfective suffix replaces the final vowel of a polysyllabic stem and normally appears as a separate syllable with monosyllabic roots, although the verb *tu* 'say' is an exception to this rule, having imperfective stem [ta], not **[tuwa].[5] In example (8.19), the combination of first person object -*hu* plus imperfective -*a* surfaces as [ha].

(8.19)   *íkamỹãw̃ãã miníthawai*
         ikam_yawaã   mini-tu-**ha**-wa-i
         jaguar   arrive-APPL-1SG.OBJ+**IPFV**-3-DECL
         'a jaguar is attacking me' (agr041005_14)

And compare (8.20a), with the imperfective stem *ta-*, with (8.20b), where the imperfective suffix follows the object marker, allowing the root to surface as *tu-*.

(8.20)   a.   *táhai*
              tu-**a**-ha-i
              say-IPFV-1SG-DECL
              'I say'

---

3 In the case of *umut* 'drink' Uwarai et al. (1998) give *uma-ha* as the perfective stem; this is not supported by my own data.
4 Corbera (1994: 253) considers what I have labelled the imperfective suffix to be a present tense marker, and states that a lexically-conditioned set of verbs do not take -*a*; however, in the examples he gives, the lack of surface /a/ can be explained by independently motivated rules of vowel elision.
5 But note one instance in my data of the form [túwamu] < *tu-a-mau* (say-IPFV-NSBJ.NMLZ) 'that which is said', used in a traditional story (agr040712_02) told by Benjamín Chamik (age approx. 70) and noted as an 'old people's pronunciation' by Pablo Santiak (aged 43); the modern pronunciation is [támau].

   b.   *túhamui*
       tu-**hama**-wa-i
       say-2.OBJ+**IPFV**-3-DECL
       '(she) says to you' (agr040721_07)

When the subject is plural, the imperfective stem is marked with the suffix *-ina*: compare (8.21a) and (8.21b).

(8.21) a.   *yúwahai*
         yu-**a**-ha-i
         eat-**IPFV**-1SG-DECL
         'I eat'

       b.   *yúinawai*
         yu-**ina**-wa-i
         eat-**PL:IPFV**-3-DECL
         'they eat'

Perfective stems mark plural subject with a separate suffix *-aha* in slot C2. Neither *-ina* nor *-aha* is obligatory, and a verb form that is not formally marked as plural is unmarked for number, and may be interpreted as having singular or plural subject. In finite verbs first and second person have distinct singular and plural subject markers in slot F, in addition to the optional plural markers.

8.3.3 The potential stem

The potential stem is formed with the potential suffix *-mai* in slot C. The potential stem makes all transitive verbs ambitransitive, of the S=O type. In (8.22a) the subject of the potential marked verb is the notional subject, while in (8.22b) it is the notional object.

(8.22) a.   *nĩ̃ wainmáinai*
         nĩ   waina-**mai**-inu=ai
         3sg   see-**POT**-NMLZ=COP:3:DECL
         'she can see'

       b.   *píshakak shíiŋ páan wainmáinai*
         pishaka=ka   shiiha   paan   waina-**mai**-inu=ai
         bird=TOP   well   clearly   see-**POT**-NMLZ=COP:3:DECL
         'the bird can be easily seen'

Potential forms very commonly appear with the nominalizer *-inu*, as in (8.23), where the nominalized verb is functioning as complement of *dikapit* 'feel' (see Chapter 17).

(8.23)   *shíiŋ antúmain dikápias'hai*
shiiiha   antu-**mai**-inu   dikapɨ-a-tsu-ha-i
well   hear-**POT**-NMLZ   feel-IPFV-NEG-1SG-DECL
'I can't hear (it) very well' lit. *I don't feel able to hear it*

Because the potential suffix occupies the same slot as the plural markers, it is incompatible with plural marking. In (8.24) the subject pronoun and the copula verb are explicitly plural, but the nominalized potential stem cannot take any plural marker.

(8.24)   *dítak wɨkaɨmáin áinatsui*
dita=ka   wɨkaɨɰa-**mai**-inu   a-ina-tsu-wa-i
3pl=TOP   walk-**POT**-NMLZ   COP-PL:IPFV-NEG-3-DECL
'they can't walk'

Although nominalized forms are more common, the potential stem may also form a finite verb, as in (8.25, 8.26).

(8.25)   *íik wɨkaɨbáitsuhi*
ii=ka   wɨkaɨɰa-**mai**-tsu-hi
1pl=TOP   walk-**POT**-NEG-1PL+DECL
'we can't walk'

(8.26)   *wíka wainmáishmaihai yakúmnak*
wi=ka   waina-**mai**-cha-maya-ha-i   yakuma=na=ka
1sg=TOP   see-**POT**-NEG-INTPST-1SG-DECL   howler.monkey=ACC=TOP
'I couldn't see the howler monkey'

8.3.4 The durative stem

The durative stem is formed with the durative suffix *-ma* in slot C. This stem only appears followed by the imperative suffix *-ta*. Imperative marking typically appears with the perfective stem; the durative stem is used in a situation where the addressee is already performing the action of the verb and the speaker is leaving the scene. Such forms thus give a sense of "keep on doing VERB (in my absence)". The most common exemplar is the usual leave-taking formula in (8.27).

(8.27)   *puhuumatá*
          puhu-**ma**-ta
          live-**DUR**-IMP
          'keep on living (in my absence)'

Although relatively uncommon aside from the formula in (8.27), there are apparently no limitations (other than contextual) on which verbs can take the durative stem.
Example (8.28) was used when the host was called away during a meal, and encour-
aged his guest to keep eating, and example (8.29) was uttered by a visitor who left
while the host was playing the guitar.

(8.28)   *yuumatá*
          yu-**ma**-ta
          eat-**DUR**-IMP
          'keep on eating (in my absence)'

(8.29)   *kitára awatuumatá*
          kitara   awatu-**ma**-ta
          guitar   hit-**DUR**-IMP
          'keep on playing the guitar (in my absence)'

The final vowel of the root is always lengthened when the durative suffix is added.

8.3.5 Periphrastic aspectual construction

In addition to the stems formed with aspect markers in slot C, progressive aspect
may be expressed with a periphrastic construction using the simultaneous subordinate verb form and an auxiliary verb. The most common auxiliary in this construction is *puhut* 'live' (example 8.30), but *wahat* 'stand' and the copula *ata* may also be
used. See §6.7 for a full description of auxiliary constructions.

(8.30)   *takákun puháhai*
          taka-ku-nu   puha-ha-i
          work+IPFV-SIM-1SG:SS   live+IPFV-1SG-DECL
          'I am working'

8.4 Tense

Aguaruna has four synthetic past tenses, plus a past tense nominalizer, and two
synthetic future tenses plus a future nominalizer. Imperative, jussive and desidera-

tive suffixes are historically based on the primary future suffix, and along with apprehensive and hortative are formally part of the tense paradigm. Lack of tense marking implies present tense. Degree of remoteness and (back/fore)grounding of the action of a verb are both relevant to the selection of tense markers. The past tenses, in particular, show a subtle interplay of degree of remoteness and grounding of the action.

Two nominalizers take part in tense marking. The narrative past nominalizer *-haku* is used in narratives to "set the scene", and the future subject nominalizer *-tinu* (etymologically composed of immediate future *-ta* and the subject nominalizer *-inu*) combines with the copula enclitic to give an indefinite future form. Although not formally part of the verbal tense paradigms, both nominalized forms are discussed here as they are functionally tense markers.

Nominalizations formed with the subject nominalizer *-u* are often used as the only lexical verb in an independent clause, and typically imply past tense and non-firsthand information source. The nominalization may appear with the enclitic copula or an auxiliary verb. In many examples the nominalized verb takes no further marking, and although this could be formally analysed as a predicate nominal, it functions as a finite verb marking non-firsthand information source (§15.5.3; and see §18.6 for further discussion of source-of-information marking).

All of the synthetic tense markers can be related historically to three basic forms, which I label the primary tense suffixes. The three primary forms are: *-ta* 'desirable future'; *-ma* 'recent past' and *-ya* 'remote past'. All three of these suffixes are used synchronically as tense markers, and also appear in historically complex morphemes. The 'desirable future' suffix *-ta* creates a future stem, which appears to have been a separate word historically. All future tense forms are based on the future stem. Past tenses are a little less straightforward. As well as explaining certain properties of historically complex morphemes, an appreciation of the historical makeup of tense suffixes helps to explain the complexities of third-person marking, as shown in §8.7 below. In the following sections I begin with present tense, followed by past and then future tenses.

8.4.1 Present tense

Present tense is formally unmarked. In conjunction with the imperfective stem, present tense expresses an ongoing or habitual action, as in (8.31).

(8.31)   *yúwahai*
           yu-a-ha-i
           eat-IPFV-1SG-DECL
           'I am eating' OR 'I eat'

While simple present imperfective forms express habitual actions or states, progressive aspect is typically expressed with constructions involving the simultaneous subordinator -*ku* and the auxiliary verb *puhut* 'live' (8.32; §6.7).

(8.32)   *máakun puháhai*
        maa-ku-nu   puha-ha-i
        bathe+IPFV-SIM-1SG:SS   live+IPFV-1SG-DECL
        'I am bathing'

A more explicitly stative sense can be expressed using a nominalization, as in example (8.33) where the use of nominalized *yuchau* 'one who does not eat' shows that this is a property of the subject. Note that in this example the finite person and mood marking is suffixed directly to the nominalized form, without a copula enclitic.

(8.33)   *bukintín yúchauhai*
        bukinti=na   yu-chau-ha-i
        palm.grub=ACC   eat-NEG.NMLZ-1SG-DECL
        'I don't eat palm grubs'

Example (8.34) shows the use of the verb *wainat* 'see' in the sense of 'get to know, know' (similar to Spanish *conocer*). This example translates not as 'I see him/her' but rather 'I know him/her'. As with (8.33), the finite person and mood marking is directly suffixed to the nominalized form (the use of verbal morphology with nominalizations is discussed further in §15.3.3).

(8.34)   *waínnuhai*
        waina-inu-ha-i
        see-NMLZ-1SG-DECL
        'I know him/her'

Just one verb, *puhut* 'live', can appear in a present tense form without being marked for imperfective aspect, as described in §6.4.3.

8.4.2 Perfective past

Just-completed actions can be expressed using the perfective form of the verb in present tense, that is, with no overt tense marker. An immediate past reading arises from the perfective aspect of the verb. First person subject is marked with the suffix -*ha* (example 8.35), second person takes the past tense form -*umɨ* (8.36, 8.37; see §8.7) and third person is marked with the suffix -*ɨ* (8.38, 8.39).

(8.35)   *máihai*
            mai-ha-i
            bathe+PFV-1SG-DECL
            'I'm done bathing' OR 'I've just bathed'

(8.36)   *wáŋka aáncha áikaumɨ*
            waŋka   aani=sha   aika-umɨ
            why   thus=Q.TOP   thus+VBLZ.TR+PFV-2SG+DECL
            'why have you done that?' (agr041005_15)

(8.37)   *taáumɨk*
            ta-a-umɨ=ka
            come-PFV-2SG=Q
            'have you come?'

(8.38)   *wɨ̃ɨ̃*
            wɨ-ɨ̃
            go+PFV-3+DECL
            's/he's gone'

(8.39)   *máinɨ̃*
            ma-ini-ɨ̃
            bathe-PFV-3+DECL
            's/he's finished bathing'

The fact that the past-tense second person suffix -*umɨ* appears with the perfective stem shows that perfective verbs are in fact treated as past tense within the grammar of Aguaruna. The third person suffix -*ɨ* does not appear elsewhere in the grammar, but may be etymologically part of the third-person recent past tense marker -*mɨ̃* (§8.4.3).

8.4.3 Synthetic past tenses

There are four true synthetic past tenses which I label RECENT PAST, INTERMEDIATE PAST, DISTANT PAST and REMOTE PAST. The NARRATIVE PAST nominalizer -*haku* is functionally part of the tense-marking paradigm. There are also a number of periphrastic strategies involving auxiliary constructions, and verbs marked with the subject nominalizer -*u* function as a non-firsthand information marker in traditional stories.

The past tense suffixes are shown in Table 8.4. Recent past, intermediate past and distant past all appear with the perfective stem, while remote past -*ya* and narrative past -*haku* are suffixed directly to the unmarked verb root.

Table 8.4: Past tense markers

form	stem	gloss	distance from present
-∅	perfective	perfective past	Just-completed action
-*ma*	perfective	recent past	Same day to a few days; relevant to present situation
-*ma…ya*	perfective	intermediate past	Same day to a few weeks; less relevance to present situation
-*ama….ya*	perfective	distant past	Months to years; relevant to event line of narrative
-*ya*	unmarked	remote past	Years; imperfective or stative sense
-*haku*	unmarked	narrative past	Years

No synthetic past tense marker takes the imperfective stem, but the nominalizer -*u* may do so, including in its role as a *de facto* finite verb marker.

Native speakers characterize the distinction between the tenses in terms of degrees of remoteness, as illustrated in Table 8.4, however actual use shows that there must be other factors involved, and it is impossible to assign a meaning for each tense purely in terms of degree of remoteness. In particular (and in spite of the formal similarity) intermediate and distant past appear in quite different contexts. Comrie (1985) warns:

> In studying degrees of remoteness in tense systems, it is essential to ensure that the distinction under discussion has degree of remoteness as part of its meaning, rather than just as an implicature deriving from other features of its meaning.
>
> (Comrie 1985: 83–84)

The major factor aside from the purely temporal is grounding of the state or event described. Recent past and intermediate past basically cover the same time periods, and are typically used in conversation. A foregrounded event is typically more recent than a backgrounded one. Intermediate past may appear on the verb 'say' marking narrative modality. In firsthand narrative (for example Text 2), distant past and remote past are typically used, again contrasting in foregrounding; clauses that are part of the main event line will take distant past tense, while those that are scene-setting or parenthetical will take remote past. The recent, intermediate and distant past forms imply firsthand information on the part of the speaker. Where the information is not firsthand (for example when telling a traditional story), verbs are typically nominalized with *-u* which functions then as a general PAST TENSE + NON-FIRSTHAND marker. Finally, narrative past marked with the nominalizer *-haku* is used for states or events furthest from the present, and does not appear to enter into the same distinctions, although it is typically used for backgrounded clauses. Table 8.5 summarizes the past tense markers on the basis of the parameters just described:

Table 8.5: Past tense markers and narrative functions

degree of remoteness	unmarked for information source		non-firsthand information source
	foregrounded	backgrounded	
–	*-ma* 'recent past'	*-ma...ya* 'intermediate past'	*-u* 'non-firsthand past tense' (nominalizer)
	-ama...ya 'distant past'	*-ya* 'remote past'	
+	*-haku* 'narrative past' (nominalizer)		

Foreground and background correlate with relative time: a backgrounded event or state is situational, and therefore typically prior to a foregrounded event. Recent past and remote past are the primary past forms, and intermediate past and distant past are apparently composed of the two primary suffixes in combination.

It is important to note that the current description may reflect limitations of the data, which consists almost entirely of narratives. The first-hand narratives are typically placed some years into the past. In normal conversation, where someone might relate a narrative about some events of the day before, presumably recent and intermediate past tenses would be used. The motivations for selecting different tenses are clearly more complex than simple degree of remoteness, and much more work is needed, along with a greater variety of data, to fully understand the system.

8.4.3.1 Recent past tense *-ma*

The recent past tense suffix is *-ma*, shown in (8.40) and (8.41). The time period covered by recent past is anywhere from earlier the same day to a few days ago, and the situation described is treated as being relevant to the present context.

(8.40) *yuwámkum*
        yu-a-**ma**=ka-umɨ
        eat-PFV-**RECPST**=Q-2
        'have you eaten?'

(8.41) *tímahai*
        ti-**ma**-ha-i
        say+PFV-**RECPST**-1SG-DECL
        'I said'

Example (8.42) is from a story in which a man kills the family dog, cooks it and feeds it to his wife. It is not until he serves her the boiled head that the wife realizes what she is eating and asks the question.[6]

(8.42) *ỹãw̃áã íinu maáshmakum*
        yawaã   ii-nau   ma-a-cha-**ma**=ka-umɨ
        dog   1pl-POSS   kill-PFV-NEG-**RECPST**=Q-2
        'have you killed our dog?' (agr041005_15)

Table 8.6 gives a paradigm for recent past with the verb *tsupit* 'cut'.

Table 8.6: Paradigm with recent past suffix *-ma*

person	singular	plural
1	*tsupíkmahai* tsupi-ka-**ma**-ha-i cut-PFV-**RECPST**-1SG-DECL	*tsupíkmahi* tsupi-ka-**ma**-hi cut-PFV-**RECPST**-1PL+DECL
2	*tsupíkmumɨ* tsupi-ka-**ma**-umɨ cut-PFV-**RECPST**-2SG+DECL	*tsupíkmuhumɨ* tsupi-ka-**ma**-uhumɨ cut-PFV-**RECPST**-2PL+DECL
3	*tsupíkmɨ̃* tsupi-ka-**mɨ̃** cut-PFV-**RECPST**:3:DECL	(same as singular)

With third person subject in declarative clauses the fusional form *-mɨ̃* appears. Perhaps this form has arisen from a fusion of recent past *-ma* with the suffix *-ɨ̃* that marks third person subject in immediate past forms (§8.4.2). The form *-mɨ̃* only appears in declarative clauses, and recent past with third person subject appears

---

6 For the use of negative polarity in this question, see discussion in Chapter 10.

as -*ma* in non-declarative clauses; this is illustrated with polar interrogative in (8.43) and counter expectation in (8.44).

(8.43)   *yuwámak*
           yu-a-**ma**=ka
           eat-PFV-**RECPST**=Q
           'did s/he eat?'

(8.44)   *timaháma*
           ti-**ma**-hama
           say+PFV-**RECPST**-CNTR.EX
           's/he said it!'

8.4.3.2 Intermediate past -*ma...ya*

Intermediate past -*ma...ya* is characterized by speakers as expressing a time longer ago than recent past. For events within the last few days, either tense may be used but recent past adds a sense of relevance to the present context that is not necessarily the case with intermediate past. In example (8.45), the speaker's wife's planting is not what is being talked about, so takes intermediate past. It is backgrounded, scene-setting or parenthetical.

(8.45)   *ánumin yúwat núnak mína núwa ukuábia*
           anumin   yu-a-t   [nu=na=ka   mi=na   nuwa
           EXPL   eat-IPFV-?   ANA=ACC=TOP   1sg=ACC   wife
           uku-a-**maya**]
           SOW-PFV-**INTPST:3**]
           'you useless thing, eating what my wife sowed!' (agr040721_07)[7]

Example (8.46) is from personal correspondence, and the addressee's daughter was born in the last day or two. The verb marked with intermediate past is backgrounded, as the focus of the interrogation is the word *piŋkiŋ* 'good'.

(8.46)   *tuhã nawanhumish piŋkihak akïinamia*
           tuhã   nawantu-hu-mɨ=sha   piŋkɨha=ka
           but   daughter-PSSD-2=Q.TOP   good=Q

---

7 It is not clear what morpheme the final /t/ of the word *yuwat* represents.

akiina-**maya**
be.born+PFV-**INTPST:3**
'so was your daughter born ok?' (personal correspondence)

Example (8.47) shows that distance in time is not the only factor conditioning the choice of tense, as the elders told this story a long time ago, when the current speaker was a child. More important is the fact that it happened in the past, and it is not what is currently the topic of discussion.

(8.47)   *núna múun áuŋmatin áhabia núna wísha táhai*

nu=na	muunta	auhumatu-inu	aha-**maya**
ANA=ACC	elder	tell-NMLZ	COP+PL-**INTPST:3**
nu=na	wi=sha	ta-ha-i	
ANAREL=ACC	1sg=ADD	say+IPFV-1SG-DECL	

'that (story) which the elders told, I also tell it (now)' (agr040723_29)

Intermediate past, like recent past, is rare in narratives. The above examples demonstrate this: (8.45) is from reported speech in a narrative, so reflects the conversational context; and (8.47) is the very last line of a narrative, a typical formula for ending stories in which the narrator addresses the audience directly, and is thus outside of the frame of the narrative itself.

The suffix itself is morphologically complex, at least historically, and is a combination of primary recent past *-ma* and primary remote past *-ya*. Three morphological effects follow from this:

– The polar interrogative enclitic *=ka* intervenes between the /ma/ and the /ya/. This enclitic always directly follows recent past *-ma*.
– Diphthong reduction when the first vowel of the suffix would be in a position to be elided suggests a morphologically complex origin (see paradigms in Table 8.7 and Table 8.8).
– The change of final /a/ to /i/ to mark third person singular subject, as happens with remote past *-ya*.

Table 8.7 and Table 8.8 show the paradigms for postconsonantal and postvocalic allomorphs, respectively, of intermediate past.

Table 8.7: Paradigm with intermediate past suffix *-ma...ya* following consonant

person	singular	plural
1	*tsupíkmaihai* tsupi-ka-**maya**-ha-i cut-PFV-**INTPST**-1SG-DECL	*tsupíkmaihi* tsupi-ka-**maya**-hi cut-PFV-**INTPST**-1PL+DECL
2	*tsupíkmayumɨ* tsupi-ka-**maya**-umɨ cut-PFV-**INTPST**-2SG+DECL	*tsupíkmaihumɨ* tsupi-ka-**maya**-uhumɨ cut-PFV-**INTPST**-2PL+DECL
3	*tsupíkmayi* tsupi-ka-**mayi** cut-PFV-**INTPST**:3:DECL	(same as singular)

Table 8.8: Paradigm with intermediate past suffix *-ma...ya* following vowel

person	singular	plural
1	*yuwábiahai* yu-a-**maya**-ha-i eat-PFV-**INTPST**-1SG-DECL	*yuwábiahi* yu-a-**maya**-hi eat-PFV-**INTPST**-1PL+DECL
2	*yuwábiumɨ* yu-a-**maya**-umɨ eat-PFV-**INTPST**-2SG+DECL	*yuwábiuhumɨ* yu-a-**maya**-uhumɨ eat-PFV-**INTPST**-2PL+DECL
3	*yuwábi* yu-a-**mayi** eat-PFV-**INTPST**:3:DECL	(same as singular)

And Table 8.9 shows a paradigm including polar interrogative (the two elements of intermediate past are glossed separately but identically).

Table 8.9: Paradigm with intermediate past *-ma...ya* and polar interrogative *-ka*

person	singular	plural
1	*untsúkmakiaŋ* untsu-ka-**ma**=ka-**ya**-ha call-PFV-**INTPST**=Q-**INTPST**-1SG	*untsúkmakiaŋ* untsu-ka-**ma**=ka-**ya**-hi call-PFV-**INTPST**=Q-**INTPST**-1PL
2	*untsúkmakium* untsu-ka-**ma**=ka-**ya**-umɨ call-PFV-**INTPST**=Q-**INTPST**-2SG	*untsúkmakiuhum* untsu-ka-**ma**=ka-**ya**-uhumɨ call-PFV-**INTPST**=Q-**INTPST**-2PL
3	*untsúkmakia* untsu-ka-**ma**=ka-**ya** call-PFV-**INTPST**=Q-**INTPST:3**	(same as singular)

Note that the forms following a vowel always contain the denasalized stop [b] – thus there exist surface minimal pairs such as (8.48) and (8.49). The phonological implications of this were discussed in §3.4.

(8.48)   *yuwámi*
             yu-a-mi
             eat-PFV-HORT
             'let's eat'

(8.49)   *yuwábi*
             yu-a-bi
             eat-PFV-INTPST:3:DECL
             'he ate'

8.4.3.3 Distant past *-ama...ya*

The distant past form consists of the syllable /a/ followed by the postvocalic allomorph of the intermediate past suffix *-ma...ya*. Table 8.10 illustrates the paradigm.

Table 8.10: Paradigm with -*ama...ya* 'distant past' following consonant

person	singular	plural
1	*untsukábiahai* untsu-ka-**amaya**-ha-i call-PFV-**DISTPST**-1SG-DECL	*untsukábiahi* untsu-ka-**amaya**-hi call-PFV-**DISTPST**-1PL+DECL
2	*untsukábiumɨ* untsu-ka-**amaya**-umɨ call-PFV-**DISTPST**-2SG+DECL	*untsukábiuhumɨ* untsu-ka-**amaya**-uhumɨ call-PFV-**DISTPST**-2PL+DECL
3	*untsukábi* untsu-ka-**amayi** call-PFV-**DISTPST**:3:DECL	(same as singular)

As with intermediate past forms, the polar interrogative enclitic =*ka* intervenes between the two elements /ama/ and /ya/. The paradigm is shown in Table 8.11.

Table 8.11: Paradigm with -*ama...ya* 'distant past' with interrogative

person	singular	plural
1	*untsukámkayaŋ* untsu-ka-**ama**=ka-**ya**-ha call-PFV-**DISTPST**=Q-**DISTPST**-1SG	*untsukámkayaŋ* untsu-ka-**ama**=ka-**ya**-hi call-PFV-**DISTPST**=Q-**DISTPST**-1PL
2	*untsukámkayum* untsu-ka-**ama**=ka-**ya**-umɨ call-PFV-**DISTPST**=Q-**DISTPST**-2SG	*untsukámkayuhum* untsu-ka-**ama**=ka-**ya**-uhumɨ call-PFV-**DISTPST**=Q-**DISTPST**-2PL
3	*untsukámkaya* untsu-ka-**ama**=ka-**ya** call-PFV-**DISTPST**=Q-**DISTPST**:**3**	(same as singular)

The distant past form has most likely arisen from a fused periphrasis, consisting of the perfective verb stem followed by the copula verb *ata* inflected with the intermediate past suffix; so for example the periphrastic form **untsu-ka a-maya-ha-i* (call-PFV be-INTPST-1SG-DECL) would fuse to form [untsúkabiahai] 'I called'.

One further oddity of distant past is in the combination with negative -*cha*. In the plural forms, the /a/ of negative -*cha* does not appear to have been elided, and epenthetic /w/ appears, as illustrated in Table 8.12. The phenomenon is apparent where level I plural -*aha* is present too, thus I have included an explicitly marked third person plural form for comparison. It is not clear what triggers this epenthesis.

Table 8.12: Paradigm with *-ama...ya* 'distant past' with negative

person	singular	plural
1	*maáchabiahai*	*maáchawabiahi*
	ma-a-cha-**amaya**-ha-i	ma-a-cha-**w-amaya**-hi
	kill-PFV-NEG-**DISTPST**-1SG-DECL	kill-PFV-NEG-**EP-DISTPST**-1PL+DECL
2	*maáchabiumɨ*	*maáchawabiuhumɨ*
	ma-a-cha-**amaya**-umɨ	ma-a-cha-**w-amaya**-uhumɨ
	kill-PFV-NEG-**DISTPST**-2SG+DECL	kill-PFV-NEG-**EP-DISTPST**-2PL+DECL
3	*maáchabi*	*maáchawahabi*
	ma-a-cha-**amayi**	ma-a-cha-**w-aha-amayi**
	kill-PFV-NEG-**DISTPST:3:DECL**	kill-PFV-NEG-**EP-PL-DISTPST:3:DECL**

Examples (8.50–8.52) illustrate distant past in discourse, where it marks foregrounded clauses on the main event line.

(8.50)   *"ayú" tusán wãỹã́w̃ãbiahai*
         [ayu   tu-sa-nu]   waĩ-aw-**amaya**-ha-i
         ok   say-SBD-1SG:SS   enter-PFV-**DISTPST**-1SG-DECL
         'saying "ok" I went in' (Text 2:22)

(8.51)   *"ayú" tíabiahai*
         ayu   ti-**amaya**-ha-i
         ok   say+PFV-**DISTPST**-1SG-DECL
         '"ok" I said' (agr040824_02)

(8.52)   *taáwabiahai*
         ta-aw-**amaya**-ha-i
         come-PFV-**DISTPST**-1SG-DECL
         'I arrived' (Text 2:15)

The multi-clause example (8.53) contrasts distant past in line (d), as the foregrounded event, with remote past in its scene-setting function in lines (a) and (c).

(8.53) a.   *volquete ... miníyi*
            volquete   mini-yi
            truck   arrive-REMPST:3:DECL
            'a truck arrived'

b. *núniakũĩ*
nu-ni-a-ku-ĩ
ANA-VBLZ.INTR-IPFV-SIM+1/3-DS
'when it did that...'

c. *iwíyahi "tɨpɨstí" tusá*

iwi-ya-hi	[tɨpɨ-sa-ti	tu-sa]
raise.hand-REMPST-1PL+DECL	lie.down-PFV-JUSS	say-SBD+1PL:SS

'we raised our hands saying "may it stop!"'

d. *túhãsh naŋkáɨtamkiabi*
tuhã=sha   naŋkaɨɰa-tama-ki-amayi
but=ADD   pass-1PL.OBJ-PFV-DISTPST:3:DECL
'but it passed us by' (agr040824_02)

8.4.3.4 Remote past -*ya*

Remote past is used in narratives to refer to situations years in the past, such as the childhood of an adult narrator, or even further into a mythological past. Unlike the other past tense suffixes, remote past is attached to the unmarked verb root, not the perfective stem. It is typically used in backgrounded, scene-setting clauses, as in example (8.54) which comes from an old man's reminiscence about taking part in vision quests as a boy, and (8.55) where a speaker steps out of the narrative to directly address the audience with some background information.

(8.54) *tunanásh kahamín áyahai*
tuna=na=sha   kahama-inu   a-**ya**-ha-i
waterfall=ACC=ADD dream-NMLZ   COP-**REMPST**-1SG-DECL
'I would dream of a waterfall too' (i.e. 'I would see visions of spirits')
(agr040723_03)

(8.55) *núna múun áuŋmatuinakũĩ "wáinkas táwa" túyahai*
nu=na   muunta   auhumatu-ina-ku-ĩ   wainakasã
ANA=ACC   elder   tell-PL:IPFV-SIM+1/3-DS in.vain+3
ta-wa   tu-**ya**-ha-i
say+IPFV-3:EXCL   say-**REMPST**-1SG-DECL
'as the elders told that (story), I would say "they're talking rubbish!"'
(agr040723_29)

Remote past, third-person singular subject and declarative mood are marked with a fusional suffix -*yi* (8.56), but the third-person singular form appears as -*ya* in non-declarative contexts as in example (8.57), where narrative modality is marked with the word *tuwahamɨ̃*.

(8.56)   *volquete ... miníyi*
          volquete   mini-yi
          truck   arrive-REMPST:3:DECL
          'a truck arrived' (repeated from example 8.53)

(8.57)   *dúik múuntak túkɨ minák áwa awatɨ̃ táya túahamɨ̃*
          duik   muunta=ka   tukɨ   [mina-kũ]
          olden   adult=TOP   always   arrive+IPFV-SIM+3:SS
          [awa   awatɨ̃]   ta-**ya**   tuwahamɨ̃
          REDUP   hit+PFV+SEQ+3:SS   come-**REMPST:3**   NARR
          'the olden-day people always hit (the tree root) as they were coming (back home), it is said' (agr040723_29)

Unlike other past tense forms, third-person plural is marked distinctly with the suffix *-numɨ̃*, and no level I plural marking is possible. The only other forms to take the third plural suffix *-numɨ̃* are jussive and apprehensive (§8.4.4, §8.5). Paradigms for remote past forms are given in Table 8.13 and Table 8.14.

Table 8.13: Paradigm with *-ya* 'remote past' following vowel

person	singular	plural
1	*máuyahai* mau-**ya**-ha-i kill-**REMPST**-1SG-DECL	*máuyahi* mau-**ya**-hi kill-**REMPST**-1PL+DECL
2	*máuyumɨ̃* mau-**ya**-umɨ kill-**REMPST**-2SG+DECL	*máuyuhumɨ̃* mau-**ya**-uhumɨ kill-**REMPST**-2PL+DECL
3	*máuyi* mau-**yi** kill-**REMPST**:3SG:DECL	*máuyanumɨ̃* mau-**ya**-numɨ kill-**REMPST**-3PL+DECL

Table 8.14: Paradigm with -*ya* 'remote past' following consonant (negative -*tsa*)

person	singular	plural
1	*máutsiahai*	*máutsiahi*
	mau-tsa-**ya**-ha-i	mau-tsa-**ya**-hi
	kill-NEG-**REMPST**-1SG-DECL	kill-NEG-**REMPST**-1PL+DECL
2	*máutsiumɨ*	*máutsiuhumɨ*
	mau-tsa-**ya**-umɨ	mau-tsa-**ya**-uhumɨ
	kill-NEG-**REMPST**-2SG+DECL	kill-NEG-**REMPST**-2PL+DECL
3	*máutsi*	*máutsianumɨ*
	mau-tsa-**yi**	mau-tsa-**ya**-numɨ
	kill-NEG-**REMPST**:3SG:DECL	kill-NEG-**REMPST**-3:PL+DECL

8.4.3.5 Nominalizers as past tense markers
Two nominalizers interact functionally with the system of past tense marking. The narrative past nominalizer -*haku* can only appear in predicate function, where it is marked with the copula enclitic. The subject nominalizer -*u* is versatile, and typically forms relative clauses. It also functions as a past tense marker in contexts of non-firsthand information source. The tense marking functions of both of these nominalizers are described in §15.5.3.

8.4.4 Future tenses, imperative, jussive and desiderative

8.4.4.1 Preliminary remarks
The primary future tense suffix is -*ta* / -*ti*. It appears as 'immediate future' in declarative verbs with first person subject, and appears to have originally had a 'desirable future' meaning. With second and third person subjects it has the sense of desirable future, as it marks imperative and jussive respectively, and does not take a mood marker in slot G. The same primary future tense can appear with all persons in interrogative and speculative clauses; but in these clause types the sense of desirability is not apparent, and it is interpreted as a simple future tense. Table 8.15 summarizes the different senses of the primary future suffix in different clause types, and the person restrictions.

Table 8.15: Interaction of primary future suffix -*ta* with mood

	declarative	imperative	jussive	other
1	immediate future	–	–	future
2	–	imperative	–	future
3	–	–	jussive	future

The immediate future appears to be the historical source of the definite and indefinite future and desiderative suffixes, as well as the intentional subordinating suffix (§13.3.2). The definite future, desiderative and intentional forms also appear to involve the verb *tuta* 'say' in their development, testifying to a considerable historical depth to the wide use of speech report constructions in Chicham languages.

The indefinite future is composed of the future subject nominalizer -*tinu* followed by the copula enclitic, and in this one can see that it has something of a potential meaning – the subject will perform some action in the future, with no specific timeframe, and this contrasts with the verbal definite future tense marker that is used when the speaker has a more-or-less specific time in mind at which the action will be performed. The future nominalizer itself is derived from the primary future -*ta* and the general subject nominalizer -*inu*.

In sum, immediate future is etymologically the only future tense morpheme in Aguaruna, and all other future forms, as well as desiderative and intentional, have arisen from grammaticalized combinations of immediate future with other elements.

8.4.4.2 Immediate future
Immediate future is marked with the suffix -*ta* (8.58).

(8.58)   *húna hukíthai*
        hu=na   hu-ki-**ta**-ha-i
        PROX=ACC   take-PFV-**IFUT**-1SG-DECL
        'I'll take this'

In declarative clauses, this form is only used with first-person singular subject – second and third-person subjects form imperative and jussive moods, respectively. The time specified is typically immediate; however, it can be used to indicate a time further into the future, such as the following day. Some examples have a more intentional or desiderative sense, such as (8.59).

(8.59) *wísha diistáhai*
        wi=sha   dii-sa-**ta**-ha-i
        1sg=ADD   see-PFV-**IFUT**-1SG-DECL
        'I want to see too!' (agr040721_07)

Examples (8.60 – 8.62) illustrate the use of intentional future in interrogative clauses, where it is compatible with subjects of all persons. Note that the third person
form in non-declarative contexts is -*ti*, the same as jussive.

(8.60) *wáŋka wahíŋmihãĩsh wɨkaɨtámɨ̃*
        waŋka   wahɨ-hu-mɨ=haĩ=sha   wɨkaɨɰa-**ta**-mɨ
        why   sister.in.law-PSSD-2=COM=Q.TOP walk+PFV-**IFUT**-2SG
        'why do you want to go with your sister-in-law?' (agr041005_14)

(8.61) *wáŋka ahápashtamɨ*
        waŋka   ahapa-cha-**ta**-mɨ
        why   give.birth+PFV-NEG-**IFUT**-2SG
        'why aren't you going to give birth?' (agr041005_16)

(8.62) *wáaŋ nĩ̃sh puhutí*
        wãã=ki   nĩ=sha   puhu-**ti**
        why=Q.RHET   3sg=Q.TOP   stay-**IFUT:3**
        'why should she stay?' (agr041005_14)

Example (8.63) shows immediate future with first person subject giving an irrealis
type sense to an interrogative clause.

(8.63) *wísha wáanuk áikathamɨ*
        wi=sha   waã-nu=ki   aika-**ta**-hamɨ
        1sg=Q.TOP   why-1SG:SS=Q.RHET   thus+VBLZ.TR+PFV-**IFUT**-1SG>2SG
        'why would I do that to you?' (agr040723_29)

Immediate future is also used in clauses with speculative modality (see §9.2.4). As
can be seen in the preceding examples, in non-declarative clauses the concept of
desirability is lost, and the suffix simply indicates future tense. In the following
sections I describe the use of the suffix -*ta* / -*ti* in mood marking.

8.4.4.3 Imperative

Imperative always appears with the perfective form of the root. There is no person suffix on a singular imperative form (as in 8.64), and the subject is second-person singular.

(8.64)   *ikɨmsata*
           ikɨma-sa-**ta**
           sit-PFV-**IMP**
           'sit down!'

In plural forms imperative takes the second person plural suffix *-humɨ* (8.65).

(8.65)   *ikɨmsatahum*
           ikɨma-sa-**ta**-humɨ
           sit-PFV-**IMP**-2PL
           'sit down!'

Two incomplete verbs appear only in the imperative form: *haásta* 'wait!' and *ɨ̈sta* 'go on!'. The latter may be used to address people or dogs; there is also a (presumably related) interjection *ɨ̈s* 'down boy!', used to scold dogs. These two incomplete verbs apparently cannot be pluralized, nor do they appear in hortative or jussive forms. I have however heard the form *haásia* 'wait!' with the familiar imperative.

The interjection *ayu* 'ok' is the expected positive response to all imperative forms and to hortative (§8.6).

8.4.4.4 Familiar imperative

The imperative second person forms sometimes appear in the familiar form, used with family and friends. The basic form is *-kia*, and this replaces the usual *-ta* (8.66 – 8.68). Unlike *-ta*, *-kia* does not take accent (compare 8.67a and 8.67b); instead, it forces accent to fall on the verb root (compare 8.68a and 8.68b).

(8.66) a.   *máikia*
             mai-kia
             bathe+PFV-**IMP:FAM**
             'have a bath!'

        b.   *máita*
             mai-**ta**
             bathe+PFV-**IMP**
             'have a bath!'

(8.67) a. *áishmaŋ ákia*
            aishmaŋku   a-**kia**
            man   COP-**IMP:FAM**
            'be a man!'

        b. *áishmaŋ atá*
            aishmaŋku   a-**ta**
            man   COP-**IMP**
            'be a man!'

(8.68) a. *húkikia*
            hu-ki-**kia**
            take-PFV-**IMP:FAM**
            'take (it)!'

        b. *hukíta*
            hu-ki-**ta**
            take-PFV-**IMP**
            'take (it)!'

In some forms, the combination of attenuative perfective suffix *-sa* and familiar imperative *-kia* fuses into *-sia*. If the vowel of the suffix *-sa* is in a position to be elided, the fusional form occurs (8.69, 8.70); otherwise, there is no fusion, as in (8.71). The fused form takes the accent (on the /i/) if the root has no inherent accent, just like imperative *-ta* (compare 8.69a with 8.70a, and see §3.7.1 for details of accent placement in verbs).

(8.69) a. *chichasía*
            chicha-**sia**
            speak-PFV+IMP:FAM
            'speak!'

        b. *chichastá*
            chicha-sa-**ta**
            speak-PFV-**IMP**
            'speak!'

(8.70) a. *uwásia*
            uwa-**sia**
            drink-PFV+IMP:FAM
            'drink!'

b. *uwásta*
    uwa-sa-**ta**
    drink-PFV-**IMP**
    'drink!'

(8.71) a. *yusákia*
           yu-sa-**kia**
           eat-PFV-**IMP:FAM**
           'eat!'

b. *awáttsakia*
    awatu-sa-**kia**
    hit-PFV-**IMP:FAM**
    'hit (it)!'

Compare the two examples in (8.72): in (8.72a), fusion occurs, but in (8.72b) the first person singular object suffix is present, and shifts the suffix *-sa* into a position where it is not a target of vowel elision, and consequently no fusion occurs.

(8.72) a. *diisía*
           dii-sia
           see-PFV+IMP:FAM
           'look!'

b. *diíŋsakia*
    dii-hu-sa-kia
    see-1SG.OBJ-PFV-IMP:FAM
    'look at me!' (agr041005_16)

The other perfective suffixes never fuse with familiar imperative (cf. 8.68a above, with *-ki* 'transferred action' perfective suffix).

8.4.4.5 Plural familiar imperative *-khua*

The plural familiar imperative has the form *-khua* (example 8.73). This suffix appears to contain the element /hu/ that forms the second person plural *-humi* within the *-kia* of singular familiar imperative, suggesting that familiar imperative is etymologically morphologically complex (singular *-ki-a*, plural *-ki-hu-a*). I have no further evidence to support this idea, as I have very few examples of plural familiar imperative.

(8.73)   *yúwakhua*
           yu-a-khua
           eat-PFV-IMP:FAM:PL
           'you~PL~ eat it!' (agr040721_07)

Although there is no evidence that familiar imperative is in the same morphological slot as imperative (because it is never followed by person suffixes), it is functionally equivalent and formally can be considered a variant of the imperative suffix.

8.4.4.6 Jussive

Primary future with third person subject is marked with the portmanteau suffix *-ti* (8.74). This form marks jussive mood.

(8.74)   *w̃ãỹắti*
           waĩ-a-**ti**
           enter-PFV-**JUSS**
           'let him enter!'

It may seem an unnecessary proliferation of terminology to label the third-person form 'jussive' when it could be considered third person imperative. There are examples such as (8.75), however, where the pragmatics of the situation preclude interpretation as a command; rather, it must be a wish or desire.

(8.75)   *wíka "yutúŋti" tusán wakɨ̧ɥahai*
           wi=ka   [yutu-ha-**ti**   tu-sa-nu]   waki-a-ha-i
           1sg=TOP   rain-PFV-**JUSS**   say-SBD-1SG:SS want-IPFV-1SG-DECL
           'I want it to rain' lit. *I want, saying "let it rain!"*

Plural jussive is marked with the suffix *-ti* followed by the third-person plural suffix *-numɨ̃* (8.76).

(8.76)   *díta kaunắ papí áusatnumɨ̃*
           dita   kaunã   papi=na   ausa-**ti-numɨ̃**
           3pl   come:PL+PFV+SEQ+3:SS   book=ACC   study+PFV-**JUSS-3PL**
           'let them come and study!' (agr040824_02)

8.4.4.7 Desiderative

The desiderative suffix is *-tata*, exemplified in (8.77).

(8.77) *yuwátatahai*
        yu-a-**tata**-ha-i
        eat-PFV-**DESID**-1SG-DECL
        'I want to eat'

Desiderative is clearly derived from the immediate future *-ta* plus the verb *tuta* 'say', so its meaning is something like 'I'm about to eat, I say'. This can be seen in the fact that the second element /ta/ is synchronically analysable as the fused combination of the verb root *tu* 'say' and the imperfective suffix *-a*. Compare (8.78), where the imperfective plural suffix *-ina* replaces imperfective *-a*, and the preceding vowel surfaces as /u/, as is the case with the verb *tuta* 'say'. Originally, the speech report construction would have given the desiderative reading, and this construction is similar to the synchronic use of speech report constructions to emphasize a speaker's own words (§17.1).

(8.78) *maátatuidau*
        ma-a-**tatuina**-u
        kill-PFV-**DESID:PL**-NMLZ
        'they wanted to kill (him)' (agr041005_19)

Corbera (1994: 266–267) gives the desiderative suffix in the form *-taŋta*, suggesting that a first-person subject suffix is still present, as in example (8.79).[8]

(8.79) nĩ   suma-ka-**taŋta**-wa-i
        3sg   buy-PFV-**DESID**-3-DECL
        'he wants to buy'

Corbera (1994: 266)

The [ŋ] in the desiderative suffix is a reflex of the first person singular suffix *-ha*. Fast & Larson (1974: 40) give the form of the desiderative suffix as *-tata* or *-tatta*; their explanation of the alternation suggests that the forms were effectively in free variation at the time the data were collected. It is quite plausible that the form *-tatta* represents an intermediate stage, where the [ŋ] has been replaced by [t] (regressive assimilation) before simplification to /tata/. Whatever the history of the desiderative

---

8 A desiderative construction involving the first person suffix and the verb 'say' as a separate phonological word is reported for Achuar-Shiwiar (Fast et al. 1996: 46). No information was available for Huambisa or Shuar.

form, it appears consistently as /tata/ in my data, even where the verb *tuta* 'say' appears as a separate phonological word (based on accent and pause) as in (8.80).

(8.80)   *dítak núna ìntsamhúkta túidau ásaŋ*

            dita=ka   nu=na   ìntsamahu-ka-**ta**   **tu**-ina-u

            3pl=TOP   ANA=ACC   have.sex-PFV-**IFUT**   **say**-PL:IPFV-NMLZ

            asã=ka

            COP+SBD+3:SS=TOP

            'they wanted to have sex with her' (agr041005_14)

The relatively recent grammaticalization of the suffix *-tata* explains the fact that it never undergoes syncope, always surfacing as /tata/ or /tatu/ when followed by the plural imperfective suffix *-ina*. See Chapter 17 for a description of speech report constructions.

    The intentional subordinating suffix *-tasa* / *-tatus* on dependent verbs is a phonologically reduced outcome of the desiderative suffix followed by the non-temporal subordinator *-sa* (see §13.3.2).

8.4.4.8 Definite future
The definite future suffix is *-tata*. It is used when the speaker has a more-or-less specific future time in mind, and is typically accompanied by a time adverb, as in (8.81, 8.82).

(8.81)   *kashín wìtathai*

            kashini   wì-**tata**-ha-i

            tomorrow   go+PFV-**FUT**-1SG-DECL

            'I will go tomorrow'

(8.82)   *dos mil seistin taáttahai*

            dos mil seis=tin   ta-a-**tata**-ha-i

            2006=TIME   come-PFV-**FUT**-1SG-DECL

            'I will come (back) in 2006'

Definite future and singular desiderative are homophonous at the underlying level, both having the form *-tata*, but contrast in the application of syncope to the surface form. Desiderative never undergoes syncope, while definite future always does (of the first or second syllable, depending upon its position in the phonological word), surfacing as /tta/ or /tat/. Like desiderative, the definite future suffix is most likely derived historically from immediate future *-ta* plus the verb *tu* 'say', but definite future is clearly a more fully grammaticalized suffix: in addition to the application of syncope already noted, forms with definite future mark plural subject with a level I suffix in the perfective stem, while desiderative verbs mark plural on the reflex of the verb *tuta* 'say'. Note however that the definite plural suffix may be followed by the simultaneous subordinator *-ku* (described in §13.4.2), as if it were an imperfective stem (8.83). It is not clear what the effect is of adding the simultaneous suffix to the definite future stem rather than the imperfective stem; perhaps it is construed as heightening the irrealis sense that the conditional marker brings to the clause.

(8.83)   *núnikchattakuik*
           nu-ni-ka-cha-tata-ku-i=ka
           ANA-VBLZ.INTR-PFV-NEG-FUT-SIM-1PL:SS=COND
           'if we won't do that' (Text 3:17)

Table 8.16 gives the paradigm for definite future. Unlike the other non-present tense markers, definite future uses the analysable third person subject marker *-wa*, because the stem etymologically terminates in the present tense imperfective stem *ta-* of the verb *tuta* 'say'.

Table 8.16: Definite future

person	singular	plural
1	*wɨtathai* wɨ-tata-ha-i go+PFV-FUT-1SG-DECL	*wɨtathi* wɨ-tata-hi go+PFV-FUT-1PL+DECL
2	*wɨtatmɨ* wɨ-tata-mɨ go+PFV-FUT-2SG+DECL	*wɨtathumɨ* wɨ-tata-humɨ go+PFV-FUT-2PL+DECL
3	*wɨtatui* wɨ-tata-wa-i go+PFV-FUT-3-DECL	(same as singular)

8.4.4.9 Indefinite future

As mentioned above, indefinite future is in fact composed of the future nominalizer *-tinu* plus the copula enclitic *=aita*. These two combine as *-tinaita* in most examples (as in 8.84), but the two parts are split if the interrogative enclitic *=ka* is present (8.85), as this enclitic always precedes the copula enclitic.

(8.84)   *dakástinaithai*
          daka-sa-**tinu**=**aita**-ha-i
          wait-PFV-**FUT**+**NMLZ**=COP-1SG-DECL
          'I will wait'

(8.85)   *taáshtinkaitam*
          taa-cha-**tinu**=ka=**ita**-mɨ
          return-NEG-**FUT**+**NMLZ**=Q=**COP**-2SG
          'aren't you going to come back?'

Semantically, the indefinite future contrasts with the definite future in that there is no specific time implied for the action of the verb. In addition, native speakers tend to consider indefinite future to indicate an action that is in the more distant future than the definite future – this most likely arises from the pragmatics, given that the precise time of occurrence is easier to know or predict for events that are closer. Synchronically, indefinite future is a nominalization rather than a verbal tense suffix. The nominal properties of the future nominalizer -*tinu* are discussed in Chapter 15.

8.4.5 Normative

Normative is a portmanteau, combining tense, person, and mood in one fix -*taya(mɨ)*, attached to the unmarked verb stem. The subject is always first person plural, and the verb is essentially timeless – a statement of "how we do things". There is no separately analysable marker of first person plural subject, but when a normative-marked verb takes a same-subject subordinate clause, its verb will be marked as first person plural, as in example (8.86).

(8.86)   *hiŋkahá hukí tsukapsá minitáyamɨ*
          [hiŋka-ha]   [hu-ki]
          tie.up-PFV+SEQ+1PL:SS   take-PFV+SEQ+1PL:SS
          [tsukapɨ-sa]   mini-tayamɨ
          carry.on.shoulder-SBD+1PL:SS arrive-NORM
          'having tied it up and taken it we arrive carrying it over our shoulder'
          (Text 3:15)

The distinction between the forms -*taya* and -*tayamɨ* is not yet understood. Both appear as finite verbs or in non-finite positions. Text 3 is a description of hunting practices, and most verbs in it take the normative form.

8.5 Apprehensive and prohibitive

8.5.1 Apprehensive -(a)i

Apprehensive is functionally the negative counterpart of jussive; unlike jussive, however, apprehensive can be used with all persons. Apprehensive is marked with the suffix -(a)i, shown with the allomorph -i in example (8.87). Apprehensive is functionally part of the mood paradigm, but is also semantically negative – see §11.1 for a discussion from the perspective of the functional domain of negation.

(8.87)   *áimak ímamkímas "intáhaiŋ" tus*
          aima-a-kũ   ímamkíma-sã   [inta-ha-**i**-ha
          fill-IPFV-SIM+3:SS take.care-SBD+3:SS break-PFV-**APPR**-1SG
          tus]
          say+SBD+3:SS
          'Filling them carefully, lest he should break them' lit. *saying "may I not break them"* (agr041006_04)

Following the high affectedness perfective suffix -*a(w)*, the long allomorph -*ai* appears (8.88).

(8.88)   *yuwáwaim*
          yu-aw-ai-mí
          eat-PFV-APPR-2SG
          'lest you eat it'

The paradigm of apprehensive combined with person suffixes is illustrated in Table 8.17.

Table 8.17: Apprehensive suffixes

person	singular	plural
1	*-i-ha* -APPR-1SG	*-i-hi* -APPR-1PL
2	*-i-mí* -APPR-2SG	*-i-humí* -APPR-2PL
3	*-í* -APPR+3SG	*-i-numí* -APPR-3PL

First and second persons are marked with the same suffixes as finite verbs. Third person, however, is marked with nasality of the preceding vowel for singular, as in subordinate verbs, and the suffix *-numĩ* for plural, as in remote past and jussive forms. The apprehensive forms cannot stand alone, and only appear in speech report constructions. The apprehensive suffix is also the basis of the prohibitive verb forms, discussed below, which can stand as independent utterances.

8.5.2 Prohibitive

Prohibitive is functionally the negative counterpart of imperative, however it is formally quite different, making use of the apprehensive suffix *-(a)i*. Prohibitive only has second and third person forms. The suffixes *-pa* and *-hupa* are used to mark second person singular (8.89a) and plural (8.89b) respectively, as in content interrogative clauses (§8.7).

(8.89) a. *achikáipa*
        achi-ka-i-pa
        touch-PFV-APPR-2SG:PROH
        'don't touch (it)!'

     b. *achikáiŋpa*
        achi-ka-i-hupa
        touch-PFV-APPR-2PL:PROH
        'don't touch (it)!'

However, second person plural may also be marked with the suffix *-pa* followed by the finite second person plural marker *-humi*, as in example (8.90); this is parallel to the positive imperative, marked with *-ta* for singular and *-ta-humi* (IMP-2PL) for plural.

(8.90)   *wáinkam ihuípahum*
         wainaka-mi   ihu-i-pa-humi
         in.vain-2   stab-APPR-PROH-2PL
         'don't stab it in vain!' (agr041005_14)

Negative jussive forms also use the apprehensive suffix, and differ from apprehensive forms only in the addition of the third-person prohibitive marker *-ka*, which follows the apprehensive suffix (8.91a and 8.91b). The *-ka* of these forms does not appear anywhere else in the grammar. One could assign it to slot G (see Figure 6.2) with the other mood/modality markers for the sake of analytic tidiness, but there is no morphological evidence for this.

(8.91) a. *hákaiŋka*
            ha-ka-ĩ-ka
            die-PFV-APPR+3SG-PROH
            'may he not die!'

        b. *hákainmiŋka*
            ha-ka-i-numĩ-ka
            die-PFV-APPR-3PL-PROH
            'may they not die!'

8.6 Hortative

Hortative expresses a suggestion or exhortation, and the subject is always first-person plural. Although functionally similar to imperative, it is formally distinct, being marked with the suffix *-mi* (8.92).

(8.92) *yuwámi*
        yu-a-**mi**
        eat-PFV-**HORT**
        'let's eat!'

Hortative fuses person and mood in its meaning, and disallows any tense specification, consequently it is impossible to say with certainty which slot it belongs to. It never co-occurs with a tense or mood suffix, and unlike imperative, it never takes a person suffix. There are, however, certain formal features that hortative shares with the suffixes of slot E. Firstly, hortative only occurs with perfective stems. This stem restriction is shared by the tense, imperative, jussive and apprehensive, but not by the mood/modality suffixes. Secondly, some slot E suffixes can impart imperative mood to the verb and thus block the addition of mood/modality suffixes, but no mood/modality suffix blocks the presence of tense suffixes. Since hortative cannot co-occur with either tense or mood suffixes, it has more in common with the other slot E suffixes that impart imperative mood than with the mood/modality suffixes. Hortative may be pluralized and negated using the same perfective plural marker *-aha* (8.93) and negative marker *-cha* (8.94) as in finite verbs.

(8.93)   *yuwáwaŋmi*
          yu-aw-**aha**-mi
          eat-PFV-**PL**-HORT
          'let's eat!' (addressing a group)

(8.94)   *wíchami*
          wi-**cha**-mi
          go+PFV-**NEG**-HORT
          'let's not go'

8.7 Person and number

8.7.1 Subject

Subject is formally marked on all finite verbs. Plural is obligatorily marked in first and second person, and level I plural suffixes may appear with all persons, although these are not obligatory. There is a tendency to interpret the obligatory SAP plural forms as paucal in contrast to the plural-marked forms, particularly in elicitation contexts, but this is not a grammatical distinction.

8.7.2 First and second person subject

Table 8.18 gives the first and second person suffixes for declarative, present tense verbs.

Table 8.18: First and second person markers on non-past declarative verbs

person	singular	non-singular
1	*-ha*	*-hi*
2	*-mɨ*	*-humɨ*

The second person non singular marker *-humɨ* can be analysed as a plural suffix **-hu* plus the second person marker *-mɨ*. By this analysis, the plural suffix has the following properties.
–   Only occurs with second person subject.
–   Always directly precedes the second person suffix *-mɨ* or *-pa* (in interrogative and prohibitive clauses).
–   Is independent of the plural suffixes *-ina* and *-aha*.

Thus the sequence -*hu-mɨ* forms a de facto second-person plural suffix, parallel to the first plural -*hi*.[9] In past tense verbs, second person is marked with -*umɨ* singular and -*uhumɨ* plural, as shown in Table 8.19.

Table 8.19: First and second person markers on past tense declarative verbs

person	singular	non-singular
1	-*ha*	-*hi*
2	-*umɨ*	-*uhumɨ*

The initial /u/ is presumably the reflex of some historical morpheme, but is synchronically unanalysable. It is independent of any past-tense marker. These forms provide a strong motivation to consider plural -*humɨ* and -*uhumɨ* to be morphologically simple suffixes synchronically: if -*hu* were synchronically a plural marker, we would expect the past tense form to surface as **-*hu-umɨ* (PL-2). In content interrogative and prohibitive clauses, second person is marked with the suffixes -*pa* (singular) and -*hupa* (plural), as in (8.95). Polar interrogative does not trigger these forms – compare (8.96) and (8.97).

(8.95) *wahúk háapa*
         wahuka   ha-a-pa
         how   be.sick-IPFV-2SG
         'in what way are you sick?' (Text 2:32)

(8.96) *yáitpa*
         ya=ita-pa
         who=COP-2SG
         'who are you?'

(8.97) *amɨkáitam*
         amɨ=ka=ita-mɨ
         2sg=Q=COP-2SG
         'is it you?' (standard greeting when not in the context of a house visit)

The same suffixes are also used to mark second person subjects in prohibitive clauses (see examples in §8.5.2).

---

9 1PL -*hi* could have arisen from an earlier sequence *-*hu* (PL) plus *-*i* (1PL), with a subsequent phonological fusion of the sequence /u-i/ to /i/. The suffix -*i* marks 1PL in conditional clauses (§13.5).

8.7.3 Third-person suffixes

In contrast to first and second person, which use the same suffixes in finite verbs almost invariably, third person subject is indexed with a range of suffixes. If we consider the variants that appear with the three primary tense markers, the situation is relatively straightforward, as laid out in Table 8.20.

Table 8.20: Third person singular subject marking with primary suffixes

primary suffix	declarative	polar interrogative, exclamatory	other
none (present tense)		-wa / -u	-∅
recent past -ma	-mɨ̄	-ma	
remote past -ya	-yi	-ya	
immediate future -ta		-ti	

There are two splits based on mood/modality of the clause: -wa / -u appears in declarative, polar interrogative and exclamatory present-tense verbs, while third person is zero-marked in other clause types. Recent past and remote past do not mark third person in non-declarative clauses. Immediate future with third person subject (i.e. jussive) always appears as -ti. The forms shown in Table 8.20 hold for whichever primary suffix appears last in a grammaticalized sequence. Thus in the definite future and desiderative forms, which have their etymological source in a construction consisting of primary future -ta followed by a present tense form of the verb tuta 'say', the final element has no primary suffix and third-person subject takes the basic form -wa ~ -u (§8.4.4).

As noted above (§8.4.3), third-person recent past may be decomposable as recent past -ma and a third person suffix -ɨ̄ (which also marks third person in perfective past forms, §8.4.2) alternating with -∅ in non-declarative clauses. Similarly, third-person remote past and immediate future forms could be decomposed as a third person suffix *-i (unattested elsewhere) added to remote past -ya only in declarative clauses, and to immediate future -ta in all clause types. It is tempting to attribute the recent past and remote past declarative forms to a fused declarative suffix -i, although there is no other evidence for this analysis.

Table 8.21 summarizes the various subject markers for all persons, and the factors conditioning the allomorphy. The forms in shaded cells are fusional, combining the tense suffix in the leftmost column with the person indicated. The forms used in same-subject subordinate verbs, described in §13.5, have been included for comparison. The symbol N represents nasalization of the stem-final vowel.

Table 8.21: Subject markers and morphological environments

	1sg	1pl	2sg	2pl	3sg	3pl
Present, definite future	-ha	-hi	-mɨ	-humɨ	-wa / -u	-wa / -u
Immediate future -ta		–			-ti	-ti-numɨ
Immediate past -∅		-hi	-umɨ	-uhumɨ	-ɨ	-ɨ
Recent past -ma					-mɨ	-mɨ
Intermediate/distant past -(a)ma...ya					-(a)mayi	-(a)mayi
Remote past -ya					-yi	-numɨ
Apprehensive			-mɨ	-mɨ	-N	-numɨ
Prohibitive	–	–	-pa	-hupa	-N-ka	-numɨ-ka
SS subordinate verb (§13.5)	-nu	-∅ / -i	-mɨ	-mɨ ~ -humɨ	-N	-N

9 Mood and modality

9.1 Preliminary remarks

Every independent clause is obligatorily marked for mood. Thirteen formally distinct markers define between them four major clause types: indicative, interrogative, imperative and exclamative; these clause types form statements, questions, commands and exclamations, respectively. Subordinate clauses are characterized by a lack of mood, but may share that of their controlling clause. Table 9.1 lays out the clause types of Aguaruna and their superordinate groups.

Table 9.1: Mood and clause types

mood type	clause type
Indicative	Declarative
	Counter-expectation
	Narrative
	Speculative
Interrogative	Polar interrogative
	Content interrogative
	Tag question
Imperative	Imperative
	Jussive
	Hortative
	Apprehensive
	Prohibitive
Exclamative	Exclamative

Traditional categories of deontic and epistemic modality are not represented directly in Aguaruna grammar. Some members of the mood/modality paradigm have epistemic meanings, and deontic modality is mostly available through implicature. The relation of Aguaruna categories to traditional modality is discussed in §9.3.

The formal marking of mood and modality in Aguaruna is somewhat disparate. Most of the imperative paradigm is marked with the 'intentional future' suffix which falls in the same morphological slot as tense markers (slot E, §8.4.4). All imperative forms select the perfective or durative verb stem (the durative stem only appears in imperative clauses), are incompatible with tense marking, and block the addition of any marking in slot G. Exclamative is characterized by a complete lack of formal marking, either on the verb or elsewhere. The other verbal mood and modality markers are in slot G. Indicative clauses are characterized by obligatory marking only on the verb, while interrogative clauses are characterized by marking throughout the clause. Two forms disrupt this patterning of form and function: tag questions and speculative. Tag questions, like indicative clauses, are marked only with a verbal suffix; morphological evidence suggests that the marking may historically incorporate the declarative suffix (see §10.6). Speculative is marked with a suffix on the verb, and also may involve an enclitic on some other constituent of the clause (§9.2.4). This double marking is a formal property of interrogative clauses.

The thirteen clause types of Table 9.1 are associated with distinct morphological markers, listed in Table 9.2.

Table 9.2: Formally marked moods/modalities

mood	clause type	marker
Indicative	Declarative	-i
	Counter-expectation	-hama
	Narrative	tuwahamɨ̄
	Speculative	-(tsa)...tai
Interrogative	Polar interrogative	=ka (or -∅ if marked elsewhere in the clause)
	Content interrogative	suppression of apocope (clause contains an interrogative word)
	Tag question	-api
Imperative	Imperative	(marked in slot E)
	Jussive	(marked in slot E)
	Hortative	(marked in slot E)
	Apprehensive	(marked in slot E)
	Prohibitive	(marked in slot E)
Exclamative	Exclamative	-∅

Of the thirteen types, eight are marked in slot G, as listed in Table 9.3.

Table 9.3: Mood/modality markers in slot G

clause type	marker
Declarative	-i
Counter-expectation	-hama
Narrative	-∅ # tuwahamȿ
Speculative	-(tsa)...tai
Polar interrogative	=ka / -∅
Content interrogative	suppression of apocope
Tag question	=api
Exclamative	-∅

In non-interrogative, non-imperative clauses, zero-marked exclamative mood marking contrasts with the segmentally marked forms, so this can be considered *zero-marked* rather than unmarked. In other clause types with no verbal marker (content interrogative and some polar interrogative clauses) there are formal indicators of clause type elsewhere in the clause – in such cases, then, the verb may be considered unmarked. Interrogative and speculative modalities may involve enclitics marking other constituents in the clause in addition to the verb, as discussed below.

9.2 Indicative clauses

Indicative clauses express statements. They are subdivided into four types, differing in their portrayal of the speaker's attitude (Table 9.4). Although there is not an evidential system, some indicative types implicitly encode information source. A general discussion of source of information marking is in §18.4.

Table 9.4: Indicative clause types

marker	gloss	remarks
-i	Declarative	functionally unmarked
-hama	Counter-expectation	first hand information source, mirative overtones
-∅ # tuwahamȿ	Narrative	hearsay information source
(-tsa)-tai	Speculative	lack of certainty

9.2.1 Declarative

Functionally the least marked statement, declarative is marked with the verbal suffix *-i*. Declarative does not imply any particular source of knowledge, but in narratives nominalizations are typically used to imply lack of first-hand knowledge, contrasting with declarative. Nominalizations may take the copula enclitic and
declarative mood, but the remaining distinction between finite declarative and nominalized clauses can be considered an evidentiality strategy (see discussion in
§15.5.3 and §18.4).

Following regular phonological rules (§3.6.1) the declarative suffix *-i* fuses with
a preceding /i/ or /ɨ/, therefore its presence is not obvious in verbs with first person
plural subject (marked with *-hi*) and second person subjects (marked with *-(u)mɨ*
or *-(u)humɨ*). However, the underlying presence of the declarative suffix means that
apocope is blocked from applying to the final CV syllable in these forms (as in 9.1),
and this is evident by comparison with non-declarative forms, in which the final
vowel of the person marker is elided (9.2).

(9.1)   *shíiŋbauchitmɨ*
          shiihama-uchi=ita-mɨ
          pretty-DIM=COP-2SG+DECL
          'you are pretty'

(9.2)   *amɨkáitam*
          amɨ=ka=ita-mɨ
          2sg=Q=COP-2SG
          'are you you?' (standard greeting formula)

9.2.2 Counter-expectation

Counter-expectation is marked with the suffix *-hama*. Third person subject is not
overtly marked in counter-expectation modality, as with speculative. The suffix
never undergoes vowel elision. Counter-expectation modality is used when the
speaker judges that the information conveyed is new, surprising or counter to the
expectation of the addressee (9.3, 9.4).

(9.3)   *kamɨ̃ núwi aikaŋháma*
          kamɨ   nu=i   aika-ha-**hama**
          truly   ANA=INS   thus+VBLZ.TR+IPFV-1SG-**CNTR.EX**
          'really, it's because of this that I do it' (agr041005_15)

(9.4)   *ámɨ húu humáinaitamhama*
          ami   hu   hu-mai-inu=aita-mɨ-**hama**
          2sg   PROX   take-POT-NMLZ=COP-2SG-**CNTR.EX**
          'you can take this' (agr041005_17)

There is no value judgement attached – the situation described may be positive or negative. It is also often used with a mirative overtone, as in (9.5), from a story in which a woman has been lost in the forest and suddenly finds herself back in her own garden; (9.6), from a story about a community whose members are being murdered, as they finally realize who is killing them; and (9.7) where a teacher is surprised to discover a child can already read.

(9.5)   *húu mína ahahuaháma*
          hu   mi=na   aha-hu=a-**hama**
          PROX   1sg=ACC   garden-PSSD:1SG=COP+3-**CNTR.EX**
          'this is my garden!' (agr040721_07)

(9.6)   *áuk amupaháma*
          au=ka   amu-pa-**hama**
          DIST=TOP   terminate-1PL.OBJ+IPFV+3-**CNTR.EX**
          '*he* is killing us!' (agr040712_02)

(9.7)   *auhaháma, dɨkaháma*
          auha-hama   dɨka-**hama**
          read+IPFV+3-CNTR.EX   know+IPFV+3-**CNTR.EX**
          'he's reading! he knows how!' (agr040824_02)

This is not a purely mirative marker, however, as shown by example (9.8), which was spoken by a shopkeeper on being asked whether he has any rice to sell. The speaker is not just discovering the fact that there is no rice; instead the counter-expectation marker relates to the addressee's state of knowledge.

(9.8)   *atsaháma*
          atsa-**hama**
          exist.NEG+IPFV+3-**CNTR.EX**
          'there isn't any!'

Counter-expectation marking implies first-hand information source. To convey the attitudinal content of counter-expectation in the absence of first-hand evidence, a speech report construction may be used, as in (9.10). The equivalent form in (9.9) could only be used if the speaker had actually witnessed the person going. This use of a speech report to mark hearsay information is very similar to narrative modality, discussed immediately below.

(9.9)   *wɨmaháma*
          wɨ-ma-**hama**
          go+PFV-RECPST:3-**CNTR.EX**
          'he's gone!'

(9.10)   *"wɨmɨ̃" tɨmaháma*
          wɨ-mɨ̃   tɨ-ma-hama
          go+PFV-RECPST:3:DECL   say+PFV-RECPST:3-CNTR.EX
          'she said "he's gone"!'

9.2.3 Narrative

Narrative modality is marked with a separate word *tuwahamɨ̃*, historically related to the verb *tuta* 'say'. Speakers typically translate it into Spanish as *así decían* 'so they would say', but the form is not synchronically morphologically decomposable. Narrative modality is used only in narratives, and indicates that the information has been received as hearsay, and this is a common grammaticalization path for speech verbs according to Aikhenvald (2004: 132ff). When a narrative marker is present there can be no bound mood marker in slot G, showing that the verb stem and the narrative marker form one grammatical word. Example (9.11) shows narrative modality combining with the non-declarative third person form of the remote past suffix *-ya*, and (9.12) shows it with a nominalized verb.

(9.11)   *yúu puháya túwahamɨ̃*
          yu   puha-ya   **tuwahamɨ̃**
          eat   live+IPFV-REMPST:3   **NARR**
          '(the boa) was eating (the man), so the story goes' (Text 1:15)

(9.12)   *núwa mákichik naŋkaín usupáŋ, hiinkíu túwahamɨ̃*
          [nuwa   makichiki]   naŋkai=na   usupa-hã
          woman   one   fruit=ACC   crave-PFV+SEQ+3:SS
          hiina-ki-u   **tuwahamɨ̃**
          go.out-PFV-NMLZ   **NARR**
          'a woman, having craved fruit, went out, so the story goes'
          (agr040721_07)

Other forms of the verb 'say' may also occasionally mark narrative modality. Example (9.13) is a simple declarative clause morphologically – the verb 'say' implies a more specific source of the information. Such a usage is related to the tendency for narrators of traditional stories to finish off with a formula like 'my father told me this story'. Crucially, the verb preceding the full speech verb in all such examples is nominalized. So the form cannot be said to be marking modality in the same way as *tuwahamĩ* does, as it does not mark finite verbs.

(9.13) *úchi nuúmpakuk ũw̃ã́ũ tímayi*
      uchi   nuumpaku=ka   uwã-u   ti-mayi
      child   grown=TOP   deny+IPFV-NMLZ say+PFV-INTPST:3:DECL
      'the eldest child denied it, so s/he said' (agr040723_29)

Example (9.14) shows another strategy for marking hearsay source of information, with a straightforward finite clause meaning 'so s/he says'.

(9.14) *túkɨ máak ɨhapɨ̃ húhaku áinawai yáunchukuk, áatus táwai*
      [tukɨ   maa-kũ   ɨhapɨ̃   hu-haku
      always   kill+IPFV-SIM+3:SS open.up+PFV+SEQ+3:SS take-NARR.PST
      a-ina-wa-i   yaunchuku=ka]   aatusã   ta-wa-i
      COP-PL:IPFV-3-DECL long.ago=TOP   thus+3   say+IPFV-3-DECL
      '(because people didn't know about giving birth) killing (the woman) they would open her up and take (the baby) out in the old days, so s/he says' (agr041005_16)

So narrative modality is fully grammaticalized in the form *tuwahamĩ*, but in some examples an actual speech verb is used to achieve the same effect, with the author of the speech report understood to be the source of the story. In the latter type of clause, the line between narrative and declarative clause types is somewhat blurred. Hearsay and other source of information marking are discussed further in §18.4 (and see also Overall 2014a).

9.2.4 Speculative

Speculative is an epistemic marker that expresses the speaker's lowered degree of commitment to the truth of the proposition expressed in the marked clause. Speculative is formally marked with a suffix *-tai* in slot G, as with other mood/modality markers. There is also a floating enclitic *=tsu* that marks a constituent of the clause as the focus of the speculation, as in (9.15). This enclitic alternates with a form *-tsa* that is suffixed to the verb and forms a complex suffix with -*tai*, as in (9.16) and (9.17).

(9.15)   *numinás tsupíktaŋtai*
            numi=na=**tsu**   tsupi-ka-ta-ha-**tai**
            tree=ACC=**SPEC**   cut-PFV-IFUT-1SG-**SPEC**
            'perhaps it's wood that I'll cut'

(9.16)   *numín tsupíktaŋtsatai*
            numi=na   tsupi-ka-ta-ha-**tsa-tai**
            tree=ACC   cut-PFV-IFUT-1SG-**SPEC-SPEC**
            'I might cut wood'

(9.17)   *túhã nĩ́ wáinchauk waináinatsuastai*
            tuhã nĩ waina-chau=ka   waina-ina-tsu-u=a-tsa-tai
            but 3sg see-NEG.NMLZ=TOP see-PL:IPFV-NEG-NMLZ=COP:3-SPEC-SPEC
            'but one who doesn't know will probably never know' (agr041005_18)

The enclitic =*tsu* can be attached to NPs (9.18) or to subordinate clauses (9.19). In example (9.19), the speaker is speculating about why the Aguaruna word for 'harmonica' is *kantash*, the name of a type of fish.

(9.18)   *numinás tsúpiatai*
            numi=na=**tsu**   tsupi-a-**tai**
            tree=ACC=**SPEC**   cut-IPFV+3-**SPEC**
            'perhaps it's wood that he's cutting'

(9.19)   *kantáshhãĩ bìtík asámtãĩs tíu áinatai*
            [kantasha=haĩ bìtìka asa-mataĩ=**tsu**]   ti-u
            macana=COM   equal   COP+SBD-1/3:DS=**SPEC**   say+PFV-NMLZ
            a-ina-**tai**
            COP-PL:IPFV+3-**SPEC**
            'they probably say that because (they think) it's the same as a *macana* fish'

The speculative enclitic =*tsu* and the verbal form -*tsa* are presumably cognate, and this is supported by the enclitic-like behaviour of -*tsa* in recent past tense, as shown below.

9.2.4.1 Tense restrictions on speculative

Speculative modality appears to be compatible only with recent past *-ma*, interme-diate past *-ma...ya*, and primary future *-ta*, in addition to the unmarked present tense.

9.2.4.2 Person marking with speculative

Speculative mood is not common in texts, and all of the forms except for third singu-lar and plural were elicited. Person is marked with *-ha* for first and *-mɨ* for second person, as in regular declarative clauses. Third person subject is unmarked in pre-sent (9.20, 9.21) and past (9.22), but the primary future suffix *-ta* appears in the third-person form *-ti* (9.23).

(9.20)   *pɨpɨnas wawiknúmak ayátai*
         pɨpɨna=tsu   wawiku=numa=ka   aya-**tai**
         macana=SPEC   Wawik.River=LOC=TOP   exist:PL+3-**SPEC**
         'perhaps there are *macana* fish in the Wawik River'

(9.21)   *mína hɨ̰a̰hũ̃ɨ̃s puhátai*
         mi=na   hɨ̰a̰-hu=ɨ̃=tsu   puha-**tai**
         1sg=ACC   house-PSSD:1SG=LOC=SPEC   live+IPFV+3-**SPEC**
         's/he's probably at my house'

(9.22)   *wainkámatai*
         waina-ka-ma-**tai**
         see-PFV-RECPST:3-**SPEC**
         's/he probably saw'

(9.23)   *wainkátitai*
         waina-ka-ti-**tai**
         see-PFV-IFUT:3-**SPEC**
         's/he will probably see'

Table 9.5 summarizes the person marking with the *-tai* form of speculative mood.

Table 9.5: Person marking with *-tai* speculative

person	singular	plural
1	*-ha*	*-hi*
2	*-mɨ*	*-humɨ*
3	*-∅*	*-∅*

In *-tsa...tai* forms first and second person marking is the same, but third-person is only unmarked in past forms. In present forms, the regular *-wa* suffix is used. In future forms, third person singular is marked with *-pa* (9.24) and third plural with *-npa* (9.25; presumably underlying /nVpa/), both suffixed to the third person form of the primary future suffix *-ti*.

(9.24)   *wainkátpastai*
          waina-ka-ti-pa-**tsa**-**tai**
          see-PFV-IFUT:3-3SG-**SPEC**-**SPEC**
          'perhaps he will see'

(9.25)   *wainkáŋtinpastai*
          waina-ka-aha-ti-npa-**tsa**-**tai**
          see-PFV-PL-IFUT:3-3PL-**SPEC**-**SPEC**
          'perhaps they will see'

In first and second person recent past forms, the person suffix intervenes between the two elements of *-tsa...tai* (9.26 and 9.27, respectively). This is reminiscent of the behaviour of the polar interrogative enclitic *=ka* which also moves from its usual position in slot G to directly follow the recent past suffix, preceding person marking (§10.4).

(9.26)   *wainkámtsaŋtai*
          waina-ka-ma-**tsa**-ha-**tai**
          see-PFV-RECPST-**SPEC**-1SG-**SPEC**
          'perhaps I saw'

(9.27)   *wainkámtsumtai*
          waina-ka-ma-**tsa**-mɨ-**tai**
          see-PFV-RECPST-**SPEC**-2-**SPEC**
          'perhaps you saw'

9.2.4.3 Speculative with copula

Example (9.28) was offered in elicitation as a possible response to a question such as "Have you seen my wife? She's wearing red." The speculative suffix *-tsa…tai* appears directly suffixed to the anaphoric pronoun *nu*, with no copula intervening. Compare (9.29), where the copula enclitic intervenes between the adjective *piŋkɨŋ* 'good' and the speculative suffix *-tai*.

(9.28)   *wainkámhai nuwán haánch kapántun nuŋkuáhun – dútsatai*

waina-ka-ma-ha-i	[nuwa=na	haanchi	kapantu=na
see-PFV-RECPST-1SG-DECL	woman=ACC	clothes	red=ACC

nuŋkua-ha-u=na]   **nu-tsa-tai**
wear-PFV-NMLZ=ACC   **ANA-SPEC-SPEC**

(in response to a question "have you seen my wife?") 'I saw a woman wearing red clothes – perhaps that's her'

(9.29)   *Suizanmayas imá pɨŋkɨhaitai*

Suiza=numa=ya=**tsu**	ima	pɨŋkɨha=ita-**tai**
Switzerland=LOC=ABL=**SPEC**	INTENS	good=COP:3:DECL-**SPEC**

'perhaps the (knife) from Switzerland is better'

9.2.5 Exclamative

Exclamative mood is formally unmarked. It is most similar to declarative types, although the lack of verbal marking is also reminiscent of some interrogatives (cf. Sadock & Zwicky's 1985: 162 observation that exclamatory sentences may show similarity to both declarative and interrogative types). Formally, exclamative clauses have no overt marker in verbal slot G, so they appear as declarative clauses without the final suffix *-i*. Third person subject is marked in exclamative mood with the suffix *-wa*, as in declarative, suggesting that exclamative is formally a subtype of declarative mood. Because the declarative suffix *-i* does not surface following the first person plural suffix *-hi* nor the second person suffixes *-mɨ* (sg), *-humɨ* (pl), there is no formal distinction in clauses with first plural or second person subjects. Exclamative is only possible in present tense.

Examples of exclamative clauses are rather scarce in my corpus, because of the nature of the materials. They are common in spontaneous speech when seeing something surprising or exciting, as in (9.30) which was uttered by a child who saw a dog on the roof of a building, or when scolding, as in example (9.31).

(9.30)   *ỹãw̃ã́ã́ yakí puháwa!*
          yawaã   yaki   puha-wa
          dog   above   live+IPFV-3+EXCL
          'there's a dog up there!'

(9.31)   *"achikáipa" táha!*
          <u>achi-ka-i-pa</u>   ta-ha
          grab-PFV-APPR-2SG:PROH   say+IPFV-1SG+EXCL
          '"don't touch it" I say!'

Example (9.32) is a rare appearance of exclamative in my corpus of narrative materials, where the narrator steps out of the story to make a commentary. Note that the exclamative form appears in a speech report, as it is a primarily conversational form.

(9.32)   *núna múun áuŋmatuinakũ̃́ĩ̃, "wáinkas táwa" túyahai*
          nu=na   muunta   auhmatu-ina-ku-ĩ   <u>wainakasã</u>
          ANA=ACC   elder   tell-PL:IPFV-SIM+1/3-DS in.vain+3
          <u>ta-wa</u>   tu-ya-ha-i
          say+IPFV-3+EXCL   say-REMPST-1SG-DECL
          'when the elders told that (story), I would say "they're talking rubbish!"' (agr040723_29)

Example (9.33) illustrates the special third person exclamative form of the copula enclitic (described in §4.14.3) and was uttered while looking through a book of photos.

(9.33)   *lanchaya!*
          lancha=ya
          boat=COP:3:EXCL
          'it's a boat!'

9.3 Deontic and Epistemic modality

As was noted above, the traditional categories of deontic and epistemic modality are not manifested in distinct formal marking in Aguaruna. There are of course ways of expressing the deontic categories of commands, suggestions, warnings and permission; and explicitly referring to the speaker's degree of commitment to the truth of the proposition in the epistemic field.

Commands and warnings are expressed with imperative and prohibitive clauses (§8.4.4). Suggestions may also be expressed by imperative mood, for example, the imperative clause in (9.34), as well as expressing a command, would be a likely translation for 'you must go' or 'you should go'.

(9.34)   *wɨtá*
            wɨ-ta
            go+PFV-IMP
            'go!'

Suggestions and permission, as well as ability, may also be expressed with the potential form. Example (9.35) illustrates this form in the context of giving permission.

(9.35)   *ámɨ húu humáinaitamhama*
            amɨ   hu   hu-mai-inu=aita-mɨ-hama
            2sg   PROX   take-POT-NMLZ=COP-2SG-CNTR.EX
            'you can take this' (agr041005_17) (repeated from example 9.4)

Another way of expressing a suggestion through implicature is by using first person singular (9.36) rather than hortative (9.37) forms; the implicature in example (9.36) is "you should come too". The first time I encountered this usage in the field I stayed home because it seemed to me that I wasn't invited.

(9.36)   *wɨɥahai*
            wɨ-a-ha-i
            go-IPFV-1SG-DECL
            'I'm going'

(9.37)   *wɨmí*
            wɨ-mi
            go+PFV-HORT
            'let's go!'

Normative verb marking (§8.4.5) expresses the way things are done, and is deontic to the extent that this is considered to be the way things *should* be done. Rhetorical questions are used widely in contexts where a deontic modal might be used in English, that is, a question of the form "is it the case that X?" is the translational equivalent of "X should not be the case", as in (9.38).

(9.38)   *kíiwish yutáiŋkaik iísh*
            kiiwi=sha   [yu-taɨ=ka=aita   ii=sha]
            ҫentipede=Q.TOP   eat-NSBJ.NMLZ=Q=COP:3   1pl=Q.TOP
            'are centipedes food we (i.e. people) eat?' (from example 10.59)

And the rhetorical question word *wããs* 'I don't know why' can also be used in an admonitive context, as in example (9.39), from the conclusion of a story about a man who followed the path of a snake which then killed him. The implied moral is that one should not follow tracks without knowing what made them.

(9.39)   *w̃ããs dúsha núnikabia muúntash*
          wããs   nu=sha   nu-ni-ka-amaya
          I.don't.know.why   ANA=Q.TOP   ANA-VBLZ.INTR-PFV-DISTPST:3
          muunta=sha
          adult=Q.TOP
          'I don't know why the man did that' (Text 1:38)

Epistemic modality is represented by a few dedicated forms: speculative, counter-expectation and exclamative all relate to speaker's knowledge. Narrative modality is used to mark traditional stories as hearsay, and this lends a higher degree of confidence to the proposition expressed. This is discussed in §18.4, along with other strategies for marking source of information.

9.4 Imperative clauses

Imperative mood is prototypically used to command or suggest. Imperative mood is marked by three formally distinct suffixes: imperative and jussive are marked with *-ta* and *-ti* respectively, cognate with the future tense suffixes; hortative is marked with *-mi*; and prohibitive is marked with the apprehensive suffix *-i*. The imperative marker itself appears in a paradigm that includes all persons; in first person it expresses intentional future, and the third person jussive expresses indirect commands and is also used to express wishes and in irrealis type clauses. The apprehensive form is used in subordinate clauses or speech reports functioning as DS purpose clauses. Prohibitive is based on the apprehensive form with two morphological changes: second person is marked with *-mi* in apprehensive, but *-pa* in prohibitive; and third person apprehensive forms add *-ka* to give the prohibitive form. All imperative forms were exemplified in §8.4.4.

9.5 Mood in subordinate clauses

Subordinate clauses are not marked for mood. They may share that of the controlling clause, and if the controlling clause is one of the types that mark constituents (interrogative or speculative), a subordinate clause may be marked (as in 9.19 above). Properties of subordinate clauses are described and exemplified in Chapter 13.

10 Questions

10.1 Preliminary remarks

Questions are morphologically distinctive in Aguaruna for their distributed morphology. The verbal markers of interrogative mood fit into the larger paradigm of mood/modality marking (Chapter 9), and NPs and other constituents in interrogative clauses may take floating enclitics that are paradigmatically related to other enclitic markers of information structure (§4.12 and §4.13). Some constituents of content interrogative clauses are marked by suppression of apocope. Aguaruna distinguishes three subtypes of interrogative clause: "tag" questions, polar questions and content questions. In the following sections, I take the declarative clause type as a starting point and describe the properties of interrogative clauses in terms of their departure from the corresponding declarative clauses.

Interrogative clauses are distinguished pragmatically from declarative clauses in that their prototypical function is to seek information from the addressee. All of the interrogative clause types expect an answer (unless used rhetorically, §10.7.2), and they share the intonational feature of a rise in the final syllable of the utterance, in addition to whatever other accent is already present. Polar and content interrogative types have in common a distributed marking, as there is (potentially) more than one marker in the clause: in addition to the verbal markers, there is also an enclitic =*sha* that may appear on one or more constituents of the clause (§10.5). This behaviour is shared by speculative modality, which similarly has a dedicated floating enclitic =*tsu* (§9.2.4). The morphological correlates of interrogative clauses fall into three general types:
(i)   Verbal affixation
(ii) Suppression of apocope
(iii) Constituent affixation with floating enclitics

Content interrogatives are described in §10.3, and polar interrogatives in §10.4. The floating enclitics associated with these two clause types are described in §10.5. "Tag" questions do not involve these enclitics, and are described in §10.6. §10.7 describes some discourse functions of clauses formally marked as questions.

10.2 Question words

Question words form a class superimposed on the other word classes, from which its members are drawn. There are three INTERROGATIVE PRONOUNS: *ya*, *tu*, and *wahĩ*, differing in specificity and humanness, and a pro-clausal form *wãã* ~ *waŋka* 'why'; the fifth root *wahu* always appears in morphologically complex adverbial words.[1] Question words are listed in Table 10.1.

Table 10.1: Question words

form	word class	gloss
ya	pronoun	who
tu	pronoun	which
tu	location word	where
wãã ~ waŋ-ka	adverb	why
wahĩ	pronoun	what
wahu-ti	time word	when
wahu-pa	quantifier	how many
wahu-k(a)	manner adverb	how

The root *wahĩ* is also used as a lexical noun meaning 'thing' or 'possession'. The suffixes associated with *wãã* and *wahu-* are not attested elsewhere, but the final *-ti* of *wahuti* 'when' could be related to the suffix *-tin* that forms time words (§12.3.4). The final *-ka* of *wahuk* 'how' could be the reflex of a perfective subordinate verb form.

There is some evidence for an interrogative verb, but examples are rare and appear to be fossilized. Example (10.1) shows one such form and its possible verbal morphological structure.

(10.1)   *wahinpa*   ?<   *wahĩ-tu-pa*
            'what did you say?'   what_VERB-APPL-2

The use of subordinate verb person marking with *wahuka* 'how' (example 10.2) also looks verbal, but as noted in §12.3, some manner adverbs are similarly inflected for person, although not necessarily etymologically derived from verb roots.

---

1 Despite the surface similarity of *wahĩ* and *wahu-*, comparative evidence suggests that they are etymologically unrelated, having originated in Proto-Chicham forms *wari* and *uru-* respectively.

(10.2)   *wíshakam wahúkanuk áanin áaŋ*
           wi=shakama   wahuka-nu=ki   aa-ni-inu   aa-ha
           1sg=ADD   how-1SG:SS=Q.RHET   thus-VBLZ.INTR-NMLZ   COP-1SG
           'how can I too be one who does that?' (agr041005_16)

There are also a few examples of the root *wahu-* 'how' with finite verbal morphology, as in (10.57) below; there too, the *-ka* suffix appears to be a perfective marker.

Finally, there is a root *utu-* which appears followed by the subordinating fix *-sa*, suggesting that it is a verbal root (10.3), but it is very rare in my data.

(10.3)   *ihapimush utusáŋ isámati*
           ihapi-mau=sha   utu-sã=ki   isama-ti
           gut+PFV-NSBJ.NMLZ=Q.TOP   how-SBD+3:SS=Q.RHET   heal+PFV-JUSS
           'how can one who has been gutted heal up?' (agr041005_16; cf. 10.60 below)

It also appears as a long form of the root *tu* 'where, which', suggesting that there may be an etymological relation.

(10.4)   *Pijuayal tabaush utunii awaa?*
           Pijuayal   ta-mau=sha   utu-ni   a-wa
           Pijuayal   say+IPFV-NSBJ.NMLZ=Q.TOP   where-ALL   exist-3
           'where is the place called Pijuayal?' (Tiinch & Danducho)

This is all suggestive evidence, but the examples all seem to be only etymologically verbal at best, and none of the productive question strategies involves a verbal interrogative.

10.3 Content interrogative

The basic identifier of the content interrogative clause type is that the clause contains a question word. Content interrogative mood is also reflected in verbal and other morphology: constituents are marked with the 'question topic' enclitic *=sha*, and the predicate shows suppression of apocope. The third person copula enclitic takes its full form *=aita* in content interrogative clauses (as in 10.16 below). Subordinate verbs with second person subject show a long form of the person marker *-mia* instead of the usual *-mi*, and finite verbs sometimes mark second person subject with *-pa* instead of the usual *-mi*.

There is no special syntax associated with questions. Question words show the same mobility as any other clausal constituent, which responds to the pragmatics

rather than the presence of the question word itself. Examples (10.5–10.19) illustrate
the use of question words in content questions.

(10.5)　　húnash ya hútihamawa
　　　　　hu=na=sha　　　　**ya**　　　hu-tika-hama-wa
　　　　　PROX=ACC=Q.TOP　**who**　　PROX-VBLZ.TR-1PL.OBJ+IPFV-3
　　　　　'who is doing this to us?' (agr040712_02)

(10.6)　　nawanhumɨsh yahãĩ awɨmabiumɨ
　　　　　nawantu-hu-mɨ=sha　　**ya**=haĩ　　　awɨma-maya-umɨ
　　　　　daughter-PSSD-2=Q.TOP　**who**=COM　　CAUS+go+PFV-INTPST-2
　　　　　'with whom did you send your daughter (to Lima)?' (Tiinch & Dandu-
　　　　　cho)

(10.7)　　w̃ãã búutmɨ
　　　　　w̃ãã　　buuta-mɨ
　　　　　why　　cry+IPFV-2
　　　　　'why are you crying?'

(10.8)　　waŋka w̃ãỹãtsua
　　　　　waŋka　　w̃ãya-tsu-wa
　　　　　why　　　enter+IPFV-NEG-3
　　　　　'why doesn't she log in (to chat)?' (personal correspondence)

(10.9)　　túu wɨmumɨ
　　　　　tu　　　wɨ-ma-umɨ
　　　　　where　go+PFV-RECPST-2
　　　　　'where did you go?'

(10.10)　　tũw̃ĩỹãĩtpa
　　　　　tu=ĩ=ya=ita-pa
　　　　　where=LOC=ABL=COP-2
　　　　　'where are you from?'

(10.11)　　húsha wahimpáya
　　　　　hu=sha　　　　wahimpaya
　　　　　PROX=Q.TOP　　what+COP:3
　　　　　'what is this?'

(10.12)   ***wahĩ*** *aikakum puhami̵ hũw̃ĩsh*
          wahĩ   aika-ku-mi̵   puha-mi̵   hu=ĩ=sha
          what   thus+VBLZ.TR+IPFV-SIM-2   live+IPFV-2   PROX=LOC=Q.TOP
          'what do you do here?' (Tiinch & Danducho)

(10.13)   ***túu*** *waki̵ɰami̵*
          tu   waki̵ɰa-mi̵
          which   want+IPFV-2
          'which do you want?'

(10.14)   ***wahúk*** *háapa*
          wahuka   ha-a-pa
          how   be.sick-IPFV-2
          'in what way are you sick?' (Text 2:32)

(10.15)   ***wahúpa*** *ákika*
          wahupa   akika
          how.much   expensive
          'how much does it cost?'

(10.16)   *edadhumish wahupaita*
          edad-hu-mi̵=sha   **wahupa**=ita
          age-PSSD-2=Q.TOP   **how.much**=COP:3
          'what is your age?' (Tiinch & Danducho)

(10.17)   *wahuti akinattawa*
          wahuti   akina-tata-wa
          when   be.born+PFV-FUT-3
          'when is the baby due?' lit. *when will she be born?* (personal correspondence)

(10.18)   *wahuti "taattahai" tawa*
          wahuti   <u>ta-a-tata-ha-i</u>   ta-wa
          when   come-PFV-FUT-1SG-DECL   say+IPFV-3
          'when does she say she'll come?' (personal correspondence)

(10.19)   *hũw̃ĩsh wahuti naŋkamsam puhami̵*
          hu=ĩ=sha   **wahuti**   naŋkama-sa-mi̵   puha-mi̵
          PROX=LOC=Q.TOP   **when**   begin-SBD-2:SS   live+IPFV-2SG
          'since when do you live here?' (Tiinch & Danducho)

Note that *wahĩ* 'what' when followed by the copula enclitic *=aita* surfaces as *wahimpáita* 'what is it?', with epenthetic /mp/. This is often reduced to *wahimpáya* in casual speech (example 10.11 above).

In a few examples the question word *wahĩ* 'what' forms time and location questions with the addition of appropriate morphology (examples 10.20 and 10.21, respectively). It is not clear to me how these forms differ from the apparently synonomous question words *wahuti* 'when' and *tu* 'where'.

(10.20) *tuhãsh dukuwa **wahin**tin naŋkamsamia apahuish tuki nimaŋkau ...*
  dusha ỹãũshkikait?

tuhã=sha	duku-wa	**wahĩ**-tin	naŋkama-sa-mia
but=ADD	mother-VOC	**what**-TIME	start-SBD-2:SS

apahui=sha	tuki	nima-hu-ka-u	...
God=Q.TOP	always	follow-APPL-PFV-NMLZ	...

nu=sha	yaunchuki=ka=it
ANA=Q.TOP	recently=Q=COP:3

'so mother, when did you start following God? (i.e. convert to christianity) ... Was it recently?' (Tiinch & Danducho)

(10.21) *amina aishumish **wahĩn**ma takawa*

ami=na	aishu-mi=sha	**wahĩ**=numa	taka-wa
2sg=ACC	husband+PSSD-2=Q.TOP	**what**=LOC	work+IPFV-3

'what does your husband work in?' (Tiinch & Danducho)

10.4 Polar questions

Polar questions are marked with the polar interrogative enclitic *=ka*. This enclitic most commonly appears on the verb in slot G (10.22); but in past tenses formed with the past formative *-ma*, polar interrogative immediately follows this suffix (10.23; and see examples of paradigms in §8.4.3).

(10.22) *amish puhámik*

ami=sha	puha-mi=**ka**
2sg=Q.TOP	live+IPFV-2SG=**Q**

'are you living?' (greeting formula)

(10.23)   *Mario Vargas Llosa Premio Nobel susaŋma dusha dikaamkum*
            [*Mario Vargas Llosa   Premio Nobel   su-sa-aha-ma*
            Mario Vargas Llosa   Nobel Prize   give-PFV-PL-RECPST
            nu=sha]   dika-a-ma=**ka**-umi
            ANA_{REL}=Q.TOP   know-PFV-RECPST=**Q**-2SG
            'did you know they gave the Nobel Prize to Mario Vargas Llosa?' (personal correspondence)

The same marker *=ka* may be encliticized to some other constituent of the clause, making it the focus of the interrogation (10.24). In this case, the verb has no mood marking.

(10.24)   *amikika minám*
            ami=ki=ka   mina-mi
            2SG=RESTR=Q   come+IPFV-2SG
            'did you come by yourself?'

The polar interrogative marker precedes the copula enclitic (if it is present), and this is the only way to form a polar interrogative clause with a predicate nominal (10.25–10.27).

(10.25)   *piŋkiŋkait*
            piŋkiha=ka=ait
            good=Q=COP:3
            'is it good?'

(10.26)   *amish múunkaitam*
            ami=sha   muunta=ka=ita-mi
            2sg=Q.TOP   adult=Q=COP-2SG
            'are you a grown-up?'

(10.27)   *amikáitam*
            ami=ka=aita-mi
            2sg=Q=COP-2SG
            'are you you?' (standard greeting when not in the context of a house visit)

In example (10.28) the marked nominal forms a complex predicate with the copula verb, and (10.29) is arguably of the same type.

(10.28)   *úchik áya wainkámaush*
        uchi=ka   a-ya   waina-ka-mau=sha
        child=Q   COP-REMPST   see-PFV-NSBJ.NMLZ=Q.TOP
        'was it a child (you) saw?'

(10.29)   *amísh píŋkɨhak puhám*
        amɨ=sha   piŋkɨha=ka   puha-mɨ
        2sg=Q.TOP   good=Q   live+IPFV-2SG
        'are you well?' (greeting formula)

Although most examples of polar interrogative marked on nominals involve predicate nominals, other arguments may also be marked, in which case the verb appears unmarked (10.30–10.32, also 10.24 above). When encliticized to a pronominal argument, the polar interrogative marker does not undergo apocope, and takes the accent (10.24, 10.30, 10.31).

(10.30)   *auká túu wɨkáɨɰam*
        au=ka   tu   wɨkaɨɰa-tu-a-mɨ
        DIST=Q   say   walk-APPL-IPFV-2SG
        'is it him you're going on about?'[2]

(10.31)   *minaká túhutuam*
        mi=na=ka   tu-hu-tu-a-mɨ
        1sg=ACC=Q   say-APPL-1SG.OBJ-IPFV-2SG
        'are you talking to me?'

(10.32)   *tsabáuk uwáŋtatam*
        tsamau=ka   uwa-ha-tata-mɨ
        chapo=Q   drink-PFV-FUT-2SG
        'will you drink *chapo* (fermented banana drink)?'

A single pronoun marked with polar interrogative may form a question, given an appropriate discourse context. Example (10.33) might be used to seek clarification in response to a request such as "give me that!" (also compare example 10.36 below, with a dependent clause).

---

2 This is a weak auxiliary construction, as described in §6.7.

(10.33)   *huká*
            hu=ka
            PROX=Q
            '(do you mean) this one?'

In example (10.34), polar interrogative appears on the full verb in an auxiliary construction (compare the use of *puhut* 'live' as auxiliary with a predicate nominal in 10.29 above), formally marked as dependent. Interrogative mood is marked only once in a clause, so the finite verb takes no mood marking.

(10.34)   *máakmik puhám*
            maa-ku-mɨ=ka   puha-mɨ
            bathe+IPFV-SIM-2:SS=Q   live+IPFV-2SG
            'are you bathing?'

In example (10.35), too, polar interrogative is enclitic to a subordinate clause, but in this case the construction is much more like the marked nominals in (10.30–10.32), in which the polar interrogative enclitic marks the focus of the interrogation.

(10.35)   *wíi numín tsupíkchau asámtaiŋ támɨ*
            [wi   numi=na   tsupi-ka-chau   asa-mataĩ=ka]
            1sg   tree=ACC   cut-PFV-NEG.NMLZ   COP+SBD-1/3:DS=Q
            ta-mɨ
            say+IPFV-2SG
            'are you saying I didn't cut wood?'

Example (10.36) shows a subordinate clause used without an overt main clause in a question and answer exchange, seeking clarification during a discussion about B's life.

(10.36) A: *muntsuhut asamka?*
            muntsuhuta   asa-mɨ=**ka**
            young.woman   COP+SBD-2:SS=**Q**
            '(was that) when you were young?'

        B: *hiʔa muntsuhut asan*
            hiʔa   muntsuhuta   asa-nu
            yes   young.woman   COP+SBD-1SG:SS
            'yes, when I was young' (Tiinch & Danducho)

Polar interrogatives are often couched in negative polarity, apparently for politeness (although this is not always entirely apparent from context). In general, politeness requires using more phonological material, and the addition of a negative marker is one way to achieve this. Example (10.37) illustrates the piling up of morphology on the verb root to soften the request.

(10.37)   *amɨsh nuhín sumákmainchaukaitam?*
          ami=sha   nuhinta   suma-ka-mai-inu-chau=ka=ita-mɨ
          2sg=Q.TOP   egg   buy-PFV-POT-NMLZ-NEG.NMLZ=Q=COP-2
          'are you not one who is able to buy eggs?' i.e. 'please buy these eggs!'

Appropriate responses to polar questions are one-word forms: *hɨʔá ~ haʔá* 'yes', *atsá* 'no', *achá* 'I don't know'. Also common is a full clause, particularly to avoid ambiguity when the question is couched in the negative.

10.5 Marking of constituents in interrogative clauses

Both polar and content interrogative clauses can mark one or more constituents with the 'question topic' enclitic *=sha*. This enclitic can be attached to NPs (10.5, 10.6, 10.16 and other examples already cited) or subordinate clauses (10.38).

(10.38)   *amɨsh Lima wɨtasamɨsh wakɨɰasmɨk*
          ami=**sha**   [Lima   wɨ-tasa-mɨ=**sha**]   wakɨɰa-tsu-mɨ=ka
          2sg=**Q.TOP**   Lima   go+PFV-INTENT-2:SS=**Q.TOP**   want+IPFV-NEG-2=Q
          'do you want to go to Lima?' (agr040824_02)

The enclitic *=sha* is used only in content and polar questions, and has the same function as the topic enclitic *=ka*, which appears only in declarative clauses (§18.2). That is, it marks the presupposed part(s) of the clause, about which the question is being asked.[3]

Subordinate clauses and speech reports can take the enclitic *=sha*, but it cannot be attached to finite verb forms. In (10.39), the speech report ends in a dependent verb, which can take the question enclitic, but the complement of *antut* 'understand' in (10.40) is notionally a finite clause: "I am writing it"; consequently, it must be relativized with the anaphoric pronoun *nu* in order to host the question topic enclitic (cf. 10.23 above).

---

3 This complementary distribution of polar interrogative *=ka* and topic marker *=ka* across clause types (interrogative and declarative, respectively), along with their formal identity, is suggestive, but at present there is no other evidence for a synchronic or diachronic connection between the two.

(10.39) *"shíiŋ aniahai witasanush" táwak*
       shiiha   ani-a-ha-i   wi-tasa-nu=**sha**
       very   desire-IPFV-1SG-DECL   go+PFV-INTENT-1SG:SS=**Q.TOP**
       ta-wa=ka
       say+IPFV-3=Q
       'is she saying "I really want to go"?'

(10.40) *antamik, yatsuta, wii aɰaŋ dusha*
       anta-mi=ka   yatsu-ta   [wi   aɰa-ha
       understand+IPFV-2SG=Q   brother-VOC   1sg   write+IPFV-1SG
       nu=**sha**]
       ANA_{REL}=**Q.TOP**
       'brother, do you understand what I'm writing?' (personal correspondence)

In content interrogative clauses, in addition to the presence of a question word and question topic enclitic and the verbal marking by suppression of apocope, there are two further effects on markers of second person subject. Firstly, second person subject in subordinate verbs may take the form *-mia*, as in (10.41, 10.42).

(10.41) *wahuti naŋkamsamia puhami hũw̃ish*
       [wahuti   naŋkam-sa-mia]   puha-mi   hu=ĩ=sha
       when   begin-PFV+SEQ-2:SS   live+IPFV-2SG   PROX=LOC=Q.TOP
       'how long have you lived here?' lit. *starting when do you live here?* (Tiinch & Danducho)

(10.42) *tikish mihana duwish wahĩ aikattsamia wakiɰami*
       [tikichi   mihan=a   nu=i=sha]   [wahĩ
       another   year=COP:3   ANA_{REL}=INS=Q.TOP   what
       aika-tu-sa-mia]   wakiɰa-mi
       thus+VBLZ.TR-APPL-SBD-2:SS   want+IPFV-2SG
       'what do you want to do next year?' (Tiinch & Danducho)

And secondly, second person singular subject in content interrogative main clause predicates may take the form *-pa* (10.43). It is not clear what conditions this – in the examples above, *-pa* appears in (10.10) and (10.14), but the usual finite form *-mi* appears in (10.7) and (10.9).

(10.43)   *yáitpa*
           ya=it-pa
           who=COP-2SG
           'who are you?'

The second person marker -*pa* can apparently be encliticized to some other constituent as the only marker of a question, and the verb then takes the usual second person suffix -*mɨ* (10.44). Such examples are rare in my corpus.

(10.44)   *nuwáhaimpa yúmi áimkum wɨkáɨɥam*
           nuwa=haĩ=**pa**   yumi   aima-ku-mɨ   wɨkaɨɥa-mɨ
           woman=COM=**2SG+Q**   water   fill+IPFV-SIM-2   walk+IPFV-2SG
           'is it with a woman that you go to get water?' (agr041006_04)

The suffix -*pa* also marks second person subject in prohibitive clauses (§8.5).

10.6 "Tag" questions

Tag questions seek confirmation or acknowledgement of something the speaker assumes to be true, and they expect a positive response, if at all. Tag questions share the final syllable pitch rise with other question types, but they do not show the same distributed morphology – the only marker is the mood suffix -*api* on the predicate (10.45, 10.46). The term "tag question" is something of a misnomer, as these questions are not formed with a phonologically separate tag element, but the function is equivalent to tag questions in a language like English, so I use the term for want of a better one.

(10.45)   *amɨsh wɨɥamɨapi*
           amɨ=sha   wɨ-a-mɨ-api
           2sg=ADD   go-IPFV-2SG-Q.TAG
           'you're going too, aren't you?'

(10.46) A: *Santa Rosa atushtapi*
              Santa Rosa   atushata=a-api
              Santa Rosa   far=COP:3-Q.TAG
              'Santa Rosa is far away, is it?'

        B: *hiʔa*
              'yes' (Tiinch & Danducho)

In (10.47) use of a tag question invites elaboration from the addressee.

(10.47) A: *aminuk apellidok apachiapi*
ami-nau=ka   *apellido*=ka   apachi=a-api
2sg-POSS=TOP   surname=TOP   non.Aguaruna=COP:3-Q.TAG
'your surname is non-Aguaruna, isn't it?'

      B: *mina dukuhuk apash*
mi=na   duku-hu=ka   apachi
1sg=ACC   mother-PSSD:1SG=TOP   non.Aguaruna
'my mother is non-Aguaruna' (Tiinch & Danducho)

And (10.48) illustrates a common conversational interjection in the form of a tag question.

(10.48)   *áaniawapi*
aa-ni-a-wa-api
thus-VBLZ.INTR-IPFV-3-Q.TAG
'is that right?'

The final /i/ of *-api* is lost when an auxiliary copula verb is present (10.49), suggesting that it may be etymologically a reflex of the copula enclitic, which also alternates with a full copula verb.

(10.49)   *dɨkás ashí aɨntsti hinátnap áinahi*
dɨkas   ashi   aɨntsu=ti   hina-tinu-**ap**
truly   all   person=SAP   die:PL-FUT+NMLZ-**Q.TAG**
a-ina-hi
COP-PL:IPFV-1PL+DECL
'truly, all of us mortals will die, won't we?' (agr040824_02)

Appropriate answers to the the tag questions given above are *hɨʔa ~ haʔa* 'yes' (10.46) or repetition of the predicate with appropriate person and TAM changes; one could respond to (10.48), for example, with *aa-ni-a-wa-i* (thus-VBLZ.INTR-IPFV-3-DECL) 'it is so'.

    Example (10.50) shows a more rhetorical use of a tag question; the speech report attributed to the subject must represent thought rather than actual speech, as the context of the story tells us that the woman was returning alone from the garden.

(10.50)   *nĩ͂sh "yuwáttahapi" tus taáuwai*
        nĩ=sha   [yu-a-tata-ha-api   tus]
        3sg=ADD   eat-PFV-FUT-1SG-Q.TAG   say+SBD+3:SS
        ta-a-u=ai
        come-PFV-NMLZ=COP:3:DECL
        'she also arrived thinking "I'm going to eat, aren't I?"' (agr041005_15)

As noted above, tag questions are not prototypical interrogatives because the speaker already has a high degree of certainty regarding the content of the clause. The somewhat less interrogative nature of these clauses is reflected in the morphology: the interrogative topic enclitic *=sha* does not appear, instead the topic marker *=ka* is used (see example 10.47), as in declarative clauses.

10.7 Discourse functions of clauses with the formal appearance of questions

It is important to distinguish illocutionary force from morphosyntactic form, and question constructions in particular find non-interrogative uses in phatic function as greetings, as rhetorical questions (which may include a dedicated rhetorical question marker *=ki*) and as complement clauses (which may also use the rhetorical question marker). Questions are not typically used with the illocutionary force of commands in Aguaruna.

10.7.1 Greetings

There are a number of formulaic question and answer pairs used in greetings. The exchange in (10.51) is used when meeting after some time; (10.52) when visiting; and (10.53) when meeting on the path.

(10.51) a.   *amɨkáitam*
           amɨ=ka=ita-mɨ
           2sg=Q=COP-2SG
           'are you you?'

      b.   *wĩithai*
           wi=ita-ha-i
           1sg=COP-1SG-DECL
           'I am I'

(10.52) a. *puhámïk*
puha-mï=ka
live+IPFV-2SG=Q
'are you living?'

b. *puháhai*
puha-ha-i
live+IPFV-1SG-DECL
'I am living'

(10.53) a. *wïkáïmïk*
wïkaïɰa-mï=ka
walk+IPFV-2SG=Q
'are you walking?'

b. *wïkáïhai*
wïkaïɰa-ha-i
walk+IPFV-1SG-DECL
'I am walking'

10.7.2 Rhetorical questions

Rhetorical questions employ the formal marking of questions to assert something that the speaker considers to be self-evident. In example (10.54) a man is scolding his son for getting distracted by a group of young women while fetching water. The (unnecessary) answer to the rhetorical question is 'no'; unmarried men were traditionally required to avoid all contact with women lest they breathe in their giggles and become weak and effeminate.

(10.54) *wïi "nuwáhãĩ yúmi áimkata" tímakham*
wi   nuwa=haĩ   yumi   aima-ka-ta
1sg   woman=COM   water   fill-PFV-IMP
ti-ma=ka-hamï
say+PFV-RECPST=Q-1SG>2SG
'did I say to you "go with the women and fill (the gourds) with water"?'
(agr041006_04)

The rhetorical question marker *=ki* appears encliticized to question words, and indicates that the speaker has no expectation of an answer (10.55).

(10.55)   *wáaŋki*
            waã=ki
            why=Q.RHET
            'why (has this happened to me)?!'

In (10.56) the question form is functioning as the complement of *diik* 'watching', a manner adverb derived from the verb *diit* 'look at'.

(10.56)   *wíi iwasán díik tipistáhai wahíŋ áikaŋmawa*
            wi   iwa-sa-nu   díik   tipɨ-sa-ta-ha-i
            1sg   be.awake-SBD-1SG:SS   watching   lie.down-PFV-IFUT-1SG-DECL
            [wahĩ=ki   aika-hama-wa]
            what=Q.RHET   thus+VBLZ.TR-2.OBJ+IPFV-3
            'I'll lie awake, watching (to see) what is doing this to you'
            (agr040723_29)

Example (10.57) shows *=ki* enclitic to a form of the interrogative word *wahuk* 'how' marked with finite verbal morphology, and in (10.58) it is enclitic to the the lexical verb *wakɨtut* 'return'.

(10.57)   *wahúkathiki*
            wahuka-ta-hi=ki
            how-IFUT-1PL=Q.RHET
            'what will we do?' (agr040824_02)

(10.58)   *wísha huní wɨkáɥunush wahúk wakítkithaki ataktú mína nuŋkahũ̃ish*
            wi=sha   hu-ni   wɨkaɨɥa-u-nu=sha   wahuka
            1sg=Q.TOP   PROX-ALL   wander+IPFV-NMLZ-1SG:SS=Q.TOP   how
            wakitu-ki-ta-ha=ki   ataktu   mi=na
            return-PFV-IFUT-1SG=Q.RHET   again   1sg=ACC
            nuŋka-hu=ĩ=sha
            land-PSSD:1SG=LOC=Q.TOP
            'having travelled all this way, how will I ever return again to my home?'
            (agr040824_02)

Examples (10.59, 10.60) illustrate reason clauses couched as rhetorical questions, introduced with the question word *waã* 'why' plus the rhetorical question marker *=ki*. This may have been calqued from the equivalent Spanish pair *por qué* 'why'/ *porque* 'because'.

(10.59)   *úchi núna yuwá, wáaŋki kíiwish yutáiŋkait iísh?, dúwi hakáu túwahami*
          uchi   nu=na   yu-ã   [waã=ki   kiiwi=sha
          child   ANA=ACC eat-PFV+SEQ+3:SS   why=Q.RHET   centipede=Q.TOP
          yu-taĩ=ka=ait   ii=sha]   nu=i   ha-ka-u
          eat-NSBJ.NMLZ=Q=COP:3   1pl=Q.TOP   ANA=INS   die-PFV-NMLZ
          tuwahamĩ
          NARR
          'the child having eaten that (centipede), because – are centipedes food
          we eat? – because of that (the child) died.' (agr040721_07)

(10.60)   *múuntak háu, wáaŋki ihapimush utusáŋ isámati?*
          muunta=ka   ha-a-u   [waã=ki   ihapi-mau=sha
          adult=TOP   die-PFV-NMLZ why=Q.RHET   gut+PFV-NSBJ.NMLZ=Q.TOP
          utu-sã=ki   isama-ti]
          how-SBD+3:SS=Q.RHET   heal+PFV-JUSS
          'that elder died, because – how can one who has been gutted heal up?'
          (agr041005_16)

There is also a special word used to mark rhetorical questions: *wããs* 'I don't know
why'. This word introduces a clause that takes the formal marking of a content interrogative clause, as in example (10.61), where interrogative markers are the enclitic
=sha on both elements of the discontinuous NP ('that man') and suppression of
apocope on the verb.

(10.61)   *w̃ããs dúsha núnikabia muúntash*
          wã ãs   nu=sha   nu-ni-ka-amaya
          I.don't.know.why   ANA=Q.TOP   ANA-VBLZ.INTR-PFV-DISTPST:3
          muunta=sha
          adult=Q.TOP
          'I don't know why that man did that' (Text 1:38)

10.7.3 Complementation

Embedded questions may function as complements of verbs *dikat* 'know' (10.62 and
10.63) and *dikapit* 'feel' (see examples in §17.2).

(10.62)   *dikahai yáa puháwa*
          dika-ha-i   [ya   puha-wa]
          know+IPFV-1SG-DECL   who   live+IPFV-3
          'I know who is there'

(10.63)   *ɨkɨ dɨkas'hai wahɨ́ áwa*
      ɨkɨ   dɨka-tsu-ha-i   [wahɨ̆   a-wa]
      not.yet   know+IPFV-NEG-1SG-DECL   what   exist-3
      'I don't yet know what there is (for dinner)'

These may include a relativizing anaphoric pronoun *nu*, as in (10.64).

(10.64)   *wahúk háaha núna tumáin dɨkáptsayahai*
      [wahuka   ha-a-ha   nu=na]   tu-mai-inu
      how   be.sick-IPFV-1SG   ANA_{REL}=ACC   say-POT-NMLZ
      dɨkapɨ-tsa-ya-ha-i
      feel-NEG-REMPST-1SG-DECL
      'I didn't feel able to say in what way I was sick' (Text 2:30; cf. 10.14 above)

These embedded questions could also be calqued from Spanish.

11 Negation

Negation in Aguaruna may be marked productively with suffixes on predicates and nominals; there is a negative deverbal nominalizer; and there are a few inherently negative lexemes. Negated clauses seem to require that at least one participant be marked with the topic enclitic =*ka*. In §11.1 I describe verbal negation, and nominal negation in §11.2. Inherently negative words are described in §11.3.

11.1 Verbal negation

Negation is marked on verbs in morphological slot D (see Figures 6.2 and 6.3 in Chapter 6). This is a level I slot, forming part of the stem that hosts level II morphology which distinguishes finite, subordinate and nominalized verbs.

There are two verbal negative suffixes for declarative and interrogative verbs: -*cha* and -*tsu*. The selection is conditioned by tense and aspect, but is not straightforward. In tensed forms, the suffix -*cha* appears with the perfective stem (11.1), while the suffix -*tsu* appears elsewhere – with the imperfective stem (11.2a, b) and also with the unmarked stem (11.2c). Note that -*tsu* has the allomorph -*tsa* when followed by the remote past suffix (as in 11.2c). Where there is any overt constituent of a negated declarative clause, one of them is typically marked with the topic enclitic =*ka* (see §18.2).

(11.1) a. *dakáschattahai*
            daka-sa-**cha**-tata-ha-i
            wait-PFV-**NEG**-FUT-1SG-DECL
            'I will not wait'

        b. *wáinkachabiahai*
            waina-ka-**cha**-amaya-ha-i
            see-PFV-**NEG**-DISTPST-1SG-DECL
            'I didn't find (any)' (Text 2:12)

(11.2) a. *wíka búuttsuhai*
            wi=ka   buuta-**tsu**-ha-i
            1sg=TOP   cry+IPFV-**NEG**-1SG-DECL
            'I am not crying'

b. *wíka yúwas'hai*
   wi=ka   yu-a-**tsu**-ha-i
   1sg=TOP   eat-IPFV-**NEG**-1SG-DECL
   'I am not eating'

c. *ɨtsɨ́ŋtsayahai*
   ɨtsɨ-hu-**tsa**-ya-ha-i
   explain-APPL-**NEG**-REMPST-1SG-DECL
   'I did not explain to them' (Text 2:33)

The remote past suffix in (11.2c) can combine with the unmarked, imperfective or perfective stem, but I have no examples of a form combining an aspect marked stem, negative, and remote past.

The negative suffix *-cha* is the default in tenseless forms, such as the simultaneous subordinate verbs in (11.3, 11.4). Note that these forms take the imperfective stem, showing that aspect is not the only factor in selection of a negative suffix.

(11.3)   *kashín yútashkuiŋ, wíka wítathai*
         [kashini   yuta-**cha**-ku-ɨ̃=ka]   wi=ka
         tomorrow   rain+IPFV-**NEG**-SIM+1/3-DS=COND   1sg=TOP
         wɨ-tata-ha-i
         go+PFV-FUT-1SG-DECL
         'if it doesn't rain tomorrow, I will go'

(11.4)   *núniashkuik*
         nu-ni-a-**cha**-ku-i=ka
         ANA-VBLZ.INTR-IPFV-**NEG**-SIM-1PL:SS=COND
         'if we don't do that...' (Text 3:13)

Either negative suffix can appear with the potential stem, which does not mark aspect – see examples in §8.3.3. There does not appear to be any semantic difference conferred by the selection of negative suffix. Further examples of both negative suffixes in combination with various tenses are in §8.4.

The suffix *-cha* is the default in nominalized forms, and has given rise to the negative nominalizer *-chau* (see Chapter 15, especially §15.4.3). In some examples, however, the suffix *-tsu* appears, typically in the specific construction illustrated in (11.5). Here the unmarked stem is negated with *-tsu* then nominalized with the subject nominalizer *-u* and followed by the topic marker =ka. In all the examples of this construction in my corpus the referent of the nominalization is the speaker (see also examples 6.55 and 15.100).

(11.5)   *yumín shíkitsuk ukúahai*
        [yumi=na   shiki-**tsu**-u=ka]   uku-a-ha-i
        water=ACC   draw-**NEG**-NMLZ=TOP   leave-IPFV-1SG-DECL
        'I'm leaving without getting water' (agr041005_14)

The suffix -*(a)i* marks apprehensive and prohibitive forms (§8.5), which are semantically the negative counterparts of jussive and imperative (§8.4.4), respectively.
Example (11.6) shows an apprehensive form couched in a speech report forming a
purpose clause, and (11.7) shows a prohibitive formed by combining the apprehensive suffix with the distinct second person suffix -*pa*.

(11.6)   *wíi numín mináahai "ámɨ iyáawaim" tusán*
        wi   numi=na   minaa-ha-i   amɨ
        1sg   tree=ACC   make.bridge+PFV-1SG-DECL   2sg
        iya-aw-**ai**-mɨ   tu-sa-nu
        fall-PFV-**APPR**-2SG   say-SBD-1SG:SS
        'I've laid a log down (as a bridge) so that you won't fall'

(11.7)   *tíipa*
        ti-**i**-pa
        say+PFV-**APPR**-2SG:PROH
        'don't say it!'

11.2 Nominal negation

Nominals are negated with the suffix -*chau*. This suffix appears on nouns (11.8),
adjectives (11.9) and derived nominals (11.10); it also appears on verb stems, functioning as a nominalizer itself (example 11.13; also see §15.4.3).

(11.8)   *húka wɨɨkchau, húka wísut*
        [hu=ka   wɨɨka-**chau**]   [hu=ka   wisuta]
        PROX=TOP   leafcutter.ant-**NEG.NMLZ**   PROX=TOP   ant.sp
        'this isn't a leafcutter ant, this is a *wisut* ant'

(11.9)   *pɨŋkɨŋchau*
        pɨŋkɨha-**chau**
        good-**NEG.NMLZ**
        'bad'

(11.10)   *húka mídauchu*
           hu=ka   mi-nau-**chau**
           PROX=TOP   1sg-POSS-**NEG.NMLZ**
           'this is not mine'

In examples (11.8) and (11.10) the negated nominals head verbless equative clauses. Negation of the predicate nominal is the only way to negate equative/attributive clauses, whether verbless or using the copula enclitic (as in 11.11 and 11.12).

(11.11)   *pákichauwaithi, íiyaithi*
           [paki-**chau**=aita-hi]   [ii=aita-hi]
           white.lipped.peccary-**NEG.NMLZ**=COP-1PL+DECL   1pl=COP-1PL+DECL
           'we're not peccaries, we're us (i.e. people)' (agr040723_12)

(11.12)   *wĩka ỹãw̃ããchuithai, ihuntáŋ suwimám átinun*
           wi=ka   yawaã-**chau**=ita-ha-i   ihũ-tu-hã
           1sg=TOP   dog-**NEG.NMLZ**=COP-1SG-DECL   gang.up-APPL-PFV+SEQ+3:SS
           suwima-ma   a-tinu-nu
           beat+PFV-NSBJ>SBJ   COP-FUT+NMLZ-1SG:SS
           'I am not a dog, to be beaten by gangs of people' (agr060816_01)

The same negative suffix also appears on verbal stems, and then functions as a nominalizer. It may appear on both unmarked and aspectualized stems, and is the negative counterpart of the other participant nominalizers (11.13, and see Chapter 15).

(11.13)   *háachu*
           ha-a-**chau**
           be.sick-IPFV-**NEG.NMLZ**
           'healthy'

The negative suffix -*chau* appears to consist of the negative suffix -*cha* plus the nominalizer -*u*, and this is supported by the fact that it appears on verb roots and performs the dual function of negation and nominalization. In addition, it undergoes the phonological process of diphthong reduction which elsewhere occurs when a suffix of the form /Ca/ is followed by the nominalizer -*u* (§3.5.2). Synchronically, however, -*chau* is clearly a distinct suffix because of its ability to appear on nominal as well as verbal stems.

11.3 Negative lexemes

11.3.1 Negative verbs

There are two inherently negative verbs, *atsut* 'not be, not exist' and *dakitut* 'refuse'. The negative existential verb *atsut* is the negative counterpart of existential *ata*, which cannot otherwise be negated. At first glance *atsut* looks like the existential verb root *a-* 'exist' plus the negative suffix *-tsu*, however the element /tsu/ is synchronically distinct from the negative suffix, as it precedes the imperfective suffix in slot C, which fuses with the final /u/ to give an imperfective stem *atsa-* (11.14).

(11.14)   *atsáwai*
           atsu-a-wa-i
           exist:NEG-IPFV-3-DECL
           'there isn't any' (agr041102_08)

This shows that /tsu/ cannot be the negative suffix *-tsu*, as that suffix appears in slot D, following the aspect markers. The formal similarity clearly indicates a relationship, but it is impossible to tell whether the negative existential represents a historical fusion of *a-* 'exist' and *-tsu* 'negative', or the negative suffix represents a grammaticalization of the verb. However, the fact that there are two negative suffixes, and the *-tsu* form is not the default, suggests that it may be a relatively more recent grammaticalization.

The verb *dakitut* 'refuse' is semantically a negative counterpart of *wakɨɰat* 'want'. Note, however, that the latter can be negated morphologically (I do not have sufficient contextualized data to tell what motivates the choice between *dakitut* and negated *wakɨɰat*). Like *wakɨɰat*, *dakitut* can take a nominal or clausal complement, the latter formed with a nominalization (see 11.16). Further discussion and examples are in §17.2. Etymologically, *dakitut* appears to consist of a nominal *daki* 'lazy, layabout' combined with the verb *tuta* 'say'.

The discourse particle *ikɨ* 'not yet' appears only in negative polarity contexts (see full details below), and thus provides a test similar to the "some/any" test for English, described by Dixon (2012: §21.4.2). That is, an inherently negative verb that imparts negative polarity to the clause should be compatible with the use of *ikɨ*, and this is indeed the case for *atsut* and *dakitut*. Example (11.15) is from an email written in the city of Nieva, in which the writer, who lives in the community of Tundusa, explains why he is in Nieva.

(11.15)   *iki Tunduzak internet atsawai*
             iki   Tunduza=ka   *internet*   atsa-wa-i
             not.yet   Tundusa=TOP   internet   exist:NEG+IPFV-3-DECL
             'there is not internet in Tundusa yet' (personal correspondence)

(11.16)   *iki witának dakitahai*
             iki   wi-ta=na=ka   dakita-ha-i
             not.yet   go-ACT.NMLZ=ACC=TOP   refuse+IPFV-1SG-DECL
             'I don't want to go yet'

Neither (11.15) nor (11.16) involves a verbal negator in slot D (although one is etymologically present in the negative existential *atsut*), showing that the negative polarity is inherent to the verb. A further correlate of their negative polarity is the presence of the topic enclitic *=ka* on clausal arguments, which is strongly preferred in negative clauses (§18.2).

11.3.2 Negative particles

The discourse particle *iki* 'not yet' appears in negative polarity clauses expressing the speaker's assessment that the proposition will or should happen. Examples (11.17) and (11.18) are from personal correspondence (see also 11.15 and 11.16 above).

(11.17)   *iki presidente shiiŋ ipiŋkiatsui utuŋchatnak*
             iki   *presidente*   shiiha   ipiŋki-a-tsu-u-i
             not.yet   president   well   resolve-IPFV-NEG-3-DECL
             utuŋchata=na=ka
             problem=ACC=TOP
             'the President still isn't really fixing the problem' (personal correspondence)

(11.18)   *yama takatnum yapahiinau asan, iki akihuinashkũĩ tahami*
             yama   taka-ta=numa   yapahiina-u   asa-nu
             recently   work-NMLZ=LOC   change+PFV-NMLZ   COP+SBD-1SG:SS
             iki   aki-hu-ina-cha-ku-ĩ   ta-hami
             not.yet   pay-1SG.OBJ-PL:IPFV-NEG-SIM+1/3-DS   say+IPFV-1SG>2SG+DECL
             'I've recently changed my job and they haven't paid me yet, I'm telling you' (personal correspondence)

The use of *iki* may have a counter-presuppositional sense to it. Example (11.19) is from an online chat, in which my correspondent had not responded to a greeting; I asked whether he was sleeping (A), and he responded with (B).

(11.19) A. *kanamik*
kana-mɨ=ka
sleep+IPFV-2SG=Q
'are you sleeping?'

    B. *atsa iki kanas'hai*
atsa iki   kana-tsu-ha-i
no   not.yet   sleep+IPFV-NEG-1SG-DECL
'no, I'm not sleeping yet' (personal correspondence)

Example (11.20) was in response to a question whether the interlocutor is planning to set up a business with his brother who has recently moved to Lima. Note that this is an incomplete clause as it lacks a predicate, but negative polarity is conferred by the presence of *atsa* 'no'.

(11.20)   *atsa duka iki*
atsa   nu=ka   iki
no   ANA=TOP   not.yet
'no, as for that, not yet' (personal correspondence)

The particle *wããs* 'I don't know why' introduces a rhetorical question (see example 10.61 in Chapter 10), and is semantically equivalent to a negated form of the verb *dɨkat* 'know', but does not seem to be compatible with the use of *iki*.

Two further negative particles are used to answer questions: *atsá* 'no', functions as a pro-clause in responses to questions, and confers negative polarity as was shown in example (11.20). The interjection *achá* 'I don't know' is a more colloquial equivalent to *dɨkas'hai* (*dɨka-tsu-ha-i* 'know+IPFV-NEG-1SG-DECL') – comparable to English *dunno*.

12 Adverbial words

12.1 Preliminary remarks

Adverbial words are a somewhat diverse category, that nevertheless share some general properties. Semantically, adverbial words can modify with clausal scope; some may have narrower scope. Syntactically they tend to precede the element they modify, or the predicate if taking clausal scope. And adverbial words are characterized by a relatively restricted range of morphology – in particular they typically lack inflectional possibilities, but may take derivational morphology and clause-level enclitics. Adverbial words fall into six major types, which differ in their derivational morphology and syntactic behaviours. These are: numerals, quantifiers, manner adverbs, ideophones, time words and location words. In §12.4 I describe a set of discourse particles that are characterized by a complete lack of morphology.

12.2 Numerals and quantifiers

Both numerals and quantifiers provide specific information about the number or quantity of an NP participant, and both are characterized by somewhat ambiguous syntactic behaviour. They may function as NP operators, and take pre-head position like pronominal determiners. But both numerals and quantifiers may also follow the NP head, and some examples appear to function adverbially, in which case they typically directly precede the verb. Numerals may also function adjectivally, and take case morphology, while quantifiers never take any morphology. There are two derivational morphological processes that are unique to numerals, deriving distributive and iterative forms. In the following sections I describe the morphological and syntactic properties of numerals and quantifiers. Their syntactic behaviour as NP constituents is described in Chapter 5.

12.2.1 Numerals

Native Aguaruna numerals have single-word forms for the numbers one to three. Above three, a system of finger counting was traditionally used. To count this way, you start with an open hand, and count of the fingers by lowering them, starting with the little finger. In this way the index finger is the fourth to be lowered, and the word for 'four' is the same as for 'index finger', which itself comes from an expression meaning 'paint with annatto' (for which the index finger is used). When the thumb is lowered you have a closed fist, and the term for five ("closed hand") and above are basically conventionalized descriptions of this counting process (cf. Gnerre 1986a). The Aguaruna numerals I recorded are listed in Table 12.1; note that only one to five are stable expressions, and the terms for six and up may be paraphrased in various ways.

Table 12.1: Aguaruna numerals

number	numeral	gloss
1	makichiki	'one'
2	himaha	'two'
3	kampaatuma	'three'
4	ipak usumɨt	'(finger used to) paint with annatto' i.e. index finger
5	uwɨha amua	'finished hand'
6	uwɨha makichiki ihuk	'one added to the hand'
7	uwɨha himaŋa ihuk	'two added to the hand'
8	uwɨha kampaatuma ihuk	'three added to the hand'
9	uwɨha ipak usumɨt ihuk	'index finger (ie. four) added to the hand'
10	uwɨha mai amua	'both hands finished'

The system can be extended as far as twenty by adding toes as well as fingers. Since the introduction of bilingual schools, Spanish numerals are used almost exclusively from four upwards, although the system of finger counting is still used. The dialogue in (12.1) illustrates the use of Spanish loans in numbers and associated terminology, here discussing someone's age. Despite the overwhelming use of Spanish numerals, Aguaruna speakers still know the traditional forms and occasionally use them in contexts where they do not want Spanish speakers to understand, such as discussing prices amongst themselves.

(12.1) A. *edadhumish wahupaita*
         edad-hu-mɨ=sha   wahupa=ita
         age-PSSD-2=Q.TOP   how.much=COP:3
         'what is your age?'

B. *dos mil trecetin cumpliamhai sesenta y cinco*
    dos mil trece-tin   *cumpli*-a-ma-ha-i
    2013-TIME   complete-PFV-RECPST-1SG-DECL
    sesenta y cinco
    sixty-five
    'in 2013 I turned sixty-five' (Tiinch & Danducho)

Syntactically, numerals may precede the noun, like demonstratives (12.2), or they may follow the head (12.3).

(12.2)　　　*hímaŋ aínts*
　　　　　　[himaha　　aintsu]NP
　　　　　　two　　　　person
　　　　　　'two people'

(12.3)　　　*tsabáu makichík yuwáta*
　　　　　　[tsamau　　makichiki]NP　　yu-a-ta
　　　　　　banana　　one　　　　　　eat-PFV-IMP
　　　　　　'eat one banana!'

The numeral *makichik* 'one' may function as an indefinite article, introducing participants into a narrative as in (12.4) (see further discussion in §5.3.1).

(12.4)　　　*iŋkúŋmahai makichík aíntsún*
　　　　　　iŋku-ha-ma-ha-i　　　　　　　　[makichiki　　aintsu=na]
　　　　　　meet-PFV-RECPST-1SG-DECL　　one　　　　　person=ACC
　　　　　　'I met a person'

Numerals typically do not function like NP constituents, as they normally do not take case marking and may take clause-initial position, as in (12.5). (Note, however, accusative case on the iterative form in example 12.6 below.)

(12.5)　　　*makishkísh wíka yuwáshmahai tsamaúnak*
　　　　　　makichiki=sha　　wi=ka　　yu-a-cha-ma-ha-i
　　　　　　one=ADD　　　　　1SG=TOP　　eat-PFV-NEG-RECPST-1SG-DECL
　　　　　　tsamau=na=ka
　　　　　　banana=ACC=TOP
　　　　　　'I didn't eat even one banana'

Numerals have two unique morphological processes: (1) partial reduplication to give distributive meaning ('*n* each') and (2) a suffix -*a* gives iterative meaning ('*n* times'); these are illustrated in Table 12.2, and in examples (12.6) and (12.7).

Table 12.2: Numeral morphology

root	distributive	iterative	gloss
makichik	*maki makichik*	*makishkia*	'one'
himaŋ	*hima himaha*	*himaha*	'two'
kampaatum	no data	*kampatuma*	'three'

(12.6) *himá himáhan tinamkáhai*
       [hima   himaha=na]   tinama-ka-ha-i
       REDUP   two+DISTRIB=ACC   share.out-PFV-1SG-DECL
       'I shared (them) out two apiece'

(12.7) *kampatumá taámĩ*
       kampatum-a   ta-a-mĩ
       three-ITER   come-PFV-RECPST:3:DECL
       'he visited three times'

See §3.8.1 for phonological details of reduplication. The iterative suffix has the same form as the nominal 'first' enclitic, which is never used with numerals, and always takes the accent (§4.12.3). These two morphological processes are unique to the numeral class.

12.2.2 Quantifiers

Quantifiers typically modify NPs but unlike adjectives and determiners cannot take case-marking morphology, so morphologically they resemble adverbs. Table 12.3 lists the quantifiers in my data.

Table 12.3: Quantifiers

quantifier	gloss
ashi	'all'
bachik	'a little', 'a little while'
bɨtɨ	'full'
dɨkasɨ	'a little, a few'
dukap	'enough' or 'a lot'
himaituk	'half'
kuwashat	'many, much'
mai	'both'
uhumak~wahumak	'a little'

Syntactically, quantifiers with NP scope typically precede that NP. Note the change of scope depending on the position of *ashi* 'all' in examples (12.8) and (12.9).

(12.8)   *ashí úchi áinau tsamaún yuwáwaŋmɨ̃*
           ashi   [uchi   a-ina-u]   [tsamau=na]
           all   child   COP-PL:IPFV-NMLZ banana=ACC
           yu-aw-aha-mɨ̃
           eat-PFV-PL-RECPST:3:DECL
           'all the children ate bananas'

(12.9)   *úchi áinau ashí tsamaún yuwáwaŋmɨ̃*
           [uchi   a-ina-u]   ashi   [tsamau=na]
           child   COP-PL:IPFV-NMLZ all   banana=ACC
           yu-aw-aha-mɨ̃
           eat-PFV-PL-RECPST:3:DECL
           'the children ate all the bananas'

In example (12.10), however, the quantifier follows the NP (note that no ambiguity is introduced by varying the position of the quantifier in this example).

(12.10)   *ukúm kuwáshat ayáwai*
           [ukumpɨ]   kuwashata   aya-wa-i
           blackfly   many   exist:PL-3-DECL
           'there are many blackflies'

Quantifiers may also function as predicate modifiers. Example (12.11) is from a story in which a man joins a herd of peccaries and turns into a peccary. After some time, the other people speculate that he must have completely changed. The sense of *ashi* is not a quantifier 'all', rather an adverbial 'completely'.

(12.11)   *ashí nahánĩstai áuk*
           ashi   nahanɨ-ɨ-tsa-tai   au=ka
           all   change+PFV-3-SPEC-SPEC   DIST=TOP
           'he'll have changed completely, that guy' (agr040723_12)

Quantifiers never take case marking, as they are not NP constituents. Lack of accusative case on the quantifier *machik* 'a little' in example (12.12) shows that it cannot be forming an NP argument.

(12.12)   *báchik unuimáhai*
           machik   unuima-a-ha-i
           a.little   learn-PFV-1SG-DECL
           'I've learned a little'

The verb *ayampa* 'look around' in example (12.13) is intransitive, and the S is singular, so the quantifier *mai* 'both' cannot refer to any NP argument.

(12.13)   *mái ayámpã...*
           mai   ayampã
           both   look.around+PFV+SEQ+3:SS
           '(the man) having looked around on both sides...' (agr040712_02)

machik 'a little' is also used in combination with *asa-* (COP+SBD-) to give the sense 'in a little while', as in (12.14).

(12.14)   *báchik asán wɨtáhai*
           [machik   asa-nu]   wɨ-ta-ha-i
           a.little   COP+SBD-1SG:SS   go+PFV-IFUT-1SG-DECL
           'I'll go in a little while'

The subordinate verb has the same subject as the controlling verb, so a literal translation would be 'I being a little bit, I will go'.

12.3 Adverbs

Adverbs in Aguaruna can be divided into three subclasses: manner, time, and location; along with a fourth subclass of ideophones, which pattern syntactically and semantically with manner adverbs but are considered by native speakers to be distinct. Adverbs modify predicates. They are almost entirely without morphological possibilities, but time and location words can take diminutive *-uchi*, and the floating topic enclitic *=ka* and additive enclitic *=sha(kama)*. An intensifier *ima* shows unique syntactic and derivational properties

12.3.1 Manner adverbs

Manner adverbs fall into two subclasses: verbal and non-verbal. The verbal type are inflected for the person of the subject, using the same person markers as same-subject subordinate verbs. Manner adverbs typically precede the predicate in a clause, as in example (12.15), spoken by the village chief when some young men were getting too boisterous at a party.

(12.15)   *diipása nantsɨmámi*
            diipasa   nantsɨma-mi
            slowly+1PL   dance+PFV-HORT
            'let's dance slowly (i.e. carefully)!'

The person markers for verbal-type adverbs are laid out in Table 12.4.

Table 12.4: Person markers in verbal-type adverbs

person	singular	plural
1	*-nu*	suppression of apocope
2	*-mɨ*	
3	nasalization of stem-final vowel	

These are the same markers as same-subject subordinate verbs (§13.5.1). Second person singular and plural are not differentiated, as example (12.16) shows; the verbal marking makes it clear that the subject is second-person plural.

(12.16)   *wáinkam ihúipahum*
            wainaka-mɨ   ihu-i-pa-humɨ
            in.vain-2   stab-APPR-2:PROH-2PL
            'don't stab it in vain!' (agr041005_14)

Table 12.5 exemplifies the adverbial person paradigm with the adverb *aatus* 'thus' (for the change of /s/ to [ts] following /t/ see §3.2.3).

Table 12.5: Paradigm of verbal-type adverb *aatusa* 'thus'

person	singular	plural
1	*áattsan*	*áattsa*
	aatusa-nu	aatusa
	thus-1sg	thus+1pl
2	*áattsam*	
	aatusa-mɨ	same as singular
	thus-2	
3	*áatus*	
	aatusã	same as singular
	thus+3	

Because of the morphological similarity, clauses subordinated with the non-temporal subordinator *-sa* (described in §13.4.1) can look like adverbs, for example *imamkima-sa-* (take.care-SBD-) 'carefully'. The few examples of true adverbs have no corresponding verb, for example *diipas* 'slowly, carefully' has no corresponding verb root ***diipa-*; it may in fact have been borrowed from Sp. *despacio* 'slowly', reanalysed to fit the native morphology. Similarly, *aatus* 'thus' has no corresponding verb root ***aatu-*, but looks as if it has come from demonstrative adverb *aa* 'thus' plus *tuta* 'say'. A further corollary of the non-verbal nature of these words is the fact that they cannot take different subject marking, unlike verbs. Table 12.6 lists the unambiguous adverbs in my corpus, that is, those that have no corresponding verb.

Table 12.6: Verbal type manner adverbs

adverb	gloss
aatus	'thus'
diipas	'slowly, carefully'
tikima	'so much'
wainak ~ wainkas	'in vain'

wainak 'in vain' occasionally appears as *wainkasa*, apparently including the non-temporal subordinating suffix *-sa*. This suggests that these adverbs are considered by speakers to be defective verbs, that only exist in same-subject subordinate form, rather than a separate word class.

Non-verbal adverbs take no morphology. Examples from the corpus are listed in Table 12.7.

Table 12.7: Non-verbal adverbs

adverb	gloss
aa	'thus'
ataktu	'again'
diik	'watching'[1]
kakahus	'easily'
shiiha	'well'
paan	'clearly'
sinchi	'strongly'[2]
titu	'still', 'quietly'
waamak	'quickly'
tsikin	'suddenly'

Examples (12.17) and (12.18) illustrate *titu* 'still' and *tsikin* 'suddenly', respectively.

(12.17)   *ámɨk titú puhustá*
           ami=ka   titu   puhu-sa-ta
           2SG=TOP   still   live-PFV-IMP
           'you stay still' (agr040721_07)

(12.18)   *íkamỹãw̃ãã tsɨkɨn wahukú, dútikam nɨ̃ máaniu*
           ikam_yawaã   tsɨkɨn   wa-hu-ka-u
           jaguar   suddenly   go.up-APPL-PFV-NMLZ
           [nu-tika-ma]BRIDGE   nɨ̃   maani-u
           ANA-VBLZ.TR+PFV-NSBJ>SBJ   3SG   fight-NMLZ
           'The jaguar suddenly came up to him; when it did that he fought (it).'
           (agr041005_14)

The adverb *waamak* 'quickly' is typically non-verbal, but as with *wainak* 'in vain', it may appear with the suffix *-sa*, as in Text 2:39, where a third-person subject form *waámkɨs* (waamakɨ-sã 'quickly-SBD+3:SS') appears. The adverb *shiiŋ* 'well' is unique in that it can also modify adverbs and adjectives, with the meaning 'very', as in examples (12.19a and 12.19b).

---

1 From *diit* 'look at, watch'.
2 *sinchi* also functions as a noun 'strength'.

(12.19) a. *shíiŋ sínchi tupikákta*
            shiiha   sɨnchi   tupika-ka-ta
            very   strong   run-PFV-IMP
            'run very fast!'

       b. *shíiŋ múun*
            shiiha   muunta
            very   big
            'very big'

12.3.2 Sound-symbolism and ideophones

The sound-symbolic forms present in my data fall into two groups. The first group is purely onomatopoetic, for example "*tu, tu, tu...*", which refers to hitting a tree's buttress root, using it like a drum to signal arrival, and "*hau, hau, hau...*" referring to a jaguar's roar. There are apparently many well-established onomatopoetic representations of bird and animal calls, which would provide an interesting field for future study. The onomatopoetic forms typically appear repeated two or three times, and some appear to be nonce formations. The second group of sound-symbolic words are IDEOPHONES. These are "marked words that depict sensory imagery" (Dingemanse 2012: 655; Dingemanse 2011), and are typically defined by native speakers as representing a sound. The ideophones attested in my corpus are listed in Table 12.8. Phonologically, the majority of ideophones are of the form CVCVC and all except one (*pauh* 'falling') are well-formed phonological words, unlike many of the purely onomatopoetic terms. A few (such as *idaim*, *pɨpiŋkasuã*) are related to verbal roots, but the majority are not. Ideophones never take any morphology, and so are syntactically and morphologically a subset of the non-verbal type manner adverbs. They are considered to be distinct by speakers, however, who typically characterize them as representing the "sound' of an action. In conversation, ideophones tend to be associated with gestures and emphatic intonation.

Table 12.8: Ideophones

form	meaning
chaát	entering (house, cave etc) (agr040723_29)
hawát	putting something over ones shoulder (bag etc) (agr041006_04)
ídaim	snake sticking out its tongue (Text 1:26) (cf. *idaimat* 'stick out tongue' < *idai* 'tongue')
kakút	hitting, breaking apart (agr040721_07)

form	meaning
kutút	vomiting (agr040723_29)
kuwɨŋkahá	unwrapping (Text 1:33)
pakɨt	solid hitting solid (agr040719_02)
panán	coming out (of a hole, doorway etc.) (Text 1:26)
páuh	falling (agr040723_29)
piípi	slapping with the hand (agr041006_04)
pɨɨt	jumping (agr040721_07)
pɨpɨŋkasuá̃	wrapping up (Text 1:10) (cf. pɨmpɨt 'wrap up with winding motion')
pisút	slashing (Text 1:32)
puhút	'splash' (agr041102_07; example 13.7)
pútit	taking small bites (Text 1:25)
pútut	taking big bites (Text 1:14)
taŋkɨt	hitting (Text 1:32)
tapít	grabbing something (agr040721_07; example 15.100)
tuhít	a part snapping off (agr040723_29)

Ideophones are used as adverbial modifiers, and typically appear directly preceding the verb. Some examples have a close relationship with particular verbs, for example the collocation in (12.20) is common.

(12.20) *tapít achík...*
tapit   achi-kã
IDEO   grab-PFV+SEQ+3:SS
'having grabbed it: "*tapit!*"...' (agr041006_04)

Ideophones need not be accompanied by a verb referring to the action depicted. Example (12.21) is from a story in which a hummingbird flies through the forest with its tail on fire, setting alight all the dry trees it hits. The sentence contains no verb referring to the hummingbird hitting the trees, but this action is understood from the use of the ideophone *pakɨt*, which always denotes something solid hitting another solid object.

(12.21) *númi kukáu átatman pakɨt pakɨt akã̃ã̃...*
[numi   kukau   a-tatamana]   pakɨt   pakɨt
tree   dry   exist-SBJ>OBJ   IDEO   IDEO
akaã
set.alight+PFV+SEQ+3:SS
'"whack! whack!" having set alight the dry trees that were there...'
(agr040719_02)

Ideophones are an important part of all the Chicham languages, and Doris Payne (2001: 596) mentions ideophones as a widespread feature of Amazonian languages, as do Epps & Salanova (2012):

> Os ideofones são um exemplo de um recurso linguístico que se encontra com frequência nas narrativas em línguas amazônicas. Na maioria dos casos, essas formas conformam uma categoria lexical distinta das demais, com estruturas silábicas ou segmentos fonéticos que não se encontram em outros lexemas, e com propriedades morfológicas diferentes.
>
> [Ideophones are an example of a linguistic resource that is often found in narratives in Amazonian languages. In most cases, these forms constitute a distinct word class, with syllable structures or phonetic segments that are not found in other lexemes, and with different morphological properties.]

(Epps & Salanova 2012: 21)

Nuckolls (1996) describes an elaborate and grammatically important system of sound-symbolic forms in Pastaza Quechua, and her characterization of their importance in the language applies equally well to Aguaruna and the other Chicham languages:

> Its pervasiveness in Quechua speakers' discursive practice suggests that sound symbolism ramifies with their larger cultural concerns by pointing their attention to what is perceptually salient, affectively suggestive, and imaginatively engaging.

(Nuckolls 1996: 5)

Nuckolls does not discuss contacts between Pastaza Quechua and neighbouring Chicham languages – this would no doubt be an extremely rewarding area for future research.

12.3.3 Demonstrative manner adverbs

Demonstrative adverbs can be used deictically, to accompany gestures, or to refer anaphorically to an earlier mentioned action. They are listed in Table 12.9. The one basic form is *aa* 'thus'; the others appear to be morphologically complex, although it is hard to be sure of the source and/or directionality of development; suggested morphological structures are indicated.

Table 12.9: Demonstrative adverbs

adverb	gloss	source
áa	'thus'	–
aá-tu-sa	'thus'	thus-say-SBD
hu-ní	'like this'	PROX-ALL (?)
imá-ni	'so much'	INTENS-VBLZ.INTR (?)
nu-ní	'like that'	ANA-ALL (?)

aatus is a verbal-type adverb, and is inflected like a same-subject subordinate verb (see above); the others are non-verbal adverbs. *aatus* is also used to signal the end of a list of coordinate NPs – see §5.11.1.

12.3.4 Time words

Time words are the most commonly encountered class of adverbs. Table 12.10 lists all the time words in my corpus. Like non-verbal type adverbs, time words are morphologically opaque, but three roots appear to be represented more than once, as indicated in the third column.

Table 12.10: Time words

time word	gloss	related form?
āhúm	later	–
díkatkau	first	–
káshi	'at night'	–
káshikmas	'early in the morning'	*kashi*
kashín(ĩ)	'tomorrow'	*kashi=nĩ* 'at.night=LOC(?)'
mihadái	'for a year'	*mihana=i* 'year=INS'
túkɨ	'always' (also NP operator meaning 'like' §5.2.3; and discourse particle meaning 'indeed' §12.4.1)	–
tsawantái	by day	*tsawanta=i* 'day=INS'
yamá	'newly, just now'	–

time word	gloss	related form?
yabái	'now, today'	yama=i 'just.now=INS'
yáū	'yesterday'	–
yáunchukɨ	long ago (also 'very recently'?)	yáū

A special time word used at the beginning of traditional stories is the compound *duwik muun* (olden.days adult) 'in the time of our ancestors'. That this originated as a compound noun is shown by the fact that it may appear with the locative enclitic -=numa. In my data this compound only ever appears introducing traditional narratives, and the first element *duwik* only ever appears in this function.

Time words function as frame-setting, and as such take positions at the periphery of the clause and often take the topic enclitic =ka. They most frequently appear in clause-initial position, as in (12.22 and 12.23).

(12.22) *kashín tũw̃í̃ wɨtatmɨ*
kashini   tu=ĩ   wɨ-tata-mɨ
tomorrow   where=LOC   go+PFV-FUT-2SG
'where will you go tomorrow?'

(12.23) *ãhúm wainiámi*
ãhum   wai-nai-a-mi
later   see-RECIP-PFV-HORT
'let's meet later' (leave-taking formula)

In example (12.27) below, there are two topic-marked constituents in the clause, the time word follows the subject NP. In (12.28) a topic marked time word takes clause-final position, and in (12.29) an additive marked time word does the same. Note in (12.28) that the initial time word *tuki* 'always' and the final *yaunchukɨk* 'long ago' have scope over the whole clause chain. Time words may also have scope over just one clause in a chain, in which case their positioning reflects this (example 12.24).

(12.24) *núniashkuik, núu dútika maáshkuik, káshish wɨtáyamɨ̃*
nu-ni-a-cha-ku-i=ka   [nu
ANA-VBLZ.INTR-IPFV-NEG-SIM-1PL:SS=COND   ANA
nu-tika]   [ma-a-cha-ku-i=ka]
ANA-VBLZ.TR+PFV+SEQ+1PL:SS   kill-IPFV-NEG-SIM-1PL:SS=COND

[kashi=sha   wɨ-tayamɨ̃]
at.night=ADD   go-NORM
'If we don't do that, if having done all that we don't kill (the animal), we even go at night.' (Text 3:18)

Constructions combining an NP referring to a period of time with a subordinate form of the copula may function as time adverbs, as in (12.25a) and (12.25b).

(12.25) a.   *dúkap tsawán ásã...*
             dukapɨ   tsawanta   asã
             many   day   COP+SBD+3:SS
             'after many days...'

       b.   *báchik asán...*
             machik   asa-nu
             little.bit   COP+SBD-1SG:SS
             'in a little while (I will...)'

Unlike non-verbal manner adverbs, time words can take the discourse enclitics =ka 'topic' (12.26–12.28) and =sha(kama) 'additive' (12.29).

(12.26)   *wíka yabáik hatánum puháhai*
          wi=ka   yamai=**ka**   ha-ta=numa   puha-ha-i
          1SG=TOP   now=**TOP**   die-ACT.NMLZ=LOC   live+IPFV-1SG-DECL
          'now I'm about to die' (agr041005_16)

(12.27)   *túhã tíkichik dúwik yáunchukuk ishámahaku áinawai*
          tuhã   tikichi=ka   duwik   yaunchuku=**ka**
          but   other=TOP   long.ago   long.ago=**TOP**
          ishama-haku   a-ina-wa-i
          be.afraid-NARR.PST   COP-PL:IPFV-3-DECL
          'but the other people long ago were afraid' (agr041005_14)

(12.28)   *túkɨ máak ɨhapɨ̃ húhaku áinawai yáunchukik, áatus táwai*
          [tukɨ   maa-kũ   ɨhapɨ̃
          always   kill+IPFV-SIM+3:SS   open.up+PFV+SEQ+3:SS
          hu-haku   a-ina-wa-i   yaunchukɨ=**ka**]
          take-NARR.PST   COP-PL:IPFV-3-DECL   long.ago=**TOP**

aatusã   ta-wa-i
thus+3   say+IPFV-3-DECL
'(because people didn't know about giving birth) killing (the woman) they would open her up and take (the baby) out in the old days, so the story goes' (agr041005_16)

(12.29)   *wɨmí dɨkás káshish*
wɨ-mi   dɨkas   kashi=**sha**
go+PFV-HORT   really   night=**ADD**
'let's go, really, even though it's night' (agr060816_01)

At least one time word, *yabai* 'now', can take the restrictive enclitic *=kI* (see example 18.15 in Chapter 18). The final /kɨ/ of *yaunchuk* 'long ago' may be a fossilized restrictive enclitic.

Some time words are formed with instrumental case, as indicated in Table 12.10. Time words can also be formed from Spanish dates and names of days with the 'time' suffix *-tin* (examples 12.30a) and (12.30b).

(12.30) a.   *dosmilcincotin*
             dos mil cinco-tin
             2005-TIME
             'in (the year) 2005' (agr040824_02)

        b.   *lunestin*
             lunes-tin
             Monday-TIME
             'on Monday'

All my examples of the suffix *-tin* are added to borrowed Spanish time expressions, but Wipio (1996: 155) gives examples of this suffix on native noun and verb roots, deriving traditional names of seasons (examples 12.31a, b).

(12.31) a.   *wachitin*
             wachi-tin
             cañabrava.flower-TIME
             'the season when the *cañabrava* reed is in flower'

        b.   *shinutin*
             shinu-tin
             call-TIME
             'the season when birds and monkeys make a lot of noise'

12.3.5 Location words

Underived location words are listed in Table 12.11 (and see also *ímau* 'right there, over there' in §12.3.6). These words never take any morphology.

Table 12.11: Location words

location word	gloss
amáin	'the other side of the river'
atú	'near'
atúshat	'far off'
yakí	'above, vertically up'

The most common position for location words is preverbal (examples 12.32, 12.33), and the complex location expression in example (12.34) is similarly positioned.

(12.32)   *ỹãw̃áá yakí áwa*
           yawaã   yaki   a-wa
           dog   above   exist-3+EXCL
           'there's a dog up there!'

(12.33)   *amáin wɨmí*
           amain   wɨ-mi
           other.side   go+PFV-HORT
           'let's cross (the river)'

(12.34)   *mina apahuk Chapisa atu, Kaŋkas tawai, ãw̃íỹã ahakuwai*
           mi=na   apa-hu=ka   chapisa=a   atu   kaŋkas
           1sg=ACC   father-PSSD:1SG=TOP   Chapisa=COP:3   near   Kagkas
           ta-wa-i   au=ĩ=ya   a-haku=ai
           say+IPFV-3-DECL   DIST=LOC=ABL   COP-NARR.PST=COP:3:DECL
           'as for my father, a place near Chapisa, called Kagkas, he was from there' (Tiinch & Danducho; cf. 15.96)

A few nouns that are semantically part of the location word set differ amongst themselves in the extent of their similarities to location words. The nouns *initak* 'inside' and *waapak* 'under' may function like location words, as in (12.35).

(12.35)   *ínitak áwai*
             initaka   a-wa-i
             inside   exist-3-DECL
             'it's inside'

But to say *what* something is inside or under, a possessed form must be used, as in (12.36, 12.37). This form then takes locative case to form a location expression.

(12.36)   *pɨɰaká waápkɨn áwai*
             pɨɰaka   waapakɨ=nɨ̃   a-wa-i
             bed+GEN   under+PSSD:1PL/3=LOC   exist-3-DECL
             'it's under the bed' lit. *it's at the bed's underside*

(12.37)   *namaká ínitkɨn*
             namaka   initakɨ̃=nɨ̃
             river+GEN   underwater+PSSD:1PL/3=LOC
             'at the bottom of the river' (agr040824_01)

úntsu 'right' and *mɨ̃na* 'left' only appear as possessed nouns, and take locative case (12.38).

(12.38)   *mína mɨ̃nahũɨ̃ áwai*
             mi=na   mɨ̃na-hu=ɨ̃   a-wa-i
             1sg=ACC   left-PSSD:1SG=LOC   exist-3-DECL
             'it's to my left'

Three other forms require the locative enclitic *=numa*: *uku=numa* 'behind'; *nuhi=numa* 'upstream' (cf. *nuhi* 'nose', also used to refer to the prow of a canoe); and *tsumu=numa* 'downstream'. The latter form is exemplified in example (12.39), from a story about a battle with a group of Huambisas from the Santiago River. They are referred to as 'enemies from downstream' because one must travel down the Marañón River from the Aguaruna area where this story was recorded to get to the Santiago River.

(12.39)   *tsumúnumia shiwáha nunú kanús anúmkauwai kayánum*
             [tsumu=numa=ya   shiwaha=a   nunu   kanusa]ₙₚ
             downriver=LOC=ABL   enemy=COP:3   ANA_REL   Santiago.River

anuma-ka-u=ai   kaya=numa
land-PFV-NMLZ=COP:3:DECL   rock=LOC
'those enemies from downriver, (those from the) Santiago River, landed
(their canoes) on the rocks' (agr041005_18)[3]

The notion of 'ahead' is represented by the verb *iimat* 'go ahead', which forms a
sequential subordinate clause in (12.40).

(12.40)   *ɨ̈mkan wɨuɑahai*
           ɨima-ka-nu   wɨ-a-ha-i
           go.ahead-PFV+SEQ-1SG:SS   go-IPFV-1SG-DECL
           'I'm going on ahead' lit. *I having gone ahead, I'm going*

Location words, like locative case-marked NPs, make no distinction between locational and directional uses. The only class to have separate locative and allative
forms is the demonstratives (§4.6.2).
    Finally, §4.4.4 discussed some inherently locational nouns that can be used
without the locative enclitic, as well as some nouns with irregular locative forms,
such as *hintá* 'in the path' < *hínta* 'path'; *naín* 'uphill' < *náin* 'hill'.

12.3.6 Intensifier *ima*

The intensifier *ima* and its derivatives are particularly flexible. The underived form
modifies nouns, where in combination with the 'restrictive' enclitic *=kI* it gives the
meaning 'only' (§4.3), or adjectives, forming a comparative construction (12.41). The
use of *ima* in comparison is perhaps motivated by its phonological similarity to
Spanish *más* 'more', which similarly form the comparative degree of a following
adjective e.g. *más grande* 'bigger'.

(12.41)   *Suizanmayas imá pɨ̨ŋkɨhaitai*
           Suiza=numa=ya=tsu   **ima**   pɨŋkɨha=i-tai
           Switzerland=LOC=ABL=SPEC   **INTENS**   good=COP:3:DECL-SPEC
           'perhaps the (knife) from Switzerland is better'

The root *ima* combines with the verbalizing suffixes *-ni* and *-tika* to produce pro-
verbs meaning 'do so much' (§6.6.2), and five words of different classes are derived
from *ima* through unproductive suffixes (Table 12.12),

---

3 Note that this example contains an 'apposed name' NP, as described in §5.7. The name *kanus* is
applied to the Santiago River and metonymically to the Huambisa people who live there.

Table 12.12: Forms based on intensifier *ima*

form	word class	gloss	translation
ímau	location word	INTENS.LOC	'over there', 'right there'
ímaŋ	adjective	INTENS.ADJ	'so big', 'so grand'
íman	pronoun	INTENS.NMLZ	'such a big one', 'such a grand one'
imáshi	manner adverb	INTENS.ADV	'so well', 'better'
imáni	demonstrative manner adverb	INTENS.DEM.ADV	'so much'

The manner adverb *imashi* (INTENS.ADV) 'so well' can be analysed as composed of *ima* plus *shiiŋ* 'well'. The demonstrative adverb *imani* may include the same /ni/ that appears in manner adverbs derived from demonstratives, which may itself be the allative suffix *-ni*. Example (12.42) illustrates the location word *imau*, and (12.43) illustrates the manner adverb *imashi*.

(12.42) *"Chúnu minámɨk?" támash, áyatak ímau ɨkɨmsau*
       [chunu   mina-mɨ=ka   ta-ma=sha]   ayatak
       Chunu   arrive+IPFV-2SG=Q   say+IPFV-NSBJ>SBJ=CONCESS   only
       imau   ɨkɨma-sa-u
       INTENS.LOC sit-PFV-NMLZ
       'although (the man) said "Chunu, are you coming?", (Chunu) just sat at a distance' (agr040721_08)

(12.43) *dakítau apahɨ́hãĩ wɨtán, túhã dukuhɨ́hãĩ imáshi wɨ̨ɨ̨au shíiŋ*
       dakita-a-u   apa-hɨ̃=haĩ   wɨ-ta=na
       refuse-IPFV-NMLZ   father-PSSD:1PL/3=COM   go-ACT.NMLZ=ACC
       tuhã   duku-hɨ̃=haĩ   **imashi**   wɨ-a-u
       but   mother-PSSD:1PL/3=COM   **INTENS.ADV**   go-IPFV-NMLZ
       shiiha
       well
       'He refused to go with his father, but went more with his mother.' (agr041005_15)

Words derived from *ima* (but not the bare root *ima* itself) can follow predicates that are marked for all finite verb categories except mood, in the same way as relativizing pronouns. In the case of derivatives of *ima* the resulting forms are adverbialized. This is illustrated for the location word *imau* in (12.44), and see §16.3 for further discussion and examples.

(12.44)   *uúbi híiya ímau tsahút íhũ*

uumi=i	[hii=a	**imau**]	tsahut
blowgun=INS	eye=COP:3	**INTENS.LOC**REL	IDEO

ihũ
stab+PFV+SEQ+3:SS

'having stabbed it right in the eye with his blowgun...' (agr041005_14)

12.4 Particles

12.4.1 Discourse particles

Discourse particles express speaker attitude and have scope over the whole clause. They do not modify any element of the clause, so can be omitted and still retain the meaning of the clause. Discourse particles are listed in Table 12.13.

Table 12.13: Discourse particles

form	gloss
áyatak	'only'
dɨkás	'really' (< *dɨkat* 'know')
íkɨ	'not yet' (see §11.3.2)
kamɨ̂	'better'
nuwiŋtú	'furthermore'
túhã	'even so', 'but'
túkɨ	'indeed' (also 'always')
úntsu	'well then'

The distal demonstrative with restrictive enclitic (*au=kI*) also functions as a discourse particle when used in its textual cataphoric function, signalling the speaker's surprised attitude towards the exclamation that follows (§4.6.2.2).

The discourse particles have the function of placing a clause in the context of the surrounding discourse, and in using them the speaker takes account of what they assume are the addressee's expectations and assumptions. In example (12.42) above, the use of *ayatak* 'only' (the clause is repeated in 12.45) explicitly guides the speaker to reject the expectation that Chunu might have moved.

(12.45)   *...áyatak ímau ɨkɨmsau*
ayatak   imau   ɨkɨma-sa-u
only   INTENS.LOC   sit-PFV-NMLZ
'[although (the man) said "Chunu, are you coming?"] (Chunu) just sat
at a distance' (agr040721_08, repeated from 12.42)

In example (12.46) the particle *dɨkas* 'really' similarly has the function of explicitly
informing the addressee that they need to override their expectations about how the
world works. Note that the additive enclitic *=sha(kama)* also appears in this example, with a similar function of overriding expectations that the addressee is pre-
sumed to hold.

(12.46)   *wɨmí dɨkás káshish*
wɨ-mi   **dikas**   kashi=sha
go+PFV-HORT   **really**   night=ADD
'let's go, really, even though it's night' (agr060816_01) (repeated from
12.29)

The additive enclitic *=sha(kama)* appears in (12.47) too, this time together with the
discourse particle *untsu* 'well then'. The effect is similar, explicitly marking a situation that is counter to what one would expect. The context here is that a jaguar is
prowling around the camp, and it is expected that nobody would go to fetch water
alone in such a situation.

(12.47)   *...ayú úntsu wikísh utithái...*
ayu   untsu   wi=kI=sha   uti-ta-ha-i
ok   well   1SG=RESTR=ADD   bring+PFV-IFUT-1SG-DECL
'[there was no water, so he said] "ok, well I'll bring it by myself" [and
went down (to the well)]' (agr041005_14)

The discourse particles typically take initial position, as they have scope over a
whole utterance. Because of their clause-initial position and counter-expectational
semantics, they may function like coordinators. In particular, *túhǎ* 'even so, but'
often functions as a contrastive coordinator 'but', and this function is described in
§14.7.1. A detailed study of the use of discourse particles, particularly in conversation, is a topic for future research.

12.4.2 Interjections

There is a semi-closed class of interjections. They typically consist of just one surface syllable of the shape CVC or CVV. Some interjections do not fit into the usual
phonological system – see §3.8.4. Table 12.14 gives an exhaustive list of conventionalized interjections present in my data.

Table 12.14: Conventional interjections

form	function
chak	'boundary marker' in narrative
waʔ	surprise
hɨʔ	surprise
chíi	'oh really?', 'I see'
áa	'thus'
ʔáɨ	surprise
pái	enough, done, ready
achá	'I don't know'
tsúwa	'well how about that?'
háu	response to someone calling one's name
sɨ́ɨ	despair
sɨ́ɨ	'thank you!'[4]
ayú	agreement, 'ok'
ái	as above – form used in women's casual register
hɨ̃ʔá ~ haʔá	'yes'
atsá	'no'
maʔ ~ máa	hesitation
chúu	defiance

As with the sound-symbolic forms, interjections can be loosely categorized into two
classes: those that are more fixed, and nonce formations, which often are not well-
formed phonological words. Three of the interjections are used pro-clausally to
answer questions: *hɨ̃ʔa ~ haʔa* 'yes'; *atsa* 'no' and *acha* 'I don't know'. These are
discussed in Chapter 10 on questions; and the latter two inherently negative forms
are discussed in §11.3.2.

---

4 *sɨ́ɨ* 'thank you' can be modified with the quantifier *kuwáshat* 'much': *sɨ́ɨ kuwáshat* 'thank you very
much' (perhaps by analogy with Spanish *muchas gracias* 'many thanks').

13 Subordinate clauses

13.1 Preliminary remarks

Clause combining is a central and highly salient feature of Aguaruna grammar. This is a clause-chaining language: narratives in particular are characterized by strings of morphosyntactically subordinate clauses, obligatorily marked for switch-reference, and relatively few finite verbs. Three general techniques are used to combine clauses: subordination; juxtaposition; and bridging constructions (or tail-head linkage). In addition, a nominalized clause can be embedded in a matrix clause, as head or modifier of an NP. The most commonly encountered clause linkage is subordination, while coordination through juxtaposition plays a relatively minor role. Bridging constructions (including tail-head linkage) are widely used in narrative, and allow the morphological resources of subordinate clauses to be used to track participants between finite clauses.

Non-finite verbs fall into two overarching groups, contrasting subordinate verbs with nominalizations. Within the subordinate verb there are two types: person marking forms contrast with non-inflecting. These groupings are schematically represented in Figure 13.1. This chapter describes the two types of subordinate verbs, contrasting their properties with finite and nominalized verbs. Nominalized verbs are described in detail in Chapter 15.

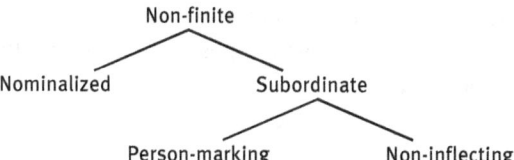

Figure 13.1: Non-finite clause types

All non-finite verbs are characterized by a reduction in the verbal grammatical categories marked, relative to finite verbs (Chapter 8 to Chapter 11 provide a detailed discussion of finite verbal categories and their marking). Non-finite verbs are incompatible with mood/modality marking, and they may share that of their controlling verb.[1] Some, but not all, are marked for aspect, and some mark temporal relations with a controlling verb. All subordinate verbs are marked for switch-reference; the person marking type are marked for person of the subject, while the non-inflecting type are not. Different-subject subordinate verbs neutralize the distinction between first and third person subject marking. Following Stirling (1993), I use the term MARKED CLAUSE for the subordinate clause whose verb carries switch-reference information, and CONTROLLING CLAUSE for the clause in relation to which switch-reference is marked. The controlling clause need not be finite: two or more subordinate clauses can form a unit that is (i) dependent on another unit and (ii) has its own internal dependencies. Table 13.1 summarizes the categories marked on finite and subordinate verbs.

Table 13.1: Comparison of categories marked on finite and subordinate verb forms

	finite	subordinate
tense	✓	–
mood/modality	✓	–
aspect	✓	some
person	✓ [a]	✓ [a]
switch reference	–	✓
floating enclitics	–	✓

[a] Different sets of person suffixes are used with finite and subordinate verbs

Table 13.2 presents the morphological distinction between the verbal categories of finite and subordinate verbs slightly differently, to highlight the gradient nature of non-finiteness: loss of verbal categories progresses from fully inflected finite verbs to fully decategorized nominalizations.

---

1 Except that nominalized verbs heading finite clauses may take narrative modality marker *tuwahamï* directly, without needing the copula enclitic, since this marker is not bound (§15.5.3).

Table 13.2: Loss of verbal properties in decategorization

	fully finite	subordinate (ss)	subordinate (DS)	non-inflecting subordinate	nominalized
Marks tense and mood	✓	–	–		–
1 and 3 subject distinct	✓	✓	–	–	–
2 subject distinct	✓	✓	✓	–	–
Marks SS/DS	–	✓	✓	✓	–

The reduction of marked categories, highlighted by the internal border of Table 13.2, can be expressed as a hierarchy of finiteness, shown in Figure 13.2.

FINITE > SUBORDINATE (SS) > SUBORDINATE (DS) > NON-INFLECTING (DS) > NOMINALIZED

Figure 13.2: Hierarchy of finiteness in clause types

This hierarchy is clearly related to Payne's (1997) cline of syntactic integration, represented in Figure 13.3. At the left extreme, there are two syntactically distinct finite clauses. At the right extreme, a nominalized clause is embedded in a matrix clause – the integration is total, and syntactically the two form a single clause.

INDEPENDENT CLAUSES > COORDINATION > SUBORDINATION > EMBEDDING

Figure 13.3: Hierarchy of syntactic integration in clause types (after T. Payne 1997: 307)

There is a general agreement between the two hierarchies, but nominalized clauses in Aguaruna are flexible: they can function at all points of the cline in Figure 13.3, from independent to embedded clauses, as described in Chapter 15. As for the distinction between subordinate and nominalized verbs, the criterial definition of a nominalized verb is the ability to form part of an NP, a property not shared by any other verbal form. As NP constituents, only nominalized verbs can take accusative, possession and vocative marking. Subordinate verbs are obligatorily marked for switch-reference while nominalizations are not, but examples do exist of nominalized verbs taking person suffixes, from both the subordinate and finite sets (§15.3.3).

    Subordinate clauses may take clause-level modality enclitics that also appear on NPs (speculative =*tsu*, question topic =*sha* and polar interrogative =*ka*), and the different subject suffix, as well as the conditional and concessive enclitics, that appear only on subordinate verbs, are historically extensions of nominal enclitics (locative, topic and additive respectively). Table 13.3 summarizes the key distinctions between subordinate verbs and nominalized verbs.

Table 13.3: Comparison of subordinate and nominalized verb forms

	can form NP	switch-reference marking
subordinate verb	no	obligatory
nominalized verb	yes	no

Clause combining has the following functions in Aguaruna:
- Complementation – a clause fills a core argument slot in a matrix clause (Chapter 17)
- Relativization – a clause modifies an NP (Chapter 16)
- Temporal clauses
- Consequence clauses
- Logical relations: conditional and concessive clauses
- Possible consequence clauses

The following sections first describe the morphological properties of the various subordinators (§13.2–§13.4), then the person and switch-reference system in §13.5. In §13.6 I describe the non-inflecting subordinators, and in §13.7 address the syntactic properties of subordinate clauses. Chapter 14 describes clause combining constructions from a semantic perspective. Speech report constructions, including their extended uses, are described in Chapter 17 along with complementation, which is a formally disparate category that makes use of subordinate, coordinate and nominalized clauses.

13.2 Morphology of subordinate verbs

Level II consists of four positions in subordinate verbs, as shown in Figure 13.4. Note that slots F and G are applicable only to inflecting subordinate verbs. Non-inflecting forms take a subordinating suffix in slot E, and may take floating enclitics in slot H.

Level I	
PFX:	Valency
	ROOT
A:	Valency
B:	Object
C:	Aspect
D:	Negative

Level II	
E:	Subordinating suffix
F:	Person
G:	Different subject -*(n)ĩ*

Floating enclitics		
H:	(i)	Conditional =*ka*
	(ii)	Concessive =*sha(kama)*
	(iii)	Mood/modality enclitics

Figure 13.4: Morphological slots in subordinate verbs

The perfective and imperfective stems can form subordinate clauses with no overt marker in slot E, and then directly take person and DS suffixes in slots F and G. The subject in subordinate verbs (slot F) is marked with a different set of suffixes from those used with finite verbs. Same subject is formally unmarked, while different subject takes a suffix in slot G. Most first and third person DS forms have fused subordinator, person and DS markers (slots E, F and G), although a reflex of the DS suffix can always be identified. In second person forms, separate person and DS marker -*(n)ĩ* can be identified in slots F and G respectively. Slot H does not host an inflectional category, but floating enclitics that can be hosted by any clausal constituent including NPs and adverbial constituents in addition to subordinate clauses. Because subordinate clauses are always verb-final, enclitics are always hosted by the verb. The topic enclitic =*ka* and additive =*sha(kama)* mark conditional and concessive clauses, respectively, when they are hosted by subordinate verbs.

Inflecting subordinate verbs fall into three groups, based on whether they appear only in same-subject clauses (four types); in both same-subject and different-subject clauses (three types) or only in different-subject clauses (one type). This three-way division is mostly reflected morphologically: SS subordinate verbs take transparent marking, but DS verb morphology is transparent only in second person. The first and third person markers are partly fusional, and may be etymologically unrelated to the second person forms (§13.2.2). Conditional and concessive express interpropositional logical relations, and are marked by enclitics that also appear on NPs marking topic and additive, respectively. Conditional and concessive markers never appear on the four SS-only clause types, although they can appear on other SS clauses (§14.6). Speculative =*tsu* (§9.2.4), polar interrogative =*ka* (§10.4), and question topic =*sha* (§10.5) may appear on subordinate clauses.

13.3 Same-subject subordinate verbs

Four subordinate verb types appear only in same-subject (SS) clauses, and encode specific semantic relations with their controlling clause. These clause types are marked by suffixes in slot E, shown in Table 13.4.

Table 13.4: SS subordinate verb markers

clause type	stem	suffix
terminative	unmarked	-*kama*-
intentional	perfective	-*tasa*- / -*tatus*
frustrative	perfective	-*takama*-
repetitive	imperfective	-*kawa*-

Same-subject subordinate verbs index their subject with one of a set of markers in slot F, described in §13.4. Note that the intentional dependent verb has an irregular third person form -*tatus*.

13.3.1 Terminative -*kama*

A terminative clause encodes an ongoing action that comes to a punctual conclusion with the action of the controlling verb. The suffix is added to the unmarked stem. Example (13.1) is from a story in which a man gets lost and his relatives are looking for him, following his tracks. After walking for some time, they come across the lost man.

(13.1)   *"wɨkaɨtáiŋ húu wɨ̃háma, hukɨɯ̨aháma" tus wɨkaɨkamã̂ wainkáuwai*
    [wɨkaɨɯ̨a-taɨ̃=ka   hu   wɨ̃-hama
    walk-NSBJ.NMLZ=TOP   PROX go+PFV+3-CNTR.EX
    hu=kɨ=a-hama   tus]   [wɨkaɨɯ̨a-**kamã̂**]
    PROX=RESTR=COP:3-CNTR.EX say+SBD+3:SS walk-**TERM+3:SS**
    waina-ka-u=ai
    see-PFV-NMLZ=COP:3:DECL
    'saying "the path went here, this is it!" and walking on they saw (the
    man's footprints)' (Text 1:19-20)

In examples such as (13.2), the word *dii-kamã̂* (see-TERM+3:SS) is consistently translated into Spanish as *al verlo* 'upon seeing it...'.

(13.2)   *anútuk diikmã̂ núna kãỹũkan pɨɨt ɨ́tsɨkɨ̃...*
    [anu-tu-kã]   [dii-**kamã̂**]   [nu=na
    approach-APPL-PFV+SEQ+3:SS look-**TERM+3:SS** ANA=ACC
    kãyuka=na   pɨɨt   i-tsɨkɨ-kɨ̃]
    agouti=ACC   IDEO   CAUS-jump-PFV+SEQ+3:SS
    'having approached, on seeing it, having made the agouti jump...'
    (agr040721_07)

13.3.2 Intentional *-tasa* / *-tatus*

The intentional suffix appears with the perfective stem. There are two allomorphs: *-tatus* is used for third person subjects with no further person marking
(example 13.3), and *-tasa-* plus person marking for first and second person subjects
(examples 13.4, 13.5).

(13.3)   *úchi akáikɨ̃, yúmiŋmat hɨ̃ɯ̨ã́tatus wɨ́tatman, ikámỹãw̃ãã tɨpɨŋkáuwai*
    [uchi akai-kɨ̃]   [yumiŋmat hɨ̃ɯ̨a-**tatus**]
    youth go.down-PFV+SEQ+3:SS well   arrive+PFV-**INTENT+3:SS**
    [wɨ-tatamana] ikam_yawaã tɨpɨ-hu-ka-u=ai
    go-SBJ>OBJ   jaguar   lie.down-APPL-PFV-NMLZ=COP:3:DECL
    'the youth, having gone down the hill, going with the intention of arriv-
    ing at the well, the jaguar pounced on him' (agr041005_14)

(13.4)   *núnika, akahú húki wɨ́ɯ̨aku, kúntin wainkátasa wahasá...*
    [nu-ni-ka]BRIDGE   [akahu   hu-ki]
    ANA-VBLZ.INTR-PFV+SEQ+1PL:SS shotgun take-PFV+SEQ+1PL:SS

[wɨ-a-ku]   [kuntinu   waina-ka-**tasa**]
go-IPFV-SIM+1PL:SS   animal   see-PFV-**INTENT+1PL:SS**
[waha-sa]   [niima-sa]
stand-SBD+1PL:SS   look-SBD+1PL:SS
'then, having taken our shotguns and gone to find animals, we stand looking' (Text 3:7)

Use of the intentional form indicates the subject's intention to perform the action denoted by the verb. This suffix is clearly a grammaticalized form of the desiderative suffix *-tata ~ -tatu* (§8.4.4.7) followed by the non-temporal subordinator *-sa*. The non-third form has undergone a haplological reduction from **-tatu-sa* (-DESID-SBD) to *-tasa*. The third-person form never appears with a final vowel in my data, but we can assume that the underlying form is *-tatu-sã* (-DESID-SBD+3:SS).

An intentional clause may function as a complement clause if the controlling verb is one of intention or desire (13.5).

(13.5)   *yuwátasan wakɨɰahai*
        [yu-a-**tasa**-nu]   wakɨɰa-a-ha-i
        eat-PFV-**INTENT**-1SG:SS   want-IPFV-1SG-DECL
        'I want to eat'

Complementation is described in detail in Chapter 17.

13.3.3 Frustrative *-takama*

Frustrative *-takama* appears with the perfective stem, and describes a thwarted intention. Typically such clauses are appropriately translated into English as "trying in vain". Example (13.6) is taken from a story in which the devil has had his arm pulled off, so he tries to pull a young woman's arm off to use in its place. The frustrative marking in the subordinate clause foreshadows the verb *tuhintut* 'be unable' in the main clause.

(13.6)   *nuúmpahun hápikĩ ahiáŋ ichiŋtakamã́ ... tuhintúk pɨmpɨ́ɨnakĩ...*
        [nuumpahu=na   hapi-kĩ]   [ahia-hã]
        young.woman=ACC tug-PFV+SEQ+3:SS knock.down-PFV+SEQ+3:SS
        [ichĩ-ka-**takamã́**]   ...   [tuhintu-kã]
        pull.off-PFV-**FRUST+3:SS**   be.unable-PFV+SEQ+3:SS

pɨmpɨɨna-kɨ̃
turn.around-PFV+SEQ+3:SS
'(the devil) tugged at the young woman and knocked her down, trying in vain to pull (her arm) off ... being unable, he turned to go...' (agr040723_29)

In example (13.7) a hunter has chased a monkey for a long time through the forest, and the monkey has become so tired that as it tries to jump from tree to tree it loses its grip and falls in the mud.

(13.7)　*pɨ̃t tsɨkɨ̃ numínum achímkatakamã akupmámak pimpikíu ásã kuchánum*
　　　　puhút ɨ̃ɰ̃ãkú

[pɨ̃t	tsɨkɨ̃]		[numi=numa	achima-ka-**takamã**]
IDEO	jump+PFV+SEQ+3:SS		tree=LOC	grab-PFV-**FRUST**+3:SS

[akupamama-kã]		[pimpi-ki-u	asã]
let.go-PFV+SEQ+3:SS		get.tired-PFV-NMLZ	COP+SBD+3:SS

kucha=numa	puhut	ɨ̃ɰ̃a-ka-u
mud=LOC	IDEO	fall-PFV-NMLZ

'(the monkey) trying in vain to jump into the tree "boing!", having let go because it was tired out, it fell "splash!" in the mud' (agr041102_07)

It is not always the case that the failure must be made explicit however. In example (13.8) the failure is implicit in the verb *awɨɨmat* 'scare off', but the only explicit indication is the frustrative suffix.

(13.8)　*dapín maátakaman awɨɨmámhai*

[dapi=na	ma-a-**takama**-nu]	awɨɨma-ma-ha-i
snake=ACC	kill-PFV-**FRUST**-1SG:SS	CAUS+go+PFV-RECPST-1SG-DECL

'trying in vain to kill the snake, I scared it off'

The typical use of frustrative in Aguaruna is with telic verbs, where the expected endpoint is clearly defined. In example (13.9) a devil has retrieved his arm from a cooking pot and is trying to stick it back on with a spell. The expected outcome is that the spell would make the arm stick on.

(13.9)　*"kusúi kusúi wíi wíithus wíithus" titakamã̃ túsã áatus kuntúhĩn iwíwakmã*
　　　　húwaknuk páuh ahɨ̃̃ɨ̃tãɨ̃...

[kusui kusui wii wiithus wiithus	ti-**takamã**]	[tu-sã
(magic formula)	say+PFV-**FRUST**+3:SS	say-SBD+3:SS

aatusã	kuntu-hĩ=na	iwiwa-kama
thus+3	arm-PSSD:1PL/3=ACC	swing-TERM+3:SS

[huwakunu-kã   pauh   ahũũ-taĩ]
come.unstuck-PFV+SEQ+3:SS   IDEO   fall-SBD:1/3:DS
'saying (in vain) "kusui kusui wii wiithus wiithus!", saying that as he swung his arm, when it came unstuck and fell "pauh!"...'
(agr040723_29)

The frustrative suffix never undergoes vowel elision, suggesting that it is a recently grammaticalized form. For Shuar, Turner (1992: 82ff) gives the frustrative construction as a two-word form: *-taj tukamá-* (/tah tukama/); this form appears to have the morphological composition shown in (13.10):

(13.10)   *-ta-h(a)*   *tu-kama-*
          -INTENTIONAL.FUTURE-1SG   say-TERMINATIVE-

That is, the verb stem is suffixed with intentional future *-ta* and first person singular *-ha*, and that verb then acts as a speech report complement to the verb *tuta* 'say', which carries the terminative suffix *-kama* followed by any person marking required. Terminative is a subordinating suffix, so the whole construction must be subordinate to a controlling verb. The frustrative sense is not apparent from the sum of the parts, which suggest only an intentional meaning.[2] Turner gives only one example, in which the controlling verb is a negative form of *umit* 'complete, fulfil' (13.11).

(13.11)   Shuar
          [taka-s-**tah**   **tukama**-n]   umi-k-cha-m-ha-i
          work-PFV-**DESID**   **'despite'**-1SG:SS   complete-PFV-NEG-RECPST-1SG-DECL
          'A pesar de haber deseado trabajar, no cumplí' [Although I wanted to work, I did not complete it]
                                                          (Turner 1992: 83)

For Achuar-Shiwiar, Fast et al. (1996: 44) give the form of the suffix as *-kamá-*, although in their examples it appears as *-tat-kamá-* (as in 13.12), looking very much like a phonologically reduced development of the Shuar periphrastic form (they do not give morphemic glosses).

---

2 In fact, [*verb*-IFUT-1SG say-] is the same periphrastic construction that gave rise to the desiderative and intentional suffixes in Aguaruna – see §8.4.4.

(13.12)   Achuar-Shiwiar
           [amɨ   wini-tat-**kama**-m]   tuhinta-mɨ̃
           2SG   arrive-?-**FRUST**-2:SS   be.unable+IPFV-2SG+DECL
           'Aunque tratas de venir, no puedes' [Although you try to come, you
           cannot]

                                        (Fast et al. 1996: 44; glosses mine)

The same authors also note that:

> El modo frustrativo aparece en el primer verbo de una expresión verbal compuesta por dos ver-
> bos, el segundo de los cuales denota la dificultad o la imposibilidad de la acción.
>
> [The frustrative mood appears in the first verb of a verbal expression composed of two verbs,
> the second of which denotes the difficulty or impossibility of the action.]
>
>   Fast et al. (1996: 44)

No grammatical information was available on Huambisa. The evidence of Turner
(1992) and of Fast et al. (1996) suggests a grammaticalization path from a periphrastic intentional construction to a subordinating intentional suffix that was always
accompanied by a controlling verb indicating an unsuccessful outcome. The association with an unsuccessful outcome then became part of the meaning of the frustrative marker itself, giving the present Aguaruna system in which the unsuccessful
outcome may remain implicit. The historical consonant cluster, evident in the
Achuar-Shiwiar form (13.12), explains the non-application of vowel elision in the
Aguaruna form (cf. §3.5.2).

Frustrative markers frequently feature in descriptions of Amazonian languages,
although rarely elsewhere (whether this is an artefact of the descriptive tradition or
indicates a genuine areal feature is as yet unclear). Overall (in press-a) proposes the
following cross-linguistically applicable definition, on the basis of a survey of morphemes labelled *frustrative* in Amazonian languages:

> Frustrative is a grammatical marker that expresses the non-realisation of some expected out-
> come implied by the proposition expressed in the marked clause.
>
>   (Overall in press-a)

Note that the proposed definition defines frustrative as marking an action performed in vain, while the Aguaruna marker implies a failure to perform the action at
all. The requirement for a semantic component of intention in the Aguaruna form
means that it is not strictly a frustrative marker, but rather a portmanteau in which
frustrative has semantic scope over an intentional construction (consistent with the
etymology described above).

13.3.4 Repetitive -*kawa*

The repetitive suffix -*kawa* is added to the imperfective stem, and expresses a repeated or prolonged action (13.13, 13.14). It is always accompanied by partial reduplication of the verb root, glossed REDUP in the examples. The phonological details of reduplication are discussed in §3.8.1.

(13.13)   *wɨkáɨ wɨkáɨkawa yapáŋki minámunum hintá kã́y̌uk bataɨ́n pɨhɨ́kɨush antútayamɨ̃*
  [wɨkaɨ   wɨkaɨɰa-**kawa**]   [yapahu-ki]
  REDUP   walk+IPFV-**REPET+1PL:SS**   get.hungry-PFV+SEQ+1PL:SS
  [mina-mau=numa   hinta   [kã̌yuka   bataɨ=na
  arrive-NSBJ.NMLZ=LOC   path+LOC   agouti   *chambira*.fruit=ACC
  pɨhɨkɨ-a-u=sha]   antu-tayamɨ̃]
  gnaw-IPFV-NMLZ=ADD   hear-NORM
  'walking and walking and getting hungry, as we arrive we hear an agouti gnawing on *chambira* fruit in the path' (Text 3:13)

(13.14)   *búu búutkã̌w̃ã́ wɨ́u*
  [buu   buuta-**kawã̌**]   wɨ-u
  REDUP   cry+IPFV-**REPET+3:SS**   go+PFV-NMLZ
  'crying and crying he went' (agr041006_01)

This suffix surfaces as -*kua* when the first /a/ is elided (see §3.5.2), as in example (13.15), referring to young men devoting themselves to preparations for warfare. This idiomatic construction, literally 'laying oneself out in the path', is commonly used to refer to young men setting out on their vision quests.

(13.15)   *hintá tɨpá tɨpákũã̌*
  hinta   tɨpa   tɨpa-**kawã̌**
  path+LOC   REDUP   lie.down+IPFV-**REPET+3:SS**
  'throwing (themselves) into the path (of preparation)...' (agr040702_01)

Corbera (1994: 297–298) suggests that the repetitive marker is composed of the simultaneous morpheme -*ku* (see §13.4.2) plus some other morpheme -*ã̌* (the nasality is actually third-person marking; Corbera analyses it as part of the phonemic form of the suffix). This analysis only works if one assumes that the basic form is /kuã/, as it cannot explain the /kawa/ alternant; it seems that Corbera's data simply did not include any examples that surfaced as [kawa].

13.4 Same or different-subject subordinate verbs

A second set of subordinate verb types can appear in both SS and different-subject (DS) clauses. They are marked by suffixes in slot E, shown in Table 13.5. The markers in the column headed "SS" are followed by the subordinate clause subject markers (§13.5.1). In DS forms the distinction between first and third person subject is neutralized, and the only person contrast is between second person and others. No number distinctions are made in first and third person, and second person plural marking is not obligatory. The DS forms fuse the suffixes from slots E, F and G, and cannot be completely decomposed but we can identify the simultaneous suffix *-ku*, second person suffix *-mi* and a DS suffix *-(n)ĩ*. All the DS forms end in /ĩ/, suggesting that the DS suffix is present in slot G, at least etymologically. The morphological breakdown of these markers is discussed in detail in §13.5.2.

Table 13.5: SS/DS dependent verb markers

clause type	stem	suffix			
		SS	**2SG DS**	**2PL DS**	**1/3 DS**
non-temporal	unmarked	*-sa-*	–	–	*-tãĩ*
simultaneous	imperfective	*-ku-*	*-kuminĩ*	*-kuminĩ ~ -kuhuminĩ*	*-kũĩ*
sequential	perfective	*-∅-*	*-minĩ*	*-minĩ ~ -huminĩ*	*-matãĩ*

In the following sections I describe these clause types in more detail. I focus on SS clauses here, and return to the DS types in §13.5.2.

13.4.1 Non-temporal *-sa*

The general adverbial subordinator *-sa* is suffixed to the unmarked stem, and is used to combine two or more clauses where the temporal relation between them is not relevant. Dependent verbs marked with *-sa* often appear in chains, as in example (13.16) from a story in which a man is trying to stay awake all night to see who (or what) keeps having sex with his wife (it turns out to be an *ĩwanch* or evil spirit, which has taken the form of a spider monkey).

(13.16) *iwás, tsaaŋkún bushútus, nahán ĩtĩmas, káhĩ maám shinták iwá tĩpáĩ...*
        [iwa-**sã**]   [tsaaŋku=na   bushutu-**sã**]   [naha=na
        be.awake-**SBD+3:SS**   tobacco=ACC   snort-**SBD+3:SS** nettle=ACC

iti-ma-**sã**]   [kahĩ   maa-ma]
beat-REFL-**SBD**+**3:SS** sleep+PSSD:1PL/3 kill+PFV-NSBJ>SBJ
[shinta-kũ]   [iwa tïpa-ĩ]
wake+IPFV-SIM+3:SS be.awake lie+IPFV+1SG/3-DS

'(lying in bed) awake, snorting tobacco and beating himself with a net-tle, when sleep overcame (lit. *killed*) him he woke up and was lying awake...' (agr040723_29)

In example (13.17), by contrast, the -*sa* marked verb appears in a string of perfective verbs, which express a sequence of events in purely temporal terms.

(13.17) *hiinúm paták, wíŋka wíŋkas, piniknúm paták...*
    [hii=numa pata-kã]   [wiŋka wiŋka-**sã**]
    fire=LOC put-PFV+SEQ+3:SS REDUP singe-**SBD**+**3:SS**
    [pinika=numa pata-kã]
    rack=LOC   put-PFV+SEQ+3:SS

    'having put (the monkey's arm) in the fire, singeing it, then having put it on the storage rack above the fire...' (agr040723_29)

Semantically, the -*sa* marked verb in (13.17) is modifying the preceding perfective clause, and not the following one. The scope and syntactic status of subordinate clauses will be discussed in detail in §13.7. The suffix -*sa* only appears in that form in SS clauses, but it has a functional counterpart in DS clauses in -*taĩ* (§13.5.2). A subclass of adverbs takes person marking similar to that of SS subordinate verbs, and there is evidence for grammaticalization of the non-temporal subordinator -*sa* into an adverb marker (see §12.3.1).

13.4.2 Simultaneous -*ku*

The simultaneous suffix -*ku* is suffixed to the imperfective stem and encodes simultaneity of the action with that of the controlling verb, as in (13.18, 13.19).

(13.18) *dúwik múuntak túkɨ minák awatĩ táya túwahamĩ*
    duwik_muunta=ka tukɨ [mina-**kũ**]   [awatĩ]
    ancestor=TOP   always arrive+IPFV-**SIM**+3:SS hit+PFV+SEQ+3:SS
    ta-ya   tuwahamɨ
    come-REMPST+3 NARR

    'our ancestors would always hit (a tree root) as they were arriving (as a signal to the people in the house)' (agr040723_29)

(13.19)   *diiyák wɨuwai*
        [dii-a-**kũ**]   wɨ-u=ai
        see-IPFV-**SIM+3:SS**   go+PFV-NMLZ=COP:3:DECL
        'he went, looking' (Text 1:7)

The suffix *-ku* is unique among the subordinators as it may appear following the future suffix *-tata* (see example 8.83 in §8.4.4.8). It is not clear what the semantic effect is of suffixing *-ku* to the future suffix rather than the imperfective stem.

Verbs subordinated with *-ku* are common in auxiliary constructions, as discussed in detail in §6.7. It suffices to say here that an auxiliary construction involves a non-finite verb form dependent upon a semantically lighter controlling verb, and the whole is reanalysed as monoclausal, as in examples (13.20, 13.21).

(13.20)   *diiyákum atá*
        dii-a-**ku**-mɨ   a-ta
        look-IPFV-**SIM**-2:SS   COP-IMP
        'watch out!' (agr040721_07)

(13.21)   *takáakun puháhai*
        taka-a-**ku**-nu   puha-ha-i
        work-IPFV-**SIM**-1SG:SS   live+IPFV-1SG-DECL
        'I'm working'

DS simultaneous clauses have only partly transparent subject marking involving the DS suffix *-(n)ĩ*, but the suffix *-ku* can be recognized throughout the paradigm, as discussed in §13.5.2.

13.4.3 Sequential *-∅*

Sequential subordinate verbs have no overt marker in slot E; person and switch-reference markers are suffixed directly to the perfective stem. In DS sequential clauses with first and third person subject, the perfective stem is followed by the suffix *-mataĩ* which is a portmanteau, combining first/third person and DS (see examples in §13.5.2).

Example (13.22) shows a simple sequential linkage: following the bridging clause, which functions much like a conjunction (see §14.8 for discussion), the sequential clause *iŋkunik* 'having met each other' can be appropriately translated with a subordinate adverbial clause in English.

(13.22)   *núnik iŋkúnik, nŵ̃ĩ naŋkámdayauwai maánitan*
          [nu-ni-kã]ʙʀɪᴅɢᴇ   [iŋku-nai-kã]   nu=ĩ
          ANA-VBLZ.INTR-PFV+SEQ+3:SS   meet-RECIP-PFV+SEQ+3:SS   ANA=LOC
          naŋkama-nai-a-u=ai   maani-ta=na
          begin-RECIP-PFV-NMLZ=COP:3:DECL   kill+RECIP-ACT.NMLZ=ACC
          'then having met, they began fighting there' (agr041005_18)

Chains of sequential clauses are a typical feature of narrative discourse. Example
(13.23) is the latter part of an even longer clause chain consisting mostly of sequential clauses, describing a man butchering and cooking a dog. In such examples,
unlike (13.22) above, it is not appropriate to translate the sequential clauses into
English with adverbial clauses (i.e. *having cut up the meat…* etc.); rather they must
be translated as a sequence of conjoined finite clauses (see further discussion of
clause chaining in Chapter 14).

(13.23)   *…nɨhɨn tsupíŋ páinak ɨkɨnák idáiyak, núna nɨhɨn akáŋkɨn ínaŋtuk*
          apúsauwai
          [nɨhɨ=na   tsupi-hã]   [paina-kã]
          meat=ACC   cut.up-PFV+SEQ+3:SS   put.in.pot-PFV+SEQ+3:SS
          [ɨkɨna-kã]   [idaiya-kã]   [nu=na   nɨhɨ=na
          put.on.fire-PFV+SEQ+3:SS   boil-PFV+SEQ+3:SS   ANA=ACC   meat=ACC
          akaŋkɨ=na   inahu-tu-kã]   apu-sa-u=ai
          abdomen=ACC   cook-APPL-PFV+SEQ+3:SS   put-PFV-NMLZ=COP:3:DECL
          '…he cut up the meat, put it in the pot, put it on the fire and boiled it, he
          cooked the meat of the abdomen (for his wife) and set it down'
          (agr041005_15)

13.4.4 Imperfective DS -∅

The imperfective stem may form a DS subordinate clause; there is no overt marker in
slot E, and person and DS marking suffixes are attached directly to the imperfective
stem. As this form only appears in DS clauses, it is described along with DS person
marking in §13.5.2.

13.5 Person marking in subordinate verbs

Subjects of subordinate verbs are obligatorily indexed with suffixes in slot F. The
suffixes used with subordinate verbs are different from those used with finite verbs
in first and third persons, but for second person the same suffix *-mɨ* is used. The
same person markers used with subordinate verbs also occasionally appear on nom-

inalized verbs (§15.3.3) and ablative-marked nouns (§4.10.7). Person marking is the same for all types of same-subject clauses, but differs slightly in the four types of different-subject clause, so there are five paradigms in total for marking person and/or different subject. In the following sections I first describe same-subject person marking, then different-subject marking.

13.5.1 Same-subject person marking

Table 13.6 shows the person markers used in same-subject clauses, marked in slot F. As with finite verbs, plural is obligatorily marked in first person, but not third; but unlike both finite and different-subject subordinate verb forms, second person can be marked with the suffix -*mɨ* in both singular and plural; an explicit second person plural suffix -*humɨ* may be used, but its use is not obligatory. All persons may optionally be marked for plurality with the level I suffix -*ina* 'plural imperfective' in the two types that take the imperfective stem (repetitive and simultaneous). The perfective plural marker -*aha* does not seem to be available in SS verb forms, unlike DS forms (see Table 13.10).

Table 13.6: Slot F subject markers on subordinate verbs in SS clauses

person	singular	plural
1	-*nu*	suppression of apocope / -*i* [a]
2	-*mɨ*	-*mɨ* ~ -*humɨ*
3	nasalization of stem-final vowel	

[a] First person plural is marked with the suffix -*i* only when followed by the conditional enclitic =*ka*.

The following sections describe each of the person markers in turn.

13.5.1.1 First person singular
First person singular is marked with the suffix -*nu* in SS clauses (13.24, 13.25).

(13.24)   *ikamỹáw̃áãn haŋkɨnum inuán achɨkhai*
           ikam_yawaã=na   [haŋkɨ=numa   inu-a-**nu**]
           jaguar=ACC   jaw=LOC   put.hand.into-PFV+SEQ-**1SG:SS**
           achi-ka-ha-i
           grab-PFV-1SG-DECL
           'having stuck my hand in its jaws, I have grabbed the jaguar'
           (agr041005_14)

(13.25)   *wíi kashín wíɰaknuk takáschattahai*
           [wi   kashini   wɨ-a-ku-**nu**=ka]   taka-sa-cha-tata-ha-i
           1sg   tomorrow   go-IPFV-SIM-**1SG:SS**=COND   work-PFV-NEG-FUT-1SG-DECL
           'if I go tomorrow, I won't work'

This suffix is apparently etymologically unrelated to other markers of first person singular: *-ha* first person singular subject in finite clauses; *-hu/-tu* first person object; *-hu* first person singular possessor (see discussion in §1.8.2); nor to the first person singular pronoun *wi*.

13.5.1.2 First person plural

First person plural subject is not marked with an overt suffix except in conditional clauses (see below), but apocope is suppressed in the surface form; this suggests that there may have been some segmental marking in the past that blocked the application of apocope, but that has since been lost. In example (13.26) the finite verb is preceded by two SS sequential clauses, and followed by a SS simultaneous clause functioning as a purpose clause.

(13.26)   *ashinká, dúwi botenum chimpimhá hiínhabiahi, iína batsámtain mininaku*
           [ashina-**ka**]   nu=i   [*bote*=numa
           finish-**PFV+SEQ+1PL:SS**   ANA=INS   boat=LOC
           chimpima-**ha**]   hiina-aha-maya-hi   [ii=na
           board:PL-**PFV+SEQ+1PL:SS**   go.out+PFV-PL-DISTPST-1PL+DECL   1pl=ACC
           batsama-taĩ=nĩ   mini-ina-**ku**]
           live:PL-NMLZ+PSSD:1PL/3=LOC   come-PL:IPFV-**SIM+1PL:SS**
           'because we had finished (the class), we boarded the boat and left, to come to our homes' (agr040824_02)

In example (13.27), three SS sequential clauses are subordinate to the final clause, which is marked 'normative' (see §8.4.5).

(13.27)   *tsawáha yuhúmkaush yuwá káshik hiinkí wɨtáyamĩ*
           [tsawa-**ha**]   [yuhumaka-uchi   yu-a]
           dawn-**PFV+SEQ+1PL:SS**   food-DIM   eat-**PFV+SEQ+1PL:SS**
           [kashik   hiina-**ki**]   wɨ-tayamĩ
           early.morning   go.out-**PFV+SEQ+1PL:SS**   go-NORM
           'having woken up, eaten a bit of food and gone out early in the morning, we go (hunting)' (Text 3:6)

When the conditional enclitic *=ka* is present, first person plural in SS clauses is marked with the suffix *-i*, as in example (13.28).

(13.28)   *kashín wɨnakuik ɨik takáschattahi*
       [kashini   wɨ-ina-ku-**i**=ka]   ɨi=ka
       tomorrow   go-PL:IPFV-SIM-**1PL:SS**=COND]   1pl=TOP
       taka-sa-cha-tata-hi
       work-PFV-NEG-FUT-1PL+DECL
       'if we go tomorrow, we won't work'

Assuming that the suppression of apocope mentioned above is triggered by the historical presence of a suffix, it follows that the suffix *-i* is most likely a reflex of the same suffix. No other persons show distinct marking only in conditional clauses. In §13.5.2.4 below, comparative evidence is presented that suggests an earlier form of the first person plural suffix in both conditional and non-conditional subordinate clauses was *-*hi*, the reflex of a Proto-Chicham suffix *-*ri*.

13.5.1.3 Second person

Second person subject is marked on subordinate verbs with the same suffixes as finite verbs: singular *-mɨ* (13.29) and plural *-humɨ* (13.30). The number distinction is not obligatory in subordinate clauses, however, and *-mɨ* can also be used with second person plural subjects (13.31, 13.32); this marking is more common in my corpus of natural data.

(13.29)   *ámɨ maátakamam awɨɨmámumɨ*
       [amɨ   ma-a-takama-**mɨ**]   awɨɨma-ma-umɨ-i
       2SG   kill-PFV-FRUST-**2:SS**   scare.off+PFV-RECPST-2-DECL
       'trying in vain to kill (the snake), you scared it off'

(13.30)   *úntsu tákuŋmɨk yúwakhua*
       untsu   [ta-ku-**humɨ**=ka]   yu-a-khua
       well.then   say+IPFV-SIM-**2PL:SS**=COND   eat-IPFV-IMP.FAM.PL
       'well then, if you say so, just eat it!' (agr040721_07)

(13.31)   *achíakum iyáitahum*
       [achi-a-ku-**mɨ**]   iya-i-ta-humɨ
       grab-IPFV-SIM-**2:SS**   fall-PFV-IMP-2PL
       'grab (the darts) and fall down' (agr040724_01; cf. 13.69)

(13.32)   *yuhúmak áusam, yúwakum dakahumatáhum*
            [yuhumaka   au-sa-**mɨ**]   [yu-a-ku-**mɨ**]
            food   put.in.pot-PFV+SEQ-**2:SS**   eat-IPFV-SIM-**2:SS**
            daka-hu-ma-ta-humɨ
            wait.for-1SG.OBJ-DUR-IMP-2PL
            'having put the food in the pot (to cook), while eating, wait for me'
            (agr041005_14)

Second person appears as *-mɨa* when the controlling clause has content interrogative mood, as in example (13.33). Content interrogative clauses also mark the main
verb with suppression of apocope, which can be seen in the verb *tukúmumɨ* in example (13.33); this is described in detail in Chapter 10.

(13.33)   *yátsuhu wahúk wɨmɨa tukúmumɨ*
            yatsu-hu   wahuka   [wɨ-**mɨa**]
            brother-PSSD:1SG+VOC   how   go+PFV+SEQ-**2:SS**
            tuku-ma-umɨ
            shoot+PFV-RECPST-2SG
            'my brother, how (i.e. where) did you go and shoot (so many mon-
            keys)?' (agr041005_28)

13.5.1.4 Third person
Third person is not marked with a suffix, but the final vowel of the stem is nasalized,
suggesting the historical presence of a suffix with a nasal component (13.34).

(13.34)   *wɨɰa wɨɰakũã hɨ̃ɰ̃áũw̃ãĩ mánchumush puhámunum*
            [wɨɰa   wɨ-a-**kawã**]   hɨ̃ɰa-u=ai
            REDUP   go-IPFV-**REPET+3:SS**   arrive+PFV-NMLZ=COP:3:DECL
            manchumuchi   puha-mau=numa
            Manchumuch   live+IPFV-NSBJ.NMLZ=LOC
            'going and going she arrived at the place where Manchumuch lives'
            (agr040721_07)

In many examples, such as (13.35), the final vowel is lost to apocope.

(13.35)   *tsampáunumin wɨhák uchín batsakɨu túwahamɨ̃*
            [tsampaunumi=na   wɨ-hu-a-**kũ**]   uchi=na
            manioc.leaf=ACC   go-APPL-IPFV-**SIM+3:SS**   child=ACC

batsa-ki-u   tuwahamɨ̃
leave-PFV-NMLZ   NARR

'going to get manioc leaves, they left the children behind, so the story goes' (agr040721_07)

The underlying nasality of the final vowel is apparent when the conditional marker =ka is added, as in (13.36). The underlying -kũ=ka (SIM+3:SS=COND) forms an NC cluster (§3.4.2) to give an intermediate representation /kuŋka/ which, after apocope, surfaces as [kuŋ] (§3.5.5.1).

(13.36)   nɨ̃ kashín wɨɰakuŋ takáschattawai
           [nɨ̆   kashini   wɨ-a-**kũ**=ka]   taka-sa-cha-tata-wa-i
           3sg   tomorrow   go-IPFV-**SIM+3:SS**=COND   work-PFV-NEG-FUT-3-DECL
           'if heᵢ goes tomorrow, heᵢ won't work'

13.5.1.5 Person marking on nominalized verbs

There are occasional examples of subordinate same-subject person suffixes appearing on forms that are nominalizations by all other criteria (in particular the ability to head or modify NPs), and as such are not expected to take person markers. In example (13.37) the nominalized verb wɨ-u (go+PFV-NMLZ) takes the SS first-person singular suffix -nu, as it is functioning as a subordinate verb, with wakɨthai 'I return' as its controlling verb.

(13.37)   "Belén wɨún wákɨthai" táwai
           [Belén   wɨ-u-nu]   wakɨta-ha-i   ta-wa-i
           Belén   go+PFV-NMLZ-1SG:SS   return+IPFV-1SG-DECL   say+IPFV-3-DECL
           'he says "I'm returning from Belén (village)"'

The suffix -u is primarily a nominalizer: it forms nominalizations that modify NPs, and crucially, the person suffix is not required – cf. example (13.38) where the nominalization has a notional first-person subject, but no person suffix. Subordinate verbs, by contrast, obligatorily mark the person of their subject.

(13.38)   yumín shíkitsuk ukúahai
           [yumi=na   shiki-tsu-**u**=ka]   uku-a-ha-i
           water=ACC   draw-NEG-**NMLZ**=TOP   leave-IPFV-1SG-DECL
           'I'm leaving without getting water' (agr041005_14)

Nominalizations may function as independent verbs, so it is to be expected that they could be readily reanalysed as subordinate verbs too. However, forms in -u are typically NP constituents and are only occasionally marked with person suffixes. Full details of the properties of nominalizations are in Chapter 15.

13.5.2 Different-subject person marking

For the four subordinate verb types that can appear in different-subject clauses (Table 13.7), person and different-subject marking are obligatory, and each of the four types shows a different marking pattern. Some distinctions are neutralized in different-subject clauses:

- In non-temporal DS verbs, person marking is neutralized, and the non-temporal marker of SS verbs *-sa* is replaced by the suffix *-taĩ*. This form is apparently incompatible with second person subjects.
- DS sequential and simultaneous verbs neutralize the distinction between first and third person subjects, while second person is marked with the usual second person suffixes *-mɨ* (singular) and *-humɨ* (plural) followed by the DS er *-(n)ĩ*.
- First and third person + DS in sequential clauses are marked with the suffix *-mataĩ*.
- First and third person + DS in simultaneous clauses are marked with the suffix *-ĩ*, presumably the DS marker *-(n)ĩ*.
- First singular and third person singular and plural + DS in imperfective DS clauses are marked with the suffix *-ĩ*.
- First person plural in imperfective DS clauses is marked with the suffix *-hi* followed by the DS marker *-(n)ĩ*.

Table 13.7 lays out the four person-marking paradigms used in DS clauses.

Table 13.7: Subject markers on subordinate verbs in SS and DS clauses

verb type	verb stem	suffix	2SG	2PL	1SG/3	1PL
non-temporal	unmarked	*-sa* [a]	–	–	*-taĩ* [a]	*-taĩ*
sequential	PFV	*-∅*	*-mɨ-nĩ* [b]	*-humɨ-nĩ* [b]	*-mataĩ*	*-mataĩ*
simultaneous	IPFV	*-ku*	*-mɨ-nĩ*	*-humɨ-nĩ*	*-ĩ*	*-ĩ*
IPFV DS	IPFV	*-∅*	*-mɨ-nĩ*	*-humɨ-nĩ*	*-ĩ*	*-hi-nĩ*

[a] The suffix *-sa* only appears with SS verbs, and is replaced by *-taĩ* on DS verbs.
[b] The DS suffix *-(n)ĩ* triggers the combining forms of the second person suffixes, so the combination surfaces as *-minĩ* (sg) and *-huminĩ* (pl).

There is asymmetrical neutralization of categories between first/third person and second person: first and third persons neutralize both person and number distinctions in DS clauses (the only exception is imperfective DS clauses, which distinguish first plural from the rest). Second person is marked distinctly and also maintains the number distinction found in finite verbs, although this distinction is probably not obligatory.[3]

Switch-reference is the phenomenon whereby a clause contains morphological indication of grammatical relations that hold in another clause. Aguaruna subordinate verbs are obligatorily marked for switch-reference, and for those in Table 13.7 this is canonical switch-reference as defined by Haiman & Munro (1983):

> Canonical switch-reference is an inflectional category of the verb, which indicates whether or not its subject is identical with the subject of some other verb.
>
> (Haiman & Munro 1983: ix)

Different subject is marked with the suffix *-(n)ĩ* (the long form appears when it is preceded by /i/ or /ɨ/, the short form elsewhere). Although not always morphologically decomposable, all DS markers end with /ĩ/, suggesting that the DS suffix is at least historically involved in their composition.

Different subject marking is triggered by a subject in the subordinate clause that is not included in that of the controlling clause. A first plural controlling clause triggers DS marking in a first singular subordinate clause (example 13.39), but a first singular controlling clause triggers SS marking in a first plural subordinate clause (example 13.40); because the subject of the controlling clause (1SG) is included in that of the subordinate clause (1PL).

(13.39)   *wíi ikiŋmáŋmatãĩ takasmí*
          [wi   ikiŋma-ha-mataĩ]   taka-sa-mi
          1sg   wash.hands-PFV+SEQ-1/3:DS work-PFV-HORT
          'after I've washed my hands, let's work'

(13.40)   *yuhúmak yuwá kánin áyahai*
          [yuhumaka   yu-a]   kanu-inu   a-ya-ha-i
          manioc   eat-PFV+SEQ+1PL:SS sleep-NMLZ   COP-REMPST-1SG-DECL
          '(we) having eaten manioc, I would sleep' (agr040824_02)

---

3 I have no examples of second person plural subjects marked with the "singular" form in DS clauses, while I do for SS clauses. This is probably a product of the data, however, since all my examples of 2PL DS are elicited, and plural marking shows up more consistently in the elicited SS forms too.

Table 13.8 shows the combinations of first singular and first plural subjects and whether they trigger SS or DS marking in the subordinate clause.

Table 13.8: SS/DS marking with combinations of first person singular and plural

subordinate clause subject	controlling clause subject	
	1SG	1PL
1SG	SS	DS
1PL	SS	SS

There are also two non-canonical switch-reference markers, *-tatamana* and *-ma*. There is no possible reflex of DS *-(n)ĩ* involved in these forms, and while the canonical switch-reference markers indicate only that the subject of the marked clause is coreferent or not with the subject of the controlling clause, *-tatamana* and *-ma* go beyond the subject pivot to encode coreference of subject and non-subject roles: *-tatamana* indicates that the subject of the marked clause is an object of the controlling clause, while *-ma* indicates that a non-subject argument of the marked clause is subject of the controlling clause. The SR relations of Aguaruna are summarized in Table 13.9.

Table 13.9: Grammatical role pivots in switch-reference markers

marker	marked clause		controlling clause
SS *-∅*	subject	=	subject
DS *-(n)ĩ /-taĩ / -mataĩ*	subject	≠	subject
-tatamana	subject	=	object
-ma	non-subject	=	subject

The crucial difference between canonical and non-canonical SR is that canonical 'different subject' gives no information on whether or not there is a common argument in the two clauses. The non-canonical markers indicate that the subject is different, but go beyond canonical DS in requiring that a common argument be a participant in both clauses. Such a requirement is outside the range of canonical switch-reference as defined by Haiman & Munro (1983), and is apparently very rare: the only reliably attested examples come from the Panoan family (Loos 1999: 237; Valenzuela 2003; Fleck 2003; Zariquiey 2011) and from the Takanan language Ese Ejja (Vuillermet 2014). The two non-canonical SR markers show some morphological properties that suggest a nominal origin, and this can also explain their non-canonical switch-reference properties (§13.6).

13.5.2.1 Non-temporal clauses

Non-temporal DS verbs are marked with the suffix *-taĩ* in first and third persons (examples 13.41 and 13.42, respectively). I have no examples with second person subject, and therefore cannot comment on the grammaticality of such a form.

(13.41)   *"hĩɰahũĩ wĩɰahai" tútãĩ "ĩtsã akɨawai hũw̃ĩ kanáham kashín wɨtá"*
         túhutkũĩ ...

[hĩɰa-hu=ĩ	wɨ-a-ha-i	tu-**taĩ**]
house-PSSD:1SG=LOC	go-IPFV-1SG-DECL	say-**SBD:1/3:DS**

[ĩtsã	akɨ-a-wa-i	hu=ĩ	kana-ha-mɨ
sun	set-IPFV-3-DECL	PROX=LOC	sleep-PFV+SEQ-2:SS

kashini	wɨ-ta	tu-hu-ta-ku-ĩ]
tomorrow	go+PFV-IMP	say-APPL-1SG.OBJ+IPFV-SIM+1/3-DS

     'when I said "I'm going home" she said to me "the sun is setting, sleep here and go tomorrow"'... (Text 2:20-21)

(13.42)   *uchín tsɨɰáŋmitkatãĩ tupikáu*

[uchi=na	tsɨɰahu-mitika-**taĩ**]	tupika-a-u
child=ACC	cry:PL-CAUS-**SBD:1/3:DS**	run-IPFV-NMLZ

     'when (the devil) made the children cry, (their father) came running' (agr040723_29)

Although the suffix *-taĩ* is semantically equivalent to the non-temporal subordinator *-sa*, they do not appear to be cognate. The suffix *-taĩ* is not morphologically decomposable, but the final /ĩ/ is presumably a reflex of the DS marker *-(n)ĩ*.

13.5.2.2 Sequential clauses

There is no explicit verbal marker of SS sequential clauses; the perfective stem is directly suffixed with person markers. In DS clauses, the second person forms take a person marker in slot F followed by the DS suffix *-(n)ĩ* in slot G. First person and third person are identically marked with the suffix *-matãĩ*; plural marking with the level I suffix *-aha* is optional. Table 13.10 shows a paradigm with the verb *antut* 'hear'.

Table 13.10: Different-subject sequential clause paradigm with *antut* 'hear'

person	singular	plural
1	*antúkmatáī*	*antúkaŋmatáī*
	antu-ka-mataī	antu-ka-aha-mataī
	hear-PFV+SEQ-1/3:DS	hear-PFV+SEQ-PL-1/3:DS
2	*antúkamin*	*antúkaŋmin*
	antu-ka-mɨ-nī	antu-ka-humɨ-nī
	hear-PFV+SEQ-2-DS	hear-PFV+SEQ-2PL-DS
3	*antúkmatáī*	*antúkaŋmatáī*
	antu-ka-mataī	antu-ka-aha-mataī
	hear-PFV+SEQ-1/3:DS	hear-PFV+SEQ-PL-1/3:DS

The suffix -*mataī* is clearly in a paradigmatic relationship with the SS forms exemplified in Table 13.6 above, and is a portmanteau marking both first/third person and DS. Given the formal similarity between -*mataī* and -*taī* it is tempting to seek an etymological relationship, but there is no evidence to support this; the historical origins of both suffixes are obscure. As with -*taī*, however, it is reasonable to consider the final /ī/ to be a reflex of the different subject marker -*(n)ī*. Although it is possible that the suffix -*mataī* contains some element that indexes the meaning 'sequential', the fact that sequential verbs are zero-marked in SS verbs and second person DS verbs strongly suggests that this is not the case.

13.5.2.3 Simultaneous clauses

In DS simultaneous clauses with second person subject, the DS suffix is simply added to the same subject form of the verb, in slot G. First and third persons are marked identically, as in sequential clauses, but in simultaneous clauses they are marked only with the DS suffix -*(n)ī*. As with the DS forms, level I plural marking is available, but not obligatory, marked with the plural imperfective suffix -*ina*. The paradigm is shown in Table 13.11.

Table 13.11: Different-subject simultaneous clause paradigm with *antut* 'hear'[4]

person	singular	plural
1	*ántakūī* anta-ku-ī hear+IPFV-SIM+1/3-DS	*ántuinakūī* antu-ina-ku-ī hear-PL:IPFV-SIM+1/3-DS
2	*ántakmin* anta-ku-mɨ-nī hear+IPFV-SIM-2-DS	*ántakhumin* anta-ku-humɨ-nī hear+IPFV-SIM-2PL-DS
3	*ántakūī* anta-ku-ī hear+IPFV-SIM+1/3-DS	*ántuinakūī* antu-ina-ku-ī hear-PL:IPFV-SIM+1/3-DS

13.5.2.4 Imperfective DS clauses

The imperfective stem forms DS subordinate clauses with person and DS marking in slots F and G. This form has no overt subordinating suffix in slot E, and has no SS counterpart. Table 13.12 gives the full paradigm for imperfective DS verb marking.

Table 13.12: Different-subject forms with imperfective stem of *puhut* 'live'

person	singular	plural
1	*puhǎī* puha-ī live+IPFV+1SG/3-DS	*puháhin* puha-hi-nī live+IPFV-1PL-DS
2	*puhámin* puha-mɨ-nī live+IPFV-2-DS	*puháŋmin* puha-humɨ-nī live+IPFV-2PL-DS
3	*puhǎī* puha-ī live+IPFV+1SG/3-DS	*puhuínāī* puhu-ina-ī live-PL:IPFV+3-DS

Imperfective DS clauses are typically ambiguous between a locative and a temporal reading, as in example (13.43).

---

4 The forms in Table 13.10 and Table 13.11 are cognates of those given for Shuar in Adelaar & Muysken (2004: 446, citing data from Juank 1982: 76).

(13.43)   *umís tɨpáĩ uchihín takáak hɨ̃ɨ̃ãmtãĩ...*
          [umi-sã   tɨpa-ĩ́]   uchi-hĩ=na
          prepare-SBD+3:SS   lie+IPFV+1SG/3-**DS**   child-PSSD:1PL/3=ACC
          taka-a-kũ   hɨ̃ɰa-mataĩ́]
          carry-IPFV-SIM+3:SS   arrive+PFV+SEQ-1/3:DS
          'when she arrived, carrying her child, at the place where he was throw-
          ing himself into preparations...'
          OR
          'as he was throwing himself into preparations, she arrived carrying her
          child' (agr041005_16)

Example (13.44) is from the story of the hero Kagkáp, and here he is preparing to
fight with a jaguar. He pulls down some vines which he uses to tie his kilt up, so that
it won't obstruct his movements, then he waits for the jaguar which suddenly arrives (*tsɨkɨn* is the ideophone used to indicate sudden arrival). Again, the verb with
the different subject suffix could be translated as locative or temporal. The locative
flavour of this construction distinguishes it from the simultaneous DS form marked
with *-ku*, and this inherent ambiguity may have originally enabled locative to be
grammaticalized into a DS marker (see below).

(13.44)   *núnik kaŋkápshakam daɨka atsuhũã́, kamisán apihík itiphũã́ wahãĩ,*
          íkamỹãw̃ãã tsɨkɨn wahakú
          [nu-ni-kã   kaŋkapɨ=shakama   [daɨka
          ANA-VBLZ.INTR-PFV+SEQ+3:SS   *Kagkap*=ADD   vine+ACC
          atsuhu-ã́]   [kamisa=na   apihi-kã́]
          pull.down-PFV+SEQ+3:SS   clothing=ACC   fold-PFV+SEQ+3:SS
          [itipa-hu-ã́]   waha-a-ĩ́]
          put.on.kilt-APPL-PFV+SEQ+3:SS   stand-IPFV+1SG/3-**DS**
          ikam_yawãã   tsɨkɨn   waha-ka-u
          jaguar   IDEO   stop-PFV-NMLZ
          'having done that, Kagkáp pulled down some vines, folded up his kilt
          and put it on, and was standing there when the jaguar suddenly ar-
          rived' (agr041005_14)

The locational reading is clear in (13.45), in which a locative-marked demonstrative
also appears, explicitly referring to the location of the action.

(13.45)   *hũw̃ɨ̃ puhãĩ́ taáta*
          [hu=ĩ̃   puha-ĩ́]   ta-a-ta
          PROX=LOC   live+IPFV+1SG/3-**DS**   come-PFV-IMP
          'come here, where I am'

In (13.46) the verb is relativized with a postposed pronoun (§16.3), which itself takes the locative suffix. It would be stretching the point to translate this example as a switch-reference construction, but it shows clear semantic and grammatical similarities with (13.45) above.

(13.46)   *áu púha nǔw̃ǐ wíųahai*
            [au   puha   nu=ǐ]   wɨ-a-ha-i
            3sg   live+IPFV+3   ANAREL=**LOC**]   go-IPFV-1SG-DECL
            'I'm going to (the place) where he is'

Rather surprisingly, first person plural in imperfective DS clauses takes the suffix *-hi* (13.47), formally identical to the suffix used with finite verbs (§8.7.2).

(13.47)   *hutíi áidauti wíųahiniŋ amɨ wáki bɨsɨmaŋ huwáktatmɨ*
            [hutii   a-ina-u=ti   wɨ-a-**hi**-nǐ=ka]   amɨ
            1pl   COP-PL:IPFV-NMLZ=SAP   go-IPFV-**1PL**-DS=COND   2sg
            wakɨ_bɨsɨmaŋ   huwa-ka-tata-mɨ-i
            sad   stay-PFV-FUT-2-DECL
            'if we go, you_SG will stay here (being) sad'

There is comparative evidence that this suffix has a different source from the finite verb first person plural marker *-hi*. In Shuar (Turner 1992: 78ff) and Achuar-Shiwiar (Fast et al. 1996: 55ff) the first plural suffix in subordinate clauses is *-ri*, which suggests that the Proto-Chicham first plural suffix on subordinate verbs was *-ri*. The expected cognate form in Aguaruna is *-hi*, but this has apparently been lost except on imperfective stems and preceding the conditional suffix (reduced to *-i* in the latter environment). The only other reflex of the Proto-Chicham suffix is in the suppression of apocope on SS verbs (§13.5.1). First person plural in finite verbs, meanwhile, is marked in Shuar and Achuar-Shiwiar with a suffix *-hi*, as in Aguaruna, suggesting a distinct Proto-Chicham suffix *-hi* for this function. The distinction between finite *-hi* and subordinate *-ri* would have been neutralized in pre-Aguaruna with the merger of Proto-Chicham */r/ and */h/ (see §3.2.4), but it is clear from the evidence just presented that in example (13.47) the suffix marking first person plural is etymologically distinct from the one which marks first person plural in finite verbs, and the homophony is due to historical accident.

13.5.2.5 Different subject *-(n)ǐ*
The different subject suffix *-(n)ǐ* (*-nǐ* following /i/ or /ɨ/; *-ǐ* elsewhere) indicates that the subject of the subordinate verb is different from that of its controlling verb (13.48, 13.49). The DS suffix triggers the combining form of the second person suf-

fixes, changing the final vowel from /ɨ/ to /i/ (example 13.49, and see §3.6.2 for details).

(13.48) *núna múun áuŋmatuinakũĩ, "wáinkas táwa" túyahai*
[nu=na   muunta   auhumatu-ina-ku-ĩ]   <u>wainakasã</u>
ANA=ACC   elder   tell-PL:IPFV-SIM+1/3-DS   in.vain+3
<u>ta-wa</u>   tu-ya-ha-i
say+IPFV-3:EXCL   say-REMPST-1SG-DECL
'as the elders told that (story), I would say "they're talking rubbish!"'
(agr040723_29)

(13.49) *ámɨ wɨmin wɨi huwákmahai*
[ami   wɨ-mɨ-**nĩ**]   wi   huwa-ka-ma-ha-i
2sg   go+PFV+SEQ-2-**DS**   1sg   stay-PFV-RECPST-1SG-DECL
'when you left, I stayed behind'

As in other parts of the grammar, four combinations of person and number are distinguished for the purposes of switch-reference: first singular, first plural, second and third. First person and third person are marked identically in different subject subordinate clauses (with the exception of first plural on imperfective stems), in contrast to the SAP versus non-SAP distinction that is commonly encountered in the grammar. The different-subject suffix appears with the simultaneous suffix -*ku* and perfective and imperfective stems.

13.5.2.6 Historical considerations

The formal similarity suggests that the different subject suffix has arisen from an earlier use of the locative enclitic =*(n)ĩ* (described in §4.10.5). Historically, it is not unlikely that switch-reference forms with different-subject -*(n)ĩ* could have arisen from causal relations marked with locative =*(n)ĩ*; cf. Heine & Kuteva (2002: 200), who say that "this appears to be an extremely widespread process whereby locative markers are grammaticalized to markers of cause." Aguaruna typically does not distinguish temporal from causal relations in clause-combining constructions (see Chapter 14). The intermediate stage is illustrated by the imperfective DS clause (described above, §13.5.2.4), which typically implies a locational sense. Table 13.13 summarizes the relationships that may be marked by -*(n)ĩ* when combined with different stems. The table also illustrates the proposed grammaticalization path from the LOCATIVE enclitic =*(n)ĩ* to DIFFERENT SUBJECT -*(n)ĩ* on verbs, via the imperfective form with its combined locational and different-subject semantics. Overall (2016a) elaborates on this discussion.

Table 13.13: Relations marked by -*(n)ī̃*

	nominal	imperfective	subordinate
location	✓	✓	–
different subject	–	✓	✓

13.6 Non-canonical switch-reference markers

The two non-canonical switch-reference markers are distinct from those discussed above, as they do not have any distinct marking for person or different-subject. In common with other subordinate verbs, these forms do indicate switch-reference relations between the marked clause and its matrix clause, as illustrated in Table 13.14. The switch-reference is not of the canonical SS/DS type, as the coreference goes beyond the subject pivot.

Table 13.14: Switch-reference in non-inflecting subordinators

marker	stem	role of common argument in:	
		marked clause	controlling clause
-*tatamana*	unmarked	subject	object
-*ma*	aspectualized	non-subject	subject

The requirement for a common argument is shared by canonical SS marking, but not by DS marking. Consider, for example, the coreference configurations in Table 13.15, illustrated in the examples that follow: all are marked with the canonical DS construction. In (13.50), there is no common argument at all. In (13.51) the subject of the marked clause is coreferent with the object of the controlling clause. In (13.52) the object of the marked clause is coreferent with the subject of the controlling clause, and in (13.53) the objects of the two clauses are coreferential.

Table 13.15: Common arguments in canonical DS linkages

example	role of common argument in:	
	marked clause	controlling clause
(13.50)	no common argument	
(13.51)	subject	object
(13.52)	object	subject
(13.53)	object	object

(13.50)   *Miguel maámi, aínts hakámtaiŋ*
        Miguel   ma-a-mi   [aintsu   ha-ka-mataĩ=ka]
        Miguel   kill-PFV-HORT   person   die-PFV+SEQ-1/3:DS=COND
        'Let's kill Miguel if the person (that Miguel beat up) dies'
        (agr060816_01)

(13.51)   *nĩshkam dɨkátatus wakɨɰau asámtãĩ, nína uháhai yamái*
        [nĩ=shakama   dika-tatus   wakɨɰa-u
        3sg=ADD   know+PFV-INTENT+3:SS   want+IPFV-NMLZ
        asa-mataĩ]   nĩ=na   uha-ha-i   yamai
        COP+SBD-1/3:DS   3sg=ACC   tell+IPFV-1SG-DECL   now
        'and because he wants to know, I am telling him now' (Text 3:3)

(13.52)   *dútihuamtãĩ, ashí hakábiahai*
        [nu-tika-hu-a-mataĩ]   ashi   ha-ka-maya-ha-i
        ANA-VBLZ.TR-1SG.OBJ-PFV+SEQ-1/3:DS   all   die-PFV-INTPST-1SG-DECL
        'when that happened to me, I almost died' (agr040824_02)

(13.53)   *ỹãw̃áã ɨkɨnmatãĩ maáhai*
        [yawaã   ɨkɨna-mataĩ]   ma-a-ha-i
        dog   flush.out+PFV+SEQ-1/3:DS   kill-PFV-1SG-DECL
        'when the dog flushed (the agouti) out, I killed it' (agr041005_15)

These examples show that canonical SR is indifferent to interclausal coreference other than 'subject = subject', while non-canonical SR makes more specific coreference distinctions within the DS category. There is some overlap: note, for example, that the configurations of (13.51) and (13.52) could be marked with non-canonical SR markers *-tatamana* 'subject = object' and *-ma* 'non-subject = subject', respectively – it is not yet clear what other factors influence which construction is chosen.

The two non-canonical SR markers are described in the following sections. There is some evidence that both *-tatamana* and *-ma* have developed through re-analysis of nominalizations, and this is discussed in §13.6.3.

13.6.1 'Subject = object' subordinator *-tatamana*

The subordinator *-tatamana* appears suffixed to the unmarked stem, and no attested example contains any derivational morphology in the stem. The action of the clause marked with *-tatamana* is simultaneous with that of the controlling clause, and the subject of the marked clause is coreferential with an object of the controlling clause. The controlling clause is always transitive.

Example (13.54) is from a story in which an *ĩwanch* (devil) detaches his penis and holding it in his hand, reaches through a gap in the wall and has sex with a sleeping woman.

(13.54)   *katín nũw̃ĩ ĭkĭnák, nuwán nihíttaman achikắ hápikĩ...*
[katĩ=na   nu=ĩ   ikĭna-a-kũ]   [nuwa=na
penis+PSSD:1PL/3=ACC   ANA=LOC   hold-IPFV-SIM+3:SS   woman=ACC
nihi-**tatamana**]   achi-kã   hapi-kĭ
have.sex.with-**SBJ>OBJ**   grab-PFV+SEQ+3:SS   tug-PFV+SEQ+3:SS
'as (the devil) was holding his penis there (in his hand) and having sex with the woman, (the man) grabbed him and tugged him (towards the wall)...' (agr040723_29)

Any type of object may take part in the coreference, including the gift-like (O) or recipient-like (E) object in a ditransitive clause, and objects added by valency-increasing derivation (see Chapter 7 for a detailed description of objects and their grammatical properties). In (13.55) the subordinate clause marked with *-tatamana* is centre-embedded in a ditransitive controlling clause, preceded by the recipient-like object (E) of the controlling clause, which is coreferent with the subject of the marked clause.

(13.55)   *núna nuwĭn, nuní wĭkáĭtatman, dútikắ suwímkan susáya túwahamĭ*
[nu=na   nuwĩ=na]ᴇ   [nuni   wĭkaĭɰa-tatamana]
ANA=ACC   woman+PSSD:1PL/3=ACC   thus   walk-SBJ>OBJ
nu-tikã   [suwimaka=na]ₒ   su-sa-ya
ANA-VBLZ.TR+PFV+SEQ+3:SS   punishment=ACC   give-PFV-REMPST:3

tuwahamɨ̃

NARR

'so he punished that wife of his when she wandered (i.e. misbehaved) so' (agr041005_15)

In example (13.56), the common argument has the role of an object added by the applicative derivation (E_{APPL}) in the controlling clause.

(13.56)   úchi akáikɨ̃ yúmiŋmat hɨ̃ɯ̃ɑ̃́tatus wɨ́tatman íkamỹãw̃ãã tɨpɨŋkáuwai
           [uchi   akai-kɨ̃]   [yumiŋmat   hɨ̃ɯa-tatus]
           child   go.down-PFV+SEQ+3:SS   well   arrive-INTENT+3:SS
           [wɨ-**tatamana**]   ikam_yawaã   tɨpɨ-hu-ka-u=ai
           go-**SBJ>OBJ**   jaguar   lie.down-APPL-PFV-NMLZ=COP:3:DECL
           'as the youth, having gone down the hill, was going to the well, the jaguar pounced on him' (agr041005_14)

Use of -*tatamana* links the action of the marked verb with that of the controlling verb through the common argument, and thus contrasts with the use of subordinate verbs marked with the 'different subject' suffix, which instead highlight the juxtaposition of two distinct actions performed by different subjects.

13.6.2 'Non-subject = subject' subordinator -*ma*

The subordinating suffix -*ma* may appear with the perfective or imperfective stem. A non-subject participant of the clause marked with -*ma* is coreferential with the subject of the controlling clause. The non-subject grammatical relation is described in §7.2. Verbs marked with -*ma* typically appear in transitive clauses, with the common argument as an object. Example (13.57) comes from a story in which the devil is captured, tied up and left in the place where people go to urinate. The verb *shikit* 'urinate on O' is transitive.

(13.57)   áishmaŋ shíkiam úmaya túwahamɨ̃
           [aishmaŋku   shiki-a-ma]   uma-ya
           man   urinate.on-IPFV-NSBJ>SBJ   drink+IPFV-REMPST
           tuwahamɨ̃
           NARR
           'when the men urinated on him, he drank it, they say' (agr040723_29)

In example (13.58) -*ma* forms a bridging clause (see §14.8). The common argument is the youth, the object of the subordinate verb *ta-ma* (say+IPFV-NSBJ>SBJ). As noted in §6.4.1, the verb *tuta* 'say' may take the addressee as an object.

(13.58)   ...*túinau, táma núu úchi chicháak...*

[...]	tu-ina-u	[ta-**ma**]BRIDGE	nu	uchi
...	say-PL:IPFV-NMLZ	say+IPFV-**NSBJ>SBJ**	ANA	youth

chicha-a-kũ
speak-IPFV-SIM+3:SS
'they said "...", when they said that to him, the youth spoke...'
(agr041005_14)

Overt objects of -*ma* clauses are not marked with accusative case, as they would be in the corresponding finite clause (similarly, non-subject nominalizations do not mark overt object NPs). In (13.59) the overt O object of the -*ma* clause is in nominative case. It is coreferent with the subject of the controlling clause, where it is restated, marked with the topic enclitic =*ka*.

(13.59)   *úchi ichinkám, dúka úchik tsɨkɨa tsɨkɨakũã hákã tɨpɨsú túwahamɨ̃*

[uchi	ichina-ka-**ma**]	nu=ka	uchi=ka	tsɨkɨa
child	pull.apart-PFV-**NSBJ>SBJ**	ANA=TOP	child=TOP	REDUP

tsɨkɨ-a-kawã	ha-kã	tɨpɨ-sa-u
jump-IPFV-REPET+3:SS	die-PFV+SEQ+3:SS	lie.down-PFV-NMLZ

tuwahamɨ̃
NARR
'when (the devil) pulled the child apart, that child jumping and jumping (i.e. having a fit) lay down dead, they say' (agr040723_29)

In example (13.60) the O object of the subordinate clause *ũhuts* 'fruit sp.' is in nominative case. Note that the common argument in this example is 'the men', and is not overtly mentioned but understood from context. The common argument is the recipient (E) object of the subordinate clause and subject of the controlling clause.

(13.60)   *ũhus súwam yúwau*

[ũhutsa	su-a-**ma**]	yu-a-u
fruit.sp	give-IPFV-**NSBJ>SBJ**	eat-IPFV-NMLZ

'as (the birds) gave (the men$_i$) fruit, they$_i$ ate it.' (agr040720_04)

Example (13.61) illustrates the use of -*ma* with an intransitive verb, *hɨ̃ɥat* 'arrive'. In the first clause the agouti is marked with locative case, and it is this locative marked argument that is coreferent with the subject of the following controlling clause.

(13.61) *kãỹṹkãĩ hĩ̃ɨ̃ɑ́ũw̃ãĩ, dútikã hĩ̃ɨ̃ɑ́m, kã́ỹũkak mamának útua utuamã́...*
         kãyuka=ĩ   hɨɨɑ-u=ai
         agouti=LOC   arrive+PFV-NMLZ=COP:3:DECL   [nu-tikã
         ANA-VBLZ.TR+PFV+SEQ+3:SS
         hɨɨɑ-**ma**]BRIDGE   kãyuka=ka   mama=na=ka
         arrive+PFV-**NSBJ>SBJ**   agouti=TOP   manioc=ACC=TOP
         utua   utuamã
         REDUP   pile.up+PFV+SEQ+3:SS
         'she arrived at the agouti's house; having done that, when she arrived,
         the agouti had piled up manioc ...' (agr040721_07)

Although possible, the use of *-ma* with intransitive verbs is very rare, and perhaps compatible only with verbs of motion, with the goal as common argument (as in 13.61). This contrasts with non-subject nominalization, which freely applies to intransitive verbs and is not limited to verbs of motion (see Chapter 15).

13.6.3 Non-canonical SR and nominalization

The requirement for a common argument in the linked clauses is a behaviour that the non-inflecting subordinators share with relative clauses formed with nominalizations. Overall (2016a) elaborates on this idea, suggesting that *-tatamana* consists etymologically of a subject nominalizer *-tatama* with the common argument as its referent, combined with the accusative case enclitic *=na* reflecting its object role in the controlling clause; meanwhile *-ma* would have its source in a non-subject nominalizer, in unmarked nominative case encoding its referent's subject role in the controlling clause. A historical origin in nominalization would thus explain the non-canonical SR properties of these two markers; it would also explain the absence of verbal person marking. Further evidence in favour of a nominal origin comes from the unmarked objects in *-ma* clauses (example 13.60 above), just as in non-subject nominalizations (and note a possible etymological connection between *-ma* and non-subject nominalizer *-mau*). A further nominal property of *-ma* is shown in examples (13.62) and (13.63), in which the clause marked with *-ma* appears to function as a copula complement. These are the only two such examples I have found, so this is clearly not a core function of *-ma*.

(13.62) *nuní dúwik múun pã́ŋkĩ yúwam asáuwai*
         nuni   [duwik_muunta]   [paŋkĩ   yu-a-**ma**]
         thus   ancestor   boa   eat-IPFV-**NSBJ>SBJ**
         a-sa-u=ai
         COP-PFV-NMLZ=COP:3:DECL
         'thus the ancestor was eaten by a boa' (Text 1:39)

(13.63)   *wíka ỹãw̃áãchuithai, ihuntáŋ suwimám átinun*

          wi=ka   yawaã-chau=ita-ha-i   [ihũ-tu-hã

          1sg=TOP   dog-NEG.NMLZ=COP-1SG-DECL   gang.up-APPL-PFV+SEQ+3:SS

          suwima-**ma**   a-tinu-nu]

          beat+PFV-**NSBJ>SBJ**   COP-FUT+NMLZ-1SG:SS

          'I am not a dog, to be beaten by gangs of people' (agr060816_01)

13.7 Syntactic status of subordinate clauses

My use thus far of the term "subordinate" has begged the question regarding the syntactic status of these clauses. While definitions of subordination necessarily rest on some structural criteria, these criteria differ among authors, typically involving some combination of dependency and embeddedness (Cristofaro 2003, Jendraschek 2009). Because of this, and the frequent mismatches between formal and functional criteria, Cristofaro (2003) takes non-assertion to be criterial. In Aguaruna, any given subordinate clause may show more or fewer of the properties traditionally associated with subordination, much like converbal clauses (Genetti 2005, Jendraschek 2009, Haspelmath 1995), and examination of such properties does not seem to be a useful criterion for making generalizations. For the purposes of this description, then, I take a structural approach to subordination: I am concerned only with those clauses that are obligatorily marked for switch-reference relations. It is not yet clear whether all of the clauses thus distinguished on structural grounds share the same pragmatic profile.

In this section I present the morphosyntactic evidence showing that Aguaruna subordinate clauses are treated as adverbial constituents of a matrix clause. An alternative analysis of clause-chaining languages holds that the non-final clauses are *cosubordinate* (Foley & van Valin 1984; van Valin & LaPolla 1997), characterized as being neither coordinate nor subordinate, but with properties of both. Cosubordinated (medial) clauses in a chain are morphologically dependent, in that they cannot form a grammatical sentence without an associated main clause; but they have the pragmatic profile of a main clause, as they are asserted and typically advance the narrative line. They are thus distinct from adverbial clauses, which are semantically modifying. The Aguaruna clauses under discussion may form part of the narrative line, but they may equally well modify a matrix clause, including expressing conditional and concessive relations (see examples in §14.6). Formally, Aguaruna subordinate clauses may be marked with floating enclitics, and they show the same flexibility of positioning as other constituents of the controlling clause. There is thus no motivation to treat the Aguaruna subordinate clauses as of a type with the cosubordinate clauses described in the literature.

Cross-linguistically, chained clauses are typically marked for switch-reference following one of two principles: (i) each clause is marked relative to the immediately following clause (the linear model); or (ii) all clauses are marked relative to the final clause (the focal model). Stirling (1993: 22, based on Oswalt 1983: 277) gives schematic representations of the two structures, shown in Figure 13.5. V_0 is the controlling verb, marked for the full range of verbal grammatical categories, and V_1 to V_n are the dependent verbs.

Linear: $V_n \ldots \longrightarrow V_2 \longrightarrow V_1 \longrightarrow V_0$

Focal: V_0 (Focus)

$V_n \ldots$, V_2, V_1

Figure 13.5: Linear and focal models of clause chaining

The clause chaining structures in Aguaruna do not straightforwardly map to either of the models in Figure 13.5. Although the switch-reference relations follow a basically linear pattern, Aguaruna clause chains share with the focal model a hierarchical structure that allows considerable flexibility in positioning: subordinate clauses may follow or be centre-embedded within their controlling clause. This is a property of chained clauses in general, that was already noted by Longacre (1972):

> [W]e may find that certain putative chains in chaining languages are not simple linear strings but are recursive nestings of sentence structure within sentence structure.

> Longacre (1972: 3)

Unexpected or non-linear SR marking (discussed in the literature under the label "clause-skipping") also suggests that subordinate clauses may be nested, with the controlling clause itself subordinated to another clause.

In the following sections I consider the properties of Aguaruna subordinate clauses as they relate to the points just described, firstly considering linear ordering of clause chains (§13.7.1); next the interaction of floating enclitics with subordinate clauses (§13.7.2); and finally the question of operator scope (§13.7.3).

13.7.1 Linear ordering in clause chains

Marking of SR relations between clauses in Aguaruna clause chains is basically linear, but some flexibility in positioning and the possibility of clause-skipping can disrupt the linear structure. Example (13.64) shows a clause chain that is straight-forwardly compatible with the linear model in Figure 13.5.

(13.64)   *tuhintúk, pɨmpɨɨnak, uchín tsɨɰáŋmitkatãĩ tupikáu*

     a.   [tuhintu-kã]
          be.unable-PFV+SEQ+3:SS

     b.   [pɨmpɨɨna-a-kũ]
          turn.around-IPFV-SIM+3:SS

     c.   [uchi=na   tsɨɰaha-mitika-taĩ]
          child=ACC   cry:PL-CAUS-SBD:1/3:DS

     d.   tupika-u
          run+IPFV-NMLZ

         'a.(the devil) was unable (to pull the child's arm off), b.turning around, c.when he made the children cry, d.(their father) came running' (agr040723_29)

The first three clauses (a, b, c) have the same subject (the devil), and the final clause (d) has a different subject (the father). Consequently, clauses (a) and (b) are marked SS and clause (c) is marked DS. The linear SR relations are represented schematically in Figure 13.6 (note that in this example the nominalized final verb functions as a finite verb, as described in §15.5.3).

	SS		SS		DS	
	[a]	→	[b]	→	[c]	→ [d]FINAL
Subject:	the devil		the devil		the devil	the children's father

Figure 13.6: Interclausal SR relations in example (13.64)

Such straightforward mapping to a linear structure is not always apparent, however. Consider example (13.65), in which four subordinate clauses are followed by a finite clause, and its schematic representation in Figure 13.7.

(13.65)   *núna húkĩ, wɨɰa wɨɰakũã "húu w̃ɨ̃ũw̃ɨ̃" tútãĩ, ɨmakmã̃ hɨɰántui ahánum*

     a.   [nu=na   hu-kĩ]
          ANA=ACC   take-PFV+SEQ+3:SS

     b.   [wɨɰa   wɨ-a-kawã]
          REDUP   go-IPFV-REPET+3:SS

     c.   [hu   wɨ-u=ɨ̃   tu-taĩ]
          PROX   go+PFV-NMLZ=NONVIS.COP:3   say-SBD:1/3:DS

     d.   [ɨma-kamã]
          take-TERM+3:SS

e. hĭʉa-tu-u=i   aha=numa
   arrive-APPL+PFV-NMLZ=COP:3:DECL   garden=LOC
   "[a.](the woman) having taken that (child), [b.]going and going, [c.]as the
   child said "she went here", [d.]on taking (the child) [e.]she arrived in a garden." (agr040721_07)

The SR marking is appropriate for clauses (a), (c), and (d) with respect to the identity or not of their subjects with that of the immediately following clause. Clause (b),
however, is marked SS despite the fact that its subject is different from that of the
following clause – the mismatch is marked in bold in Figure 13.7. If clause (c) were
absent, this clause chain would fit the linear model – the DS marked clause is
"skipped" for the purposes of SR marking (Reesink 1983).

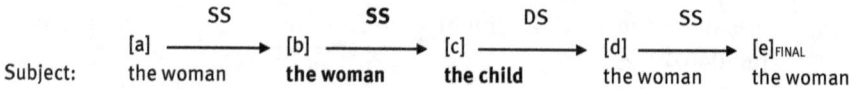

Figure 13.7: Interclausal SR relations in example (13.65)

In fact, it is not clear that the skipped DS clause should be analysed as having a
single controlling clause; instead, one could treat it as being adjoined to the rest of
the chain as a whole, comparable to the English subordinate clause in (13.66),
which modifies all three coordinate finite clauses (Matthiessen & Thompson 1988).

(13.66)   While Ed was coming downstairs, *Mary slipped out the front door, went
            around the house, and came in the back door.*
                                          (Matthiessen & Thompson 1988: 281)

Such an analysis is consistent with Longacre's (1972: 10) observation that unexpected SS marking is associated with the presence of a DS temporal clause, which is
backgrounded by being skipped. This approach is not always semantically appropriate, however. In example (13.67) clause (d) is skipped, but does not form a background for the whole chain, as it is semantically associated only with waking up
(clause c) and eating a meal (clause e; and note that the skipped clause (d) is
grouped intonationally with (e)). As in (13.66), however, the skipped clause is a
backgrounded temporal clause. So it seems that skipped clauses may be semantically associated with the whole clause chain or with just some subset of it. Example
(13.67) is discussed in detail in Overall (2014b).

(13.67)   *núnik kanáŋ tsawák atásh shináĩ yuhúmkan kukáŋmã wɨuwai nĩ̃shkam*
   a.   [nu-ni-kã]BRIDGE
            ANA-VBLZ.INTR-PFV+3:SS

    b.   kana-hã
            sleep-PFV+3:SS
    c.   tsawa-kũ
            wake.up+IPFV-SIM+3:SS
    d.   atash   shina-ĩ
            chicken   call+IPFV+1SG/3-DS
    e.   yuhumka=na kukaŋmã
            food=ACC   eat.lightly+PFV+3:SS
    f.   wɨ-u=ai   nĩ=shakama
            go+PFV-NMLZ=COP:3:DECL   3sg=ADD
            '[a.]Having done that (i.e. prepared blowdarts for the following day's hunting), [b.]he went to sleep, [c.]and waking up [d.]as the rooster was crowing [e.]he ate a light meal and [f.]he too went out.' (agr041005_28)

Now, the SR marking in example (13.67) would be compatible with the focal model of clause chaining in Figure 13.5, as all of the clauses are marked appropriately for SR with respect to the final clause. But this analysis would not be possible for other clause chains, such as (13.64) above – in that example all of the subordinate clauses have a different subject from the finite clause, but only the one directly preceding the finite clause is actually marked DS, reflecting a linear structure. Furthermore, the focal model does not adequately reflect the semantic structure, as clause chains typically relate a sequence of events (as in 13.67). As noted above, the linear structure is a more useful model, once we admit the possibility of skipping DS clauses in a sequence of SS clauses.

    Although skipped clauses are always DS, it is also possible for DS clauses to take part in linear clause chains with no skipping. This was the case in (13.64), with just one DS clause, and in (13.68) two DS clauses in a chain (a and b) encode linear SR relations with their immediately following clause. Note that clause (13.68d) is a subordinate purpose clause, and follows its controlling clause (c), as discussed below.

(13.68)   *túhã piípish ãĩ, mína apáŋ papí múun áuŋbaunum áuhak wɨɰakũĩ, sínchi wakɨyin áyahai wísha áusatasan*

    a.   [tuhã   piipichi   a-ĩ]
            but   small   COP+1/3-DS
    b.   [mi=na   apa-hu   papi   muunta   auhu-mau=numa
            1SG=ACC father-PSSD:1SG book   adult   study-NMLZ=LOC
            auha-kũ   wɨ-a-ku-ĩ]
            study+IPFV-SIM+3:SS   go-IPFV-SIM+1/3-DS
    c.   sɨnchi   wakɨɰa-inu a-ya-ha-i   wi=sha
            strongly want-NMLZ   COP-REMPST-1SG-DECL   1sg=ADD

    d.   [au-sa-tasa-n]
        study-PFV-INTENT-1SG:SS

        '[a.]But when I was small, [b.]when my father was going to study at the school for adults, [c.]I too really wanted [d.]to study.' (Text 2:3-5)

The SR relations of (13.68) are schematized in Figure 13.8.

Figure 13.8: Interclausal SR relations in example (13.68)

Although long chains of subordinate clauses tend to be ordered sequentially, more flexible ordering is possible when dealing with shorter chains. A subordinate clause may be centre embedded in a matrix clause, in the sense that it intervenes between constituents of that clause. In example (13.69), a man is planning to trick his foster father into believing that he has killed all the birds, so he explains to the birds that he will fire darts towards them from his blowgun, and they must catch the darts and pretend to fall down dead.

(13.69)   *átum, tsíntsak minákũĩ, achíakum iyáitahum*
        atumɨ   [tsɨntsaka   mina-ku-ĩ]   achi-a-ku-mɨ
        2PL   dart   arrive-SIM+1/3-DS   grab-IPFV-SIM-2:SS
        iya-i-ta-humɨ
        fall-PFV-IMP-2PL
        'you, when the darts arrive, grab them and fall down' (agr040724_01)

The first word *atum* 'you[PL]' is the subject of both the following subordinate and finite clauses: 'you[PL] grab them and fall down'. Centre-embedded in that chain is a different-subject subordinate clause, 'the darts arrive'. It is not possible to say whether the DS clause is syntactically a constituent of the subordinate clause ('you grab them') or the finite clause ('fall down'), and semantically it relates to both (similarly to the skipped DS temporal clause in 13.65 above).

    Example (13.70) shows a non-inflecting subordinate *-ma* clause centre-embedded in its controlling clause, following the subject NP [*nunú namák áina dúka*] 'those fish'.

(13.70) *nunú namák áina dúka, nunú datsáuch áwantak hiiyám, máma*
         naháni̇aku áinawai

   nunu   namaka   a-ina   nu=ka   [nunu   datsauchi
   ANA   fish   COP-IPFV.PL+3 ANAREL=TOP   ANA   youth
   awantaka   hii-a-**ma**]   mama   nahani̇a-ka-u
   on.the.surface take.out-IPFV-**NSBJ>SBJ** manioc   become-PFV-NMLZ
   a-ina-wa-i
   COP-PL:IPFV-3-DECL
   'Those fish, when the youth took them out of the water at the surface,
   turned into manioc.' (agr040824_01)

Subject NPs are the most frequently encountered constituents preceding centre-
embedded subordinate clauses, but not the only possibility. Example (13.71) shows a
centre embedded SS clause. Here the accusative-marked NP *ikam_yawaã=na*
(jaguar=ACC) is the object of the final verb, and the subordinate sequential temporal
clause intervenes.

(13.71) *ikámyawan haŋki̇num inuán achíkhai*
   ikam_yawaã=na [haŋki̇=numa inu-a-nu]
   jaguar=ACC   jaw=LOC   put.hand.in-PFV+SEQ-1SG:SS
   achi-ka-ha-i
   grab-PFV-1SG-DECL
   'I've stuck my hand in its jaws and grabbed the jaguar' (agr041005_14)

When a shared subject precedes a SS subordinate clause this could be analysed
similarly as centre embedding, but there is no morphological or syntactic evidence
available to decide the question. Example (13.72) shows such a construction, bracketed according to the centre-embedding analysis: the NP *nuwa makichik* "a woman"
is subject of the finite verb, and the subordinate clause has no overt subject. Alternatively, the NP could be analysed as part of the subordinate clause. It remains an
open question whether such examples should be analysed as centre-embedded. In
any case, the possibility of centre embedding, as demonstrated by examples
(13.69)–(13.71), clearly shows that subordinate clauses are treated syntactically as
constituents of a matrix clause.

(13.72) *núwa mákichik naŋkaín usupáŋ hiinki̇u túwahami̇*
   nuwa   makichiki [naŋkai=na usupa-hã]
   woman   one   fruit=ACC   crave-PFV+SEQ+3:SS

> hiina-ki-u   tuwahamĩ
> go.out-PFV-NMLZ   NARR
> 'a woman, having craved fruit, went out (to get it), they say'
> (agr040721_07)

There is a general preference for finite clauses to be final in multiclausal constructions, in keeping with Aguaruna's predicate-final profile; as such, subordinate
clauses typically precede the predicate of their controlling clause. However, just as
constituents such as NP arguments and adverbs may follow the predicate in some
circumstances, subordinate clauses also may follow their controlling verb. That this
should be the case is hardly surprising: complement clauses are core arguments and
other subordinate clause types are treated as adverbial constituents of a matrix
clause, so it is to be expected that they should show the same positioning possibilities as their non-clausal counterparts. The difference lies in the fact that clauses
express states or actions, and as such there is a motivation to order them iconically
if those states or actions show any chronological ordering amongst themselves. In
particular, chains of sequential clauses describing actual (not hypothetical) events
are obligatorily iconically ordered. The clause type most commonly found postposed to the verb of a finite controlling clause are purpose clauses (see examples in
§14.5). This ordering is iconic, as the action of the purpose clause necessarily follows
that of the controlling clause chronologically. Complement clauses are also often
postposed to the controlling verb; indeed, many complement clauses are morphologically identical to purpose clauses (see example 13.68 above, and further discussion in §17.2).

As noted above, the principle of iconicity requires that sequential temporal
clauses should not be postposed to their controlling verb when they describe actual
events. But the sequential clause in example (13.73) appears with the conditional
enclitic, and is postposed to the controlling clause. In this case the unrealized nature of the conditional construction renders iconity of ordering irrelevant – the person had not actually died at the time of speaking.

(13.73)   *Miguel maámi, aínts hakámtaiɲ*
           Miguel   ma-a-mi   [aintsu   ha-ka-mataĩ=ka]
           Miguel   kill-PFV-HORT   person   die-PFV+SEQ-1/3:DS=COND
           'Let's kill Miguel if the person (that Miguel beat up) dies'
           (agr060816_01)

In example (13.74), the action of wrapping up expressed in the postposed sequential
clauses must precede the killing, since that is precisely how a boa kills; but the subordinate clause represents a manner linkage, not a temporal one, and a better translation might be 'it killed the man by wrapping him up'. The repetition of the subor-

dinate clause also suggests it is being treated as semantically modifying the action – while repetition of subordinate clauses is not common, ideophones are adverbial elements which are often repeated, and in some cases show formal similarities to semantically related verbs (§12.3.2).

(13.74)   *maáuwai pȋmpȋáŋ pȋmpȋáŋ*
           ma-a-u=ai   [pȋmpȋa-hã]
           kill-PFV-NMLZ=COP:3:DECL   wrap.up-PFV+SEQ+3:SS
           [pȋmpȋa-hã]
           wrap.up-PFV+SEQ+3:SS
           '(the boa) killed (the man) by wrapping him up' (Text 1:11)

To summarize: the switch-reference marking shows that subordinate clauses are typically marked with respect to linear order, but with the possibility of clause skipping, whereby a DS temporal clause in a chain of clauses that share a subject has no effect on the marking of the preceding verb. The freedom of positioning of subordinate clauses shows that there is a more hierarchical structure in Aguaruna than is found with cosubordinate constructions. While iconic ordering of temporal clauses is the norm, those examples that depart from iconic ordering can be shown to have properties that suggest they are not considered purely temporal clauses by speakers. Overall (2014b) goes into more detail regarding the discourse motivations for the different clause chaining structures.

13.7.2 Marking of subordinate clauses with floating enclitics

Mood/modality marking offers further evidence for the subordinate status of chained clauses. Mood/modality is marked on finite verbs (Chapter 9) and has clausal scope. Three clause types assign mood/modality marking to the verb, marked with a suffix, and also involve floating enclitics: (i) speculative marks a constituent of the clause as the locus of speculation with enclitic *=tsu*; (ii) polar interrogative assigns 'question topic' enclitic *=sha* marking to constituents; and (iii) content interrogative also assigns 'question topic' marker *=sha*. Crucially, the enclitic markers may be hosted by subordinate verbs as well as by NP and adverbial constituents, evidence that all have equal syntactic status. The following illustrative examples are repeated from Chapter 9 and Chapter 10. In (13.75) the speculative enclitic *=tsu* is hosted by the subordinate verb, and in (13.76) the subject NP and the subordinate verb in a polar interrogative clause are both marked with the enclitic *=sha*.

(13.75)   *kantáshhãĩ bɨtɨk asámtãĩs tíu áinatai*
           [kantasha=haĩ   bɨtɨka   asa-mataĩ=**tsu**]   ti-u
           macana=COM   equal   COP+SBD-1/3:DS=**SPEC**   say+PFV-NMLZ
           a-ina-**tai**
           COP-PL:IPFV+3-**SPEC**
           'they probably say that because (they think) it's the same as a *macana*
           fish'

(13.76)   *amɨsh Lima wɨtasamɨsh wakɨɰasmɨk?*
           amɨ=**sha**   [*Lima*   wɨ-tasa-mɨ=**sha**]   wakɨɰa-a-tsu-mɨ=**ka**
           2sg=**Q.TOP**   Lima   go+PFV-INTENT-2=**Q.TOP**   want-IPFV-NEG-2SG=**Q**
           'do you want to go to Lima?' (agr040824_02)

13.7.3 Operator scope and subordinate clauses

While subordinate clauses may be marked with floating mood/modality enclitics,
they are characterized by an absence of mood/modality marking of their own, and
do not necessarily share that of the controlling clause. This situation can be compared to Genetti's (2005) discussion of "participial" (=converbal) forms in Dolakhā
Newar:

> [O]ne cannot predict scope of illocutionary force simply on the basis of syntax; non-structural
> factors must also be taken into account.
>
> Genetti (2005: 68)

Since most narrative is couched in declarative mood there is little to say that the
subordinate clauses in chains do not share this with the finite verbs which overtly
mark mood. It is in questions and commands that variation can be more readily
assessed, and although a full study of the pragmatics of such clauses has yet to be
undertaken, the following generalizations can be made:

– SS clauses typically share the mood of their controlling clause, especially imperative and hortative. This can be seen in example (13.77), where imperative
  mood has scope over the subordinate clause – in fact this construction is preferred to repeating the imperative marking on both verbs.

(13.77)   *húw̃ɨ kanáham kashín wɨtá*
           [hu=ĩ   kana-ha-mɨ]   kashini   wɨ-ta
           PROX=LOC   sleep-PFV+SEQ-2:SS   tomorrow   go+PFV-IMP
           'sleep here and go tomorrow' lit. *having slept here, go tomorrow* (Text
           2:21)

- DS clauses typically express a precondition. Compare (13.77) with (13.69) above, in which the imperative marking of the controlling clause does not have scope over the DS subordinate clause.
- Overtly marked conditional and concessive clauses express preconditions and block shared mood, as in (13.73) above.
- Interrogative clauses may include marking on a subordinate clause (§13.7.2), which may be presupposed or within the scope of interrogation. Presupposed clauses may also be nominalized in questions, as in (13.78) – also see (10.23).

(13.78)　　*ihapimush utusáŋ isámati*
　　　　　　ihapɨ-mau=sha　　　　　utu-sã=ki　　　　　　isama-ti
　　　　　　gut+PFV-NSBJ.NMLZ=Q.TOP　how-SBD+3:SS=Q.RHET　heal+PFV-JUSS
　　　　　　'how can one who has been gutted heal up?' (agr041005_16; cf. 10.60)

- Speculative modality may also be marked on subordinate clauses with the enclitic =*tsu* (13.75 above). Examples such as (13.79), repeated from Chapter 9, suggest that the speculative enclitic marks the constituent over which the modality has scope. Example (13.75) above, where the marked constituent is a subordinate clause, can be interpreted similarly.

(13.79)　　*numinás tsupíktaŋtai*
　　　　　　numi=na=**tsu**　　　tsupi-ka-ta-ha-**tai**
　　　　　　tree=ACC=**SPEC**　　cut-PFV-IFUT-1SG-**SPEC**
　　　　　　'perhaps it's wood that I'll cut' (cf. 9.15)

So while subordinate clauses in Aguaruna are not completely predictable with respect to their pragmatic status, there are some generalizations to be made.

With respect to the linear ordering of subordinate clauses described above, Gordon (1983, 1986: 266ff.) reports similar syntactic flexibility for dependent clauses in Maricopa (Yuman), but also shows that dependent clauses differ in their positioning possibilities according to the semantics of the linkage:

> Clauses which are temporally related to a reference clause or which are expressing a kind of loose conjunction of events between the dependent and the reference clauses cannot be center-embedded. Dependent clauses which serve as complement clauses, as modifying clauses, and as reason clauses can be center-embedded within their reference clauses.
> Gordon (1983: 89)

The data presented above suggest that Aguaruna subordinate clauses may similarly differ in their syntactic possibilities depending on their function, but since relevant data is rare in texts, further detailed elicitation will be required in order to move beyond the generalizations made here.

14 Clause chaining and clause combining

14.1 Preliminary remarks

Having described the formal morphological and syntactic properties of subordinate clauses in Chapter 13, the present chapter focuses on the semantics of the various clause linking constructions. The chapter is arranged along semantic lines, describing the formal structures that are used to encode the semantic types. The semantic types themselves are basically the subset of those described in Dixon (2009) that are relevant to the grammar of Aguaruna.[1] Conditional and concessive clauses are described in §14.6, coordination in §14.7, and bridging constructions (tail-head linkage) in §14.8.

14.2 Temporal clauses

Temporal linkages explicitly indicate the relative timing of events in two linked clauses. They are typically formed with sequential or simultaneous clauses, two of the basic subordinate clause types described in §13.4; but a range of other options is also available.

In linkages involving sequential clauses, no distinction is made between temporal and consequence linkages; that is, there is no explicit indication as to whether the temporally prior action is to be understood as causing or merely preceding the subsequent action. Thompson, Longacre & Hwang (2007) note that such a neutralization is not unexpected:

> [T]wo events which are mentioned together as being simultaneous or adjacent in time are often inferred to be causally related.
>
> Thompson, Longacre & Hwang (2007: 247)

The distinction can be made explicit, however, using a case-marked pronoun to form a bridging construction, where locative case indicates a temporal relation and instrumental case a consequence relation (§14.8). The following description divides the temporal clause types on the basis of whether the action of the subordinate clause is prior to that of the controlling clause (§14.2.1); simultaneous with that of the controlling clause (§14.2.2); or follows that of the controlling clause (§14.2.3).

---

1 See Overall (2009) for a description of Aguaruna that follows Dixon's (2009) typology more closely.

14.2.1 Temporal clauses expressing prior action

Prior action may be marked with one of the following five constructions:

(i) Terminative *-kama* indicates that termination of an ongoing action in the subordinate clause coincides with the start of a new action in the controlling clause. This marker only appears in SS clauses (14.1).

(14.1) *chapáȳã diikmá, aintsún ... wainák ...*
      [chapayã   dii-kamã]   aintsu=na ...
      look.over.edge+PFV+SEQ+3:SS   look-TERM+3:SS   person=ACC ...
      waina-kã
      see-PFV+SEQ+3:SS
      'looking over the edge, on looking they saw a person ...' (agr040712_02)

(ii) A sequential clause formed on the perfective stem, which may be SS (example 14.2) or DS (14.3).

(14.2) *naŋkimá̃ namaká ahuŋkuí*
      [naŋkimã]   namaka   ahũ-ka-u=i
      throw+PFV+SEQ+3:SS river+LOC   throw.in.water-PFV-NMLZ=COP:3:DECL
      'having thrown it, he let it drop into the water' (agr040824_01)

(14.3) *ȳã̃ẘã́ã̃ ikínmatã̃ı̃ maáhai*
      [yawaã   ikina-mataĩ]   ma-a-ha-i
      dog   flush.out+PFV+SEQ-1/3:DS   kill-PFV-1SG-DECL
      'when the dog flushed (the agouti) out, I killed it' (agr041005_15)

(iii) The non-inflecting subordinator *-ma* (NSBJ>SBJ) with perfective stem (14.4).

(14.4) *ípinim, nı̃́ ikámȳã̃ẘã́ã̃ "tru tru tru" waháu*
      [ipini-ma]   nĩ   ikam_yawaã   <u>tru</u>   <u>tru</u>   <u>tru</u>
      trap+PFV-NSBJ>SBJ   3sg jaguar   IDEO IDEO IDEO
      waha-a-u
      call-IPFV-NMLZ
      'when (they) trapped (it), the jaguar was going "roar roar roar!"'
      (agr041005_14)

(iv) Where the controlling clause represents a stretch of time rather than a point in time (i.e. 'since'), this is expressed with a subordinate form of the verb *naŋkamat* 'begin' (14.5).

(14.5)   *mína apáŋ hakámtãĩ naŋkámsan, bitáik huwákuithai*
      [mi=na   apa-hu   ha-ka-mataĩ]   [naŋkama-sa-nu]
      1sg=ACC father-PSSD:1SG die-PFV+SEQ-1/3:DS begin-SBD-1SG:SS
      bitaik   huwa-ka-u=ita-ha-i
      orphan   stay-PFV-NMLZ=COP-1SG-DECL
      'since my father died, I remain an orphan'

(v) A bridging construction (SS or DS) – see §14.8 below.

14.2.2 Temporal clauses expressing simultaneous action

Where a temporal subordinate clause expresses a state or event that is simultaneous with that expressed by the controlling clause, one of the following six constructions is used:

(i) Repetitive subordinate clause with *-kawa* (accompanied by partial reduplication in the verb root). This form is only used in SS clauses (14.6).

(14.6)   *búu búutkãw̃ã w̃ɨu*
      [buu   buuta-kawã]   wɨ-u
      REDUP cry+IPFV-REPET+3:SS go+PFV-NMLZ
      'crying and crying he went' (agr041006_01)

(ii) Simultaneous clause marked with *-ku*, in SS (14.7) or DS (14.8) clauses.

(14.7)   *antuínaku w̃ɨɥaŋmi*
      [antu-ina-ku]   wɨ-aha-mi
      hear-PL:IPFV-SIM+1PL:SS go+PFV-PL-HORT
      'when we hear, let's go'

(14.8)   *núna múun áuŋmatuinakũĩ, "wáinkas táwa" túyahai*
      [nu=na   muunta   auhumatu-ina-ku-ĩ]   <u>wainakasã</u>
      ANA=ACC elder   tell-PL:IPFV-SIM+1/3-DS in.vain+3
      <u>ta-wa</u>   tu-ya-ha-i
      say+IPFV-3+EXCL say-REMPST-1SG-DECL
      'when the elders were telling that (story), I would say "they're talking rubbish!"' (agr040723_29)

(iii) Imperfective DS clause. These clauses have a locative nuance, as can be seen in examples (14.9, 14.10); also see §13.5.2.4.

(14.9)   *kabisán apihík itiphũã̄ wahã́ĩ, íkamỹãw̃ãã̄ tsíkɨn wahaukú*
             [kabisa=na   apihi-kã   itipahu-ã
             kilt=ACC   fold-PFV+SEQ+3:SS   put.on-PFV+SEQ+3:SS
             waha-ĩ   ikam_yawaã   tsíkɨn   wahau-ka-u
             stand+IPFV+1SG/3-DS   jaguar   suddenly   stop-PFV-NMLZ
             'having folded his kilt and put it on, he was standing when the jaguar
             suddenly arrived' (agr041005_14)

(14.10)   *hṹw̃ĩ puhã́ĩ taáta*
            [hu=ĩ   puha-ĩ]   ta-a-ta
            PROX=LOC   live+IPFV+1SG/3-DS   come-PFV-IMP
            'come here, where I am'

(iv) Non-inflecting subordinator *-tatamana* (SBJ>OBJ), with unmarked stem.

(14.11)   *úchi akáikĩ, yúmiŋmat hɨ̃ɰ̃ã́tatus wɨ́tatman, ikámỹãw̃ãã̄ tɨpɨŋkáuwai*
            [uchi   akai-kĩ   yumiŋmat
            youth   go.down-PFV+SEQ+3:SS   well
            hɨɰa-tatus   wɨ-tatamana]   ikama_yawaã
            arrive+PFV-INTENT+3:SS go-SBJ>OBJ   jaguar
            tɨpi-hu-ka-u=ai
            lie.down-APPL-PFV-NMLZ=COP:3:DECL
            'the youth having gone down the hill, while he was going to the well,
            the jaguar pounced on him' (agr041005_14)

(v) Non inflecting subordinator *-ma* (NSBJ>SBJ) with imperfective stem (14.12).

(14.12)   *táma, núu úchi chicháak...*
            [ta-ma]   nu   uchi   chicha-a-kũ
            say+IPFV-NSBJ>SBJ   ANA   child   speak-IPFV-SIM+3:SS
            'when they said that to himᵢ, that youthᵢ was saying...' (agr041005_14)

(vi) Relative clause formed with the imperfective stem and the subject nominalizer *-u* (see §15.5.2).

(14.13)   *yakí wakã́ ɨkɨ́tun yunúmtukui*
            [yaki   wa-kã   ɨkɨ-ta-u=na]
            above   go.up-PFV+SEQ+3:SS   sit-APPL+IPFV-NMLZ=ACC

yunuma-tu-ka-u=ai
approach-APPL-PFV-NMLZ=COP:3:DECL
'(The man) approached (the boa) that had gone up and was sitting up above him.' (Text 1:8)

14.2.3 Temporal clauses expressing future action

Where the action of the subordinate clause follows that of the controlling clause, one of the following four constructions is used.

(i) Speech report with future controlling clause gives the sense of 'until' as in (14.14).

(14.14)   *"mína dukúŋ tsau̯áŋti" tusán kuitámkun puhúttahai*
[mi=na   duku-hu   tsau̯a-ha-ti   tu-sa-nu]
1sg=ACC   mother-PSSD:1SG   recover-PFV-JUSS   say-SBD-1SG:SS
kuitama-ku-nu   puhu-tata-ha-i
care.for+IPFV-SIM-1SG:SS   live-FUT-1SG-DECL
'I will stay here looking after my mother until she gets well' lit. *...saying "may my mother recover"*

(ii) A sequential clause formed on the perfective stem, with future controlling clause, gives the sense of 'until' (note that the DS subordinate clause in example 14.15 is skipped, and the preceding verb is marked SS – see §13.7).

(14.15)   *hǔw̃ĩ puhusán, Wawík kǔy̌ǔmatãĩ wítathai*
[hu=ĩ   puhu-sa-nu]   [wawiku   kǔyu-a-matãĩ]
PROX=LOC   live-SBD-1SG:SS   Wawik   subside-PFV+SEQ-1/3:DS
wi-tata-ha-i
go+PFV-FUT-1SG-DECL
'I will stay here until the Wawik river subsides, then I'll go'

(iii) An imperfective DS subordinate clause with negative polarity gives the sense of 'before', that is, 'while not yet'.

(14.16)   *taáuwai Kaŋkáp táatsiŋ*
ta-a-u=ai   [kaŋkapɨ   ta-a-tsu-ĩ=ka]
come-PFV-NMLZ=COP:3:DECL   Kagkap   come-IPFV-NEG-1/3:DS=TOP
'(the jaguar) arrived before Kagkap (a legendary hero) had arrived' (agr041005_14)

(iv) A frustrative subordinate clause may also give the sense of 'before'.

(14.17) *ahánum núwa wíu wáutakamã...*
         [aha=numa   nuwa   wɨ-u   wau-takamã]
         garden=LOC   woman   go+PFV-NMLZ   arrive-FRUST+3:SS
         'before the woman who had gone to the garden arrived ... (her husband
         butchered and cooked her dog)' (agr041005_15)

14.3 Consequence clauses

Consequence clauses express a relation of causality; the action or state expressed by
the controlling clause is a consequence of that expressed by the subordinate clause.
As noted above, consequence blurs with temporal succession when the action of the
subordinate clause is prior to that of the controlling clause. Consequence linkage
can be divided into two groups: prior action (§14.3.1); and non-prior action (§14.3.2).

14.3.1 Prior action consequence clauses

Where the situation described by the subordinate clause is prior to that of the controlling clause, the same set of markers is used as for prior temporal above.

(i) SS sequential temporal clause (14.18) – DS clauses expressing prior action are
     typically encoded with bridging constructions (§14.8).

(14.18) *núwa mákichik naŋkaín usupáŋ hiinkíu túwahamɨ̃*
         [nuwa   makichiki naŋkai=na   usupa-hã]
         woman   one   fruit=ACC   crave-PFV+SEQ+3:SS
         hiina-ki-u   tuwahamɨ̃
         go.out-PFV-NMLZ   NARR
         'a woman craved fruit, so she went out (to get it), they say'
         (agr040721_07)

(ii) Non-person-marking subordinator -*ma* (NSBJ>SBJ) with perfective stem.

(14.19) *suwimám búutua*
         [suwima-ma]   buuta-wa
         beat+PFV-NSBJ>SBJ   cry+IPFV-3:EXCL
         'he's crying because he was beaten!'

14.3.2 Non-prior action consequence clauses

Where the situation described by the subordinate clause is simultaneous to or follows that of the controlling clause, four construction types may be used.

(i) Non-temporal subordinate clause.

(14.20) *waámak hĩ̃ɰ́átatau asá, "ayú" tusá wáhabiahi*

[waamakɨ hĩɰa-tata-u   asa]   [ayu

quickly   arrive+PFV-DESID-NMLZ   COP+SBD+1PL:SS ok

tu-sa]   wa-aha-maya-hi

say-SBD+1PL:SS go.up+PFV-PL-INTPST-1PL+DECL

'(the driver told us we had to pay him and) because we wanted to get home quickly, we said "ok" and got onto the truck' (agr040824_02)

Contrast the following two elicited examples; in (14.21) a DS imperfective clause indicates a temporal relation, and in (14.22), a similar situation is described using a non-temporal subordinate clause, highlighting the causal nature of the linkage.

(14.21) *wíi hṹw̃ãĩ, shintáŋ tɨpáu wáitukmɨ̃*

[wi   hu-a-ɨ̃]   shinta-hã   tɨpa-u

1sg   collect-IPFV+1SG/3-DS wake-PFV+SEQ+3:SS lie.down+IPFV-NMLZ

wai-tu-ka-mɨ̃

see-1SG.OBJ-PFV-RECPST:3:DECL

'as I was taking (things), someone who was awake saw me'

(14.22) *áu shintáŋ tɨpáu ásã mínak wáitukmɨ̃*

[au   shinta-hã   puha-u   asã]

DIST wake-PFV+SEQ+3:SS live+IPFV-NMLZ COP+SBD+3:SS

mi=na=ka   wai-tu-ka-mɨ̃

1sg=ACC=TOP see-1SG.OBJ-PFV-RECPST:3:DECL

'because he was awake, he saw me'

(ii) Speech report (see §17.1).

(14.23) *búutui, "Simón wɨ́ɰawai" tus*

buuta-wa-i   [Simón wɨ-a-wa-i   tus]

cry+IPFV-3-DECL Simon go-IPFV-3-DECL say+SBD+3:SS

'It's crying because Simon's going' lit. *...saying "Simon's going"*

The subordinate clause (typically a rhetorical question) may be introduced with *waŋki* 'because' < 'why'; in the same construction the controlling clause may be introduced with bridging anaphoric *nu* + instrumental case (as above).

(14.24) *úchi núna ỹũw̃ǎ́, wáŋki kíiwish yutáiŋkait íish, dúwi hakáu túwahamɨ̃*

    uchi   nu=na   yu-ã   [wãã=ki   kiiwi=sha

    child   ANA=ACC   eat-PFV+SEQ+3:SS   why=Q.RHET   centipede=Q.TOP

    yu-taĩ=ka=ita   ii=sha]   [nu=i]BRIDGE   ha-ka-u

    eat-NSBJ.NMLZ=Q=COP   1pl=Q.TOP   ANA=INS   die-PFV-NMLZ

    tuwahamɨ̃

    NARR

    'the child having eaten that (centipede), because – are centipedes food we eat? – because of that (the child) died.' (agr040721_07)

(iii) Non-inflecting subordinator *-tatamana* (SBJ>OBJ).

(14.25) *nuní núna nuwɨ́n nuní wɨkáɨtatman dútikã suwímkan susáya túwahamɨ̃*

    nuni   [nu=na   nuwɨ=na   nuni

    thus   ANA=ACC   wife+PSSD:1PL/3=ACC   thus

    wɨkaɨɨa-tatamana]   [nu-tikã   suwimaka=na

    walk-SBJ>OBJ   ANA-VBLZ.TR+PFV+SEQ+3:SS   punishment=ACC

    su-sa-ya   tuwahamɨ̃]

    give-PFV-REMPST+3   NARR

    'and so he punished (lit. *gave punishment to*) that wife of his who had done such a thing (lit. *who had wandered thus*) (agr041005_15)

(iv) Juxtaposition of finite clauses may also encode consequence linkage, as in (14.26a and b).

(14.26) a. *wɨka ỹãw̃ǎ́ãchuithai ihúntuhã suwímam átinun,*

        [wi=ka   yawaã=chau=ita-ha-i]   [ihũ-tu-hã

        1sg=TOP   dog=NEG.NMLZ=COP-1SG-DECL   gang.up-APPL-PFV+SEQ+3:SS

        suwima-ma   a-tinu-nu]

        beat+PFV-NSBJ>SBJ   COP-FUT+NMLZ-1SG:SS

     b. *wɨka wakɨ́tkittahai mína nuŋkahɨ́ɨ̃*

        wi=ka   wakɨtu-ki-tata-ha-i   mi=na   nuŋka-hu=ɨ̃

        1sg=TOP   go.back-PFV-FUT-1SG-DECL   1sg=ACC   land-PSSD:1SG=LOC

        'a.I am not a dog, to be beaten by gangs of people, b. (so) I will go back to my land' (agr060816_01)

14.4 Possible Consequence

Possible consequence is marked with two constructions.

(i) It may use the apprehensive form (14.27); the consequence alluded to is always an undesirable one.

(14.27)   *wakítkita ámɨk mantámawainum*
          wakitu-ki-ta   amɨ=ka   [mantama-aw-ai-numɨ̃]
          go.back-PFV-IMP   2sg=TOP   kill+2.OBJ-PFV-APPR-3PL
          'you go back, lest they kill you' (agr060816_01)

The apprehensive verb is typically embedded in a speech report construction, as in example (14.28) from a story about a woman who finds an egg and takes it home to hatch.

(14.28)   *takímpaŋ kuitámkauwai shíiŋ, "hákãĩ" tus*
          takimpa-hã   kuitama-ka-u=ai   shiiha
          hatch-PFV+SEQ+3:SS   care.for-PFV-NMLZ=COP:3:DECL   well
          [ha-ka-ĩ]   tus]
          die-PFV-APPR+3SG   say+SBD+3:SS
          'having hatched it, she cared for it well, lest it should die' lit. *...saying "lest it die"* (agr040724_01)

Note that this example differs structurally from the DS purpose clause (§14.5) only in its use of the apprehensive suffix. But unlike purpose, possible consequence is expressed with a speech report even when the two clauses have the same subject (14.29).

(14.29)   *shíiŋ yúwamɨ "hákaiŋ" túsam*
          shiiha   yu-a-mɨ   [ha-ka-i-ha   tu-sa-mɨ]
          well   eat-IPFV-2SG+DECL die-PFV-APPR-1SG   say-SBD-2:SS
          'you eat well so that you won't die' lit. *you$_i$ eat well, saying "lest I$_i$ die"*

(ii) Possible consequence may also be implied with a direct speech report, without apprehensive marking; example (14.30) could be translated "they hid his right hand *lest he finish them all*".

(14.30)   *"aúk amúktathama!" tákuŋ untsuhín uhúk awasám...*
          [au-kI   amu-ka-tata-hama   ta-kũ=ka]
          DIST-RESTR   finish-PFV-FUT+3-CNTR.EX say+IPFV-SIM+3:SS=TOP

> untsu-hĩ=na   uhu-kã   awa-sa-ma
> right.hand-PSSD:1PL/3=ACC   hide-PFV+SEQ+3:SS   put-PFV-NSBJ>SBJ
> 'saying "hey, he'll finish them all!" they restrained his right hand…'
> (agr040724_01)

Unlike other clause combining constructions, the subordinate clause typically follows the controlling clause in a possible consequence linkage, as in examples (14.27–14.29). This ordering is iconic, as the possible consequence is chronologically subsequent to the finite controlling clause; the preference for iconic ordering can override the usual preference for a finite clause to be final. However, the ordering is reversed in (14.30), and the apprehensive-marked construction may also be ordered with the subordinate clause first, as in (14.31). This example comes from a myth about young Etsã (the sun) and Ajaim, a cannibal who killed and ate Etsã's mother and raised the boy as his own. When Etsã goes out hunting every day, Ajaim brings out the skull of the mother and plays it as one would blow a jug. He makes Etsã wear a necklace that rattles loudly, so that Ajaim will hear him coming home and have time to hide the skull before Etsã catches him playing with it.

(14.31)   *"ĩtsã antúkãĩ" tus tíŋkapin nahátũã dĩtuáya túwahamĩ*
            [ĩtsã   antu-ka-ĩ   tus]   tiŋkapi=na
            Etsã   hear-PFV-APPR+3SG   say+SBD+3:SS   necklace=ACC
            naha-tu-ã   dĩ-tu-a-ya   tuwahamĩ
            make-APPL-PFV+SEQ+3:SS   hang-APPL-PFV-REMPST+3   NARR
            'lest Etsã should hear, (Ajaim) made him a necklace and hung it on him'
            (agr040724_01)

14.5 Purpose clauses

Two types of clause explicitly indicate purpose: intentional clause (SS) and speech report (DS). Both are also used in complementation; in fact there is no surface grammatical distinction between a purpose clause and a complement clause (§17.2). A simultaneous clause can also encode purpose.

(i) Intentional dependent clause (SS).

(14.32)   *wĩkaĩɰák wĩuwai kuntínun mantumaátatus*
            wĩkaĩɰa-kũ   wĩ-u=ai   [kuntinu=na
            walk+IPFV-SIM+3:SS   go+PFV-NMLZ=COP:3:DECL   animal=ACC

mantu-ma-a-tatus]
kill+APPL-REFL-PFV-INTENT+3:SS
'he went walking to kill animals for himself' (i.e. 'he went hunting')
(Text 1:3)

(ii) Speech report (DS).

(14.33) *iwíyahi "tɨpɨstí" túsa*

iwi-ya-hi	[tɨpɨ-sa-ti	tu-sa]
raise.hand-REMPST-1PL+DECL	lie.down-PFV-JUSS	say-SBD+1PL:SS

'we raised our hands so that it (the truck) would stop' lit. *saying "let it lie down"* (agr040824_02)

(iii) A simultaneous clause may also indicate purpose, as in example (14.34).

(14.34) *hiínhabiahi iína batsámtãĩ minínaku*

hiina-aha-maya-hi	[ii=na	batsama-taĩ
go.out+PFV-PL-INTPST-1PL+DECL	1pl=ACC	live-NSBJ.NMLZ

mini-ina-ku]
arrive-PL:IPFV-SIM+1PL:SS
'we set off to go back to our homes' (agr040824_02)

In all three types, there is no strict ordering of subordinate and controlling clauses, although it seems that the subordinate clause is more commonly final, as in examples (14.32–14.34). As in the possible consequence linkage described above, this ordering is iconic.

14.6 Conditional and concessive clauses

Conditional and concessive clauses mark logical relations between clauses. Both are formed from subordinate clauses, and they are formally marked with the topic *=ka* and additive *=sha(kama)* enclitics, respectively. These enclitics also appear on NPs and some adverbial words.

14.6.1 Conditional clauses

The protasis in a conditional linkage is normally a simultaneous (14.35–14.37) or sequential clause (14.37, 14.38; see §13.4 for details of these clause types), and takes the topic enclitic *=ka* (glossed COND when used in this function). See §18.2 for further discussion of the link between topic and conditional markers. The protasis may be

SS (14.35, 14.37) or DS (14.36, 14.37. 14.38). The form of the apodosis is constrained, but perhaps only by pragmatics: all examples in my corpus are future, potential or imperative forms.

(14.35)   *wakɨɰakmɨk, yuwáta*
           [wakɨɰa-a-ku-mɨ=ka]   yu-a-ta
           want-IPFV-SIM-2:SS=COND   eat-PFV-IMP
           'if you want, eat!'

(14.36)   *kashín yútashkuiŋ, wɨtathai mína aháhuiŋ takáakun*
           [kashini   yuta-cha-ku-ĩ=ka]   wɨ-tata-ha-i
           tomorrow   rain+IPFV-NEG-SIM+1/3-DS=COND   go+PFV-FUT-1SG-DECL
           mi=na   aha-hu-ĩ=ka   taka-a-ku-nu
           1sg=ACC garden-PSSD:1SG=LOC=TOP   work-IPFV-SIM-1SG:SS
           'if it doesn't rain tomorrow, I will go to work in my garden'

(14.37)   *kúntin kaútu wainkáik, piníha áushkam dakáka, kúntin minítkuiŋ*
           mantúmtayamɨ̃
           [kuntinu   kau-ta-u   waina-ka-i=ka]
           animal   assemble-APPLIC+IPFV-NMLZ   see-PFV+SEQ-1PL:SS=COND
           pini-ha   au=shakama   daka-ka
           build.hide-PFV+SEQ+1PL:SS   DIST=ADD   wait.for-PFV+SEQ+1PL:SS
           [kuntinu   mini-ta-ku-ĩ=ka]   mantu-ma-tayamɨ̃
           animal   arrive-APPL+IPFV-SIM+1/3-DS=COND   kill+APPL-REFL-NORM
           'if we have seen animals gathering (to eat), having built a hide and waited for them too, if the animals come we kill them' (Text 3:17)

(14.38)   *Miguel maámi, aɨnts hakámtaiŋ*
           Miguel   ma-a-mi   [aintsu   ha-ka-mataĩ=ka]
           Miguel   kill-PFV-HORT   person   die-PFV+SEQ-1/3:DS=COND
           'Let's kill Miguel if the person (that Miguel beat up) dies' (agr060816_01)

Examples of conditional clauses formed on other subordinate clause types are rare, but there is no reason to assume that it is not possible with all types. Example (14.39) shows a conditional clause formed on the non-inflecting subordinator -*ma*, and (14.40) shows an imperfective DS clause marked as a conditional clause.

(14.39)   *núwa shíkiamak wapíkmau túwahamɨ*
           [nuwa   shiki-a-ma=ka]   wapikama-u
           woman   urinate.on-IPFV-NSBJ>SBJ=COND   close.mouth+PFV-NMLZ

tuwahamɨ

NARR

'if a woman urinated (on the devil), he closed his mouth, they say'
(agr040719_13)

(14.40)　*hutíi áidauti wɨɰahiniŋ amɨ wákɨ bɨsɨmaŋ huwáktatmɨ*

[hutii　a-ina-u=ti　　　　　wɨ-a-hi-nɨ̃=ka]　　　amɨ

1pl　　COP-PL:IPFV-NMLZ=SAP　go-IPFV-1PL-DS=COND　2sg

wakɨ_bɨsɨmaŋ　　huwa-ka-tata-mɨ-i

sad　　　　　　stay-PFV-FUT-2-DECL

'if we go, you~SG~ will stay here (being) sad'

Counterfactual conditional linkages have the same form, but the apodosis takes the potential stem (14.41).

(14.41)　*núna washín dushíkiashkunuk tukúmain awakáhai*

[nu=na　　washi=na　　　　　dushiki-a-cha-ku-nu=ka]

ANA=ACC　spider.monkey=ACC　laugh.at-IMFPV-NEG-SIM-1SG:SS=COND

tuku-mai-inu　　awakɨ-ka-ha-i

shoot-POT-NMLZ　overcome-PFV-1SG-DECL

'if I hadn't laughed at that monkey, I would have been able to shoot it'
(agr041102_07)

Typically the protasis precedes the apodosis, but this is not always the case, as is shown by (14.38) above.

14.6.2 Concessive clauses

Concessive clauses are marked with the additive enclitic *=shakama ~ =sha* (glossed CONCESS when used in this function). They are formed on various kinds of subordinate clauses. Example (14.42) is from a story in which a young man goes to the river alone, even though he knows there is a man-eating jaguar in the vicinity.

(14.42)　*ímau ã̃ish, wɨɰak ukukíuwai*

[imau　　　a-ĩ=sha]　　　　　　wɨ-a-kũ

INTENS.LOC　exist+1/3-DS=CONCESS　go-IPFV-SIM+3:SS

uku-ki-u=ai

leave-PFV-NMLZ=COP:3:DECL

'although (the jaguar) was right there, he went (outside) and left'
(agr041005_14)

Example (14.43) is from the story of a man who tames a bear cub, naming it Chunu.

(14.43)   *"Chúnu minámɨk?" támash, áyatak ímau ɨkɨmsau*
          [chunu   mina-mɨ=ka   ta-ma=sha]   ayatak
          Chunu   arrive+IPFV-2=Q   say+IPFV-NSBJ>SBJ=CONCESS   only
          imau   ɨkɨma-sa-u
          INTENS.LOC   sit-PFV-NMLZ
          'although (the man) said "Chunu, are you coming?", (Chunu) just sat at
          a distance' (agr040721_08)

In examples (14.44) and (14.45) the concessive enclitic appears on a pro-verb forming a bridging construction, as discussed in §14.8.

(14.44)   *"wáamak huhuktáhum!" waháu, núnitãĩshkam antúkchahu áinawai*
          [waamakɨ   hu-hu-ki-ta-humɨ   waha-a-u]
          quickly   take-1SG.OBJ-PFV-IMP-2PL   call-IPFV-NMLZ
          [nu-ni-taĩ=shakama]BRIDGE   antu-ka-cha-aha-u
          ANA-VBLZ.INTR-SBD:1/3:DS=CONCESS   listen-PFV-NEG-PL-NMLZ
          a-ina-wa-i
          COP-PL:IPFV-3-DECL
          'he called out "quickly take me away!", but although he did that, they
          didn't listen' (agr041005_14)

(14.45)   *áshanta, washín iŋkuáŋhai, núniknush tukúshhai, ishiákhai*
          ashanta   washi=na   iŋkuã-ka-ha-i
          wife+VOC   spider.monkey=ACC   meet-PFV-1SG-DECL
          [nu-ni-ka-nu=sha]BRIDGE   tuku-cha-ha-i
          ANA-VBLZ.INTR-PFV+SEQ-1SG:SS=CONCESS   shoot+PFV-NEG-1SG-DECL
          ishia-ka-ha-i
          CAUS+flee-PFV-1SG-DECL
          'honey, I found a spider monkey, but I didn't shoot it; I scared it off'
          (agr041102_07)

The same marker *=sha(kama)* also appears on nominals and adverbs marking additive, and in that function also may give a concessive reading, as in example (14.46)
with the time word *káshi* 'at night'.

(14.46)   *wɨmí dɨkás káshish*
          wɨ-mi   dɨkas   kashi=sha
          go+PFV-HORT   really   night=ADD
          'let's go, really, even though (it is) night' (agr060816_01)

14.7 Coordination

There is no coordinating conjunction ('and'); clauses may be coordinated by asyndetic parataxis, but subordination is far more common than coordination. The advantage of subordination is that it offers richer options for expressing temporal and aspectual relations between the linked clauses. Bridging constructions (discussed in §14.8) also function as coordinators.

Two particles are used to link clauses but neither is a true coordinator. The particle *atsa* is used only in questions, typically to disjoin NPs, with the sense 'or'. A second particle *tuhã* can be used as a contrastive conjunction ('but') to link clauses but also appears in the absence of a clause linkage expressing counter-to-expectation, and is analysed as a discourse particle in §12.4.1.

14.7.1 Contrastive coordination

Contrast is expressed by two finite clauses, of which the second is introduced with *tuhã* 'but', often marked with the concessive enclitic *=sha(kama)*. Example (14.47) is illustrative.

(14.47)   *sĩnchi wakɨyahai wĩtasan, túhãsh kákahus wĩmáin atsúyi*
      sɨnchi   wakɨɯa-ya-ha-i   wɨ-tasa-nu
      strongly   want-REMPST-1SG-DECL   go+PFV-INTENT-1SG:SS
      tuhã=sha   kakahus   wɨ-mai-inu   atsu-yi
      but=CONCESS   easily   go-POT-NMLZ   exist:NEG-REMPST:3:DECL
      'I really wanted to go, but it was not easy to go' lit. *...it was not easily goable*' (agr040824_02)

Use of *tuhã* is not always strictly contrastive, and there is some semantic overlap with consequence linkage. There is an implication of unexpectedness in example (14.48): the subject knew that there was a jaguar prowling around so it is surprising that he decided to go outside alone.

(14.48)   *yúmi atsutáĩ túhãsh "ayú úntsu wikísh utithái" tus akaikíuwai*
      [yumi   atsu-taĩ]   **tuhã**=sha   [ayu   untsu
      water   exist:NEG-SBD:1/3:DS   **but**=CONCESS   ok   well
      wɨ-kĩ=sha   uti-ta-ha-i   tus]
      1sg-RESTR=ADD   bring+PFV-IFUT-1SG-DECL   say+SBD+3:SS

akai-ki-u=ai
go.down-PFV-NMLZ=COP:3:DECL
'there was no water, so he said "ok, well I'll bring it by myself" and
went down (to the well)' (agr041005_14)

The same particle may also mark a rejection linkage, of the type 'instead of x, y', as
in example (14.49).

(14.49) *dakítau apahĩhãĩ wĩtán, túhã dukuhĩhãĩ imáshi wĩɯau shíiŋ*
         [dakita-a-u   apa-hĩ=haĩ   wĩ-ta=na]   [**tuhã**
         refuse-IPFV-NMLZ father-PSSD:1PL/3=COM go-ACT.NMLZ=ACC   **but**
         duku-hĩ=haĩ   imashi   wĩ-a-u   shiiha]
         mother-PSSD:1PL/3=COM   INTENS.ADV   go-IPFV-NMLZ   well
         'He refused to go with his father, but went more with his mother.'
         (agr041005_15)

The particle *tuhã* must have originated as a marker of speaker's attitude, and is used
widely in speech reports in narrative. In example (14.50), a woman wants to bury
her dead baby, but every time she selects a spot, the villain Manchumush tells her
she cannot bury it there – the woman doesn't know that Manchumush is a cannibal,
and wants to eat the corpse. Use of *tuhã* reflects the woman's surprise that every
spot she asks about should turn out to be unsuitable.

(14.50) *"túhãsh tũwĩ́ ukumáinaitha?" tútãĩ...*
         tuhã=sha   tu=ĩ   uku-mai-inu=aita-ha   tu-taĩ
         but=CONCESS where=LOC bury-POT-NMLZ=COP-1SG   say-SBD:1/3:DS
         'saying "but where can I bury it?"...' (agr040721_07)

The fact that discourse markers such as *tuhã* typically appear in clause-initial position would have facilitated a reanalysis of [CLAUSE] [*tuhã* CLAUSE] as a contrast linkage [[CLAUSE] *tuhã* [CLAUSE]].

14.7.2 Disjunctive coordination

Disjunction uses *atsa* 'or' (14.51). It is only used in questions.

(14.51) *nihamánch wakĩɯamĩk, atsá tsabáu wakĩɯamĩk?*
         [nihamanchi   wakĩɯa-mĩ=ka]   **atsa** [tsamau   wakĩɯa-mĩ=ka]
         masato   want+IPFV-2=Q   **or**   *chapo*   want+IPFV-2=Q
         'Do you want *masato* (manioc beer) or *chapo* (plantain beer)?'

The verb of the second clause is typically the same, and can be omitted – so the construction is effectively NP disjunction. The word *atsa* also means 'no', and is related to the negative existential verb *atsut*; the use in questions can be considered as "thinking aloud", where the asker answers their own question (the first option) in the negative and then asks a second question: *do you want masato? ...no... do you want chapo?* This type of disjunction is very rare in my corpus, although probably more common in conversation.

14.8 Bridging constructions

As discussed above, Aguaruna lacks coordinating conjunctions, instead linking clauses by subordination, or occasionally juxtaposition. Bridging constructions constitute a third strategy, which can be considered a "best of both worlds" amalgam of subordination and coordination. There are two formally distinct bridging constructions in Aguaruna. The first uses a subordinate form of one of the pro-verbs described in §6.6.2, most commonly *nunit* and *dutikat* (both derived from the anaphoric pronoun *nu*). The pro-verb follows and recapitulates a finite clause, and is subordinate to a following clause. Such constructions have been labelled tail-head linkage in the literature, although Thompson, Longacre and Hwang (2007: 274) label this type that does not repeat the same lexical verb "summary-head" linkage. The second, less common, construction uses an oblique case-marked form of the anaphoric pronoun *nu* itself, which may follow a finite or subordinate verb. In the examples below, the pro-forms involved in bridging constructions are bracketed separately and labelled BRIDGE.

14.8.1 Verbal bridging constructions

Bridging pro-verbs appear immediately following a finite verb. The pro-verb refers anaphorically to the preceding clause, and indicates temporal/causal and switch-reference relations between it and the following clause. In example (14.52), the bridging construction shows that the action of the preceding clause is prior to that of the following clause, and that the subject is different; neither of these useful pieces of information is marked in the preceding clause itself, because it is an independent clause.

(14.52) *yunúmtukui, núnikmatãĩ núna achikúi aĩntsún páŋkĩ*
  [yunuma-tu-ka-u=i]   [nu-ni-ka-mataĩ]BRIDGE
  approach-APPL-PFV-NMLZ=COP:3:DECL   ANA-VBLZ.INTR-PFV+SEQ-1/3:DS

> [nu=na   achi-ka-u=i   aɨntsu=na   paŋkĩ]
> ANA=ACC   grab-PFV-NMLZ=COP:3:DECL   person=ACC   boa
> '(the person) approached (the boa), then the boa grabbed that person'
> (Text 1:8–9)

The bridging verb forms a separate clause syntactically, subordinate to and intonationally grouped with the following finite clause, and functions much like a conjunction. In example (14.53), a bridging nmlz construction indicates a consequence relation between the two clauses.

(14.53)   *mína apáŋ maŋkaŋtuáu áyi, núnikmatã̃́ áuhtsuk papínak puhúyahai*
           [mi=na   apa-hu   maŋkahatu-a-u   a-yi]
           1sg=ACC   father-PSSD:1SG   kill+1PL.OBJ-PFV-NMLZ COP-REMPST:3:DECL
           [nu-ni-ka-matã̃́]BRIDGE   [auhu-tsu-u=ka   papi=na=ka
           ANA-VBLZ.INTR-PFV+SEQ-1/3:DS   study-NEG-NMLZ=TOP   book=ACC=TOP
           puhu-ya-ha-i]
           live-REMPST-1SG-DECL
           'my father killed a person, and because of that, I was unable to study
           (because the family had to go into hiding for fear of retribution)'
           (agr040824_02)

A bridging verb may take the conditional enclitic, as in example (14.54), where the bridging verb functions as a disjunctive coordinator.

(14.54)   *miercolestin wɨ́tathai, núniashkunuk viernestin wɨ́tathai*
           [*miercoles*-tin   wɨ-tata-ha-i]
           Wednesday-TIME   go+PFV-FUT-1SG-DECL
           [nu-ni-a-sha-ku-nu=**ka**]BRIDGE   [*viernes*-tin
           ANA-VBLZ.INTR-IPFV-NEG-SIM-1SG:SS=**COND**   Friday-TIME
           wɨ-tata-ha-i]
           go+PFV-FUT-1SG-DECL
           'I'll go on Wednesday, or if not, I'll go on Friday'

Examples (14.44) and (14.45) above showed that bridging verbs also may take concessive marking. As mentioned, the most commonly used pro-verbs in bridging constructions are those derived from the anaphoric pronoun *nu*. Example (14.55) illustrates the transitive form *dutika-* < *nu-tika-* 'ANA-VBLZ.TR-'.

(14.55)   *nṹwĩ háta múun achiŋkábi, dútihuamtã̃́ ashí hakábiahai*
           [nu=ĩ   ha-ta   muunta   achi-hu-ka-mayi]
           ANA=LOC   be.sick-ACT.NMLZ big   grab-1SG.OBJ-PFV-INTPST:3:DECL

[nu-tika-hu-a-mataĩ]ʙʀɪᴅɢᴇ   [ashi   ha-ka-maya-ha-i]
ANA-VBLZ.TR-1SG.OBJ-PFV+SEQ-1/3:DS   all   die-PFV-INTPST-1SG-DECL
'a big sickness grabbed me, when that happened to me, I almost died'
(agr040824_02)

Example (14.56) illustrates an intransitive pro-verb formed from the intensifier *ima*, giving *imanit* 'do so much'.

(14.56)   *nuŋkának kuwíŋ ĩmau, imánitãĩ titú díis, titú díis...*
        [nuŋka=na=ka   kuwiha   ima-u]
        ground=ACC=TOP   soft   take+IPFV-NMLZ
        [ima-ni-taĩ]ʙʀɪᴅɢᴇ   [titu   dii-sã   titu
        INTENS-VBLZ.INTR-SBD:1/3:DS   still   look-SBD+3:SS   still
        dii-sã]
        look-SBD+3:SS
        '(as the jaguar roared) it made the ground shake, as it did that so much, they just kept watching quietly...' (agr041005_14)[2]

Bridging verbs are very common in narrative, providing textual cohesion by linking finite clauses. The discourse functions of bridging constructions are discussed further in §18.5.

14.8.2 Pronominal bridging constructions

Unlike the verbal type, bridging anaphoric pronoun *nu* normally appears directly following a subordinate clause, and serves to specify that clause's relation with the controlling clause. Bridging *nu* appears either with locative or instrumental case, marking a temporal or causal relation respectively. This is the only marking strategy that explicitly differentiates these two semantic types in constructions where a subordinate clause expresses an action prior to that of the controlling clause. Example (14.57) illustrates the locative case-marked form, and example (14.58) illustrates instrumental case marking.

---

2 This example is not entirely straightforward. The context is that a group of men are trying to trap and kill a jaguar, and are hiding as they watch it go into the trap they have made. The jaguar roars loud enough to shake the ground, expressed literally as "taking the ground (to a state of being) soft" while the men remain in hiding.

(14.57)   *Arias Pablohãĩ máimtãĩ, núw̃ĩ máithai*
            [*Arias   Pablo=haĩ   mai-mataĩ*]   [nu=ĩ]BRIDGE
            Arias   Pablo=COM   bathe+PFV+SEQ-1/3:DS   ANA=LOC
            [mai-ta-ha-i]
            bathe+PFV-IFUT-1SG-DECL
            'After Arias and Pablo have bathed, then I'll bathe'

(14.58)   *ashinká, dúwi botenum chimpimhá...*
            [ashina-ka]   [nu=i]BRIDGE   [*bote*=numa
            finish-PFV+SEQ+1PL:SS   ANA=INS   boat=LOC
            chimpima-ha]
            board:PL-PFV+SEQ+1PL:SS
            'because we had finished (the class), we boarded the boat (to go
            home)...' (agr040824_02)

Although typically used to relate a subordinate clause to its controlling clause, the
pronominal bridging construction can also function as a coordinator linking finite
clauses, as in example (14.59). Pronominal bridging is much less common in narrative than the verbal type.

(14.59)   *sïmahai, dúwi kaháŋ puhúŋtawai*
            [sïma-a-ha-i]   [nu=i]BRIDGE   [kaha-hu
            sweat-IPFV-1SG-DECL   ANA=INS   sleepiness-PSSD:1SG
            puhu-hu-ta-wa-i]
            live-APPL-1SG.OBJ+IPFV-3-DECL
            'I'm hot, so I'm tired'

14.8.3 Functions of bridging constructions

Bridging constructions are a conspicuous and distinctive feature of Aguaruna narrative, and play an important role in discourse organization. The widespread use of
bridging constructions underscores the pervasiveness of overt verbal markers of
reference tracking (i.e. switch-reference) in Aguaruna discourse, as it functionally
extends the phenomenon to the linkage between finite clauses. Pronominal bridging plays a useful role in eliminating the ambiguity that is inherent in prior action
linkages between temporal and consequence linkage.

15 Nominalization

15.1 Preliminary remarks

I assume a definition of nominalization as an operation that forms a nominal grammatical unit from some non-nominal unit; the resulting form has the same syntactic properties as other nominals, in particular the ability to constitute an NP and function as an argument of a predicate. Nominalizations take the morphology appropriate to the nominal class, with a few restrictions; and some nominalizations can be marked for a restricted set of verbal grammatical categories. Morphological details are described in §15.3. The class of nominals in Aguaruna encompasses both nouns and adjectives (see Chapter 4), and nominalizations share the syntactic properties that are common to this class; nominalizations vary in the extent to which they can be possessed (§15.3), a key feature that sets nouns apart from adjectives. Also unlike adjectives, nominalizations are not gradable. The nominalizations described in this chapter are all derived from verbal roots, and nominals cannot be derived from other word classes. Among deverbal nominalizations we can distinguish between lexical and clausal nominalization, the former taking only the verb as its target, the latter taking a whole clause. In the case of clausal nominalization, there is no evidence that the nominalized verb is functioning as a noun heading an NP; instead, the whole clause headed by the nominalized verb functions as an NP.[1] Applying this distinction to the data discussed below, we find that Aguaruna nominalizations are generally more like the clausal model, but the distinction between clausal and lexical nominalization is not clear-cut. Firstly, some of the same suffixes that form clausal nominalizations also form lexical nominalizations, with corresponding syntactic differences: as derived nouns, lexical nominalizations head NPs, and any notional arguments and modifiers must conform to the internal syntax characteristic of NPs (§15.2). Secondly, although clausal nominalizations typically constitute whole NPs, they may take preposed determiners and postposed modifiers, suggesting that this is not simply a case of a nominalized clause filling an NP slot. Clausal nominalizations also function as relative clauses, modifying an NP with a lexical head (Chapter 16).

There are eight nominalizing suffixes in Aguaruna, all of which are completely productive. The suffixes are listed in Table 15.1 along with their meanings, that is,

---

1 Similarly, Comrie and Thompson (2007: 377), describing nominalization in Mojave, say that "it is more appropriate … to view clauses as undergoing certain modifications which allow them to function as noun phrases rather than to think of the verb itself as having become a noun in such nominalizations."

the referent of the nominalization, and the stem(s) that each suffix can combine with.

Table 15.1: Nominalizing suffixes

suffix	referent	stem(s) selected
-ta	action	unmarked
-inu	subject participant	unmarked or potential
-taĩ	non-subject participant	unmarked
-u	subject participant	perfective or imperfective[2]
-mau	non-subject participant or action	perfective or imperfective
-tinu	participant + FUTURE	perfective
-chau	participant + NEGATIVE	perfective, imperfective or unmarked
-haku	subject participant + REMOTE PAST	unmarked

The resulting nominalizations differ according to (i) whether they refer to the verbal action itself or to a participant; (ii) the verbal grammatical categories marked in the nominalized verb; and (iii) treatment of overt arguments of the nominalized verb. The nominalizers are briefly presented in the remainder of this section, and their properties are described more fully in the following sections.

The action nominalizer *-ta* is suffixed to the unmarked stem and forms an abstract nominal referring to the action of the verb. The remaining six nominalizers all refer to participants. The four most commonly encountered are those in rows 2–5 of Table 15.1, which form a natural grouping with the distinction between them defined by the two parameters of the referent – subject or non-subject – and the stem to which they may be attached – unmarked or aspect-marked. These parameters are laid out in Table 15.2.

Table 15.2: Participant nominalizers: referent and stem selection

	subject referent	non-subject referent
unmarked stem	*-inu*	*-taĩ*
aspect marked stem	*-u*	*-mau*

---

2 A few examples show *-u* attached to an unmarked stem, always in a specific construction of the form: *unmarked.stem*-NEG-NMLZ=TOP, with first-person singular referent (see example 15.100 below). This construction is described in §11.1.

Two further participant nominalizers are transparently morphologically complex, although they cannot be treated as synchronically compositional. These are the future participant nominalizer *-tinu* < *-ta* FUTURE (§8.4.4) + *-inu*; and the negative participant nominalizer *-chau* < *-cha* NEG (§11.1) + *-u*. The non-subject participant nominalizer *-mau* and the remote past subject nominalizer *-haku* (see below) both also may historically involve the subject nominalizer *-u*.

The remote past subject nominalizer *-haku* appears in narratives and is functionally part of the tense marking system. Although I have labelled this form a nominalizer, it is not entirely so: unlike other nominalizations, NPs formed with *-haku* can only appear in copula complement function; in other words, these forms never refer, but only predicate. This syntactic restriction means that *-haku* does not fit the definition of nominalization given above, as it does not have the same syntactic distribution as other nominals. By morphological criteria, however, forms with *-haku* do behave as nominals, and as such are most appropriately described in this chapter. The suffix *-haku* must be a nominalizer etymologically, and its range of syntactic freedom has reduced as it grammaticalized into a verbal tense marker. In §15.5 I discuss further the interaction of nominalizations with the verbal TAM marking system.

In the following sections I first describe the internal syntax of nominalizations and show that this is consistent with the clausal nature of the construction. Next I describe the morphology of nominalized verbs, in terms of verbal and nominal grammatical categories associated with them, and finally I describe the range of functions associated with nominalizations in Aguaruna.

15.2 Internal syntax of nominalizations

I noted above that Aguaruna nominalization is typically a clause-level process. Genetti (2011: 164) represents clausal nominalization schematically as in (15.1).

(15.1)   [(NP) ... V-NMLZ]$_{NP}$

The operation applies to a clause and results in an NP. Crucially, there is no evidence that the resulting NP is headed by a derived noun, and the internal syntax is that of a clause, rather than that of an NP headed by a noun. The standard model of deverbal lexical nominalization (derivational nominalization, in Genetti's 2011 terminology), meanwhile, involves the change of a verb to a noun through the addition of nominalizing morphology (15.2).

(15.2)   [V-NMLZ]$_N$

For such a constituent to head an NP, notional arguments of the verb and any adverbial material must take on the morphological and syntactic properties appropriate to NP internal syntax.

Givón (2001) represents lexical nominalization as the adjustment of clausal to NP syntax – the finite clause in (15.3a) is nominalized to give (15.3b).

(15.3) a. She *knew* mathematics well.
        b. Her good *knowledge* of mathematics.

(Givón 2001: 25)

In addition to the loss of finite verbal categories (past tense in this example) and the overt morphological marking of nominalization (*know → know-ledge*), the morphosyntactic adjustments noted by Givón (2001: 25) include "subject and/or object acquiring *genitive* case-marking" (*she → her*; *mathematics → of mathematics*) and "conversion of adverbs into *adjectives*" (*well → good*). These two criteria are relevant to the distinction I shall make between lexical and clausal nominalizations in Aguaruna. In distinguishing between lexical and clausal nominalization, the morphological and syntactic properties of notional clausal constituents become diagnostic criteria; consequently, when a nominalization consists only of the nominalized verb, it is impossible to test whether it is lexical or clausal. Given the relative scarcity of unambiguously lexical nominalizations in Aguaruna, it seems reasonable to assume that they are ultimately lexicalized from reanalysed clausal nominalizations in which only the verb is overt (15.4).

(15.4)   [Ø V-NMLZ]$_{NP}$ →   [V-NMLZ]$_N$

All arguments of clausal nominalizations may be overtly realized, although typically they are not. When the aspect-marked nominalizations formed with *-u* and *-mau* function as relative clauses, the common argument is typically (but apparently not obligatorily) omitted ("gapped").

Overt subjects of clausal nominalizations take nominative case. Objects take accusative case in the subject nominalizations formed with *-inu* (15.5), *-u* (15.6), *-tinu* (15.7), *-chau* (15.8) and *-haku* (15.9) and nominative case in non-subject nominalizations formed with *-taĩ* (15.10) and *-mau* (15.11).

(15.5)   *wíi uchín chicháhin atáhai*
            wi   [uchi=**na**   chicha-hu-**inu**]   a-ta-ha-i
            1sg   child=ACC   speak-APPL-**NMLZ**   COP-IFUT-1SG-DECL
            'I will be the children's advisor' (agr040723_29)

(15.6)   *núna kaŋkapín nuwín íntsámhuinaushkam*
          [[nu=**na**   kaŋkapɨ=**na**   nuwĩ=**na**]
          ANA=**ACC**   *Kagkap*=**ACC**   woman+PSSD:1PL/3=**ACC**
          ɨntsamahu-ina-**u**=shakama]ₙₚ
          have.sex-PL:IPFV-**NMLZ**=ADD
          'also those who were having sex with Kagkap's wife' (agr041005_14)

(15.7)   *ápa ámina "míhãĩ nuwínati" tus suhustíñĩ*
          apa   ami=**na**   [mi=haĩ   nuwina-ti
          father:PSSD:2   2sg=ACC   1sg=COM   marry+PFV-JUSS
          tus]
          say+SBD+3:SS   su-hu-sa-**tinu**=ɨ
                           give-1SG.OBJ-PFV-**FUT+NMLZ**=NONVIS.COP:3
          'your father will give you to me in marriage' (see §17.1 for an explana-
          tion of the semi-direct speech report)

(15.8)   *bukintín yúchauwaithai*
          bukinti=**na**   yu-**chau**=aita-ha-i
          palm.grub=**ACC**   eat-**NEG.NMLZ**=COP-1SG-DECL
          'I don't eat palm grubs'

(15.9)   *datɨmá amúhakun...*
          [datɨma   amu-**haku**-nu]
          ayahuasca+**ACC**   drink-**NARR.PST**-1SG:SS
          'I used to drink ayahuasca...' (agr040723_03)

(15.10)   *buukɨa pakátãĩnum ɨhɨ̃ɰ̃ãũ*
          [buukɨa   paka-**taĩ**=numa]   i-hɨɰa-u
          skull   peel-**NSBJ.NMLZ**=LOC   CAUS-arrive+IPFV-NMLZ
          'he brought them to the place where skulls were skinned (to make
          shrunken heads)' (agr040712_02)

(15.11)   *mína núwa chíŋkim tsupíŋkamun wainkáttawai*
          [mi=na   nuwa   chiŋkimi   tsupi-hu-ka-**mau**=na]
          1sg=ACC   wife   firewood   cut-APPL-PFV-**NSBJ.NMLZ**=ACC
          waina-ka-tata-wa-i
          see-PFV-FUT-3-DECL
          'he will see my wife, for whom firewood was cut'
          OR
          'he will see the firewood that was cut for my wife'

Note that the accusative-marked objects follow the same split as in finite clauses; where the subject is first person plural or second person, third person object NPs are not marked with accusative case (§7.3). This is the case in example (15.49) below. Example (15.83) below shows that SAP objects do receive accusative case marking in nominalized clauses even where third person objects are unmarked.

All five of the major nominalizers appear to form lexical nouns, as in examples (15.12–15.16), and -*u* may also form lexical adjectives as in (15.17). These lexicalized forms are the exception rather than the rule, however, as nominalization is productive only as a clause level operation in Aguaruna.

(15.12) *háta*
         ha-ta
         be.sick-ACT.NMLZ
         'sickness'

(15.13) *hintínkaŋtin*
         hintintu-kahatu-inu
         teach-1PL.OBJ-NMLZ
         'teacher' lit. *one who teaches us*[3]

(15.14) *yutã̃ĩ*
         yu-taĩ
         eat-NSBJ.NMLZ
         'food'

(15.15) *wáimaku*
         waima-ka-u
         see.vision-PFV-NMLZ
         'a person who has received spirit power from seeing a vision'

(15.16) *aúŋmatbau*
         auhuma-ta-mau
         tell.story-APPL+IPFV-NSBJ.NMLZ
         'traditional story'

---

3 Note also that the verb *hintintut* 'teach' is formed with the possessed noun *hintĩ* 'our path' and a verbalizing suffix -*tu*.

(15.17)   *mamukú*
          mamu-ka-u
          wear.out-PFV-NMLZ
          'worn out'

By the definition given above, the derived lexical nouns can head NPs, and any overt arguments and modifiers must conform to NP internal syntax. When such elements are overt, therefore, their form becomes diagnostic of lexical as opposed to clausal nominalization.

In Aguaruna, notional subjects of lexical nominalizations appear as possessors, and are marked on the nominalized verb itself (15.18–15.20) and with appropriate form if the possessor is overt, in conformity to NP internal syntax (15.19, 15.20). If the notional subject is represented as an overt NP, it is marked as possessor, with accusative case if it is pronominal (15.19, 15.20) or genitive case if it is a noun (15.21, the title of a collection of traditional stories; see §4.10.3 for a description of genitive forms and §5.6 on the possessive NP).

(15.18)   *shinutáĩhĩ*
          shinu-**taĩ**-hĩ
          sing-**NSBJ.NMLZ**-PSSD:1PL/3
          'its song (i.e. of a bird)' (agr041005_17)

(15.19)   *mína puhutáiŋ*
          mi=na   puhu-**taĩ**-hu
          1sg=ACC   live-**NSBJ.NMLZ**-1SG
          'where I live', 'my home'

(15.20)   *húwai mína puhúthuk*
          hu=ai   [mi=na   puhu-**ta**-hu=ka]
          PROX=COP:3:DECL   1sg=ACC   live-**ACT.NMLZ**-1SG=TOP
          'this is my life' (agr040824_02)

(15.21)   <duik muunta pujuti augbatbau>
          [duwik_muunta   puhu-**tĩ**]
          ancestor+GEN   live-**ACT.NMLZ+PSSD:1PL/3**
          auhuma-ta-mau
          tell.story-APPL+IPFV-NSBJ.NMLZ
          'stories of the ancestors' lives'
                                                    (Kasen Elena et al. 1992)

In example (15.22) the possession relation is not marked on the possessed noun, but the notional subject is marked with the possessive suffix. Given that this is a usual second strategy for marking possession in an NP (§5.6), presumably this should also be analysed as an example of lexical nominalization with possessive-marked subject.

(15.22)   *mídau takát atsáwai*
          [mi-nau   taka-**ta**]   atsa-wa-i
          1sg-POSS   work-**ACT.NMLZ**   exist:NEG+IPFV-3-DECL
          'I have no work' lit. *my work does not exist*

There does not appear to be any possibility of including overt notional objects with lexical nominalizations: if an object appears, the whole nominalization takes the clausal form, with the subject taking nominative case and the object taking accusative or nominative case as described above.

With respect to the second criterion mentioned above, namely conversion of adverbs into adjectives, examples are much more scarce. It is certainly the case that clausal nominalizations can include adverbs (15.23) and subordinate clauses (15.24), neither of which appears in NPs headed by underived nouns.

(15.23)   *yamá nahánɨtnumak*
          yama   nahanɨ-**ta**=numa=ka
          newly   create-**ACT.NMLZ**=LOC=TOP
          'in the beginning' (formula used to introduce traditional stories)
          (agr040720_04)

(15.24)   *nihámchi nampɨká̃ hiínunashkam húwau*
          [nihamchi   nampɨ-kã̃   hiina-**u**=na=shakama]
          [masato.ACC   get.drunk-PFV+3:SS   go.out+IPFV-**NMLZ**=ACC=ADD]NP
          hu-a-u
          take-PFV-NMLZ
          '(the devil) also took (people) who left the house having got drunk on *masato*' (agr040719_13)[4]

A lexical nominalization would be modified by an adjective, rather than an adverb. In my corpus I have come across only one such example (15.25), in which the adjective *muun* 'big' modifies the nominalization *hata* 'sickness'.

---

4 The final word of this example is a nominalization functioning as a finite verb, described in §15.5.3. The same is the case in example (15.26).

(15.25)   *nŭw̃ĩ háta múun achiŋkábi*
          nu=ĩ   [ha-**ta**   muunta] achi-hu-ka-mayi
          ANA=LOC be.sick-**ACT.NMLZ** big   grab-1SG.OBJ-PFV-INTPST:3:DECL
          'then I got really sick' lit. *a big sickness took hold of me* (agr040824_02)

Although I have no other examples of nominalizations directly modified by adjectives, there is evidence that the lexical nominalization in (15.18) above is a derived noun, as it shows the discourse property of persistence (see §5.10). Example (15.26) appears later in the same narrative, where the adjective *muun* 'big' forms a headless NP, and it is clear from context that the understood head is the nominalization *shinutaĩ* 'song'.

(15.26)   *níŋka muúntan shináu*
          nĩ=ka   [muunta=na]ₙₚ   shina-u
          3sg=TOP big=ACC   sing+IPFV-NMLZ
          'it (the *kúgkup* bird) sang a big (song)' *i.e. it sang loudly* (agr041005_17)

In Table 15.3 the distinct syntactic properties of clausal and lexical nominalizations are contrasted. In the remainder of this section I address some less clear-cut aspects of the distinction.

Table 15.3: Properties of clausal and lexical nominalizations

	clausal	lexical
marking of subject	nominative	possessor
marking of object	accusative or nominative	–
modifier	adverb	adjective

As noted above, possession marking associated with nominalized verbs can be analysed as a reflex of the notional subject argument. Some nominalizations, however, show a combination of syntactic properties. Aspectualized non-subject nominalizations may take possession marking as in (15.27), but an overt subject NP remains in nominative case, as in the clausal nominalization in (15.28).

(15.27)   *nĩ puhámuhin w̃ĩ wainkámhai*
          [nĩ   puha-**mau**-hĩ=na]   wi   waina-ka-ma-ha-i
          3sg live+IPFV-**NSBJ.NMLZ**-PSSD:1PL/3=ACC   1sg see-PFV-RECPST-1SG-DECL
          'I saw where he lives'

(15.28)   *Pablo puhámunmaya mináwai*
          [*Pablo*   puha-**mau**=numa=ya]   mina-wa-i
          Pablo   live+IPFV-**NSBJ.NMLZ**=LOC=ABL   arrive+IPFV-3-DECL
          '(someone) from where Pablo lives is coming'

As shown above, action nominalizations with *-ta* are readily possessed, and the possessor may be the notional subject of the verb, as in (15.20). However, the morphological possessor of a *-ta* nominalization need not be a notional argument of the verb at all. Consider (15.29), in which the second person possessor marked on the verb is not the notional subject, rather it is the expected or intended subject. And in (15.30), the possessor *apahui* 'God' is similarly a beneficiary but presumably not expected to be the one who does the work.

(15.29)   *umiŋkáthamɨ takathúmin*
          umi-hu-ka-ta-hamɨ   [taka-ta-hu-mi=na]
          complete-APPL-PFV-IFUT-1SG>2SG+DECL   work-ACT.NMLZ-PSSD-2=ACC
          'I'll do your work (for you)'

(15.30)   *apahúi takatḯ idáyas...*
          [apahui   taka-tḯ]   idaya-sã
          God+GEN   work-ACT.NMLZ+PSSD:1PL/3+ACC   leave-SBD+3:SS
          'abandoning God's work...' (agr060816_01)

In sum, it is not straightforwardly the case that lexical nominalizations involve possession morphology marking the subject relation, although the pattern is clearly apparent. The evidence from internal syntax shows that the nominalizing suffixes *-ta* and *-taḯ* are used for both clausal and lexical nominalization, with different syntactic structures associated with the two types. The examples given above suggest that the same holds true for the other nominalizers, but the scarcity of examples with overt arguments or modifiers means that there is no evidence available to support this hypothesis.

15.3 Morphology of nominalizations

The morphology associated with nominalizations can be described in three categories: firstly, the verbal stem to which the nominalizing suffix is attached may include verbal suffixes. Secondly, nominalizations take nominal morphology following the nominalizing suffix. And thirdly, despite their nominal status, nominalizations occasionally take verbal morphology following the nominalizing suffix. The appearance of verbal morphology on nominalizations is sporadic and not fully productive, and never combines with nominal morphology. Both of these factors suggest that this is a byproduct of reanalysis of the nominalization as an inflected verb. The three sets of phenomena are described in order below.

15.3.1 Verbal grammatical categories in nominalizations

In §13.1, nominalizations and other verb forms were arranged as a cline of decategorization, manifested in a reduction of verbal grammatical categories. Finite, independent verbs are at one extreme, and nominalizations at the other, manifesting a reduced set of verbal grammatical categories with respect to both finite and subordinate verbs. Categories that may be marked in all nominalizations are those in the derivational slots: valency changing in slot A and object markers in slot B. These form the unmarked stem. Some nominalizations also take aspect marking (slot C); imperfective aspect marks plural with a portmanteau suffix in slot C1, while perfective aspect in slot C1 can combine with plural subject marking in slot C2 (see §8.3 for details). Slots A to C form the aspect marked stem. The two stems are illustrated schematically in Figure 15.1. Negation, in slot D, may combine with unmarked and aspect marked stems, but has some idiosyncratic restrictions as discussed below.

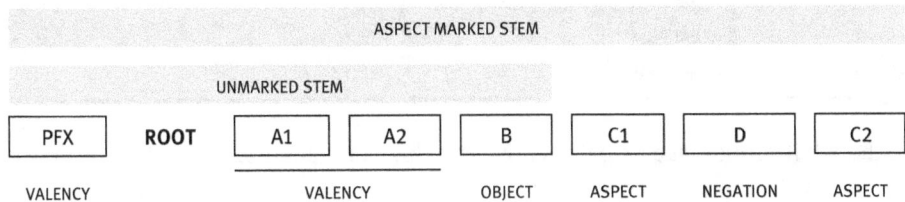

Figure 15.1: Unmarked and aspectualized stems

In addition to the unmarked stem, the subject nominalizer *-inu* may be suffixed to the potential stem with *-mai* (example 15.31); this option is not available to the other nominalizers. The potential suffix takes slot C, replacing aspect marking, but is incompatible with plural marking.

(15.31) *wainmáinaithai*
         waina-mai-**inu**=aita-ha-i
         see-POT-**NMLZ**=COP-1SG-DECL
         'I can see'

Negation in slot D can be included in unmarked or aspectualized stems, but does not combine with the subject nominalizer *-inu* or the remote past nominalizer *-haku*. The negative nominalizer *-chau* is etymologically a combination of negative *-cha* and nominalizer *-u*, but is analysed as a distinct suffix synchronically because of its non-combinatorial properties, in particular the ambiguity of participant reference (§15.4.3). This means that synchronically, negative *-cha* is also incompatible with subject nominalizer *-u* and the negative nominalizer *-chau* (very rarely, the negative suffix *-tsu* combines with the subject nominalizer *-u*, with no aspect marking – this construction is described in §11.1). Table 15.4 summarizes the combinatorial possibilities of potential and negative marking with nominalizations.

Table 15.4: Combinations of nominalizers with potential and negative stems

nominalizer	gloss	potential -mai	negative -cha
-ta	ACTION	–	✓
-inu	SUBJECT	✓	–
-taɨ	NON-SUBJECT	–	✓
-u	SUBJECT	–	(✓)
-mau	NON-SUBJECT	–	✓
-tinu	FUTURE	–	✓
-chau	NEGATIVE	–	–
-haku	REMOTE PAST	–	–

Although it cannot take verbal negative marking, a nominalization with *-inu* may be negated with the addition of *-chau* (15.32), which attaches to nominal as well as verbal stems.

(15.32) *wɨmáinchau*
wɨ-mai-inu-chau
go-POT-NMLZ-NEG.NMLZ
'one who is unable to go'

Nominalizations formed on the aspectualized stems have the semantic effect of locating the state of affairs described in time as an actual event, whereas that of an unmarked nominalization is a habitual or potential action that becomes a property of the referent. Compare the pairs of examples in (15.33a, b) and (15.34a, b).

(15.33) a. *úmau*
uma-**u**
drink+IPFV-**NMLZ**
'one who is drinking'

b. *úmin*
   umu-**inu**
   drink-NMLZ
   'a drinker'

(15.34) a. *yuwámu*
   yu-a-**mau**
   eat-PFV-**NSBJ.NMLZ**
   'what was eaten'

b. *yútãĩ*
   yu-**taĩ**
   eat-NSBJ.NMLZ
   'food'

Examples (15.35) and (15.36) illustrate the semantic effect of the selection of aspectualized stems, imperfective and perfective respectively.

(15.35)   *támaun antúkmahai*
   ta-**mau**=na   antu-ka-ma-ha-i
   say+IPFV-**NSBJ.NMLZ**=ACC   hear-PFV-RECPST-1SG-DECL
   'I heard what was being said'

(15.36)   *tímaun antúkmahai*
   ti-**mau**=na   antu-ka-ma-ha-i
   say+PFV-**NSBJ.NMLZ**=ACC   hear-PFV-RECPST-1SG-DECL
   'I heard (secondhand) what had been said'

The negative nominalizer *-chau* is the only one that may appear with either aspectualized (15.37a) or unmarked stems (15.37b); recall from Table 15.4 that the nominalizer *-inu* cannot co-occur with the negative marker – negative *-chau* fills this gap.

(15.37) a. *yuwáchu*
   yu-a-**chau**
   eat-PFV-**NEG.NMLZ**
   'one who has not eaten'

b. *yúchau*
   yu-**chau**
   eat-NEG.NMLZ
   'one who does not eat'

The negative nominalizer can function as the negative counterpart for all subject nominalizations. Object nominalizations are negated by combining negative *-cha* with a nominalizer, as in example (15.38), a common term used to describe a visitor who arrives unannounced.

(15.38)   *páchiashbau*
           pachi-a-cha-mau
           consider-IPFV-NEG-NSBJ.NMLZ
           '(one who is) unexpected'

15.3.2 Nominal morphology associated with nominalizations

Nominalizations take nominal morphology following the nominalizing suffix. They vary in the nominal morphology they can take, as shown in Table 15.5. All can take the copula enclitic and function as copula complement. All the participant nominalizations except remote past *-haku* can take nominative, accusative and oblique cases. Vocative and possession marking are in complementary distribution, and this can be ascribed to the semantics of the nominalizations: subject nominalizations typically have human referents, and can therefore take vocative marking but cannot be possessed, while non-subject forms typically have non-human referents, and can be possessed but are not compatible with vocative marking. The action nominalizer *-ta* can take nominative and accusative cases, but cannot take oblique cases except for locative case in an aspectual construction described in §15.4.5 below.

Table 15.5: Nominal morphology with nominalizations

suffix	core cases	oblique cases	vocative	possession	copula
-ta	yes	only locative	no	yes	yes
-inu	yes	all	yes	no	yes
-taí	yes	all	no	yes	yes
-u	yes	all	yes	no	yes
-mau	yes	all	no	yes	yes
-tinu	yes	all	yes	no	yes
-chau	yes	all	no data	no	yes
-haku	no	none	no	no	yes

All of the non-subject nominalizations and the action nominalization can be possessed using the suffixing possession morphology. Only *-ta* action nominalizations are sometimes declined as vowel-changing, sometimes as suffixing (see §4.8 for details of nominal possession marking).

15.3.3 Verbal morphology

In addition to the verbal grammatical categories that are marked in the nominalized stem, verbal markers of first person singular subject occasionally appear on nominalized verbs, suggesting that they have been reanalysed as predicates of subordinate or finite clauses. This reanalysis can also affect constituent ordering and NP marking within relative clauses (cf. examples with *-mau* in §15.4.2). The verbal suffixes involved are the subordinate verb first person singular subject marker *-nu* and the finite first person singular subject marker *-ha* (followed by declarative *-i*). In (15.39) a subject nominalization with *-inu* and is followed by the same-subject subordinate-clause first-person subject marker *-nu* and the concessive enclitic *=sha(kama)*; and in (15.40) the same nominalizer is followed by the main-clause first-person subject suffix *-ha* and declarative mood marker *-i*.

(15.39)   *wáŋka wíi húninchinush uchín imátikan puháha*

    waŋka   [wi   hu-ni-inu-uchi-**nu**=sha]   uchi=na

    why   1SG   PROX-VBLZ.INTR-NMLZ-DIM-**1SG:SS**=CONCESS   child=ACC

    ima-tika-nu   puha-ha

    INTENS-VBLZ.TR+PFV+SEQ-1SG:SS   live+IPFV-1SG

    'why, although I am so insignificant, do I have so many children?' (agr041005_16)

(15.40)   *"dakítnuhai" tímahai*

    <u>dakitu-inu-**ha**-i</u>   ti-ma-ha-i

    refuse-NMLZ-**1SG**-DECL   say+PFV-RECPST-1SG-DECL

    'I said I didn't want (it)'

The negative nominalizer *-chau* typically takes the copula enclitic when it is functioning predicatively, but may take main-clause person marking directly, without the copula enclitic, as in example (15.41).

(15.41)   *bukintín yúchauhai*

    bukinti=na   yu-chau-**ha**-i

    palm.grub=ACC   eat-NEG.NMLZ-**1SG**-DECL

    'I don't eat palm grubs'

The form in (15.41) is apparently stylistically preferred to the equally grammatical (15.42), with the copula enclitic.

(15.42)   *bukintín yúchauwaithai*
            bukinti=na   yu-chau=**aita-ha**-i
            palm.grub=ACC   eat-NEG.NMLZ=**COP-1SG**-DECL
            'I don't eat palm grubs'

The aspectualized subject nominalizer *-u* can take subordinate-clause person marking as in (15.43).

(15.43)   *"Belén wɨún wákɨthai" táwai*
            [*Belen*   wɨ-u-**nu**]   wakɨta-ha-i
            Belén   go+PFV-NMLZ-**1SG:SS**   return+IPFV-1SG-DECL
            ta-wa-i
            say+IPFV-3-DECL
            'he says: "I'm returning from Belén (village)"'

Finally, the remote past subject nominalizer *-haku* also occasionally appears with subordinate clause first person singular subject marking. Example (15.44) is taken from a man's description of the preparation for battle he underwent as a youth. The idiom 'follow the path' refers to the metaphorical path of preparation for battle that young men traditionally undertook, and 'dreamed of a waterfall' means he went to a waterfall and had dreams, that is, hallucinations produced by the plant preparations he was drinking. Of particular note is the fact that the consultant felt that each of these nominalized verbs should be transcribed as two phonological words – this is reflected in the word division of the first line.

(15.44)   *wíthai hintá aintú hakún, datɨmá amú hakún, baikuá amú hakún,*
            tsaaŋkú amú hakún, tunanásh kahamín áyahai
            wi=ita-ha-i   [hinta   aintu-**haku**-nu]
            1sg=COP-1SG-DECL   path+ACC   follow-**NARR.PST**-1SG:SS
            [datɨma   amu-**haku**-nu]   [baikua
            ayahuasca+ACC   drink-**NARR.PST**-1SG:SS   angels.trumpet+ACC
            amu-**haku**-nu]   [tsaaŋku   amu-**haku**-nu]
            drink-**NARR.PST**-1SG:SS   tobacco+ACC   drink-**NARR.PST**-1SG:SS
            tuna=na=sha   kahama-inu   a-ya-ha-i
            waterfall=ACC=ADD   dream-NMLZ   COP-REMPST-1SG-DECL
            'it is I, following the path, drinking ayahuasca, drinking angel's trumpet, drinking tobacco, I dreamed of a waterfall' (agr040723_03)

Table 15.6 summarizes the appearance of verbal person marking from the finite and subordinate paradigms with nominalized verbs. As noted above, only first person singular markers are attested in this function. It bears repeating here that this marking is not obligatory, and is relatively uncommon in my corpus.

Table 15.6: Attested combinations of verbal person marking with nominalized verbs

nominalizer	finite	subordinate
-inu	yes	yes
-chau	yes	–
-u	–	yes
-haku	–	yes

In §15.5.2 I discuss further the clause-chaining function of nominalizations, and note there that the use of verbal subject marking is clear evidence that nominalized clauses have been reanalysed as subordinate clauses. Of course the use of verbal morphology with nominalized verbs is not unexpected, as these are after all verbal roots, often in predicating function.

15.4 Referential and attributive uses of nominalizations

In the following sections I discuss the various uses to which nominalizations are put. Nominals function referentially, forming NPs that can then fulfil core or oblique argument roles in a clause; by definition, nominalizations function in this way, either naming objects and concepts or as complement clauses. Nominalizations in Aguaruna may also modify NPs, and this is the typical function of the aspect-marked participant nominalizers -u and -mau. And nominalizations have found their way into verbal paradigms: the remote past nominalizer -haku appears to have lost most nominal properties and can only function as a predicate, in the copula complement role, where it forms part of the tense marking paradigm; however it is incompatible with finite verbal inflection, showing that it is still treated morphologically as nominal. Nominalizations with -u may also function as finite clauses (a "standalone" nominalization), and unlike those with -haku, these forms may appear with or without a copula. The use of a nominalized clause in this context gives a reading of non-firsthand evidentiality, adding a new verbal category to the grammar, and is described in §15.5.3.

Table 15.7 summarizes the functions of the nominalizations identified in Aguaruna. In the following sections they are described in more detail.

Table 15.7: Functions of nominalizations

form	concrete N	abstract N	RC	CC	standalone
-ta	–	✓	–	✓	–
-inu	✓	–	–	–	–
-taĩ	✓	✓	–	–	–
-u	✓	–	✓	–	✓
-mau	✓	✓	✓	limited	–
-tinu	✓	–	?	✓	–
-chau	✓	–	?	–	–

15.4.1 Subject nominalizers

There are three subject nominalizers: *-inu* takes the unmarked stem and is an agent nominalization, naming entities for their typical or habitual actions. *-u* takes the imperfective or perfective stem and is also an agent nominalization; the resulting forms have an actualized reading. *-haku* is only used in remote past contexts, typically in backgrounded clauses in traditional stories. The three subject nominalizers share two important properties: (1) their object arguments take accusative case; and (2) the nominalized form occasionally appears with verbal subject marking suffixes, as described above.

The subject nominalizer *-inu* ascribes a propensity or habitual action to the referent, as subject of the nominalized verb, as in examples (15.45–15.47).

(15.45) *iwishín*
iwishi-**inu**
bewitch-**NMLZ**
'shaman'

(15.46) *hintínkaŋtin*
hintina-kahatu-**inu**
teach-1PL.OBJ-**NMLZ**
'teacher'

(15.47) *mántin*
mantu-**inu**
kill+APPL-**NMLZ**
'killer' (typically applied to hunting dogs)

Object arguments may be overt, and are marked with accusative case as in finite clauses (15.48, 15.49).

(15.48) *nunú kaŋkapín nuwín intsámhin áidaushkam*
         [nunu [[kaŋkapi=na   nuwɨ=**na**]ₙₚ:ₒ   intsamahu-**inu**]
         ANA   *Kagkap*=ACC   woman:1PL/3=ACC   have.sex-**NMLZ**
         a-ina-u=shakama]ₙₚ
         COP-PL:IPFV-NMLZ=ADD
         'those who were having sex with Kagkap's wife too' (agr041005_14)

(15.49) *núna múun áuŋmatin áhabia núna wísha táhai*
         [nu=**na**   muunta auhumatu-**inu**]   aha-maya
         ANA=**ACC**   elder   tell-**NMLZ**   COP:PST-INTPST:3
         nu=na   wi=sha   ta-ha-i
         ANA_REL=ACC   1sg=ADD   say+IPFV-1SG-DECL
         'what the elders told, I also tell' lit. *I also tell that which the elders were tellers of it* (agr040723_29)

Note in example (15.50) that the object NP *mina uchiŋ* 'my children' takes nominative case, as the subject is second person (see §7.3).

(15.50) *ámɨ mína uchíŋ yuhútnaitmɨ*
         amɨ   [[mi=na   uchi-hu]ₙₚ:ₒ   yu-hu-tu-**inu**=aita-mɨ]
         2sg   1sg=ACC child-PSSD:1SG   eat-APPL-1SG.OBJ-**NMLZ**=COP-2.DECL
         'you eat my children' (agr040720_04) [*tayu* (oilbird) speaking to a man who became trapped in their cave while collecting nestlings]

In addition to internal object arguments, nominalized clauses may include adverbs, as in (15.51) and subordinate clauses, as in (15.24) above.[5]

(15.51) *hápak sínchi tupikáinai*
         hapa=ka   [sɨnchi   tupikau-**inu**=ai]
         deer=TOP   strongly   run-**NMLZ**=COP:3:DECL
         'the deer is a fast runner'(agr041005_26)

In example (15.52) the speech report complement is included in a nominalization headed by the verb *tuta* 'say'. This could be literally translated as *in the place about which they said "let's meet"*.

---

5 The word *sinchi* functions as an adverb 'strongly, very' and an adjective 'strong, powerful'. In (15.50) it is clearly functioning as an adverb.

(15.52)   *"iŋkúnikmi" tímaunum*
           [iŋku-nai-ka-mi   ti-**mau**=numa]
           meet-RECIP-PFV-HORT   say+PFV-**NSBJ.NMLZ**=LOC
           'in the place where they had agreed to meet' (agr041005_17)

Both subject and non-subject aspect-marked nominalizations, formed with suffixes -*u* and -*mau* respectively, form referential NPs. They also form relative clauses
modifying NPs, and those NPs which consist only of a nominalization can be considered headless relatives. Such examples, as with other nominalizations, can include object arguments, adverbs and subordinate clauses.

(15.53)   *ikámyawã̃ aɨntsún yuwáuk*
           ikam_yawã=ka   [aɨntsu=na   yu-a-**u**=ka]
           jaguar=TOP   person=ACC   eat-PFV-**NMLZ**=TOP
           'the jaguar that ate a person' (agr041005_14)

(15.54)   *wainkábiahai kuwáshat aɨnts háu áinaun*
           waina-ka-bia-ha-i   [kuwashata   aɨntsu   ha-a-**u**
           see-PFV-INTPST-1SG-DECL   many   person   be.sick-IPFV-**NMLZ**
           a-ina-**u**=na]
           COP-PL:IPFV-**NMLZ**=ACC
           'I saw many sick people' (agr040824_02)

Note in particular the form *a-ina-u* 'COP-PL:IPFV-NMLZ', which functions as a plural
marker. Relative clauses may be headless, in that the understood subject of the
nominalized verb is not overt. In both of (15.55) and (15.56) the subject can be recov-
ered from the preceding discourse context.

(15.55)   *nihámchi nampɨká̃ hiínunashkam huwáu*
           [nihamchi   nampɨ-kã   hiina-**u**=na=shakama]NP
           masato+ACC   get.drunk-PFV+SEQ+3:SS   go.out+IPFV-**NMLZ**=ACC=ADD
           hu-a-u
           take-PFV-NMLZ
           '(the devil) also took (people) who left the house having got drunk on
           masato' (agr040719_13)

(15.56)   *yakɨ́ wakã̃ ɨkɨtun yunúmtukui*
           [yaki   wa-kã   ɨkɨ-ta-**u**=na]NP
           above   go.up-PFV+SEQ+3:SS   sit-APPL+IPFV-**NMLZ**=ACC

yunuma-tu-ka-u=ai
approach-APPL-PFV-NMLZ=COP:3:DECL
'(The man) approached (the boa) that had gone up and was sitting up above him.' (Text 1:8)

Although -*u* nominalizations typically have an immediate sense, there are examples with more of a habitual sense (15.57).

(15.57)   *wíka uchíŋmauwaithai, húnak wíi díkahai*
           [wi=ka   uchi-hǐ-ma-**u**=aita-ha-i]   [hu=na=ka
           1sg=TOP   child-PSSD:1PL/3-VBLZ+IPFV-**NMLZ**=COP-1SG-DECL   PROX=ACC=TOP
           wi   díka-a-ha-i]
           1sg   know-IPFV-1SG-DECL
           'I am a child-bearer – I know this (i.e. *I know how to bear children*)'
           (agr041005_16)

More typically, such a habitual sense is conveyed with the subject nominalizer -*inu*.
   The negative nominalizer -*chau* and future nominalizer -*tinu* appear to be formed from -*u* and -*inu*. The latter does not refer exclusively to the subject participant; rather, it is ambiguous in its referent between subject and object. These portmanteau nominalizers are discussed in §15.4.3 and §15.4.4, respectively.

15.4.2 Non-subject nominalizations

The non-subject nominalizer -*taǐ* forms a noun whose referent is a non-subject participant; typically an object of a transitive verb or location of an intransitive verb. Typical examples are commonly-encountered nouns referring to everyday cultural artefacts or activities, as in (15.58–15.62).

(15.58)   *ikímtãǐ*
           ikima-taǐ
           sit-NSBJ.NMLZ
           'seat' (intransitive; referent = location)[6]

---

6 cf. *ikǚma-sa-ta chimpui=numa* (sit-PFV-IMP stool=LOC) 'sit on the stool!', with an overt locative-marked participant.

(15.59)   *yutấĩ*
            yu-taĩ
            eat-NSBJ.NMLZ
            'food' (transitive; referent = object)

(15.60)   *umpútấĩ*
            umpu-taĩ
            blow-NSBJ.NMLZ
            'flute' (transitive; referent = object)

(15.61)   *shikitấĩ*
            shiki-taĩ
            urinate.on-NSBJ.NMLZ
            'urinal, place where people go to urinate' (transitive; referent = location? object?) (agr040723_29)

(15.62)   *atúshat wáintấĩ*
            atushat   waina-taĩ
            far   see-NSBJ.NMLZ
            'binoculars' (transitive; referent = instrument)

The use of *-taĩ* contrasts with the aspect-marked non-subject nominalizer *-mau* in that it refers to a non-specific, typical object. So while *yu-taĩ* (eat-NSBJ.NMLZ) is best translated with the general term 'food', *yu-a-mau* (eat-PFV-NSBJ.NMLZ) is 'that which was eaten', with reference to a specific event. Although many examples are fully lexicalized (and appear in dictionaries), the productivity of the suffix is apparent from such forms as *aɰa-taĩ* (write-NSBJ.NMLZ), which can mean 'pen' (instrument), 'notebook' (instrument) or 'writing desk' (location), depending on the context.

   -taĩ nominalizations tend to be used without their arguments. Object arguments may, however, be included, and are then unmarked (examples 15.63, 15.64). In both of these examples the referent of the nominalization is the location, not the overt object.

(15.63)   *buukɨa pakátãĩnum ɨhɨ́ɰ̃ãũ*
            [buukɨa   paka-**taĩ**=numa]   ɨ-hɨɰ̃a-u
            skull   peel-**NSBJ.NMLZ**=LOC   CAUS-arrive+IPFV-NMLZ
            'he brought them to the place where skulls were skinned (to make shrunken heads)' (agr040712_02)

(15.64)   *áishĩ dakatã̃inum wakáuwai*
           [aishĩ   daka-**taĩ**=numa]
           husband+PSSD:1PL/3   wait.for-**NSBJ.NMLZ**=LOC
           wa-ka-u=ai
           go.up-PFV-NMLZ=COP:3:DECL
           'she went up to the place where she always waited for her husband'
           (agr041005_28)

In example (15.65) the referent of the nominalization is the object, and the subject
NP (*yacha* 'wise people') is overt.

(15.65)   *ãhántiahai yácha áuhtain áuhu asán*
           ãhantu-ya-ha-i   [yacha   auhu-**taĩ**=na]
           be.shy-REMPST-1SG-DECL   wise   study-**NSBJ.NMLZ**=ACC
           auha-u   asa-nu
           study+IPFV-NMLZ   COP+SBD-1SG:SS
           'I was shy, because I was studying what wise people study'
           (agr040824_02)

When an intransitive verb is nominalized with *-taĩ* the referent is typically the location cf. *kanu-taĩ* (sleep-NSBJ.NMLZ) 'dormitory for guests'. And *-taĩ* may also refer to
the action rather than a participant (15.66).

(15.66)   *wiyá uhaktáhamɨ mína uwɨmtã̃ihun*
           wi=a   uha-ka-ta-hamɨ   [mi=na
           1sg=FIRST   tell-PFV-IFUT-1SG>2SG+DECL   1sg=ACC
           uwɨ-ma-**taĩ**-hu=na]
           defend-REFL-**NSBJ.NMLZ**-1SG=ACC
           'I'll tell you about my method of self-defence first' (agr041005_21)

Corbera (1994: 149) suggests that the nominalizer *-taĩ* is composed of the action
nominalizer *-ta* and the instrumental *-i* (note that he transcribes the suffix without a
nasal vowel). But this could not be a synchronically analysable combination, as a
nominalization with *-taĩ* can itself be followed by case markers including instrumental. Similarly, one could speculate that the source is the action nominalizer plus the
locative *-(n)ĩ*, which would explain the nasal quality of *-taĩ*, but this would again
have to be considered synchronically opaque. So the suffix *-taĩ* is not synchronically
decomposable, and there is no strong evidence regarding its etymology.

   The aspectualized non-subject nominalizer *-mau* is similar to *-taĩ* in its referent,
but does not appear to refer to instruments. Instead, the referent is the object of

transitive verbs (15.67) and the goal or location (i.e. arguments that would take locative case) of intransitive verbs (15.68).

(15.67)   *ihapimush utusáŋ isámati*
         [ihapi-**mau**=sha]   utu-sã=ki   isama-ti
         gut+PFV-**NSBJ.NMLZ**=Q.TOP   how-SBD+3:SS=Q.RHET   heal+PFV-JUSS
         'how can one who has been gutted heal up?' (agr041005_16; cf. 10.60)

(15.68)   *wákitu, dukuhĩ́ wimaunum wiɯ̯au*
         wakita-u   [duku-hĩ   wi-**mau**=numa]
         return+IPFV-NMLZ   mother-PSSD:1PL/3   go+PFV-**NSBJ.NMLZ**=LOC
         wi-a-u
         go-IPFV-NMLZ
         '(the dog) returning, he went to (the place) where his mother had gone'
         (agr041005_15)

The nominalizer *-mau* may also function as an action nominalizer, as in (15.69) where the action nominalization is subject of a verbless clause.

(15.69)   *kuwáshat yúwamu piŋkiŋchau*
         [kuwashata   yu-a-**mau**]ₙₚ:ᵥ꜀ₛ   piŋkiha-chau
         a.lot   eat-IPFV-**NMLZ**   good-NEG.NMLZ
         'eating a lot is bad'

In this function it is used for titles of stories, for example (15.70) and (15.71) are titles given to me for stories I recorded, and (15.72, 15.73) are headings of sections in the Bible.

(15.70)   *páŋkĩ aínts yuwámu*
         paŋkĩ   aintsu   yu-a-**mau**
         boa   person   eat-PFV-**NSBJ.NMLZ**
         '(the story of) a person's getting eaten by a boa' (title given for Text 1)

(15.71)   *ikámỹãw̃ãã aínts hintá wikáiɯu hitíkbau*
         ikam_yawãã   [aintsu   hinta   wikaiɯa-a-u]
         jaguar   person   path+LOC   walk-IPFV-NMLZ
         hiti-ka-**mau**
         attack-PFV-**NSBJ.NMLZ**
         '(the story of) a man attacked by a jaguar as he was walking the path (of preparation)' (title given for agr041006_01)

(15.72) <Pablo Jerusalén webau>
        *Pablo   Jerusalén   wɨ-**mau***
        Paul   Jerusalem   go+PFV-**NSBJ.NMLZ**
        'Paul goes to Jerusalem' (Acts 21:1)

                                               (YCA 2008: 254)

(15.73) <Jisus jakamu>
        *Jisus   ha-ka-**mau***
        Jesus   die-PFV-**NSBJ.NMLZ**
        'Jesus' death' (Matthew 27:45)

                                             (YCA 2008: 67)

Note that both transitive and intransitive verbs may enter into this function, and both imperfective and perfective aspects. Constituent ordering is AOV, as in finite clauses, and this contrasts with relativization in which the referent, the notional O, is syntactically external and typically precedes or follows the nominalization (§16.2).

15.4.3 Negative nominalizer

The negative nominalizer *-chau* is a subject participant nominalizer, and has the added semantic value of negative polarity. It appears to consist of the negative suffix *-cha* plus the subject nominalizer *-u*, but I analyse it as a single suffix, because of its spread beyond verbs to nominal stems.

(15.74) *nɨ̃ wáinchauk*
        [nɨ̃   waina-**chau**=ka]ɴᴘ
        3sg   see-**NEG.NMLZ**=TOP
        'one who doesn't know' (agr041005_18; cf. example 9.17)

(15.75) *yúchau ásã hakáu*
        yu-**chau**   asã   ha-ka-u
        eat-**NEG.NMLZ**   COP+SBD+3:SS   die-PFV-NMLZ
        '(a child ate a centipede and) being one who does not eat that, it died' (agr040721_07)

The same form may be suffixed to nominals to negate them. Such forms typically appear as predicates, and this is the only way to negate clauses with nominal predicates. Examples are given in Chapter 11.

15.4.4 Future participant nominalizer

As mentioned above, the subject nominalizer *-inu* combines with a future stem formed from the perfective stem and the future suffix *-ta* to give a future participant nominalizer *-tinu*.

(15.76)   *wítin*
         wɨ-**tinu**
         go+PFV-**FUT+NMLZ**
         'one who will go'

(15.77)   *wɨaŋtin*
         wɨ-aha-**tinu**
         go+PFV-PL-**FUT+NMLZ**
         'those who will go'

(15.78)   *áu takáak puháwai ahán mídau átinun*
         au   taka-a-kũ   puha-wa-i   aha=na
         3sg   work-IPFV-SIM+3:SS   live+IPFV-3-DECL   garden=ACC
         [mi-nau   a-**tinu**=na]
         1sg-POSS   be-**FUT+NMLZ**=ACC
         'he is working on the garden that will be mine'

(15.79)   *húnak kamɨ uchiŋmáktinnak umiŋkáhamɨ*
         hu=na=ka   [kamɨ   uchi-hĩ-ma-ka-**tinu**=na=ka]
         PROX=ACC=TOP   indeed   child-PSSD:1PL/3-VBLZ-PFV-**FUT+NMLZ**=ACC=TOP
         umi-hu-ka-hamɨ
         prepare-APPL-PFV-1SG>2SG+DECL
         'I have prepared this for you, who are indeed about to give birth'
         (agr041005_16)

Although clearly etymologically derived from future *-ta* + subject nominalizer *-inu*, the form *-tinu* is a distinct suffix synchronically. The crucial difference is in the referent: the future nominalizer may be interpreted as referring to the object of the verb, as in (15.80).

(15.80)   *uwáŋtinchakam áwai*
         uwa-ha-**tinu**=shakama   a-wa-i
         drink-PFV-**FUT+NMLZ**=ADD   exist-3-DECL
         'there's also drink (i.e. *that which will be drunk*)'

This shows that the form *-tinu* has been reanalysed from FUTURE STEM + SUBJECT NOMI-NALIZER > PERFECTIVE STEM + FUTURE NOMINALIZER. As the meaning of the suffix has shifted to futurity, the sense of subjecthood has been lost, allowing the referent in individual examples to be interpreted as context allows.[7] A suffix *-tinu* also appears on nouns (marked as possessed) to form an attributive, i.e. 'one who has NOUN'. This is most likely traceable historically to the verb root *tu-* 'say' and the nominalizer *-inu*; so the meaning would be something like 'one who says "my NOUN"' (see further discussion in §4.9.1).

15.4.5 Action nominalizer

The action nominalizer forms an abstract noun referring to the action of the verb. Typically nominalizations with *-ta* function as lexical nominalizations, for example *hata* 'sickness', *takat* 'work, job'. Subject and object arguments may be overt, however, and all appear in nominative case. Example (15.81) shows an overt subject NP.

(15.81)   *wíka ɨháphut*
            [wi=ka   ɨhapahu-**ta**]ₙₚ
            1sg=TOP   give.birth-**ACT.NMLZ**
            'my giving birth' (agr041005_16)

Example (15.82) comes from a story about a man who was swallowed by a giant boa, and tried to kill it by cutting up its heart. The notional object NP is overt, and note that it is not marked with the accusative case enclitic.

(15.82)   *naŋkámauwai anɨntãĩ tsupíŋtan*
            naŋkama-a-u=ai   [anɨntaĩ   tsupi-hu-**ta**=na]
            begin-PFV-NMLZ=COP:3:DECL   heart   cut-APPL-**ACT.NMLZ**=ACC
            'he began to cut (the boa's) heart' (agr040721_01)

An exception to this lack of accusative marking arises when there is a first person pronominal object: compare (15.83) with (15.84).

---

7 A possible source of analogy is the commonly encountered combination of the potential stem formed with the potential suffix *-mai* + subject nominalizer *-inu*; the potential stem is always S=O ambitransitive (§7.6.3).

(15.83) *máma suhután dakítawai*
        [mama   su-hu-**ta**=na]   dakita-wa-i
        manioc   give-1SG.OBJ-**ACT.NMLZ**=ACC   refuse+IPFV-3-DECL
        'he refuses to give me manioc'

(15.84) *mína suhután dakítawai*
        [mi=na   su-hu-**ta**=na]   dakita-wa-i
        1sg=ACC   give-1SG.OBJ-**ACT.NMLZ**=ACC   refuse+IPFV-3-DECL
        'he refuses to give (it) to me'

Other material may be overt, including adverbs and oblique NPs (15.85).

(15.85) *dakítau apahíhãĩ wɨtán*
        dakita-u   [apa-hí=haĩ   wɨ-**ta**=na]
        refuse+IPFV-NMLZ   father-PSSD:1PL/3=COM   go-**ACT.NMLZ**=ACC
        'he refused to go with his father' (agr041005_15)

Action nominalizations are used to form complement clauses, particularly of the verbs *naŋkamat* 'begin', as in example (15.82) above, and *dakitut* 'refuse', as in examples (15.83–15.85). Verbs of wanting and desire, however, take intentional clauses or speech reports as complements (see §17.2).

    Complement clauses formed with action nominalizations are typically objects of the complement taking verb, but can also function as A; this is the case in example (15.86).

(15.86) *háta naŋkámhuawabi*
        ha-**ta**   naŋkama-hu-aw-amayi
        be.sick-**ACT.NMLZ**   begin-1SG.OBJ-PFV-DISTPST:3:DECL
        'I became ill' lit. *to be sick began me* (Text 2:27)

Action nominalizations also appear as NP arguments expressing abstract concepts, such as *puhu-ta* (live-ACT.NMLZ) 'life'; *ha-ta* (be.sick-ACT.NMLZ) 'sickness', and the examples in (15.87–15.89).

(15.87) *takát áwai*
        taka-**ta**   a-wa-i
        work-**ACT.NMLZ**   exist-3-DECL
        'there is work' (Text 2:16)

(15.88) *inímtanash inimáinchau dɨkapɨyahai*
        inima-**ta**=na=sha   inima-mai-inu-chau   dɨkapɨ-ya-ha-i
        ask-**ACT.NMLZ**=ACC=ADD   ask-POT-NMLZ-NEG.NMLZ   feel-REMPST-1SG-DECL
        'I couldn't even ask a question' (Text 2:13)

(15.89) *ipáamatai*
        ipaama-**ta**=i
        thunder_VERB-**ACT.NMLZ**=COP:3:DECL
        'it's thunder (that you hear)'

A locative-marked *-ta* nominalization is used with the verb *puhut* 'live' to express the sense of 'about to do' something, as in examples (15.90, 15.91).

(15.90) *wíka yabáik hatánum puháhai*
        wi=ka   yamai=ka   ha-**ta**=numa   puha-ha-i
        1sg=TOP   now=TOP   die-**ACT.NMLZ**=LOC   live+IPFV-1SG-DECL
        'now I'm about to die' (agr041005_16)

(15.91) *Arias wɨtánum puháwai*
        Arias   wɨ-**ta**=numa   puha-wa-i
        Arias   go-**ACT.NMLZ**=LOC   live+IPFV-3-DECL
        'Arias is about to go'

Nominalizations with *-ta* are used as the citation form of verbs in dictionaries (Wipio 1996; Uwarai et al. 1998) as well as in this grammar.

15.4.6 Nominalization as copula complement or verbless clause complement

The predicative function is available to all nominals, including deverbal nominalizations, provided the appropriate morphosyntactic structure is present. Nominalizations are formed on verbal roots, and predication is a prototypically verbal function; consequently, when a nominalized verb is used to predicate, the resulting construction is apt to be reanalysed as a straightforward verbal clause, as described in §15.5. In Aguaruna, the narrative past *-haku* can only predicate, in copula complement function; it is never used referentially. Consider *maani-haku=i* (fight-NARR.PST=COP:3:DECL) '(they) used to fight'. There are no examples of a hypothetical nominal **maani-haku (fight-NARR.PST) 'one who used to fight', although there is no apparent pragmatic reason why a sentence like 'the one who used to fight was my grandfather' should not be possible. Because of this restriction to predicating function, narrative past is functionally a member of the tense marking paradigm.

15.4.6.1 Narrative past *-haku*

The narrative past nominalizer appears suffixed to the unmarked stem. It typically appears in narratives dealing with the remote past, particularly in a scene-setting function, as in example (15.92) where it appears in the first clause of a story, and (15.93) from the beginning of a story about one such battle.

(15.92) *bakichík múun ahakuí*
     makichiki   muunta   a-**haku**=i
     one   adult   exist-**NARR.PST**=COP:3:DECL
     'there was a man' (Text 1:2)

(15.93) *maanihakúi hũw̃ĩỹã aínts kanús'hãĩ*
     maani-**haku**=i   [hu-ĩ=ya   aĩntsu]
     fight-**NARR.PST**=COP:3:DECL   PROX=LOC=ABL   person
     [kanusa=haĩ]
     Santiago.River=COM
     'the people from here used to fight with (the people from) the Santiago River (i.e. Huambisas)' (agr041005_18)

A *-haku* nominalization typically functions as the main verb of a sentence, and requires a copula, either encliticized or verbal. Examples (15.94) and (15.95) illustrate the use of a separate copula verb to mark plural subject, as the enclitic copula is not compatible with plural marking. Note that the nominalizer is suffixed to the auxiliary verb *ata* in example (15.95).

(15.94) *túhã tíkichik dúik yáunchukuk ishámahaku áinawai*
     tuhã   tikichi=ka   duik   yaunchuku=ka   ishama-**haku**
     but   other=TOP   long.ago   long.ago=TOP   be.afraid-**NARR.PST**
     a-ina-wa-i
     COP-PL:IPFV-3-DECL
     'but the other people long ago were afraid' (agr041005_14)

(15.95) *"tsampáunum" múuntak túu ahakú áinawai*
     tsampaunumi   muunta=ka   tu   a-**haku**   a-ina-wa-i
     tsampaunum   adult=TOP   say COP-**NARR.PST**   COP-PL:IPFV-3-DECL
     'the elders used to call (those manioc leaves) "*tsampaunum*"' (agr040723_29)

As with nominalizations in *-u*, those with *-haku* occasionally appear marked for first person singular subject as in subordinate verbs, as shown above (§15.3.3).

Narrative past has a sense of discontinuous past, that is, a situation that held in the past but no longer holds at the time of speaking (Plungian & van der Auwera 2006). This is shown in example (15.96), where speaker B's use of narrative past when talking about their father alerts the interlocutor to the fact that he must no longer be alive.

(15.96) A: *apash tũw̃ĩỹãmpaita*

        apa=sha   tu=ĩ=ya=mp=aita

        father:PSSD:2=Q.TOP   where=LOC=ABL=EP=COP:3

        'where is your father from?'

   B: *mina apahuk Chapisa atu, Kaŋkas tawai, ãw̃ĩỹã ahakui*

        mi=na   apa-hu=ka   chapisa=a   atu

        1sg=ACC   father-PSSD:1SG=TOP   Chapisa=COP:3   near

        kaŋkas   ta-wa-i   au=ĩ=ya   a-**haku**=ai

        Kagkas   say+IPFV-3-DECL   DIST=LOC=ABL   COP-**NARR.PST**=COP:3:DECL

        'as for my father, a place near Chapisa, called Kagkas, he was from there'

    A: *atsawak apa*

        atsa-wa=ka   apa

        exist:NEG+IPFV-3=Q   father:PSSD:2

        'is your father not living?' (Tiinch & Danducho)

In §15.5.3 I take up again the question of nominalizations functioning in lieu of finite verbs.

15.5 Non-referential functions of nominalizations

I identify the following non-referential functions of nominalizations, some of which involve reanalysis:
− Complementation (Chapter 17)
− Relativization (Chapter 16)
− Auxiliation (§6.7; §15.5.1)
− Clause chaining (Chapter 14; §15.5.2)
− Standalone nominalizations (§15.5.3)

The use of nominalizations as complement and relative clauses is discussed in Chapters 17 and 16, respectively, and will not be addressed in detail here. In the following sections I discuss the use of nominalizations as main verbs in auxiliary constructions (§15.5.1), clause chaining using relative clause constructions (§15.5.2), and standalone nominalizations functioning as finite verbs (§15.5.3).

As described above, nominalized verbs in predicate function are ripe for reanalysis as verbal predicates. The nominalizing morphology, along with any nominal morphology, may then in turn be reanalysed as verbal morphology. This type of diachronic change has been described for Tibeto-Burman languages (see e.g. Matisoff 1972; DeLancey 2011) and for Cariban languages (Gildea 2008), among others, where it results in new main clause structures. Nominalizations may also be reanalysed as dependent verbal clauses, via relativization. This has been described for Hup (Epps 2009) and Cavineña (Guillaume 2011). Both of these historical processes are attested for Aguaruna, as described below.

15.5.1 Nominalizations in auxiliary constructions

The full verb in an auxiliary construction may be nominalized. In this case there is no overt morphosyntactic indication that the clause is anything other than a copula clause. The whole process described in (15.97) is habitual, as the narrator is describing his life when he worked for a *mestizo* family for a year. The nominalization combines with the copula as auxiliary to form a complex predicate with a progressive aspectual reading. The auxiliary construction could be read literally as "I was a sleeper."

(15.97)   *káshik hiinkí taká takákua ɨtsã shíiŋ akãṹ̯ãɨ̃ kíihitutu wahãɨ̃ taá mái*
          yuhúmak yuwá kánin áyahai
          [kashiki   hiina-ki]   [taka   taka-a-kawa]
          early   go.out-PFV+SEQ+1PL:SS   REDUP   work-IPFV-REPET+1PL:SS
          [ɨtsã   shiiha   akai-a-ɨ̃]   [kiihitutu   waha-ɨ̃]
          sun   well   set-IPFV+1SG/3-DS   IDEO   stand+IPFV+1SG/3-DS
          [ta-a]   [mai]   [yuhumaka
          come-PFV+SEQ+1PL:SS   bathe+PFV+SEQ+1PL:SS   manioc
          yu-a]   [kanu-**inu**   a-ya-ha-i]
          eat-PFV+SEQ+1PL:SS   sleep-**NMLZ**   COP-REMPST-1SG-DECL
          '(we) having gone out early, working, when the sun was well set, as it was getting dark, (we) having come back, having bathed, having eaten a meal, I would sleep' (agr040824_02)

Such constructions are frequent in bridging constructions, as in example (15.98), where the complex predicate forms a bridging construction translating as 'therefore'. Again, this construction literally reads as a copula clause: "you being thus-doers." Auxiliation is described in more detail in §6.7.

(15.98)   <...nunin asajum imá senchi suwimak jukitin ainagme>

[nu-ni-**inu**   **asa**-humɨ]BRIDGE   ima   sɨnchi

ANA-VBLZ.INTR-**NMLZ**   **COP**+SBD-2PL:SS   INTENS   strongly

suwimaka   hu-ki-tinu   a-ina-humɨ

punishment   take-PFV-FUT+NMLZ   COP-PL:IPFV-2PL+DECL

'(Woe to you, scribes and Pharisees, hypocrites, because you devour widows' houses, and for a pretense you make long prayers;) therefore you will receive greater condemnation.' lit. *you are more strongly future takers of punishment* (Matthew 23:14)

(YCA 2008: 54; English translation
from New American Standard Bible)

15.5.2 Nominalizations in clause chaining

It was already noted in §13.5 that nominalizations may function as clause chaining constructions. Example (15.99) is simple enough, and can be analysed as involving an NP headed by *paŋkɨ* 'boa', and containing a nominalized relative clause that itself has three subordinate clauses. This NP is then marked with accusative case as it is the object of the matrix verb *yunumtukui* 'approached'.

(15.99)   *páŋkiŋ ímau wɨ̃ iíkuakɨ yakí wakã̂ ɨkɨ́tun yunúmtukui*

[paŋkɨ̃=ka   [[imau   wɨ̃]   [iikua-kɨ̃]

boa=TOP   INTENS.LOC   go+PFV+SEQ+3:SS   come.back-PFV+SEQ+3:SS

[yaki   wa-kã̃]   ɨkɨ-ta-**u**=na]]NP?

above   go.up-PFV+SEQ+3:SS   sit-APPL+IPFV-**NMLZ**=ACC

yunuma-tu-ka-u=i

approach-APPL-PFV-NMLZ=COP:3:DECL

'(the man) approached the boa that had gone away, come back and gone up (a tree) and was sitting above'

OR

'the boa went away then came back and went up (a tree), and as it was sitting there (the man) approached it' (Text 1:8)

The problem with the relative clause analysis is that it is not appropriate to the pragmatic status of the clauses: the information is not serving to further specify the head noun *paŋkɨ̃* 'boa', instead these clauses are part of the event line of the narrative. The length and internal complexity of this nominalization also suggest that it is functioning as a clause-chain rather than as an argument NP.

In (15.100), the relative clause analysis would again be inappropriate; the nominalized clause is not functionally part of a subject NP ("I who didn't tell my brother-in-law"). In fact, it is semantically of equal status to the following subordinate clause: "[without telling my brother-in-law], [saying "I have no father], I went".

(15.100)   *mína saíŋnakɨsh uhátsuk "mína apáhuk atsáwai" tusán wɨ̨uʉabiahai*
           [mi=na   sai-hu=na=kI=sha   uha-tsu-**u**=ka]
           1sg=ACC   brother.in.law-1SG=ACC=RESTR=ADD   tell-NEG-**NMLZ**=TOP
           [mi=na   apa-hu=ka   atsa-wa-i   tu-sa-nu]
           1sg=ACC   father-PSSD:1SG=TOP exist:NEG+IPFV-3-DECL   say-SBD-1SG:SS
           wɨ-amaya-ha-i
           go+PFV-DISTPST-1SG-DECL
           '(my father was away and) without even telling my brother-in-law, I said "I have no father," and went' (agr040824_02)

Epps (2009) and Guillaume (2011) argue similarly for the reanalysis of nominalized relative clauses as adverbial clauses in Hup and Cavineña, respectively.

   In same-subject linkages, the nominalization will take unmarked nominative case, as in (15.100). As shown above, the occasional presence of subordinate verb subject markers on nominalizations is clear evidence of the reanalysis as a subordinate clause. In different-subject linkages, the nominalization cannot take nominative case. It may take accusative case if the subject of the nominalized clause is coreferent with an object of the matrix clause (as in 15.99). This requirement for a common argument that is not subject of both clauses is reminiscent of the non-inflecting subordinators, and Overall (2016a) shows that the two non-canonical switch-reference clause types described in §13.6 also probably originated as nominalizations. In (15.101) the subordinate clause headed by the non-inflecting subordinator -*tatamana* functions in the same way as the accusative marked nominalization in (15.99).

(15.101)   *uchihɨ́ tsɨkɨtátutatman dakáku ásã tapít achík...*
           [uchi-hĩ   tsɨkɨ-tatu-**tatamana**]   daka-ka-u
           child-PSSD:1PL/3   jump-DESID-**SBJ>OBJ**   wait.for-PFV-NMLZ
           asã   tapit   achi-kã
           COP+SBD+3:SS   IDEO   grab-PFV+3:SS
           '(the agouti's) child tried to jump, but as she was lying in wait she grabbed it...' (agr040721_07)

Example (15.102) illustrates even more clearly how the accusative marking on a nominalization can functionally simulate switch-reference. The example is part of a sequence involving conversation, where switch-reference markers show the change of speaker at each turn. The first verb is nominalized and takes the accusative enclitic, which indicates the change of speaker equally as well as the different subject marking in the following clauses. (The context is that the woman has arrived at the agouti's house, and found piles of food, so she decides to stay.)

(15.102) *"ímaŋnum puhustáhai" tus puháun, "maʔ ahánum wɨ́uɂahai" túsã wɨ́tãĩ, "wɨ́sha minithái" tútãĩ...*

[imaŋ=numa   puhu-sa-ta-ha-i   tus
INTENS.ADJ=LOC   live-PFV-IFUT-1SG-DECL   say+SBD+3:SS

puha-**u**=**na**   [maʔ   aha=numa   wɨ-a-ha-i
live+IPFV-**NMLZ**=**ACC**]   HESIT   garden=LOC   go-IPFV-1SG-DECL

tu-sã   wɨ-taĩ]   [wɨ=sha   mini-ta-ha-i
say-SBD+3:SS   go-SBD:1/3:DS   1sg=ADD   come+PFV-IFUT-1SG-DECL

tu-taĩ]
say-SBD:1/3:DS

'the woman said "I'm going to stay in this great place", and the agouti said to her "well, I'm going to the garden", then the woman said "I want to come too"...' (agr040721_07)

Where there is no coreference, a nominalization cannot be used, and a different-subject marked canonical switch-reference clause must be used instead. As described above (§13.5.2), the DS marker itself has developed from locative case marking. Overall (2014b) gives a more detailed analysis of the use of case-marked nominalizations as switch-reference marked subordinate clauses.

15.5.3 Nominalizations in finite clauses

Nominalizations may function in lieu of finite verbs. The use of such standalone nominalizations (Noonan 1997; also known as non-embedded nominalizations, Matisoff 1972) marks non-firsthand information source, and can be considered an evidentiality strategy (Aikhenvald 2004). The construction is very frequent in traditional stories, as in (15.103, 15.104).

(15.103) *ditáshkam uminás, ditáshkam minínau; hũwĩ́yãshkam akaɨháu*

dita=shakama   umina-sã   dita=shakama
3pl=ADD   get.ready-SBD+3:SS   3pl=ADD

mini-ina-**u**   hu=ĩ=ya=shakama   akaɨɥa-ha-**u**
come-PL:IPFV-**NMLZ**   PROX=LOC=ABL=ADD   go.down-PFV-**NMLZ**

'(following a declaration of war between Aguarunas and Huambisas) they (the Huambisas) also got ready, they also came this way, and the people from here (Aguarunas) also went downriver' (agr041005_18)

(15.104) *itáhak ȋ̃w̃ãnch utuáu, yakahȋ̃ atsáu*
itahaka   ȋ̃wanchi   utu-a-**u**   yaka-hȋ̃
empty.house   devil   enter-PFV-**NMLZ**   arm-PSSD:1PL/3
atsa-**u**
exist.NEG+IPFV-**NMLZ**
'the devil went into the empty house, and his arm was missing'
(agr040723_29)

An unmarked standalone nominalization is formally similar to same-subject clause chaining, with relativization as the source construction, as described above. But examples (15.103, 15.104), which show a change of subject following the standalone nominalization, are possible only if the nominalization is treated as chain-final, that is, functionally equivalent to a finite verb. A further property setting standalone nominalizations and finite clauses apart from subordinate clauses is that the latter are obligatorily verb-final, while the former are not. Example (15.105) illustrates this with a standalone nominalization.

(15.105) *dakítau apahȋ̃hãȋ̃ wɨtán*
dakita-a-**u**   [apa-hȋ̃=haȋ̃   wɨ-ta=na]NP:O
refuse-IPFV-**NMLZ**   father-PSSD:1PL/3=COM   go-ACT.NMLZ=ACC
'he refused to go with his father' (agr041005_15)

A standalone nominalization may take the copula enclitic. The use of the copula allows the nominalization to host finite verbal morphology.

(15.106) *tupikákȋ̃ wɨɰa wɨɰakũã hȋ̃ɰ̃ɑ̃ũ̃w̃ãȋ̃ mánchumush puhámunum*
tupika-kȋ̃   wɨɰa   wɨ-a-kuã
run-PFV+3:SS   REDUP   go-IPFV-REPET+3:SS
hɨɰa-**u**=**ai**   manchumuchi   puha-mau=num
arrive+PFV-**NMLZ**=**COP:3:DECL**   Manchumuch   live+IPFV-NMLZ=LOC
'having run, going and going, she arrived at the place where Manchumuch lives' (agr040721_07)

(15.107) *shȋ̃iŋ anɨachuhai, aɨnts wɨɰaun "núwa uhathúkta mína dáahuk Sántiakui" tíuwaithai*
shiiha   ani-a-chau-ha-i   aɨntsu   wɨ-a-u=na
well   remember-IPFV-NEG.NMLZ-1SG-DECL   person   go-IPFV-NMLZ=ACC
nuwa   uha-tu-hu-ka-ta   mi=na   naa-hu=ka
woman   tell-APPL-1SG.OBJ-PFV-IMP   1sg=ACC   name-PSSD:1SG=TOP

santiaku=i   ti-**u**=**aita**-ha-i

Santiago=COP:3:DECL   say+PFV-**NMLZ**=COP-1SG-DECL

'I don't remember very well, apparently I said to people passing by "tell my wife for me, my name is Santiago".' (agr040824_02)

(15.108)   \<Herodes Judea nugka apuji wajas pujai, nunú nugkanmag yaakat Belegnum Jisus akiinauwai\>

Herodes   Judea   nugka   apu-hĩ   waha-sã

Herod   Judea   land+GEN   chief-PSSD:1PL/3   stand-SBD+3:SS

puha-ĩ   nunu   nugka=numa=ka   yaakata

live+IPFV+1SG/3-DS   ANA   land=LOC=TOP   town

*Beleŋ=numa   Jisus   akiina-**u**=**ai***

Bethlehem=LOC   Jesus   be.born+PFV-**NMLZ**=COP:3:DECL

'When Herod was King of Judea, in that land, in the town of Bethlehem, Jesus was born.' (Matthew 2:1)

(YCA 2008: 8)

When a standalone nominalization combines with the narrative modality marker *tuwahamĩ* (described in §9.2.3) it does not require the copula enclitic, as the narrative modality marker is not morphologically bound (15.109).

(15.109)   *núwa mákichik naŋkaín usupaŋ, hiinkíu túwahamĩ*

nuwa   makichiki   naŋkai=na   usupa-hã

woman   one   fruit=ACC   crave-PFV+SEQ+3:SS

hiina-ki-**u**   **tuwahamĩ**

go.out-PFV-**NMLZ**   **NARR**

'A woman having craved fruit, (she) went out they say.' (agr040721_07)

While the structure of such clauses is much like a copula or verbless equative clause, there is a semantic distinction: standalone nominalizations are used in past tense contexts, while equative clauses formed with the enclitic copula (15.110) or a verbless construction (15.111) are necessarily interpreted as present tense.

(15.110)   *apahĩ mina primohui*

apa-hĩ   mi=na   *primo*-hu=**i**

father-PSSD:1PL/3   1sg=ACC   cousin-PSSD:1SG=**COP:3:DECL**

'her father is my cousin' (personal correspondence)

(15.111)   *húka wísut*

hu=ka   wisut

PROX=TOP   ant.sp

'this is a *wisut* ant'

Standalone nominalizations are very common in traditional narratives, and feature in many of the examples in this grammar. As a non-firsthand evidentiality strategy, their use is appropriate in narratives that relate events that the speaker has not personally witnessed. Example (15.103) above is from a more "historical" account of warfare, while examples (15.104–15.106, 15.109) are from more myth-like stories, which include supernatural elements. Example (15.108) is from a translation of the Bible. Example (15.107) is especially interesting, as it comes from an autobiographical narrative (from which Text 2 is extracted). Because the speaker witnessed the events of his life, the vast majority of this text is couched in finite past tense verb forms; but example (15.107) explicitly relates an episode that the speaker doesn't remember because he had been injured. As such, the use of non-firsthand marking is appropriate. It is important to reiterate that this is an EVIDENTIALITY STRATEGY in Aikhenvald's (2004) terms, and not a fully grammatical evidentiality system. Firstly, the marker is primarily a nominalizer, and there is no dedicated evidentiality marking morphology. Secondly, there is no paradigmatic opposition involved: although standalone nominalizations contrast with finite verbs, it is not the case that a finite verb necessarily signals firsthand information. This is shown by example (15.112), in which the speaker relates events that happened while he was unconscious, having fainted from illness.

(15.112)   *túhãsh waámak yutúnhabiahai, núnitãĩ, waámkɨs mediconum*
            ɨhɨtuawahamayi
            tuhã=sha   waamakɨ   yutuna-ha-amaya-ha-i
            but=ADD   quickly   get.worse-PFV-DISTPST-1SG-DECL
            [nu-ni-taĩ]BRIDGE   waamakɨsã   *medico*=numa
            ANA-VBLZ.INTR-SBD:1/3:DS   quickly+3   doctor=LOC
            ɨhɨ-tu-aw-aha-amayi
            take-1SG.OBJ-PFV-PL-DISTPST:3:DECL
            'I quickly got worse. When I did that, they quickly took me to a doctor.'
            (Text 2:38–39)

It is not yet clear what other factors influence the selection of a standalone nominalization over a finite verb form. Overall (2014a) discusses the phenomenon in more detail.

15.6 Unproductive nominalization patterns

A few apparently cognate pairs of nouns and verbs show the presence of unproductive derivational morphology on the noun. Table 15.8 lists all such pairs that I am aware of. Likely morpheme boundaries between the root and the nominalizing morphology have been marked.

Table 15.8: Unproductive nominalizations

nominal	verb
hapi-muk(u) 'broom'	*hapimat* 'sweep', *hapit* 'pull'
yuhu-mak(a) 'food'	*yuta* 'eat' and compare *ayuhut* 'feed' with prefixed causative, suggesting a historical root **yuhu-* 'eat'
tsawan-(ta) 'day'	*tsawaut* 'dawn'
kapan-tu 'red (adj.)'	*kapaut* 'burn'
anɨn-(ta) 'magic song'	*anɨit* 'love, miss, think about (a person)'

Two patterns are suggested by these few forms. Firstly, the two words with final /mVkV/ suggest an old suffix of that form. Secondly, the other three nominals have final /ntV/. This suggests the presence of a suffix /tV/ and epenthetic /n/, similar to the verb *maut* 'kill' which gains an epenthetic nasal when consonant initial suffixes are added (see §3.4.2).

15.7 Summary of nominalization

The evidence presented above shows that the same nominalizers form both lexical and clausal nominalizations, although the latter are more productive and are the diachronic source for the former. When functioning as a relative clause, a nominalization may be externally headed, but in other functions all overt arguments are internal to the nominalization. This raises the issue of the psychological reality of nominalized clauses, or rather, of the NPs they head or modify. Where a large number of such clauses are nested or combined, the function is basically that of clause-chaining. Do native speakers of Aguaruna really consider such constructions to constitute NPs? This is an important area for future research, along with the mechanics of clause-chaining and reference tracking in general.

16 Relative clauses

16.1 Preliminary remarks

Relative clauses were introduced in Chapter 5, where their role in the internal syntax of the NP was described. In this chapter I describe in more detail the internal syntax of relative clauses. There are two relativizing constructions in Aguaruna; one makes use of nominalizations and the other makes use of relativizing pronouns. Relative clauses of both types are frequently headless. Headed relative clauses formed with nominalizations are externally headed (with a gapping strategy), but headed pronominal relative clauses are typically internally headed. In the following sections I first describe relative clauses formed with nominalizations, then those formed with pronouns.

16.2 Nominalized relative clauses

Relative clauses are formed with the two aspect marked participant nominalizers, -*u* 'subject nominalizer' and -*mau* 'non-subject nominalizer'. Nominalization operates at the level of the clause, and the nominalized verb may be accompanied by overt NP arguments, oblique NPs, adverbial elements and subordinate clauses. Either the subject or a non-subject argument can be nominalized (as in 16.1 and 16.2, respectively). When the referent of the relative clause is overt, as in these examples, it is external to the nominalization and heads the NP.

(16.1)   *ikámyawaŋ aíntsún yuwáuk*
        [ikam_yawaã=ka   [aíntsu=na   yu-a-**u**=ka]RC]NP
        jaguar=TOP   person=ACC   eat-PFV-**NMLZ**=TOP
        'the jaguar that ate a person' (agr041005_14)

(16.2)   *nihamánch yahámushkam*
        [nihamanchi   [yaha-**mau**=shakama]RC]NP
        masato   prepare+PFV-**NSBJ.NMLZ**=ADD
        'also *masato* (manioc beer) that had been prepared' (agr040721_07)

A number of syntactic and morphological phenomena show that these relative clauses are externally headed. Firstly, the head typically precedes, but may follow, the relative clause. In example (16.3) the relative clause precedes the head noun.

(16.3)   *íw̃ãnch yáunchuk húkimu núwa*
           [[ĩwanchi   yaunchukɨ   hu-ki-**mau**]ᵣ𝒸   nuwa]ₙₚ
           devil   long.ago   take-PFV-**NSBJ.NMLZ**   woman
           'women that the devil had taken long ago' (agr040723_29)

Secondly, morphological marking shows that the head noun is treated as an NP constituent separate from, not internal to, the relative clause. As noted in Chapter 5, the NP is a rather loose constituent in Aguaruna, and morphology that is typically enclitic to it may in some examples appear on more than one constituent of the phrase. Example (16.1) above showed this with the topic enclitic *=ka*, which appears on the head and on the nominalized relative clause, but not on the internal object argument of the nominalization. Example (16.4) shows the additive enclitic *=shakama* on the head, but not the relative clause.

(16.4)   *dúshakam múun áuŋmatbau áatus hiináawai*
           [nu=shakama   [muunta   auhumata-**mau**]ᵣ𝒸]   aatusã
           ANA=ADD   elder   tell+IPFV-**NSBJ.NMLZ**   thus+3
           hiina-a-wa-i
           come.out-IPFV-3-DECL
           'and that (story) that was told by the elders goes like that'
           (agr041005_18)

Further examples are provided by accusative case marking. Examples where an NP consisting of a noun plus a relative clause takes accusative marking are very rare except with plural marking *a-ina-u* (COP-PL:IPFV-NMLZ), which behaves like any regular modifier in that it takes the accusative enclitic while the head noun remains unmarked (16.5).

(16.5)   *hiŋkái áinaun utuák...*
           [hiŋkai   a-ina-u=**na**]ₙₚ:ₒ   utua-kã
           fruit   COP-PL:IPFV-NMLZ=**ACC**   pile.up-PFV+SEQ+3:SS
           'having piled up fruits...' (agr040721_07)

However, among the few other examples of relative clauses in object NPs, marking is variable, and both the head and the relative clause may be marked accusative, as in (16.6). Again, this demonstrates that the head is external to the nominalized clause.

(16.6)   *saɨpɨn iyáhun yuwáu túwahamɨ̃*
           [saɨpɨ=**na**   iyã-ha-u=**na**]NP:O   yu-a-u   tuwahamɨ̃
           peel=**ACC**   fall-PFV-NMLZ=**ACC**   eat-PFV-NMLZ   NARR
           '(the child) ate the (manioc) peelings that had fallen (on the ground),
           they say' (agr040721_07)

And example (16.7) consists of a demonstrative determiner, head noun, and nominalized relative clause. Again, all three constituents of the NP receive accusative
case marking, as is expected in a determined NP (see §5.2.1).

(16.7)   *húna saɨpchíhin iyaunakɨ́sh yuwáwaiŋka*
           [hu=**na**   saɨpɨ-uchi-hɨ̃=**na**   [iya-**u**=**na**=kI=sha]RC]NP:O
           PROX=**ACC**   peel-DIM-PSSD:1PL/3=**ACC**   fall+PFV-**NMLZ**=**ACC**=RESTR=ADD
           yu-aw-aɨ̃-ka
           eat-PFV-APPR+3SG-PROH
           'and make sure (the child) doesn't eat these (manioc) peelings that have
           fallen (on the floor)!' (agr040721_07)

Example (16.8) shows a locative-marked participant included in the nominalized
clause.

(16.8)   *núwa áidau ahánum ashinkáu*
           [nuwa   a-ina-u   [aha=numa   ashina-ka-**u**]RC]NP
           woman   COP-PL:IPFV-NMLZ   garden=LOC   go:PL-PFV-**NMLZ**
           'women who had gone to the garden' (agr041005_19)

Adverbs and subordinate clauses may also be included in nominalizations (§15.2).
     Nominalizations formed from ditransitive verbs are ambiguous with respect to
which object is the referent. In (16.9) the nominalization *su-sa-mau* (give-PFV-
NSBJ.NMLZ) refers to 'the things that were given', while in (16.10), the same form refers to 'the one who was given things'.

(16.9)   *susámu áidaun oficinanum ukúkmɨ̃*
           [su-sa-**mau**   a-ina-u=na]   *oficina*=numa
           give-PFV-**NSBJ.NMLZ**   COP-PL:IPFV-NMLZ=ACC office=LOC
           uku-ki-mɨ̃
           leave-PFV-RECPST:3:DECL
           'he left the donations in the office'

(16.10)   *susámuhãĩ chichastáhai*
           [su-sa-**mau**=haĩ]   chicha-sa-ta-ha-i
           give-PFV-**NSBJ.NMLZ**=COM   speak-PFV-IFUT-1SG-DECL
           'I'll talk with (the person) who received things'

In example (16.11), both objects of a nominalized derived ditransitive verb are overt. The preferred reading out of context takes the initial argument as the external head of a nominalized relative clause.

(16.11)   *mína núwa chíŋkim tsupíŋkamun wainkáttawai*
           [mi=na   nuwa   [chiŋkimi   tsupi-hu-ka-**mau**=na]ᵣ꜀]ₙₚ:ₒ
           1sg=ACC   wife   firewood   cut-APPL-PFV-**NSBJ.NMLZ**=ACC
           waina-ka-tata-wa-i
           see-PFV-FUT-3-DECL
           'he will see my wife, for whom firewood was cut'

However, consultants also accept a reading in which the firewood is the referent of the nominalization, that is, *he will see the firewood that was cut for my wife*. This reading implies an internally headed relative clause. It is important to note, however, that I have no examples of internally headed nominalized relative clauses from spontaneous speech.

When an intransitive verb is nominalized with *-mau* the referent is typically the location (as in 16.12 and 16.13). I have no examples in which a location common argument is an overt external head; these could be analysed as headless relative clauses.

(16.12)   *hĩɰ́áũw̃áĩ mánchumush puhámunum*
           hĩɰa-u=ai   [manchumuchi   puha-**mau**=numa]
           arrive+PFV-NMLZ=COP:3:DECL   Manchumuch   live+IPFV-**NSBJ.NMLZ**=LOC
           'she arrived (at the place) where Manchumuch (a mythical cannibal)
           lives' (agr040721_07)

(16.13)   *aák atsámunum tɨpɨsá...*
           [aaka   atsa-**mau**=numa]   tɨpɨ-sa
           hut   exist:NEG+IPFV-**NSBJ.NMLZ**=LOC   lie.down-PFV+1PL:SS
           '(we) having lain down (in the place) where there was no hut...'
           (agr060816_01)

The non-subject nominalizer *-mau* thus has two functions that are somewhat distinct: when its referent is an object, the common argument is typically subject or object of the matrix clause; but when its referent is location, the common argument is typically also location in the matrix clause. The referent of the subject nominalizer *-u* is typically subject or object of the matrix clause. These coreference patterns are summarized in Table 16.1.

Table 16.1: Coreference patterns in nominalized relative clauses

nominalizer	role in relative clause	role in matrix clause
-u	subject	subject or object
-mau	object	subject or object
-mau	location	location

To include a relative clause in an NP that plays any other oblique role in the matrix clause, a pronominal relativizer may be used, as described in the next section.

16.3 Relativization with postposed relativizer

The postposed relativizer construction in Aguaruna consists of a partially finite clause: tense and SAP subject are always marked, and there is never mood/modality marking; third person subjects are typically unmarked (as in example 16.16), but may be marked in present tense (as in examples 16.14, 16.15); it is not clear what conditions the presence of third-person marking. The relative clause must be predicate-final, and is directly followed by a relativizer that then takes the full range of NP morphology appropriate to its role in the matrix clause. The relative marker may be one of: anaphoric pronoun *nu*; proximal demonstrative *hu*; distal demonstrative *au*. Derivatives of the intensifier *ima* (see the list in §12.3.6) enter into the same construction, forming adverbial expressions. There are no restrictions on the role of the common argument in the relative clause or the matrix clause, and it may appear overtly in either clause (compare examples 16.19 and 16.20). In fact, there is no requirement for a common argument at all, as discussed below. In the glosses, postposed relativizers are labelled with subscript REL.

Example (16.14) is straightforward: the common argument is O object of both the relative and matrix clauses.

(16.14)   *nĩ́ táwa núnak wíi díkahai*
          [nĩ   ta-wa   nu=na=ka]$_{NP:O}$ wi   dɨka-a-ha-i
          3sg   say+IPFV-3   ANA$_{REL}$=ACC=TOP   1sg   know-IPFV-1SG-DECL
          'I (already) know what he's saying'

In (16.15), the relativized clause is a copula clause, and the enclitic copula takes the non-declarative form. This construction is commonly used to focus NPs (§18.2). The common argument is subject of the relativized copula clause and object of the matrix clause.

(16.15) *puhúwa húna hukíthai*
         [puhu=a   hu=na]~NP:O~   hu-ki-ta-ha-i
         white=COP:3 PROX~REL~=ACC   take-PFV-IFUT-1SG-DECL
         'I'll take this white one'

In (16.16), the common participant would be an oblique (locative) NP if it were overtly included in the relativized clause. Given that oblique NPs are not core arguments, it is not clear that this can be treated as a "common argument", strictly speaking. Note, however, that the pattern of a common participant being a location in both relative and matrix clause is the same as we saw for the non-subject nominalization above (Table 16.1).

(16.16) *áu púha ấw̃ĩ w̃ɨµahai*
         [au puha   au=ĩ]~NP~   wɨ-a-ha-i
         DIST live+IPFV+3   DIST~REL~=LOC go-IPFV-1SG-DECL
         'I'm going to where he lives'

The relativizer is inflected for its role in the matrix clause, and may take any role. It can even be verbalized with one of the pro-verb forming suffixes *-ni* or *-tika*, as in (16.17), in which the layers of morphology function to make the referent *aints* 'person' more vague.

(16.17) *aíntsua núnin mináu*
         [aɨntsu=a   nu-ni-inu]   mina-u
         person=COP:3 ANA~REL~-VBLZ.INTR-NMLZ arrive+IPFV-NMLZ
         'something like a person (is) coming' lit. *someone who does being-a-person* (agr060816_01)

In example (16.18) the relative clause is verbalized with the suffix *-tika* and becomes a sequential subordinate clause.

(16.18)   *kánu apɨaku ituŋtáya dútikã...*
          [kanu   apɨ-a-ku   ituhu-taya
          canoe   burn-IPFV-SIM+1PL:SS make-NORM
          nu]-tikã
          ANA~REL~-VBLZ.TR+PFV+SEQ+3:SS
          '(they) having done what we do, burning out a canoe...' (agr040723_29)

There are no restrictions on which participant of a pronominal relative clause is shared with its matrix clause. In example (16.19) the O argument of the relative clause functions as the S argument of the matrix clause.

(16.19)   *wɨi aɨntsún wainkámha dúka chapínum puhúwai*
          [wi aɨntsu=na   waina-ka-ma-ha   nu=ka]~NP:S~ chapi=numa
          1sg person=ACC   see-PFV-RECPST-1SG   ANA~REL~=TOP Chapi=LOC
          puhu-wa-i
          live-3-DECL
          'the person that I saw lives in Chapi (village)'

In (16.20), what would be an oblique instrumental participant in the relative clause is a copula subject in the matrix clause. As with (16.16) above, it is not entirely appropriate to think of this as a "common argument", and there is no indication in the relative clause of which participant is shared with the matrix clause. A literal translation would be *"The knife [that I killed a pig] is yours"*; clearly context and real-world knowledge are crucial to the interpretation.

(16.20)   *wɨi kuchín maámha dúka kuchík áminuwɨ̃*
          [[wi   kuchi=na   ma-a-ma-ha   nu=ka]~RC~   kuchi=ka]~NP:CS~
          1sg   pig=ACC   kill-PFV-RECPST-1SG   ANA~REL~=TOP   knife=TOP
          ami-nau=ɨ̃
          2sg-POSS=NONVIS.COP:3
          'the knife I killed the pig with was yours'[1]

The role that the relativized referent plays in the matrix is similarly unconstrained, although here case-marking limits the potential for ambiguity. We have already seen nominative, accusative and locative marked examples as well as those with derivational morphology. The following examples show instrumental (16.21) and locative + ablative case marking (16.22).

---

1 Note that *kúchi* 'pig' and *kuchí* 'knife' are distinguished by underlying accent placement, so are not homophonous, despite the similarity of form.

(16.21)   *kuchí suhúsmumɨ dúwi kuchín maámhai*
          [kuchi   su-hu-sa-ma-umɨ   nu=i]_{NP:INS}   kuchi=na
          knife   give-1SG.OBJ-PFV-RECPST-2SG   ANA_{REL}=INS   pig=ACC
          ma-a-ma-ha-i
          kill-PFV-RECPST-1SG-DECL
          'I killed the pig with the knife you gave me'

(16.22)   *ámɨ namák wainkúmɨ nŭ̃wĩ̃yã̃ɨ̃thai*
          [amɨ   namaka   waina-ka-umɨ   nu]=ĩ=ya=aita-ha-i
          2sg   river   see-PFV-2SG   ANA_{REL}=LOC=ABL=COP-1SG-DECL
          'I am from the river you saw' (i.e. *I live there*)

A headless demonstrative construction formed on a copula-marked noun is often used to focus the noun, without adding any modificational information. See (16.15) above, and (16.23, 16.24).

(16.23)   *papín múunta núu wiŋkayai*
          [papin   muunta=a   nu]_{NP}   wiŋka=ai
          book   big=COP:3   ANA_{REL}   blue=COP:3:DECL
          'that big book is blue'

(16.24)   *ĩ̃wãnchia núu*
          [ĩwanchi=a   nu]_{NP}
          devil=COP:3   ANA_{REL}
          'the devil' lit. *that which is the devil*

Examples (16.25) and (16.26) illustrate the use of the relativized copula construction in marking pragmatic status: in (16.25) the chicken is indefinite, while in (16.26) the relativized copula construction is used to mark the chicken as identifiable in the discourse context. This focussing strategy is discussed further in §18.2.

(16.25)   *atásh muúntan maáthai*
          [atashu   muunta=na]_{NP:O} maa-ta-ha-i
          chicken big=ACC   kill+PFV-IFUT-1SG-DECL
          'I'll kill a big chicken'

(16.26)   *atásh múunta núna maáthai*
          [atashu [muunta=a   nu=na]_{RC}]_{NP:O} maa-ta-ha-i
          chicken big=COP:3   ANA_{REL}=ACC   kill+PFV-IFUT-1SG-DECL
          'I'll kill the big chicken' (addressee knows which chicken I mean)

The examples given above suggest that although some examples appear to be headed relative clauses, in fact the postposed relativizer construction is always headless. Consider example (16.27).

(16.27)   *amina apahui tukɨ puhuwa nuu yaimpakti*
           [ami=na]~NP:O~   [apahui   tukɨ   puhu-wa   nu]~NP:A~
           2SG=ACC   God   always   live-3   ANA~REL~
           yaĩ-pa-ka-ti
           help-2.OBJ-PFV-JUSS
           'may God, who is eternal, help you' (personal correspondence)

Although it looks as if *apahui* 'God' heads an NP, with a following relative clause ('who always lives'), by analogy with the other examples presented above this is better analysed as a whole clause that is relativized, in which the common argument just happens to be clause-initial. There is no evidence to suggest that in this example the common argument is extraposed.

Various words formed from the intensifier *ima* (see §12.3.6) enter into similar constructions; in that case the postposed form is not case-marked. The bare root *ima* itself cannot function in this way. In example (16.28) the verb *hapit* 'drag' is nominalized, then the copula enclitic is added and the resulting equative clause is followed by the word *iman* (INTENS.NMLZ) 'such a big one' (labelled REL, although not strictly forming a relative clause). Although the resulting form has a nominal referent, it cannot take any case marking.

(16.28)   *kánu hapikbáuwa íman tahák akaikíuwai*
           [kanu   hapi-ki-mau=a   iman]
           canoe   pull-PFV-NSBJ.NMLZ=COP:3   INTENS.NMLZ~REL~
           taha-kũ   akai-ki-u=ai
           clear+IPFV-SIM+3:SS   go.down-PFV-NMLZ=COP:3:DECL
           '(something) as big as a canoe being dragged had come down clearing a path through the undergrowth' (Text 1:6)

In (16.29) again a copula clause is followed by a derivative of *ima*, in this case *imau* 'right there'. The resulting form functions adverbially.

(16.29)   *uúbi híiya ímau tsahút íhũ...*
           uumi=i   [hii=a   imau]   tsahut   ihũ
           blowgun=INS   eye=COP:3   INTENS.LOC~REL~   IDEO   stab+PFV+SEQ+3:SS
           'having stabbed it right in the eye with his blowgun...' (agr041005_14)

16.4 Summary of relative clauses

We have seen that nominalizations may function as externally headed relative clauses. Nominalized relative clauses, like other modifiers, typically follow their head noun, but may precede it. The nominalized form *a-ina-u* (COP-PL:IPFV-NMLZ) is used as a plural marker and shows signs of being somewhat grammaticalized. Nominalizations may also head NPs, and although these constructions could be analysed as involving headless relative clauses there is no language-internal motivation to do so.

Relative clauses formed with pronouns are internally headed, and apparently have no restrictions on the role of the common argument in the relative clause or the matrix clause. These constructions are also used as a focus construction, and similar constructions based on the intensifier *ima* form adverbial expressions.

17 Speech reports and complement clauses

In this chapter I discuss two multiclausal constructions that involve one clause functioning as a core argument of another. Speech reports are always direct quotes in Aguaruna, aiming for a more-or-less verbatim repetition of the original speaker's words. Because speech reports are typically full clauses, they find extended uses as complements of verbs expressing thought, purpose and desire. Complement clauses are primarily functionally defined (unlike speech reports, which are formally distinct from any other construction), and may be expressed with a variety of formal structures including nominalizations, embedded questions, and finite clauses, as well as with speech reports.

17.1 Speech reports

Speech report constructions are of great importance in Aguaruna discourse, both in reporting actual speech and vocalizations, and in complementation strategies relating to thought and intentionality. They also play an important role in narrative structure, where major events may be related through the speech of a main character rather than directly reported by the narrator (Larson 1978; and see §18.5). In its basic form, a speech report construction is not strictly clause combining: the quoted speech is an argument, and does not express a proposition to be related to the matrix verb. However, a speech report is typically a grammatical utterance that expresses one or more propositions, so it is inevitable that the speech report construction has been extended into clause-linking uses, in particular complementation. In all of the extended uses, a subordinated form of the verb *tuta* 'say' is used, and seems to be developing in the direction of a general speech report marker and complementizer. In addition, a number of verbal suffixes have apparently developed from periphrastic constructions with *tuta* 'say' – see Chapter 8.

The speech report itself is a more-or-less verbatim quote, and the deictic centre is that of the original speaker (OS), except that overt pronouns referring to the current speaker (CS) and current addressee (CA) are shifted to the deictic centre of the CS – what Aikhenvald (2008) calls "Current-Speaker-oriented semi-direct speech". There is only one speech-report construction in Aguaruna; one cannot adjust the deictic centre of a speech report for stylistic purposes. The speech report always precedes the speech verb. The subject of the speech verb is not usually expressed, being recoverable from morphology or context (as in example 17.1). When it is expressed, the most common position is preceding the speech report (as in 17.2). Rarely, the subject of the speech verb may intervene between the speech report and the

speech verb (as in 17.3). The subject of the speech verb is apparently the only constituent that may come between the speech report and the speech verb. In all examples, speech reports are underlined.

(17.1) *"yutúpis nuwanúĩ áwai" tímayi*
      <u>yutupisa</u> <u>nuwanu=ĩ</u> <u>a-wa-i</u>   ti-mayi
      Yutupis ANA=LOC   exist-3-DECL say+PFV-INTPST:3:DECL
      '"It's there, at Yutupis (a community on the Santiago River)" he said.'
      (agr040723_29)

(17.2) *núwa "ái" tíuwai*
      nuwa   <u>ai</u>   ti-u=ai
      woman ok   say+PFV-NMLZ=COP:3:DECL
      'The woman said "ok".' (agr041005_14)

(17.3) *"dakahúumata" yatsúŋ túhutmĩ*
      <u>daka-hu-ma-ta</u>   yatsu-hu
      wait-1SG.OBJ-DUR-IMP brother-PSSD:1SG
      tu-hu-ti-mĩ
      say-APPL-1SG.OBJ+PFV-RECPST:3:DECL
      '"Wait for me" my brother said to me.' (agr041005_14)

17.1.1 Semi-direct speech

As noted above, speech reports are essentially verbatim quotes, and the deictic centre is that of the OS. When a pronoun or verb references a current speech act participant (i.e. CS or CA), however, the deictic centre shifts to that of the CS. So CS is always referred to as first person and CA is always referred to as second person,
regardless of their status in the original quote. Such a shift never happens with non
SAP participants, so shifted and unshifted reference may appear within the same
quote. To put it another way, a single speech report may contain pronominal and
verbal reference from the deictic centre of the OS and the CS simultaneously. The
incompleteness of the shift makes this semi-direct speech (Aikhenvald 2008). Table
17.1 summarizes the deictic centre indexed by pronouns and possession marking (in
the first column) and verbal marking (in the second column) for first, second and
third person (all singular – I have no data on plural persons).

Table 17.1: Deictic shift in speech reports

person	pronoun/possession	verbal marking
1sg	CS	OS
2sg	CS	CS/OS
3sg	OS	OS

Below I discuss some examples to illustrate the shifts. To begin with, (17.4) is a straightforward example of semi-direct speech. The speech report attributed to the OS (Pablo) is literally "I saw your child." But that is not what Pablo is understood to have said: he saw the CA's child, not the CS's. The possession marking is shifted to the CS's deictic centre, but the verbal marking is not shifted; the two translations given, using indirect and direct speech, show how the partial deictic shift gives the Aguaruna construction properties of both.

(17.4)   *Pablo "uchíŋmin wainkámhai" tímĩ*
          pablo   uchi-hu-mi=na   waina-ka-ma-ha-i
          Pablo   child-PSSD-2=ACC   see-PFV-RECPST-1SG-DECL
          ti-mĩ
          say+PFV-RECPST:3:DECL
          'Pablo said that he saw your child'
          OR
          'Pablo said "I saw his_{CA} child"'

Example (17.5) shows a similar shift of possession marking to the CS's deictic centre, this time with a first-person possessor. Again the verb is still marked from the OS's deictic centre, so the first person subject refers to the OS.

(17.5)   *Pablo túhutmĩ "uchíhun wainkámhai" tus*
          pablo   tu-hu-ti-mĩ   [uchi-hu=na
          Pablo   say-APPL-1SG.OBJ+PFV-RECPST:3:DECL   child-PSSD:1SG=ACC
          waina-ka-ma-ha-i   tus]
          see-PFV-RECPST-1SG-DECL   say+SBD+3:SS
          'Pablo told me that he saw my child' lit. *Pablo_(OS) said to me_(CS): "I_(OS) saw my_(CS) child"*

This example is ambiguous: it could just as well be interpreted as 'Pablo told me he saw his own child', where the speech report is treated entirely as a direct quote. It seems to be the case, however, that the applicative marking on the speech verb means the interpretation as referring to the CS's child is preferred.

Examples (17.6, 17.7) illustrate purpose clauses couched as speech reports, with apprehensive marked verbs (see §8.5). In both examples, the speech report is the same, and the subordinate clause translates literally as '...saying "may I not fall"'. This is clearly direct speech, as the deictic centre is that of the OS. In example (17.6), OS and CS are the same, so deictic shift is irrelevant, and in (17.7), neither CS nor CA is involved.

(17.6)   *wíi numín mináahai "iyáhaiŋ" tusán*
            wi   numi=na   minaa-ha-i   [iyaa-ha-i-ha
            1sg   tree=ACC   lay.down+PFV-1SG-DECL   fall-PFV-APPR-1SG
            tu-sa-nu]
            say-SBD-1SG:SS
            'I've laid a log down (across the stream) so as not to fall'

(17.7)   *numín mináamɨ̃ "iyáahaiŋ" tus*
            numi=na   minaa-mɨ̃   [iyaa-ha-i-ha
            tree=ACC   lay.down+PFV-RECPST:3:DECL   fall-PFV-APPR-1SG
            tus]
            say+SBD+3:SS
            'he laid a log down (across the stream) so as not to fall'

Example (17.8) shows the different treatment of a CA subject of the apprehensive-marked verb. Here the second person pronoun and subject marking refer to CA, not OA. This sentence is basically indirect speech, as the entire contents of the speech report are shifted to the deictic centre of the CS.

(17.8)   *numín mináamɨ̃ "ámɨ iyáaimɨ" tus*
            numi=na   minaa-mɨ̃   [amɨ   iyaa-i-mɨ
            tree=ACC   lay.down+PFV-RECPST:3:DECL   2sg   fall+PFV-APPR-2SG
            tus]
            say+SBD+3:SS
            'he laid a log down so that you wouldn't fall' lit. *he laid a log down saying "may you not fall"*

When the CS is subject of the speech report, however, the verbal marking does not shift, as in example (17.9).

(17.9)   *numín mináamǐ "mína ǐỹǎǎǐ" tus*
         numi=na   minaa-mǐ   [mi=na   iyaa-ǐ
         tree=ACC   lay.down+PFV-RECPST:3:DECL   1sg=ACC(CS) fall+PFV-APPR+3SG
         tus]
         say+SBD+3:SS
         'he laid a log down so that I wouldn't fall'

Here the verb of the speech report is third person, literally '...saying "may he not fall"', while the pronominal subject has shifted. Note also that the first person pronoun, although it is the subject, is marked with accusative case.

Table 17.1 showed that second person verbal marking is variable. In example (17.8) above, the verbal marking shifts to mark the CA subject as second person. But in example (17.10), the verb of the quote is third person, although its subject too is the CA.

(17.10) *ápa ámina "míhǎǐ nuwǐnati" tus suhustǐnǐ*
         apa   ami=na   [mi=haǐ   nuwǐna-ti   tus]
         father:PSSD:2   2sg=ACC 1sg(CS)=COM marry+PFV-JUSS say+SBD+3:SS
         su-hu-sa-tinu=ǐ
         give-1SG.OBJ-PFV-FUT+NMLZ=NONVIS.COP:3
         'your father will give you to me in marriage'

Here the purpose clause translates literally as '...saying "may she(CA) marry me(CS)"'. The first-person pronoun shows a shift to the CS's deictic centre, while the verb does not. It is likely that the modality of the speech report plays a role. Both (17.8) and (17.10) are functionally purpose clauses, and are not necessarily intended to convey actual quotes. Apprehensive modality is available for all persons, so can be shifted in (17.8). Jussive mood, however, is only possible with a third-person subject. The same form (at least etymologically) marks imperative when combined with a second-person subject. It is possible then that the third person marking in (17.10) has been retained to enable marking of jussive mood, as imperative marking would imply a direct quote. Clearly more work is required to ascertain the full range of deictic centre shift in speech reports, contrasting in particular actual quotes with purpose clauses and the like. It should also be borne in mind that all of these examples are elicited, and (17.10) in particular is grammatically unusual in having two SAP objects. Future collection and analysis of more natural conversational data will, I hope, provide more examples.

The final point to make about semi-direct speech is that it is in no way a distinct construction from direct speech. There is only one speech report construction in Aguaruna, which surfaces as:

(i) Direct speech when all pronouns and verbal markers index non SAP participants from the CS's point of view.

(ii) Indirect speech if all pronouns and verbal markers index SAP participants.

(iii) Semi-direct speech if there is a mix of SAP and non-SAP referents.

17.1.2 Bracketing of the Speech Report

The speech report is only rarely preceded by a speech verb. It often begins with an interjection such as *ma?* (hesitation), *ayu* 'ok', *naa* (uncertainty), as is common in normal speech. There is not typically any intonational marker of the speech report. Although sometimes the report is delivered at a higher pitch, typically it is not apparent until the speech verb that the preceding material is in fact a speech report. There may be a clear intonation break between the speech report and the following constituent; in other cases, the speech verb follows closely.

Example (17.11) shows an apparently discontinuous speech report. However, in all such cases, there must be one speech verb for every section of speech. So although this may be one discontinuous speech report in the sense of reporting one speech act, syntactically there are two speech reports.

(17.11) *Kaŋkáp ikám ashinkáuwai, "wɨmí" tus "kúntin maá yuwámi" tus ashinkáuwai*

kaŋkapɨ   ikama   ashina-ka-u=ai   w<u>ɨ-mi</u>
Kagkap   forest+LOC go:PL-PFV-NMLZ=COP:3:DECL   go+PFV-HORT
tus   <u>kuntinu</u>   <u>ma-a</u>   <u>yu-a-mi</u>
say+SBD+3:SS animal   kill-PFV+SEQ+1PL:SS   eat-PFV-HORT
tus   ashina-ka-u=ai
say+SBD+3:SS go:PL-PFV-NMLZ=COP:3:DECL
'Kagkap went to the forest saying "let's go", saying "let's kill animals and eat" he went.'(agr041005_14)

Speech reports can be nested within other speech reports. Example (17.12) is an extreme example: the quoted speaker quotes his brother's words, which themselves include a speech report.

(17.12) *ɨtsã tahímtãɨ, "ɨtsã tahímui, "ɨɨsta mína nuwáhãɨ uyúntusta tusám, yúmi shikisám iwakám, máma áusam, yúwakum dakahuumatá" tíuwai, táma núwa "ái" tíuwai*

[ɨtsã tahima-taɨ]   ɨtsã tahima-a-wa-i
sun reach.noon-SBD:1/3:DS sun reach.noon-IPFV-3-DECL

ɨɨsta [mi=na nuwa=haɨ [ũyu-tu-sa-ta]
come.on 1SG=ACC wife=COM accompany-1SG.OBJ-PFV-IMP

tu-sa-mɨ yumi shiki-sa-mɨ i-wa-ka-mɨ
say-SBD-2:SS water draw-SBD-2:SS CAUS-go.up-PFV+SEQ-2:SS

mama au-sa-mɨ   yu-a-ku-mɨ   daka-hu-ma-ta]
manioc put-PFV+SEQ-2:SS eat-IPFV-SIM-2:SS wait-1SG.OBJ-DUR-IMP

yatsu-hu   tu-hu-ti-mĩ   nunu
brother-PSSD:1SG say-APPL-1SG.OBJ+PFV-RECPST:3:DECL ANA

nu-tika-mi   ti-u=wai]   [[ta-ma]
ANA-VBLZ.TR+PFV-HORT say+PFV-NMLZ=COP:3:DECL say+IPFV-NSBJ>SBJ

nuwa ai ti-u=wai]
woman ok say+PFV-NMLZ=COP:3:DECL

'When it reached noon, he said "it's noon, come on, my brother said to me "go with my wife, saying "*come with me*", draw the water and bring it up, put the manioc in, and eat it while you wait for me" - let's do that"; when he said that, the woman said "ok".' (agr041005_14)

See §17.1.5 below for discussion of the development of *tus* < *tu-sã* (say-SBD+3:SS) as a speech report marker.

17.1.3 Speech Verbs

The most common speech verb by far is *tuta* 'say', the use of which is illustrated in examples (17.13, 17.14).

(17.13) *"wáinkas táwa" túyahai*
wainakasã ta-wa   tu-ya-ha-i
in.vain+3 say+IPFV-3:EXCL say-REMPST-1SG-DECL
'"He's lying!" I used to say.' (agr040723_29)

(17.14)   *"wíka yabáik hatánum puháhai" tíuwai*
wi=ka   yamai=ka   ha-ta=numa   puha-ha-i
1sg=TOP   now=TOP   die-ACT.NMLZ=LOC   live+IPFV-1SG-DECL
ti-u=wai
say+PFV-NMLZ=COP:3:DECL
'"Now I'm about to die" she said.' (agr041005_16)

The only other verb that can be used with a speech report is *wahat*, which has the primary meaning 'stand', and can be used as a copula (§7.8) and an auxiliary verb (§6.7). In addition, *wahat* may be used to represent animal vocalizations, as in (17.15), and to report shouted human speech (17.16). In the latter two senses, I gloss *wahat* as 'call'.

(17.15)   *ímau wakïïnĩã "háu, háu!" wahatãĩ*
imau   wakïï=nĩ=ya   hau   hau   waha-taĩ
INTENS.LOC   cliff=LOC=ABL   ONOM   ONOM   call-SBD:1/3:DS
'when (the puma) called "hau, hau" from a distant cliff...' (agr041006_01)

(17.16)   *"Kaŋkapí!" waháidau, "yatsúmin ikámỹãw̃ã yúwawai!" waháidau*
kaŋkapï   waha-ina-u   yatsu-mi=na
Kagkap+VOC   call-PL:IPFV-NMLZ   brother+PSSD-2SG=ACC
ikama yawaã   yu-a-wa-i   waha-ina-u
jaguar   eat-IPFV-3-DECL   call-PL:IPFV-NMLZ
'"Kagkap!" they were calling, "a jaguar is eating your brother!" they were calling.' (agr041005_14)

Other speech verbs are never accompanied directly by a speech report, but may be accompanied by a subordinate form of the speech verb *tuta* 'say' which itself introduces a speech report; this is illustrated in examples (17.17, 17.18) for the verbs *aimat* 'reply' and *untsumat* 'call'. Other verbs that can take such subordinate clause complements are listed in Table 17.2.

(17.17)   *"ayú" tus aimkáuwai*
[ayu   tus]   aima-ka-u=ai
ok   say+SBD+3:SS   reply-PFV-NMLZ=COP:3:DECL
'He replied "ok".' lit. *he replied saying "ok"* (agr041005_14)

(17.18)   *"ikámỹãw̃ã tukúhui, ayamhútkata!" tus untsúmu*
           [ikama yawaã   tuku-hu-a-wa-i   ayamhu-tu-ka-ta
           jaguar   attack-1SG.OBJ-IPFV-3-DECL   defend-1SG.OBJ-PFV-IMP
           tus]   untsuma-u
           say+SBD+3:SS   call+IPFV-NMLZ
           '"A jaguar is attacking me! Help me!" he was calling' (agr041005_14)

Table 17.2: Verbs of speech

verb	gloss
aimat	'reply'
auŋmat	'relate (a story)'
buut	'cry'
chichat	'speak'
ìtsìhūt	'tell'
untsumat	'call (for help)'

17.1.4 The Syntactic Status of Speech Reports

From their position preceding the reporting verb, direct speech reports appear to function as objects. However, the intonation break that may follow a speech report sets it apart from other objects (including nominalized clauses), which typically are more closely linked intonationally to the verb. Examples of textual anaphora, where a speech verb takes a pronominal object referring to a stretch of discourse (§4.6.2), also suggest that the speech itself is an object of the speech verb. Example (17.19) illustrates this.

(17.19)   *núna múun áuŋmatin áhabia núna wísha táhai*
           [nu=na   muunta   auhuma-tu-inu   aha-maya
           ANA=ACC   elder   tell.story-APPL-NMLZ   COP:PL-INTPST+3
           nu=na]   wi=sha   ta-ha-i
           ANAREL=ACC 1sg=ADD   say+IPFV-1SG-DECL
           'I also say that which the elders told' (agr040723_29)

A speech report is not obligatory with *tuta* 'say', which, unlike other verbs, is of indeterminate underlying transitivity (§7.6.3). *wahat* 'stand' / 'call' is only interpreted as a speech verb when a speech report is present.

17.1.5 Speech report marker *tus*

The dependent form *tu-sã* (say-SBD+3:SS) is often used as a kind of speech report marker, directly following the speech report and then followed by another speech verb. In this context, it generally appears in the phonologically reduced form *tus* – this reduction does not follow the usual rule of apocope, as the underlying form has only two syllables. The examples in §17.1.3 above showed this use of *tus*; in (17.20), the verb *tuta* 'say' itself is the speech verb.

(17.20) *"ayú" tus tímatãĩ*
       [ayu   tus]   ti-mataĩ
       ok   say+SBD+3:SS   say+PFV+SEQ-1/3:DS
       'when (the child) said "ok"...' lit. *when (the child) said, saying "ok"*
       (agr040721_07)

It looks as if *tus* is heading towards grammaticalization as a speech report marker, whereby the construction schematized in (17.21) will become general. The phonological reduction of *tusã* > *tus* is clear evidence of a grammaticalization process.

(17.21)   [<u>speech report</u> *tus*] speech.verb

Importantly, however, *tus* is still transparently a subordinated form of *tuta* 'say'. This is clear from the fact that it is only used with third person subject. In addition, a construction with a speech report followed by *tus* does not require any other speech verb, which shows that *tus* retains the semantic content of a full speech verb.

17.1.6 Functions of Speech Reports

The primary use of speech reports is for quoting speech. Dialogue is common in Aguaruna narratives, and speech reports may be used as a narrative device to highlight important plot points (Larson 1978). The extended functions of the speech report construction can be divided into:
(i) Emphasis
(ii) Expressing thoughts non-vocally
(iii) Intention and purpose clauses
(iv) Complement clauses

The first three of these functions are described in turn below, and complement clauses formed with speech reports are described in §17.2.

(i) Emphasis

In conversation, a speech report construction can be used to emphasize the speaker's own words, as in (17.22, 17.23). In such examples the speech verb typically takes exclamative mood.

(17.22)   *"achikáipa" táha!*
            <u>achi-ka-i-pa</u>   ta-ha
            grab-PFV-APPR-2SG:PROH   say+IPFV-1SG:EXCL
            '"Don't touch it" I say!'

(17.23)   *ma?, "antúkta" táha! wáŋka ántasmi? "wáamak witáhai" táha!*
            [ma?   <u>antu-ka-ta</u>   ta-ha]   [waŋka
            hey   listen-PFV-IMP   say+IPFV-1SG:EXCL   why
            anta-tsu-mi]   [waamaki   <u>wi-ta-ha-i</u>
            listen+IPFV-NEG-2   quickly   go+PFV-IFUT-1SG-DECL
            ta-ha]
            say+IPFV-1SG:EXCL
            'Hey, "listen" I say! Why don't you listen? "I'm in a hurry" I say!'
            (agr041006_04)

See also example (17.24) (repeated from Chapter 11); the context here is that the speaker is asking for a loan, so finds it important to highlight the fact that he is expecting to be paid. In this case it is not clear how much of the preceding discourse is being treated as a speech report.

(17.24)   *yama takatnum yapahiinau asan, iki akihuinashkũĩ tahami*
            <u>yama</u>   <u>taka-ta=numa</u>   <u>yapahiina-u</u>   <u>asa-nu</u>
            recently   work-NMLZ=LOC   change+PFV-NMLZ   COP+SBD-1SG:SS
            <u>iki</u>   <u>aki-hu-ina-cha-ku-ĩ</u>   <u>ta-hami</u>
            not.yet   pay-1SG.OBJ-PL:IPFV-NEG-SIM+1/3-DS   say+IPFV-1SG>2SG+DECL
            'I've recently changed my job and they haven't paid me yet, I'm telling you' (personal correspondence)

(ii) and (iii) Expression of thoughts, intention and purpose clauses

In addition to reporting speech, the speech report construction has been generalized to cover non-verbal vocalizations and extended to express thoughts and intentions. The speech report construction is used to represent both human (17.25) and non-human (17.26) vocalizations. For animal vocalizations the verb *wahat* 'stand/call', is used. The same verb used with a verbal speech report indicates shouting (cf. 17.16).

(17.25)   *búu búutkãw̃ã "si̇̃" tus*

	buu	buuta-kawã	**si̇̃**	tus
	REDUP	cry+IPFV-REPET+3:SS	alas	say+SBD+3:SS

'crying and crying, saying "alas!".' (agr041006_04)

(17.26)   *ikámỹãw̃ã "tru tru tru!" wahau*

ikama_yawaã	**tru tru tru**	waha-a-u
jaguar	ONOM	call-IPFV-NMLZ

'The jaguar was calling "roar roar roar!".' (agr041005_14)

Onomatopoetic representations of non-vocal sounds can appear with verbs describing their production in a construction similar to speech reporting (17.27), as can ideophones (17.28); however these forms are never accompanied by speech verbs, and are syntactically manner adverbs rather than verbal arguments.

(17.27)   *tu! tu! awáttãĩ...*

tu tu	awatu-taĩ
ONOM	hit-SBD:1/3:DS

'When he hit it: "tap! tap!"...' (agr040723_29)

(17.28)   *pakɨt anuhúk...*

pakɨt	anuhu-kã
IDEO	stick.on-PFV+SEQ+3:SS

'Having stuck it on with a slap...' (agr040723_29)

Some examples of speech report constructions are ambiguous as to whether the author of the speech report actually spoke aloud. Example (17.29) comes from a story about a woman who goes out alone to look for fruit and gets lost. As she was alone, it is unlikely that the words couched as a speech report were actually spoken aloud.

(17.29)   *hiinkɨ́ wɨuwai, wɨɯa wɨɯakũã "tupikáktahai" tus tupikákɨ̃, wɨɯa wɨɯakũã hɨ̃ɯ̃ã́ũ̃w̃ãĩ Mánchumush puhámunum*

hiina-kɨ̃	wɨ-u=ai	wɨɯa
go.out-PFV+SEQ+3:SS	go+PFV-NMLZ=COP:3:DECL	REDUP

wɨ-a-kawã	**tupika-ki-ta-ha-i**	tus
go-IPFV-REPET+3:SS	run-PFV-IFUT-1SG-DECL	say+SBD+3:SS

tupika-kĩ	wĩɥa	wɨ-a-kawã
run-PFV+SEQ+3:SS	REDUP	go-IPFV-REPET+3:SS

hĩɥa-u=ai	manchumuchi	puha-mau=numa
arrive+PFV-NMLZ=COP:3:DECL	Manchumuch	live+IPFV-NSBJ.NMLZ=LOC

'Having gone out she kept going, saying "I will run", and she went on running and arrived at the place where Manchumuch (a mythical cannibal) lives.' (agr040721_07)

Other cases more clearly involve thought rather than actual spoken words. Example (17.30) comes from a story in which a man camping out in a hut hears a puma growling outside and wonders what the noise is.

(17.30)   *"wahĩ túhãsh wahĩ táwa?" tus anɨntaimá puhãĩ...*

[wahĩ	tuhã=sha	wahĩ	ta-wa	tus]	anɨntaima
what	BUT=ADD	what	say+IPFV-3	say+SBD+3:SS	think

puha-ĩ
live+IPFV+1SG/3-DS

'as he was thinking "what's making that noise?"...' lit. *as he was thinking, saying "what says that?"* (agr041006_01)

The same construction is used to express intention in (17.31). This type of construction is the historical source of the desiderative suffix *-tata* (§8.4.4).

(17.31)   *yuwáta táma nuní áyamhumak...*

[yu-a-ta-ha	ta-ma]	nuni
eat-PFV-IFUT-1SG:EXCL	say+IPFV-NSBJ>SBJ	thus

ayamhu-ma-kã
defend-REFL-PFV+SEQ+3:SS

'when (the puma) tried to eat him, he defended himself like that...' lit. *when (the puma) said "I will eat him!"...* (agr041006_01)

Example (17.32) also expresses intention.

(17.32)   *áimak ɨmamkɨmas, "intáhaiŋ" tus...*

aima-a-kũ	ɨmamkɨma-sã	[inta-ha-i-ha
fill-IPFV-SIM+3:SS	be.careful-SBD+3:SS	break-PFV-APPR-1SG

tus]
say+SBD+3:SS

'Filling it carefully, lest he should break it...' lit. *...saying "may I not break it"* (agr041006_04)

Example (17.33) expresses reason; it refers to a cow that was mooing as we passed it in a canoe. This example is grammatically parallel to example (17.25) above, in which the same verb *buutut* 'cry' appears, and the speech report is an actual representation of the vocalization; here, however, the speech report is clearly not intended to represent the cow's vocalization.

(17.33)   *búutui "Simón wɨuawai" tus*
       buuta-wa-i   [*Simón*   wɨ-a-wa-i   tus]
       cry+IPFV-3-DECL Simon   go-IPFV-3-DECL say+SBD+3:SS
       'It's crying because Simon's going' lit. *...saying "Simon's going"*

Example (17.34) is ambiguous, as it is functionally a purpose clause but at the same time is a believable representation of an actual utterance.

(17.34)   *nuwán "yúmi shikiktá" tus awɨmám...*
       nuwa=na   [yumi   shiki-ki-ta   tus]   awɨma-ma
       woman=ACC water   draw-PFV-IMP say+SBD+3:SS send+PFV-NSBJ>SBJ
       'when they sent a woman to draw water...' lit. *...saying "draw some water"* (agr040712_02)

The extended used of speech reports in Aguaruna are analogous to those of the Quechua verb *ni-* 'say', as reported by Adelaar (1990):

> [T]he meaning of *ni-* to a large extent extends beyond that of a verb of communication. And...the verb *ni-* demands a message complement in directly quoted speech... The above combination of facts compels speakers to use quotations in sentences which do not refer to actual speaking in order to render the content of a mental activity.
>
> Adelaar (1990: 4–5)

As described above, there is evidence that the form *tus* is developing into a speech report marker. In these examples of speech reports as complement clauses, we see a further development of *tus* into a complementizer. This is not unexpected: Lord (1993) describes such a grammaticalization path in African languages, and Heine & Kuteva (2002: 261ff) give examples of 'say' verbs developing into cause and purpose markers and complementizers. Similar grammaticalization of speech report constructions in Aguaruna has very likely led to many verbal suffixes expressing futurity, desire and intention, that appear to have developed form forms of *tuta* 'say' – see discussion in §8.4.4.

17.2 Complementation

Complementation is the embedding of an entire clause as a core argument of a matrix clause (Dixon 2006). In Aguaruna there is no single construction that has complementation as its primary function. All of the clause types used as complement clauses also have other functions; these are COMPLEMENTATION STRATEGIES in Dixon's (2006) terminology. Complement clause types in Aguaruna can be distinguished according to whether the subject of the complement clause is the same or different from that of the matrix verb. Complement clauses with the same subject as the matrix clause take the following forms:
- Nominalization
- Subordinate intentional clause
- Rhetorical question

Where the subject of the complement clause is different from that of the matrix verb, another set of constructions are used:
- Speech report
- Nominalization
- Embedded question
- Juxtaposition of finite clause(? – see below)

The type of complement clause selected also depends upon the matrix verb. The complementation strategies are described below; the juxtaposition strategy is marginal, hence the question mark. Table 17.3 lists the main complement taking verbs and the strategies employed for SS and DS complement clauses.

Table 17.3: Complement-taking verbs and their complement clause types

verb	gloss	complement clause type SS	DS
wakiujat	'want'	intentional clause	speech report
dakitut	'refuse'	-ta nominalization; juxtaposition	–
wainat	'see'	–	nominalization; juxtaposition
antut	'hear'	–	nominalization
dikat	'know'	–	nominalization; indirect question
dikapit	'try'	non-temporal subordinate clause	–
dikapit	'feel'	nominalization	–

verb	gloss	complement clause type	
		SS	DS
naŋkama(na)t	'begin'	*-ta* nominalization; other nominalization	–
umit	'complete'	*-ta* nominalization	–

Juxtaposition of a finite clause can occasionally function as a complementation strategy, as in example (17.35) with the verb *dakitut* 'refuse'.

(17.35)   *wíka ubáŋnak awɨmchattahai, dakítahai*
           [wi=ka   uma-hu=na=ka   awɨma-cha-tata-ha-i]
           1sg=TOP   sibling-PSSD:1SG=ACC=TOP   send+PFV-NEG-FUT-1SG-DECL
           [dakita-a-ha-i]
           refuse-IPFV-1SG-DECL
           'I will not send my sister away; I refuse to do it (male speaker)'
           (agr060816_01)

It seems to be stretching the point to call this a complement clause (i.e. *I refuse [to send my sister away]*), as there are two juxtaposed finite clauses. But note that the complement taking predicate *dakitut* 'refuse' is semantically incomplete without the preceding clause, as it is transitive and requires an understood object. And compare example (17.61) below, where a juxtaposed finite clause is clearly functioning as the complement of the verb *wainat* 'see'. The conclusion to be drawn here is that the distinction between complementation and other types of clause-combining is not always syntactically clear-cut, and this can be ascribed to the absence of a dedicated complementation construction in Aguaruna.

Although most attested examples of complement clauses are in O function, this is not a grammatical requirement. Example (15.85) in Chapter 15 shows a complement clause formed with the action nominalizer *-ta* in A function, and example (17.59) below shows an embedded question complement clause in S function.

17.2.1 Same-subject complement clauses

17.2.1.1 Subordinate intentional clauses
The intentional subordinating suffix is used to form complements of verbs of wanting and intention, as in (17.36).

(17.36)   *yuwátasan wakɨɰahai*
     [yu-a-**tasa**-nu]   wakɨɰa-a-ha-i
     eat-PFV-**INTENT**-1SG   want-IPFV-1SG-DECL
     'I want to eat'

This is structurally identical to a purpose clause (cf. Dixon 2006: 39). Purpose can also be encoded using a simultaneous temporal subordinate clause marked with the suffix -*ku*, as in (17.37).

(17.37)   *wɨtathai mína ahahuíŋ takákun*
     wɨ-tata-ha-i   [mi̱=na   aha-hu=ĩ=ka
     go+PFV-FUT-1SG-DECL   1sg=ACC garden-PSSD:1SG=LOC=TOP
     taka-a-ku-nu]
     work-IPFV-SIM-1SG:SS
     'I will go to work in my garden'

The example translates literally as *I will go, working in my garden*. This construction provides a useful test for distinguishing complement clauses from purpose clauses: although both types can be encoded with the intentional suffix, only the purpose clause can be encoded using a -*ku* subordinate clause.

17.2.1.2 Action nominalizer -*ta*

A verb nominalized with the action nominalizer -*ta* can fill the same types of functions as any noun, including subject and object roles. When a nominalization is an argument of a complement-taking verb, as in (17.38–17.40), it functions as a complement clause. Note in examples (17.39, 17.40) that the internal object of the nominalized clause does not take accusative marking, as is normal for this type of nominalization (§15.2).

(17.38)   *dakítau apahĩ́hãĩ wɨtán*
     dakita-a-u   [apa-hĩ=haĩ   wɨ-**ta**=na]ₙₚ:ₒ
     refuse-IPFV-NMLZ   father-PSSD:1PL/3=COM **go-ACT.NMLZ**=ACC
     'he refused to go with his father' (agr041005_15)

(17.39)   *naŋkámauwai anɨntãĩ́ tsupíŋtan*
     naŋkama-a-u=ai   [anɨntaĩ   tsupi-hu-**ta**=na]ₙₚ:ₒ
     begin-IPFV-NMLZ=COP:3:DECL heart   cut-APPL-**ACT.NMLZ**=ACC
     'he began to cut (the boa's) heart' (agr040721_01)

(17.40)   *naŋkámau áyahai papí áuhtan*

        naŋkama-a-u   a-ya-ha-i   [papi   auhu-**ta**=na]NP:O

        begin-IPFV-NMLZ   COP-REMPST-1SG-DECL   book   study-**ACT.NMLZ**=ACC

        'I began to study' (agr040824_02)

The use of *-ta* in discourse is rather rare, and the most common *-ta* complement taking verbs are the two illustrated: *dakitut* 'refuse' and *naŋkamat* 'begin'. The verb *umit* 'complete (a task)' can also take a *-ta* nominalization object argument. In (17.41), however, this appears to be a lexical nominalization rather than a complement clause.

(17.41)   *takatán umíkhai*

        [taka-**ta**=na]NP:O   umi-ka-ha-i

        work-**ACT.NMLZ**=ACC   complete-PFV-1SG-DECL

        'I've completed the work'

For other uses of *-ta* nominalizations, see Chapter 15.

17.2.1.3 Non-temporal subordinate clause

The verb *dikapit* 'try', a derivative of *dikat* 'know' (see §7.7.4.5), can take a SS complement clause formed with the non-temporal subordinator *-sa* (17.42).

(17.42)   *yanasán dikapsáthai*

        [yana-**sa**-nu]   dikapi-sa-ta-ha-i

        carry.on.shoulder-**SBD**-1SG:SS   try-PFV-IFUT-1SG-DECL

        'I'll try carrying it'

The same verb *dikapit* also functions as a copula, with the meaning 'feel', and then takes a nominalization as complement, as described in the following section.

17.2.1.4 Participant nominalizations

Complements may be formed with the non-subject nominalizer *-mau*, which functions as an action nominalizer. In example (17.43), the Marañón river is the subject of the verb 'begin', and the nominalized clause is the object, literally '*the Marañón began a flooding*'.

(17.43) *naŋkámnawabi mahanú abáuhamun*
    naŋkamana-a-amai   mahanu [amauha-**mau**=na]_{NP:O}
    begin-PFV-DISTPST:3:DECL Marañón rise+IPFV-**NSBJ.NMLZ**=ACC
    'the Marañón River began to rise' (agr040824_02)

Example (17.44) shows a *-mau* nominalization complement of *wakɨɰat* 'want'.

(17.44) *papí áuŋbaunak sínchi wakɨɰau asán...*
    [papi auha-**mau**=na=ka]_{NP:O}   sinchi wakɨɰa-a-u
    book study+IPFV-**NSBJ.NMLZ**=ACC=TOP strongly want-IPFV-NMLZ
    asa-nu
    COP+SBD-1SG:SS
    'Because I really wanted to study...' (agr040824_02)

In example (17.45), the verb *tukut* 'shoot' is nominalized with *-mau*, functioning as an action nominalization, and this form is then relativized with the postposed relativizer construction as a focussing strategy. This whole construction forms the complement of the verb *naŋkamat* 'begin'.

(17.45) *naŋkámauwai píshakush áidau tukuámua núna*
    naŋkama-a-u=ai   [[pishaka-uchi a-ina-u]
    begin-PFV-NMLZ=COP:3:DECL bird-DIM   COP-PL:IPFV-NMLZ
    tuku-a-**mau**=a   nu=na]_{NP:O}
    shoot-PFV-**NSBJ.NMLZ**=COP:3 ANA_{REL}=ACC
    'he began to shoot small birds' lit. *he began [that which is the shooting of small birds]* (agr040724_01)

The verb *dikapɨt* 'feel' is a copula, taking two nominative case-marked arguments. In example (17.46), the copula complement clause is functioning as a complementation strategy.

(17.46) *ashí aɨnts áidau ikámyawanak kákahus maanimáinchau dikapɨdau*
    [ashi aɨntsu a-ina-u]_{NP:CS}   [ikama_yawaã=na=ka
    all person COP-PL:IPFV-NMLZ jaguar=ACC=TOP
    kakahus maani-mai-inu-chau]_{NP:CC} dikapɨ-ina-u
    easily fight-POT-NMLZ-NEG.NMLZ feel-PL:IPFV-NMLZ
    'all the people felt (that they were) unable to fight a jaguar' (agr041005_14)

17.2.1.5 Rhetorical question embedded in speech report

Rhetorical questions have a variety of uses (see §10.7); in example (17.47), a rhetorical question couched as a speech report functions as the complement of the verb *wakɨɰat* 'want'.

(17.47) *"wísha wahúkanuk unuimáhan aánkaŋ chicháu áha?" tusán sínchi wakíyahai*
[wi=sha   wahuka-nu=ki   unuima-ha-nu   aankaŋ
1sg=Q.TOP how-1SG=Q.RHET   learn-PFV+SEQ-1SG:SS   thus
chicha-a-u   a-ha   tu-sa-nu]   sínchi
speak-IPFV-NMLZ COP-1SG   say-SBD-1SG:SS   strongly
wakɨɰa-ya-ha-i
want-REMPST-1SG-DECL
'I really wanted to learn to speak like that (i.e. in Spanish)' lit. *I wanted saying "how will I speak like that, having learned (it)?"* (agr040824_02)

17.2.2 Different-subject complement clauses

17.2.2.1 Speech report

Where its subject differs from that of the main clause, a speech report construction is used for the complement clause of *wakɨɰat* 'want'. In example (17.48), the speech report construction itself forms a subordinate clause dependent on the verb *wakɨɰat* 'want'.

(17.48) *"nĩ yuwáti" tusán wakíɰahai*
[nĩ   yu-a-ti   tu-sa-nu]   wakɨɰa-a-ha-i
3sg   eat-PFV-JUSS say-SBD-1SG:SS   want-IPFV-1SG-DECL
'I want him to eat' lit. *I want, saying "let him eat"*

Note in example (17.49) that the matrix verb *wakɨɰat* 'want' is marked with applicative and first person singular object.

(17.49) *dita áidau wakíɰaŋtuinawai "ápu atí" tus*
dita   a-ina-u   wakɨɰa-hu-tu-ina-wa-i   [apu
3pl   COP-PL:IPFV-NMLZ   want-APPL-1SG.OBJ-PL:IPFV-3-DECL   chief
a-ti   tus]
COP-JUSS   say+SBD+3:SS
'they all want me to be chief' lit. *they want (for my benefit) saying "let him be chief"*

17.2.2.2 Nominalization

For the verbs *wainat* 'see' and *antut* 'hear', a nominalization may function as a DS complement clause. The construction in (17.50) is effectively a relative clause.

(17.50)   *uchíhum mináun wainkámhai*
           [uchi-hu-mi   mina-**u**=na]NP:O   waina-ka-ma-ha-i
           child-PSSD-2   arrive+IPFV-**NMLZ**=ACC   see-PFV-RECPST-1SG-DECL
           'I saw your child coming' OR 'I saw your child, who was coming'

But complement clauses of *antut* and *wainat* are more typically expressed with a non-subject nominalization, marked with -*mau*; in (17.51) this functions as an action nominalizer.

(17.51)   *minák kantámun antúkmahai*
           [mina-kũ   kanta-a-**mau**=na]NP:O
           arrive+IPFV-SIM+3:SS   sing-IPFV-**NSBJ.NMLZ**=ACC
           antu-ka-ma-ha-i
           hear-PFV-RECPST-1SG-DECL
           'I heard him singing as he came' lit. *I heard the singing-while-arriving*

In (17.52) the verb is also marked for second person object, a kind of "raising" construction.

(17.52)   *ámɨ takámunak wíi wainkámhamɨ*
           [amɨ   taka-a-**mau**=na=ka]   wi   waina-ka-ma-hamɨ
           2sg   work-IPFV-**NSBJ.NMLZ**=ACC=TOP   1sg   see-PFV-RECPST-1SG>2SG+DECL
           'I saw you working' lit. *I saw you, your working*

A non-subject nominalization can also function as complement of *dɨkat* 'know', as in example (17.53). Note that this example could be parsed as relativization (*I know myself who was seen by you*), as the common argument of the relative clause (first person singular) is also marked as (reflexive) object on the verb of the matrix clause, but it is better analysed as complementation, with the reflexive marking representing the same object-raising as in (17.52).

(17.53)   *dɨkámhai ámɨ wáitkamunak*
           dɨka-a-ma-ha-i   [amɨ   wai-tu-ka-**mau**=na=ka]
           know-IPFV-REFL-1SG-DECL   2sg   see-1SG.OBJ-PFV-**NSBJ.NMLZ**=ACC=TOP
           'I know you saw me'

In example (17.54), a participant nominalization is the object of *wainat* 'see'. Note that -*inu* normally forms a subject nominalization, but the potential form of the verb is always S=O ambitransitive.

(17.54)   *dushíkmainun wainkáuwai*
           [dushiki-mai-**inu**=na]ₙₚ:ₒ   waina-ka-u=ai
           laugh.at-POT-**NMLZ**=ACC   see-PFV-NMLZ=COP:3:DECL
           'he saw that it was funny' lit. *he saw the one that was able to be laughed at* (agr041102_07)

This is similar to the subject nominalization exemplified above (17.50), as the distinction between a nominalization functioning as a complement clause and one functioning as a nominal argument (as in 17.55), is not clear cut.

(17.55)   *máaninun wainkámhai*
           [maani-**inu**=na]ₙₚ:ₒ   waina-ka-ma-ha-i
           fight-**NMLZ**=ACC   see-PFV-RECPST-1SG-DECL
           'I saw a warrior'

Example (17.56) shows a relative clause formed with a pronoun functioning as the complement of *dikat* 'know', here better translated as 'find out'.

(17.56)   *dikáwahui tsuŋkí aíshĩ datsáuchia núna dukuhĩ́ kukáŋ nuŋkánum*
           puhúwa núnak
           dika-aw-aha-u=i   [tsuŋki   aishĩ
           know-PFV-PL-NMLZ=COP:3:DECL mermaid+GEN   husband+PSSD:1PL/3
           datsauchi=a   nu=na   duku-hĩ   kukaŋ
           youth=COP:3   ANA=ACC mother-PSSD:1PL/3   by.land+LOC
           nuŋka=numa   puhu-wa   **nu**=na=ka]ₙₚ:ₒ
           land=LOC   live-3   ANA=ACC=TOP
           'they found out that the mermaid's young husband's mother lived on land' (agr040721_07)

17.2.2.3 Embedded questions

The verb *dikat* 'know' takes a DS complement clause formed with an embedded question (17.57, 17.58). The question takes the same form as it would if it were direct: there is no overt mood marking on the verb, but apocope is suppressed (see Chapter 10 for morphological details).

(17.57) *wíka íkɨ díkas'hai wahǐ áwa*

        wi=ka   íkɨ   díka-a-tsu-ha-i   [wahǐ   a-wa]

        1SG=TOP   not.yet   know-IPFV-NEG-1SG-DECL   what   exist-3

        'I don't know yet what there is (for dinner)'

(17.58) *díkahai yáa puháwa*

        díka-a-ha-i   [ya   puha-wa]

        know-IPFV-1SG-DECL   who live+IPFV-3

        'I know who is there'

In example (17.59) the embedded question is an S argument, as the construction takes advantage of the S=O ambitransitivity of all verbs marked with the potential suffix *-mai* (see §7.6.3).

(17.59) *túu wakɨɥamɨ díkamáitsui*

        [tu   wakɨɥa-a-mɨ]   díka-mai-tsu-u-i

        which   want-IPFV-2   know-POT-NEG-3-DECL

        '(I) can't know which one you want' lit. *which (one) you want is unknowable*

In example (17.60) the indirect question is a complement to a complex predicate consisting of the adverb *diik* 'watching' and the auxiliary verb *tipit* 'lie down' (note that the adverb *diik* itself is derived from the verb *diit* 'look at').

(17.60) *wíi iwasán díik tɨpɨstáhai wahíŋ áikaŋmawa*

        wi   iwa-sa-nu   diik   tɨpɨ-sa-ta-ha-i

        1SG   be.awake-SBD-1SG:SS   watching   lie.down-PFV-IFUT-1SG-DECL

        [wahǐ=ki   aika-hama-a-wa]

        what=Q.RHET   thus+VBLZ.TR-2.OBJ-IPFV-3

        'I'll lie awake, watching (to see) what is doing this to you' (agr040723_29)

The examples illustrate that the same construction can be used for subject or object complement clauses, and with both positive and negative polarities of the matrix verb. There do not appear to be any restrictions on which interrogative words can take part in such constructions.

17.2.2.4 Juxtaposition

DS complementation can be achieved by juxtaposition of clauses, as in example (17.61).

(17.61)　*wainkáuwai kánu hapikbáuwa íman tahák akaikíuwai*
　　　　　waina-ka-u=ai　　　　　[kanu　hapi-ki-mau=a
　　　　　see-PFV-NMLZ=COP:3:DECL　canoe　drag-PFV-NSBJ.NMLZ=COP:3
　　　　　iman　　　　　taha-kũ　　　　　akai-ki-u=ai]
　　　　　INTENS.NMLZ_{REL}　clear+IPFV-SIM:3:SS　come.down-PFV-NMLZ=COP:3:DECL
　　　　　'he saw (that) something as big as a canoe being dragged had come
　　　　　down clearing a path through the undergrowth' (Text 1:5–6)

There is no overt object of the verb 'see', but the following finite clause describes what was seen, and thus functions as a complement clause. The meaning of the verb would be incomplete without the juxtaposed clause. See also example (17.35) above.

17.2.3 Other uses of complement clause constructions

All of the constructions illustrated above as complement clauses are also used in other functions. Because there is no single complement clause construction, nor any construction with complementation as its sole function, these forms can be described as complementation strategies, that is, appropriation of various clause combining and subordinating constructions in complementation function, due to the absence of any dedicated complementation device in the grammar (cf. Dixon 1995, 2006).

18 Discourse organization

This grammar is organized on the traditional "ascending" grammar model (Mosel 2006), which can be broadly characterized as working from smaller to larger units: beginning with phonology and progressing to multiclausal syntactic constructions. I have tried throughout the description to acknowledge the importance of pragmatic and linguistic context to the morphosyntactic phenomena under discussion, and the present chapter builds on that recognition to draw together the various discourse-pragmatic motivations that have been identified as underpinning the grammar in the preceding chapters. The aim of this chapter is to sketch some of the morphological, syntactic, and lexical choices that speakers of Aguaruna make in order to situate their speech in the discourse and extralinguistic context and provide thematic cohesion to their narratives. I characterize these choices in terms of the speaker explicitly guiding the addressee towards the intended interpretation of utterances; in other words, the speaker makes these choices (at least in part) on the basis of their assumptions about the addressee's state of knowledge.

In the following sections, I first describe the role of constituent order in marking information structure (§18.1), then in §18.2 address the overt morphological marking of information structural status. In §18.3 I provide a more integrated account of the various reference tracking devices than was possible in previous chapters. §18.4 describes the grammatical strategies available for marking source of information, and discusses how this fits in with wider cultural concerns. In §18.5 I describe the uses of speech reports and other devices for foregrounding and backgrounding clauses and allowing speakers to explicitly signpost the narrative structure. Finally, §18.6 briefly addresses some aspects of linguistic interaction in Aguaruna that remain to be investigated.

18.1 Constituent order and syntactic marking of information structure

Basic constituent order in Aguaruna is predicate final; this is obligatory in subordinate clauses and the unmarked ordering in finite clauses. Within the predicate-final structure, the object typically immediately precedes the verb, giving an AOV structure to a transitive clause with two overt arguments (of course, clauses in which one or both arguments are ellipted are more common). Only a few constructions strictly require a fixed constituent order:

- Temporal/causal subordinate clauses must be iconically ordered, and precede (subordinate or finite) clauses describing chronologically subsequent actions or events (§13.7, §14.2)
- The semantically full verb in an auxiliary construction must precede the auxiliary verb (§6.7)
- A genitive-marked possessor NP must directly precede the possessum, with no intervening material (§5.6)

In keeping with the verb-final preference, a main clause is normally the last in a clause-chain; departures from this tendency are restricted to a few semantic linking types (see §13.7 and discussion in Chapter 14).

Although the OV order is most common and unmarked, the clause-initial and clause-final positions are both used to highlight constituents. There does not seem to be a strong association of position with information structural status; rather, clause-initial and clause-final position are both used to highlight constituents, and morphological marking used to specify whether they are to be interpreted as given, new, or contrastive. Having said that, clause initial position does seem to be more commonly associated with presupposed information, often overtly marked as topical. The subject argument normally takes the clause-initial position, giving AOV/SV ordering. Some adverbs, question words, focussed and pronominal object arguments take clause-initial position. When an overt object NP is neither focussed nor pronominal, there is a strong preference for OV ordering, with no intervening material between object and verb. An overt full subject NP may take postverbal position if the object is initial, giving an OVA order. In clauses with two objects, one may appear in preverbal position and the other postverbal, but this is not obligatory. In examples (18.1, 18.2), pronominal object NPs take clause initial position, and the subject NPs, also pronominal, follow.

(18.1)   *mína ámɨ dakumhúkta*
         [mi=na]_{NP:O}   [amɨ]_{NP:A}   dakuma-hu-ka-ta
         1sg=ACC   2sg   imitate-1SG.OBJ-PFV-IMP
         'take a photo of me'

(18.2)   *núna wísha táhai*
         [nu=na]_{NP:O}   [wi=sha]_{NP:A}   ta-ha-i
         ANA=ACC   1sg=ADD   say+IPFV-1SG-DECL
         'I also tell that (story)' (agr040723_29)

In example (18.3), the pronominal determiner of a discontinuous object NP is clause initial, while the head follows the verb, as does the subject.

(18.3)   *núna achikuí aintsún páŋkĩ*
        [nu=na]ₙₚ:ₒ   achi-ka-u=i   [aintsu=na]ₙₚ:ₒ [paŋkĩ]ₙₚ:ₐ
        ANA=ACC   grab-PFV-NMLZ=COP:3:DECL   person=ACC   boa
        'the boa grabbed that person' (Text 1:9)

Example (18.4), from online chat, illustrates post-predicate position marking contrast. I asked about the Vargas Llosa novel "La casa verde," and my correspondent replied with (18.4), where "La ciudad y los perros" is another novel by the same author.

(18.4)   *wika ausamiahai 'La ciudad y los perros'*
        wi=ka   au-sa-maya-ha-i   *La ciudad y los perros*
        1sg=TOP read-PFV-INTPST-1SG-DECL   <book title>
        'I have read *La ciudad y los perros*' (personal correspondence)

Example (18.5) shows AOV constituent order, where both NPs are marked with 'question topic' enclitic *=sha*, as they represent presupposed information.

(18.5)   *amish final de mundial sudafricash diismakum*
        amɨ=sha   *final de mundial*   sudafrica=sha
        2sg=Q.TOP   world cup final   South Africa=Q.TOP
        dii-sa-ma=ka-umɨ
        look.at-PFV-RECPST=Q-2SG
        'did you watch the world cup final (that was held in) South Africa?' (personal correspondence)

In (18.6b) the subject marked with topic enclitic *=ka* appears in post-predicate position.

(18.6)   *atsá, áuk wáinak túhamui, áuk pɨ́ŋkɨhai híntak*
    a. atsa   au=ka   wainakã   tu-hama-u-i
        no   DIST=TOP in.vain+3   say-2.OBJ+IPFV-3-DECL

    b. au=ka   pɨŋkɨha=i   [hinta=ka]ₙₚ:cs
        DIST=TOP good=COP:3:DECL path=TOP
        'ᵃ·no, she's lying to you, ᵇ·the path is good' (agr040721_07)

Discourse particles and question words typically take clause-initial position (Chapter 12), while time words and oblique NPs take either clause-initial or clause-final position. Subordinate clauses normally precede the main clause, but this position is not fixed (Chapter 13). The principle of iconicity motivates the position of subordinate clauses, as temporal clauses representing chronologically ordered events are always ordered iconically, and purpose clauses, which are necessarily subsequent to the controlling clause, typically follow the latter. Where these principles do not apply, the general preference is for the controlling verb to be sentence-final. As noted above, subordinate clauses are always verb-final.

18.2 Morphological marking of information structure

Various strategies are available to foreground or background the events, actions and states represented by clauses. The past tense system reflects this, as shown in §8.4.3, as the selection of tense functions to foreground or background the events or states represented. It seems to be the case that switch-reference marking can also be manipulated in accordance with a preference for different-subject backgrounded clauses and same-subject foregrounded clauses (see Overall 2014b for discussion). Reported speech was shown in §17.1 to have a number of important functions beyond quoting, and reported speech may be used to highlight important events in a narrative; this is addressed in §18.5 below. All of these techniques help to structure narratives and other discourse genres in such a way as to ensure that the addressee is able to keep track of the main narrative line distinct from the backgrounded clauses, and they interact with the NP marking and reference tracking strategies to be described below.

This section describes the morphological resources available for signalling the pragmatic status of a particular NP, beyond the marking of grammatical role. The most important and frequent of these resources is the topic enclitic =*ka*, which has the general function of marking identifiable referents or backgrounded constituents within a clause; these are the elements about which, or in relation to which, the rest of the clause is predicated. The same marker is used to form conditional clauses, as expected since they also provide a framing function for the rest of the clause (Haiman 1978). In interrogative clauses the function of =*ka* is played by a different marker, =*sha*. And =*ka* is in complementary distribution with the additive enclitic =*sha(kama)* 'also', which I discuss in §18.2.4 below. Prior to that, I describe the various functions of =*ka* in §18.2.1, the use of determiners in NPs in §18.2.2 and the relativized copula construction in §18.2.3. I do not go into detail here regarding the phenomenon of covert arguments. This is frequent in discourse and correlates with highly topical referents, either available from the immediate extralinguistic context or an active discourse topic.

18.2.1 Topic enclitic *=ka*

The topic enclitic can be attached to any NP. It typically marks identifiable referents (and as such has been labelled a definiteness marker), but its use is also expected in certain syntactic environments.
– Reintroducing participants
– In verbless copula clauses, marking the subject
– Contrasting NPs
– In parenthetical and elaboration clauses
– In negated clauses

Like the other discourse enclitics, this marker shows a certain ambiguity of scope. Although it typically has scope over the marked constituent, its almost obligatory use in certain types of clause means that effectively it is the whole clause that is being marked. The five contexts of use are described in the following sections.

A. Reintroducing participants
When major participants in a narrative are reintroduced as core arguments, they are typically restated as full NPs and receive topic marking, as in example (18.7). The boa and its victim, the man, are the main characters of the story, but the preceding context had another man as subject, who found the boa wrapped around the dead man and killed it. Now both the boa and the first man are taken up again as subject and object respectively (note that the boa is also in a determined NP).

(18.7) *dúka páŋkiŋ kuwiŋkahá atihǎ, aíntsnak shitákĩ ahápauwai*
  [nu=**ka** paŋkĩ=**ka**] kuwiŋkaha ati-hã
  ANA=**TOP** boa=**TOP** IDEO unwrap-PFV+SEQ+3:SS
  [aíntsu=na=**ka**] shita-kĩ ahapa-a-u=ai
  person=ACC=**TOP** push-PFV+SEQ+3:SS throw.out-PFV-NMLZ=COP:3:DECL
  '(when the boa was killed), that boa unwrapped the person "*kuwiŋkaha*!", pushed him out and discarded him.' (Text 1:33)

Example (18.8) follows a crucial point in the story of the origin of manioc and masato, when the protagonist goes to visit his mother. This line reorients us to the story as we begin a new episode.

(18.8) *núnik dukuhín ihás datsáuchik wakítkiuwai*
  nu-ni-kã duku-hĩ=na
  ANA-VBLZ.INTR-PFV+SEQ+3:SS mother-PSSD:1PL/3=ACC

iha-sã   [datsauchi=**ka**] wakitu-ki-u=ai
visit-PFV+SEQ+3:SS youth=**TOP**   return-PFV-NMLZ=COP:3:DECL
'then, having visited his mother, the youth went back' (agr040824_01)

As in the translations above, this function correlates with definiteness, as the speaker is signalling that the referent of the NP is identifiable through having been activated in the discourse context.

B. Verbless clause subjects

When a nominal functions as a predicate without the enclitic or independent copula, its subject is typically marked with the topic enclitic, as in (18.9).

(18.9)   *mina dukuhuk apash*
     [mi=na duku-hu=**ka**]_{NP:VCS} [apachi]_{NP:PRED}
     1sg=ACC mother-PSSD:1SG=**TOP** non.Aguaruna
     'my mother is non-Aguaruna' (Tiinch & Danducho)

Further examples are in (18.11) and (18.13) below.

C. Contrasting NPs

When a contrast is explicitly indicated, the enclitic *=ka* normally appears on each of the contrasted NPs, as in (18.10, 18.11).

(18.10) *tíkichik nuwínas batsátinaĩ, dúka nuwínchaush áhakui*
     [tikichi=**ka**] nuwina-sã   batsata-ina-ĩ   [nu=**ka**]
     other=**TOP** marry-PFV+SEQ+3:SS live:PL-PL:IPFV+3-DS ANA=**TOP**
     nuwina-chau-uchi a-haku=i
     marry-NEG.NMLZ-DIM COP-NARR.PST=COP:3:DECL
     'while the others were married, that guy remained unmarried' (agr041005_19)

(18.11) *húka wïïkchau, húka wísut*
     [hu=**ka**] wiika-chau   [hu=**ka**] wisuta
     PROX=**TOP** leafcutter.ant-NEG.NMLZ PROX=**TOP** ant.sp
     'this isn't a leafcutter ant, this is a *wisut* ant'

Example (18.12) is a speech report attributed to a character in a traditional story, so it has the form of interpersonal conversation rather than narrative.

(18.12)   *atsá, ámɨk miníipa, wíka ishámainnum wíɰahai, ámɨk titú puhustá*

atsa   [amɨ=**ka**]   mini-i-pa   [wi=**ka**]

no   2sg=**TOP**   come+PFV-APPR-2SG:PROH   1sg=**TOP**

ishama-mai-inu=numa   wɨ-a-ha-i   [amɨ=**ka**]   titu

fear-POT-NMLZ=LOC   go-IPFV-1SG-DECL   2sg=**TOP**   still

puhu-sa-ta

live-PFV-IMP

'no, don't you come, I'm going into danger, you stay still'

(agr040721_07)

It is difficult to say for sure that *=ka* is marking contrast in these examples, as there are other factors that favour its appearance, such as verbless clause subjects and negative polarity. There does appear to be a strong correlation, however, of *=ka* marking each of a set of contrasted NPs. Incidentally, (18.12) shows that *=ka* is not simply marking definiteness or identifiability, as it appears on SAP pronouns which are of course inherently identifiable.

D. In parenthetical clauses

Narratives often contain asides in which the narrator explains some point that may be misunderstood. Use of the topic marker here anchors the digression to the narrative context. Example (18.13) elaborates on the particular type of boa that is eating the man, explaining why it made a hole in his abdomen; the subject takes topic marking. As was noted for examples above, there is another possible motivation for the topic marking in this example, as subjects of verbless equative clauses also typically receive such marking.

(18.13)   *dúka shukuím, akapɨn yúwa nunú*

[nu=**ka**]   [shukuima   akapɨ=na   yu-a   nunu]

ANA=**TOP**   boa.sp   liver=ACC   eat-IPFV:3   ANAREL

'that was a *shukuim* boa, that eats livers' (Text 1:13)

Example (18.14) is taken from a recording of a traditional story; the narrator had used the archaic word *tsampaunum* 'manioc leaves' in a speech report attributed to one of the protagonists, and broke out of the narrative to briefly clarify its meaning. The subject NP *muun* 'adult' takes the topic marker, as it is one of these elders who used the potentially confusing word. The use of topic marking with this NP does not seem to have any other factor favouring its appearance, and this could be considered an instance of the marker effectively having scope over the whole clause, marking it as background information that is not part of the main event line.

(18.14)   *núna tsanímpan dukɨ́n "tsampáunum" múuntak túu ahakú áinawai*
        [nu=na   tsanimpa=na   dukɨ̃=na]   <u>tsampaunumi</u>
        ANA=ACC   manioc.plant=ACC leaf+PSSD:1PL/3=ACC *tsampaunum*
        muunta=**ka**   tu   a-haku   a-ina-wa-i
        adult=**TOP**   say   COP-NARR.PST COP-PL:IPFV-3-DECL
        'the elders used to call those manioc leaves *"tsampaunum"*'
        (agr040723_29)

Example (18.15) directly follows a description of fish turning into manioc. This clause specifies that it is the manioc that we now have in the jungle.

(18.15)   *dúka yabáikish hũ̃ĩ ikám áwa nunú núnikui*
        [nu=**ka**]   [yabai=kI=sha   hu=ĩ   ikama   a-wa
        ANA=**TOP**   now=RESTR=ADD PROX=LOC forest+LOC exist-3
        nunu]   nu-ni-ka-u=i
        ANA_{REL}   ANA-VBLZ.INTR-PFV-NMLZ=COP:3:DECL
        'it was that which we have now, here in the forest' (agr040824_01)

Example (18.15) can also be read as elaborating, and this is also the case in (18.16). Here a list of food types includes topic marking on each item. This example is immediately preceded by a description of the woman arriving at the agouti's house, and immediately followed by the woman saying she intends to live there. So while it does not provide the same kind of meta-commentary as the parenthetical comments described above, it does have the function within the narrative of providing background and explanation for the subsequent events.

(18.16)   *kãỹũkak mamának útua útuamã, paámpanak, piríanak, ashí yutã̃ĩ*
        aídaunak...
        [kãyuka=**ka**]   [mama=na=**ka**]   utua   utuama-ã
        agouti=**TOP**   manioc=ACC=**TOP**   REDUP   pile.up-PFV+SEQ+3:SS
        [paampa=na=**ka**]   [piria=na=**ka**]   [ashi   yu-taĩ
        plantain=ACC=**TOP** banana.sp=ACC=**TOP** all   eat-NSBJ.NMLZ
        a-ina-u=na=**ka**]
        COP-PL:IPFV-NMLZ=ACC=**TOP**
        'the agouti, having piled up manioc, plantains, bananas, all kinds of food...' (agr040721_07)

E. In negated clauses

Topic marking of at least one constituent is typical with negative polarity. In example (18.17) the S argument is marked.

(18.17)   *mína apáhuk atsáwai*
            [mi=na   apa-hu=**ka**]   atsa-wa-i
            1sg=ACC   father-PSSD:1SG=**TOP**   exist:NEG+IPFV-3-DECL
            'I have no father' (agr040824_02)

And in example (18.18), the O argument is marked.

(18.18)   *ashí aínts áidau ikámyawanak kákahus maanimáinchau dɨkapɨdau*
            [ashi   aɨntsu   a-ina-u]NP:CS   [ikama_yawaã=na=**ka**
            all   person   COP-PL:IPFV-NMLZ   jaguar=ACC=**TOP**
            kakahus   maani-mai-inu-chau]NP:CC   dɨkapɨ-ina-u
            easily   fight-POT-NMLZ-NEG.NMLZ   feel-PL:IPFV-NMLZ
            'all the people felt (that they were) unable to fight a jaguar'
            (agr041005_14)

Negative always has a counter-suppositional nuance, as it is marked with respect to positive polarity, and is therefore the pragmatic focus of its clause, as the asserted new information. The topic marked constituent then provides the pragmatic anchor about which the negation is predicated.

18.2.1.1 Conditional clauses

The enclitic *=ka* appears on subordinate clauses, forming conditional clauses (see examples in §14.6.1). The conditional clause typically precedes its associated finite clause, consistent with the clause-initial tendency for topics and with the typical positioning of subordinate and main clauses. Haiman (1978) demonstrates the relation between conditional and topic marking in terms of functional similarity:

> Conditionals, like topics, are givens which constitute the frame of reference with respect to which the main clause is either true (if a proposition), or felicitous (if not).
>
> Haiman (1978: 564)

18.2.1.2 Question topic enclitic *=sha*

The topic marker *=ka* does not appear in questions, where its function is filled by the enclitic *=sha*. The distribution of *=sha* is similar to that of *=ka*, appearing on clausal constituents including arguments, modifiers and subordinate clauses. Neither the main predicate of the question nor question words themselves are marked – this is of course consistent with the pragmatics of question words, which are inherently focal. Use of *=sha* is apparently obligatory in any question that has a potential host constituent. Examples of the use of *=sha* are in Chapter 10. The tendency is for the constituents marked with *=sha* to appear either clause-initially or clause-finally.

As has already been noted, the question topic marker can also have a clausal rather than constituent scope, and it can be used as the only marker of a question, showing that it can confer interrogative mood.

18.2.2 Determined NPs

The addition of the anaphoric pronoun *nu* to an NP as determiner can function as definiteness marking, showing that the referent has been activated in the discourse. In addition, the numeral *makichik* 'one' may function as an indefiniteness marker, when activating a referent that will be important in the discourse. Examples of such NPs are found §5.3.

18.2.3 Relativized copula

The relativized copula construction makes use of the postposed demonstrative type of relative clause formation described in detail in Chapter 16. Its typical function is overt marking of identifiable referents. In example (18.19), the subject NP *datsa-uchi=a nu* (youth-DIM=COP:3 ANA_REL) could be translated literally as '(he) who is a youth'; in the context of the narrative, the youth is the protagonist, and the marking explicitly indicates that this NP has an identifiable referent.

(18.19) *datsáuchia núu puyathús wakɨ̃hus diiyák...*
 [datsa-uchi=a   nu]   puyathu-sã
 youth-DIM=COP:3   ANA_REL   take.interest-SBD+3:SS
 wakɨɰa-hu-sã   dii-a-kũ
 want-APPL-SBD+3:SS   look-IPFV-SIM+3:SS
 'that youth, watching with great interest and desire...' (agr040824_01)

The function of marking an identifiable referent is clearly similar to that of the topic enclitic =ka, and it is not entirely clear how the effects of the two strategies differ. In (18.20) a relativized copula construction is itself marked with the topic enclitic =ka.

(18.20) *nuwɨnmauwa dúka shíiŋ pɨ́ŋkɨhush naŋkáɨmkiuwai*
 [nuwɨna-mau=a   nu=**ka**]   shiiha   pɨŋkɨha-uchi
 marry-NSBJ.NMLZ=COP:3   ANA_REL=**TOP**   well   good-DIM
 naŋkaɨma-ki-u=ai
 pass-PFV-NMLZ=COP:3:DECL
 'that wedding passed very beautifully' (agr040824_01)

The functions of the markers just described are far from being fully understood, and a detailed study of their roles in discourse is an important future undertaking.

18.2.4 Focus marking

A set of enclitics with various meanings also have the pragmatic effect of focussing their host. These enclitics do not form a single paradigm: additive *=sha(kama)* is in complementary distribution with topic marker *=ka*; restrictive *=kI* may co-occur with either of them. Polar interrogative *=ka* only appears in interrogative clauses, it typically appears on the predicate as part of the mood marking paradigm but also may mark a questioned constituent; speculative *=tsu* has the least semantic content, and appears to have the sole function of marking the focus of speculative modality. Like polar interrogative, it alternates with a verbal marker.

Table 1: Focus enclitics

enclitic	gloss	described in
=sha(kama)	additive	§4.12.2
=kI	restrictive	§4.11
=ka	polar interrogative	§10.4
=tsu	speculative	§9.2.4

A feature of these focus enclitics is a certain ambiguity of scope, which may be clausal or phrasal. Polar interrogative *=ka* forms part of the mood marking paradigm, the rest of whose members are strictly verbal markers. While *=ka* may appear on the predicate, taking the mood slot, it may also appear on an NP or subordinate clause constituent. Speculative *=tsu* appears on a constituent that may be considered the focus of the epistemic modality being conveyed. Alternatively, there may be no constituent marked and instead the verbal marking includes an element /tsa/: presumably this arrangement, as with polar interrogative, reflects different scope effects. Additive *=sha(kama)* always appears on NP constituents, but its scope in some instances is clearly clausal. The same marker appears on subordinate clauses marking concessive clauses (§14.6.2).

18.3 Reference tracking

Reference tracking is a fundamental concern in discourse organization: without effective means of keeping track of the grammatical roles associated with participants there is no way to ensure effective communication. While case marking of NPs is an effective way to explicitly mark their grammatical roles, many clauses in Aguaruna have no overt NP arguments, instead using a variety of predicate-marking strategies to keep track of arguments between clauses. Switch-reference marking is obligatory in all subordinate verbs, and case-marking on nominalized verbs may approximate the same function. Bridging constructions (also known as tail-head linkage) allow all the categories marked in subordinate verbs to be applied to the nexus between finite clauses, and the choice of pro-verb in such constructions also conveys information about the anticipated pragmatic status of its core arguments. In this way, head-marking reference tracking strategies pervade even the loosest of paratactic clause-combining constructions. Table 18.2 summarizes the constructions that have been described in previous chapters.

Table 18.2: Reference-tracking strategies

strategy	described in
Canonical switch-reference (SS/DS marking)	Chapter 13
Non-canonical switch-reference	§13.6
Nominalization	Chapter 15
Bridging constructions (tail-head linkage)	§14.8
Pro-verb selection	§6.6.2, §14.8

Canonical switch-reference indicates whether the subject of a subordinate clause is the same as or different from that of the controlling clause. This marking is obligatory in most subordinate clause types. Non-canonical switch-reference conveys information about the role of a common argument in both clauses. This marking appears only in two types of subordinate clause, and is typologically unusual, otherwise described only for Panoan languages (Valenzuela 2003; Fleck 2003; Zariquiey 2011) and Ese Ejja (Vuillermet 2014) – see further discussion in Overall (2016a).

The use of nominalized clauses is a common and highly effective reference tracking strategy: the choice of nominalizer indicates the grammatical role of the shared argument in the relative clause, and NP case-marking indicates its role in the matrix clause. As discussed in §15.5.2, nominalization constructions probably underlie the two non-canonical switch-reference marking subordinators (see also Overall 2014b, 2016a).

The final strategy is bridging constructions, also known as tail-head linkage. These are a very distinctive feature of Aguaruna narratives and serve to illustrate the pervasive nature of head-marking reference tracking strategies. Bridging constructions typically follow finite clauses in narratives, and are formally subordinate to the following clause. Switch-reference marking is obligatory in subordinate clauses, but not in finite clauses. A bridging construction links two finite clauses, and involves "summing up" the action of the first clause with a pro-verb that is formally subordinate to the second. Because it is subordinate, the bridging pro-verb marks switch-reference and temporal/causal relations between the two clauses. This phenomenon serves to demonstrate just how important reference tracking through switch-reference marking is to the grammar of Aguaruna: typically almost every finite clause in a narrative is followed by a bridging pro-verb, so that although reference tracking markers are formally restricted to subordinate verbs, in practice they appear on every clause. The choice of pro-verb in a bridging construction is an important cue to anticipated discourse prominence of one of the participants. As described in §6.6.2, pro-verbs are formed with one of two verbalizers: -*ni* or -*tika*, of which the former indicates subject prominence and the latter object prominence. Bridging constructions were described in detail in §14.8.

Highly topical participants are typically ellipted, and tracked only through verbal marking. When there is a change in the core participants, the new NP taking the subject or object role may be overtly stated, either with a pronoun or full NP. When an already activate referent is reactivated, the NP typically also takes topic marking with the enclitic =*ka*.

Full NP arguments are associated with the pragmatic function of introducing participants, where they may be accompanied by the numeral *makichik* 'one' functioning as an indefinite article. They are also used to reintroduce participants as subjects or objects where they did not have that role in the preceding clause.

The fragment of narrative in (18.21) shows how participants can be tracked through morphology and lexical choices. The two key participants here are the devil, which has just attacked a child, and the child's father, who has come running upon hearing the child's cries.

(18.21) *pɨmpɨ̈nun tahũã́ húkɨ̃ tupikámtikɨ̃ waánum chaát akunáu túwahamɨ̃*
[[pɨmpɨ̈na-u=na]   ta-hu-ã̃]   [hu-kɨ̃]
turn+IPFV-NMLZ=ACC   arrive-APPL-PFV+SEQ+3:SS   take-PFV+SEQ+3:SS
[tupika-mitika-kɨ̃]   wãã̃=numa   chaat
run-CAUS-PFV+SEQ+3:SS   cave=LOC   IDEO
akuna-u   tuwahamɨ̃
CAUS+enter.hole+PFV-NMLZ   NARR
'as (the devil) was turning to leave, (the man) arrived, grabbed him and made him run, sent him "zip!" into his cave, they say' (agr040723_29)

The first verb is nominalized: the devil is the referent of the nominalization and semantic actor, and the nominalization is marked with accusative case, indicating that the devil is the object of the following verb. For the following four verbs, the devil is the object and the man the subject. Note that the man is not restated with an overt NP when he becomes subject, as he is already active as a participant. Of interest is the fact that the second verb *tahuã* 'arrived' is applicativized, with the devil as object; and the third and fourth are causativized, with the devil as the semantic actor. All three would be intransitive without this valency increasing morphology. So in addition to the inflectional morphology that has the primary purpose of reference tracking, derivational morphology can also be used to keep participants active as subjects and objects.

18.4 Source-of-information marking

As I mentioned in the introduction to this chapter, all of the phenomena discussed here can be considered to relate to the negotiation of knowledge between speaker and addressee. Thus far we have considered the grammatical resources that speakers use to guide the addressee towards the intended meaning. In this and the following section we consider two areas that relate to how a speaker positions themselves with respect to their assumptions about the speaker's knowledge (see also Chapter 9 on mood and modality).

Aguaruna does not have a grammaticalized system of evidentiality marking, in that marking of information source is not an obligatory category. There are, however, two important strategies that supply such information. The first evidentiality strategy is the distinct narrative modality, used in traditional stories (§9.2.3). Use of narrative modality necessarily implies that the information being related is not firsthand – in fact the usual narrative modality marker *tuwahamĩ* is derived from the verb *tuta* 'say', and finite forms of the speech verb may also be used to mark narrative modality (§9.2.3). This conforms to Aikhenvald's (2004) observation that reported evidentiality may arise from a speech report construction:

> Reported speech and quotations may develop epistemic and other overtones similar to those of reported evidentials.
>
> Aikhenvald (2004: 132)

In contrast to the rejection of "hearsay" evidence in modern Western legal contexts, narrative modality in Aguaruna renders the information conveyed *more* reliable, as it adds the authority of previous generations to that of the current speaker – in effect it marks the information as being wisdom received from the ancestors (Overall 2014a).

The second technique for marking source of information is to use the nominalizer *-u* as a marker of non-firsthand evidentiality. This strategy is most noticeable in traditional stories, where the majority of verbs heading independent clauses – the usual domain of finite verbs – are marked with *-u*. Such forms often combine with narrative modality. Although both narrative modality and nominalization as evidentiality strategy have similar functions in marking reduced personal involvement of the speaker, they are not synonymous. Nominalized verbs are used in conversation and even in first-person contexts where the speaker has not personally witnessed the events being reported, and there may be an epistemic overtone of speaker's reduced commitment to the truth of the proposition; by contrast, the narrative form implies a high confidence in the validity and veracity of the propositional content. Example (18.22) comes from a story in which a group of people were forced to flee their home after being attacked, and were hiding out in the forest during the night. One of the refugees hears movement and says:

(18.22) *aíntsua núnin mináu*
         [aintsu=a   nu-ni-inu]$_{NP:S}$ mina-u
         person=COP:3   ANA$_{REL}$-VBLZ.INTR-NMLZ   come+IPFV-NMLZ
         'something like a person (is) coming' (agr060816_01)

This is clearly not hearsay, rather it appears to be functioning as an inferred or non-visual evidential (also see examples of nominalizations with first person subject in §15.5.3, and Overall 2014a). Again, this type of evidentiality strategy is attested cross-linguistically:

> Deverbal nominals of all sorts, including deverbal nouns, participles, gerundives, gerunds, converbs, and infinitives, can all acquire evidential overtones.
>
> Aikhenvald (2004: 118)

Desubordination of a non-finite verb form to mark non-firsthand information source is iconic, as the reduction in categories marked on the verb corresponds to a reduced firsthand information on the part of the speaker.

18.5 Speech reports and rhetorical questions

We have seen the grammatical markers of information structure and the strategies speakers employ to position their statements with respect to the source of information. In this section I describe two commonly used rhetorical devices that relate to the speaker's attitude: speech reports and rhetorical questions. The functions of speech reports are described in detail in Chapter 17. In addition to their use in the straightforward reporting of direct quotations, speech reports find extended uses both as a grammatical device and a rhetorical device. We have seen that the main grammatical extensions of speech reports are in complementation (§17.2) and clauses expressing intention (§14.5). They also play an important role in narrative structure, where crucial plot points may be narrated in the form of a speech report attributed to a protagonist (Larson 1978). The use of self-quotation to reinforce the speaker's words has been noted (§17.1). This occurs in situations where the speaker wants to be certain of having the addressee's attention: in admonitions, and as a hedging device when asking questions or favours. The common theme is that using reported speech alerts the addressee to pay attention to particular parts of the message with which the speaker feels more personally involved.

Questions, like speech reports, have both grammatical and rhetorical extended uses. Embedded questions may function as complements of verbs of knowledge (§17.2), and non-embedded questions may be used rhetorically to make a point more forcefully. Both embedded and rhetorical content questions may make use of a dedicated enclitic =ki, which appears on the interrogative word or the predicate, and indicates that the speaker does not expect an answer to the question.

18.6 Future research

Much work remains to be done in the area of discourse organization. In particular, the subtle interplay of morphological marking, zero anaphora and constituent ordering in signalling information structural status requires further study. Collection and analysis of much more conversational data will be an important step in understanding how source-of-information marking works. A major aspect of contemporary Aguaruna discourse that lies mostly outside the scope of this grammar is code-switching and calquing from Spanish. Bilingual schools have been in operation among the Aguaruna since the mid 1950's, and it is estimated that only 35% of the population is monolingual (Wise 1999: 309). We have seen various examples of Spanish verbs that have been nativized to greater or lesser extent, and of various lexical items that are freely interpolated in Aguaruna language interactions (for example, number terminology). Example (18.23) is another such example, from an exchange where bilingual speakers were discussing a conflict with non-Aguaruna people. Note that the first Spanish verb *atacar* 'attack' is suffixed with the Aguaruna non-inflecting subordinator *-ma*, while the second *retrocede* 'retreats' is inflected entirely in Spanish (Spanish material is enclosed in braces in the gloss line).

(18.23) *apásh atacam retrocede*
apachi *ataca*-ma *retrocede*
non.Aguaruna {attack}-NSBJ>SBJ {retreat.3SG.PRS}
'a non Aguaruna, when attacked, retreats'

I have touched upon language contact issues in a few parts of the grammar: §3.4 discusses some effects of Spanish on the Aguaruna phonological system, and §3.9 mentions some nativization strategies in borrowed words; §12.2.1 mentions the use of Spanish for numerals and associated concepts, and see example 12.1; and Text 2 includes an autobiographical description of contact with Spanish speakers. A detailed study of the effects of language contact with Spanish remains to be undertaken, however.

My corpus consists almost entirely of narratives, mostly traditional stories. More recently I have collected some examples from online chat conversations with native speakers, which illustrate some of the patterns of natural conversational interaction. Example (18.24) illustrates two common features of conversation. The discourse particle *waa* is used to express mild surprise, and appears here as a response to A's statement. B then asks a rhetorical question formed with the pro-verb *aanit* 'do thus', a common backchannelling strategy. Note that A is the author, a non-native speaker of Aguaruna, and B is a native speaker. The context is that B has just told A the weather in Lima is nice.

(18.24) A: *huhuiŋ ataktu tsɨtsɨkai*
        huhu=ĩ=ka   ataktu   tsɨtsɨka=i
        PROX=LOC=TOP again   cold=COP:3:DECL
        'here it's cold again'

    B: *waa*
        waa
        'wow'

    B: *aniatsuak*
        aa-ni-a-tsu-wa=ka
        thus-VBLZ.INTR-IPFV-NEG-3=Q
        'is that right' (personal correspondence)

Gnerre (1986b) discusses a historical change in discourse practices among the Shuar and Achuar, from primarily one-to-one dialogue to a culture of public life involving frequent one-to-many interactions. He suggests that some of the grammatical features of Shuar that are built around a privileging of second person (among which is the split object marking described in Chapter 7) are in a state of change in the contemporary languages because of this change in interactional practices.

Many questions about these and other aspects of Aguaruna grammar and language practices remain to be answered, and I hope that this work will provide a foundation for future research.

Texts

Text 1: A man is eaten by a boa

agr041005_27
Recorded in Centro Wawik, 5 October 2004. About 3 min 40 sec.
Told by Tito Nanchijam Pegas, age about 50, resident of Nuevo Belén, Wawik River

The following story is a typical "cautionary tale" type traditional story. It tells the story of a man who was out hunting and came across the trail of some large animal, which turned out to be a boa. He followed the trail, and was killed by the boa. The man's family then went to look for him, found the boa eating his corpse, killed the boa and took the corpse home. A brief moral at the end questions why the man followed the trail without knowing what had made it.

(T1.1)   *ya dúshakam*
          ya   nu=shakama
          ok   ANA=ADD
          'ok, this (story) too'

(T1.2)   *bakichík múun ahakuí*
          makichiki   muunta   a-haku=i
          one   adult   exist-NARR.PST=COP:3:DECL
          'There was a man.'

(T1.3)   *núnin wɨkáɨ ̶aḳ wɨúwai kuntínun mantumaátatus*
          nu-ni-inu   [wɨkaɨɯa-kũ   wɨ-u=ai]
          ANA-VBLZ.INTR-NMLZ   walk+IPFV-SIM+3:SS   go+PFV-NMLZ=COP:3:DECL
          [kuntinu=na   mantu-ma-a-tatus]
          animal=ACC   kill+APPL-REFL-PFV-INTENT+3:SS
          'That very (man) went walking to kill animals for himself.'[1]

(T1.4)   *núnik wɨkáɨ wɨkáɨkawã ɨ́tsã akã́ɯ́ã̃ɨ ̃ yapáŋkɨ miníuwai*
          nu-ni-kã   [wɨkaɨ   wɨkaɨɯa-kawã]
          ANA-VBLZ.INTR-PFV+SEQ+3:SS   REDUP   walk-IPFV-REPET+3:SS
          [ɨtsã   akaɯa-í]   [yapahu-kɨ̃]
          sun   set-IPFV+1SG/3-DS   be.hungry-PFV+SEQ+3:SS

---

1 The idiom "go walking to kill animals" is the standard way of referring to going hunting.

mini-u=ai
arrive+PFV-NMLZ=COP:3:DECL
'Having done that, walking and walking, as the sun was setting he was arriving (home) having got hungry.'

(T1.5)   *núnik hi̵n taátatus minikmá̰ wainkáuwai*
nu-ni-kã   [hĩ̵=nĩ
ANA-VBLZ.INTR-PFV+SEQ+3:SS   house+PSSD:1PL/3=LOC
ta-a-tatus]   [mini-kamã̰]   waina-ka-u=ai
come-PFV-INTENT+3:SS   arrive-TERM+3:SS   see-PFV-NMLZ=COP:3:DECL
'Having done that, as he arrived wanting to get to his house he saw (that)...'

(T1.6)   *kánu hapikbáuwa íman tahák akaikíuwai*
[kanu   hapi-ki-mau=a   iman]
canoe   pull-PFV-NSBJ.NMLZ=COP:3   INTENS.NMLZREL
[taha-kṵ]   akai-ki-u=ai
clear.undergrowth+IPFV-SIM+3:SS   come.down-PFV-NMLZ=COP:3:DECL
'something as big as a canoe being dragged had come down clearing a path through the undergrowth.'[2]

(T1.7)   *núnikmataĩ "wahĩ̵ húnikĩ" tus patá̵tus diiyák wi̵uwai*
nu-ni-ka-mataĩ   [wahiĩ   hu-ni-ka-i̵
ANA-VBLZ.INTR-PFV-1/3:DS   what   PROX-VBLZ.INTR-PFV-3
tus]   [patá̵-tu-sã]   [dii-a-kṵ]
say+SBD+3:SS   follow-APPL-SBD+3:SS   see-IPFV-SIM+3:SS
wi̵-u=ai
go+PFV-NMLZ=COP:3:DECL
'After it did that, following it, saying "what did this?", he went looking.'

(T1.8)   *núnik wi̵kamá̰ nuwanúĩ páɲkiɲ ímau wĩ̵ iíkuakĩ yakí waká̰ i̵ki̵tun yunúmtukui*
nu-ni-kã̰   [wi̵-kamã̰]   nuwanu=ĩ   [paɲki̵=ka
ANA-VBLZ.INTR-PFV+SEQ+3:SS   go-TERM+3:SS   ANA=LOC   boa=TOP
[imau   wĩ̵]   [iikua-ki̵]
INTENS.LOC   go+PFV+SEQ+3:SS   come.back-PFV+SEQ+3:SS
[yaki   wa-kã̰]   i̵ki̵-ta-u=na]
above   go.up-PFV+SEQ+3:SS   sit-APPL+IPFV-NMLZ=ACC

---

2 This is a finite clause, but it functions as a complement clause to the preceding finite predicate *wainkauwai* 'he saw' – see §17.2.2.4.

yunuma-tu-ka-u=i
approach-APPL-PFV-NMLZ=COP:3:DECL
'Having done that, when he went there, (there was) a boa that had gone away, come back and gone up (a tree) and was sitting, and he approached it.'

(T1.9)   *núnikmatãĩ núna achikuí aĩntsún páɲkĩ*

nu-ni-ka-mataĩ	nu=na	achi-ka-u=i
ANA-VBLZ.INTR-PFV+SEQ-1/3:DS	ANA=ACC	grab-PFV-NMLZ=COP:3:DECL
aĩntsu=na	paɲkĩ	
person=ACC	boa	

'When he did that, the boa grabbed that person.'

(T1.10)   *núnik kaŋkaŋnúm náŋkamã pɨpɨŋkasuã́ ihĩ́ã́ iwakuí buúkchinum ɨtsapɨ́s atúsui*

nu-ni-kã	[kaŋkahĩ=numa	
ANA-VBLZ.INTR-PFV+SEQ+3:SS	lower.leg+PSSD:1PL/3=LOC	
naŋkamã]	[pɨpɨŋkasuã	ihi-ã]
begin+PFV+SEQ+3:SS	IDEO	wrap.up-PFV+SEQ+3:SS
i-wa-ka-u=i	[buukɨ-uchi=numa	
CAUS-go.up-PFV-NMLZ=COP:3:DECL	head-DIM=LOC	
ɨtsapɨ-sã]	atu-sa-u=i	
poke.out-SBD+3:SS	lean.against-PFV-NMLZ=COP:3:DECL	

'Having done that, starting at his lower leg it wrapped him up and worked its way up to his head, so that only a little bit poked out, and it leaned him (up against a tree).'

(T1.11)   *dútikã maáuwai pɨmpɨáɲ pɨmpɨáɲ*

nu-tikã	ma-a-u=ai
ANA-VBLZ.TR+PFV+SEQ+3:SS	kill-PFV-NMLZ=COP:3:DECL
[pɨmpɨa-hã]	[pɨmpɨa-hã]
wrap.up-PFV+SEQ+3:SS	wrap.up-PFV+SEQ+3:SS

'Having done that to him, it killed him by wrapping him up.'

(T1.12)   *núnik mã́ã́ hṹw̃ĩ akápchinum chíɲkãĩ*

nu-ni-kã	[ma-ã]	[hu=ĩ
ANA-VBLZ.INTR-PFV+SEQ+3:SS	kill-PFV+SEQ+3:SS	PROX=LOC
akapɨ-uchi=numa	chiŋka-ĩ]	
liver-DIM=LOC	make.hole-PFV+SEQ+3:SS	

'Having done that, having killed him, having made a hole in his liver here...'

(T1.13)   *dúka shukuím akapɨn yúwa nunú*

nu=ka	[shukuima	akapɨ=na	yu-a	nunu]
ANA=TOP	boa.sp	liver=ACC	eat-IPFV+3	ANAREL

'that was a *shukuim* boa, that eats livers'[3]

(T1.14)   *nunú nũ̃wĩ̃ akápchinum chíŋkãĩ utúk akapnúm utukã́ akapɨn yuhák pútut pútut awáhak*

[nunu	nu=ĩ	akapɨ-uchi=numa	chiŋka-ĩ]
ANA	ANA=LOC	liver-DIM=LOC	make.hole-PFV+SEQ+3:SS

[utu-kã̃]		[akapɨ=numa	utu-kã̃]
go.in-PFV+SEQ+3:SS		liver=LOC	go.in-PFV+SEQ+3:SS

[akapɨ=na	yu-ha-kũ̃]	[putut	putut
liver=ACC	eat-APPL+IPFV-SIM+3:SS	IDEO	IDEO

a-waha-kũ̃]
CAUS-stand+IPFV-SIM+3:SS

'That one there, having made a hole in the liver, having entered into the liver, it was eating his liver, (taking bites) making the sound "*putut putut!*"...'

(T1.15)   *aɨntsún pɨduáŋ níŋka ímaŋ ũ̃ũ̃ wahás buúkchinum ɨ́tsapɨs puhús yúu puháya túwahamɨ̃*

[aɨntsu=na	pɨnua-hã̃]		[nɨ̃=ka	imaŋ
person=ACC	wrap.up-PFV+SEQ+3:SS		3sg=TOP	INTENS.ADJ

ũ̃ũ̃	waha-sã̃]	[buukɨ-uchi=numa	ɨtsapɨ-sã̃]
smother	stand-SBD+3:SS	head-DIM=LOC	poke.out-SBD+3:SS

puhu-sã̃]	yu	puha-ya	tuwahamɨ̃
live-PFV+3:SS	eat	live+IPFV-REMPST:3	NARR

'having wrapped up the man, it was completely smothering him up to his head so only a little bit poked out, and it was eating (him).'

(T1.16)   *núnikmatãĩ mɨŋkaɨkámtãĩ*

nu-ni-ka-mataĩ	[mɨŋkaɨ-ka-mataĩ]
ANA-VBLZ.INTR-PFV+SEQ-1/3:DS	disappear-PFV+SEQ-1/3:DS

'When (the boa) did that, when (the man) disappeared...'

---

3 This clause is a parenthetical aside, to explain the fact that the snake went for the dead man's liver. The narrative is taken up again in the following line. See §18.2 for a discussion of the grammatical correlates of such constructions.

(T1.17)   *"dúsha wáaŋ muúntash mɨŋkaɨkã́ɨ̃ wahúkamkɨ" tus*
      nu=sha   waã=ki   muunta=sha   mɨŋkai-ka-ɨ̃
      ANA=Q.TOP   why=Q.RHET   adult=Q.TOP   disappear-PFV-3
      wahuka-ma=ki   tus
      how-RECPST:3=Q.RHET   say+SBD+3:SS
      'saying "why did that guy disappear? what can have happened?"...'

(T1.18)   *patahɨ̃́ áinau ashintúk*
      pata-hɨ̃   a-ina-u   ashina-tu-kã
      family-PSSD:1PL/3   COP-PL:IPFV-NMLZ   go:PL-APPL-PFV+SEQ+3:SS
      'the man's family having gone...'

(T1.19)   *"wɨkaɨtáiŋ húu wɨ̃háma, hukɨɰaháma" tus*
      wɨkaɨɰa-taɨ̃=ka   hu   wɨ̃-hama
      walk-NSBJ.NMLZ=TOP   PROX   go+PFV+3-CNTR.EX
      hu-kɨ=a-hama   tus
      PROX-RESTR=COP:3-CNTR.EX   say+SBD+3:SS
      'saying "the path went here, this is it"...'

(T1.20)   *wɨkaɨkamã́ wainkáuwai*
      [wɨkaɨɰa-kamã]   waina-ka-u=ai
      walk-TERM+3:SS   see-PFV-NMLZ=COP:3:DECL
      'and walking on, they saw (the man's footprints).'[4]

(T1.21)   *núnik wainák nawɨn waitúk patáɨtuk iní inímkãw̃ã itám nṹw̃ɨ̃ hɨ̃ɰãũsh*
      taáttak tsɨŋkɨkɨ̃́ nu akaɨtúkbaun diís
      nu-ni-kã   [waina-kã]   [nawɨ̃=na
      ANA-VBLZ.INTR-PFV+SEQ+3:SS   see-PFV+SEQ+3:SS   foot+PSSD:1PL/3=ACC
      wai-tu-kã]   [patai-tu-kã]   [ini
      see-APPL-PFV+SEQ+3:SS   follow-APPL-PFV+SEQ+3:SS   REDUP
      inima-kawã]   [[i-ta-a-ma]   [nu=ɨ̃
      take.with-REPET+3:SS   CAUS-come-PFV-NSBJ>SBJ   ANA=LOC
      hɨ̃ɰa-uchi   ta-a-tata-kɨ̃]   [tsɨŋkɨ-kɨ̃]
      house-DIM   come-PFV-FUT-SIM+3:SS   branch.off-PFV+SEQ+3:SS

---

4 That the zero-marked object of the verb 'see' is 'the man's footprints' is not made clear until the
following line; without the following clarification, it would be assumed that they saw the man.

[nu   akaɨ-tu-ki-mau=na]]   [dii-sã]
ANA   go.down-APPL-PFV-NSBJ.NMLZ=ACC   look-SBD+3:SS
'After doing that, after seeing (that), after they saw his foot(prints), after following him, taking (the footprints?) with them, when they brought (them), (the footprints) branched off there, going to the house, as they were looking at the place where the footprints went down that way...'[5]

(T1.22)   *"hu akáikɨhama" tus*
hu   akai-kɨ-hama   tus
PROX   go.down-PFV+3-CNTR.EX say+SBD+3:SS
'saying "he's gone down here"...'

(T1.23)   *diikmã́ páŋkɨ̃ shukuím nunú yúwak pɨduáŋ aɨntsún puhúhun ɨhɨɨ̨ahu*
[dii-kamã]   [paŋkɨ̃   shukuima   nunu   yu-a-kũ]
look-TERM+3:SS   boa   boa.sp   ANA   eat-IPFV-SIM+3:SS
[pɨnua-hã]   [aɨntsu=na   puhu-ha-u=na]
wrap.up-PFV+3:SS person=ACC   live-APPL+IPFV-NMLZ=ACC
ɨhɨɨ̨a-aha-u
discover+PFV-PL-NMLZ
'upon looking, they discovered that *shukuim* boa that was there eating, having wrapped up the man.'[6]

(T1.24)   *núnik ɨhɨ̃ɨ̨ã́ diiyám nunú páŋkɨ̃ hṹɨ̃̃ akapnúm utukã́ akapɨ́n yuhák*
nu-ni-kã   [ɨhɨɨ̨ã]
ANA-VBLZ.INTR-PFV+SEQ+3:SS   discover+PFV+SEQ+3:SS
[dii-a-ma]   [nunu   paŋkɨ̃   hu=ɨ̃]
look-IPFV-NSBJ>SBJ   ANA   boa   PROX=LOC
akapɨ̃=numa   utu-kã]   [akapɨ̃=na
liver+PSSD:1PL/3=LOC enter-PFV+SEQ+3:SS liver+PSSD:1PL/3=ACC

---

5 This passage is a little confused; 'the man's tracks' is the object of the verb 'see', but then the verbs 'take with' and 'cause to come' seem as if they should have the man as the object – although they have not seen him yet. Then the idea of 'branching off for home' also fits better with a human subject. It seems that 'footprints' is being treated like a human subject, and that the verbs 'take with' and 'cause to come' are being used figuratively, referring to following the tracks. It should be noted that native speakers who helped with transcription and translation also found the wording slightly odd.

6 The verb *puhu* 'live' appears to be acting as an auxiliary for the preceding two verbs.

yu-ha-kũ]
eat-APPL+IPFV-SIM+3:SS

'Having done that, having discovered (the boa), as they were looking at it, that boa having entered here into his liver, it was eating (the man's) liver...'

(T1.25)   *pútit pútit awáhak*

putit   putit   a-waha-kũ
IDEO   IDEO   CAUS-call+IPFV-SIM+3:SS

'(taking bites) making the sound "*putit putit*"...'[7]

(T1.26)   *panán hiínak ídaim ídaim ídaim aták ỹãũshmatũã yúwak aták hiínak ídaim ídaim ídaim wahá puhutãĩ*

[panan   hiina-kũ]   [idaim   idaim   idaim   atak
IDEO   go.out+IPFV-SIM+3:SS   IDEO   IDEO   IDEO   again

yaunchma-tu-ã]   [yu-a-kũ]   [atak
dive.in-APPL-PFV+SEQ+3:SS   eat-IPFV-SIM+3:SS   again

hiina-kũ]   [idaim   idaim   idaim   waha
go.out+IPFV-SIM+3:SS   IDEO   IDEO   IDEO   stand

puhu-taĩ]
live-SBD:1/3:DS

'coming out "*panan!*", (sticking out its tongue) "*idaim! idaim! idaim!*" and having dived in (to the corpse) again (it was) eating, then coming out again (sticking out its tongue) as it made the sound "*idaim! idaim! idaim!*"...'[8]

(T1.27)   *diiyá diiyákũã "wahúpa asáŋ hiínũã, ánik utukấsh" tus*

[diiya   dii-a-kawã]   [wahupa   asã=ki
REDUP   look-IPFV-REPET+3:SS   how.much   COP+SBD+3:SS=Q.RHET

hiina-wa   [a-ni=kã   utu-kã=sha]
go.out+IPFV-3   thus-VBLZ.INTR-PFV+SEQ+3:SS   go.in-PFV+SEQ+3:SS=Q.TOP

tus]
say+SBD+3:SS

'(the family members were) looking and looking, saying "after how much time does it come out, after it's gone in?"...'

---

7 *wahat* 'stand' / 'call' is used with speech reports to represent vocalizations of animals or shouting etc. of humans (§17.1). The causative form here takes the sound symbolic *putit* as a speech-report-like object, so can be translated as 'causing the noise *putit* to be produced'.

8 The sound-symbolic word *idaim* is related to the verb *idaimat* 'stick out one's tongue' and the noun *idai* 'tongue'.

(T1.28)   *diiyám dúkap ásã núna akapín yuhák utúk puhutãí̃*
[dii-a-ma]   [dukapɨ   asã]   [nu=na
look-IPFV-NSBJ>SBJ   enough   COP+SBD+3:SS   ANA=ACC
akapɨ=na   yu-ha-kũ]   [utu-kã
liver+PSSD:1PL/3=ACC   eat-APPL+IPFV-SIM+3:SS   go.in-PFV+SEQ+3:SS
puhu-taĩ]
live-SBD:1/3:DS
'as they were looking at it, after enough time it had gone in to eat his liver...'[9]

(T1.29)   *"ayú" tus*
<u>ayu</u>   tus
<u>ok</u>   say+SBD+3:SS
'saying "ok"...'

(T1.30)   *idaiyás diiyá diiyákũã bachítan shíiŋ ɨtsa ɨtsakɨs ututãí̃ huwátkiuwai*
[idaiya-sã]   [diiya   dii-a-kawã]   [bachita=na
leave-SBD+3:SS   REDUP   look-IPFV-REPET+3:SS   machete=ACC
shiiha   ɨtsa   ɨtsaki-sã]   [utu-taĩ]
well   REDUP   sharpen-SBD+3:SS   go.in-SBD:1/3:DS
huwa-tu-ki-u=ai
approach-APPL-PFV-NMLZ=COP:3:DECL
'leaving, watching and watching, sharpening a machete well, as (the boa) went in they approached it.'

(T1.31)   *núnik huwátkĩ hɨᵤantáuwai*
nu-ni-kã   [huwa-tu-kĩ]
ANA-VBLZ.INTR-PFV+SEQ+3:SS   approach-APPL-PFV+SEQ+3:SS
hɨᵤã-ta-u=ai
arrive-APPL+IPFV-NMLZ=COP:3:DECL
'Having done that, having approached, they got close.'

(T1.32)   *núnik hɨᵤantún kuntúchihia húka anánchish wãí̃ ĩỹã́ puhúttaman bachítai*
          pisút awatĩ́ taŋkɨ́t tsupɨ́kui
nu-ni-kã   [[hɨᵤã-ta-u=na]
ANA-VBLZ.INTR-PFV+SEQ+3:SS   arrive-APPL+IPFV-NMLZ=ACC
[kuntu-uchi-hi=a   hu=ka   ananchi=sha
neck-DIM-PSSD:1PL/3=COP:3   PROX=TOP   thin=ADD

---

9 The word *ásã* (COP+SBD+3:SS) was added during transcription.

wɨ̃ iyã puhu-tatamana]
go+PFV+SEQ+3:SS fall.forward live-SBJ>OBJ
[bachita=i pisut awatĩ] taŋkɨt
machete=INS IDEO hit+PFV+SEQ+3:SS IDEO
tsupi-ka-u=i
cut-PFV-NMLZ=COP:3:DECL
'Having done that, as (the boa's) thin neck went falling towards the person who was approaching, having hit it "slash!" with the machete, he cut (the boa) "whack!".'[10]

(T1.33) *dútikam dúka páŋkiŋ kuwɨŋkahá atihã́ aɨ́ntsnak shitákĩ ahápauwai*
nu-tika-ma [nu=ka paŋkĩ=ka kuwɨŋkaha
ANA-VBLZ.TR+PFV-NSBJ>SBJ ANA=TOP boa=TOP IDEO
ati-hã] [aɨntsu=na=ka shita-kĩ]
unwrap-PFV+SEQ+3:SS person=ACC=TOP push-PFV+SEQ+3:SS
ahapa-a-u=ai
throw.out-PFV-NMLZ=COP:3:DECL
'When he had done that (to the boa), that boa unwrapped (the person) "*kuwɨŋkaha*!", pushed the person out and discarded him.'

(T1.34) *dútikam nu aɨ́nts puhú wahás hákã iyántui*
nu-tika-ma [nu aɨntsu puhu waha-sã]
ANA-VBLZ.TR+PFV-NSBJ>SBJ ANA person white stand-SBD+3:SS
[ha-kã] iyã-ta-u=i
die-PFV+SEQ+3:SS fall.forward-APPL+IPFV-NMLZ=COP:3:DECL
'When it did that to him, the man who was very pale, fell forward having died.'

(T1.35) *núnikmatãĩ dapíshkam dúshakam paŋkĩ́shkam atíhui*
nu-ni-ka-mataĩ dapi=shakama nu=shakama
ANA-VBLZ.INTR-PFV+SEQ-1/3:DS snake=ADD ANA=ADD
paŋkĩ=shakama ati-ha-u=i
boa=ADD unwrap-PFV-NMLZ=COP:3:DECL
'When (the man) did that, the snake, that one, the boa, also unwrapped him.'[11]

10 *bachita=i* (machete=INS) was corrected during translation from the original *bachita=haĩ* (machete=COM).

11 This sentence was considered to be unnecessary and repetitious by consultants working on transcription.

(T1.36) *dútikam núnikmatãĩ nũw̃ĩ paŋkín mãã́ nuwadúi núna aɨntsún ĩỹǎshín*
         hukíuwai

nu-tika-ma | [nu-ni-ka-mataĩ] | [nu=ĩ
ANA-VBLZ.TR+PFV-NSBJ>SBJ | ANA-VBLZ.INTR-PFV+SEQ-1/3:DS | ANA=LOC

paŋkĩ=na | ma-ã] | nuwanu=i | nu=na | aɨntsu=na
boa=ACC | kill-PFV+SEQ+3:SS | ANA=INS | ANA=ACC | person=ACC

iyãshĩ=na | hu-ki-u=ai
body+PSSD:1PL/3=ACC | take-PFV-NMLZ=COP:3:DECL

'When (the boa) did that (to the man), after (the man) did that, (the family) having killed the boa there, then they took the man's body.'

(T1.37) *núnin ásã anɨnhás kamĩ́ núninuk patáɨtus diimáinchui*

nu-ni-inu | asã | [anɨnhasã | kamĩ
ANA-VBLZ.INTR-NMLZ | COP+SBD+3:SS | thoughtlessly+3 | truly

nu-ni-inu=ka | patáɨ-tu-sã
ANA-VBLZ.INTR-NMLZ=TOP | follow-APPL-SBD+3:SS

dii-mai-inu-chau=i
see-POT-NMLZ-NEG.NMLZ=COP:3:DECL

'That being the case, really he was one who acted thoughtlessly, following (the boa's tracks) he couldn't see (the danger).'

(T1.38) *w̃ãã́s dúsha núnikabia muúntash áan umímkatin ásã áankachabiasha*

wãã́s | nu=sha | nu-ni-ka-amaya
I.don't.know.why | ANA=Q.TOP | ANA-VBLZ.INTR-PFV-DISTPST:3

muunta=sha | [aan | umim-ka-tinu | asã]
adult=Q.TOP | MED | be.doomed-PFV-FUT.NMLZ | COP+SBD+3:SS

aa-ni-ka-cha-amaya=sha
thus-VBLZ.INTR-PFV-NEG-DISTPST:3=Q.TOP?

'I don't know why that man acted like that, did that although he was doomed to die.'

(T1.39) *nunú dúshakam nuní dúwik múun páŋkĩ yúwam asáuwai*

nunu | nu=shakama | nuni | duik_muunta | [paŋkĩ
ANA | ANA=ADD | thus | ancestor | boa

yu-a-ma] | a-sa-u=ai
eat-IPFV-NSBJ>SBJ | COP-PFV-NMLZ=COP:3:DECL

'That also (happened), so the ancestor was eaten by a boa.'[12]

---

12 This use of a clause subordinated with *-ma* as a copula complement is unusual – see §13.6.3.

(T1.40) *dúshakam áuŋmatbau nuní áwai dúshakam*

        nu=shakama   auhuma-tu-mau   nuni   a-wa-i

        ANA=ADD   tell-APPL-NSBJ.NMLZ   thus   exist-3-DECL

        nu=shakama

        ANA=ADD

        'That story also exists.'

Text 2: Extracts from Pablo's autobiography

agr040824_02
Recorded in Centro Wawik, 24 August 2004. Total text is about 18 min.
Told by Pablo Santiak Kajekui, age 42, resident of Centro Wawik

This text consists of three extracts from a relatively long narrative recounting Pablo's life. Pablo was born in Chikais, a community located on the Marañón River about 8km due north of Centro Wawik, and moved to Wawik at a young age.

Section 1 starts at the beginning of the narrative. Pablo introduces himself and tells about how he was first exposed to education as his father was learning to read and write at the school for adults.

(T2.1)   *mína dáahuk Pabloi*
           mi=na   naa-hu=ka   *Pablo*=i
           1sg=ACC   name-PSSD:1SG=TOP   Pablo=COP:3:DECL
           'My name is Pablo.'

(T2.2)   *wíka akínauwaithai comunidad chikáis*
           wi=ka   akina-u=aita-ha-i   *comunidad*   Chikais
           1SG=TOP   be.born+PFV-NMLZ=COP-1SG-DECL community   Chikais
           'I was born in the community Chikais.'

(T2.3)   *túhã piípish ã́ĩ*
           tuhã   piipichi   a-ĩ
           but   small   COP+1SG/3-DS
           'But when I was small...'

(T2.4)   *mína apáŋ papí múun áuŋbaunum áuhak wíᶣakũ̃ĩ*
           mi=na   apa-hu   [papi   muunta   auhu-mau=numa]
           1sg=ACC   father-PSSD:1SG   book   adult   study-NSBJ.NMLZ=LOC
           auha-kũ   wɨ-a-ku-ĩ
           read+IPFV-SIM+3:SS   go-IPFV-SIM+1/3-DS
           'when my father went to study at the school for adults...'

(T2.5)   *sínchi wakíyin áyahai wísha áusatasan*
           sinchi   wakɨᶣa-inu   a-ya-ha-i   wi=sha
           strongly   want-NMLZ   COP-REMPST-1SG-DECL   1sg=ADD

auhu-sa-tasa-nu
read-PFV-INTENT-1SG:SS
'I too really wanted to study.'

(T2.6) *núniau asán patáikan wɨyahai mína apáŋ wɨɰakũĩ*
nu-ni-a-u   asa-nu   patai-ka-nu
ANA-VBLZ.INTR-IPFV-NMLZ   COP+SBD-1SG:SS   follow-PFV+SEQ-1SG:SS
wɨ-ya-ha-i   [mi=na   apa-hu   wɨ-a-ku-ĩ]
go-REMPST-1SG-DECL   1sg=ACC   father-PSSD:1SG   go-IPFV-SIM+1/3-DS
'Because I was doing that (i.e. wanting), having followed (him) I went
when my father went.'

(T2.7) *imaní wɨkáɨ asán papí mína apáŋ áuŋbaun unuimátiahai díkasɨ*
imani   wɨkaɨɰa   asa-nu   [papi   mi=na
INTENS.DEM.ADV   walk   COP+SBD-1SG:SS   book   1sg=ACC
apa-hu   auhu-mau=na]   unuima-tu-ya-ha-i
father-PSSD:1SG   read-NSBJ.NMLZ=ACC   learn-APPL-REMPST-1SG-DECL
díkasɨ
a.few
'Doing that so much, I learned a few of the books that my father was
studying.'

(T2.8) *núniu asámtãĩ mína apáŋ "áuŋduwĩ" túsã hintínkaŋtinu uhakábi*
nu-ni-a-u   asa-mataĩ   mi=na   apa-hu
ANA-VBLZ.INTR-IPFV-NMLZ   COP+SBD-1/3:DS   1sg=ACC   father-PSSD:1SG
[auhu-inu=ɨ   tu-sã]   hintina-kahatu-inu
read-NMLZ=NONVIS.COP:3   say-SBD+3:SS   teach-1PL.OBJ-NMLZ+ACC
uha-ka-amayi
tell-PFV-DISTPST:3:DECL
'When I was doing that, my father told the teacher "he can read!".'

(T2.9) *dútikam "áusakia" tákũĩ áuhiahai wi unuimáthamun*
du-tika-ma   auhu-sa-kia   ta-ku-ĩ
ANA-VBLZ.TR+PFV-NSBJ>SBJ   read-PFV-IMP.FAM   say+IPFV-SIM+1/3-DS
auhu-ya-ha-i   [wi   unuima-tu-ha-mau=na]
read-REMPST-1SG-DECL   1sg   learn-APPL-PFV-NSBJ.NMLZ=ACC
'When he did (i.e. said) that (to him), (the teacher) saying "read!", I
read what I had learned.'

(T2.10)   *núnitãĩ "auhaháma, dɨkaháma" túsã "kashín naŋkámsamɨk áusattamɨ*
          papík" túhutiabi

nu-ni-taĩ		auha-hama	dɨka-hama
ANA-VBLZ.INTR-SBD:1/3:DS		read+IPFV+3-CNTR.EX	know+IPFV+3-CNTR.EX

tu-sã	kashini	naŋkama-sa-mɨ=ka
say-SBD+3:SS	tomorrow	begin-SBD-2:SS=TOP

auhu-sa-tata-mɨ	papi=ka
read-PFV-FUT-2SG+DECL	book=TOP

tu-hu-ti-amayi
say-APPL-1SG.OBJ+PFV-DISTPST:3:DECL

'When I did that, saying "he's reading! he knows how!", (the teacher)
said to me "starting tomorrow you will study".'

The narrative continues with Pablo describing the problems that forced his family to
move and prevented him from continuing his study until he moved to Wawik.
Meanwhile, he had a great desire to learn Spanish and see the city, but nobody
could take him as his father spoke no Spanish. In section 2 he tells about how he left
home as a child to look for work in the *mestizo* settlements.

(T2.11)   *wíi tíkish wɨnakũĩ wɨɰabiahai Chiriaco*

wi	[tikichi	wɨ-ina-ku-ĩ]		wɨ-amaya-ha-i
1sg	other	go-PL:IPFV-SIM+1/3-DS		go+PFV-DISTPST-1SG-DECL

Chiriaco
Chiriaco

'When others were going, I went to Chiriaco.'

(T2.12)   *núnikan ɨɰãknush wáinkachabiahai*

nu-ni-ka-nu		ɨɰa-ka-nu=sha
ANA-VBLZ.INTR-PFV-1SG:SS		look.for-PFV-1SG:SS=CONCESS

waina-ka-cha-amaya-ha-i
see-PFV-NEG-DISTPST-1SG-DECL

'Having done that, although I looked, I didn't find (any work).'

(T2.13)   *nuwiŋtúsh kistián chíchaman dɨkachu asán chichasán inímtanash*
          inimáinchau dɨkápiahai

nuwiŋtu=sha	[kistian_chichama=na	dɨka-chau
furthermore=ADD	Spanish=ACC	know+IPFV-NEG:NMLZ

asa-nu]	[chicha-sa-nu]	inima-ta=na=sha
COP+SBD-1SG:SS	speak-SBD-1SG:SS	ask-ACT.NMLZ=ACC=ADD

inima-mai-inu-chau   dɨkapɨ-ya-ha-i
ask-POT-NMLZ-NEG.NMLZ   feel-REMPST-1SG-DECL

'Furthermore, not knowing Spanish, I couldn't even ask a question by speaking.'

(T2.14)   *núniau asán wakítkin midíyahai*

nu-ni-a-u   asa-nu   [wakitu-ki-nu]
ANA-VBLZ.INTR-IPFV-NMLZ   COP+SBD-1SG:SS   return-PFV-1SG:SS

mini-ya-ha-i
arrive-REMPST-1SG-DECL

'Because of my being that way, having turned back I arrived.'

(T2.15)   *nawɨnum miná minákuan Mesones taáwabiahai*

[nawɨ=numa   mina   mina-kawa-nu]   *Mesones*
foot=LOC   REDUP   arrive+IPFV-REPET-1SG:SS   Mesones.Muro

ta-aw-amaya-ha-i
come-PFV-DISTPST-1SG-DECL

'Arriving on foot, I came to Mesones Muro (a settlement in Imaza district).'

(T2.16)   *núnikan nũ̃wĩ "takát áwai" tákũ̃ĩ, "haánchin ukukíu asán mína hĩ̃ũãh̃ũ̃ĩ̃yã utithái" tusán midíu áyahai*

nu-ni-ka-nu   nu=ĩ   [taka-ta   a-wa-i]
ANA-VBLZ.INTR-PFV-1SG:SS   ANA=LOC   work-ACT.NMLZ   exist-3-DECL

ta-ku-ĩ]   [haanchi=na   uku-ki-u   asa-nu
say+IPFV-SIM+1/3-DS   clothes=ACC   leave-PFV-NMLZ   COP+SBD-1SG:SS

mi=na   hĩũa-hu=ĩ=ya   uti-ta-ha-i
1sg=ACC   house-PSSD:1SG=LOC=ABL   fetch+PFV-IFUT-1SG-DECL

tu-sa-nu]   mini-u   a-ya-ha-i
say-SBD-1SG:SS   arrive+PFV-NMLZ   COP-REMPST-1SG-DECL

'Having done that, there they said to me "there is work", I said "I left my clothes behind, so I'll get them from my house" and was coming back.'

(T2.17)   *núnikan miná minákuan Campamento Unión táu áyahai*

nu-ni-ka-nu   [mina   mina-kawa-nu]
ANA-VBLZ.INTR-PFV-1SG:SS   REDUP   arrive+IPFV-REPET-1SG:SS

Campamento Unión   ta-a-u   a-ya-ha-i
Campamento.Union   come-IPFV-NMLZ   COP-REMPST-1SG-DECL

'Having done that, coming and coming I was arriving at Campamento Unión (a settlement in Imaza district).'

(T2.18)   *ɨtsã akã́ɨ̨̃ãĩ nṹw̃ĩ makíchik hɨ̃ɨ̨̃ã kistián puhámu aún dɨisán naŋkã́ɨ̨̃ãĩ*
[ɨtsã   akaɨɨ̨a-ĩ]   nu=ĩ   [makichiki   hɨɨ̨a   kistian
sun   set+IPFV+1SG/3-DS   ANA=LOC   one   house   *mestizo*
puha-mau   au=na]   dɨi-sa-nu
live+IPFV-NSBJ.NMLZ   DIST=ACC   look-SBD-1SG:SS
naŋkaɨɨ̨a-ĩ
pass.by+IPFV+1SG/3-DS
'As the sun was going down, I was looking at a house there that *mesti-zos* lived in as I passed by...'

(T2.19)   *nṹw̃ĩ núwa puháu "tu wɨɨ̨amɨ" tuhútĩ*
nu=ĩ   nuwa   puha-u   tu   wɨ-a-mɨ
ANA=LOC   woman   live+IPFV-NMLZ   where   go-IPFV-2
tu-hu-tĩ
say-APPL-1SG.OBJ+PFV+3:SS
'a woman who lived there having said to me "where are you going?"...'

(T2.20)   *tákṹĩ "hɨɨ̨ahṹĩ wɨɨ̨ahai" tútãĩ*
ta-ku-ĩ   hɨɨ̨a-hu-ĩ   wɨ-a-ha-i
say+IPFV-SIM+1/3-DS   house-PSSD:1SG=LOC   go-IPFV-1SG-DECL
tu-taĩ
say-SBD:1/3:DS
'when she said that, I said "I'm going home"...'

(T2.21)   *"ɨtsã akɨawai, hṹw̃ĩ kanáham kashín wɨtá" túhutkṹĩ*
ɨtsã   aki-a-wa-i   hu=ĩ   kana-ha-mɨ   kashini
sun   set-IPFV-3-DECL   PROX=LOC   sleep-PFV-2:SS   tomorrow
wɨ-ta   tu-hu-ta-ku-ĩ
go+PFV-IMP   say-APPL-1SG.OBJ+IPFV-SIM+1/3-DS
'she said to me "the sun is setting, sleep here and go tomorrow"...'

(T2.22)   *"ayú" tusán w̃ãỹã́w̃ãbiahai*
ayu   tu-sa-nu   waɨ-aw-amaya-ha-i
ok   say-SBD-1SG:SS   enter-PFV-DISTPST-1SG-DECL
'saying "ok" I went in.'

(T2.23)   *núnikan ã́ĩ yumáinun ahampúsmatãĩ yuwán kánãĩ*
nu-ni-ka-nu   a-ĩ   yu-mai-inu=na
ANA-VBLZ.INTR-PFV+SEQ-1SG:SS   COP+1/3-DS   eat-POT-NMLZ=ACC

ahampu-sa-mataĩ   yu-a-nu   kana-ĩ
give.food-PFV+SEQ-1/3:DS   eat-PFV+SEQ-1SG:SS   sleep+IPFV+1SG/3-DS
'Having done that, she offered me food, and having eaten I was sleeping...'

(T2.24)   *"dɨkás hṹwĩ puhusmí wíi haánchin sumáŋkathamɨ" tákũĩ*
          <u>dɨkas</u>   <u>hu=ĩ</u>   <u>puhu-sa-mi</u>   <u>wi</u>   <u>haanchi=na</u>
          truly   PROX=LOC   live-PFV-HORT   1sg   clothes=ACC
          <u>suma-hu-ka-ta-hamɨ</u>   ta-ku-ĩ
          buy-APPL-PFV-IFUT-1SG>2SG+DECL   say+IPFV-SIM+1/3-DS
          'when she said "better, let's live (together) here, I'll buy you clothes"...'

(T2.25)   *"ayú" tusán nuní níina hḯn huwákan takákun puhúyahai mihadái*
          <u>ayu</u>   tu-sa-nu   nuni   nĩ=na   hḯ=nĩ
          ok   say-SBD-1SG:SS   thus   3sg=ACC   house+PSSD:1PL/3=LOC
          huwa-ka-nu   taka-ku-nu   puhu-ya-ha-i
          stay-PFV+SEQ-1SG:SS   work+IPFV-SIM-1SG:SS   live-REMPST-1SG-DECL
          mihana=i
          year=INS
          'so saying "ok" I stayed in her house and worked for a year.'

The young Pablo was still very keen to travel to the city and learn Spanish, and one
day an opportunity arose – an officer in the local garrison was going back to Lima
and his wife wanted to take a local orphan to raise and educate in the city. Pablo's
father was not around to ask permission, so young Pablo told the officer he was an
orphan and went with them. He describes the drive to Lima and his amazement at
seeing the cities of Bagua, Chiclayo and Lima for the first time. Section 3 begins
when Pablo has recently arrived in the city and is set to work washing dishes in the
officer's wife's parents' house. He still only knows a few phrases of Spanish.

(T2.26)   *subteniente mína Lima iwaŋkáuk ikám wákɨtak ukúŋkiabi nína wɨɰahḯ*
        hḯn
          [*subteniente*   mi=na   *Lima*   i-wa-hu-ka-u=ka]
          second.lieutenant   1sg=ACC   Lima   CAUS-go.up-1SG.OBJ-PFV-NMLZ=TOP
          ikama   wakɨta-kũ   uku-hu-ki-amayi
          jungle+LOC   go.back+IPFV-SIM+3:SS   leave-1SG.OBJ-PFV-DISTPST:3:DECL
          [nĩ=na   wɨɰa-hĩ   hḯ=nĩ]
          3sg=ACC   father.in.law-PSSD:1PL/3+GEN   house+PSSD:1PL/3=LOC
          'The second lieutenant who had brought me to Lima left me at his fa-
ther-in-law's house when he went back to the jungle.'

(T2.27)   *núnikmatã͏̃ puhã͏̃í háta naŋkámhuawabi*

nu-ni-ka-mataĩ   puha-ĩ   ha-ta

ANA-VBLZ.INTR-PFV+SEQ-1/3:DS   live+IPFV+1SG/3-DS   be.sick-ACT.NMLZ

naŋkama-hu-aw-amayi

begin-1SG.OBJ-PFV-DISTPST:3:DECL

'After he did that, while I was there, I became ill.'

(T2.28)   *dúka sahampíum ã͏̃í*

nu=ka   sahampium   a-ĩ

ANA=TOP   measles   COP+1SG/3-DS

'That was measles...'

(T2.29)   *túhãsh nuní "háahai" tusán*

tuhã=sha   nuni   <u>ha-a-ha-i</u>   tu-sa-nu

but=ADD   thus   be.sick-IPFV-1SG-DECL   say-SBD-1SG:SS

'but saying only "I'm sick"...'

(T2.30)   *wahúk háaha núna tumáin dɨkáptsayahai*

[wahuka   ha-a-ha   nu-na]   tu-mai-inu

how   be.sick-IPFV-1SG   ANA_REL=ACC   say-POT-NMLZ

dɨkapɨ-tsa-ya-ha-i

feel-NEG-REMPST-1SG-DECL

'I didn't feel able to say in what way I was sick.'

(T2.31)   *núniau asán áyatak "háahai" túyahai*

nu-ni-a-u   asa-nu   ayatak

ANA-VBLZ.INTR-IPFV-NMLZ   COP+SBD-1SG:SS   only

<u>ha-a-ha-i</u>   tu-ya-ha-i

be.sick-IPFV-1SG-DECL   say-REMPST-1SG-DECL

'Because of that, I only said "I'm sick".'

(T2.32)   *tútã͏̃í "wahúk háapa" tuhútianumɨ̃*

tu-taĩ   <u>wahuka</u>   <u>ha-a-pa</u>

say-SBD:1/3:DS   how   be.sick-IPFV-2SG

tu-hu-tu-ya-numɨ̃

say-APPL-1SG.OBJ-REMPST-3PL+DECL

'when I said that, they said to me "in what way are you sick?".'

(T2.33)   *túhãsh nuní "háahai" tusánuk ɨtsíŋtsayahai*

tuhã=sha   nuni   <u>ha-a-ha-i</u>   tu-sa-nu=ka

but=ADD   thus   be.sick-IPFV-1SG-DECL   say-SBD-1SG:SS=TOP

itsɨ-hu-tsa-ya-ha-i
explain-APPL-NEG-REMPST-1SG-DECL
'But saying only "I'm sick" I did not explain to them."

(T2.34)   *núnitãĩ "dakɨmak táwai" tuhútĩ*
nu-ni-taĩ   dakima-kũ   ta-wa-i
ANA-VBLZ.INTR-SBD:1/3:DS   be.lazy+IPFV-SIM+3:SS   say+IPFV-3-DECL
tu-hu-tĩ
say-APPL-1SG.OBJ+PFV+SEQ+3:SS
'When I did that, they said about me "he says that because he's lazy"...'

(T2.35)   *túhãsh nuní sɨnchi waųą́ntuyi háta*
tuhã=sha   nuni   sɨnchi
but=ADD   thus   strongly
waųa-hu-tu-yi   ha-ta
overcome-APPL-1SG.OBJ-REMPST:3:DECL   be.sick-ACT.NMLZ
'but the sickness more strongly overcame me.'

(T2.36)   *núniakũĩ plato niháktasan wɨtakamán winchaínhan iyáutãĩ*
nu-ni-a-ku-ĩ   [plato   niha-ka-tasa-nu]
ANA-VBLZ.INTR-IPFV-SIM+1/3-DS   plate   wash-PFV-INTENT-1SG:SS
[wɨ-takama-nu]   winchaina-ha-nu   iyau-taĩ
go+PFV-FRUST-1SG:SS   faint-PFV-1SG:SS   fall-SBD:1/3:DS
'When it did that, I was trying to go and wash the plates but I fainted
and fell down...'

(T2.37)   *yamá dɨ́ká́ntuawabi dɨkás háamun*
yama   dɨka-hu-tu-aw-amayi   dɨkas
now   know-APPL-1SG.OBJ-PFV-DISTPST:3:DECL   truly
ha-a-mau=na
be.sick-IPFV-NSBJ.NMLZ=ACC
'now they really knew about my illness.'

(T2.38)   *túhãsh wáamak yutúnhabiahai*
tuhã=sha   waamak   yutuna-ha-amaya-ha-i
but=ADD   quickly   get.worse-PFV-DISTPST-1SG-DECL
'I quickly got worse.'

(T2.39)   *núnitãĩ wáamkɨs médiconum ɨhɨ́tuawahabi*
nu-ni-taĩ   waamakɨsã   *médico*=numa
ANA-VBLZ.INTR-SBD:1/3:DS   quickly+3   doctor=LOC

ɨhɨ-tu-aw-aha-amayi
take-1SG.OBJ-PFV-PL-DISTPST:3:DECL
'When I did that, they quickly took me to a doctor.'

(T2.40) *nɯ̃w̃ɨ̃ médico "hospital ɨmáta" tútãɨ̃*

nu=ĩ   médico   <u>hospital</u>   <u>ɨma-ta</u>   tu-taĩ
ANA=LOC   doctor   hospital   take+PFV-IMP   say-SBD:1/3:DS
'There, when the doctor said "take him to a hospital"...'

(T2.41) *huhukɨ̃́ ɨ́tiahabi*

hu-hu-kɨ̃́   ɨ-tu-i-aha-amayi
take-1SG.OBJ-PFV+SEQ+3:SS   take-1SG.OBJ-PFV-PL-DISTPST:3:DECL
'having picked me up, they took me there.'

Text 3: Hunting

agr040708_03
Recorded in Centro Wawik, 8 July 2004. About 2 min 35 sec.
Told by Arias Chamik Ukuncham, age 37, resident of Centro Wawik

The following text was recorded in response to my request to hear about hunting techniques. After the first three introductory lines, it is entirely couched in the 'normative' verb form (see §8.4.5), with first person plural subject as can be seen from the subordinate verb forms.

(T3.1)   *yatsún Simón wakɨɰawai ii hutíi iiniáti kúntin maá maátasa wahúk wɨkáɨtayamɨ̃ nunúna*

yatsu-hu		Simón	wakɨɰa-wa-i	[ii	hutii
brother-PSSD:1SG		Simon	want+IPFV-3-DECL	[1pl	1pl
iinia=ti		kuntinu	maa	ma-a-tasa		wahuka
one.of.us=SAP		animal	REDUP	kill-PFV-INTENT+1PL:SS		how
wɨkaɨɰa-tayamɨ̃]		nunu=na				
walk-NORM		ANA=ACC				

'My brother Simon wants (to know): how do we, (people) from around here, go hunting?'

(T3.2)   *núniu asámtãĩ nɨ́hãĩ chichákun puháhai*

nu-ni-a-u		asa-mataĩ		nɨ̃=haĩ
ANA-VBLZ.INTR-IPFV-NMLZ		COP+SBD-1/3:DS		3sg=COM
chicha-ku-nu		puha-ha-i		
converse+IPFV-SIM-1SG:SS		live+IPFV-1SG-DECL		

'Because he does (i.e. wants) that, I am conversing with him now.'

(T3.3)   *nɨ̃́shkam dɨkátatus wakɨɰau asámtãĩ nína uháhai yamái*

nɨ̃=shakama	dɨka-tatus		wakɨɰa-u
3sg=ADD	know+PFV-INTENT+3:SS		want+IPFV-NMLZ
asa-mataĩ	nɨ̃=na	uha-ha-i		yamai
COP+SBD-1/3:DS	3sg=ACC	tell+IPFV-1SG-DECL		now

'And because he wants to know, I am telling him now.'

(T3.4)   *huní ɨɰamtayamɨ̃*

hu-ni	ɨɰama-tayamɨ̃
PROX-ALL	look.for-NORM

'We search (for game) like this.'

(T3.5) *dɨkatkau nuwáhãĩ chichasá "kashín wɨkáɨkun wɨtathai" tusá*

dɨkatkau   nuwa=haĩ   chicha-sa   [kashini

first   woman=COM   converse-PFV+SEQ+1PL:SS tomorrow

<u>wɨkaɨɰa-ku-nu</u>   <u>wɨ-tata-ha-i</u>   tu-sa]

walk+IPFV-SIM-1SG:SS   go+PFV-FUT-1SG-DECL   say-SBD+1PL:SS

'First, having spoken to our wives, saying "tomorrow I will go walking (i.e. hunting)"...'

(T3.6) *tsawáha yuhúmkaush yuwá káshik hiinkí wɨtáyamɨ̃*

[tsawa-ha]   [yuhumaka-uchi   yu-a]

dawn-PFV+SEQ+1PL:SS   food-DIM   eat-PFV+SEQ+1PL:SS

[kashik   hiina-ki]   wɨ-tayamɨ̃

early.morning   go.out-PFV+SEQ+1PL:SS   go-NORM

'having woken up, eaten a bit of food and gone out early in the morning, we go.'

(T3.7) *núnika akahú húki wɨaku kúntin wainkátasa wahasá niimsá*

nu-ni-ka   [akahu   hu-ki]

ANA-VBLZ.INTR-PFV+SEQ+1PL:SS   shotgun   take-PFV+SEQ+1PL:SS

[wɨ-a-ku]   [kuntinu   waina-ka-tasa]   [waha-sa]

go-IPFV-SIM+1PL:SS   animal   see-PFV-INTENT+1PL:SS   stand-SBD+1PL:SS

[niima-sa]

look-SBD+1PL:SS

'Having done that, having taken our shotguns and gone to find animals, we stand looking...'

(T3.8) *nũ̃ĩ wahasá niimsá wákɨ̃ ákuiŋ ɨsáa diisá ukuáku wɨtáyamɨ̃*

[nu=ĩ   waha-sa]   [niima-sa]   [wakɨ̃

ANA=LOC   stand-PFV+SEQ+1PL:SS   look-PFV+SEQ+1PL:SS   cliff

a-ku-ɨ̃=ka]   [ɨsa-a]

exist+IPFV-SIM-1/3.DS=COND   stretch.neck-PFV+SEQ+1PL:SS

[dii-sa]   [uku-a-ku]   wɨ-tayamɨ̃

look-PFV+SEQ+1PL:SS   leave-IPFV-SIM+1PL:SS   go-NORM

'having stood there looking, if there is a cliff, having stretched out our necks and looked, we leave and go.'

(T3.9) *apiihánum hɨɰantá nṹw̃ĩ waíttsa hiínki wɨkamá imániaku kúntin*
      waintáyamɨ̃

[apiiha=numa	hɨɰã-ta]		[nu=ĩ́
thicket=LOC	arrive-APPL+PFV+SEQ+1PL:SS		ANA=LOC
[waitu-sa]	hiina-ki]		[wɨ-kama]
suffer-SBD+1PL:SS	go.out-PFV+SEQ+1PL:SS		go-TERM+1PL:SS
[ima-ni-a-ku]		kuntinu	waina-tayamɨ̃
INTENS-VBLZ.INTR-IPFV-SIM+1PL:SS		animal	see-NORM

'Having arrived in thick brush, after getting out of there with difficulty, on going, doing this so much we see an animal.'

(T3.10) *núnika antúki wɨkamá waintáyamɨ̃ kúntin mináushkam*

nu-ni-ka	[antu-ki]	[wɨ-kama]
ANA-VBLZ.INTR-PFV+SEQ+1PL:SS	listen-PFV+SEQ+1PL:SS	go-TERM+1PL:SS
waina-tayamɨ̃	kuntinu	mina-u=shakama
see-NORM	animal	arrive-IPFV-NMLZ=ADD

'Having done that, going on listening we see animals coming.'

(T3.11) *núnika wainká máutayamɨ̃*

nu-ni-ka	waina-ka	mau-tayamɨ̃
ANA-VBLZ.INTR-PFV+SEQ+1PL:SS	see-PFV+SEQ+1PL:SS	kill-NORM

'Having done that, having seen it, we kill it.'

(T3.12) *núnika maá huhúmkuik yúpichu huhumtáyamɨ̃*

nu-ni-ka	[ma-a]
ANA-VBLZ.INTR-PFV+SEQ+1PL:SS	kill-PFV+SEQ+1PL:SS
[hu-hu-ma-ku-i=ka]	[yupichu	hu-hu-ma-tayamɨ̃]
take-APPL-REFL-SIM-1PL:SS=COND	easy	take-APPL-REFL-NORM

'Having done that, having killed it, if we take it away, we easily take it away.'

(T3.13) *núniashkuik íi wáinkash táakuik wɨkáɨ wɨkáɨkawa yapáŋki minámunum*
      hintá kã́y̆ŭk bataín pɨhɨkɨush antútayamɨ̃

nu-ni-a-cha-ku-i=ka	[ii	wainaka=sha
ANA-VBLZ.INTR-IPFV-NEG-SIM-1PL:SS=COND	1pl	in.vain+1PL=ADD
ta-a-ku-i=ka]	[wɨkaɨ	wɨkaɨɰa-kawa]
come-IPFV-SIM-1PL:SS=COND	REDUP	walk+IPFV-REPET+1PL:SS
[yapahu-ki	mina-mau=numa]	hinta
be.hungry-PFV+1PL:SS	arrive+IPFV-NSBJ.NMLZ=LOC	path+LOC

kãyuka   batai̱=na   pihi̱ki̱-a-u=sha   antu-tayamĩ
agouti   *chambira*.fruit=ACC   gnaw-IPFV-NMLZ=ADD   hear-NORM
'If we don't do that, if we come empty-handed, walking and walking and getting hungry, as we arrive we hear an agouti gnawing *chambira* fruit in the path.'

(T3.14)   *núnika antúka nũ̃w̃ĩ shitá shitámhakua "itsi̱ki̱shtahash" túsa*
           ani̱ntáimtakua tsapúhi puháu wáinkaik dúshakam máutayamĩ
           nu-ni-ka   [antu-ka]   [nu=ĩ   shita
           ANA-VBLZ.INTR-PFV+SEQ+1PL:SS   hear-PFV+SEQ+1PL:SS   ANA=LOC   REDUP
           shitama-ha-kawa]   [[i̱-tsi̱ki̱-cha-ta-ha=sha
           crawl-APPL+IPFV-REPET+1PL:SS   CAUS-jump+PFV-NEG-IFUT-1SG=ADD
           tu-sa]   ani̱ntaima-ta-kawa]
           say-SBD+1PL:SS   think-APPL+IPFV-REPET+1PL:SS
           [[tsapu-hi   puha-u]   waina-ka-i=ka]
           lift.head-APPL+PFV+3:SS   live-IPFV-NMLZ   see-PFV+SEQ-1PL:SS=COND
           nu=shakama   mau-tayamĩ
           ANA=ADD   kill-NORM
           'Having done that, having heard that, crawling and crawling there, thinking "I won't startle it", if we have seen it there having lifted its head to look around, we kill that too.'

(T3.15)   *dútika maá dúwi hiŋkahá hukí tsukapsá minitáyamĩ*
           nu-tika   [ma-a]   nu-i
           ANA-VBLZ.TR-PFV+SEQ+1PL:SS   kill-PFV+SEQ+1PL:SS   ANA=INS
           [hiŋka-ha]   [hu-ki]
           tie.up-PFV+SEQ+1PL:SS   take-PFV+SEQ+1PL:SS
           [tsukapi̱-sa]   mini-tayamĩ
           carry.on.shoulder-SBD+1PL:SS   arrive-NORM
           'Having done that, having killed it, consequently having tied it up and taken it we arrive carrying it over our shoulder.'

(T3.16)   *núnia núniakua i̱tsã aká̱ĩũ̯ã̱ĩ iina nũ̃w̃ĩ puhámunum iina hi̱uchíhiŋ*
           tatáyamĩ
           nunia   nu-ni-a-kawa   [i̱tsã   akai̱ɰa-ĩ]
           REDUP   ANA-VBLZ.INTR-IPFV-REPET+1PL:SS   sun   set+IPFV+1SG/3-DS
           [ii=na   nuw̃ĩ   puha-mau=numa]   ii=na
           1pl=ACC   woman+PSSD:1PL/3   live+IPFV-NSBJ.NMLZ   1pl=ACC

hĩ̀-uchi-hĩ=ka	ta-tayamĩ
house+PSSD-DIM-PSSD:1PL/3=TOP	come-NORM

'Going on doing that, as the sun is setting we come to our home, where our wife is.'

(T3.17)   *túhã nu núnikchattakuik kúntin kaútu wainkáik piníha áushkam dakáka kúntin minítkuiŋ mantúmtayamĩ*

tuhã	[nu	nu-ni-ka-cha-tata-ku-i=ka]	[[kuntinu
but	ANA	ANA-VBLZ.INTR-PFV-NEG-FUT-SIM-1PL:SS=COND	animal
kau-ta-u]		waina-ka-i=ka]	
assemble-APPL+IPFV-NMLZ		see-PFV+SEQ-1PL:SS=COND	
[pini-ha]		[au=shakama	daka-ka]
build.hide-PFV+SEQ+1PL:SS		DIST=ADD	wait.for-PFV+SEQ+1PL:SS
[kuntinu	mini-ta-ku-ĩ=ka]		mantu-ma-tayamĩ
animal	arrive-APPL+IPFV-SIM+1/3-DS=COND		kill+APPL-REFL-NORM

'But if we don't do that, if we have seen animals gathering (to eat), having built a hide and waited for them too, if the animals come we kill them.'

(T3.18)   *núniashkuik núu dútika máashkuik káshish wɨtáyamĩ*

nu-ni-a-cha-ku-i=ka	[nu
ANA-VBLZ.INTR-IPFV-NEG-SIM-1PL:SS=TOP	ANA
nu-tika]	[ma-a-cha-ku-i=ka]
ANA-VBLZ.TR+PFV+SEQ+1PL:SS	kill-IPFV-NEG-SIM-1PL:SS=TOP
kashi=sha	wɨ-tayamĩ
night=ADD	go-NORM

'If we don't do that, if having done all that we don't kill (the animal), we even go at night.'

(T3.19)   *núnika káshi wɨ̃ wɨkáɨ wɨkáɨkawa*

nu-ni-ka	[kashi	wɨ]	[wɨkaɨ
ANA-VBLZ.INTR-PFV+SEQ+1PL:SS	night	go+PFV+SEQ+1PL:SS	REDUP
wɨkaɨɰa-kawa]			
walk+IPFV-REPET+1PL:SS			

'Having done that, having gone at night, walking and walking…'

(T3.20)   *íi wainkáttakuik kúhi wainká yuwíchu wainká máakuik*

ii	waina-ka-tata-ku-i=ka	[kuhi	waina-ka]
1pl	see-PFV-FUT-SIM-1PL:SS=COND	kinkajou	see-PFV+SEQ+1PL:SS

[yuwichu   waina-ka]   ma-a-ku-i=ka
deer.sp   see-PFV+SEQ+1PL:SS   kill-IPFV-SIM-1PL:SS=COND
'if we see something, having seen a kinkajou, having seen a *yuwichu* deer, if we kill it...'

(T3.21)   *áattsa shushuikísh wainkáttakuik núu maá*
aatusa   [shushui=kI=sha   waina-ka-tata-ku-i=ka]
thus+1PL   armadillo=RESTR=ADD   see-PFV-FUT-SIM-1PL:SS=COND
nu   ma-a
ANA   kill-PFV+SEQ+1PL:SS
'thus if we if we see even just an armadillo, having killed that...'

(T3.22)   *wáittsa itaá íina nũw̃ı̃ũchíhı̃hã̃ı̃ akáha ína patahı̃́ ipása aátsa húsha kuntínchakam yutáyamı̃*
[waitu-sa]   [i-ta-a]   [ii=na
suffer-SBD+1PL:SS   CAUS-arrive-PFV+SEQ+1PL:SS   1pl=ACC
nuwı̃-uchi-hı̃=haı̃   ii=na
woman+PSSD-DIM-PSSD:1PL/3=COM   butcher-PFV+SEQ+1PL:SS
[ii=na   pata-hı̃   ipa-sa]   aatusa
1pl=ACC   family-PSSD:1PL/3   invite-PFV+SEQ+1PL:SS   thus+1PL
hu=sha   kuntinu=shakama   yu-tayamı̃
PROX=ADD   animal=ADD   eat-NORM
'having brought it with difficulty, having butchered it with our wives, having invited our family, thus we eat that animal too.'

(T3.23)   *ı̃ik aáttsa wáittsa ıɰamsá yúwaithi*
ii=ka   aatusa   [waitu-sa]   [ıɰama-sa]
1pl=TOP   thus+1PL   suffer-SBD+1PL:SS   search-SBD+1PL:SS
yu-u=aita-hi-i
eat-NMLZ=COP-1PL-DECL
'And so, suffering while searching, we are ones who eat.'

References

Adelaar, Willem F.H. 1990. The role of quotations in Andean discourse. In W.F.H. Adelaar (ed.), *Papers presented to Simon C. Dik on his 50th birthday*, 1–12. Dordrecht: Foris.

Adelaar, Willem F.H. 2006. The Quechua impact in Amuesha, an Arawak language of the Peruvian Amazon. In A.Y. Aikhenvald & R.M.W. Dixon (eds.), *Grammars in Contact: A Cross-linguistic Typology*, 290–312. Oxford: Oxford University Press.

Adelaar, Willem F.H. with Pieter C. Muysken. 2004. *The Languages of the Andes*. Cambridge: Cambridge University Press.

Aikhenvald, Alexandra Y. 1996. Words, pauses and boundaries: Evidence from South-American languages. *Studies in Language* 20: 487–517.

Aikhenvald, Alexandra Y. 2002. *Language Contact in Amazonia*. Oxford: Oxford University Press.

Aikhenvald, Alexandra Y. 2004. *Evidentiality*. Oxford: Oxford University Press.

Aikhenvald, Alexandra Y. 2006. Grammars in contact: A cross-linguistic perspective. In A.Y. Aikhenvald & R.M.W. Dixon (eds.), *Grammars in Contact: A Cross-linguistic Typology*, 1–66. Oxford: Oxford University Press.

Aikhenvald, Alexandra Y. 2007a. Typological dimensions in word-formation. In T. Shopen (ed.), *Language Typology and Syntactic Description: Vol. 3, Grammatical categories and the lexicon* (second edition), 1–65. Cambridge: Cambridge University Press.

Aikhenvald, Alexandra Y. 2007b. Languages of the Pacific coast of South America. In O. Miyaoka, O. Sakiyama & M.E. Kraussof (eds.) *The Vanishing Languages of the Pacific Rim*, 183–205. Oxford: Oxford University Press.

Aikhenvald, Alexandra Y. 2008. Semi-direct speech: Manambu and beyond. *Language Sciences* 30 (4): 383–422.

Aikhenvald, Alexandra Y. 2012. *The languages of the Amazon*. Oxford: Oxford University Press.

Aikhenvald, Alexandra Y. and R.M.W. Dixon. 2001. Introduction. In A.Y. Aikhenvald & R.M.W. Dixon (eds.), *Areal Diffusion and Genetic Inheritance: Problems in comparative linguistics*, 1–26. Oxford: Oxford University Press.

Appel, René and Pieter Muysken. 1987. *Language Contact and Bilingualism*. London: Edward Arnold.

Beuchat, Henri and Paul Rivet. 1909. La langue Jibaro ou Šiwora. *Anthropos* 4: 805–822.

Beuchat, Henri and Paul Rivet. 1910. La langue Jibaro ou Šiwora. *Anthropos* 5: 1053–1064 and 1109–1124.

Bhat, D.N.S. 1994. *The Adjectival Category: Criteria for Differentiation and Identification*. Amsterdam: John Benjamins.

Blust, Robert. 1998. Seimat vowel nasality: A typological anomaly. *Oceanic Linguistics* 37(2): 298–322.

Bruno, Ana Carla, Frantomé Pacheco, Francesc Queixalós, and Leo Wetzels. (eds.). *La structure des langues amazoniennes, Amérindia* 32.

Campbell, Lyle. 1988. Review of Greenberg (1987) *Language in the Americas. Language* 64(3): 591–615.

Castner, James L. 2004. *Shrunken Heads: Tsantsa Trophies and Human Exotica*. Gainesville, FL: Feline Press.

Chen, Matthew Y. and William S-Y. Wang. 1975. Sound change: Actuation and implementation. *Language* 51: 255–281.

Colini, G. A. 1883. Osservazioni etnografiche sui Givari. *Atti della R. Accademia dei Lincei (3rd series)* 11: 337–380.

Comrie, Bernard. 1976. *Aspect*. Cambridge: Cambridge University Press.

Comrie, Bernard. 1985. *Tense*. Cambridge: Cambridge University Press.

Comrie, Bernard and Sandra A. Thompson. 2007. Lexical Nominalization. In T. Shopen (ed.), *Language Typology and Syntactic Description: Vol. 3, Grammatical Categories and the Lexicon* (second edition), 334–381. Cambridge: Cambridge University Press.

Corbera Mori, Angel. 1994. *Fonologia e gramática do Aguaruna (Jívaro)*. PhD dissertation, University of Campinas.

Corbett, Greville G. 2000. *Number*. Cambridge: Cambridge University Press.

Cristofaro, Sonia. 2003. *Subordination*. Oxford: Oxford University Press.

DeLancey, Scott. 2011. Finite structures from clausal nominalization in Tibeto-Burman. In F.H. Yap, K. Grunow-Hårsta and J. Wrona (eds.), *Nominalization in Asian Languages: Diachronic and typological perspectives*, 343–359. Amsterdam: John Benjamins.

Dik, Simon C. 1989. *The Theory of Functional Grammar: Part I: Structure of the Clause*. Dordrecht and Providence, RI: Foris.

Dingemanse, Mark. 2011. *The meaning and use of ideophones in Siwu*. PhD dissertation, Radboud University.

Dingemanse, Mark. 2012. Advances in the Cross-Linguistic Study of Ideophones. *Language and Linguistics Compass* 6/10: 654–672.

Dixon, R.M.W. 1994. *Ergativity*. Cambridge: Cambridge University Press.

Dixon, R.M.W. 1995. Complement clauses and complementation strategies. In F.R. Palmer (ed.) *Grammar and Meaning: Essays in Honour of Sir John Lyons*, 175–220. Cambridge: Cambridge University Press.

Dixon, R.M.W. 2004a. Adjective classes in typological perspective. In R.M.W. Dixon & A.Y. Aikhenvald (eds.), *Adjective Classes: A Cross-linguistic Typology*, 1–49. Cambridge: Cambridge University Press.

Dixon, R.M.W. 2004b. *The Jarawara Language of Southern Amazonia*. New York: Oxford University Press.

Dixon, R.M.W. 2006. Complement clauses and complementation strategies in typological perspective. In R.M.W. Dixon & A.Y. Aikhenvald (eds.), *Complementation*, 1–48. Cambridge: Cambridge University Press.

Dixon, R.M.W. 2009. The semantics of clause linking in typological perspective. In R.M.W. Dixon & A.Y. Aikhenvald (eds.) *The Semantics of Clause Linking: A cross-linguistic typology*, 1–55. Oxford: Oxford University Press.

Dixon, R.M.W. 2010. *Basic Linguistic Theory, Vol. 2: Grammatical topics*. Oxford: Oxford University Press.

Dixon, R.M.W. 2012. *Basic Linguistic Theory, Vol. 3: Further grammatical topics*. Oxford: Oxford University Press.

Dixon, R.M.W. and Alexandra Y. Aikhenvald. 1999. Introduction. In R.M.W. Dixon & A.Y. Aikhenvald (eds.), *The Amazonian Languages*, 1–21. Cambridge: Cambridge University Press.

Dixon, R.M.W. and Alexandra Y. Aikhenvald. 2000. Introduction. In R.M.W. Dixon & A.Y. Aikhenvald (eds.), *Changing Valency: Case studies in transitivity*, 1–29. Cambridge: Cambridge University Press.

Durie, M. 1986. The grammaticization of number as a verbal category. *Proceedings of the Berkeley Linguistic Society* 12: 355–70.

Epps, Patience. 2009. Escape from the noun phrase: From relative clause to converb and beyond in an Amazonian language. *Diachronica* 26(3): 287–318.

Epps, Patience and Andrés Salanova. 2012. A linguística amazônica hoje. *LIAMES* 12: 7–37.

Fabre, Alain. 2005. *Diccionario Etnolingüístico y Guía Bibliográfica de los Pueblos Indígenas Sudamericanos [Updated version of Manual de las Lenguas Indígenas Sudamericanas. Munich:*

Lincom Europa, 1998]. Accessed at:
http://butler.cc.tut.fi/~fabre/BookInternetVersio/Alkusivu.html

Fast, Gerhard and Mildred L. Larson. 1974. *Introducción al Idioma Aguaruna*. [Documento de Trabajo 3]. Lima: Instituto Lingüístico de Verano.

Fast, Gerhard, Ruby Warkentin and Daniel Fast. 1996. *Diccionario Achuar-Shiwiar – Castellano*. Lima: Instituto Lingüístico de Verano.

Fleck, David W. 2003. *A grammar of Matses*. PhD dissertation, Rice University.

Flornoy, Bertrand. 1953. *Jivaro: Among the Headshrinkers of the Amazon*. London: The Travel Book Club.

Foley, William A. and Robert D. van Valin, Jr. 1984. *Functional Syntax and Universal Grammar*. Cambridge: Cambridge University Press.

Genetti, Carol. 2005. The participial construction of Dolakhā Newar. *Studies in Language* 29(1): 35–87.

Genetti, Carol. 2011. Nominalization in Tibeto-Burman Languages of the Himalayan Area: A typological perspective. In F.H. Yap, K. Grunow-Hårsta & J. Wrona (eds.), *Nominalization in Asian Languages: Diachronic and typological perspectives*, 163–193. Amsterdam: John Benjamins.

Gildea, Spike. 2008. Explaining similarities between main clauses and nominalized clauses. In A.C. Bruno, F. Pacheco, F. Queixalos, & L. Wetzels (eds.), *La structure des langues amazoniennes*, 57–75. *Amérindia* 32.

Givón, Talmy. 2001. *Syntax: An introduction* [2 volumes]. Amsterdam/Philadelphia: John Benjamins.

Gnerre, Maurizio. 1973. Sources of Spanish *Jívaro*. *Romance Philology* 27(2): 203–204.

Gnerre, Maurizio. 1975. L'utilizzazione delle fonti documentarie dei secoli XVI e XVII per la storia linguistica Jíbaro. In E. Cerulli & G. Della Ragione (eds.), *Atti del XL Congresso Internazionale degli Americanisti* (vol. 3), 79–86. Genoa: Tilgher.

Gnerre, Maurizio. 1976. American Spanish *palta* 'avocado': The diffusion of a Quechua word, viewed in relation to its etymology. *Romance Philology* 29(3): 297–310.

Gnerre, Maurizio. 1986a. Some notes on quantification and numerals in an Amazon Indian language. In M.P. Closs (ed.), *Native American Mathematics*, 71–91. Austin: University of Texas Press.

Gnerre, Maurizio. 1986b. The decline of dialogue: Ceremonial and mythological discourse among the Shuar and Achuar of Eastern Ecuador. In J. Sherzer & G. Urban (eds.), *Native South American Discourse*, 307–341. Berlin/New York: Mouton de Gruyter.

Gnerre, Maurizio. 1999. *Profilo Descrittivo e Storico-comparativo di una Lingua Amazzonica: Lo Shuar*. Naples: Istituto Universitario Orientale.

Gordon, Lynn. 1983. Switch reference, clause order, and interclausal relationships in Maricopa. In J. Haiman & P. Munro (eds.), *Switch-Reference and Universal Grammar*, 83–104. Amsterdam: John Benjamins.

Gordon, Lynn. 1986. *Maricopa Morphology and Syntax*. Berkeley: University of California Press.

Greenberg, Joseph H. 1987. *Language in the Americas*. Stanford: Stanford University Press.

Guallart, José María. 1990. *Entre Pongo y Cordillera: Historia de la Etnia Aguaruna – Huambisa*. Lima: Centro Amazónico de Antropología y Aplicación Práctica.

Guillaume, Antoine. 2011. Subordinate clauses, switch-reference, and tail-head linkage in Cavineña narratives. In R. van Gijn, K. Haude & P. Muysken (eds.), *Subordination in Native South-American Languages*, 109–128. Amsterdam/Philadelphia: John Benjamins.

Haiman, John. 1978. Conditionals are topics. *Language* 54(3): 564–589.

Haiman, John and Pamela Munro (eds.). 1983. *Switch-Reference and Universal Grammar*. Amsterdam: John Benjamins.

Harner, Michael J. 1973. *The Jívaro: People of the Sacred Waterfalls*. New York: Anchor Books.

Haspelmath, Martin. 1995. The converb as a cross-linguistically valid category. In M. Haspelmath & E. König (eds.), *Converbs in Cross-Linguistic Perspective*, 1–55. Berlin: Mouton de Gruyter.

Haspelmath, Martin. 2007. Ditransitive alignment splits and inverse alignment. In A. Siewierska & W.B. Hollmann (eds.), *Ditransitivity: Special issue of Functions of Language* 14(1): 79–102.

Heine, Bernd and Tania Kuteva. 2002. *World Lexicon of Grammaticalization*. Cambridge: Cambridge University Press.

Hengeveld, Kees. 1992. *Non-verbal Predication: Theory, typology, diachrony*. Berlin: Mouton de Gruyter.

Hornberger, Esteban and Nancy Hornberger 1977. *Diccionario Tri-lingue: Quechua of Cusco-English-Spanish/Tri-lingual Dictionary: Quechua de Cusco-Ingles-Español*. Cusco: LCA.

Hyman, Larry M. 2009. How (not) to do phonological typology: the case of pitch-accent. *Language Sciences* 31: 213–238.

INEI [Instituto Nacional de Estadística e Informática] 2009. *Resumen Ejecutivo: Resultados definitivos de las comunidades indígenas*.
    <http://www1.inei.gob.pe/biblioineipub/bancopub/Est/Lib0789/Libro.pdf>

Jakway, Martha, Horacio Lorenzo C. and Arturo Antonio A. 1987. *Vocabulario Huambisa* [Serie Lingüística Peruana 24]. Lima: Instituto Lingüístico de Verano.

Jendraschek, Gerd. 2009. Switch-reference constructions in Iatmul: Forms, functions and development. *Lingua* 119: 1316–1339.

Jernigan, Kevin. 2006. *An Ethnobiological Exploration of Sensory and Ecological Aspects of Tree Identification among the Aguaruna Jívaro*. PhD dissertation, University of Georgia, Athens.

Jespersen, Otto. 1958 [1924]. *The Philosophy of Grammar*. London: Allen & Unwin.

Jijón y Caamaño, J. 1919. Contribución al conocimiento de las lenguas indígenas, que se hablaron en el Ecuador interandino y occidental, con anteriodad a la Conquista Española. *Boletín de la Sociedad Ecuatoriana de Estudios Históricos Americanos*, 340–413.

Jiménez de la Espada, Marcos (ed.) 1965 [1586]. *Relaciones Geográficas de Indias: Perú*. [Biblioteca de Autores Españoles, vols. 183–185]. Madrid: Atlas.

Jimpikit, Carmelina and Gladys Antun'. 2000. *Los Nombres Shuar: Significado y conservación* (second edition). Quito: Abya Yala.

Juank, Aij^{íu}. 1982. *Aujmatsatai, Yatsuchi: Manual de Aprendizaje de la Lengua Shuar* (vol. 1). Ecuador: Mundo Shuar.

Karsten, Rafael. 1935. *The Head-hunters of Western Amazonas: The Life and Culture of the Jibaro Indians of Eastern Ecuador and Peru* [Commentationes Humanarum Litterarum 7(1)]. Helsingfors: Societas Scientiarum Fennica.

Kasen Elena, Moisés, Mateo Anag Untsum, Filemón Apiquey Yunuica, Rector Ugkum Ampam, Jorge Apikai Yamanua, Timías Akuts Nugkai, and Samuel Nanantai. 1992. *Duik Muunta Pujuti Augbatbau: Relatos sobre la vida de nuestros abuelos* [Colección Literaria y Cultural 7]. Lima: Instituto Lingüístico de Verano.

Katan Jua, T. 2011. Ii chichame unuimiamu/Investigando nuestra lengua/Investigating our language: Shuar Chicham. In M. Haboud & N. Ostler (eds.), *Endangered Languages: Voices and images* [Proceedings of the FEL XV conference], 103–105.

Kemmer, Suzanne. 1993. *The Middle Voice*. Amsterdam/Philadelphia: John Benjamins.

Krasnoukhova, Olga. 2012. *The Noun Phrase in the Languages of South America*. Utrecht: LOT.

Larson, Mildred L. 1963. Emic classes which manifest the obligatory tagmemes in major independent clause types of Aguaruna (Jivaro). In V.G. Waterhouse (ed.), *Studies in Peruvian Indian languages* (vol. 1), 1–36. Texas: SIL International.

Larson, Mildred L. 1978. *The Functions of Reported Speech in Discourse*. Texas: SIL International.

Larson, Mildred L. and Lois Dodds. 1985. *Treasure in Clay Pots: An Amazon People on the Wheel of Change*. California and Texas: Person to Person Books.

Lehmann, Christian. 1988. Towards a typology of clause linkage. In J. Haiman & S.A. Thompson (eds.), *Clause combining in grammar and discourse*, 181–225. Amsterdam/Philadelphia: John Benjamins.

Longacre, Robert E. 1972. *Hierarchy and Universality of Discourse Constituents in New Guinea Languages: Discussion*. Washington, D.C.: Georgetown University Press.

Loos, Eugene E. 1999. Pano. In R.M.W. Dixon & A.Y. Aikhenvald (eds.), *The Amazonian Languages*, 227–250. Cambridge: Cambridge University Press.

Lord, Carol. 1993. *Historical Change in Serial Verb Constructions*. Amsterdam/Philadelphia: John Benjamins.

Loukotka, Čestmír (edited by Johannes Wilbert). 1968. *Classification of South American Indian Languages*. Los Angeles: University of California.

Maldonado, Pedro. 1750. *Carta de la Provincia de Quito y de sus adjacentes*. Paris.

Matisoff, James A. 1972. Lahu nominalization, relativization, and genitivization. In J.P. Kimball (ed.), *Syntax and Semantics* (vol. 1), 237–257. New York: Academic Press.

Matisoff, James A. 1975. Rhinoglottophilia: the mysterious connection between nasality and glottality. In C.A. Ferguson, L.M. Hyman & J.J. Ohala (eds.), *Nasálfest (Papers from a Symposium on Nasals and Nasalization)*, 265–287. Stanford: Stanford University Press.

Matthews, P.H. 1997. *The Concise Oxford Dictionary of Linguistics*. Oxford: Oxford University Press.

Matthiessen, Christian and Sandra A. Thompson. 1988. The structure of discourse and 'subordination'. In J. Haiman & S.A. Thompson (eds.), *Clause combining in grammar and discourse*, 275–329. Amsterdam/Philadelphia: John Benjamins.

Mosel, Ulrike. 2006. Grammaticography: The art and craft of writing grammars. In F. Ameka, A. Dench & N. Evans (eds.), *Catching Language: The standing challenge of grammar writing*, 41–68. Berlin: Walter de Gruyter.

Noonan, Michael. 1997. Versatile Nominalizations. In J. Bybee, J. Haiman & S.A. Thompson (eds.), *Essays on Language Function and Language Type. Dedicated to T. Givón*, 373–394. Amsterdam: John Benjamins.

Nuckolls, Janis B. 1996. *Sounds like Life: Sound-symbolic Grammar, Performance, and Cognition in Pastaza Quechua*. Oxford: Oxford University Press.

O'Connor, Loretta and Pieter Muysken (eds.) 2014. *The native languages of South America: Origins, development, typology*. Cambridge: Cambridge University Press.

Olawsky, Knut J. 2006. *A Grammar of Urarina*. Berlin: Mouton de Gruyter.

Oswalt, Robert L. 1983. Interclausal reference in Kashaya. In J. Haiman & P. Munro (eds.), *Switch-Reference and Universal Grammar*, 267–290. Amsterdam: John Benjamins.

Overall, Simon E. 2007. *A grammar of Aguaruna*. PhD dissertation, RCLT, La Trobe University.

Overall, Simon E. 2008. On the non-phonemic status of the velar nasal [ŋ] in Jivaroan. *LIAMES* 8: 45–59.

Overall, Simon E. 2009. The semantics of clause linking in Aguaruna. In R.M.W. Dixon & A.Y. Aikhenvald (eds.), *The Semantics of Clause Linking*, 167–192. Oxford: Oxford University Press.

Overall, Simon E. 2014a. Nominalization, knowledge and information source in Aguaruna (Jivaroan). In R.M.W. Dixon & A.Y. Aikhenvald (eds.), *The Grammar of Knowledge*, 227–244. Oxford: Oxford University Press.

Overall, Simon E. 2014b. Clause-chaining, switch-reference and nominalisations in Aguaruna (Jivaroan). In R. van Gijn, D. Matić, J. Hammond, S. van Putten & A.V. Galucio (eds.), *Information Structure and Reference Tracking in Complex Sentences*, 309–340. Amsterdam/Philadelphia: John Benjamins.

Overall, Simon E. 2016a. Switch-reference and case-marking in Aguaruna (Jivaroan) and beyond. In R. van Gijn & J. Hammond (eds.), *Switch-Reference 2.0*, 453–472. Amsterdam/Philadelphia: John Benjamins.

Overall, Simon E. 2016b. Who were the Antipas? A linguistic and ethnohistorical investigation of a forgotten tribe. *LIAMES* 16(1): 59–69.

Overall, Simon E. In press (a). A typology of frustrative marking in Amazonian languages. In A.Y. Aikhenvald & R.M.W. Dixon (eds.), *Cambridge Handbook of Linguistic Typology*. Cambridge University Press.

Overall, Simon E. In press (b). Attributive adjectives and the internal syntax of the NP in Jivaroan. In F. Queixalós & D.M. Gomes (eds.), *A estrutura do sintagma nominal em línguas amazônicas*.

Parker, Steve. 1996. Toward a universal form for 'yes': or, rhinoglottophilia and the affirmation grunt. *Journal of Linguistic Anthropology* 6(1): 85–95.

Payne, David L. 1978. *Nasalidad en Aguaruna* (second edition) [Serie Lingüística Peruana 15]. Lima: Instituto Lingüístico de Verano.

Payne, David L. 1981a. *The phonology and morphology of Axininca Campa*. Arlington: Summer Institute of Linguistics.

Payne, David L. 1981b. Bosquejo fonológico del Proto-Shuar-Candoshi: Evidencias para una relación genética. *Revista del Museo Nacional* 45: 323–377.

Payne, David L. 1990a. Some widespread grammatical forms in South American languages. In D. Payne (ed.), *Amazonian Linguistics*, 75–87. Dallas: University of Texas Press.

Payne, David L. 1990b. Accent in Aguaruna. In D. Payne (ed.), *Amazonian Linguistics*, 161–184. Dallas: University of Texas Press.

Payne, Doris L. 1990. *The pragmatics of word order: Typological dimensions of verb initial languages*. Berlin/New York: Mouton de Gruyter.

Payne, Doris L. 1993. Nonconfigurality and discontinuous expressions in Panare. In D. A. Peterson (ed.), *Proceedings of the Nineteenth Annual Meeting of the Berkeley Linguistic Society, February 12-15, 1993: Special session on syntactic issues in native American languages*, 121–138. Berkeley: Berkeley Linguistics Society.

Payne, Doris L. 2001. Review of R.M.W. Dixon & A.Y. Aikhenvald (eds.) (1999) *The Amazonian Languages. Language* 77(3): 594–598.

Payne, Thomas E. 1997. *Describing Morphosyntax: A guide for field linguists*. Cambridge: Cambridge University Press

Pellizaro, Siro and Fausto Osvaldo Náwech. 2005. *Chicham: Diccionario Shuar–Castellano*. Quito: Abya-Yala.

Pike, Kenneth L. and Mildred L. Larson. 1964. Hyperphonemes and non-systematic features of Aguaruna phonemics. In A.H. Marckwardt (ed.), *Studies in Languages and Linguistics in Honor of Charles C. Fries*, 55–67. Ann Arbor: English Language Institute.

Plungian, Vladimir A. 2001. Agglutination and flection. In M. Haspelmath, E. König, W. Österreicher & W. Raible (eds.), *Language Typology and Language Universals* (vol. 1), 669–678. Berlin/New York: Walter de Gruyter.

Plungian, Vladimir A. and Johan van der Auwera. 2006. Towards a typology of discontinuous past marking. *Sprachtypologie und Universalienforschung* 59(4): 317–349.

Reesink, Ger P. 1983. Switch-reference and topicality hierarchies. *Studies in Language* 7(2): 215–246.

Regan, Jaime, Anfiloquio Paz Agkuash, Abel Uwarai Yagkug, and Isaac Paz Suikai. 1991. *Chichasajmi: Hablemos Aguaruna 1*. Lima: Centro Amazónico de Antropología y Aplicación Práctica.

Rivet, Paul 1907. Les indiens Jíbaro. Étude géographique, historique et ethnographique. *L'Anthropologie* 18: 333–368 and 583–618.

Rodríguez, Manuel. 1684. *El Marañón y Amazonas: Historia de los descubrimientos, entradas, y reducción de naciones*. Madrid: Imprenta de Antonio Gonçalez de Reyes.

Rubenstein, Steven. 2002. *Alejandro Tsakimp: A Shuar Healer in the Margins of History*. Lincoln: University of Nebraska Press.

Sadock, Jerrold M. and Arnold M. Zwicky. 1985. Speech act distinctions in syntax. In T. Shopen (ed.), *Language Typology and Syntactic Description: Vol. 1, Clause Structure*, 155–196. Cambridge: Cambridge University Press

Stark, Louisa R. 1985. Indigenous languages of lowland Ecuador: History and current status. In H.E. Manelis Klein & L.R. Stark (eds.), *South American Indian Languages: Retrospect and Prospect*, 157–193. Austin: University of Texas Press.

Stark, Louisa R. and Pieter C. Muysken. 1977. *Diccionario Español–Quichua, Quichua–Español*. Guayaquil: Publicaciones de los museos del banco central del Ecuador.

Stirling, M. W. 1938. *Historical and Ethnographical Material on the Jivaro Indians* [Smithsonian Institution Bureau of American Ethnology Bulletin 117]. Washington: U.S. Government Printing Office.

Stirling, Lesley. 1993. *Switch-reference and Discourse Representation*. Cambridge: Cambridge University Press.

Surrallés, Alexandre. 2007. Los Candoshi. In F. Santos & F. Barclay (eds.), *Guía etnográfica de la alta amazonía* (vol. 6), 243–380. Lima: Smithsonian Tropical Research Institute/Instituto Francés de Estudios Andinos.

Taylor, Anne-Christine. 1988. *Al Este de los Andes: Tomo II*. Quito: Abya-Yala.

Taylor, Anne-Christine and Ernesto Chau. 1983. Jivaroan magical songs: Achuar anent of connubial love. *Amerindia 8* [no page numbering] <http://celia.cnrs.fr/FichExt/Am/A_08_04.pdf>

Taylor, Anne-Christine and Philippe Descola. 1981. El conjunto Jívaro en los comienzos de la conquista Española del Alto Amazonas. *Bull. Inst. Fr. Et. And.* 10(3–4): 7–54.

Thompson, Sandra A., Robert E. Longacre, & Shin Ja J. Hwang. 2007. Adverbial clauses. In T. Shopen (ed.), *Language Typology and Syntactic Description: Vol. 2, Complex Constructions* (second edition), 237–300. Cambridge: Cambridge University Press.

Tuggy, John C. 1992. Algunos aspectos de la morfofonémica del Candoshi. In S.G. Parker (ed.), *Estudios etno-lingüísticos II* [Documento de Trabajo 23], 322–337. Yarinacocha: Ministerio de Educación/Instituto Lingüístico de Verano.

Turner, Glen D. (edited by Stephen H. Levinsohn). 1992. *Una Breve Gramática del Shuar* [Cuadernos Etnolingüísticos 19]. Quito: Instituto Lingüístico de Verano.

Up de Graff, F. W. 1923. *Head-hunters of the Amazon: Seven Years of Exploration and Adventure*. London: Herbert Jenkins Ltd.

Uwarai Yagkug, Abel, Isaac Paz Suikai and Jaime Regan. 1998. *Diccionario Aguaruna–Castellano: Awajún Chícham Apáchnaujai*. Lima: Centro Amazónico de Antropología y Aplicación Práctica.

Valenzuela, Pilar. 2003. *Transitivity in Shipibo-Konibo grammar*. PhD dissertation, University of Oregon.

Van Valin, Robert D. and Randy J. LaPolla. 1997. *Syntax: Structure, Meaning, and Function*. Cambridge: Cambridge University Press.

von Hagen, Victor Wolfgang. 1937. *Off With Their Heads*. New York: Macmillan.

von Murr, C.G. 1785. *Reisen einiger Missionarien der Gesellschaft Jesu in Amerika*. Nuremberg: Johann Eberhard Zeh.

Vuillermet, Marine. 2014. The multiple coreference systems in the Ese Ejja subordinate clauses. In R. van Gijn, D. Matić, J. Hammond, S. van Putten & A.V. Galucio (eds.), *Information Structure and Reference Tracking in Complex Sentences*, 341–371. Amsterdam/Philadelphia: John Benjamins.

Wipio Deicat, Gerardo (revised by Alejandro Paati Antunce Segundo and Martha Jakway). 1996. *Diccionario Aguaruna–Castellano* [Serie Lingüística Peruana 39]. Lima: Instituto Lingüístico de Verano.

Wise, M. R. 1999. Small language families and isolates in Peru. In R.M.W. Dixon & A.Y. Aikhenvald (eds.), *The Amazonian Languages*, 307–340. Cambridge: Cambridge University Press.

YCA 2008. *Yyamajam* [sic] *Chicham Apajuinu* [New Testament in Aguaruna] (5th edition). La Liga Bíblica.

Zariquiey Biondi, Roberto. 2011. *A grammar of Kashibo-Kakataibo*. PhD dissertation, RCLT, La Trobe University.

Zúñiga, Fernando. 2006. *Deixis and Alignment: Inverse systems in indigenous languages of the Americas*. Amsterdam/Philadelphia: John Benjamins.

Index

www.ingramcontent.com/pod-product-compliance
Lightning Source LLC
Chambersburg PA
CBHW081330090726
47907CB00011B/2439